The Arctic

Deanna Swaney

LONELY PLANET PUBLICATIONS
Melbourne • Oakland • London • Paris

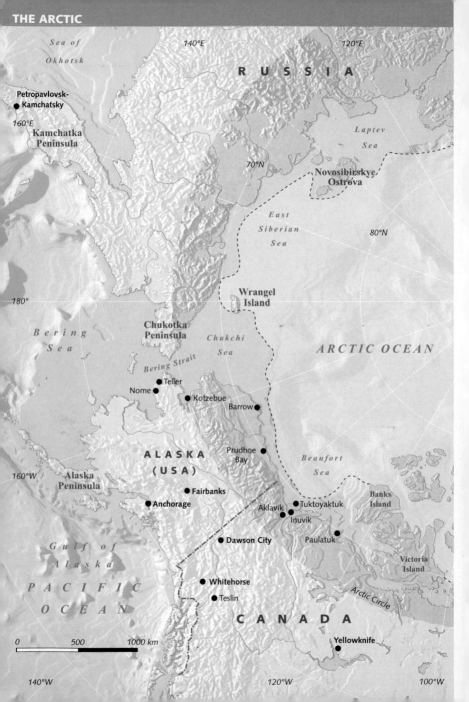

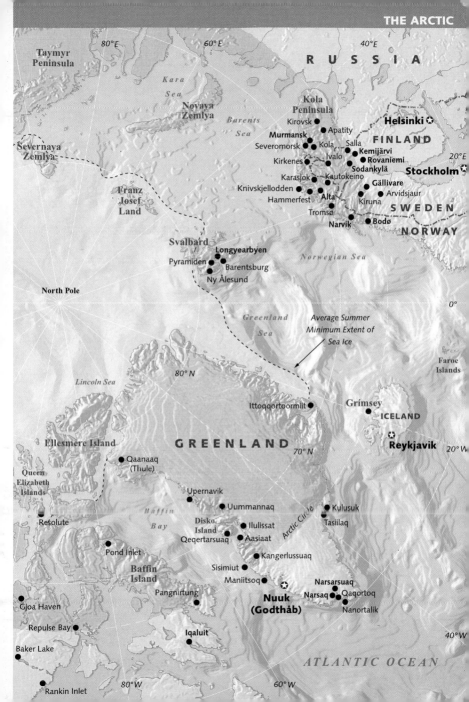

The Arctic
1st edition – November 1999

Published by
Lonely Planet Publications Pty Ltd A.C.N. 005 607 983
192 Burwood Rd, Hawthorn, Victoria 3122, Australia

Lonely Planet Offices
Australia PO Box 617, Hawthorn, Victoria 3122
USA 150 Linden St, Oakland, CA 94607
UK 10a Spring Place, London NW5 3BH
France 1 rue du Dahomey, 75011 Paris

Photographs
Many of the images in this guide are available for licensing from
Lonely Planet Images.
email: lpi@lonelyplanet.com.au

Front cover photograph
Polar Bear, Baffin Bay (Nicholas Reuss)

ISBN 0 86442 665 8

Printed by The Bookmaker Pty Ltd
Printed in China

**Although the authors
and Lonely Planet try
to make the informa-
tion as accurate as
possible, we accept
no responsibility for
any loss, injury or
inconvenience sus-
tained by anyone
using this book.**

Contents – Text

2 Contents – Text

ARCTIC SWEDEN 383

ARCTIC FINLAND 392

ARCTIC RUSSIA 407

INDEX 451

MAP LEGEND back page

METRIC CONVERSION inside back cover

Contents – Maps

ARCTIC MAP INDEX

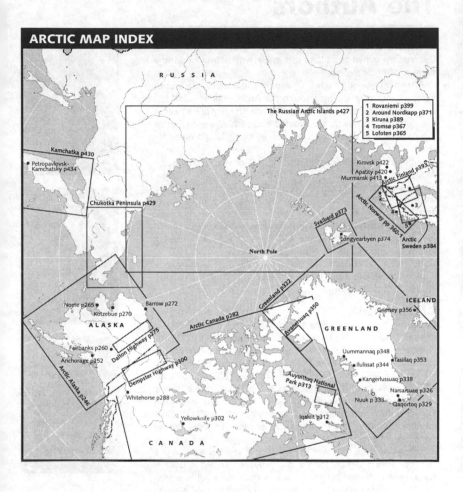

The Authors

Deanna Swaney

Deanna researched and wrote this guide with assistance from a number of Arctic experts.

After her university studies, Deanna made a shoestring tour of Europe – including a jaunt through the Arctic regions – and has been addicted to travel ever since. Despite an erstwhile career in computer programming, she avoided encroaching yuppiedom in the Arctic wastes of midtown Anchorage by making a break for South America, where she wrote Lonely Planet's *Bolivia* guide.

Subsequent travels led through a circuit of island paradises – Arctic and tropical – and resulted in three more guides: *Tonga, Samoa* and *Iceland, Greenland & the Faroe Islands*. Back on dry land, she wrote *Zimbabwe, Botswana & Namibia* and *Norway* and, in between, contributed to Lonely Planet's guides to *Brazil, Mauritius, Réunion & Seychelles, Madagascar & Comoros, Southern Africa*, and *Russia, Ukraine & Belarus*, as well as shoestring guides to Africa, South America and Scandinavia.

Her time is now divided between travelling, writing and working on various construction projects around her home base in Alaska's Susitna Valley.

Graham Bell

Graham Bell wrote the Arctic Nature Guide. He is a well known naturalist based in Northumberland, north-east England. Educated at Manchester Grammar School and Durham University, he took Honours in French and English and a Diploma in Education. He has travelled widely, studying and photographing wildlife on all continents, but his favourite area is the Arctic, which he has visited regularly for 35 years. He has been Ornithological Recorder for north-east England, a member of the British Birds Rarities Committee and the Council of the Royal Society for the Protection of Birds, a consultant to various organisations and has accompanied cruises all over the world as guest lecturer. He is a specialist in bird identification and is actively involved in wildlife conservation, as well as lecturing and writing on wildlife topics. He is also Guided Walks Leader for the Northumberland National Parks and Countryside Service, leading wildlife walks at home and abroad. Graham is committed to his lifelong passion of helping people to understand and enjoy nature.

Lawson W Brigham

Lawson Brigham wrote the Arctic Research chapter. He has had a lifelong involvement with the sea and the polar regions. As a US Coast Guard officer (1970-95) he has sailed on all oceans and has extensive experience in Arctic and Antarctic waters. As Captain of the Coast Guard polar icebreaker *Polar Sea*, he was part of the

US/Canada Arctic Ocean Section Expedition that crossed the Arctic Ocean for science in July and August 1994. Since the 1970s his research has focused on the Soviet and Russian Arctic, investigating all aspects of the Northern Sea Route. Author of more than 75 papers, Captain Brigham is an adviser to the US Arctic Research Commission and an elected Fellow of the Arctic Institute of North America. He is currently a doctoral candidate at the Scott Polar Research Institute, University of Cambridge, UK.

Liz Cruwys & Beau Riffenburgh

Liz Cruwys and Beau Riffenburgh wrote the sections on Environment & Ecology, Icebreakers, Nanavut and the Russian Arctic Islands. They are based at the Scott Polar Research Institute at the University of Cambridge, UK. Liz is a marine biologist working on environmental contamination in the polar regions and the biology of seals, fur seals and sea lions. Beau is the editor of the institute's journal *Polar Record* and is a polar historian, with interests in the popular press, exploration and imperialism. Both have written a number of books on subjects as diverse as biology, the press and exploration, cathedrals and castles, and medieval history.

Robert Headland

Robert Headland wrote the Arctic History & Exploration chapter. He has worked in both polar regions with the Scott Polar Research Institute, the British Antarctic Survey, and several other organisations since 1977. His research has largely involved historical geography and the principles of sovereignty exercised over the Arctic and Antarctic. Since 1991, when it became possible, he has been invited to lecture on many occasions aboard Russian icebreaker vessels out of Murmansk and Vladivostok. These have visited most parts of the Arctic but especially the Eurasian regions and North Pole. This has allowed the theoretical information from the institute to be combined with the practical experience of visiting the regions. In 1984 he was decorated with the Polar Medal. He is a fellow of the Royal Geographical Society and a member of the Arctic Club and Antarctic Club. He is based in Cambridge, UK, where he is the Archivist of the Scott Polar Research Institute.

Mark Nuttall

Mark Nuttall wrote the Indigenous Peoples & Cultures of the Arctic chapter. He is a social anthropologist and specialises in the peoples and cultures of the Arctic and North Atlantic. He travels regularly and extensively throughout the region. He is author of *Arctic Homeland* and *Protecting the Arctic*, co-author of *White Settlers* and co-editor of *The Arctic: environment, people policy*. When not in the field, he teaches anthropology at the University of Aberdeen, Scotland.

Norbert Schurer

Norbert Schurer wrote the Arctic Literature chapter. He travelled continuously before he even had a choice in the matter. He moved back and forth between the United States and Germany every other of his first 10 years. In a career slalom, Norbert went on to study classical music, arts management, pedagogy, as well as German and English literature in Berlin and Manchester. He is currently pursuing a PhD in Literature at Duke University, Durham, North Carolina. Norbert has visited many parts of the Arctic and subarctic, but his favourite northern hangout is Greenland.

FROM THE AUTHOR

Deanna Swaney In Norway, invaluable help was provided by Ingalill Sandal, Jens Riis-Næs, Steinar Lindås, Ulf Prytz, Andreas Umbreit and Graeme Cornwallis. For the Greenland chapter, Søren Thalund helped immeasurably with the latest updates. For the Russia section, Steve Kokker graciously kept me up to date with all the latest happenings and wrote an excellent report on the Laplandsky Zapovednik. Valentin Petrov in Apatity, Tatiana Bolod in Murmansk, Rune Rafaelsen in Kirkenes, and Audhild and Børge at Sovjetrejser all provided invaluable and hard-to-find information.

I must also acknowledge and thank the several specialists and Lonely Planet authors who have made contributions to this book: Ryan ver Berkmoes; Jim DuFresne; Clem Lindenmayer; Jennifer Brewer; Graeme Cornwallis; Dr Mark Nuttall at the University of Aberdeen; Norbert Schurer at Duke University; Dr Robert Keith Headland; Dr Graham Bell; Dr Liz Cruwys; Lawson Brigham and Dr Beau Riffenburgh at the Scott Polar Research Institute; Dr Fred Peterson and Kathleen Cartwright.

Finally, love and best wishes to Earl, Dean, Kim, Jennifer and Lauren Swaney, in Fresno; to Keith and Holly Hawkings in Anchorage and to Dave Dault, who most admirably continues to keep things humming back home.

This Book

Material from Lonely Planet's guides to Canada; Iceland, Greenland and the Faroe Islands; Norway; Scandinavian & Baltic Europe; Finland; Russia, Ukraine & Belarus and USA was used for this book.

FROM THE PUBLISHER

This first edition of The Arctic was edited in Lonely Planet's Melbourne office by Helen Yeates with the assistance of Shelley Muir, Susie Ashworth, Ron Gallagher, Anne Mulvaney, Chris Wyness, Ada Cheung and Clay Lucas. Lisa Borg was responsible for the design and layout of the book and coordinated the mapping. Cartographers Celia Wood, Joelene Kowalski, Ann Jeffree and Mark Griffiths assisted. Adrian Persoglia compiled the climate charts. Mick Weldon supplied the new illustrations. Maria Vallianos designed the cover. Thanks also to Tim Uden, Matt King and Tamsin Wilson for their advice.

Foreword

ABOUT LONELY PLANET GUIDEBOOKS

The story begins with a classic travel adventure: Tony and Maureen Wheeler's 1972 journey across Europe and Asia to Australia. Useful information about the overland trail did not exist at that time, so Tony and Maureen published the first Lonely Planet guidebook to meet a growing need.

From a kitchen table, then from a tiny office in Melbourne (Australia), Lonely Planet has become the largest independent travel publisher in the world, an international company with offices in Melbourne, Oakland (USA), London (UK) and Paris (France).

Today Lonely Planet guidebooks cover the globe. There is an ever-growing list of books and there's information in a variety of forms and media. Some things haven't changed. The main aim is still to help make it possible for adventurous travellers to get out there – to explore and better understand the world.

At Lonely Planet we believe travellers can make a positive contribution to the countries they visit – if they respect their host communities and spend their money wisely. Since 1986 a percentage of the income from each book has been donated to aid projects and human rights campaigns.

Updates Lonely Planet thoroughly updates each guidebook as often as possible. This usually means there are around two years between editions, although for more unusual or more stable destinations the gap can be longer. Check the imprint page (following the colour map at the beginning of the book) for publication dates.

Between editions up-to-date information is available in two free newsletters – the paper *Planet Talk* and email *Comet* (to subscribe, contact any Lonely Planet office) – and on our Web site www.lonelyplanet.com. The *Upgrades* section of the Web site covers a number of important and volatile destinations and is regularly updated by Lonely Planet authors. *Scoop* covers news and current affairs relevant to travellers. And, lastly, the *Thorn Tree* bulletin board and *Postcards* section of the site carry unverified, but fascinating, reports from travellers.

Correspondence The process of creating new editions begins with the letters, postcards and emails received from travellers. This correspondence often includes suggestions, criticisms and comments about the current editions. Interesting excerpts are immediately passed on via newsletters and the Web site, and everything goes to our authors to be verified when they're researching on the road. We're keen to get more feedback from organisations or individuals who represent communities visited by travellers.

Lonely Planet gathers information for everyone who's curious about the planet – and especially for those who explore it first-hand. Through guidebooks, phrasebooks, activity guides, maps, literature, newsletters, image library, TV series and Web site we act as an information exchange for a worldwide community of travellers.

Research Authors aim to gather sufficient practical information to enable travellers to make informed choices and to make the mechanics of a journey run smoothly. They also research historical and cultural background to help enrich the travel experience and allow travellers to understand and respond appropriately to cultural and environmental issues.

Authors don't stay in every hotel because that would mean spending a couple of months in each medium-sized city and, no, they don't eat at every restaurant because that would mean stretching belts beyond capacity. They do visit hotels and restaurants to check standards and prices, but feedback based on readers' direct experiences can be very helpful.

Many of our authors work undercover, others aren't so secretive. None of them accept freebies in exchange for positive write-ups. And none of our guidebooks contain any advertising.

Production Authors submit their raw manuscripts and maps to offices in Australia, USA, UK or France. Editors and cartographers – all experienced travellers themselves – then begin the process of assembling the pieces. When the book finally hits the shops, some things are already out of date, we start getting feedback from readers and the process begins again ...

WARNING & REQUEST

Things change – prices go up, schedules change, good places go bad and bad places go bankrupt – nothing stays the same. So, if you find things better or worse, recently opened or long since closed, please tell us and help make the next edition even more accurate and useful. We genuinely value all the feedback we receive. Julie Young coordinates a well travelled team that reads and acknowledges every letter, postcard and email and ensures that every morsel of information finds its way to the appropriate authors, editors and cartographers for verification.

Everyone who writes to us will find their name in the next edition of the appropriate guidebook. They will also receive the latest issue of *Planet Talk*, our quarterly printed newsletter, or *Comet*, our monthly email newsletter. Subscriptions to both newsletters are free. The very best contributions will be rewarded with a free guidebook.

Excerpts from your correspondence may appear in new editions of Lonely Planet guidebooks, the Lonely Planet Web site, *Planet Talk* or *Comet*, so please let us know if you *don't* want your letter published or your name acknowledged.

Send all correspondence to the Lonely Planet office closest to you:

Australia: PO Box 617, Hawthorn, Victoria 3122
USA: 150 Linden St, Oakland, CA 94607
UK: 10A Spring Place, London NW5 3BH
France: 1 rue du Dahomey, 75011 Paris

Or email us at: talk2us@lonelyplanet.com.au

For news, views and updates see our Web site: www.lonelyplanet.com

HOW TO USE A LONELY PLANET GUIDEBOOK

The best way to use a Lonely Planet guidebook is any way you choose. At Lonely Planet we believe the most memorable travel experiences are often those that are unexpected, and the finest discoveries are those you make yourself. Guidebooks are not intended to be used as if they provide a detailed set of infallible instructions!

Contents All Lonely Planet guidebooks follow roughly the same format. The Facts about the Destination chapters or sections give background information ranging from history to weather. Facts for the Visitor gives practical information on issues like visas and health. Getting There & Away gives a brief starting point for researching travel to and from the destination. Getting Around gives an overview of the transport options when you arrive.

The peculiar demands of each destination determine how subsequent chapters are broken up, but some things remain constant. We always start with background, then proceed to sights, places to stay, places to eat, entertainment, getting there and away, and getting around information – in that order.

Heading Hierarchy Lonely Planet headings are used in a strict hierarchical structure that can be visualised as a set of Russian dolls. Each heading (and its following text) is encompassed by any preceding heading that is higher on the hierarchical ladder.

Entry Points We do not assume guidebooks will be read from beginning to end, but that people will dip into them. The traditional entry points are the list of contents and the index. In addition, however, some books have a complete list of maps and an index map illustrating map coverage.

There may also be a colour map that shows highlights. These highlights are dealt with in greater detail in the Facts for the Visitor chapter, along with planning questions and suggested itineraries. Each chapter covering a geographical region usually begins with a locator map and another list of highlights. Once you find something of interest in a list of highlights, turn to the index.

Maps Maps play a crucial role in Lonely Planet guidebooks and include a huge amount of information. A legend is printed on the back page. We seek to have complete consistency between maps and text, and to have every important place in the text captured on a map. Map key numbers usually start in the top left corner.

Although inclusion in a guidebook usually implies a recommendation we cannot list every good place. Exclusion does not necessarily imply criticism. In fact there are a number of reasons why we might exclude a place – sometimes it is simply inappropriate to encourage an influx of travellers.

Introduction

Let us probe the silent places
Let us seek what luck betides us
Let us journey to a lonely land I know.
There's a whisper on the night wind,
There's a star agleam to guide us
And the Wild is calling, calling ... let us go.

Robert Service *(The Spell of the Yukon)*

What traveller hasn't dreamed of venturing beyond the beaten track – and even beyond the unbeaten track – where one can feel as if they're truly pioneering in untrodden territory? While there may be a few corners of the Sahara or the Amazon that remain too inhospitable for mass tourism, apart from the depths of the sea, there's no more wild country on earth than the polar regions.

Antarctica is generally considered the ultimate destination for globetrotters, and its wildlife can only be called spectacular, but the uninhabited continent surrounded by water misses out on the colour and interest that can only be created by human cultures and their interactions. The northern polar regions, the Arctic, on the other hand, form a nearly perfect negative of the Antarctic – an ocean surrounded by continents, where pristine seas, incredible otherworldly landscapes and ragged mountains of ice merge through the region into a vast white mirage.

Thanks to its relatively inhospitable climate and remote expanses, the Arctic enjoys not only broad horizons and rich wildlife communities, but also a complement of human cultures that have interacted with this boreal country and its seas from time immemorial. Against all odds, they've thrived and developed into some of the hardiest societies on earth.

Definitions of exactly what comprises the Arctic region are diverse, and few agree on where the Arctic ends and more temperate zones begin. The most popularly defended delimiter is probably the Arctic Circle, the 66.5° line of latitude, on which the sun never sets on the longest day of the year and never rises on the shortest day. However, that designation includes the forested and relatively balmy northern coast of Norway, yet excludes the decidedly polar-like regions of south Greenland and the bleak tundra expanses around Canada's Hudson Bay.

Another common delimiter is the 10°C isotherm, the line north of which the average temperature doesn't rise above 10°C in any month of the year, which would exclude many areas of Scandinavia, Russia, Alaska and Canada that lie well north of the Arctic Circle. A third definition would include only the Arctic cultural area – that is, those areas inhabited by indigenous Arctic peoples – the Inuit, Athapaskans and Sami, as well as the Chukchi, Samoyed and other indigenous groups of northern Russia, plus the polar seas where they've traditionally hunted.

For this book, we've chosen the Arctic Circle as the logical guideline for defining the Arctic region, but we've also decided to recognise other areas south of that magic line that are Arctic in nature and will provide visitors with a suitably polar experience. That means that this book includes not only the 'Arctic banana belt' of northern Scandinavia, which lies well north of the circle, but also Canada's Hudson Bay region, Alaska's Seward Peninsula, south Greenland and Russia's Chukotka and Kamchatka peninsulas, to the south of it.

In contrast with most guidebooks, our purpose isn't to provide exhaustive practical information for travellers, detailing every lodge, hotel and flight possibility. Rather, our objective is to thoroughly introduce the region to prospective visitors and provide enough background information to choose a destination and plan an Arctic adventure.

Whatever their approach, anyone who's feeling adventurous and looking for an unusual destination is sure to find this otherworldly land more incredible than they'd ever imagined, and after one visit, they're sure to start planning another.

Facts about the Arctic

HISTORY
The Inuit

The Inuit (pronounced INN-ooit) are sometimes called Eskimos ('eaters of raw meat' in the Athapaskan language), however this name is now out of favour. They are the predominant population group in Arctic Alaska, northern Canada and Greenland and there's also a small population on Russia's Chukotka Peninsula. Although the American Indians are descendants of the Siberian peoples who are thought to have migrated into North America across the Bering Land Bridge some 25,000 to 23,000 years ago (or earlier), there is evidence that the Inuit first arrived in Alaska by *umiaq* (skin boat), between 7000 and 8000 years ago. This was long after the presumed land bridge had disappeared beneath Bering Strait.

Because the Alaskan Athapaskans had already occupied the most productive lands in central and southern Alaska, the latecoming Inuit were relegated to the barren Arctic coastlines. As the population grew, people began to move eastward, into the more productive hunting grounds of Canada's Arctic Archipelago and southward to Hudson Bay and northern Labrador.

It's likely that the first Greenlanders migrated from Ellesmere Island in northern Canada some 5000 years ago during a warm climatic period. Evidence of this Stone Age culture, known as Independence I (after Independence Fjord in Peary Land, north Greenland), has been uncovered only around the northernmost tip of Greenland. It probably consisted of no more than 500 nomadic individuals who eked out a meagre existence at the frontier of human endurance. These people sustained themselves by hunting polar bears, muskoxen, Arctic hares and other animals.

At this stage, about 3800 years ago, there's evidence that the Independence I people were either supplanted by or developed into the culture known as Independence II, which inhabited northern Greenland from about 3400 to 2600 years ago. It's thought that they eventually migrated southward and probably replaced another culture, the Saqqaq. Around 2500 years ago, however, the climate turned colder and the Saqqaq culture mysteriously disappeared. It's possible that they combined with the southward-moving Independence II people, and developed into the Dorset culture. It's also suggested that when faced with the climatic change and invasion from the north, they retreated westward, back into Canada.

Evidence of the subsequent culture, the Thule, has been found from western Alaska all the way east to Greenland, indicating that the most recent eastward migration occurred very rapidly. The generally accepted theory is that the Thule culture migrated directly from Alaska to Canada during a warming trend in the 10th century and continued spreading eastward until it had occupied much of the Greenlandic coast in less than 150 years, absorbing or supplanting all other cultures.

However, alternative theories suggest that the Independence II culture didn't migrate south but merely stayed in place and developed into the Thule culture, which eventually moved south across Greenland; or that the Dorset culture met up with the Independence II in north-west Greenland and combined to form the Thule culture.

Whatever the case, it was the Thule culture that developed the *qajaq* (kayak), the harpoon and the dogsled, all of which are still used. A climatic shift in the 12th century forced the Thule to migrate southward and fragment into a number of subcultures. There's conclusive archaeological evidence that the modern-day Greenlandic Inuit – known as the Inussuk culture – have descended from the Thule.

Inuit Religion

Early Inuit belief systems were characterised by belief in familiar spirits who helped or hindered individuals. The Inuit did not fear death but they were wary of the *toornot*, the spirits of the dead; the *tupilat*, the hideous creatures that populate nightmares; and the *qivittoq*, the glacier spirits that could take possession of a person who reported seeing one.

Hunters believed that the earth and its creatures should be treated with respect, believing that a successful hunter had not conquered an animal, but that the animal had willingly sacrificed its life. Prior to European influences, the Inuit believed that success in hunting – the most essential of human endeavours – was monitored by a water spirit, an old woman who sat by the shore and would punish blundering humans by combing her hair over the surface of the water, thus preventing seals from surfacing. The services of an *angaqqoq*, or shaman, were required to rectify the problem.

The people also took special care not to upset the *sila*, the delicate natural balance of the universe. For example, to kill an animal that had been inhabited by a *toornoq* (singular of 'toornot') would indicate such a blunder, and only with the death of the hunter could the balance be restored.

When the first Europeans arrived in the far north, the Inuit people surmised that the newcomers were the product of a union between Inuit women and dogs. However, that didn't prevent their acceptance of the relatively simplistic religious philosophy offered by the outsiders. Even before the arrival of Christianity, the Inuit believed in an all-pervading soul or a 'breath', that survived death. The souls of those whose bodies lay on the earth were relegated to the cold and unpleasant sky, while those who were thrown into the sea lived underground in warm, rich hunting grounds. The Middle Eastern notion that hell is a hot place must have inspired amusement and confusion in Arctic dwellers! Although most of the region was converted to Christianity over two centuries ago and most of the rest had converted by the early 20th century (the Russian Inuit were converted to Communism instead!), many Inuit still adhere to certain aspects of their traditional shamanistic religion, especially in times of hardship.

The North Atlantic

Early European Perceptions Between 330 and 325 BC, the Greek navigator Pytheas embarked on a voyage from Massilia (Marseille), through the Pillars of Heracles, and then northward to investigate trade routes to the amber and tin markets of northern Europe. In the process, he circumnavigated Britain, 'discovered' Orkney (and possibly Shetland), and visited the west coast of Norway.

In his report on the journey, Pytheas mentioned the island of Ultima Thule, six days sailing north of Britain, beyond which the sea congealed into a viscous jelly. This was almost certainly a reference to Iceland.

Given the description, it seems unlikely he actually visited the island, but it is significant that the Celts or the Norse knew of its existence at such an early date.

Non-Nordic European perceptions of the North Atlantic region before and after Pytheas' journey, however, were even more shrouded in rumour and myth. The great northern ocean, *oceanus innavigabilis*, or the Hyperborean Sea, was a place of maelstrom where the fierce winds of Boreas howled through the Rhipæan mountains and guarded idyllic lands of plenty like Vinland, the Elysian fields, Avalon, the Hesperides and other enigmatic, but mythical, locales. The borders of paradise were inhabited, they believed, by barbaric dog-headed people (the Cynocephali and the Scythians) who ate raw meat and behaved like bears. To venture northward, they presumed, would invite all sorts of grisly eventualities. Their fears of the irksome, unknown entities were overcome by economic opportunism when amber and tin deposits beckoned.

The Monks Some of the myths about Arctic regions were dispelled during the 6th century when Ireland was seized by the religious fervour that accompanied its adoption of Roman Christianity and the first Irish monks set sail for fabled lands to the north-west. Some were hermits in search of a solitary environment for religious contemplation. Others undoubtedly observed sea birds flying in from the north-west and concluded that countries awaiting Christian enlightenment lay in that direction.

While some of the Irish zealots were settlers, some were merely voyagers. In the early 6th century the Irish abbot St Brendan embarked on a seven year voyage through the region in a *curraugh*, an open skin boat. Unfortunately, the account of his journey, *Navigatio Sancti Brendani Abbatis*, wasn't written down until the 9th century and the time lapse surely caused some distortion of fact. Although no conclusive proof of his itinerary has been established, his references to 'sheep islands', the 'paradise of birds', 'flaming mountains' and 'crystal columns' have been construed as references to the Faroes, Iceland and the Greenland icebergs.

Some traditions state (although they are hardly backed by evidence) that St Brendan and later voyagers pushed on to eastern Canada and even made their way up the St Lawrence River toward the North American heartland.

Others brought back to Ireland tales of the land of Thule where there was no daylight in winter, but on summer nights, according to the clergyman Dicuil in 825, 'whatever task a man wishes to perform, even picking lice from his shirt, he can manage as well as in clear daylight'. This almost certainly describes Iceland and its midnight sun.

To the first monks to settle in the Faroes and Iceland (around the year 700), it would have been apparent that the islands were uninhabited and therefore more suitable as a hermitage than a mission. They built monasteries along the coast, and it's likely that some remained in Iceland and the Faroes and mixed with the Norse people who began arriving in the early 9th century. Nordic accounts, however, state that these *papar* (fathers) fled during the period of Norse settlement.

The Norse Although much Norse pride is derived from notions that they're 'children of the Vikings', most Nordic settlers in Iceland and other North Atlantic lands were ordinary Scandinavian citizens: farmers, herders, merchants and opportunists. The reasons for the westward expansion were undoubtedly complex but Scandinavian politics and tyranny, population growth, shipbuilding prowess, commercial potential and even sheer boredom and wanderlust have been cited as catalysts of the Nordic 'explosion' that nurtured both the Viking rampages and the westward migrations.

However, Norse tradition credits the settlement of Iceland and the Faroe Islands to a single mainland phenomenon. From the middle to late 9th century, the tyrannical Harald Haarfager (Harald Finehair), the king of the Vestfold district of south-eastern Norway, was taken with expansionist aspirations. In 890, he won a significant naval victory at Hafrsfjord (Stavanger), and the deposed chieftains and landowners chose to flee rather than submit. Many wound up in Iceland and the Faroes, some via Orkney and Shetland, which in turn also fell to the indefatigable King Harald.

Much of Europe at this time was being subjected to Nordic mischief and entrepreneurial spirit. Storming through the British Isles, sacking, looting, plundering and murdering, the Viking hordes struck terror wherever they went and, by the middle of the 9th century, they controlled most coastal regions of Britain and Ireland. Over the next 200 years they raided their way across the continent as far east as the Volga and south to the Mediterranean and north Africa. They might have continued in both directions had King Harald Hardraada (known as Harald Hard-Ruler) not fallen to the Saxons in 1066. Throughout the Viking Age (800-1066), violent Norse advances were marked by an exodus into the North Atlantic, not only of Scandinavians but also of Britons, Westmen (Irish) and Scots who had intermarried with the fleeing victims of Nordic despotism. Slaves and kinsfolk also migrated with these mixed families, introducing a heterogeneous stock into Iceland and the Faroes. The sagas (fact-based literary accounts of the settlement and subsequent development of these new lands), written mostly after the Viking Age had passed, have much to say about events in the colonies and the slow march of European civilisation toward the Arctic regions. The opening lines of the *Færeyingar Saga* are:

There was a man called Grim Kamban. It was he who first colonised the Faroe Islands in the time of Harald Haarfager. There were many people at that time who fled from the tyranny of the King, of whom some settled down in the Faroes and made their abode there; but others sought out other deserted countries.

Another work, the Icelandic *Landnámabók* or *The Book of Settlement*, explains the renaming of Thule far less romantically:

… at a place called Vatnsfjörður on Barðaströnd … the fjord teemed with fish of all kinds … The spring was extremely cold. Flóki climbed a high mountain and looked north toward the coast, and saw a fjord full of drift ice; so they called the country Ice-land and that has been its name ever since.

In the *Íslendingabók*, the *Book of the Icelanders*, the earliest settlement of that island is also recounted:

A Norwegian called Ingólfur is reliably reported to have been the first man to leave Norway for Iceland … He settled in the south, at Reykjavík.

The settlement of Greenland by the Norse people is dealt with in two works, the *Saga of Eiríkur Rauðe* or *Erik the Red's Saga* and the *Grænlendinga Saga* or *Tale of the Greenlanders*. The first European contact with Greenland was probably in the 10th century by Norwegian Gunnbjörn Ulfsson. It was first colonised from the east in 982 by Eiríkur Rauðe (Erik the Red), an exile from Iceland and a murderer.

After bestowing Greenland's lovely name, which has come to be regarded as history's first great real-estate scam, he returned to Iceland and enticed 500 other settlers to bring their expertise and livestock and follow him. They established two settlements, the Østerbygd or 'eastern settlement' on Eiríks Fjord in south Greenland and the Vesturbygd or 'western settlement' several hundred kilometres north near the present-day Greenlandic capital, Nuuk. The *skrælings* (Eskimos) they encountered appeared to be far less advanced than modern archaeology indicates the Thule people were. Based on this, it can be assumed that southern Greenland at the time was inhabited by survivors from earlier Eskimo cultures, who possibly resettled from Labrador or north Greenland before the arrival of the Thule people. Forays from these two colonies led to the European 'discovery' of Helluland (the 'land of flat stones', probably Baffin Island), Markland (the 'land of woods', most likely Labrador) and Vinland (the 'land of wine', probably somewhere between Newfoundland and New Jersey).

Eiríkur's son, Leif the Lucky, set foot in the New World as early as the year 999. Europeans had reached the Americas, but permanent settlement was thwarted by the skrælings, who were anything but welcoming. For more on the Norse colonisation of Greenland, see the boxed text 'Greenland Norse Colonies' in the Greenland chapter.

Later European Exploration Between the 13th and 15th centuries, European knowledge of North Atlantic geography

Norse Seafaring

Realising the vast distances covered by the early voyagers through difficult seas, one can only wonder what sort of ships and technology the Norse people used to travel so far abroad through uncharted territory. Archaeological evidence suggests that Viking longboats, low vessels over 30m long, were used primarily in war and raiding. The majority of the settlers travelled in smaller cargo boats called *knerrir* (singular: *knörr*). These sturdy little craft, scarcely 18m in length and sitting low in the water, were designed to carry great loads. Journeys in them must have been crowded, uncomfortable and often frightening.

Perhaps the most interesting aspect of these early voyages, however, is the method of navigation employed. The sagas mention a mysterious device known as a *solarsteinn*, or 'sunstone', which allowed navigation even when the sky was overcast or the sun was below the horizon and celestial navigation was impossible.

It is now generally agreed that the solarsteinn was a crystal of cordierite, which is found in Scandinavia and has natural polarising qualities. When the crystal is observed from below and rotated, light passing through it is polarised blue when the long axis is pointed toward the source of the sunlight.

This same principle is used today. Jet planes flying over the polar regions, where magnetic compasses are unsuitable and celestial navigation is difficult, use a sky compass that determines the position of the sun by filtering sunlight through an artificial polarising lens.

A Norse *knörr* boat

extended as far north as Iceland. Although Europeans had colonised and occupied Greenland in the late 10th century, the place had been effectively forgotten and, unknown to most people, the Greenland colonies had disappeared. On maps, this island was normally represented as a vast peninsula connected to the Scandinavian mainland.

Although fishing boats from the British Isles were already reaping the harvests of Newfoundland at the time, John Cabot's voyage to that coast in 1497 was considered a mission of discovery. Potential colonies and the possible existence of a Northwest Passage to the trading grounds of the East Indies were too much for the British to ignore. It didn't take long for much of the rest of Europe – the French, Portuguese, Spanish and Italians – to show interest in becoming the first to make something of it. The Portuguese, suspecting that Cabot's landfall may have been east of the Pope's line of demarcation (making it Portuguese territory), sent João Fernandes, a *lavrador* or private landholder, to determine its position. In 1500, he happened instead upon southern Greenland, which he modestly named Lavrador, after himself. Later, a confused cartographer evidently shifted the name south-westward to present-day Labrador. For more on later attempts to navigate the presumed Northwest Passage, see the Arctic History & Exploration chapter.

Northern Russia
Northern Siberia & the Far East The first known Siberians were Palaeolithic (early Stone Age) tribes who lived around Lake Baikal and the headwaters of the Ob and Yenisey rivers. Remains of Neolithic (late Stone Age) settlements have been found all over Siberia. Indeed, many northern tribes were still basically at the Neo-lithic stage when the Russians arrived. As late as the Iron Age, the steppes and forests from the Ural Mountains to Lake Baikal were populated by tribes of herders whose origins lay in the Caucasus (Abakan's regional museum contains relics from burial mounds of this period). Soon afterwards the earliest Mongolians arrived in the area.

The first Russians in Siberia were fur traders from Novgorod who reached the northern Ob River in the late 11th century. Although the 13th century warlord Jenghiz Khan confederated his Tatar armies and subdued most of Asia, he never did push northward into the Arctic regions. If the Russians appreciate Ivan the Terrible for anything, it is for his seizure of the Tatar strongholds of Kazan (in 1552) and Astrakhan (in 1556), which put the entire Volga in Russian hands and swung open the door to the north and east. Seeing the writing on the wall, Yediger, the Khan of the Sibir Tatars, offered Ivan a tribute of sable pelts and became his vassal.

In 1558, the tsar authorised the powerful Stroganov family to open trading posts east of the Ural Mountains under the protection of Cossack mercenaries. When Yediger's successor, Kuchum, began plundering these settlements, a band of Cossacks and soldiers led by a convict named Yermak Timofeevich set out to teach him a lesson and in 1582, they took the Tatar capital of Kashlyk (now Tobolsk). In recognition of this achievement, Ivan pardoned Yermak for his

Ivan (IV) the Terrible (1530-84) was crowned as the first tsar of Russia in 1547.

past crimes and this bandit is now honoured as the 'conqueror of Siberia'. Three years later Yermak plunged into a river to escape a Tatar ambush and was drowned.

Nevertheless, the settlement of Siberia had begun and the next half-century saw one of history's most explosive expansions. Fuelled by a lust for furs, waves of Cossacks, trappers, traders and misfits had reached the Ob River by the 1580s. Until then this had represented the eastern limit of the known world. They had pushed on to the Yenisey by the end of the 16th century, the Lena by the 1620s and, in 1639, they reached the Pacific coast at Okhotsk. Behind the pioneers came the tsar's officials and soldiers to exact tributes (known as *yassak*) in the form of pelts. The export of furs became Russia's biggest money-maker. Indigenous tribes may have found the newcomers a welcome change from the Tatars but, despite their greater numbers, with only bows and arrows against Russian muskets they had no choice in the matter anyway.

Only the Tatars, the Buryats (who lived around Lake Baikal) and the Chukchi of Chukotka put up much resistance.

By the late 17th century there were as many settlers, traders, soldiers and missionaries as there were indigenous Siberians. As expeditions began to size up Siberia's huge mineral wealth, Peter the Great also sent engineers and geologists. In 1648, the Cossack Semyon Dezhnev had been the first to sail round the northeast corner of Asia, from the Pacific Ocean into the Arctic. However, the glory went to Vitus Bering, a Danish officer in the Russian navy, who discovered the strait (which now bears his name) all over again in 1728. Four years later, the tsar called Bering to head the Great Northern Expedition. This was ostensibly a scientific survey of Kamchatka (claimed for the tsar in 1697 by the explorer Atlasov) and the eastern seaboard, but in reality its aim was to expand Russia's Pacific sphere of influence as far south as Japan and across to North America.

Bering succeeded in discovering Alaska, landing in 1741 but unfortunately, on the return voyage his ship was wrecked off an island just 250km east of the Kamchatka coast. Bering died on the island, and it, too, now carries his name. Survivors of Bering's crew brought back reports of an abundance of foxes, fur seals and otters inhabiting the islands off the mainland, triggering a fresh wave of fur-inspired expansion. An Irkutsk trader, Grigory Shelekhov, landed on Kodiak Island (in present-day Alaska) in 1784 and, 15 years later, his successor founded Sitka (originally called New Archangel), which was the capital of Alaska until 1906.

From about 1650, the authorities began dumping criminals in Siberia and the Russian Arctic. In the 1700s, as the region's natural wealth became obvious, the 'dumpees' were put to work digging it up. As demand for labour increased, so did the list of punishable offences: prize-fighting, prostitution, vagrancy, even fortune-telling all became grounds for banishment.

The death penalty was abolished and replaced with exile and forced labour, and soon people were being sent to Siberia and northern Russia without trial. POWs, religious dissenters and, more or less, anyone with an irritating opinion were soon joining the criminals on the long trail east. Exile had become big business. The Great Siberian Trakt, or Post Road, long the only route through the Ural Mountains and the taiga beyond, was developed to include a complex system of exile stations and holding prisons.

Soviet rule was proclaimed in Siberia's major towns soon after the October Revolution of 1917, but in spite of all those exiled dissidents, this was not fertile ground for the Bolsheviks. Cossacks, merchants and a fairly contented peasantry were uneasy about Lenin's promises. Local heroes tended to be upper-class explorers and scientists, rather than revolutionary politicians. In May 1918, a general counter-revolution swept across Siberia, sparked by a force of 45,000 Czechoslovakian POWs. Convinced that the new Soviet government was going to hand them over to the Germans, the Czechoslovaks seized virtually the entire Trans-Siberian Railway. The regional Bolshevik government in the Far East was thrown into retreat and by mid-September all Siberia was 'White'.

The exile system was abolished at the turn of the century, but Stalin brought it back with a vengeance, expanding it into a full-blown, home-grown slave trade. He established a vast bureaucracy of resettlement programs, labour colonies, concentration camps and special psychiatric hospitals all over Russia, commonly known as the Gulag (Glavnoe Upravlenie Lagerey, or Main Administration for Camps). Its inmates – often their only 'offence' was to be Jewish or a modern artist or a high-profile Buryat, or simply to have shaken the hand of such a person – cut trees, dug canals, laid railway tracks and worked in factories in remote areas of northern and eastern Russia. A huge slice of the north-east was set aside exclusively for labour camps, and cities such as Magadan were developed as Gulag centres. It was during Stalin's rule that

Siberia became synonymous with death, and during his rule, an estimated 20 million people died in the wilds of eastern and northern Russia.

Following Stalin's death in 1953, amnesties freed up to two-thirds of the prisoners, but exile labour camps remained 'corrective' tools of the state right up until the dissolution of the USSR, in 1991. The word 'Gulag' was replaced with 'gigantomania', and the 1950s brought about a proliferation of Olympian schemes that were variously bigger, wider, taller or more powerful than anything ever seen before (and in many cases costlier, less efficient and more environmentally disastrous, too). A series of hydroelectric power plants was constructed along the Angara and Yenisey rivers to supply power for the huge *kombinaty* (plants), such as aluminium smelters and pulp mills, that sprang up in their wake. At one point, Soviet planners even proposed building a barrage of mammoth dams along the Arctic coast to reverse the flow of the rivers and flood parts of central Siberia. Fortunately, that scheme never got off the drawing board.

Shielded from foreign attention, Siberia and Arctic Russia became major centres of Cold War activity, and Novaya Zemlya and Kamchatka were used for thermonuclear testing. To attract a workforce to Siberia and the Arctic regions, the government offered salaries three times higher than those in European Russia, as well as bonus schemes, longer holidays and tax exemptions. By the late 1980s, however, wages failed to keep up with inflation, bonuses were cut and, perhaps most significantly, the work dried up. Protesting miners either went on strike or loudly voiced complaints that the central government was less interested in developing the region than in simply milking it.

The collapse of the Soviet empire has given Russia's back of beyond a greater degree of self-determination but has also left it underdeveloped, sparsely populated and short of investment capital. The region is rich in resources – oil, gas, coal, diamonds, bauxite, gold and other precious metals, fish and timber – and is, in fact, the potential saviour of Russia. However, most of this eldorado lies in remote regions, deep below the surface and securely locked in ice. How to get at it, and to whom the spoils (Moscow? The local inhabitants? Foreign investors?) are the questions that currently dominate the region. They're the same questions that have always dominated. Even now, more than 350 years after the first explorations, the northern areas of Siberia and the Russian Far East remain untamed frontier territory.

The Kola Region Early Russian incursions into the Kola region came from Novgorod, which by the 12th century was a European political and commercial centre that began expanding aggressively up Karelia's rivers and lakes to the White Sea. Today most of the north's permanent Russians are descendants of Novgorodian merchants, adventurers, hunters and fishermen, and are known as Pomory (the phrase *po more* means 'up to the sea').

The Swedes, who at the time held sway in most of present-day north-western Russia, up to and including the Kola Peninsula, began to feel the effects of the Pomory expansion. The friction, at first economic, became ostensibly religious as Swedish crusaders tried to push back the Orthodox 'heathens'. Novgorod's Prince Alexandr Nevsky is considered a Russian hero for thrashing the Swedish and Teutonic crusaders in the 1240s, putting an end to Western Christian intentions in Russia. The Norwegians were more easily persuaded to give up claims to the Kola Peninsula. For several centuries Russians, Norwegians, Finns and Swedes exploited fish, fur and the indigenous Lapp reindeer-herders on the peninsula.

The first Western European visitors to the region were Dutch and English explorers who crashed into the Arctic island of Novaya Zemlya in the 16th century. During the Time of Troubles (1606-13), a period of domestic anarchy and foreign invasions, Sweden again took over a swathe of territory from the Baltic to the White Sea.

Determined to defeat the Swedes and reach the Baltic, Peter the Great made an alliance with Poland and Denmark, and forced his way to the Gulf of Finland, pausing only to lay the foundations of St Petersburg. With his new navy, he won the Great Northern War (1700-21), winning everything back from Sweden, plus Vyborg and the Baltic coastline down to Riga. The Swedes were pushed back even further, and in 1809 they forfeited Finland.

The north rose to prominence again as a WWI supply route. An Arctic port was built at Murmansk and a rail line laid down to Petrozavodsk and St Petersburg. After the October Revolution, the Allies occupied Murmansk and Arkhangelsk for two years, advancing south almost to Petrozavodsk.

Stalin invaded Finland and the Baltic states in 1939-40, confident from his secret pact with Hitler that they were 'his'. Finland, having achieved independence after the revolution, fought the Red Army to a standstill but had to give up its entire Arctic coastline and Vyborg. Hoping to retrieve this territory, Finland allied itself with Germany during WWII, and Hitler launched attacks along the entire Soviet-Finnish border. Murmansk again became a supply port, a lifeline from the Allies to Russia's defenders, and was later bombed to rubble by the Allies lest it become a Nazi stronghold.

Arctic Canada

The Arctic Archipelago of northern Canada has been inhabited for anywhere between 4000 and 8000 years (see Inuit History in this chapter), but the earliest known inhabitants of the Northwest Territories, the Dene (Athapaskans) are thought to have arrived between 10,000 and 40,000 years ago.

The Vikings were the first Europeans to see northern Canada, landing on Helluland (Baffin Island) and Markland (Labrador) around 1000 AD. After the Norse influence vanished from the region, Europeans concentrated on exploring the area and finding the legendary Northwest Passage – a sea passage between the Atlantic and Pacific, via the Arctic Ocean – which would shorten

the trip to and from the Far East and its trade riches. From 1524, British, French and Dutch adventurers joined the search and mapped the formerly uncharted region, but it wasn't until 1906 – after 330 years of effort – that Norwegian Roald Amundsen successfully navigated the Northwest Passage (Robert McClure had done most of it from west to east in 1854, but not in a single ship; after walking part of the way, he hitched back to England with Sir Edward Belcher). The route was later used by military vessels, but is now largely ignored, except as a summer cargo route and a thrilling icebreaker cruise for tourists (for the whole story on the Northwest Passage, see the Arctic History & Exploration chapter).

In the 1840s Robert Campbell, a Hudson's Bay Company trader, explored the region that is now north-western Canada, followed by fur traders, prospectors and whalers. With the prospect of wealth from whaling and the fur trade, Europeans, such as Alexander Mackenzie, began to explore in earnest during the 18th and 19th centuries. In their wake came missionaries who built churches, schools and hospitals. Until 1870, when the Canadian government took over, administration of the territories was shared between the Hudson's Bay Company and the British government.

In 1870 the area that would become the Yukon was amalgamated into the region known as the Northwest Territories (NWT), but real changes didn't take hold until 1896 when gold was discovered along a tributary of the Trondoick River (now Klondike) near what became Dawson City. As you can imagine, all hell broke loose, and the ensuing gold rush attracted hopefuls from around the world. Dawson's population boomed to around 38,000 – quite a bit higher than today's 1300 – and transport routes opened up. Towns sprang up overnight as service centres for the rough-and-ready prospectors, and it was the merchants, suppliers, entertainers and prostitutes who raked in most of the money. In 1898 the Yukon became a separate territory with Dawson as the capital, but after the gold ran out and the Alaska

Highway was constructed, the territorial focus shifted to Whitehorse, and in 1953 the capital was moved south.

Through the 19th and most of the 20th centuries, the Canadian government was primarily interested in the eastern Arctic for its mineral wealth and strategic position. Following the discovery of oil in the 1920s near Fort Norman, a territorial government was set up. In the 1930s the discovery of radium around Great Bear Lake marked the beginning of more rapid change and 20th century development. When gold was discovered near Yellowknife in 1934, the town's population swelled, and by 1967 it had become the capital of the Northwest Territories (which at that stage still included Nunavut). WWII brought airfields and weather stations. In the 1950s the Canadian government implemented health, welfare and education programs, and additional social schemes in the 1960s forcibly resettled most of the Inuit people in villages, where the government could keep an eye on them.

In 1982, 56% of NWT voters approved splitting the Northwest Territories in two to create a homeland for the Inuit people, which was followed by several years of wrangling over where to draw the boundaries and split up the bureaucracy and infrastructure. In 1993, the Canadian Parliament approved the Nunavut Land Claims Agreement Act, which paved the way for the official creation of Nunavut in 1999.

Unlike Nunavut, which is largely populated by the Inuit, the new Northwest Territories population of 40,000 is split almost equally between Native and non-Native people, and in addition to English and French, seven local languages are spoken. As a result, choosing a name for the new territory has been a real bone of contention. A 1996 government survey revealed that over 90% of the people preferred to stick with the old name, but some political factions continue to agitate for change. Many aboriginal names have been suggested, causing animosity between groups. One faction – apparently fed up with the entire question – advocates calling it Bob.

Alaska

Most indigenous Alaskans (the Athapaskans, Aleuts, and the coastal Tlingit, Haida and Tsimshian tribes) are descended from people who migrated over the Bering Land Bridge, while the Inuit peoples (the Yup'ik and Inupiat of the Bering Sea and Arctic Ocean coasts) arrived by boat much later (see Inuit History earlier in this chapter).

Early Spanish, British and French explorers touched on Alaska's coasts, but Russia became the dominant power. Russian fur merchants overran the Aleutian Islands and Kodiak Island in the 18th century, competing murderously between themselves and nearly annihilating the peaceful Aleuts.

When the fur colonies were depleted, the Russians moved to the south-east, ruthlessly subduing the Tlingit peoples and using the substantial profits from the fur trade to turn Sitka into 'an American Paris in Alaska'.

By the 1860s, the Napoleonic Wars had left the Russians seriously overextended, and the fur industry was declining. As a result, in 1867 Russia signed a treaty with the US Secretary of State William H Seward, which sold the territory for a meagre US$7.2 million – less than 2¢ an acre. There was a public uproar over the 'foolish' purchase of 'Seward's Folly' (also nicknamed 'Walrussia' and 'Uncle Sam's Attic'), but Congress eventually approved the deal. Much to the glee of Seward and most other US citizens, the riches of remote Alaska gradually emerged: first whales, then phenomenal salmon runs and crabbing grounds, and finally, unimaginable quantities of gold and oil.

Gold-rush towns such as Juneau and Douglas sprang up in the 1880s and Circle City appeared on the banks of the Yukon River in 1893. Shortly thereafter, the town of Skagway sprang up as a launching point for 30,000 hopeful prospectors heading for the Klondike gold fields (named for the Trondoick River) immediately east of the Alaska-Yukon border. They lugged their grubstakes up the steep Chilkoot Trail into Canada, then travelled downstream by barge or bathtub to the Klondike. In the 1900s, gold was also discovered in the beach sands at Nome, turning that Seward Peninsula backwater into a booming city before the miners shifted their focus to the alluvial gold that ran through the river valleys around Fairbanks. After that rush, attention turned to the rich copper deposits around Kennicott, which is now Alaska's best-loved ghost town.

In 1913, the first territorial legislature met at Juneau, which had become the capital in 1906. During WWII, when the Japanese attacked and occupied the Aleutian islands of Attu and Kiska, the US military became a prominent presence in Alaska as thousands of personnel arrived to defend the territory.

Fearing future naval and air attacks, the military constructed the renowned Alcan (Alaska-Canada) Highway to supply its troops, and thus linked the remote territory with the rest of the USA. This above all else contributed to the post-war development of Alaska, which became the 49th state of the USA on 3 January 1959.

On Good Friday in 1964, a powerful earthquake (9.2 on the Richter scale – the strongest quake ever recorded in a populated area) hit South-Central Alaska, leaving the new state in a shambles and destroying the towns of Anchorage, Valdez, Seward and Kodiak. However, economic recovery was boosted in 1968 when massive oil deposits were discovered beside the Arctic Ocean at Prudhoe Bay.

The 1971 Alaska Native Claims Settlement Act opened the way for construction of a 1100km pipeline between Prudhoe Bay and the icefree port of Valdez, and the following boom years of pipeline construction saw rampant economically inspired population growth and the emergence of Anchorage as a fully fledged – if rather desultory – city.

For a time the Alaskan economy boomed, but the party ended in 1986 when oil prices plummeted and caused a mass exodus combined with bank failures due to a profound real estate bust. The hangover came in 1989 when the *Exxon Valdez*, under the command of Captain Joseph Hazelwood, struck a rock reef in Valdez Arm and spilled 11 million gallons of crude oil into Prince William Sound. The spill contaminated 790km of shoreline, and a massive – unimaginably expensive – clean-up effort recovered only 14% of the oil.

Although the economy has diversified since then – and grown on a par with that of the other US states – the fishing and forestry industries have just about gone belly-up, the Prudhoe Bay oil reserves continue to decline, and the oil companies are merging and laying off management and blue-collar employees. Current hopes for a brighter economic future lie in tourism, retail sales and service, and international transport.

GEOGRAPHY

Unlike Antarctica, which is a continent surrounded by oceans, the Arctic is essentially an ocean surrounded by continents and islands. Despite the fact that most of this ocean is frozen for much of the year, the presence of water has a moderating effect on the climate, and makes the Arctic regions more hospitable to human and animal life than the ice-locked Antarctic. In short, the geography of the Arctic – as well as its proximity to heavily populated regions of Europe, Asia and North America – has allowed the northern polar regions to enjoy more of the influences of the modern world than its southern counterpart.

While numerous nations have claims on bits of the Antarctic (which are recognised by no one but themselves), the lands north of the Arctic Circle are shared by eight countries: Norway, Sweden, Finland, Russia, the USA (Alaska), Canada, Denmark (Greenland) and Iceland (whose only Arctic toeholds are the tiny islands of Grímsey and Kolbeinsey).

(continued on page 29)

The North Poles

Four corresponding poles may be defined in the Arctic (and, of course, the Antarctic as well). The geographic pole and the pole of inaccessibility are relatively fixed, while the geomagnetic pole wanders slightly, depending mainly on solar influences, and the magnetic pole migrates many kilometres annually.

- Geographic North Pole (90°N) – a fixed location on the surface of the Arctic Ocean, which is the northern axis of the earth's rotation. It was first seen on 12 May 1926 from the airship *Norge*.
- Magnetic North Pole (1996 position: 78°30'N, 104°10'W) – a wandering location where conventional lines of magnetic force converge and exit vertically; the north point of a compass needle points to this pole. It was first measured by Captain James Ross on 1 June 1831 when it was on the Boothia Peninsula, and has subsequently migrated northward to near Ringnes Island.
- Geomagnetic North Pole (78°30'N, 69°W) – the north end of the axis of the geomagnetic field that surrounds the earth and extends into space as the magnetosphere. It's currently situated west of the north-west Greenland village of Qaanaaq. The aurora borealis occurs principally within a stratospheric torus of 23° around this pole.
- Northern Pole of Inaccessibility (84°03'N, 174°51'W) – this is the point on the surface of the Arctic Ocean which is most distant from land – about 1100km from the nearest coast – and is therefore (theoretically, anyway) the most difficult location to attain. It was first reached on 8 April, 1941, by I Cherevichniy, by aircraft. Although some sources claim that Sir Hubert Wilkins was in fact the first to reach this spot, in the late 1920s.

Visiting the North Poles The Geographic North Pole, the point at the northern tip of the earth's axis and about 800km north of Ellesmere Island, lies in neutral territory – an area of permanently frozen Arctic Ocean sea water without national jurisdiction. But the Magnetic North Pole, the direction to which a compass needle points, spends most of its time in Canadian territory. Its exact location, however, varies from day to day. These days, it generally hovers just north of Bathurst Island and west of Cornwallis Island at about 100°W longitude, moving in elliptical circles that can extend over 100km in a 24 hour period. In recent years, its migration has tended to be north-westward.

From Resolute, it's possible to visit both of the main poles (for a price, of course). The magnetic pole currently lies only about 500km away by air and there are frequent flights in spring and summer. The scenery is quite similar to Resolute – lots of rocks and ice – and given that there is definitely no *there* there when it comes to finding the exact location of the pole this is really just an excuse for a jaunt through the High Arctic and the chance to see your compass behave oddly.

In contrast, the Geographic North Pole more or less stays put, thankfully. Reaching the pole for most people involves a series of charter plane flights to prepositioned fuel and supplies for the 1700km journey north of Resolute. You have to really want to go, however, because weather instability means that a one hour glimpse of the top of the world can involve seven to 10 days of travel and delays, and cost C$9000 to C$14,000 per person.

And then there's the Fairbanks, Alaska, suburb called North Pole, which is nowhere near the North Pole. In fact, it isn't even north of the Arctic Circle!

Arctic Phenomena

Aurora Borealis There are few sights as mesmerising as an undulating aurora. Although these appear in many forms – pillars, streaks, wisps and haloes of vibrating light – they're most memorable when they take the form of pale curtains, wafting on a gentle breeze. Most often, the Arctic aurora appears as a faint green or light yellow or rose colour, but in periods of extreme activity it can change to bright yellow or crimson.

The visible aurora borealis is also known as the northern lights (in the southern hemisphere, the corresponding phenomenon is called the aurora australis). The aurora borealis is caused by streams of charged particles from the sun, the solar winds, flowing past and elongating the earth's magnetic field in the polar regions. Because the field curves downwards in a halo surrounding the magnetic poles, the charged particles are drawn earthward. Their interaction with electrons in the upper atmosphere (about 160km above the surface) releases the energy creating the visible aurora. During periods of high activity, a single auroral storm can produce one trillion watts of electricity with a current of one million amps. The colour variations are a product of the altitude of the storm, and the density of ions at that altitude. A white aurora suggests that storms are occurring at a range of altitudes, and the entire spectrum of colours is revealed as white light. The undulations in the aurora are due to eddies, fluctuations and changes of direction in the earth's magnetosphere, or magnetic field.

The Inuit call the lights *arsarnerit* (to play with a ball), as they were thought to be celestial ancestors playing ball with a walrus skull. It was also believed that the lights could be attracted by whistling or repelled by barking like a dog (and indeed, in some cases, this seems to be borne out). The Inuit also attach spiritual significance to the lights, and some believe that they represent the capering of unborn children; others consider them gifts from the dead to light the long polar nights or as a storehouse of events, past and future.

Although science dismisses it as imagination, many people also report that the aurora is often accompanied by a crackling or whirring sound. Don't feel unbalanced if you hear it – it's the sort of sound you'd expect to hear from such a dramatic display, and if it's an illusion it's a very convincing one.

The best time of year to catch the northern lights in most of the Arctic region is between October and March, although you may well see them as early as August in the far south. Oddly enough, Svalbard, far northern Greenland, Ellesmere Island and Franz Josef Land are actually too far north to catch the greatest activity.

Midnight Sun & Polar Night Because the earth is tilted on its axis, the polar regions are constantly facing the sun at their respective summer solstices and are tilted away from it in winter. The Arctic and Antarctic circles, at 66½° north and south latitude respectively, represent the southern and northern limits of constant daylight on the longest day of the year.

In any place north of the Arctic Circle – indeed, anywhere north of about 60°N latitude – the summer sun is never far below the horizon. Between late May and mid-August, nowhere in the region experiences true darkness and at 60°N, the first stars aren't visible until mid-August. Although many visitors initially find it difficult to sleep while the sun is shining brightly outside, most people quickly get used to it, even if that simply means joining the locals in their summer nocturnal hyperactivity.

Conversely, winters here are dark and dreary, with only a few hours of twilight to break the long polar nights. In the northernmost parts of the Arctic – Svalbard, Ellesmere Island,

Arctic Phenomena

Franz Josef Land and Avanersuaq (Greenland) – not even a twilight glow can be seen for over a month, and most far northern communities make a ritual of welcoming the sun the first time it peeks above the southern horizon. During this period, many people suffer from SAD, or 'seasonal affective disorder', which results from a deprivation of the vitamin D provided by sunlight. Its effects may be minimised by taking dosages of vitamin D (as found in cod-liver oil) or with special solar spectrum light bulbs.

Fata Morgana If the aurora inspires wonder, the Fata Morgana and related phenomena common in the polar regions may inspire a visit to a shrink. The clear and pure Arctic air means that distant features appear in focus. As a result, depth perception becomes impossible and the world takes on a strangely two-dimensional aspect in which distances are indeterminable. An amusing example of distance distortion is described in the enigmatic book *Arctic Dreams*, by Barry Lopez:

A Swedish explorer had all but completed a written description in his notebook of a craggy head-land with two unusually symmetrical valley glaciers, the whole of it a part of a large island, when he discovered what he was looking at was a walrus.

The Fata Morgana, a special type of mirage, is also common in the vast expanses of sand, ice and tundra found in the Arctic. Early explorers laid down on maps and charts careful documentation of islands, headlands and mountain ranges that were never seen again.

Fata Morganas are apparently caused by reflections off water, ice and snow, and when combined with temperature inversions, create the illusion of solid, well-defined features where there are none. On clear days along the Arctic Ocean coastlines, you may well see nonexistent archipelagos of craggy islands resting on the horizon. It's difficult indeed to convince yourself, even with an accurate map, that they aren't really there!

Also unsettling are the sightings of ships, large cities and forests where there could clearly be none. Normal visibility at sea is just under 18km, but in the Arctic, sightings of islands and other features hundreds of kilometres distant are frequently reported.

Arctic scenery in south-west Greenland

Glacier & Ice Glossary

Glaciers have forged much of the Arctic landscape and, even today, the land area in the region is dominated by ice caps, valley glaciers, icebergs and sea ice. The following is a list of terms relating to these icy phenomena:

arête – a sharp ridge between two valley glaciers

bergschrund – the crevasse at the top of a valley glacier separating the moving ice from the parent ice field

bergy bits – icebergs rising less than 5m above the surface of the sea

calving – breaking off of icebergs from tidewater glaciers

cirque – an amphitheatre-like basin scoured out by a glacier

crevasse – a fissure in moving ice, which may be hidden under snow, caused by various strains as the ice flows downhill

dead glacier – a valley glacier that stops short of the sea

erratic – a stone or boulder which clearly was transported from elsewhere, possibly by a glacier

fast ice – solid pack ice

firn limit – the level on a glacier below which the snow melts each year; the snow that remains above this limit is called firn (or névé)

frazil – needle-shaped ice crystals which form a slush in the sea

glacial flour – the fine, talcum-like silt which flows in glacial streams and is deposited in glacial river valleys; it is formed by the abrasion of ice on rock

growler – a small iceberg floating just on the surface which is difficult to see, thereby causing a hazard for ships

hanging valley – a valley formed when a tributary valley glacier flows into a larger valley glacier

horn – the sharp peak that remains after glaciers have scoured all faces of a mountain peak

hummock – a place where ice floes have piled atop one another

icecap or ice field – a stable zone of accumulation and compression of snow and ice, and a source of valley glaciers. An icecap generally covers a larger area than an ice field. When the entire interior of a landmass is covered by an icecap (as in Greenland or Antarctica), it's often called a continental glacier.

ice floe – a flat chunk of floating sea ice, normally pack ice, but it may also be a small iceberg

jökulhlaup – Icelandic word meaning 'glacial burst'; refers to a sudden and often catastrophic release of water from a glacier, caused by a broken ice dam or by glacial lifting due to volcanic activity beneath the ice

moraine – deposit of material transported by a glacier; rock and silt pushed ahead of the glacier is called a terminal moraine, that deposited along the sides is a lateral moraine, and that deposited down the centre of a glacier is a medial moraine

moulin – French word meaning 'mill'; refers to a pond or stream inside a glacier, often evidenced by a deep round hole in the ice

névé – hard granular snow on the upper part of a glacier which hasn't yet turned to ice

nilas – thin crust of sea ice that moves up and down with wave action but doesn't break

nunatak – Greenlandic word referring to a mountain peak that protrudes through a glacier or icecap

pack ice – floating ice formed by frozen sea water, which often creates an impenetrable barrier to navigation

piedmont glacier – a slumped glacier at the foot of a steep slope, caused by the confluence of two or more valley glaciers

polynya – Russian word referring to an area of open water surrounded by pack ice

postholing – what hikers do when crossing fields of rotten or melting snow, sinking up to their thighs at every step

roche moutonée – French word for 'sheep rock'; refers to a glacier-scoured boulder, often resembling sheep grazing on the mountainsides

sastrugi – wind-blown furrows in snow

suncup – a mushroom-shaped snow formation caused by irregular melting on sunny slopes

tarn – a lake in a cirque

tide crack – a crack separating sea ice from the shore, caused by the rise and fall of tides

tidewater glacier – a valley glacier that flows into the sea and calves icebergs

valley glacier – a river of ice which flows downward through a valley from an ice field or icecap

(continued from page 24)

Alaska

With an area of 1.53 million sq km, Alaska is the largest and least densely populated state in the USA, and with 17 of the country's 20 highest peaks (including the highest, Mt McKinley at 6096m); over 5000 glaciers and icecaps (one of which, the Bering, is larger than Switzerland); and the third longest river in North America (the Yukon), it's a land of superlatives in a country known for its self-proclaimed superlatives. The latitude ranges from 52°N (the same as London!) at Adak Island in the Aleutians to 72°N at Point Barrow (the same as Nordkapp, Norway), and the longitude, from 130°W (the same as the Gambier Islands in French Polynesia) at Hyder to 172°E (the same as Christchurch, New Zealand) at Attu Island in the Aleutians. Even Anchorage lies as far west as Papeete, in French Polynesia.

The state is conveniently divided into six major geographic regions. The panhandle, commonly known as 'Southeast', is a narrow forested strip of mountains and islands along the eastern shore of the Gulf of Alaska. The mostly mountainous birch and spruce-forested South-Central region includes Alaska's largest city, Anchorage, and also the Kenai Peninsula and the Prince William Sound area. South-west Alaska is a largely treeless region dominated by the volcanoes and islands of the 1500km-long Aleutian Range, as well as rugged Kodiak Island. The Bering Sea coast region takes in the flat, marshy and lake ridden bog lands of the Yukon and Kuskokwim deltas, while the Arctic coast/North Slope, which stretches from the Seward Peninsula to the Canadian border, is mainly more of the same, but flatter and even harsher. Finally, the vast Inter-ior, which takes in nearly half the area of the state, is characterised mainly by birch and taiga forest dotted with thousands of lovely lakes and cut by countless wild rivers. (Most of the Arctic areas covered in this book lie within these last two regions.)

Canada

Canada, which measures 7730km from east to west, is the world's second largest country, but it's only neighbour is the USA, with which it shares a 5000km border (including the border with Alaska, in the north-west). Canada's northern territories make up a vast tract of land stretching from the 60th parallel to within 800km of the North Pole, and bordered by the Atlantic on the east and the Arctic Ocean on the north and west.

In 1999 this vast region underwent a major political change with the creation of the 2.2 million sq km territory of Nunavut, which was carved off the Northwest Territories, leaving the latter with 1.17 million sq km in the western Canadian Arctic. The designation of Canada's three Arctic entities – the Northwest Territories, Nunavut and the Yukon – as territories, as opposed to provinces, prevents their relatively small populations from having a disproportionate voice in the Canadian Parliament (and as if to reinforce their location in the country, their shared telephone area code of 867 spells out T-O-P on the dial!).

Much of the Northwest Territories (the former District of Mackenzie) lies on the formation known as the Canadian Shield, a vast glaciated plain covered with lakes and taiga forests and rich in deposits of oil, gas, diamonds and gold. The territory is home to the mighty Mackenzie River (known to the Athapaskans as the Dene, or De Cho – the Big River), which flows 1800km from Great Slave Lake in the south-east to the Beaufort Sea near Inuvik. Near its mouth, it fans out into one of the world's largest deltas, with hundreds of channels and islands covering an area of 16,000 sq km.

Most of mainland Nunavut (the former District of Keewatin) lies on the Canadian Shield, but the territory's prominent geographical feature is the vast Arctic Archipelago (the former District of Franklin), which is made up of enormous islands: Baffin, Ellesmere, Victoria, Banks, Prince of Wales, Somerset, Southampton, Devon, Cornwallis, Bathurst, Melville and dozens of others.

The Yukon, a triangular slice wedged between the Northwest Territories and Alaska, is bordered on the south by British Columbia and on the north by the Beaufort Sea of the Arctic Ocean. The territory is covered by several dramatic mountain ranges including the Wrangell-St Elias range, which features Canada's highest peak, Mt Logan (5950m).

Canada's Arctic climatic regions also extend southward from Nunavut along the shores of Hudson Bay into the northern portions of Manitoba and Ontario (which are both home to substantial numbers of polar bears), and farther east, into northern Quebec and Labrador (where the population is dominated by several Inuit groups).

Greenland

Greenland, with a total area of 2,175,600 sq km and a 40,000km coastline, is the world's largest island – over 2½ times the size of the second largest island, New Guinea, and 52 times the size of mainland Denmark. It's also the northernmost country in the world. Its southernmost point, Cape Farewell (Nunaap Isua), lies at 59° 45' north latitude while the northernmost point of the mainland, Cape Morris Jesup, is at 83° 20' north. Oodaaq Island, a tiny scrap of rock off the north coast, is the world's most northerly land at 83° 40' north.

Although Greenland is vast, 1.8 million sq km (that's all but 375,600 sq km of the total area) lies beneath a sheet of ice up to 3000m thick – a burden so great that the island's interior has sunk beneath its weight into an immense concave basin that reaches a depth of 360m below sea level. This vast ice sheet, which can be spotted from trans-Atlantic flights, measures 2500km from north to south and up to 1000km from east to west. It contains over four million cubic km of ice, which amounts to one billion litres of water for every person on earth. If Greenland were to melt, the global sea level would rise an estimated 6m!

Around its edges, this icecap spills down in thousands of valley glaciers, which have sculpted the coast into deep fjords and dramatic landscapes. The largest, the Humboldt Glacier in the north-west, measures 120m high by 80km wide. All but the southern quarter of Greenland lies north of the Arctic Circle. In the far north, the sun is visible for nearly three months during the summer but nowhere on the island is there darkness between late May and mid-July. During midwinter, southern Greenland experiences several hours of real daylight. On the Arctic Circle, which passes just south of Kangerlussuaq, the sun doesn't rise at all on 21 December. The far north experiences true polar night with several weeks of constant darkness and two months of little more than a hazy twilight before the sun returns and builds up to its summer marathon.

Greenland's nearest neighbour is Canada, whose Ellesmere Island lies only 26km away across Kennedy Channel from the north-west coast. At its nearest point, Iceland is about 300km away across Denmark Strait and Svalbard (Norway) lies about 500km east of the north-east coast.

Geologically, Greenland and neighbouring Iceland could scarcely be farther apart. While Iceland's landscape is the world's youngest and most dynamic, Greenland's is

How the Greenland Ice Cap was formed

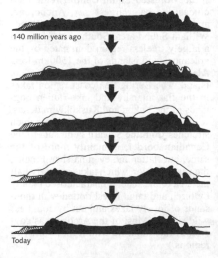

140 million years ago

Today

the oldest yet discovered and you don't have to be a geologist to wonder at its compressed, scraped, ground and tortured surface. The Illua formation near Nuuk dates back at least 3.7 billion years and when the airport was constructed at Nuuk, the tarmac was blasted out of metamorph-ic rock that had been around for over three billion years.

Norway

With a land area of 323,878 sq km, Norway stretches along the western coastal strip of the Scandinavian peninsula and shares borders with Sweden, Finland and Russia. The northern one-third of the country – which includes most of the county of Nordland, plus Troms, Finnmark and the Svalbard archipelago – lies north of the Arctic Circle. The Nordland coast is indented with hundreds of relatively small fjords and flanked by numerous islands, including the wedge-shaped archipelagos of Lofoten and Vesterålen. Farther north, the coastline alternates between vast fjords and great, nearly treeless peninsulas. Mountain ranges, some capped with Europe's largest glaciers and ice fields, cover more than half of the land mass, and the only relatively level area is the lake-studded and taiga-forested Finnmarksvidda Plateau, which occupies most of southern Finnmark.

Svalbard, 1000km north of the mainland, is about the size of Ireland and extends from 74°N at Bjørnøya in the south to over 80°N on northern Spitsbergen and Nordaustlandet. Svalbard is gripped in sea ice for most of the year and much of the interior is covered in glaciers and ice fields.

Sweden

Sweden covers an area of 450,000 sq km and measures over 1500km from north to south. This extent provides some climatic diversity, but the landscape is derived mainly from the most recent glacial periods. As a result, most of the country is covered by lakes (about 100,000 of them, by the latest count) and forests, which are dominated by Norway spruce, Scots pine and birch. In the far north, however, the trees thin out

into a taiga landscape. A prominent mountainous spine along the Norwegian border forms a natural frontier between the two countries, with the most dramatic fells rising in Sweden's far north-west.

Swedish geopolitical divisions are rather complicated, but in general, the country is divided into three regions: Götaland in the south, Svealand in the centre, and Norrland in the north. Regional administration is based on the 23 *län* (counties) plus the northernmost region, which is known as Lappland.

Finland

Finland, with an area of 338,000 sq km, is the seventh largest country in Europe, and the Arctic portion shares borders with Sweden, Norway and Russia. Much of the country, including Arctic Finland, is dominated by water: ponds, marshes, muskeg bogs, rivers, creeks, rapids, waterfalls, and most promin-ently, 187,888 lakes (at least that's the official number). Altogether, these inland waters cover about 10% of the country. Approximately 70% of Finland is covered by forest – the highest proportion in the world – but there are no real mountainous areas. The highest hills, or *tunturi*, are in the far north, adjacent to the highlands of northern Norway and Sweden. The highest point, Halti, in the far north-west, rises to only 1328m.

Russia

In the north, Russia faces six seas of the Arctic Ocean, which are created by five major island groups off the northern shore. Norway's Svalbard archipelago, and the Russian archipelagos of Franz Josef Land (Zemlya Franca-Iosifa) and Novaya Zemlya create the Barents Sea, while the Kola Peninsula encloses a large inlet known as the White Sea. The rest of the northern Russian coastline (which is commonly known as the Northeast Passage) stretches eastward across Asia along the coastlines of the Kara, Laptev, East Siberian and Chukchi seas, which are created by the archipelagos of Novaya Zemlya, Severnaya Zemlya, the New Siberian Islands (Novosibirskye Ostrova) and Wrangel Island (Ostrov Vrangelya).

The European portion of Arctic Russia has a short border with Norway and a longer one with Finland. In the Far East, the Chukotka Peninsula reaches out and almost touches Alaska's Seward Peninsula (in fact, the Russian island of Big Diomede and Alaska's Little Diomede lie only 3km apart, across the International Dateline), while the vast Kamchatka Peninsula dangles between the Bering Sea and the Sea of Okhotsk (both of which belong to the Pacific Ocean).

Thanks to the final gasp of the North Atlantic Gulf Stream, the vegetation of northwestern Russia from the Kola to the Taymyr peninsulas is characterised mainly by low coniferous forest known as taiga. In the far west, the trees can grow to a respectable size (although environmental contamination creates big problems for any sort of vegetation there), but as one moves eastward, the trees diminish in size and eventually give way to the tundra plains that dominate all of north-eastern Russia and the various archipelagos.

All the major rivers of northern Russia – the Pechora, Ob, Yenisey, Lena and Kolyma – flow northward into the Arctic Ocean, making them of little use for transportation. In spring when the weather begins to warm up and the ice melts in the south, the northern coasts remain blocked by ice. Because the waters can't be flushed out to sea, they back up into the vast swamps and marshes that cover much of western Siberia (one of these covers about one-third the area of the USA!).

CLIMATE
Alaska
As would be expected, the Alaskan Interior experiences greater climatic extremes than the milder coastal areas.

The south-eastern portions of the state and much of the Prince William Sound area experience cool and rainy weather in summer and cooler and snowy weather in winter. Farther west, on the Alaska Peninsula, Kodiak Island and the Aleutian Islands, the weather is more blustery, but still very mild temperature-wise.

The Anchorage area experiences a more stable climate, with colder and longer winters and generally warmer but shorter summers than the southern coastal regions. In the Interior, winters are much colder (-40°C isn't at all uncommon) but shorter, while summers are generally quite hot and lovely (30°C is a common high temperature). Around the Bering Sea and Arctic coasts, the winters range from bitterly cold to relatively mild, while summer days may be anywhere from cool to mild.

In high alpine areas, winters are generally cold and snowy, and in summer, any sort of weather can be expected at any time.

Canada
Most of Canada enjoys four distinct seasons, all of which occur right across the country, but it's the latitude that determines the definitions of these 'seasons'. That is, springtime on Ontario's Niagara Peninsula will bring wildflowers, new greenery and temperatures approaching 15°C to 20°C, while in Whitehorse, Iqaluit and Yellowknife, springtime means daytime temperatures marginally above 0°C, when the snow begins to melt. In Ontario, autumn is a two month burst of colour, while in the north, it's a two week period of yellow birch or red tundra (the latter signifies ripe blueberries!).

Along the US border, particularly in southern British Columbia and southern Ontario, summer temperatures can climb to between 25°C to 30°C, but each year, a few days even see temperatures in the 30°Cs. The regions between Manitoba and central British Columbia receive the warmest summer temperatures as well as the most sunshine, while the Atlantic and Pacific coasts receive up to 2500mm of precipitation annually (mostly in the winter months).

Summers in the Yukon, Northwest Territories and Nunavut can be pleasantly warm and enjoy the added benefit of extremely long daylight hours. On the other hand, Canadian winters are long, especially in the Arctic regions, where the icy weather can hang on from late September to early May.

In fact, over two-thirds of the country sees average January temperatures of -18°C or lower.

Greenland

Although most other North Atlantic regions enjoy the wet and tempering effects of the Gulf Stream, Greenland misses out entirely

and experiences a more continental climate. In summer, maximum daytime temperatures average between 10°C and 18°C in the south and between 5°C and 10°C in the north. In winter in the far south, temperatures of -20°C can be expected but, farther north and on the inland ice, the legendary bitter temperatures of the Arctic become

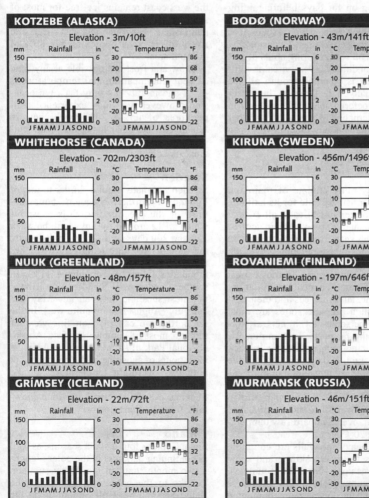

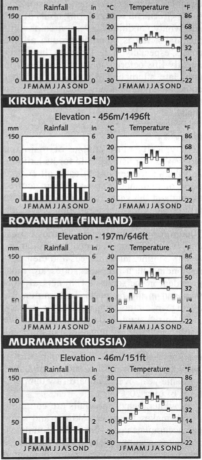

reality. It's not unusual for the thermometer to hover at a chilling -40°C for weeks. The good news is that the coldest days are also the clearest and calmest, and the seemingly unearthly beauty of such an Arctic winter day (or night!) is indescribable.

At times, the south-western coast blocks warm air masses moving up from North America and captures storm systems that seem to hang on for days before raining themselves out. This is especially true around the Nuuk area, which experiences Greenland's foulest weather. Occasionally, south Greenland sees enduring bouts of wet and windy conditions. Even on calm summer days, fog is common around all the coasts, especially in the far south, but it frequently lifts before noon, or doesn't roll in until late afternoon. In short, the weather could do anything at any time; in July, you may see anything from snow to 25°C in the shade.

Norway

The typically rainy climate of mainland Norway is surprisingly mild for its latitude, and thanks to the Gulf Stream, all coastal ports of mainland Norway remain icefree throughout the year. The coastal mountain ranges block the moisture-laden prevailing south-westerly winds, and can reach 5000mm annually. Bergen is the wettest city, with 2250mm of annual precipitation.

The continental influences and their corresponding high pressure zones are most prevalent in the south-east, in central Norway and in the far north. In summer, the average maximum temperatures for July are 16°C in the south and around 11°C in the north. However, summer temperature extremes are also possible, even in the Arctic region; in July 1998, the temperature in Narvik rose to over 30°C and in August of the same year, even Svalbard saw temperatures of over 20°C.

In winter, heavy snowfalls are common, which makes for superb skiing, and snow can accumulate up to 10m in the mountains. However, accumulations of 2m to 3m are more usual in the lower, more populated

areas. In January, the average maximum temperature in the south is 1°C and in the north, -3°C. It can get much colder, however; in January 1999, the temperature in Kirkenes dropped for a short time to a decidedly chilly -56°C.

Most of Svalbard enjoys a brisk polar desert climate, and receives only 200mm to 300mm of precipitation annually. Although the west coast remains ice-free for most of summer, pack ice hovers just north of the main island year-round and vast sheets and rivers of ice cover approximately 60% of the land area.

Snow and frost are possible at any time of year; the mean annual temperature is -4°C, and in July it's only 6°C. On occasion, however, you may experience temperatures of up to 20°C or higher. In January, on the other hand, the mean temperature is -16°C, but temperatures of -30°C aren't uncommon.

Sweden

Sweden's climate is quite similar to that of Finland. In northern Sweden, about one-third of the precipitation falls as snow, which sticks around for anywhere between 150 and 200 days of the year. In the south, the monthly average temperature reaches about 17°C in July, while in the Arctic mountains it rarely rises above 11°C. In southern and central Sweden, you'll have the most sunshine between late May and late July (August can be quite wet). In the far north, you can plan on fine weather through most of summer (in fact, Abisko National Park in Arctic Sweden enjoys the most hours of sunshine in the country), but note that overnight temperatures in the higher mountain areas can drop below freezing, even in summer, and June snowfalls aren't that uncommon.

Finland

Finland enjoys four distinct seasons, as well as continuing darkness in the polar night to a two month 'day' in the Arctic summer. Thanks to the tempering effects of the Baltic Sea and the Gulf Stream along the

Norwegian coast, Finland's climate is, on average, much warmer than in other places of similar latitude, such as Siberia, Greenland and Alaska.

Naturally, the winters are cold, but it's generally dry and not as uncomfortable as one might expect. In the southern part of the country, snow first falls in October and melts by the end of March, but in the Arctic regions, snow may fall as early as September and linger until late May. In higher altitudes in the northernmost regions, snow may last even into late June.

Summer sees hot spells and weeks of little rain, although temperatures can be as low as 10°C at any time in summer, and freak snowstorms have occurred as late as June. Occasionally, however, Finland experiences the highest daytime temperatures in Europe (normally in July or August), and in January the mercury may rise as high as 5°C. In general, however, yearly averages follow a logical curve: the shorter the nights, the warmer the days, and vice versa.

Russia

The interior portions of Arctic Russia enjoy a continental climate and experience climatic extremes, with hot sultry summers and bitterly cold winters. However, along the Arctic Ocean coast and in the islands, summers are cool and short, and winters cold but relatively dry.

Though Kola Peninsula winters are bitter, the Gulf Stream, which sporadically affects the area, creates changeable conditions in Murmansk. Average temperatures in Petrozavodsk are only about 5°C lower than St Petersburg during all seasons, while Murmansk and Apatity can be wintry as early as the first week in September.

The maritime effects along Russia's Pacific coast cause Kamchatka (and to a lesser extent, Chukotka) to experience milder and stormier conditions year-round.

ENVIRONMENT & ECOLOGY

To many, mention of the Arctic environment summons up images of frigid winds screaming over snow-clad mountains and barren rocks, months of complete darkness when the sun never appears over the horizon, temperatures that seldom rise above freezing, and endless expanses of ice-choked sea. To an extent, this is true, but the Arctic covers a vast geographical area, and it boasts a wide and diverse array of habitats.

At the fringes of the Arctic is the taiga, vast forests of spruce and birch that are home to a variety of bird and animal species (see the Arctic Nature Guide). North of this lies the tundra, great treeless swaths of land that are home to sedges, herbs and dwarf shrubs. These meadows are often boggy, and blaze with colour each summer as saxifrage and Arctic poppies bloom in carpets of yellow, red and pink. Farther north again is the Arctic Basin, with its frozen sea fringed with a polar desert of bare, shattered bedrock and barren gravel plains. And throughout the region rise vast ranges of mountains – great jagged spines of rock that have been gouged and carved by glaciers and weathered over the centuries by the wind, ice and rain.

Yet even in the most inhospitable and barren of places, there is often life. Lichens paint bare rock with patches of green, yellow and red, and seals and polar bears hunt for food in the fertile waters that lie under the sea ice that stretches down from the North Pole. Because the Arctic is so varied, so is its range of inhabitants. The seas teem with plankton, which provide the basis for all marine life in the north. Fish and shellfish have adapted to the cooler polar seas to take advantage of this wealth of food, and in turn, they become prey for walruses and seals. And at the very top of the food web is the largest carnivore in the world – the magnificent polar bear, which is as much at home swimming in the sea as it is lumbering across hundreds of kilometres of sea ice hummocks.

On land, the diverse plant life provides food for some large herbivores, such as reindeer (known as caribou in North America), which are superbly adapted for travelling across snow and soft, marshy ground.

They feed on a variety of tundra plants and, in winter, they scrape the snow from rocks in search of lichens. Another impressive tundra beast is the muskox, which has long, thick hair to combat the polar cold and bony horns that form a formidable deterrent to predators. Wolves and foxes stalk these herds, as well as taking smaller mammals like hares, ground squirrels, beavers and lemmings.

Besides the animals that are permanently resident in the Arctic, there are many seasonal visitors. Birds flock north in their millions to breed, and to take advantage of the brief summer, when there is plentiful food and a rich diversity of nesting sites. However, the Arctic can be a cruel, as well as a welcoming, host. Sudden storms, early winters and unpredictable weather can mean an unsuccessful breeding season. Humans can also have an impact on this harsh environment, and in places where oil has been spilled or factories built, the damage caused might take many centuries to repair. Despite the variety of life in the Arctic, the environment is a fragile one, and it takes very little to destroy its delicate balance.

Wilderness Pollution

Pollutants can reach the Arctic in a number of ways. Many rivers, particularly in Russia, are flanked by factories or other industrial sites that pump waste directly into them. This, along with pesticides and other agricultural chemicals that find their way into the drainage system, eventually ends up in the sea. The Arctic Ocean sits in an enclosed basin, which means any contaminants deposited there tend to persist. Once in the water, pollutants like heavy metals and PCBs enter the food web, becoming more concentrated as they pass from plankton to fish to top-level predators like seals and bears. Elevated levels of man-made contaminants have been found in birds and animals throughout the Arctic, and even in human milk. It is not known what the long-term effects of these pollutants will be, although there is some suggestion that they reduce breeding efficiency and compromise

the immune systems of the young, leaving them more vulnerable to disease.

Perhaps more obvious than the sinister but largely invisible contamination of the oceans is the pollution of the land. Around Nikel, Monchegorsk and Norilsk in north-western Russia, some areas have been designated 'technogenic barrens', where high levels of sulphur dioxide from copper and nickel processing plants have destroyed the natural vegetation surrounding them.

In addition, the huge oil and gas reserves in the Arctic mean that accidents are inevitable. In 1989, the tanker *Exxon Valdez* spilled some 11 million gallons of heavy crude oil into the environmentally sensitive Prince William Sound in Alaska. The resulting oil slick smeared along 790km of shoreline, killing birds, fish and marine mammals. Because salmon stocks were damaged, the people who relied on fishing for their livelihood were also affected. In some cases, the clean-up operation did more harm than good, and some beaches remain sterile and barren.

Another pollution problem in the north is Arctic haze. The haze comprises largely sulphates, soot and dust, and most of it originates in Eurasia and is carried high in the atmosphere to the Arctic. Travellers to the north in spring and summer may notice a brown-yellow sheen in what should be clear blue skies.

The Nuclear Threat

Radioactivity in the far north comes from events within and outside the Arctic. The major source of human-produced radioactivity came from the testing of nuclear weapons. Novaya Zemlya in Russia was used for the detonation of a number of weapons in the 1950s and 1960s, and underground nuclear tests were also carried out in Amchitka Island in Alaska. Weapons production plants at Mayak, Krasnoyarsk and Tomsk south of the Russian Arctic have also introduced large quantities of nuclear waste into the environment, some of which has been transported through the drainage system into the Kara Sea.

The Chernobyl explosion of 1986 also spewed a lethal cocktail of radionuclides into the environment – including radiocaesium, iodine-131, caesium-137 and strontium-90. The radioactive cloud was carried by winds to the Baltic states, then to Scandinavia, and the Russian Arctic. There was concern that the lichen-reindeer-human food chain was compromised, although no part of the Arctic was seriously contaminated. This had major health and financial implications for peoples like the Sami, who rely heavily on reindeer for subsistence. Future problems may result from the fact that Russia has scuttled a number of decommissioned nuclear-powered submarines off the coast of Novaya Zemlya. Although there is no suggestion that any of these are currently leaking, it is not inconceivable that they will do so in the future.

Besides weapons testing and accidents, nuclear reprocessing plants in Europe (where plutonium is recovered from spent nuclear fuel) are also a source of radioactive contamination. In Europe, three reprocessing plants pose a threat to the Arctic, because they are located where ocean currents transport the contaminants northward. These are Sellafield and Dounreay in the UK and La Hague in France, although since the 1970s, levels have declined dramatically.

Giants of the Sea

Whaling has been a way of life for the indigenous peoples of the Arctic for thousands of years. Commercial whaling by Europeans is also an ancient tradition, and there are communities in the Faroe Islands (where the controversial *grindadráp* or pilot whale drive is still carried out) and Norway that insist the current international ban on whaling is destroying their cultures.

Although whaling was a successful, if dangerous, industry for many years, it was only in the 19th century that it really began to expand. The development of the mounted harpoon in the 1860s by a whaler named Sven Foyn meant that more whales could be caught – previously, whales were shot, but

their bodies sometimes sank before the ships could reach them. Temperate-water and Antarctic stocks were quickly eradicated, and the whaling ships began to move farther and farther north. In Newfoundland and in places like Whitby on the north coast of England, whaling became an important source of employment, with entire communities being built around it.

The large baleen whales, particularly the blubber-rich, slow-swimming right whales and bowheads, were targeted first, with blues and greys next. Grey whale stocks in the Pacific were wiped out in the 18th century, and the Atlantic populations almost went the same way in the 19th and 20th centuries. However, the grey whale is the success story of the cetacean world. It received International Whaling Commission protection in 1946, and numbers immediately began to increase. Although some greys are still harvested each year by indigenous peoples, the population seems to have reached pre-exploitation numbers.

Whether the international ban on commercial whaling should be lifted is a contentious issue. Many marine biologists agree that some species of whale are no longer at risk, and even that some are more numerous now than they were prior to the golden age of whaling. Whaling cultures argue that they should be allowed to resume whaling in order to preserve their heritage and so that they can be independent of southern welfare hand-outs. Indigenous peoples are exempted from the whaling moratorium, which the Faroese and Norwegian communities regard as unfair.

There is no easy answer. Perhaps the most salient question that should be asked is not 'can the whale population withstand hunting?' or 'will whaling further damage the ecological balance?' but 'is whaling humane?'. Although exploding harpoon heads can kill whales quickly, death is not instant and can be protracted and painful. Killing an animal is one thing, but causing it distress and suffering as it dies is another matter entirely.

Seals & Sealing

Like whaling, sealing is an ancient tradition. For many indigenous people, a seal kill means meat for food, blubber for fuel, skin for clothes, tents and blankets, sinews for sewing and sled traces, and teeth and bones for needles, knives, tools and even toys.

European cultures have also killed seals for subsistence, although commercial exploitation came later. Northern fur seals were decimated in Alaska's Pribilof Islands in the 19th century, while populations of harp and hooded seals came under serious threat in the Atlantic simultaneously.

Commercial sealing was halted in the 1980s, partly because the populations were declining and furs were becoming increasingly expensive, and partly because public opinion objected to the notion of pups being 'knocked down' with clubs. Today, virtually no commercial sealing takes place, although some subsistence sealing is permitted for indigenous peoples.

A greater threat for seals, however, is the fishing industry. Fish stocks are declining all over the world, and while fishing boats often blame the seals, the seals doubtless would blame the fishing boats. Not only is there less food for seals, but they often become entangled in fishing nets and drown. Seals are curious animals, and brightly coloured nets or other gear interests them. It is not uncommon to see seals with plastic looped around necks or flippers, which might either bite into their skin and cause infections, or reduce their hunting ability and cause them to starve. It is not known how many seals die each year from entanglement, but the number is likely to be high.

The increase of pollutants in the food chain is also problematic for seals. In Greenland and Canada, increased levels of heavy metals and PCBs have been detected in seal livers and blubber, which have a negative impact on their general health. It was suggested that the phocine distemper that killed so many harbour seals in northern Europe was aggravated by environmental contamination that compromised the seals' immune systems.

Oil spills also pose a risk to marine mammals. Seals have a layer of blubber to insulate them from the cold, but fur seals and sea otters rely on fur. When their fur becomes oiled, the animals lose heat and can die of hypothermia. When they try to groom away the oil, they ingest it, and can be poisoned.

Tourism in the North

These days, people are more interested in seeing whales, seals and other Arctic animals in their natural environment than in hunting them. Each year, thousands of visitors travel north, keen to see this magnificent wilderness for themselves. Tourism in the Arctic, however, has its negative points. First, there is the issue as to whether human presence disturbs the birds or animals they have come to see – either because they frighten them away from breeding or feeding sites, or because creatures like polar bears become used to humans, resulting in encounters that can be lethal (usually for the bears).

There is also the problem that the Arctic vegetation is extremely sensitive, and a footprint on the tundra or muskeg might remain for literally hundreds of years. In addition, these visitors need an infrastructure to accommodate them – roads across the permafrost, air strips and heliports if they travel by plane or helicopter, hotels or camp sites, and imported food and fuel supplies. And there is also the local population to be considered; what impact will these visitors have on traditional lifestyles?

Yet, despite all this, many people feel that tourism has a place in the far north. Few who experience the fragile beauty of the Arctic are unmoved by it, and hopefully, they will become ambassadors for its continued survival. Only with awareness of the importance of this vast, diverse and fascinating region will it be safe from potentially harmful development. Public opinion is a powerful force in world politics, and it is public opinion that will speak out against careless exploitation and industry in these northern wildernesses in the future.

ARCTIC NATIONAL PARKS

Although they may seem redundant in the Arctic wilderness, the region does include a range of spectacular national parks.

Alaska

Denali Although it lies south of the Arctic Circle, Denali National Park and its centrepiece, Mt McKinley, is Alaska's contribution to the 'overloved-US-national-park' syndrome. It may be lovely – the wildlife and scenery are truly spectacular – but with well over a million visitors each season (June to August), you'll need a long fuse to cope with the crowds, the queues, and the reservations system. If you do manage to get a camp site, a backcountry permit or a seat on the shuttle bus to the Eielson Visitor Center or Wonder Lake, count yourself very lucky indeed. In fact, the best time to visit is probably on or immediately after Labor Day weekend (the first weekend in September), when you're taking risks with the weather, but when the summer visitors have gone, tundra turns into a carpet of brilliant colours and the bears are fat and happy. You'll find guidelines and information on the Web site www.nps.gov/dena.

Gates of the Arctic Thanks to its inaccessibility, Gates of the Arctic has escaped the ravages of Denali, but it's every bit as scenic and inspiring. Most people fly in via Bettles for hiking, rafting or canoeing, but you can also undertake several hikes from roads leading west from the Dalton Highway. For information, call up the Web site www.nps.gov/gaar.

Kobuk Valley This true wilderness national park is best-known for its 65 sq km of Arctic sand dunes, which rise south of the Kobuk River. Most visitors to the park are participating in expensive commercial river floats or cross-country treks.

Noatak National Preserve The vast Noatak National Preserve protects the largest wilderness river basin in North America. In summer, 200,000 migrating caribou cross the park, but it's also home to large numbers of moose, wolves, grizzly bears and smaller mammals. As with Kobuk Valley, most visitors arrive on commercial rafting, kayaking or trekking trips.

Wrangell-St Elias North America's largest national park protects two of the continent's highest and most spectacular mountain ranges, as well as the classic Kennicott ghost town. It's popular with wilderness hikers and white-water enthusiasts, who come to tackle the Kennicott, Chitina and Copper rivers.

Canada

Aulavik Established in 1992, Aulavik, 'the place where people travel', covers 12,275 sq km on the northern central coast of Banks Island. This pristine Arctic wilderness protects the Thomsen River, which is considered the world's northernmost navigable stream, as well as a landscape of gently undulating hills, upland plateaux and steep canyons.

Auyuittuq Covering an area of 21,500 sq km, Auyuittuq (pronounced 'ah-you-EE-tuk), the 'land that never melts', is a beautiful, pristine wilderness of granite fells, valleys, fjords and meadows. Most visitors hike along the 97km Akshayuk Pass and climbers flock to Mount Thor (1500m), which boasts one of the world's highest cliff faces.

Ellesmere Island At the northern end of Ellesmere Island – the real top of the world – this park features Cape Columbia (the northernmost point of North America); the lovely Lake Hazen; numerous glaciers and ice fields; and one of the last habitats of the enigmatic Arctic wolf. Around the park's thermal oases, plants and animals can survive despite the harsh conditions.

Ivvavik Bordering the Beaufort Sea at the northern end of the Yukon Territory, Ivvavik takes in 10,170 sq km of mountains, foothills, river valleys and coastal plains.

The name means 'place for giving birth' and in early summer it serves as a calving ground for the Porcupine caribou herd.

Kluane Kluane (pronounced klu-AH-nee), 'many fish', covers 22,015 sq km at the south-western corner of the Yukon Territory. This rugged but accessible UN World Heritage Site consists mainly of the expanding St Elias Mountains and the world's largest nonpolar ice fields. The park also encompasses valleys, glacial lakes, forests, meadows and tundra.

Nahanni This magnificent World Heritage Site in the south-western corner of the Northwest Territories protects a superb stretch of the Mackenzie Mountains and the spectacular canyons of the turbulent South Nahanni River. Canoeists can challenge the white waters of the renowned 322km Canadian Heritage River and climbers can attack the awe-inspiring Cirque of the Unclimbables.

Wood Buffalo One of the world's largest national parks, 45,000 sq km Wood Buffalo National Park was established in 1922 to protect the few remaining wood bison, which once numbered in the millions. Now a World Heritage Site, its broad landscapes are largely characterised by boreal forest dappled with a myriad of bogs and crisscrossed with the shallow delta channels of the Peace and Athabasca rivers.

Greenland
North-East Greenland The world's largest national park, established in 1974 and expanded in 1988 to encompass a total of 972,000 sq km, takes in the north-eastern quarter of Greenland and extends 1400km from south-east to north-west. UNESCO has recently named it a Man and the Biosphere Reserve. Described as an 'Arctic Riviera' its tundra expanses provide a haven for muskoxen, polar bears, caribou, Arctic wolves, foxes, hares and a variety of delicate plant life, while the fjords shelter seals, walruses and whales.

Norway
Ånderdalen This tiny park on the island of Senja protects the bogs and the pine and birch coastal forests typical of Troms county. Some of the trees are over 500 years old.

Forlandet This park takes in the 86km-long island, Prins Karls Forlandet, off the west coast of Spitsbergen. It exists mainly to protect breeding grounds for eider ducks, geese and pinnipeds.

Nordvest Spitsbergen This wild corner of Spitsbergen Island takes in not only the fabulous Kongsbreen ice field, but also lovely Magdalenefjord, a number of archaeological sites and some of the world's finest breeding grounds for sea birds, caribou and marine mammals.

Øvre Anarjåkka This little-known park adjoins Finland's wild Lemmenjoki National Park and protects a vast expanse of birch and pine forests, bogs and lakes.

Øvre Dividal This lovely and wild park lies at the heart of a complex network of trekking routes in northern Norway, Sweden and Finland. It's known for the Arctic rhododendron and heather, and is also home to the rare wolverine.

Øvre Pasvik This park, tucked between Finland and Russia, protects a lovely area of boreal forest as well as large areas of muskeg and the last habitat of the brown bear in Norway.

Rago Lonely and dramatic Rago National Park is characterised by high mountain peaks divided by waterfalls and plunging valleys. It abuts the Padjelanta, Sarek and Stora Sjöfallet national parks in Sweden, forming a combined protected area of 5700 sq km.

Reisa The most prominent feature of this park is the dramatic Reisa gorge, its lovely waterfalls, varied wildlife and intriguing hiking.

Saltfjellet-Svartisen The two-part Saltfjellet-Svartisen National Park, which straddles the Arctic Circle, combines the upland moors of Saltfjellet with the two vast Svartisen icecaps. It also includes a number of Sami archaeological relics and sacred sites.

Sør Spitsbergen By far Norway's largest national park, Sør Spitsbergen takes in Spitsbergen's entire southern peninsula. About 65% is covered in ice, but there are several nesting sites for barnacle geese and eider ducks, and the coastal cliffs attract millions of nesting sea birds.

Stabbursdalen The main reason for preserving Stabbursdalen is its pine forest, which is the world's most northerly. In addition, it offers excellent wild hiking and broad vistas well off the trodden track.

Sweden
Abisko This small but fabulous national park offers numerous easy hiking routes. Here you'll find the lovely lake Törnetrask, the landmark Lapporten pass, and the northern gateways to the famed Kungsleden and Ofoten hiking tracks.

Muddus This 493 sq km park features the lake Muddusjaure and the surrounding ancient forests and muskeg bogs. It also has several deep and impressive gorges, such as the Måskoskårså, and superb bird-watching opportunities.

Padjelanta This park consists mainly of a high moorland surrounding the lakes Vastenjaure and Virihaure. It's favoured by grazing reindeer and also hosts a range of Swedish wildlife. Hikers especially like the renowned Kvikkjokk-Akka track.

Pieljekaise Just south of the Arctic Circle, this park features moorlands, birch forests, flowering meadows and lakes rich in Arctic char.

Sarek With its vast plateaux, glaciers, deep valleys, sharp peaks and vast tracts of birch and willow forest, Sweden's best-loved national park, Sarek, represents the wild essence of the country's far north. There's no road access, but hikers can reach the park on the Kungsleden route.

Stora Sjöfallet This park is dominated by the lake Akkajaure and the lofty Mt Akka. It's readily accessible by road.

Vadvetjåkka Sweden's northernmost national park protects a large river delta with bogs, lakes, limestone caves and a variety of bird species. The easiest access is on foot from Abisko.

Finland
Lemmenjoki At 2855 sq km, Lemmenjoki (Sami: Leammi) is the largest national park in Finland. Its diverse experiences include sloshing through desolate wilderness rivers, exploring the rough Arctic landscape and perhaps even meeting up with isolated gold prospectors.

Urho Kekkonen The Saariselkä Wilderness – which includes Urho Kekkonen National Park, the Sompio Strict Nature Reserve, Nuortti Recreational Fishing Area and large tracts of protected forestry lands – is by far the most popular trekking area in Finland.

One reason is the wild beauty of the landscape, but another is the network of excellent hikers' huts.

Pallas-Ounastunturi Pallas-Ounastunturi National Park, established in 1938, is one of the oldest national parks in Finland. It protects the area surrounding Pallastunturi Fell. The main attraction is the superb 60km trekking route through the park from the village of Hetta to Hotel Pallastunturi.

Russia
Kronotsky Zapovednik This reserve protects 10,990 sq km of the Kamchatka Peninsula and features bears, seals and sea eagles.

It also contains the spectacular Valley of Geysers and Uzon Caldera.

Laplandsky Zapovednik South of ecologically disastrous Monchegorsk, the UNESCO-protected Laplandsky Zapovednik (☎ 81536-5 00 80, fax 81536-5 71 99, email GilyasovaEV@monch.mels.ru) consists of 2784 sq km of biologically rich wilderness including virgin tundra, alpine grasslands, marshes, rivers, lakes and peaks up to 1114m high. It's home to 33 mammal species, 201 bird species and 15 species of fish, as well as 900 species of plants, mosses and lichens.

Taymyr-Poluostrovsky Zapovednik North of Norilsk, jutting into the Arctic Ocean, this 13,483 sq km of protected tundra shelters a host of wildlife, including the rare red-breasted goose and the muskox.

Ust-Lensky Zapovednik Russia's largest national park covers 14,330 sq km of wild tundra at the mouth of the Lena River.

Vrangelya Ostrovsky Zapovednik Since 1976, Wrangel Island, 140km off the north-east coast of Russia, has been a haven for polar bears, walruses and snow geese.

Facts for the Visitor

PLANNING
What Kind of Trip?
Your style of travel will derive from your budget, curiosity and adventurous spirit. The first decision you'll have to make is whether to visit the Arctic on your own or as part of a tour. Some places lend themselves well to independent travel – specifically most of northern Scandinavia; along the air, road and rail systems in Alaska and parts of northern Canada; and the air and ferry routes in Greenland. Further information on getting around on your own is provided in the Getting Around sections of the individual country chapters.

If you are going alone, the first thing to remember is that transport is limited (except in northern Scandinavia), so it's extremely important to book ferries and flights as far in advance as possible. If you decide to travel independently with others, bear in mind that travel can strain relationships as few other experiences can. You can minimise this by either formulating a rigid itinerary before the trip, or agreeing to remain flexible about everything. When planning your route, it's wise to consider the costs involved. In most Arctic regions, transport costs are so high that many independent travellers will just want to hole up for awhile in one place and spend some time getting to know the local way of life, observing the local way of life and discovering lesser-known sites.

Alternatively, you can take a tour organised by an outfitter or cruise company. If you're heading for the wilds, the High Arctic or the polar seas and don't want to mount a serious expedition, this is probably the way to go. In addition, seniors, travellers with children, inexperienced travellers and those wanting to reach very remote areas tend to appreciate such options because they minimise hassles, uncertainties and the complicated logistics involved in organising expeditions. They also shelter inexperienced would-be adventurers from the region's inherent risks, and obviate the headaches independent travellers face when sorting out timetables and booking transport.

There are plenty of tour options (the Organised Tours & Adventures chapter will provide some direction), some of which will take you to spectacular, otherworldly places straight out of nature documentaries. In the Arctic region, you can choose between cruising, kayaking, hiking, dogsledding and sightseeing packages, but note that package tours leave little time for independent exploration and discovery.

While longer tours can become experiments in social cohesion and friction can develop, for anyone who's not flush with cash, the ample costs involved in reaching the Arctic will probably preclude a mad dash that crams a once-in-a-lifetime Arctic experience into a week-long holiday. Those sorts of trips may be fine in Europe or the Caribbean, but here, that style is definitely not recommended.

Maps
In the UK, good map sources include The Map Shop (☎ 01684-593146, fax 01684-594559), 15 High St, Upton-upon-Severn, Worcs, WR8 0HJ; and Stanfords (☎ 020-7836 1321, fax 020-7836 0189), 12-14 Long Acre, London, WC2E 9LP. Either can provide detailed listings of available maps and both offer mail order services.

In Australia, try Map Land (☎/fax 03-9670 4383), 372 Little Bourke St, Melbourne, VIC 3000; or the Travel Bookshop (☎ 02-9241 3554), 20 Bridge St, Sydney, NSW 2000.

Alaska & the USA Your best map source for Alaska is the *Alaska Atlas & Gazetteer*, published by DeLorme (toll-free ☎ 1-800 227 1656), PO Box 298-7200, Freeport, ME 04032. Otherwise, the state Division of Tourism (DOT; see Tourist Information later in this section) distributes a respectable road map free of charge.

Much of the state is also covered by US Geological Survey (USGS) maps at a scale of 1:62,500, making them excellent for hiking (most of the northern reaches, however, are covered only by the 1:250,000 series). You can request a catalogue or order maps from the USGS, Denver Federal Center, PO Box 25286, Denver, CO 80225. The US Forest Service also publishes detailed maps of the Tongass and Chugach National Forests which cost around US$6 each. Also worth contacting is Maplink (☎ 805-965 4402), 25 E Mason Street, Santa Barbara, CA 93101.

Canada The Canada Map Office (☎ 613-952 7000, toll-free ☎ 1-800 465 6277) produces topographic maps of the entire country. The Web site, www.nrcan.gc.ca, lists its dealers across Canada. World of Maps & Travel Books (☎ 613-724 6776, toll-free ☎ 1-800 214 8524), 1235 Wellington St, Ottawa, ON K1Y 3A3, stocks thousands of road maps and topographic maps of Canada and the world. The store accepts orders by email and the Web site, www.worldofmaps.com, reviews new maps and publications.

The Canada Map Company (☎ 416-362 9297, toll-free ☎ 1-800 844 9377), 63 Adelaide St, Toronto, ON, M5C 1K6, has a wide selection of maps of all kinds. Standard highway maps, city maps, fishing maps, nautical and aviation charts and topographic maps are all available. The company will fill phone and mail orders. Also worth contacting is Worldwide Books & Maps (☎ 604-687 3320), 552 Seymour Street, Vancouver, BC.

Greenland Greenland's coastal areas are covered by 1:250,000 series topographical sheets by the Danish national mapping institute, Kort og Matrikelstyrelsen (KOM). The scale makes them of limited use to trekkers, but for much of Greenland, they're the only maps available. To order maps or catalogues, contact Kort og Matrikelstyrelsen (☎ 45-35 87 53 10, fax 45-35 87 50 51),

Kortsalget, Rentemestervej 8, DK-2400 Copenhagen NV, Denmark. Saga Maps has taken the KOM mapping and patched contiguous sheets into 20 regional maps that cover all populated areas. To order, contact Tage Schjött (☎/fax 33-628 35848), La Coma del Colat 22, La Massana, Andorra.

In addition, Greenland Tourism has produced an excellent series of hiking maps covering the most popular areas at a scale of 1:100,000; they're available through www.greenland-guide.dk.

Iceland Landmælingar Íslands (the Iceland Geodetic Survey), with its monopoly on map production in Iceland, offers high quality topographic sheets, a small road atlas, and various thematic maps. The best general country map is the Ferðakort (touring map), at a scale of 1:500,000. For a catalogue, price list and order form, contact Landmælingar Íslands (☎ 354-533 4000, fax 354-533 4011), Laugavegur 178, PO Box 5060, 125 Reykjavík.

Norway For drivers, the best road maps are the Cappelens series, which are sold in Norwegian bookshops. The 1:325,000 series divides the Arctic portion of the country into two sections: No 4 Nordland and No 5 Troms og Finnmark. Another excellent Cappelens sheet is the 1:700,000 No 20 Nordkalotten, which covers all of northern Scandinavia, including north-western Russia. For all travellers, Nortrabooks has produced the colourful and popular Bilkart over Norge, which includes excellent topographic shading and depicts the entire country on one sheet at a scale of 1:1,000,000. The national mapping agency Statens Kartverk (☎ 32-11 81 00, fax 32-11 81 01, email firmapost@statkart.no), Kartverksveien 21, N-3500 Hønefoss, covers Norway in 21 sheets at a scale of 1:250,000, and also produces hiking maps at a scale of 1:50,000. Its Web site is at www.statkart.no.

Sweden Sweden's standard topographical maps are Lantmäteriverket's red 1:100,000 (Skr98) and red 1:250,000 (Skr110) series, available in larger bookshops. To order maps directly, contact Kartförlaget, Lantmäteriverket (☎ 026-63 33 00 0), Lantmäterigaten 2, SE-80264 Gävle. The Fjällkartan series covers mountain areas at a scale of 1:100,000 (Skr98) while the more detailed green series, at a scale of 1:50,000, costs Sk475 per sheet. Motorists can compare the half a dozen Sweden road atlases, from the spring-bound *Vägatlas Sverige* (Sk4220) to Reader's Digest's (Det Bästa) hardcover *Sverige Vägvisaren* for Skr495.

Finland The national mapping agency, Karttakeskus (☎ 204-45 144, fax 204-45 5919, email info@karttakeskus.fi), PO Box 40, FIN-01511, Vantaa, publishes the 1:800,000 *Autoilijan Tiekartta* (AT) road map of Finland, which costs Fmk55. Additionally, the series of 19 GT road maps at a scale of 1:200,000 (Fmk55 each) show practically all the places that might interest travellers, including hostels and wilderness huts. Karttakeskus has also produced approximately 40 titles for trekking areas, including urban walking tracks, at scales of 1:25,000 to 1:50,000, and national park maps (1:50,000 to 1:100,000). For the highest level of detail and accuracy, pick up the 1:20,000 series maps, which cost from Fmk55 to Fmk85 each. You'll find the Web site at www.karttakeskus.fi.

Russia The Soviet Union may have been the only country in the world with a black market in maps. Stalin put the state cartographic office under the control of the NKVD, forerunner of the KGB, which began systematically distorting maps for the sake of secrecy. Streets, neighbourhoods, whole towns were erased, rivers and highways were rerouted, mountain ranges disappeared. In 1989 the cartographic office began to produce the first proper maps in almost 60 years. Though inexpensive and accurate Russian maps of many cities and regions are now published, availability is very patchy. You'll also find a lot of inaccurate 'tourist maps' of cities, mostly called *Turisticheskaya Skhema* or *Plan Goroda*.

Pick up a useful map whenever you see one, as you may never see it again!

The Russian-language *Atlas avtomobil~nykh dorog (Road Atlas)* (Trivium, Minsk, 1993), with 120 pages of regional road maps covering the whole ex-USSR, and some city maps, is reasonably compact and worthwhile. In Russia, it costs around US$5. The *CIS* map from the German publisher Hallwag is one of the clearest all-Russia maps, covering the whole country and the rest of the CIS (main roads and railways included) on one sheet at a scale of 1:7,000,000 (1cm to 70km). *Hildebrand's Travel Map CIS* is also good.

What to Bring

The amount of stuff you'll need to carry on an Arctic trip will be determined by your budget and your intended activities. Those who want to travel cheaply will unfortunately need to load themselves down with a lot of things that more upmarket travellers won't need to worry about – a good case for bringing a vehicle where applicable. Under ideal circumstances, such things as tents, stoves and cooking implements can be divided among members of a group, but lone travellers may find themselves struggling beneath a good deal of weight.

Some general items which will be required by almost everyone (except those staying in hotels and eating in restaurants) include a synthetic-fibre sleeping bag which is preferably rated to at least -10°C; a Swiss army-style knife; a towel; a torch (flashlight); a water bottle (at least one litre); lighters or waterproof matches; a couple of thick paperbacks to read during inclement weather (English-language books are very expensive in Scandinavia and practically unavailable in Russia and Greenland); a copy of medical and optical prescriptions; and any film or camera equipment you may need.

Clothing Warm clothing will be of utmost importance to everyone, at any time of year. Given the range of weather possibilities in summer (yes, including warm and sunny!), the layering method seems to work best. The items on the following list should be sufficient to keep you comfortable anywhere in the region between May and September (winter travellers will obviously need to prepare for severe Arctic conditions):

• thermal underwear made of polypropylene or similar material
• several pairs of thick wool and/or polypro socks
• heavy windproof ski gloves
• high-protection sunglasses
• wool hat with ear protection
• a T-shirt or two
• at least one woollen pullover
• hiking shorts (canvas or polyester)
• wool shirt and trousers (jeans are comfortable when dry, but cumbersome and uncomfortable when wet!)
• windproof and waterproof jacket and trousers – Gore Tex may not provide sufficient protection. As disagreeable as it can be, light treated nylon is probably better, though it can trap sweat and cause chills when removed.
• strong hiking shoes with ankle support or (preferably) boots
• swimsuit – well, this isn't really essential, but Scandinavia and Russia have lots of swimming pools and the northern countries (especially Iceland) also enjoy some very appealing hot springs.

Camping Equipment In addition to the previously mentioned sleeping bag, campers should carry:

• a tent – easily assembled (due to wind), sturdy, waterproofed and preferably free-standing. It's a good idea to get one with some kind of annexe (vestibule) outside for storage of wet clothing, boots and cooking implements.
• a light stove and aluminium fuel bottle – a Peak II or MSR mountain stove (which can burn unleaded petrol, as well as white gas/Shellite/ Coleman fuel) or an alcohol stove would be preferable to butane stoves that are rather unstable and don't work well in wind. In some countries, butane cartridges are very hard to come by.
• cooking pots, cups and utensils – a nesting kit is probably the best way to go if you want to keep weight and volume to a minimum.
• waterproof ground cover or space blanket
• water filter and/or purification tablets

If you plan on hiking or trekking, add the following items:

• gaiters
• GPS system
• compass and magnetic deviation figures – this is vital in the far north since deviation from magnetic north in the region can be as high as 80°.
• if fishing is your bag, a fishing line, hook and lures (this is a great way to supplement your diet on long hikes)
• medical kit (see Health later in this chapter)
• applicable maps

TOURIST INFORMATION
Many Arctic countries have national and regional tourist organisations which can help you with your trip planning. Some also have tourist offices abroad.

Alaska
The Alaska Division of Tourism (☎ 907-465 2010), Dept 901, PO Box 110801, Juneau, AK 99811-0801, USA, isn't particularly helpful, but does produce a free annual vacation planner and a state highway map. It can also provide ferry and rail timetables (note, however, that none of the ferry or railway routes extend north of the Arctic Circle). On the Web it can be found at www.travelalaska.com and www.state.ak.us/tourism.

Canada
Each of Canada's provinces and territories has its own visitor information centres. The following are for those included in this book:

Manitoba
    Travel Manitoba (toll-free ☎ 1-800 665 0040), Department SM5, 7th Floor, 155 Carlton St, Winnipeg, Manitoba R3C 3H8, www.gov.mb.ca
Northwest Territories
    NWTAT-MP (toll-free ☎ 1-800 661 0788), PO Box 610, Yellowknife, NT X1A 2N5, www.nwttravel.nt.ca
Nunavut
    Nunatour (toll-free ☎ 1-800 491 7910 or ☎ 867-979 6551, fax 867-979 1261, email nunatour@nunanet.com), PO Box 1450, Iqaluit, Nunavut X0A 0H0, www.nunatour.nt.ca

Yukon
Tourism Yukon (☎ 867-667 5340, email info@touryukon.com), PO Box 2703, Whitehorse, YT, Y1A 2C6, www.touryukon.com

Greenland

For tourist information, contact either Greenland Tourism (☎ 299-32 28 88, fax 299-32 28 77, email tourism@greennet.gl), PO Box 1552, DK-3900 Nuuk, Greenland; or Greenland Tourism Copenhagen (☎ 45-33 13 69 75, fax 45-33 93 38 83, email greenfo@inet.uni2.dk), Pilestræde 52, PO Box 1139, DK-1010 Copenhagen K, Denmark. You can also check out the Web site, www.greenland-guide.dk.

Iceland

For tourist information, contact the Tourist Information Centre, or Upplýsingamiðstöð Ferðamála (☎ 562 3045, fax 562 3057, email tourinfo@simnet.is), at Bankastræti 2, Reykjavík. You can also access its Web site at www.icetourist.is.

France
(☎ 01 47 42 54 87, fax 01 42 65 17 52) 9 Boulevard des Capucines, F-75002 Paris
Germany
Isländisches Fremdenverkehrsamt (☎ 6102-25 44 84, fax 6102-25 45 70) Stadtmitte, Karl-Ulrich-Straáe 11, D-63263 Neu-Isenburg 1; or (☎ 069-29 99 78, fax 069-28 38 72) Rossmarkt 10, D-60313 Frankfurt a/M 1
Japan
(☎ 03-5820 0773, fax 03-5820 0780) 6th Floor Harada Building, No 1-1-15, Asakusabashi, Taitoh-Ku, Tokyo 111
UK
(☎ 020-7388 4499, fax 020-7387 5711) 172 Tottenham Court Rd, 3rd Floor, London W1P 9LG
USA
Iceland Tourist Board (☎ 212-949 2333, fax 212-983 5260) 655 Third Ave, New York, NY 10017; or (☎ 212-967 8888, fax 212-330 1456) 610B Fifth Ave, Rockefeller Centre, New York, NY 10020

Norway

The Norges Informasjonsenter tourist office (☎ 22-83 00 50, fax 22-83 81 50) in Oslo offers nationwide tourist information. Its Web site is at www.oslopro.no. For useful general brochures and books on travel in Norway, contact the Norwegian Tourist Board (NORTRA; ☎ 22-92 52 00, fax 22-56 05 05, email Webmaster@nortra.no), PO Box 2893, Solli, Drammensveien, N-0239 Oslo. Its Web site is at www.tourist.no. There are also several international offices which can help you plan a trip:

Australia
Royal Norwegian Embassy (☎ 02-6273 3444, fax 02-6273 3669), 17 Hunter St, Yarralumla, ACT 2600
France
Office National du Tourisme de Norvège (☎ 01 53 23 00 50, fax 01 53 23 00 59), 28 rue Bayard, F-75008 Paris
Germany
Norwegisches Fremdenverkehrsamt (☎ 040-22 71 08 10, fax 040-22 71 08 15), Mundsburger Damm 45, D-22087 Hamburg
Netherlands
Noors Verkeersbureau (☎ 20-671 2854, fax 20-679 8886), Saxen Weimarlaan 58, NL-1075 CE Amsterdam
UK
Norwegian Tourist Board (☎ 020-7839 6255, ski hotline 020-7321 0666, fax 020-7839 6014), Charles House, 5 Lower Regent St, London SW1Y 4LR
USA
Norwegian Tourist Board (☎ 212-885 9700, fax 212-885 9710), 655 Third Ave, Suite 1810, New York, NY 10017

Sweden

Sweden has about 350 local tourist information offices. Members of the Svenska Turistföreningen (Swedish Mountain Touring Club; ☎ 08-463 21 00), Box 25, 10120 Stockholm, receive discounts on mountain huts and hostels (vandrarhem). Its Web site is at www.stfturist.se. Several international offices also promote tourism in Sweden:

Australia
Scandinavian Airlines System (SAS; ☎ 02-9299 9800), 5th floor, 350 Kent St, Sydney, NSW 2000
France
Office Suédois du Tourisme et des Voyages (☎ 01 53 43 26 27), 18 Boulevarde Malesherbes, F-75008 Paris

Germany
  Schweden-Werbung für Reisen und Touristik
  (☎ 040-32 55 23 55, email info@swe-
  tourism.de), Lilienstrasse 19, 20095 Hamburg
UK
  Swedish Travel & Tourism Council (☎ 020-
  7724 5868, email info@swedish-tourism
  .org.uk), 11 Montague Place, London W1H
  2Al
USA
  Swedish Travel & Tourism Council (☎ 212-
  885 0700, email info@gosweden.org), Grand
  Central Station, New York, NY 10017-5617

Finland

All major Finnish towns have a tourist office with helpful, English-speaking staff,
English-language brochures and excellent
free maps. The national tourist information
organisation is the Finnish Tourist Board, or
Matkailun Edistämiskeskus (☎ 09-4176
9300, fax 09-4176 9301, email mek@
mek.fi), PO Box 249, SF-00131 Helsinki,
Finland. There are also the following offices in foreign countries:

Australia
  Finnish Tourist Board (☎ 02-9290 1950, fax
  02-9290 1981), Level 4, 81 York Street, Syd-
  ney, NSW 2000
Canada
  Finnish Tourist Board (toll-free ☎ 1-800 346
  4636), PO Box 246, Station Q, Toronto, ON
  M4T 2M1
France
  Office National du Tourisme de Finlande (☎ 01
  42 66 40 13, fax 01 47 42 87 22), 13 rue Auber,
  75009 Paris
Germany
  Finnische Zentrale für Tourismus (☎ 069-7 19
  19 80, fax 069-7 24 17 25), Lessingstrasse 5,
  60325 Frankfurt
Japan
  Finnish Tourist Board (☎ 03-3501 5207, fax
  03-3580 9205), Imperial Hotel, Room 505, 1-
  1-1 Uchisaiwai-cho, Chiyoda-ku, Tokyo 100-
  0011
UK
  Finnish Tourist Board (☎ 020-7930 5871, fax
  020-7321 0696, email mek.lon@mek.fi), 30-
  35 Pall Mall, 3rd Floor, London SW1Y 5LP
USA
  Finnish Tourist Board (☎ 212-885 9700, fax
  212-885 9710), PO Box 4649, Grand Central
  Station, New York, NY 10163-4649

Russia

Unfortunately, none of the tourist offices in
Arctic Russia can offer much assistance,
and finding information on Russia from
abroad may prove an exercise in futility. Although Intourist, Russia's national tourism
agency, has offices abroad (the one in London is probably the best), they're essentially
just travel sales agencies and not information offices. There is a Russian National
Tourist Office (☎ 212-758 1162), 800 Third
Avenue Suite 3101, New York, NY 10022,
USA, which is purportedly independent of
Intourist, but don't expect any miracles. It's
better to phone than to write.

The telephone-only Russian Tourist Information Service (☎ 0891-516 951), in
London, UK, can advise you on visas, accommodation, tourist attractions, climate,
transport, health and money. Calls are
charged at £0.48 per minute.

VISAS & DOCUMENTS
Alaska

As Alaska is a state of the USA, US visa
regulations apply. Canadians can enter
without a passport, but do require proof of
their citizenship. Countries whose citizens
can stay for up to 90 days without a visa on
the Visa Waiver Program include Andorra,
Argentina, Australia, Austria, Belgium,
Brunei, Denmark, Finland, France, Germany,
Iceland, Ireland, Italy, Japan, Liechtenstein,
Luxembourg, Monaco, Netherlands, New
Zealand, Norway, San Marino, Slovenia,
Spain, Sweden, Switzerland and the UK.
However, everyone needs a non-refundable
return ticket and you may be required to
show financial solvency.

If you're not eligible for the Visa Waiver
Program, you'll need a US Non-Immigrant
Visitor Visa issued by a US consulate
abroad. To apply, you need a passport that's
valid for at least six months longer than
your intended stay, a recent photo (37 by
37mm) and a US$35 fee. If you look all
right to the admitting immigration officer,
you'll probably get a six-month stay; if not,
you'll immediately get to use your return
ticket.

There are all sorts of complicated regulations which require utmost care and thought to sort out. Anyone who has been involved in genocide, terrorism, smuggling, drug-trafficking, drug-addiction, prostitution, communism or Nazism; has been convicted of a crime or has a communicable disease, may be 'excluded' from visiting the USA. The INS (Immigration & Naturalization Service) isn't the most easy-going organisation so honesty is the best policy, especially when it comes to previous criminal convictions or communicable diseases. In these two cases, it's often possible to sort out an 'exclusion waiver' after two months or so of trying encounters with US bureaucracy.

The latest US visa regulations are available at the Web site travel.state.gov/visa_services.html.

Canada

Visitors from all countries except the USA need a passport. Two exceptions are residents of Greenland (Denmark), and the islands of St Pierre & Miquelon (France), who don't need a passport if they are entering from their areas of residence. However, all the above do require some proof of citizenship (in the case of the USA, a drivers' licence may suffice, but there are no guarantees and it's wise to carry a birth certificate or passport). Visitors from most western countries don't need visas, but those from South Africa, Korea, Taiwan, most of Eastern Europe, all communist countries and most developing countries do need them. Visitor visas are valid for six months (extendable for a fee) and cost C$75; apply at a Canadian Immigration Centre in your home country.

Immigration officers have the right to refuse anyone who they consider suspicious. Visitors need to be in good health, have sufficient funds for their intended stay, and perhaps even hold a ticket out of the country. Having said that, few westerners who are clearly legitimate travellers will be refused entry. If you are refused entry but have a visa, you have the right of appeal at the Immigration Appeal Board at the port of entry.

If you've rented a car, trailer or any other vehicle in the USA and are driving it into Canada, bring a copy of the rental agreement to save any aggravation from border officials. The rental agreement should stipulate that taking the vehicle to Canada is permitted. Similarly, drivers of US-registered vehicles must present a yellow insurance card (technically, a Canadian Non-Resident Inter-Provincial Motor Vehicle Liability Insurance Card) verifying that their insurance is valid in Canada.

Greenland

Citizens of countries who require visas for Denmark (and Greenland) include many African countries, Turkey, Jordan, Vanuatu, Tonga, Independent Samoa, Papua New Guinea, Taiwan, China, Russia and the other former Soviet republics, Myanmar, India, Iraq, Pakistan, Bangladesh, Iran, Sri Lanka, Indonesia, the Philippines, Belize, Egypt and South Africa. Visitors from other Nordic countries – Norway, Finland, Iceland, Sweden, the Åland and Faroe islands and, of course, Denmark – only need valid identification cards. Citizens of other countries not requiring visas only need valid passports for stays of up to three months.

Technically, you must be able to show sufficient funds for your intended length of stay, but customs and immigration formalities are normally cursory, especially since the vast majority of visitors enter Greenland from Denmark or Iceland.

Iceland

Citizens of Austria, Belgium, France, Germany, Italy, Liechtenstein, Luxembourg, the Netherlands and Switzerland need only a valid identity card to enter Iceland for tourist visits. Norwegians, Swedes, Danes, Faroese and Finns must only carry proof of citizenship when entering Iceland from another Nordic country. Other Western Europeans and citizens of many other countries, including Australia, New Zealand, Japan, Canada and the USA, need just a valid passport to enter as tourists. Others need a visa from an Icelandic consulate before arriving.

Tourist visits of up to 90 days during any nine-month period are normally granted if you can show proof of sufficient funds for your visit. Officials are fairly liberal with this requirement – they're used to shoestring travellers – but they may ask to see an onward ticket if they think you may run short of cash. Lengths of stay can be easily extended at police stations.

Norway

Citizens of Denmark, Finland, Iceland and Sweden may enter Norway freely without a passport. Citizens of the USA, Canada, the UK, Ireland, Australia and New Zealand need a valid passport to visit Norway, but do not need a visa for stays of less than three months. The same is true for EU and EEA countries, most of Latin America and most Commonwealth countries (except South Africa and several other African and Pacific countries).

Sweden

Citizens of the EU, Norway or Iceland do not need passports or work permits for Sweden, but will need identification (a passport is recommended). Temporary residency visas *(uppehållstillstånd)* are generally required only for stays of more than three months in Sweden and are issued free for specified periods. However, citizens of South Africa, Hong Kong residents with Chinese passports and citizens of many African, Asian and some eastern European countries require tourist visas for entry, which are valid for 90 days.

Finland

For most foreign visitors, a valid passport is required to enter Finland. Citizens of the EU countries (except Greece), as well as Liechtenstein, San Marino and Switzerland may use either a national identity card or a passport. Citizens of Denmark, Iceland, Sweden and Norway do not need a passport to visit Finland.

Russia

All foreigners visiting Russia need visas. To get one you must technically have confirmed accommodation for every night you'll be in the country, though in practice there are countless ways around this. At the time of writing, a Russian visa is a passport-sized paper document; nothing goes into your passport (but this may soon change to stamps). It lists entry/exit dates, your passport number, any children travelling with you, and your visa type, as well as cities you intend to visit – although this isn't as much of a limitation as it once was. It's also an exit permit, so don't lose it because leaving the country can be harder than getting in.

When you check in to any accommodation, you must surrender your passport and visa so the hotel can register you with OVIR (Otdel Viz i Registratsii), the Department of Visas and Registration. Your documents will be returned the next morning. It's essential that independent travellers register their Russian visas with OVIR within three working days after entering Russia – no ifs or buts about it – and this may involve a registration fee of US$5 to US$10.

If you're not sure which organisation invited you (that is, if the sponsorship line – on tourist visas this begins with the words *V uchrezhdenie* – has a name you've never heard of), one option is to spend a night at one of the major (expensive) hotels, which will register your visa for you.

To apply for any Russian visa, you need a passport that's valid for at least one month beyond your intended stay; three passport-sized (4 by 4.5cm), full-face photos not more than a year old; a completed application form, including entry/exit dates; and a handling fee which will vary from country to country and according to your citizenship. In addition, how long you wait for your visa depends on how much you're willing to pay. As an example, the Russian consulate in San Francisco charges US$40 for service in seven to eight days, US$50 for five to six-day service, US$60 for three to four-day service and US$80 for next-day service. A two-hour rush visa (or one that is mailed back to you the same day) costs US$120. Rush fees vary not just by country but by individual consulate.

Most visitors will be interested in a Tourist Visa, which is the most straightforward but also the most inflexible. In theory you're supposed to have booked accommodation for every night you'll be in the country, but in practice you can often get away with booking only a few, even just one – ask the travel agent, hotel or hostel through which you book. In addition, you'll need confirmation of hotel reservations, which can be a faxed copy on hotel letterhead signed and stamped by the hotel, or confirmation of bookings from Intourist or a travel agent. If you're booking your flight or accommodation through a travel agency, they'll also get your visa for an extra fee, usually between US$5 and US$30.

Alternatively, you could apply for a business visa, which requires an invitation from a Russian company (these are fairly easy to get, and numerous companies and organisations will issue them for a fee). One-month On-the-Spot visas are available for between US$150 and US$250 at St Petersburg's Pulkovo-2 and Moscow's Sheremetevo-2 airports.

Prebooked cruise passengers can visit Russian ports for up to four days without a visa if they sleep aboard the ship. In 1994, the Russian government added a 2 am curfew to that restriction, but this may change in the future. This won't work for return passengers on ordinary scheduled sailings.

The Russian government wavers on the issue of HIV/AIDS testing, but at the time of writing, only visitors who intend to stay more than three months require a test. If you're getting your visa in the USA, however, that requirement may be enforced regardless of your length of stay.

MONEY
Alaska
As with the rest of the USA, the unit of currency is the US dollar, which is divided into 100 cents. Coins in circulation include 1¢

(penny), 5¢ (nickel), 10¢ (dime), and 25¢ (quarter), as well as the rarer 50¢ and $1 coins. Notes come in denominations of US$1, $2 (rare), $5, $10, $20, $50 and $100. The $20s, $50s and $100s have recently been changed, so two versions are in use; the newer ones have much larger, off-centre portraits.

Changing foreign currency in Alaska – especially Arctic Alaska – would be a real headache (few Americans are even aware that foreign currency exists!). Either bring US dollar cash, US dollar travellers cheques (which are accepted like cash nearly everywhere), or a credit card (note that Eurocard is not accepted). Automatic teller machines are also common in cities and towns, and most accept the Cirrus, Plus, Exchange and Excel card formats (or some combination of these).

Canada
The Canadian unit of currency is the dollar, which is divided into 100 cents. Coins come in 1¢ (penny), 5¢ (nickel), 10¢ (dime), 25¢ (quarter), $1 (loonie) and $2 (twoonie) pieces. There is also a 50¢ coin but it's rarely used. Notes come in denominations of C$5, $10, $20, $50 and $100.

Changing money is best done at companies such as Thomas Cook or American Express which specialise in international transactions, or at banks. Although hotels and other businesses may change US dollars, the rates are unlikely to be in your favour.

Automatic teller machines (ATMs) with Interac are ubiquitous, and in some businesses, bank debit cards may be used instead of cash by swiping the card through a scanner at the checkout. Known in Canada as banking machines, these can be used day or night, any day of the week. Most Canadian ATMs will take cards from most foreign countries. Credit cards are also accepted throughout the country and are especially useful for making reservation deposits or securing car hire charges.

The GST (General Sales Tax, better known as the Gouge & Screw Tax) adds 7%

to just about every product, service and transaction and is applied on top of the usual provincial or territorial sales tax, which in some cases amounts to a total sales tax of 15%.

Greenland

The Danish krone (Dkr) is used throughout the Kingdom of Denmark – that is, on the mainland and in the Faroe Islands and Greenland. One krone is equal to 100 øre. Coins come in 25 and 50 øre denominations, as well as Dkr1, 2, 5, 10 and 20. Notes come in denominations of Dkr50, 100, 500 and 1000.

Greenland's two banks, Nuna Bank and Grønlandsbanken, have branches in most towns; in villages, foreign exchange is handled by KNI. Major currencies and travellers cheques can be exchanged for Dkr in any bank or KNI office, as well as larger hotels. As yet, ATMs are only available to holders of Danish bank accounts or Danish-issued credit cards, but that will probably change. Note that there are no bank exchange services at Kangerlussuaq or Kulusuk airports; be sure to bring enough Danish currency to reach your next destination. Those arriving at Narsarsuaq can exchange currency at the hotel.

Iceland

The Icelandic unit of currency is the króna (Ikr) which equals 100 aurar. Coins come in 1, 5, 10, 50 and 100 krónur denominations. Notes come in 500, 1000, 2000 and 5000 krónur denominations. You may also occasionally encounter 5, 10 and 50 aurar denominations, which are practically worthless.

Foreign-denomination postal cheques, travellers cheques and banknotes may be exchanged for Icelandic currency at any bank, most of which charge a commission of around Ikr150 per transaction, but Landsbanki Íslands takes no commission on foreign exchange. After-hours currency exchange is available at Keflavík international airport (open daily 6.30 am to 6.30 pm), and at The Change Group in Reykjavík.

Norway

Norway's unit of currency, the krone (Nkr), equals 100 øre. Coins come in denominations of 50 øre and Nkr1, 5, 10 and 20, and notes in denominations of Nkr50, 100, 200, 500 and 1000.

Post offices and banks exchange major foreign currencies and travellers cheques, which command a better exchange rate than cash by about 1%. Post offices offer the best exchange rates, but charge a service fee of Nkr10 per travellers cheque or Nkr20 per cash transaction. Some banks, including Kreditkassen and Den Norske Bank, match those rates, but others charge a rather steep Nkr20 per travellers cheque (which means you're better off with higher denomination travellers cheques). 'Mini-Bank' ATMs, found adjacent to many banks and shopping districts, accept major credit cards as well as Cirrus and/or Plus format bank cards. Visa, Eurocard, MasterCard, American Express and Diners Club cards are widely accepted throughout Norway.

Sweden

The Swedish krona (plural kronor) comes in coins of 50 öre and Skr1, 5 and 10 denominations. The notes are Skr20, 100, 150, 500, and 1000. Prices are rounded to the nearest 50 öre.

You should encounter few problems if you carry cash in any convertible currency or travellers cheques. Although not all machines are fully connected, the national Minuten and Bankomat ATM networks provided by Swedish banks accept international Visa, Plus, EC, Cirrus, Eurocard or MasterCard ATM cards. Forex, found in the biggest cities and some ferry terminals, is one of the cheapest and easiest places to exchange money. Forex charges Skr20 to buy any amount of kronor and charges Skr15 per travellers cheque. Banks and post offices charge Skr50 per transaction, but offer better exchange rates.

Finland

The Finnish unit of currency is the markka (plural markkaa), or Fmk. One markka is equal to 100 penniä. Coins come in one, five and 10 markkaa, and 50 and 10 penniä, while notes come in denominations of 20, 50, 100, 500 and 1000 markkaa. Fmk5 is often called *vitonen*; Fmk10, *kymppi*; and Fmk100, *satanen*.

ATMs are the best way to obtain local currency, but you can also go the traditional route, with travellers cheques and cash. Finland has three national banks with similar rates and charges. In the big cities independent exchange facilities such as Forex usually offer better rates and charge lower fees or commissions than banks. Finnish post offices also provide some banking services and normally keep longer hours than banks.

Russia

The Russian currency is the rouble, which is divided into 100 kopecks or kopeki. There's no point in running through the denominations of rouble notes. Due to massive inflation, new banknotes – either in higher denominations or in lower denominations because a few zeros have been lopped off – are likely to appear at any time. The Russian law that all transactions must be in roubles was clearly made to be broken, as many businesses advertise their rates in – and happily accept – US dollars.

If you're taking cash, US dollars are the best, followed by Deutschmarks. In Arctic Russia, you may also get away with Norwegian kroner, but travellers cheques aren't recommended. To safeguard your cash, divide it up and carry it in several different places on your person and in your baggage. When you enter the country, all your cash must be declared on a customs *deklaratsia*, and you won't be allowed to leave the country with more than that; the difference will be confiscated. However, roubles may normally be changed back into foreign currency.

Credit cards are also making inroads, especially in larger cities, but can't be relied upon exclusively.

Banks and exchange offices are competitive and representative rates are printed in major newspapers and also posted in offices with exchange services. Generally, rates in private exchange offices are a bit better than in the banks. In small towns, it's wise to bring along your passport, visa and customs declaration to the exchange office. Word of reform in Russia filters down slowly, and bureaucrats are most efficiently handled with valid paperwork.

INTERNET RESOURCES

Lonely Planet's own Web site, www.lone lyplanet.com, provides extensive information and updates on destinations all over the world. For a peek at the world's weather, check www.intellicast.com. For a rundown of tourist offices around the world, try www.towd.com. Pan European rail info is detailed on www.raileurope.com and airline info is available on www.trave locity.com. If you're coming from the USA and want to bid on airline seats, call up www.priceline.com. You'll get the lowdown on the latest currency exchange rates on www.xe.net/currency&pacific.commer ce.ubc.ca/xr.

Alaska

A great source of information is the Alaska Internet Travel Guide at www.alaskaone .com, while you'll find transport schedules and background information on www .alaskan.com.

All units of the US National Park Service, including those in Alaska's Arctic region, have Web pages which are accessed through the US National Park Service Web site, www.nps.gov. The Web site www .alaskanadventureguide.com offers tips and suggestions for visitors, including sightseeing, hotels and lodges, fishing, and state and national parks.

Canada

For current general news try www .canoe .com. You'll find information on some of Canada's best-known sites at www.attrac tionscanada.com and the Parks Canada National Parks Web site, parkscanada.pch .gc.ca, has an exhaustive array of information on the national parks.

Greenland

The wonderful www.greenland-guide.dk includes numerous tourism-related links, courtesy of Greenland Tourism, and the useful Greenland Home Rule Web site www.gh.gl reveals all they want you to know about what's happening in the government.

Iceland

The most useful online resources are probably at www.icetourist.is and www.zocalo.net/iceland/iceice.htm.

Norway

Both general and tourism-related information about Norway can be accessed on the Internet at www.norway.org. NORTRA, the Norwegian Tourist Board, has a particularly useful Web site at www.tourist.no. The Norwegian Ministry of Foreign Affairs Web site, www.odin.dep.no, provides all sorts of general information and documentation, as well as daily news updates. Go to the bottom of the Norwegian intro page and click on the British flag for the English-language version, (this also provides access to the German and French versions).

Sweden

The best English-language Web sites include the general tourist information sites, www.sverigeturism.se and www.visit-sweden.com; the Swedish Environmental Protection Agency site, www.environ.se; the Sport & Outdoor Activities site, www.svenskidrott.se; and the Swedish Institute site at www.si.se/eng/eindex.html.

Finland

Finnish Web sites usually offer an English-language translation page or pages. A few good ones are the MEK, or Finnish Tourist Board at www.mek.fi; the SRM, or Finnish Youth Hostel Association at www.srmnet.org; and the Metsähallitus, or Forest and Park Service at www.metsa.fi. Virtual Finland, virtual.finland.fi/, is an excellent site maintained by the Finnish Ministry of Foreign Affairs.

Russia

These days you can search the Web for just about any Russian town and come up with something, but whether it has been updated in the last year or is accessible in English is another story. A few sites that might be useful include www.halcyon.comwistar/rus sites.html that has maps and links to various sites in eastern Russia, though some are outdated; and www.touritel.ru/hotels.htm that lists many Russian hotels, including those in the north. Then there's www.ex press.tsi.ru, which lists railway schedules; the only catch is that you have to enter the station names in Cyrillic. For weather forecasts, call up meteo.infospace.ru. If you have problems finding these sites, try again as they can be difficult to access.

BOOKS

Books and literary efforts about the Arctic, and those by Arctic writers, are covered in the Arctic Literature chapter later in the book. The following list includes guidebooks and other publications that will provide background information or help you plan a trip.

Lonely Planet

For more in-depth coverage of any of the countries discussed in this book, Lonely Planet publishes individual guides to *Alaska, Canada, Finland, Iceland, Greenland & the Faroe Islands, Norway, Russia, Ukraine & Belarus*, and a forthcoming guide to Sweden. If your focus is Scandinavia, you may want to check out *Scandinavian & Baltic Europe* and the *Scandinavian Europe Phrasebook* (with language background and phrases in Danish, Finnish, Icelandic, Norwegian and Swedish). Hikers headed for Alaska may also want to check out *Backpacking in Alaska*, which discusses hikes around the state.

General

For independent explorers along the highway systems in Alaska and northern Canada, an indispensable companion is *The

Milepost (toll-free ☎ 1-800 726 4707 or 907 272 6070, fax 907 258 5360, email books@themilepost.com), which has been through over 50 editions and covers practically every business, service and wide spot in the road along every mile/kilometre of the way. If you're heading beyond the highways, the same publisher also produces the *Alaska Wilderness Guide*, which presents an exhaustive array of possibilities in Alaska's roadless areas. You can find the Web site at www.themilepost.com.

If you're heading farther east in Arctic Canada, be sure to get hold of the comprehensive *Nunavut Handbook*, which can be ordered for US$21.50 from Nunatour, the Nunavut territorial tourist office; for contact details, see Tourist Information earlier in this chapter.

Anyone hoping to strike off into the Arctic wilderness on their own will thoroughly appreciate a copy of *Planning a Wilderness Trip in Canada & Alaska*, by Keith Morton. It contains information on everything you'll want to know, from chartering a bush flight and surviving bears, insects and inclement weather to gutting fish, cooking a palatable meal and dealing with such wilderness plagues as constipation and flatulence. It focuses on the wilderness areas of Alaska and Canada, but the information is applicable anywhere in the Arctic regions.

The Svalbard section in the Norway chapter of this book is intended for tourists and casual independent travellers only. Those who want more background information or wish to mount a longer expedition can check out one of the three books which are dedicated only to Svalbard. The German-language *Spitsbergen Reisehandbuch*, by longtime Svalbard resident Andreas Umbreit, is the most comprehensive. An abridged English translation of this book has been published by Bradt Publications as the *Guide to Spitsbergen*. Lastly, the French tour agency Grand Nord Grand Large has published the French-language *Spitzberg – L'Archipel du Svalbard*.

For Russia information and background, you can't beat Zwemmer (☎ 020-7379 6253) at 28 Denmark St, London WC2H 8NJ, which is a bookshop devoted entirely to Russia, the former USSR and Eastern Europe. You can send for a comprehensive catalogue.

Bird-watchers, botanists, and other wildlife enthusiasts have a wide choice of natural history publications about the Arctic regions. You may want to look at *A Naturalist's Guide to the Arctic*, published by Chicago University Press; *The Vanishing Arctic* by B & C Alexander; or *The Arctic Guide* by Chester and Oetzel. *One Season in the Taiga*, by Russian ornithologist Vadim Ryabitsev, describes the birds of Russia's vast taiga forests and *Alaska's Wildlife*, by Tom Walker, deals with the incredible wildlife of the 'American Serengeti'. In Britain, these and thousands of other natural history titles are available from Subbuteo Natural History Books Ltd (☎ 01352-756551, fax 01352-756004, email sales@subbooks.demon.co.uk) Pistyll Farm, Nercwys, near Mold, Flintshire, North Wales CH7 4EW. The company also takes international orders. On the Web it can be found at www.subbooks.demon.co.uk.

For a list of hiking, trekking, mountaineering and other adventure guides, see the Activities chapter.

PHOTOGRAPHY & VIDEO

Photographers worldwide sing the praises of the magical Arctic light. The crystalline air combined with the long, red rays cast by a low sun create excellent effects on film. Add spectacular scenery and colourful human aspects and you have a photographer's paradise. Quite a few tour companies offer photography tours and instruction, so check with your travel agent or a tourist office if you're interested.

Due to the clear Arctic light and glare from water, ice and snow, photographers may want to use a UV filter or a skylight filter and a lens shade. In winter, especially in the High Arctic, mechanical cameras should be polar oiled so the mechanism doesn't freeze up. In temperatures below approximately -20°C, electronic cameras may fail altogether.

As usual, subjects for interesting people shots are to be found throughout the region and most individuals will enjoy being photographed. As a courtesy, however, ask permission of the subject before snapping away, especially in Sami and Inuit areas where tourism is commonplace and people may have tired of photographic attention.

For wildlife photography and in places where your sightseeing will be done aboard ship, it's a good idea to bring a telephoto or zoom lens if you hope for any recognisable shots. Conversely, there will also be plenty of opportunities throughout the region to use a wide-angle 28mm lens for broad vistas, dramatic skies and urban landscapes.

Throughout the Arctic region, film, videotape and camera equipment are expensive and in most places, hard to find (the exception is in the larger towns of northern Scandinavia, where it's just expensive). If you're headed anywhere else in the Arctic, be sure to bring everything you'll be needing from home. When it comes to film, make sure that you bring twice as much as you plan on using – and then try to use restraint in the face of celluloid-swallowing scenery!

TIME

Because the Arctic is a circumpolar region, all time zones are represented. Norway and Sweden are one hour ahead of GMT/UTC, but summer time (from the end of March to the end of September) is another hour ahead. Otherwise, at noon in Norway and Sweden, it's 6 pm the previous day in New York and Toronto, 3 pm the previous day in San Francisco, 11 am in London, 9 pm in Sydney, 11 pm in Auckland, noon in Copenhagen and Berlin, and 1 pm in Helsinki (Finland is one hour later all year round). The 24 hour clock is used.

Russia stretches nearly halfway around the world and has the time zones to prove it. While the Kola Peninsula lies two hours later than Norway and Sweden and one hour later than Finland – that is, noon in Norway is 1 pm in Finland and 2 pm in Murmansk – the Chukotka and Kamchatka

peninsulas, in the Russian Far East, are nine hours later still.

Canada stretches across six time zones, and all provinces and territories except Saskatchewan use daylight-saving time during summer. It begins on the last Sunday in April and ends on the last Sunday in October. Some examples for time comparisons are: if it's noon in Toronto (UST/GMT), it is 9 am in Vancouver or Los Angeles, 1 pm in Halifax, 5 pm in London, 2 am (the following day) in Tokyo, and 3 am (the following day) in Sydney.

Most of Alaska remains four hours earlier than New York all year round, as both areas go onto daylight-saving time between April and October; the far western reaches of Alaska, including St Lawrence Island and the western Aleutian Islands, are five hours earlier than New York.

From 25 October to 24 March, Greenland is two hours earlier than London, two hours later than New York and 14 hours earlier than Sydney, while for the rest of the year, it's an hour earlier than these times. From 25 October to 24 March, Iceland is on the same time as London, five hours later than New York, and 11 hours earlier than Sydney; for the rest of the year, subtract one hour from these times.

ELECTRICITY
Alaska & Canada

Canada and Alaska use 110V, 60-cycle electric power. Non-North American visitors should bring a plug adaptor and a transformer if they wish to use their own small appliances such as razors and hairdryers. In Canada and Alaska, electrical goods come with a plug with two flat prongs or with two flat prongs and one round one (which is ground or earth). Most sockets can accommodate both types of plugs, but those that don't can be used with an adaptor.

Scandinavia

The electric current in Denmark (including Greenland), Norway, Sweden, Finland and Iceland is 220V AC, 50Hz. Plugs have two round pins and often clip in. Some hotels have 110V sockets or suitable adaptors. Note that US plugs, sockets and voltages are used at Kangerlussuaq and Thule Airbase in Greenland.

Russia
Standard voltage is 220V, 50 cycles AC, though a few places still have an old 127V system. Sockets require a continental or European plug with two round pins. Travel adaptors will enable many appliances from countries with different electrical set-ups to work in Russia. Look for voltage (V) and frequency (Hz) labels on your appliances. Some trains and hotel bathrooms have 110V and 220V shaver plugs.

WEIGHTS & MEASURES
The metric system applies in all of the Arctic except Alaska, where imperial measurements are used. Norway and Sweden use the term *mil*, which is a nautical mile, or 10km; don't confuse it with an imperial mile! In most areas, decimals are indicated by commas and thousands by points; in Alaska and Canada, the reverse system is used.

To convert between metric and imperial units, see the table on the inside back cover of the book.

HEALTH
Most Arctic residents (outside of Russia) enjoy one of the world's most pollution-free environments and healthiest – although admittedly often unpleasant – climates. As a result, travellers face few health hazards, but preparation is essential, as good medical care is only available in larger cities and towns, and those who do suffer from an accident or acute illness will need enough cash, insurance and time to reach it.

Travel Insurance
Citizens of Iceland, Denmark, Norway, Finland, Sweden and the UK have reciprocal health-care agreements, which entitles them to health care coverage in those countries. Local rates for ambulance services and prescriptions still apply. Citizens of other countries pay only minimal charges for

Medical Kit Check List

Following is a list of items you should consider including in your medical kit – consult your phamacist for brands available in your country.

☐ **Aspirin** or **paracetamol** (acetaminophen in the US) – for pain or fever.

☐ **Antihistamine** – for allergies, eg hay fever; to ease the itch from insect bites or stings; and to prevent motion sickness.

☐ **Antibiotics** – consider including these if you're travelling well off the beaten track; see your doctor, as they must be prescribed, and carry the prescription with you.

☐ **Loperamide** or **diphenoxylate** – 'blockers' for diarrhoea; **prochlorperazine** or **metaclopramide** for nausea and vomiting.

☐ **Rehydration mixture** – to prevent dehydration, eg due to severe diarrhoea; particularly important when travelling with children.

☐ **Insect repellent, sunscreen, lip balm** and **eye drops.**

☐ **Calamine lotion, sting relief spray** or **aloe vera** – to ease irritation from sunburn and insect bites or stings.

☐ **Antifungal cream** or **powder** – for fungal skin infections and thrush.

☐ **Antiseptic** (such as povidone-iodine) – for cuts and grazes.

☐ **Bandages, Band-Aids (plasters)** and other wound dressings.

☐ **Water purification tablets** or **iodine.**

☐ **Scissors, tweezers** and a **thermometer** (note that mercury thermometers are prohibited by airlines).

☐ **Syringes** and **needles** – in case you need injections in a country with medical hygine problems. Ask your doctor for a note explaining why you have them.

☐ **Cold** and **flu tablets, throat lozenges** and **nasal decongestant.**

☐ **Multivitamins** – consider for long trips, when dietary vitamin intake may be inadequate.

medical services and non-discounted rates on prescriptions. Greenland extends free health care to everyone, regardless of citizenship, but prescription medicines may be unavailable in smaller towns and villages.

Even for those who are entitled to covered treatment, it's a good idea to take out a travel insurance policy to cover theft, loss and medical problems. There is a wide variety of policies available and your travel agent will make recommendations. The international student travel policies handled by STA Travel or other student travel organisations are usually good value. Some policies offer lower and higher medical expenses options but the higher one is chiefly for countries like the USA with extremely high medical costs.

Note that some travel insurance policies specifically exclude 'dangerous activities' which can include mountain climbing, kayaking, motorcycling and even canoeing and trekking. If these activities are on your agenda, you don't want that sort of policy. You may prefer a policy which pays doctors or hospitals directly rather than requiring you to pay now and claim later. If you do have to claim later, make sure you keep all documentation. Some policies ask you to call back (reverse charges) to a centre in your home country where an immediate assessment of your problem is made. Check if the policy covers ambulances or an emergency flight home. If you have to stretch out, you will need more than one seat and somebody will have to pay for it!

Water Purification

The water from taps in all Arctic countries except Russia is safe to drink and, for the most part, surface water is potable except in urban areas and much of Arctic Russia. Water from glacial rivers may appear murky but you may drink it, if necessary, in small quantities. The murk is actually fine particles of silt scoured from the rock by the glacier and drinking too much of this has been known to clog up internal plumbing.

Those who are concerned about contamination, however, should purify their drinking water. The simplest way is to thoroughly boil it. Technically, this means for 10 minutes although most people can't be bothered to wait that long. Remember that at higher altitudes water boils at lower temperatures so germs are less likely to be killed. Simple filtering will not remove all organisms so, if you cannot boil water, it may be treated chemically. Chlorine tablets (Puritabs, Steritabs or other brand names) will kill many, but not all organisms.

Iodine is very effective in purifying water and is available in tablet form (Potable Aqua) but follow the directions carefully and remember that too much iodine can be harmful.

Giardia

Although most unpopulated lands throughout the Arctic regions serve as sheep pastures, giardia is widespread only in Alaska and Canada, making it unwise to drink untreated surface water. Giardia, sometimes called 'beaver fever', is an intestinal parasite that lives in the faeces of humans and animals and is normally contracted through drinking water.

Problems can start several weeks after you have been exposed to the parasite and symptoms may sometimes remit for a few days and then return; this can go on for several weeks or even longer. The first signs are a swelling of the stomach, pale-coloured faeces, diarrhoea, frequent gas and headache, followed by nausea and depression.

You should seek medical advice if you think you have giardiasis or amoebic dysentery, but where this is not possible, tinidazole or metronidazole are the recommended drugs. Treatment is a 2g single dose of tinidazole or 250mg of metronidazole three times daily for five to 10 days.

Sunburn & Windburn

Sunburn and windburn should be primary concerns for anyone planning to trek or travel over snow and ice. The sun will burn you even if you feel cold and the wind will

SAD – Seasonal Affective Disorder

The seasonal effects on human moods and behaviour is an established phenomenon, and the syndrome known as seasonal affective disorder (SAD) represents the morbid extreme of the spectrum of seasonality.

SAD is characterised by recurrent depressive episodes in the autumn and winter months, followed by hypomania (excessive activity) or mania (extreme excitement) in summer. Classic symptoms include carbohydrate cravings, increased sleep time, fatigue, loss of libido, weight gain and a profound sense of loneliness. Those most affected by SAD include a subgroup of hypersensitive, often depressed individuals with tendencies towards emotional sensitivity and the likelihood of entertaining unconventional beliefs and ideas.

People with SAD have a 'biological clock' that is significantly phase-delayed and less tuned to the 24 hour daily cycle. The presence of melatonin seems to be an indicator of this disturbance, but not a cause.

SAD differs from classical affective disorders (depression, melancholy, schizophrenia and manic depression) in its frequency, severity, symptoms and typical seasonal variation. More women are affected than men and the incidence has been estimated as high as 10% of the population residing north of 45°N or south of 45°S latitude. However, some studies have suggested similar incidences in more tropical climes where seasonal variations may be minimal (such as India).

There is also a tendency for seasonal changes in mood and behaviour to run in families, largely due to biological predispositions. Genetic effects exert a global influence across all behavioural changes, accounting for at least a third of the seasonal variance in both men and women.

Classic treatment has consisted of bright light, administered for up to 45 minutes just after waking (6am to 9 am). The response in people with SAD is contingent on the exposure of the individuals' eyes to light, and it's worth noting that 40% of patients are resistant to this therapy.

In addition, the timing of phototherapy remains controversial. Some data show that the antidepressant effect of a single pulse of light was similar in the morning, at noon and in the evening, and the level of the neurotransmitter serotonin (a mood-mediating chemical) is usually suppressed. Treatment with its precursor L-tryptophan (no longer available in the USA) and antidepressants (such as fluoxitene, better-known as Prozac) have also proven beneficial, especially to those resistant to phototherapy. Additionally, relapse occurs more slowly after withdrawal of pharmacological therapy than phototherapy.

These treatments have also been applied to school-age children: the treatment appears to improve cognition and alertness but no change in intellect or improvement in attendance is seen.

Current studies include the roles of other neurotransmitters (catacholamines), endocrine agents (cortisol) and vitamins (primarily D, as found in cod-liver oil). Others are examining the inverse relationships with latitude and geomagnetic field decreasing melatonin function; and the size of one's pituitary gland in relation to duration of sunlight.

Further resources are available on the Internet (at www.outside.co.uk, www.pho tothera.com or www.truesun.com) or through your local doctor.

Dr Fred Peterson, MD

cause dehydration and chafing of skin. Use a good sun block and a moisture cream on exposed skin, even on cloudy days. A hat provides added protection and zinc oxide or some other barrier cream for your nose and lips is recommended.

Reflection and glare from ice and snow can cause snow blindness, so high-protection sunglasses are essential for any sort of glacier visit or ski trip.

Hypothermia

Perhaps the most dangerous health threat in the Arctic regions is hypothermia. This occurs when the body loses heat faster than it can produce it and the core temperature falls. It is surprisingly easy to progress from very cold to dangerously cold due to a combination of wind, wet clothing, fatigue and hunger, even if the air temperature is above freezing. It is best to dress in layers; silk, wool and polypropylene are all good insulating materials. A hat is important as a lot of heat is lost through the scalp. A strong, waterproof and windproof outer layer is essential since keeping dry is of utmost importance. Carry basic supplies including food containing simple sugars to generate heat quickly and be sure plenty of fluids are always available.

Symptoms of hypothermia include exhaustion; numb skin (particularly toes and fingers); shivering; slurred speech; irrational, confused or violent behaviour; lethargy; stumbling; dizzy spells; muscle cramps; and violent bursts of energy. Irrationality may include sufferers claiming they are warm and trying to remove clothing.

To treat hypothermia, first get out of the wind and/or rain. If possible, remove wet clothing and replace with dry, warm clothing. Drink hot liquids, not alcohol, and eat some high-calorie, easily digestible food. This should be enough for the early stages of hypothermia but, if it has gone further, it may be necessary to place the victim in a warm sleeping bag and get in with them. Do not rub the patient, or place them near a fire, or remove wet clothing while they're exposed to wind. If possible, place them in a warm (not hot) bath but, if that is not available, remember that the body heat of another person is immediately more important than medical attention, so do not leave the victim alone under any circumstances.

Rabies

Rabies exists in all Arctic countries except Iceland, and is caused by a bite or scratch from an infected animal. Dogs are noted carriers. Any bite, scratch or even lick from a mammal should be cleaned immediately and thoroughly. Scrub with soap in running water, then clean with an alcohol solution. If there is any possibility that the animal is infected, medical help should be sought immediately. Even if the animal is not rabid, all bites should be treated seriously as they can become infected or can result in tetanus. A rabies vaccination is now available.

Bugs

The sheer density of bugs and pests in the Arctic rivals that of the Amazon. For survival guidelines, see Dangers & Annoyances later in this chapter.

Sexually Transmitted Diseases

Infection with the human immunodeficiency virus (HIV) may lead to acquired immune deficiency syndrome (AIDS), which is a fatal disease. Any exposure to blood, blood products or body fluids may put the individual at risk. The disease is often transmitted through sexual contact or dirty needles - vaccinations, acupuncture, tattooing and body piercing can be potentially as dangerous as intravenous drug use. HIV/AIDS can also be spread through infected blood transfusions. If you do need an injection, ask to see the syringe unwrapped in front of you, or take a needle and syringe pack with you. Fear of HIV infection should never preclude treatment for serious medical conditions.

Motion Sickness

Since a great deal of Arctic travel is by boat or ship and much of the overland travel is on rough, unsurfaced roads, those prone to motion sickness may have problems. Eating lightly before and during a trip will reduce the chances of motion sickness. If you know you are likely to be affected, try to find a place that minimises disturbance –

near the wing on aircraft, close to midships on boats and near the centre on buses. Fresh air almost always helps, but reading or cigarette smoking (or even being around someone else's smoke) normally makes matters worse.

Commercial motion-sickness preparations, which can cause drowsiness, have to be taken before the trip – it's too late after you've begun feeling ill. Dramamine tablets should be taken three hours before departure. Ginger and peppermint are excellent natural preventatives and are available in capsule form.

Health Care

Alaska In case you haven't heard, health care in the USA is extremely expensive, and Alaska has among the highest health costs in the country (only Alaska Natives receive free government health care). If you can pay for it, excellent care is available in Anchorage and Fairbanks, and evacuation services from the bush to these cities are generally very well organised (and formidably expensive). In short, a good travel insurance policy is essential.

Canada Medical, hospital and dental care is excellent but very expensive in Canada and for non-residents, the standard rate for a bed in a city hospital is at least $500 a day and up to $2000 a day. Therefore, it's essential to buy an insurance policy that covers you in Canada and to carefully check the precise details, limitations and exclusions of that coverage.

The largest hospital and medical insurer for visitors is John Ingle Insurance (☎ 416-340 0100, toll-free ☎ 1-800 387 4770), 438 University Ave, Suite 1200, Toronto, ON M7Y 2Z1. It offers hospital medical care (HMC) policies from a minimum of seven days to a maximum of one year with a possible renewal of one additional year. The 30-day basic coverage costs $90 for an adult under the age of 55, $110 for ages 55 to 64, and $130 above that. Family rates are available. Coverage includes the hospital rate, doctors' fees, extended health care and

other features. Visitors are not covered for conditions they had prior to arrival.

Greenland Greenland extends free health and dental care to everyone, regardless of citizenship (courtesy of Danish taxpayers!). While all towns have hospitals or health clinics and access to medications, many villages lack pharmacy services and may only have a health worker. Serious cases will be transferred to the main hospital in Nuuk, or in extreme cases, to Copenhagen.

Iceland Iceland has no private medical services; they are available only through the National Health system. By reciprocal agreement, citizens of Nordic countries and the UK are automatically covered by Icelandic National Health. Other travellers need private or travel insurance coverage. Dental care is handled privately, but charges are lower than in the USA and comparable to those in most European countries.

Norway For a medical emergency, dial ☎ 113; for nonemergency medical needs, visit the local tourist office, your accommodation, or a pharmacy for a referral.

EU citizens may be required to pay a service fee for emergency medical treatment, but presentation of an E111 form will certainly expedite matters and minimise paperwork. Inquire about these at your national health service or travel agent well in advance; you may be able to pick one up from a local post office. Travel insurance is still advisable, however, because it allows treatment flexibility and will also cover any ambulance and repatriation costs.

Sweden Apoteket pharmacies provide prescription and non-prescription medicines as well as advice on how to deal with common ailments. The *nattapotek* are open 24 hours. For emergencies and casualty services, local medical centres *(vårdcentraler)* or hospitals *(sjukhus* or *lasarett)* are the best places to go (you must show your passport). These are operated by the public health system and duty doctors *(distriktsläkare* or *jourhavande läkare)* are standing by. Ordinary casualty visits cost Skr300.

The general emergency number, including the ambulance, is ☎ 112. Sweden's health system can be expensive and travel insurers recommend top levels of coverage. Private doctors *(läkare)* are also listed in telephone books, but check that they are affiliated with the national health scheme (UK citizens enjoy reciprocity). All EU citizens will require an E111 form (see Norway earlier in this chapter for details). Dentists *(tandläkare)* are quite expensive when compared with the rest of Europe, but are a bargain by US standards.

Finland From anywhere in Finland dial ☎ 112 for emergency ambulance service and ☎ 10023 for 24-hour emergency medical advice. Local pharmacies *(apteekki)* and neighbourhood health-care centres are fine for minor medical problems. Tourist offices and hotels can recommend doctors or dentists, and your embassy will probably know one who speaks your language.

Visitors whose home countries have reciprocal medical-care agreements with Finland and can produce a passport or insurance card – or an E111 form for EU citizens – are charged the same subsidised rates as Finns. These are Fmk50 for a doctor visit and Fmk125 per day for hospitalisation. Others pay the full cost of treatment.

Russia Hotels and guides can call a doctor; in fact, some hotels keep one on call. Polyclinics *(polikliniki)*, which are like district surgeries or health centres, provide free medical attention, though you may have to pay a little for medications. Having said that, the Russian medical system is in a dismal state due to lack of funds, poor equipment and poor training, and some common medications are unavailable.

In Moscow and St Petersburg there are some expensive western-run medical services and pharmacies as well as some higher-quality Russian clinics and hospitals which are used to dealing with foreigners. Otherwise, the average Russian pharmacy

(apteka) lacks many medications which are considered standard in most western countries, and when it comes to supplies, the Arctic region lies at the back of the queue. When medical treatment is required, foreigners should have a contingency plan for evacuation back home.

For problems beyond first-aid (including hospitalisation) contact your embassy or consulate for advice. If your condition requires evacuation, most will probably help to organise it, but unless you have medivac insurance, you'll need either mountains of cash or a credit card with a very generous credit limit.

WOMEN TRAVELLERS

The Arctic presents few concerns specific to women. However, throughout the region, menstruating women may want to avoid venturing into the wilds, as it's believed that menstrual fluids can attract bears. Similarly, avoid carrying strong-smelling toiletries, such as deodorants, colognes or minty toothpaste; when it comes to human goodies, if it smells nice, bears may well be happy to sample a taste of it.

Alaska

The bush areas of northern Alaska are still very much man's country. Although two women, Libby Riddles and Susan Butcher (residents of the rural communities of Teller and Manley Hot Springs, respectively) won the Iditarod dogsled race four years running, it will be a long while before feminism is taken very seriously. Similarly, in Native communities, traditional male and female roles are more emphasised than they are in most towns and non-Native areas.

As a sort of end-of-the-road destination for the rest of the USA, Alaska also attracts some pretty marginal characters, and women should never hitch lifts. Similarly, bars in the USA play a different role than most of their counterparts in Europe or Australasia, and it's unwise to wander into such a place unaccompanied unless you're looking to be picked up.

Canada

More and more, women are travelling alone in Canada for both business and holidays, and there are few cultural or traditional pitfalls of which females need to be aware. However, women may well face some sexism, and the threat of violence is certainly felt more by women than by men.

When travelling alone, try to arrive at your destination before dark. If driving, keep your vehicle well maintained and don't get low on petrol. If you do break down on the highway, especially at night, a large pre-made sign reading 'Call Police' to place in the window may be useful and – unless you're in the back of beyond – will quickly result in a police car on the way. Away from busy areas, especially at night, women should remain in their car with the doors locked.

Greenland

With its Scandinavian veneer, Greenland presents few problems for women travellers. However, it would be decidedly unwise to venture alone into a night spot frequented by locals unless you're prepared for a lot of attention – and more.

Scandinavia

Throughout Scandinavia, sexual equality is emphasised and there should be no question of discrimination. Women often travel alone or in pairs around the region, which should pose no problems, but women do tend to attract more unwanted attention than men, and common sense is the best guide to dealing with potentially dangerous situations like hitchhiking and walking alone at night. Most bars and night spots in the region are both fine and fun, but in some places (particularly in Finland) solo women may be vulnerable to harassment.

Russia

Women travellers are unlikely to experience sexual harassment on the streets, though sexual stereotypes remain prevalent and in remoter areas, the idea that women are somehow less capable than men may persist. Women travellers may also be treated rudely or ignored by female service bureau staff while a man standing next to you is getting smiles and answers to his questions. Perseverance is the only answer. Interacting with Russian women outside the unreal world of tourist hotels can be enjoyable. Among other places, markets provide a chance to communicate with local people. Even with minimal Russian language skills, you'll get by and penetrate those unsmiling facades.

Anywhere in the country, revealing clothing will probably attract unwanted attention, and is unsuitable for nights out or visits to Russian Orthodox churches. With lawlessness and crime on the rise, you need to be wary; a woman alone should certainly avoid private taxis at night. In addition, any young or youngish woman alone in or near flashy bars frequented by foreigners risks being mistaken for a prostitute. Clearly stating your status will defuse most situations.

You'll now find tampons in most pharmacies but the prices are shocking, so that's one item to bring from home.

DISABLED TRAVELLERS

Scandinavia (including Greenland), Canada and Alaska all have regulations requiring businesses, public transport and government offices to be wheelchair accessible, and in North America, car parks have special disabled parking spots with ramps, which are near the entrance to the building. This will be useful if you're limiting your explorations to cities and towns, but unfortunately, the Arctic wilderness areas that most people are after – as well as Arctic Russia – will mostly be the domain of the able-bodied.

However, some parts of the Arctic are accessible by private vehicle; Arctic cruises are available to just about everyone (although people with limited mobility will probably have to forego Zodiac landings); dogsled trips are always a possibility; and many tour operators do cater for disabled travellers. When booking your trip, be sure to specify your individual needs and ascertain whether the operator is equipped to accommodate you.

Whether travelling independently or on a tour, you're limited only by your creativity and willingness to push your limits. Wheelchair users have rafted Arctic rivers, blind people have climbed Mt McKinley, and thousands of people with limited mobility travel in private vehicles to northern Alaska, Canada and Scandinavia every year.

For general travel information, disabled travellers may want to contact one of the following organisations:

Australia
National Communication & Recreation Network, (☎/TTY 02-6285 3713, TTY toll-free ☎ 1-800 806 769, fax 02-6285 3714, email nican@spirit.com.au), PO Box 407, Curtin, ACT 2605
Canada
The Canadian Paraplegic Association (☎ 416-422 5640), 520 Sutherland Drive, Toronto, ONT M4G 3V9
Finland
Rullaten Ry (☎ 09-694 1155), Malminkatu 38, 00100 Helsinki
Iceland
Icelandic League of Handicapped Persons (☎ 551 2517), Hátún 10, Reykjavík
Ireland
National Rehabilitation Board (☎ 01-874 7503), 44 North Great George's St, Dublin 1
New Zealand
Disability Information Service (☎ 03-366 6189, fax 03-379 5939), 314 Worcester St, PO Box 32-074, Christchurch
Norway
Norges Handikapforbund (☎ 22 95 28 60, fax 22 95 21 51), Folke Bernadottes vei 2, N-0862 Oslo
Sweden
De Handikappades Riksförbund (☎ 08-18 91 00, fax 08-645 65 41), Katrinebergsvägen 6, 11743 Stockholm
UK
Royal Association for Disability & Rehabilitation (☎ 020-7250 3222), 12 City Forum, 250 City Rd, London EC1V 8AF
USA
Access Alaska (☎ 907-248 4777)
Mobility International USA (☎ 541-343 1284, fax 451-343 6812, email miusa@igc.apc.org), PO Box 10767, Eugene, OR 97440
Society for the Advancement of Travel for the Handicapped (☎ 212-447 7284), 347 Fifth Ave No 610, New York, NY 10016

SENIOR TRAVELLERS

In Arctic North America, seniors make up a significant percentage of the visitor population, mainly because they often have sufficient time and money to make such a trip worthwhile and rewarding. While many of these arrive on all-inclusive holiday packages, huge numbers travel independently in private vehicles, especially motor homes (see Dangers & Annoyances later in this chapter). Similarly, in Europe, a growing number of seniors are either driving or organising their own itineraries through northern Scandinavia.

If you're signing onto an organised tour, try to ascertain in advance what sort of activities will be included. Many Arctic-region tours are activity-oriented and may involve a lot of walking or other physical effort. Even cruises normally include landings, which require some measure of agility to climb in and out of the tenders. Note that some adventure tour companies may have an upper age limit – most often around 70 or 75 – so be sure to ask.

Throughout Scandinavia, Canada and Alaska, senior travellers are entitled to discounts on museum admission, ferries, rail travel and often, accommodation as well. In North America, some restaurants even offer discounts on meals. However, these aren't always advertised, so it often pays to ask and to have some proof of your age. In Europe, the definition of 'senior' is normally anyone older than 60 to 67, while in North America, that is more often 55 to 60.

TRAVEL WITH CHILDREN

If you're organising a self-drive 'family holiday' in the Arctic, it pays to remember that distances in northern North America and Europe are long – you'll be on the road for weeks rather than days – so it's wise to plan stops and activities along the way to keep the kids occupied and interested. Bring a few small travel games; take short walks off the highway with a bird or plant book, identifying species you encounter; and stop for picnics in wild spots rather than at restaurants or roadhouses, to give the children a chance to run off some energy. Note that northern camping grounds are great places to meet other families with children.

If you're using public transport, trains are preferable to buses, as they allow children to get up and stretch their legs (or run rampant, as the case may be) or go for a snack. Ferries and ships are also comfortable but you'll obviously have to keep a very close watch on younger children.

Many tour companies also welcome children, but on activity tours – hiking, rafting, kayaking, wildlife-viewing and even cruises – there may be a lower age limit. This would normally be anywhere from 12 to 18, depending on the risk level.

As with seniors, children almost always receive discounts on attractions, activities and transport. The age cut-off will vary, but in Scandinavia, it may be anywhere from six to 12 and in North America, from six to 16.

DANGERS & ANNOYANCES
Crime
The good news is that the Arctic regions – even the cities – are generally far less risky than areas farther south.

The Scandinavian countries are some of the safest in the world, crimes perpetrated against travellers are fairly rare, and in the Arctic regions, you won't even have to worry about the Neo-Nazis, drug-related crime and obnoxious panhandlers that infest the larger cities of southern and central Europe. In Arctic North America, the risks are slightly greater, especially in larger Alaskan and Canadian towns, but overall, they're still quite safe by urban Australian, European and contiguous US standards.

Unfortunately, the same can't be said about Russia, which suffers from increasing poverty and some of the world's most pervasive organised crime. While most of it is aimed at local entrepreneurs, visitors still need to keep their wits about them and remain vigilant with their belongings.

RVs & Caravans
In summer, folks from the USA and southern Canada head north by the thousands in enormous self-contained motor homes (RVs). They are usually equipped with everything under the sun – gravel/bug shields, TVs, satellite dishes, VCRs, showers, bicycles, lawn chairs, microwave ovens, rowboats, canoes, 25 jerry cans full of petrol, and yes, even the kitchen sink – followed by a spindly trailer burdened with the family car and perhaps a couple of four-wheelers (all-terrain vehicles or ATVs) or jet skis. The obvious snail analogy is enhanced by the fact that with all this stuff, they can't reach speeds over about 60km/h. While this is about the right speed for serious highway sightseeing, the typically narrow northern highways become chronically constipated and anyone in more of a hurry will become frustrated as they attempt to overtake a train of these things that may stretch for hundreds of kilometres. And it's a well-known law of the north country that it doesn't matter how many you overtake – there's always another one ahead.

The European equivalents are the caravan (camper trailer) and a strange German breed of home-built motor home. When these are encountered in Scandinavia, they'll almost invariably be headed for Nordkapp, but at speeds that suggest very little conviction and in a manner that indicates either paranoia or concurrent sightseeing. Unfortunately, few European drivers have ever before seen the likes of the typically narrow and twisting Norwegian highways, and many decide that the safest bet is to opt for the middle half of the road. This makes them not only impossible to overtake, but also impossible to pass when coming from the opposite direction.

In both these cases, drivers of lesser vehicles will have to work on keeping calm and always exercise extreme caution. For those who are actually driving motor homes and caravans, please be courteous; if you're holding up a string of five vehicles or more, pull off to the side and let them overtake.

Alcohol

Alcohol is a serious problem throughout the Arctic, and is strictly controlled in Scandinavia and marginally regulated in Greenland and parts of Arctic Alaska and Canada. Alcohol abuse has created myriad problems, including violence, social decay, suicide, child and spouse abuse and the breakdown of families. In an attempt to get a grip on things, many Alaskan and Canadian villages have voted themselves dry, but a thriving black market and access to home brews mock any local attempts at alcohol control and in many places, weekend or pay day evenings see rampant partying and all its associated strife. At such times, it's probably wise to keep a low profile until you can assess the general demeanour.

Alcohol in the Arctic

All indigenous Arctic populations suffer from similar social, cultural and physical maladjustment, and it's widely believed that the high incidence of alcohol abuse and alcohol dependence among the 26 recognised Arctic Mongoloid peoples may be mediated by their unique environmental and genetic characteristics. These aboriginal peoples (the Inuit, Chukchi, Sami, Yakut, etc) have a shorter average life span and sustain a disproportionate amount of physical disease and mental illness.

Manifestations such as alcohol amnesia, withdrawal and alcohol poisoning are seen in upwards of 50% of some adult populations, and infant mortality rates among the Canadian Inuit are more than double the national average. Of the adult Native population in Canada, a third suffer chronic health problems. There are also higher rates of homicide, suicide and diseases such as pneumonia.

Studies have shown that those who respond less intensely to alcohol are at greater risk of developing alcohol related problems. Despite the 'firewater' myth, a higher rather than lower alcohol tolerance predisposes one to the risk of alcoholism. The biologic and genetic risk factors are not thoroughly understood. Native American men show altered responses to alcohol influenced by the presence of polymorphism in the alcohol metabolising enzyme alcohol dehydrogenase (ADH). As with Caucasians, there is a positive association between the incidence of alcoholism and a family history of alcoholism.

What little research has been done shows significant subjective differences, but not objective effects of alcohol. Research with aboriginal Arctic peoples also suggests a tendency to blame illness and alcoholism on natural and supernatural causes.

Treatment is problematic: counselling and education heighten awareness but enjoy only marginal success, and in fact the most successful strategy thus far has been the limitation of the availability of alcohol. However, alcohol related mortality did not differ significantly between Native American reservations where alcohol was prohibited and those where alcohol was legal.

Although national policies in Arctic countries have been uniformly aimed at reducing the overuse and abuse of alcohol, Scandinavian countries with the highest taxes and strictest regulations on alcohol tend to have higher incidences of alcoholism than countries without such controls, and among aboriginal peoples, the controls are mitigated by the relative governmental autonomy of Arctic Natives, perceptions of a 'Big Brother' threat, and a general apathy towards the problem.

Dr Fred Peterson, MD

Environmental Dangers

Weather & Climate The first thing to remember about weather and climate in the Arctic is that anything can happen at any time. I've seen convection thunderstorms and temperatures more appropriate for the tropical rainforests in Arctic Norway; July snowstorms in Greenland; T-shirt weather in Svalbard; winter sunshine and 5°C temperatures in Siberia; and -50° for weeks on end in Alaska.

The bottom line is that the weather is unpredictable, to say the least, and can be unimaginably harsh or just as surprisingly pleasant. If you set off on a hiking or trekking trip in 15°C sunshine without a full complement of protective winter gear, you're risking hypothermia or worse if the weather dishes up a torrential downpour or a howling blizzard. In fact (and this is the annoyance factor here), sunny-to-sour weather changes, at least in my experience, are more the rule than the exception! In short, hope for the best and plan for the worst.

Wild Animals Most visitors to the region will want to observe bears in the wild, but few creatures inspire more fear and trepidation than the boreal bruin.

Three species of bears inhabit the Arctic regions. Polar bears, which are exclusively carnivorous (although they do occasionally eat seaweed in times of food shortages), keep mainly to the sea ice and the immediately adjoining tundra coastlines around the Arctic Ocean and Hudson Bay, as well as most of east Greenland. To humans, they're by far the most dangerous bear species, and will happily attack and eat a defenceless hiker or camper. For that reason, when visiting their domain, it's always wise to carry a suitable weapon and know how to use it if necessary.

The other circumpolar species is the brown bear, which lives mainly in the taiga forests and adjoining tundra areas of Alaska, Canada, northern Scandinavia and Russia (small populations are also found in the western USA and mountainous areas of Central Europe). The largest brown bears are those living along the coastlines, where they enjoy a high-protein diet rich in fish. The size and weight record goes to Alaska's Kodiak Island bears, which can stand nearly 4m high. Inland bears, on the other hand, tend to be smaller due to a more vegetable-dependent diet. In North America, this smaller sub-species is commonly known as the grizzly bear.

The third Arctic ursine is the American black bear, whose range just extends northward into the southernmost taiga forests, mainly in areas dominated by birch and other hardwoods. It's considerably smaller than the brown or polar bear, but can still be extremely dangerous and shouldn't be underestimated.

While paranoia isn't warranted in dealing with brown and black bears, some precautions are worth considering. Around populated areas, some bears may have become accustomed to humans and their edible scraps and goodies, and they're perfectly happy to stroll into towns or public camping grounds, hang around garbage tips and even break into vehicles and homes if it means a free meal. These are not the sort of bears you want to encounter!

Hikers and campers should take special precautions. In forested areas, place your food in nylon bags, tie them to a rope and sling them over a branch well away from your tent. Hoist it up high enough (about 3m) so a standing bear can't reach it and if you're in black bear country, keep it away from the tree trunk, as black bears are pretty good climbers. If you're on the open tundra, pack your food in a string container and deposit it well away from your tent – at least 100m. Don't leave food scraps around your campsite and never keep food (or any strong-smelling item) in your tent.

Don't try to get close-up photographs of bears and never come between a bear and its cubs. If you see cubs, quietly and quickly disappear. If you do see a bear, try to get upwind to warn it of your presence and avoid startling it. While hiking through woods or the mountains in bear country, some people dangle a bell or tin full of pebbles which will rattle and ostensibly warn bears that people are around, but singing or speaking loudly works just as well. Whatever you do, don't feed bears – they lose their fear of people and, especially in national parks, may become nuisances and eventually have to be destroyed (also see Women Travellers earlier in this chapter).

Blackflies, Midges & Mosquitoes During the short boreal summers, tundra bogs and ponds turn into prolific nurseries for insects – mosquitoes, midges, blackflies and gnats – which hatch in numbers that will boggle the imagination. While they're an essential part of the ecosystem and provide nourishment for migrating and nesting birds, they're also hell on earth for the warm-blooded mammals that are their main food source. There's no way to escape the swarms and there are tales of caribou being driven insane or utterly drained of blood.

Although some of the peskiest bugs are actually non-biting midges, most are perfectly happy to drill anywhere and through anything, and some can even penetrate denim jeans. For humans, the effects of the bites and stings are usually small itchy bumps in the case of mosquitoes and midges, and larger swollen areas in the case of blackflies. While there's little pain during the bite, the cumulative effect of hundreds of bites can be very annoying indeed. Fortunately, there's no malaria this far north and in most cases the hazards are mainly psychological.

As a rule, darker clothing is thought to attract biting insects more than lighter clothing. Apparently, perfumes and colognes also attract the wrong kind of attention. The need for a good repellent can't be stressed enough; carry plenty of 'jungle juice' liquid or spray repellents with a good percentage of that bug bane, DEET (diethylmetatoluamide). It's nasty stuff to put on your skin (and shouldn't be used on young children), but is eminently preferable to insanity. However, it doesn't work on the tiny but vicious Alaskan and Canadian gnats locally called 'no-see-ums'. For these, the only proven repellent is a skin cream known as Skin-so-Soft, produced by Avon; it's normally diluted in water and applied liberally.

Other measures include minimising the amount of exposed skin by wearing long-sleeved shirts and long trousers. In extreme cases, you'll also need a head net, which is a hat with a veil-like net which fastens around the neck and keeps the kamikaze divers out of your eyes, nose, mouth and lungs.

In most places, June is the worst month, but in northern Scandinavia and Russia, they endure into mid-August. The worst places are open boggy tundra or in forested areas, but fortunately, even a light breeze will send most of them diving for cover (or heading for shelter downwind of any obstruction, such as a hiker). If you're camping, a tent with a zippered insect screen is essential.

If you do run out of repellent and find yourself being eaten alive – and this can happen – you'll get some temporary relief by submerging your body in water. At least this will give you a moment to think clearly and make a plan, but the bottom line is, don't run out of repellent!

SPECIAL EVENTS

All around the Arctic, a celebration – and a sigh of relief – marks the end of the polar night, when the sun returns after its sojourn below the horizon. With considerably less fanfare, it's also bid farewell as it descends below the horizon for the last time before the polar night.

Throughout Scandinavia and in Greenland, the summer solstice, or Midsummer, is celebrated as one of the year's most festive occasions with midnight sun games and barbecues on the beach or in the forests and mountains. It may fall anywhere from 20 to 23 June.

Every year, one of the four Inuit countries holds the Inuit Circumpolar Conference, a week-long cultural meeting where

(continued on page 70)

The Arctic's Most Prominent Citizen

The legend of Father Christmas, or Santa Claus (Noel Baba in Turkish), is said to have begun in Demre, Turkey in the 4th century. A poor peasant who lacked the money for his three daughters' dowries decided to ensure that at least two could find husbands by selling the youngest into slavery. However, the night before the sale, the now famous Christian bishop of Myra (Kale), later canonised as St Nicholas, filled a sock with gold coins while the family was sleeping and dropped it down the chimney. This 'gift from heaven' provided the girls with some dowry clout, and made them 'worthy'.

As a result, St Nicholas became the patron saint of virgins, and went on to also represent sailors, poor children, pawnbrokers, moneylenders, merchants, wanderers, gift-givers, judges, murderers, thieves, paupers, scholars, Mother Russia, and just about anyone else who might have found themselves in a heap of trouble. On 9 May 1087, upon hearing that Venetian merchants were about to carry the saint's body off to Venice, the merchant seamen of Bari, Italy, raided Myra and carried the remains back to Bari, where they're now ostensibly interred in the Cathedral of St Nicholas. As it happens, the anniversary of the death of St Nicholas, 6 December (345 or 352 AD), was also near the Christmas holiday.

After the Protestant Reformation, efforts throughout northern Europe attempted to eradicate the St Nicholas legends, but they were unsuccessful. It was said in that period that he had been seen to ride through the sky on a horse, wearing bishop's robes and bearing gifts. In the Netherlands, Sinter Klaas and his Moorish helper, the elf Black Peter, exchanged sweets and nuts for hay to feed their sky horses, and in Germany, Sankt Nikolaus was credited with surreptitiously placing gifts of nuts, apples and sweets in children's shoes. Parents quickly caught on to the obvious disciplinary tool this offered, and children who hadn't behaved properly were presented with switches rather than goodies. The Protestant churches, on the other hand, who perceived that the popular myth challenged clerical authority, encouraged the replacement of the Catholic St Nicholas with the Christ Child or *Christkindl* (hence the modern moniker, Kris Kringle).

Another facet of the story unfolded in medieval Scandinavia, where the pagan god of war, Oðinn, spent his days riding across the world on his eight footed horse Sleipnir, giving out rewards and punishment, and the god Þór travelled across the sky in a goat-drawn chariot, battling the forces of cold, ice and snow with his red sword of lightning. The third member of the Norse trinity, Freyr, served as the purveyor of love and fertility, and with the advent of Christianity in Scandinavia, the pagan fertility feast, *joulu* or *lol*, syncretised nicely with the holiday to honour the birth of Christ. Modern Scandinavia has developed several unique traditions; in the countryside, gifts of oat cheaves are left out for the birds and a bowl of porridge is left in the barn for the *nisse*, or Christmas elf.

Eventually, all these traditions merged into the modern concept of Santa Claus, a jolly old elf dressed in red who flies through the air in a reindeer-sleigh and distributes gifts to those who have behaved themselves. His modern image and identity were further honed thanks to Clement Moore's popular poem *The Night Before Christmas*.

The notion of Santa's Arctic residence has been traced back to several sources, including the aforementioned Norse myths; his penchant for flying around with reindeer (the modern equivalent of Oðinn's eight footed horse and Þór's goats); the wintry nature of the Christmas environment in the northern hemisphere; and an assertion by the 1930s Finnish radio personality, Uncle Markus, that Santa Claus was at home at Korvatunturi Fell on the Russian-Finnish border.

The Arctic's Most Prominent Citizen

Well, that may have once been the case, but these days it's clear that Santa Claus is wealthy enough to maintain homes all around the Arctic, and there seems to be some dispute about his official residence (perhaps for tax purposes). The Finns have him dividing his time between Korvatunturi Fell and Rovaniemi, Icelanders believe he's at home in Hveragerði and Vopnafjörður, the Swedes have him somewhere around Kiruna, and for the Norwegians, he commutes between the Oslofjord village of Drøbak and the Arctic town of Finnsnes. It comes as no surprise then that Danes and Greenlanders cite his official address as Spraglebugten, DK-3961 Uummannaq, Greenland. And naturally the Turks also have a claim on him, as St Nicholas was born in Patara, Turkey. Well, I've always been told he was a fellow Alaskan, from the village of North Pole, near Fairbanks. Perhaps everyone is right!

Finland According to the aforementioned Uncle Markus, Santa Claus' home is Korvatunturi Fell, a remote fell near the Russian border, but he also has a city residence where the Arctic Circle (Napapiiri) crosses the main Rovaniemi-Sodankylä road, about 8km north of Rovaniemi. Here you'll find an Arctic Circle marker and the 'official' Santa Claus Village and gift shops. (Mrs Claus, however, has her 'official' headquarters and workshop at the Joulupukin Muorin Tupa shop in distant Savukoski, farther north, which sells local handicrafts and holiday paraphernalia.) The Santa Claus Main Post Office (address: Santa Claus, SF-96930 Arctic Circle, Finland) receives nearly a million letters a year from children all over the world.

For kids, there are computerised portraits with St Nick, and for adults, a hokey 'Arctic Circle Initiation Ceremony', which scores them an Arctic Circle certificate. (Note, however, that the Arctic Circle can shift several metres daily, and by 2000, it will approach the Rovaniemi airport.)

Santapark (www.santapark.com), a Christmas-themed amusement park built inside a cavern, opened in 1998 at Syvasenvaara Mountain, 2km west of the Rovaniemi airport. It features a Magic Sleigh Ride, a Christmas Carousel, a theatre, a cafeteria and, of course, Santa Claus himself. Admission is FMk95/65 for adults/children.

Alaska In Fairbanks, Alaska, suburb of the North Pole, which isn't even north of the Arctic Circle, Santa enjoys the sort of celebrity that only the USA can bestow. But even if the North Pole falls short on the latitudinal scale, this odd little place (which incidentally has a penchant for recalling its local politicians – they haven't yet persuaded Santa to run for mayor) has taken Christmas to new heights. Not only can you stroll down Mistletoe Lane, Kris Kringle Drive and Santa Claus Lane (where you'll find the post office that receives about half a million Santa letters annually), but you can do your holiday shopping year-round at the enormous Santa Claus House gift shop, be photographed in front of a candy-striped

(continued from page 68)

Inuit from Greenland, Canada, Alaska and Russia gather and discuss Arctic issues which affect them all. The official proceedings are accompanied by cultural exhibitions, and visitors are welcome. Check out the Web site at www.inusiaat.com. Similarly, the Arctic Winter Games, which feature Arctic sports, attract athletes from Alaska, northern Canada, and Russia (the northern parts of Magadan and Tyumen provinces). They're held in even-numbered years; the 2000 games will be hosted by Whitehorse, Yukon, and in 2002, by Nuuk, Greenland, and Iqaluit, Nunavut, Canada.

The Arctic's Most Prominent Citizen

North Pole, eat at the Elf's Den Diner, moor your Winnebago at the Santaland RV Park, and wash your clothes at the Santa Suds Laundrette. And if you have a particular Christmas wish, you can make it known to the big man himself by writing to Santa Claus (St Nicholas, Kris Kringle, Father Christmas, et al), North Pole, AK 99705, USA, or you can fax him at 907-488 HOHO.

Lest you be tempted to assume that North Pole has left the Christ out of Christmas, a rival organisation there has set up a log-cabin community known as Jesus Town, which revolves around radio station KJNP, the 'Gospel Station at the Top of the Nation'.

Greenland Since the Santa Claus House in Nuuk closed down, all that remains of Santa's legacy in Greenland's capital city are Rudolph's Café, a large artificial spruce tree full of children's dummies (pacifiers) that have been outgrown; and a Christmas-theme post office where tourists can send off specially postmarked holiday greetings at any time of the year.

However, Santa still has a strong presence in Greenland. On a short hike from the beautifully situated high Arctic town of Uummannaq, you can visit his Royal Castle, a traditional sod hut on the shore at Spraglebukten. Now, if I needed a secluded place where I could mastermind an annual worldwide distribution expedition and direct elfin gift production, I couldn't think of a better spot to collect my thoughts and get on with the work!

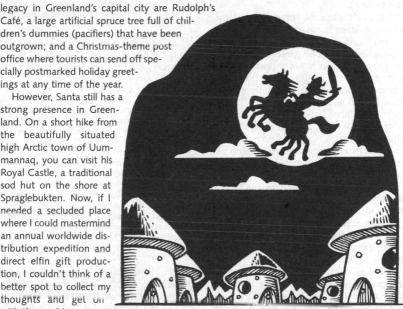

Oðinn and his eight footed horse

You can learn more about the games at www.yukon.net/awg/default.htm.

Greenland's popular two-week cultural festival and political gathering known as Aasivik was first held in 1976 as a forum for musical, artistic, traditional and political expression, and subsequently became an annual event. It always features presentations of traditional theatre, drum dances and folk music but, in recent years, the scope has been extended to electronically synthesised Greenlandic rock music! It starts around 15 July and is held in a different location each year.

In Canada, the provincial and territorial governments publish lists of annual events – including musical performances and ethnic festivals – as part of their tourism promotion packages and local tourist offices print up more detailed information. Major provincial and national holidays are usually cause for some celebration throughout the country, especially in summer when events often wrap up with a fireworks display. The 1 July Canada Day festivities are particularly worthwhile, with the skies lit up from coast to coast.

Alaska celebrates the 4th of July in similar fashion, even in small Arctic communities, and Fairbanks marks the occasion with a midnight-sun baseball game. On the summer solstice, Nome holds a festival dedicated to the Midnight Sun (although technically, Nome doesn't actually see the midnight sun) and around 10 May, Barrow cranks up a local festival dedicated to the fact that the sun won't set for 83 days.

In late February and early March, Russians in St Petersburg and Karelia celebrate the end of the Russian winter with troika (sleigh) rides and folk programs. At the end of March, Murmansk and other Kola Peninsula towns hold the Festival of the North with reindeer races and ski marathons. Also in the spring, Easter *(Paskha)*, the main festival of the Orthodox Church year, begins with celebratory midnight services, after which people eat special dome-shaped cakes called *kulichy* and curd cakes called *paskha*, and may exchange painted wooden Easter eggs. The devout deny themselves meat, milk, alcohol and sex in the 40-day pre-Easter fasting period of Lent.

COURSES

A number of universities around the world offer courses in Arctic studies, which may focus on anything from auroral research and petroleum exploitation to Arctic ecology or Inuit languages and anthropological studies. For an almost complete list of universities all over the world offering Arctic-oriented courses, call up the Web site of the Arctic Council at arctic-council.usgs.gov/

knowledge/academic.html. For information on Arctic-theme courses and studies, contact the following:

Arctic Studies Center, Alaska Regional Office (☎ 907-343 6162, fax 907-343 6130, email aronc@muskox.alaska.edu, Web site www.mnh.si.edu/arctic), Anchorage Museum of History & Art, 121 W 7th Ave, Anchorage, AK 99501, USA

Association of Canadian Universities for Northern Studies (☎ 613-362 0515, fax 613-562 0537, email acuns@cyberus.ca, Web site aix1.uottawa.ca/associations/aucen-acuns), 17 York St, Suite 405, Ottawa, ONT K1N 9S6, Canada

Polar Science Center, University of Washington (☎ 206-543 6613, fax 206-616 3142, Web site psc.apl.washington.edu), Applied Physics Laboratory, 1013 NE 40th St, Seattle, WA 98105-6698, USA

The Arctic Centre, University of Groningen (email arctisch@let.rug.nl, Web site odin.let.rug.nl/arctic), PO Box 716, 9700 AS, Oude Kijk in't Jatstraat 26, Groningen, Netherlands

The Roald Amundsen Centre for Arctic Research (☎ 77 64 52 40, fax 77 67 66 72, email frits.jensen@arctic.uit.no, Web site www.arctic.uit.no), University of Tromsø, N-9037 Tromsø, Norway

University of Alaska Fairbanks (☎ 907-474 7112, Web site info.alaska.edu or www.uaf.edu), PO Box 757500, Fairbanks, AK 99775, USA

University of Svalbard (UNIS; email webmaster@unis.no, Web site www.unis.no), N-9171 Longyearbyen, Norway

If you're interested in Arctic languages, particularly Inupiaq, good sources of information and courses include the University of Minnesota (☎ 612-627 1872, fax 612-627 1875, email lctl@maroon.tc.umn.edu), UTEC Suite 111, 1313 5th St SE, Minneapolis, MN 55414, USA; and the Alaska Native Language Center, University of Alaska Fairbanks (☎ 907-474 7874, fax 907-474 6586, email fyanlp@aurora.alaska.edu), PO Box 757680, Fairbanks, AK 99775-7680, USA.

One of the best courses in outdoor and wilderness studies is the Alaska Wilderness Studies program, offered by the College of Community & Continuing Education, University of Alaska Anchorage (☎ 907-786 1468, fax 907-786 4069, email afda @uaa.alaska.edu), 3211 Providence Dr, Anchorage, AK 99508, USA.

WORK

The first thing to say about finding work in the Arctic region is that it's considerably easier than in the Antarctic, where projects are dominated by governments and stuffy research organisations, and there are throngs of applicants for every position. If you've given up finding a job in the southern polar regions, it's worth noting that any EU citizen is eligible to work anywhere in Sweden or Finland (or even Norway, with a bit more effort); citizens of any country that is a signatory to the Svalbard treaty – if they can find a job – are permitted to work in Svalbard; any US, Canadian, Swedish, Finnish, Danish or Russian citizen may work in the Arctic regions of their own countries; and young British, Australian and New Zealand citizens are eligible for working holidays in Arctic Canada. However, working in Arctic Russia may be a bit more difficult for foreigners and will normally involve contract labour with an overseas firm in partnership with a Russian development company.

While most outside workers in the Arctic regions are involved in seasonal fishing, fish processing and tourism-related jobs, other possibilities are available. School districts in Arctic Alaska and Canada are frequently looking for qualified teachers, and health workers are always in demand, especially in northern Canada. In larger Arctic towns – Tromsø, Narvik, Kirkenes and Hammerfest, Norway; Rovaniemi, Finland; Gällivare and Kiruna, Sweden; Iqaluit, Yellowknife, Whitehorse, Dawson, Inuvik and Churchill, Canada; and Barrow, Kotzebue and Nome, Alaska – you will find local service infrastructures similar to those in population centres anywhere in the world, and you'll have little trouble finding casual (and low-paying) work in shops, bars, restaurants, fast food outlets and other local businesses.

If you'd prefer to work at a research station in the Arctic, or volunteer in an Arctic National Park (note that most of these parks are little-visited, so few positions are available), it's worth contacting one of the following entities to learn what's currently available:

Danish Polar Center (☎ 45-32 88 01 00, fax 45-32 88 01 01, email dpc@dpc.dk, Web site www.dpc.dk), Strandgade 100H, DK-1401 Copenhagen K, Denmark

Scott Polar Research Institute (☎ 01223-337733, fax 01223-336549, Web site www.spri .cam.ac.uk), Lensfield Rd, Cambridge CB2 1ER, UK

Parks Canada (Web site parkscanada.pch.gc.ca), 25 Eddy St, Hull, PQ K1A 0M5, Canada

US National Park Service (Web site www .nps.gov/pub_aff/jobs.htm or www.nps.gov/ volunteer); or for the Alaska Region (☎ 907-297 2687, fax 907-297 2533, email AKRO_Regional_Director@nps.gov), 2225 Gambell St, Room 107, Anchorage, AK 99503-2892

USA Alaska Public Lands Information Office (☎ 907-271 2737, fax 907-271 2744, email anch_superintendant@nps.gov), 605 W 4th Ave, Anchorage, AK 99501, USA

For a complete directory of polar research facilities all over the world, check out the Scott Polar Research Institute Web site link at www.spri.cam.ac.uk/lib/organ/keyindex .htm.

ACCOMMODATION

Accommodation options for the various countries are covered in the individual country chapters.

FOOD

Instead of launching into an in-depth description of the national cuisines of Scandinavia, Russia and North America, this discussion is limited to the traditional and natural foods available in the Arctic regions.

Meat & Seafood

Although visitors may be put off by traditional Arctic fare for sentimental or ideological reasons, remember that whales and seals have dominated the Inuit subsistence hunting culture for thousands of years with no adverse effects on the populations, and that the current declines in cetacean numbers were brought about by European commercial whalers.

Traditional Inuit practise neither commercial nor recreational whaling or sealing, and animals are only hunted on a small scale for subsistence purposes. When an animal is killed, every bit of it is used, including the blubber, oil, skin and bones. While some may assume that the meat-rich Inuit diet is unhealthy, in fact, the Arctic region has one of the world's lowest rates of cardiovascular disease, due to the consumption of unsaturated fatty acids found in marine mammals.

Traditionally among the Inuit, whales, seals, walrus, caribou and other wild animals are respected beings, and people are grateful to the creatures that willingly give up their lives for human sustenance. Traditional hunters wouldn't decimate the population of any species, lest they deplete their children's inheritance, and if a person is accidentally injured or killed during the hunt, it's considered a fair balance.

Having said that, the increasingly western outlook of most Inuit has brought changes. For native hunters, there's no quota on subsistence seal hunting, provided that they take no more than they can use, but in reality, the commercial value of many marine mammals and other polar creatures has inspired liberal interpretations of that regulation. Modern young people may well shoot at birds and seals for fun rather than food, and for the most part, only older people keep to traditional foods. In fact, the youngsters consume at least as much ice cream, sweets, hamburgers and junk food as the rest of the western world, and respect for hunting traditions seems to be fading quickly.

Currently, commercial whaling takes place only in northern Norway. In Greenland, Alaska and Canada, each predominantly Inuit district is allowed an annual whale quota, and whenever a whale is taken, people clamour to buy the blubber and the choice cuts. Fresh whale steaks, which are readily available in Greenland and to a lesser extent in northern Norway, are rich and filling fare. Whale blubber (*mattak* or *muktuk*), which is relatively tasteless and difficult to chew, is rich in vitamins and fats which the body uses efficiently to retain heat. Even a thin slice will provide several hours of jaw work!

For visitors who want to try the local fare, frozen seal meat is sold in Greenlandic supermarkets and fresh seal and whale are sold at harbour markets, and may also be sampled (for a price!) in tourist restaurants in northern Norway. Seal is tougher than whale and tastes more fishy. It can be cooked by cutting it into chunks and boiling it for an hour; it's popular to prepare the resulting stock as brothy soup with rice and onions.

In addition to marine mammals, many people supplement their diet by hunting sea birds, caribou and muskoxen. Fishing also provides nourishment, and the seas, lakes and streams are inhabited by a range of delicious cold-water fish. Some, particularly capelin, are dried for the winter while salmon is normally salted and smoked. Although many native peoples enjoy subsistence rights on their traditional lands, visitors will need a local licence to fish in all inland waters (see Fishing in the Activities chapter).

At low tide, it's also possible to collect blue mussels in sheltered areas which aren't exposed to direct sunlight. They're excellent steamed or fried with butter and garlic. However, avoid collecting near towns where they may be tainted by sewage or other pollution.

Wild Edible Plants

Throughout the Arctic, particularly in areas where taiga and muskeg predominate, people also pick, collect and preserve wild foods like berries, mushrooms and greens which appear during the short summers. From August to early September, dry tundra areas are carpeted with huckleberries (small blueberries). The tundra offers a bounty of bitter black crowberries, which improve greatly with the addition of sugar. Occasionally, you'll also find bright red lowbush cranberries growing alongside them.

In more forested areas, you'll also find such treats as highbush cranberries, wild currants (which need a bit of sugar to be palatable), watermelonberries (in Alaska and Canada), and a number of other berries, including wild raspberries, blackberries and strawberries. In Scandinavia and Arctic Russia, cloudberries grow in areas of boggy tundra and are a real treat; the Alaskan and Canadian version is called the salmonberry, which grows on bushes in areas exposed to a lot of sunshine.

Angelica grows in many areas, wild chamomile is abundant and wild thyme makes an excellent tea, as well as seasoning. In late summer, common harebells *(Campanula greseckiana)* and rosebay willow herb are common in the North Atlantic region, and the sweet, slightly fragrant flowers are delicious. Many varieties of Arctic seaweed are delicious as well, especially the slimy species known as 'sea lettuce'.

Several types of edible mushrooms grow in the region, and in Arctic Russia, mushroom hunting is economically essential for many people. The most delicious Arctic mushroom is a large, chocolate-coloured one with a spongy centre known as 'slippery jack', which reaches its peak in early August. It grows mainly in damp tundra and scrub forest all over the North Atlantic region. In well drained taiga areas of Alaska and Canada, springtime brings a good crop of morels; this convoluted mushroom has a strong and delicious flavour (beware, however, of the false morel, which looks similar but is poisonous). Never eat any mushroom that hasn't been positively identified!

Tupilak

Inuit *tupilak*, now produced and sold as art and souvenirs, had their origins in east Greenland around the town of Ammassalik. They were made from bone, skin and chunks of peat as a bad luck charm against an enemy. They were originally intended to bring misfortune and even death to that person, so one had to be particularly careful when casting harm with a tupilak. If the victim's power was greater than the maker's, the spell would backfire and harm its maker instead.

Modern tupilak are carved from caribou antler, soapstone, driftwood, narwhal tusk, walrus ivory and bone. These carvings are small and meant to be held in the hand. Some represent polar bears, birds or marine mammals, but most are just hideous imaginary beings. They are no longer intended to project misfortune, only to satisfy the artistic urge of and stimulate financial good fortune for the artists.

A tupilak carving

SHOPPING

The indigenous peoples of the Arctic regions are renowned for their traditional arts and crafts, most of which are derived from a range of natural materials: grasses, bark, roots, soapstone, bone, walrus and narwhal ivory, caribou antler, whale baleen, muskox hair *(qiviut)* and skins of seals, beavers, otters, foxes, caribou/reindeer, polar bears and other fur-bearing animals. The Sami also use iron, silver and other metals.

Among the most popular souvenirs in Inuit areas are baskets made of bark and grasses; soapstone, bone or ivory carvings (especially *tupilak* – see the boxed text in this chapter); natural material dolls; *ulus* (knives with semicircular blades, used for chopping); and clothing knitted or woven from qiviut. In the Sami regions of northern Scandinavia, you'll also find fabulous jewellery and decorative knives.

Given the fact that many items are derived from internationally protected species, it's important to get a certificate stating the origin of the product and that it is indeed genuine. In most cases, import restrictions do not apply to art items or crafts produced by indigenous peoples, but you should check with your home customs authority to ensure that you can import such items into your home country. Note that in all Arctic countries the export of historical artefacts – in most cases, anything made prior to 1940 – is prohibited without an export licence.

In Canada, those who fall under the 'Spell of the Yukon' can indulge in the local fashions. The first thing to buy is a classic checked flannel lumberjack shirt, followed by an Elmer Fudd hunters' hat with fuzzy ear flaps and a pair of Baffin boots (felt-lined Canadian wellies); these will ensure you look locally elegant. For those nights beneath the northern lights, traditional Hudson's Bay blankets and coats of 100% wool are available at The Bay department stores run by Canada's oldest company (the genuine articles bear tell-tale green, red, yellow and black stripes on a white background).

The trademark Russian souvenir is the *matryoshka*, the set of wooden dolls within dolls. After glasnost, they became something of a folk art, and now feature all manner of painted designs (you'll even find kitschy representations of Russian leaders, the Keystone Cops and other characters). They're available in pracally every town, as is some very acceptable lacquerware.

Getting There & Away

Most visitors to the Arctic regions arrive by air, not only because much of the area is essentially roadless, but also due to the vast distances involved in reaching the far north from the more populated areas of the world. If you are intent on travelling by road, you'll be limited to Scandinavia, Alaska, north-western Russia and north-western Canada, where slim tendrils of highway reach northward to the Arctic Ocean. Alternatively, you may want to consider one of the three world-famous ferry systems that can get you to the Arctic (or at least within striking distance): the Greenland ferries, Norway's Hurtigruten coastal steamer and the Alaska Marine Hwy.

This chapter concentrates on how to reach Arctic countries from other parts of the world. For information on travelling between Arctic countries, see the Getting Around chapter. Details on travelling within individual countries are found in the Getting Around sections at the beginning of each country chapter.

ALASKA
Air
Currently, Aeroflot flies between Anchorage and the Russian Far East, and there are plans to add direct flights between Anchorage and Tokyo, Taipei, Hong Kong, and other Asian cities. Most visitors to Alaska, however, arrive from the 'Lower 48' (the 48 contiguous states of the USA). Most flights depart from Seattle and nearly all use Anchorage as a gateway, although some flights call in at Anchorage and continue to Fairbanks.

Alaska Airlines has the most flights, but Delta, Northwest, United, TWA, Sun Country, Reno Air and several charter airlines also fly the route. Sun Country and Reno Air generally offer the lowest fares; for the current scoop, check with www.lowestfare.com. While full fares start at around US$450 return from Seattle and climb to well over US$1000 for most other major cities (including some on the west coast), all the airlines occasionally offer better-value deals and with some research and good timing, you'll probably find something for US$500 to US$600 from any other US city. From Canada, the best deals are with Canada 3000, which offers excellent fares between Vancouver and Anchorage.

Sea
The Alaska Marine Hwy (☎ 907-277 4829, toll-free ☎ 1-800 642 0066), 1591 Glacier Ave, Juneau, AK 99801-1427, USA, which connects Bellingham, Washington, with Haines, Alaska, is a three-day trip, stopping en route at Prince Rupert, in British Columbia, and Ketchikan, Wrangell, Petersburg, Sitka, and Juneau, all in Alaska. Smaller ferries connect the main route with other Southeast Alaska communities, such as Metlakatla, Prince of Wales Island, Hyder, Skagway and other places.

From Haines, those who brought their vehicles can drive through Canada's Yukon to the rest of Alaska, and others can board a bus to Haines Junction and on to either Anchorage or Fairbanks (see the Getting Around chapter). From either city, you'll find plenty of tours and flights into Arctic Alaska, or perhaps even connect with another traveller with a vehicle who is looking for passengers to share expenses driving the Dalton Hwy towards Prudhoe Bay. For more information, check the Alaska Marine Hwy Web site www.dot.state.ak.us/amhs home.html.

Conditions on ferries are ideal for backpackers, as the top deck is actually an open-air solarium with heat lamps and astroturf on which you can roll out a sleeping bag or, space permitting, pitch a tent for privacy. If you're bringing a vehicle in summer, book the trip as far in advance as possible; even six months wouldn't be too much. (Note that the Alaska Marine Hwy also has a Southwestern Network, which connects the towns on Prince William Sound with Seward, Homer, Seldovia, Kodiak, the Alaska Peninsula and Dutch Harbor, in the Aleutian Islands.)

Alternatively, Alaska's Inside Passage is one of the world's most popular and inexpensive cruising destinations, and nowadays, many of these cruises extend north to Seward, where there's a railhead and opportunities to extend your trip into Interior and Arctic Alaska. It's beyond the scope of this book to list all the cruise lines, but among the most popular are Carnival, Celebrity, Crystal, Holland America, Norwegian, Royal Caribbean, and Princess. For further information, see the Web site www.cruise2.com, which provides links to all the world's major cruise lines.

CANADA
Air
Major gateway cities (main entry points) are Dorval airport, Montreal; Pearson airport, Toronto; and Vancouver international airport, Vancouver. Major British, European, Australian and American airlines all fly into Canada as do the two domestic carriers, Air Canada and Canadian Airlines.

The most common way to enter Canada is via the USA. Many overseas flights to North America go to the USA (but they often cost only slightly less than flying directly to Canada), with New York, San Francisco and Los Angeles being the major destinations. You can then either fly to a major Canadian city such as Montreal or Vancouver, or catch a bus or train.

Flights between US and Canadian cities are abundant and frequent; Montreal, Toronto and Vancouver are the busiest Canadian destinations but all major cities are plugged into the extensive North American system. Canadian Airlines flies from Los Angeles to Vancouver from US$205 plus taxes, one way.

Air Canada and American Airlines fly from New York City to Montreal and Toronto (US$330). Canadian Airlines has

London, Amsterdam and Frankfurt as major cities although they serve many other European cities, too. From Frankfurt midweek, midsummer the return ticket to Toronto costs DM1706. The low-season rate for this fare is about 30% less. Prices are highest between 15 June and 15 August.

Continental Airlines, Canadian Airlines, United Airlines, Qantas and Air New Zealand offer regular flights to Vancouver from Australia and New Zealand. Qantas offers standard economy air fares from Australia to Canada; a return ticket to Vancouver is a whopping A$4966 all year. However, there are much cheaper advance-purchase tickets available with varying conditions attached. These fares range from A$1752 in the low season to a high of A$2145. From Auckland the regular return economy fare with Air New Zealand is also huge at NZ$5468, but like Qantas it offers discounted advance-purchase air fares. These start from NZ$2019 in the low season, for a minimum stay of five days and must be purchased seven days in advance.

Coming from Australia, New Zealand or Asia, it may be easier and/or cheaper to travel via the USA, arriving in Los Angeles, San Francisco, or possibly Seattle (which has good bus connections with Vancouver). In addition, Qantas and Air New Zealand flights from Australia to US cities (in California), often include many Pacific stopovers – Fiji, Rarotonga, Hawaii and even Tahiti. Those coming from Australasia may want to consider a Round-the-World (RTW) ticket. Outside of Canada, Air Canada offers RTW tickets in conjunction with other airlines, such as Cathay Pacific, Qantas and Singapore Airlines. Expect to pay from around C$3500.

To reach Arctic Canada, the main gateways are Whitehorse, Yellowknife and Iqaluit, all of which are most easily accessed from Vancouver, Calgary, Ottawa and/or Montreal on First Air (☎ 613-839 3340, fax 613-839 5690, email reservat@firstair.ca), 3257 Carp Rd, Carp, ON X0A 1L0. Try its Web site at www.firstair.ca for further information. First Air also connects these three towns with all major villages throughout Arctic Canada. Air Canada flies between Vancouver and Yellowknife and Canadian Airlines has connections to Whitehorse and Yellowknife from all over the country. Their Web addresses are www.aircanada.ca and www.cdnair.ca, respectively.

Land

The US Greyhound bus network (toll-free ☎ 1-800 231 2222) connects the major continental US cities with most major destinations in Canada but with a bus transfer at the border or nearest town to it. In Canada, Montreal, Toronto and Vancouver may be accessed on the US Greyhound system routes. Main routes include Chicago to Toronto (15 hours, US$76), New York to Montreal (eight hours, US$74) and Seattle to Vancouver (four hours, US$20). Other US bus lines run directly to some Canadian cities with no stop or need for a bus change. Alaskon Express connects Fairbanks, Anchorage, Skagway and Haines in Alaska with Whitehorse in the Yukon, as does Alaska Direct Busline; for details, see Alaska in the Getting Around chapter.

Amtrak has four routes between the USA and Canada. In the east, these are New York City to Montreal (10 hours, $US54 to $62 one way), New York City to Toronto (12 hours via Niagara Falls, $US65 to $US99 one way) and Chicago to Toronto (11½ hours, $US98 one way). On the west coast, Amtrak connects Seattle to Vancouver (four hours, $US21 to $32 one way). For information about fares and schedules contact Amtrak (toll-free ☎ 1-800 872 7245), 60 Massachusetts Ave NE, Washington, DC 20002, USA or try its Web site at www.amtrak.com.

The only rail route to the northern region is the link between Winnipeg and Churchill, Manitoba; details are provided in the Churchill section of the Canada chapter.

Sea

Alaska Marine Hwy car ferries from Bellingham, Washington, call in at Prince Rupert, British Columbia. For information on that ferry system, see Alaska, earlier in this chapter. There are also east coast ferries between Bar Harbor, Maine, and Yarmouth, Nova Scotia, but they're of little use for reaching the Arctic regions.

Leaving Canada

Canada has a departure/airport tax that is levied on all departing international flights, but it's normally built into the ticket price. In Vancouver there is an additional tax known as the airport improvement tax. Flights to the US are taxed at C$10 per person and other international flights at C$15. Remember, too, that if you intend to apply for any GST rebate this is your last chance to pick up a form.

GREENLAND

Air

Scheduled air travel to Greenland is through five airports: Narsarsuaq, Kangerlussuaq, Pituffik (Thule Air Base), Kulusuk and Nerlerit Inaat. From 15 June to 15 August, SAS, in conjunction with Greenlandair, flies three times weekly between Copenhagen and Kangerlussuaq or Narsarsuaq; in winter, there are two weekly flights. In the low season, you'll pay from Dkr3495 return (Dkr7620 without restrictions). Every second week, the Kangerlussuaq flight continues north to Pituffik (but note that only 14 'tourist' tickets are available on each flight, and Thule air base permits are required unless you're transiting to Qaanaaq). Student fares for these flights start at Dkr5790 return from Copenhagen. Try the SAS and Greenlandair Web sites for further information at www.sas.dk and www.greenland guide.dk/gla.

Sea

There are currently no passenger boat services to Greenland but a growing number of cruise lines are including it as a stop on their trans-Atlantic crossings. Other companies offer exclusively Arctic cruises, which may also call in at Iceland, Norway, Jan Mayen and Svalbard; navigate the Russian or Canadian Arctic; or even ice-break their way to the North Pole. Private boat owners will need the *Faroes, Iceland & Greenland Cruising Notes*, by RCC Pilotage Foundation and Oz Robinson, published by Imray, Laurie Norie & Wilson Ltd, St Ives, Cambridgeshire, UK.

For information on reaching Greenland from Iceland and Canada, see the Getting Around chapter. To learn more about the Greenland ferries, which ply the west coast from Aapillattoq in the south to Upernavik in the north, see the Greenland chapter.

ICELAND
Air
Most air travellers coming from Europe or North America will arrive on the national flag carrier Icelandair (USA toll-free ☎ 1-800 223 5500, UK ☎ 020-7338 5599), which flies between Iceland and Luxembourg starting at US$600 return; from London for around UK£300 return (with numerous restrictions); and from Baltimore/Washington, New York JFK, Orlando, Boston, Halifax or Minneapolis starting from around US$350 return in the off-season and considerably more in summer. Try its Web site www.icelandair.is for further information. Greenlandair (☎ 570 3030, fax 570 3001), SAS (☎ 562 2211, fax 562 2281) and Air Atlanta Icelandic (☎ 566 7700, fax 566 7766) all have offices in Reykjavík and offer limited services between Iceland and Greenland, Europe and North America. The Web site for Air Atlanta Icelandic can provide further details at www.atlanta.is.

Sea
Smyril Line runs weekly vehicle and passenger ferries from Hanstholm, Denmark, or Bergen, Norway, which involve a two-day layover at Torshavn in the Faroe Islands and landfall at Seyðisfjörður, on Iceland's east coast. For details, contact Smyril Line (☎ 298-315 900, fax 298-315 707, email bookings@smyril-line.fo), J Broncksgøta 37, PO Box 370, FR-110, Torshavn, Faroe Islands, or try the Web site at www.smyril-line.fo.

SCANDINAVIA
Air
Although you may not find a cheap direct flight to Norway, Sweden or Finland from outside Europe, plenty of European companies sell inexpensive flights to Oslo, Stockholm or Helsinki via whatever European hub they use, and the result is some good value deals to/from Delhi, Tokyo, Hong Kong, Bangkok and North America. As airlines go, SAS provides the most direct international flights to Scandinavia (including from New York Newark, Chicago O'Hare and Seattle-Tacoma). Note that Copenhagen's Kastrup airport, which is more of a hub than Oslo, Stockholm or Helsinki, lies 45 minutes from Sweden by hydrofoil. The discount carrier Ryanair flies between London Stansted and Nyköping, Sweden, or Torp (south of Oslo), Norway, from UK£99 return.

Icelandair (USA toll-free ☎ 1-800 223 5500) flies from New York, Baltimore-Washington, Boston, Minneapolis, Fort Lauderdale and Orlando via Reykjavík to many European destinations including Glasgow, Helsinki, Oslo, Stockholm, and Copenhagen. On all its transatlantic flights it allows a free three-day stopover in Reykjavík.

Land
At present the only direct access to Arctic Scandinavia is by domestic air routes or overland by car, bus or train from the larger hubs in the southern parts of Norway, Sweden and Finland – Oslo, Bergen, Stockholm, Göteborg, and Helsinki (see the Getting Around chapter). To reach Scandinavia from Britain and the Continent, you have numerous choices, and in many cases, trains and buses drive right onto the ferries so you'll hardly even notice the short sea crossings. However, travelling by train from the UK to Scandinavia can be more expensive than flying. From London a return 2nd class train ticket will cost UK£228 to Copenhagen, UK£281 to Stockholm and UK£367 to Oslo. Note that the lowest equivalent air fares are UK£99!

Construction of the Öresund tollway bridge between Copenhagen and Malmö (scheduled for completion in late 2000) will open up a handy direct rail/road link with Denmark.

Norway Travel by bus between Denmark and Norway normally involves a hop across the strait between Copenhagen and Malmö (Sweden), and an express bus between there and Oslo. Twice weekly, Nor-Way Bussekspress buses connect Oslo with Berlin (14¾ hours, Nkr600), via Göteborg, Sweden, and Rostock, Germany. They run on Monday and Thursday southbound and on Tuesday and Friday northbound.

If you like arduous journeys, you can bus it between London and Oslo in about 38 hours, but that trip involves changing buses up to four times. The service operates two or three times weekly, year-round, via Amsterdam and Hamburg. Reservations are compulsory. In the UK, contact National Express (☎ 01990-505050) or Nor-Way Bussekspress (☎ 23 00 24 40, fax 23 00 24 49) in Oslo. The return fare is Nkr2000, so it may be cheaper to fly! For further information try its Web site at www.nbe.no.

Trains run three times daily from Oslo to Copenhagen (9½ hours, Nkr790), including a night train that leaves at 10.40 pm. At Helsingborg, Sweden, the train boards a rail ferry across the Øresund to Helsingør, Denmark.

Hamburg is the central European gateway for Scandinavia, with several daily trains daily to Copenhagen and a few to Stockholm; in either city, you'll readily find connections into Norway. The train from Hamburg to Copenhagen travels between Puttgarden and Rødby Havn by ferry, which is included in the ticket price; there's also a 20-minute ferry segment between Copenhagen, Denmark, and Malmö, Sweden.

Sweden Eurolines runs four services weekly from London to Stockholm (29 hours, Skr1065) and Göteborg (26½ hours, Skr895); five times weekly between Göteborg and Berlin (10 hours, Skr505); and

four times weekly to and from Brussels (18 hours, Skr840). In Stockholm, Eurolines is represented by Busstop (☎ 08-440 8570) at the Cityterminalen, and its Göteborg office (☎ 031-10 02 40) is at Kyrkogatan 40. For general information, contact Eurolines (☎ 020-98 73 77). Swebus (☎ 020-64 06 40) runs the Continentbus services throughout Europe to Swedish cities, and is also represented in Stockholm by Busstop. The Göteborg office is at Kruthusgatan 7. You can also check out the Web sites for Eurolines and Swebus at www.eurolines.se and www.express.swebus.se.

From Denmark, Kustlinjen runs a roughly hourly bus service from Copenhagen (and Kastrup airport), which crosses by ferry to/from Helsingborg (Skr110) and Halmstad (Skr150). Buses No 109 and 999 run a 24 hour service between Copenhagen via Malmö to Lund (both Skr110). Eurolines runs to/from Copenhagen and Stockholm (Skr390) five times weekly and to Göteborg (Skr390) daily.

Kustpilen trains run four times daily between Copenhagen and Hässleholm and the cost is Skr206. Rail passes apply, and the ferry price is included. There are also two direct trains daily between Stockholm and Copenhagen, and four daily between Copenhagen and Oslo (via Helsingborg and Göteborg). Direct trains from Berlin run twice daily to Malmö (nine hours), via Sassnitz and Trelleborg.

Finland All road and rail links into Finland are from Norway, Sweden or Russia, and are covered in the Getting Around chapter.

Sea
Norway Ferry connections between Norway and Denmark, Germany, Iceland, the Faroe Islands, Sweden and the UK provide a straightforward link, especially for anyone bringing their own vehicle. Note that in most cases, the quoted fares for vehicles also include the driver.

DFDS Scandinavian Seaways (☎ 22 41 90 90, bookings ☎ 66 81 66 00) runs daily overnight ferries from Oslo to Copenhagen.

It's also recently started a new service between Harwich and Kristiansund. You could try its Web site www.scansea.com for further information.

The Color Line (☎ 22 94 44 00, fax 22 83 07 76, email colorline@colorline.no) runs three to four ferries daily between Kristiansand and Hirtshals. The journey takes four hours and is the shortest ferry connection between Norway and Denmark. From 19 June to 16 August, Color Line also has one or two daily ferry services on the M/S *Peter Wessel* between Fredrikshavn, Moss and Larvik (once daily the rest of the year). Its three-hour M/S *Pegasus II* route between Larvik and Skagen runs twice daily and costs from Nkr195 to Nkr250, plus Nkr200 for a car; many people use this route as a duty-free day trip.

To and from Germany, the Color Line has a daily 19-hour ferry link between Oslo and Kiel, departing either city at 2 pm. The Color Line (☎ 55 54 86 60) also sails from Bergen to Newcastle, via Stavanger, twice weekly in winter and thrice weekly in summer. Summer sailings are on Tuesday, Friday and Sunday from Bergen and on Monday, Wednesday and Saturday from Newcastle. The trip takes 21 hours. For further information try the Web site at www.colorline.no.

From 19 June to 30 August, Stena Line (☎ 22 33 50 00) operates ferries between Oslo and Frederikshavn daily and at other times from three to six times weekly. They leave Oslo at 8 pm and from Frederikshavn at 10.30 am (6.30 pm on some Mondays) and take 12 hours. Check out its Web site at www.stenaline.se. The Fjord Line (☎ 55 32 37 70) sails from Bergen to Hanstholm on Monday, Wednesday and Friday afternoons, stopping en route in Egersund. It returns from Hanstholm on Tuesday, Thursday and Sunday. Try its Web site at www.fjord line.dk if you want further details.

The Larvik Line (☎ 22 52 55 00) has a daily ferry from Larvik (via Moss) to Frederikshavn. It takes six hours and costs from Nkr240 to Nkr380 for passengers and Nkr325 to Nkr530 for a car. It also operates a three-hour daily catamaran service between Larvik and Skagen for the same fares.

For information on the Hurtigruten coastal steamers, see Getting Around in the Norway chapter.

Sweden There are about 200 launches daily either way between Denmark and Sweden (providing a convenient, unregulated 'booze cruise' for many local imbibers). The most frequent and quickest services are between Helsingør and Helsingborg (Skr20 to Skr23). In Copenhagen boats depart from the Havnegade/Nyhavn area, and in Malmö from just near the train station. The Direkten service between Copenhagen (Havnegade) and Landskrona runs up to seven times daily (Skr70, bicycles Skr35). Passenger cars up to 6m can carry five people. The Helsingør to Helsingborg ferry charges Skr295 one way (Skr445 return). The Copenhagen-Malmö route is dearer: Skr395 (Skr595/695 off-peak/peak) and runs between Limhamn and Dragør.

There are also services between Jutland and Sweden. Stena Line cruises between Göteborg and Frederikshavn up to 10 times daily and the journey takes about three hours, while the SeaCat catamaran service is twice as fast. Lion Ferries from Grenå travel four hours to reach Varberg and Halmstad.

From Germany, Trelleborg is the main gateway, and more than a dozen ferries arrive daily from Travemünde, Rostock and Sassnitz. Stena Line cruises between Gothenburg and Kiel daily, taking 10 hours. From Malmö, Nordö-Link (☎ 040-6111 670) sails to Travemünde.

You can also come from Poland. There are daily services from Swinoujscie to Ystad and Malmö, from Gdynia to Karlskrona and less frequent services from Gdansk to Nynäshamn and from Oxelösund.

If you're combining Scandinavia with Arctic Russia, you may want to check out the Nordic Trucker Line (☎ 08-522 201 00), which operates a cargo ferry from Stockholm to St Petersburg twice weekly, with a few passenger berths (32 hours, Skr1000). To Tallinn, in Estonia, Estline (☎ 08-667 00 01) runs daily ferries (seats Skr350) and Ånedinlinjen (☎ 08-456 22 00) sails three times weekly to Riga, in Latvia (seats Skr280), from Frihamnen in Stockholm (take bus No 41 from Cityterminalen). Ånedinlinjen also has weekend cruises in August to Saaremaa (Ösel) for Skr1195/ 1395 single/return.

From June to August, there's also a direct ferry from the UK. DFDS Scandinavian Seaways sails weekly between Göteborg and Newcastle (22 hours, UK£136/162 or Skr825/1125 low/high season).

Finland The Baltic ferries are some of the world's most impressive seagoing craft and could accurately be described as floating hotels-cum-casinos-and-shopping plazas. Many lines offer 50% discounts for holders of Eurail, ScanRail and Inter-Rail passes, as well as senior, youth and student discounts. Make ferry reservations well in advance when travelling in July, especially if you plan to bring a car.

Currently, a staggering number of ferries, catamarans and hydrofoils ply between Tallinn and Helsinki, just 80km apart. Car ferries cross in 3½ hours, catamarans and hydrofoils in about 1½ hours. Ferries are cheapest, with return fares from Fmk125 in summer – Tallink, Silja Line and Eckerö Linjen all have daily departures. Catamarans and hydrofoils cost Fmk150 to Fmk270 return. Note that a return ticket from Helsinki is often cheaper than a one-way fare from Tallinn.

It is advisable to reserve a seat in advance during summer, particularly if you wish to travel on Saturday or Sunday. You may purchase tickets at the Helsinki city tourist office, at the ferry line's office in central Helsinki or from the ferry terminal itself.

Silja Line offers a ferry service between Helsinki and Travemünde, connecting with direct buses to Hamburg. The sea passage takes about 23 hours one way. Departures are three times weekly from mid-April to mid-September. Rates are from US$130 to US$660 one way, depending on season and class of service. The one-way rate for car transport starts at US$155. Beginning in 1999, Finnlines plans to offer year-round service between Helsinki and Travemünde, as well as year-round service between Helsinki and Lübeck.

RUSSIA

In general, getting to Russia and getting to Arctic Russia are two different matters, but if you're coming from anywhere except Scandinavia or Alaska, your trip will probably begin with a flight, bus or train ride to Moscow or St Petersburg.

Air

There are daily services to Moscow from all major European capitals and New York, as well as from Hong Kong and other Asian travel centres. There are also daily services from several European cities to St Petersburg. From Australasia, you'll have to get to an Asian, European or North American gateway.

Airlines with daily service to Moscow, and at least several weekly flights to St Petersburg, include British Airways, Lufthansa, Finnair, Delta and SAS. Other airlines with regular flights to one or both main Russian cities include Aeroflot, Air China (CAAC), Air France, Air India, MIAT-Mongolian Airlines, Alaska Airlines, Alitalia, ANA (All Nippon Airways), Balkan, CSA, JAL, KLM, Korean Air, LOT Polish Airlines, MALEV Hungarian Airlines, Pakistan International Airlines, Sabena, SAS, Swissair, Turkish Airlines and Transaero. Major airlines all have offices in Moscow, and there are also many in St Petersburg. Samples of the lowest fares from Moscow include: Los Angeles with Delta, Lufthansa and many others (US$764); New York with Aeroflot, Delta and others (US$618); London with Sabena (US$213) and Aeroflot (US$485); Sydney with Qantas/British Airways/Thai/Aeroflot, via Singapore (US$1636); Paris with various airlines (US$545); Frankfurt with Lufthansa and other airlines (US$665); Tokyo with several airlines (US$2630); and Hong Kong with several airlines (US$2500).

Otherwise, only a few places have direct flights from outside the former USSR. These include Petrozavodsk (from Helsinki and Joensuu, Finland), Murmansk (from Tromsø and Kirkenes, Norway), and several cities in the Russian Far East (all from Anchorage or Nome, Alaska, or several Asian cities): Provideniya, Khabarovsk, Vladivostok, Magadan, Yuzhno-Sakhalinsk and Petropavlovsk-Kamchatsky.

For more information on the Arctic region options, see Russia in the Getting Around chapter.

Land

Note that you may need tourist or transit visas for any countries you're passing through en route to Russia from Europe or Asia, including China, Mongolia, Belarus, Ukraine, Moldova, the Baltic States or the Central Asian countries.

Bus Daily at 9.45pm, a bus leaves Autobussijaam in Tallinn, Estonia, for St Petersburg; you'll arrive, much worse for wear, about nine hours later. Finnord and Sovtransavto Express Bus have daily services between Helsinki, Vyborg and St Petersburg, stopping in the city centre and at several hotels. Farther north, from Ivalo, a postbus heads to Kostamuksha in western Karelia, where you can get connecting ground transport to Petrozavodsk. The Kola Peninsula has a short Arctic border with Norway, and from the town of Kirkenes, bus connections to Nikel, Zapolyarny and Murmansk are available three times weekly. (For more on the routes from Norway and Finland, see the Getting Around chapter.) If you're approaching from the east, buses link Ürümqi, in China, with Almaty, in Kazakhstan, where you can pick up a train to Moscow or elsewhere.

Train The main western rail gateways to Russia are Helsinki (about eight hours,

US$110 to St Petersburg), Warsaw (24 hours, US$60 to Moscow; 29 hours, US$60 to St Petersburg), Prague (38 hours, US$140 to Moscow) and Budapest (41 hours, US$170 to Moscow). Through trains or through carriages also run from Tallinn, Riga, Vilnius, Chisinau, Kiev, Athens, Berlin, Brussels, Bucharest, Frankfurt and Venice to Moscow, and from Berlin and Brussels to St Petersburg. Daily services are also available from Paris and Amsterdam to Moscow, with a change at Warsaw.

Coming from the east, most opt for the Trans-Manchurian and Trans-Mongolian routes from China or Mongolia, or they take a ferry from Japan to Vladivostok and catch the Trans-Siberian eastbound toward Moscow. The very adventurous may want to check out the Turkestan-Siberia (Turk-Sib) route from Almaty in Kazakhstan, which runs north via Barnaul to Novosibirsk in western Siberia. A service from Tashkent (Uzbekistan) to Barnaul and Novosibirsk also uses this line, as do trains to Krasnoyarsk from Almaty and Bishkek (Kyrgyzstan). Another railway runs from Tashkent to Yekarerinburg, through the heart of Kazakhstan via Almaty and Bishkek, and yet another (for the very keen only!) connects Ussuriysk (between Khabarovsk and Vladivostok) with the North Korean capital of Pyongyang (the amount of red tape required to go this route is probably mind-boggling).

Car & Motorcycle Foreigners can now drive legally into Russia and travel most highways, however, driving in Russia, while truly an unfiltered Russian experience, is *truly* an unfiltered Russian experience. Poor roads, maddeningly inadequate signposting, poor-quality petrol (usually 76 octane, though better grades are increasingly available), rampant car theft and overly keen highway cops may well lead to frustration, dismay and serious hair-pulling.

The undaunted will need a driving licence and either an international driving permit with a Russian translation or a certified Russian translation of your full licence (you can certify translations at a Russian embassy or consulate). You'll also need vehicle registration and proof of insurance that is valid in Russia. Russian insurance should be available at the border through Ingosstrakh (☎ 095-233 17 59, ☎ 095-233 05 50, ☎ 233 20 70, fax 095-230 25 18), Pyatnitskaya ulitsa 12, Moscow; through your home insurance agent; or through a Finnish agent, which may be able to organise Russian coverage. Of course you'll also need an official customs declaration promising to take your vehicle with you when you leave, so don't let anyone steal it!

Sea

The Baltic Shipping Company runs visa-free cruises from Helsinki to St Petersburg aboard the *Konstantin Simonov* and between Stockholm, Kiel and St Petersburg aboard the *Anna Karenina*. In the UK, CTC Lines (☎ 020-7896 8844, fax 020-7839 2483), 1 Lower Regent St, London SW1Y 4NN, offers a 14-day cruise that stops in several ports en route to St Petersburg. Cabins for the return route start at £873.

A rather unreliable ferry system links Vladivostok with Niigata (the most popular route), Toyama, Fushiki and Tokyo, all in Japan, and also Pusan, in South Korea. The voyage to Niigata takes 42 hours and 1st/2nd/3rd class passage is US$730/300/280. In Tokyo, you can organise it through the Japan-Russia Travel Bureau (☎ 03-3432 6161, fax 03-3436 5530) in the Kamiyacho Building, 3rd Floor, 5-12-12, Toranomon, Minato-ku, Tokyo 105. A cheaper option from Japan may be to take the ferry to Shanghai and ride the rails via Beijing. You might also be able to catch a ship from Japan to Korsakov, the southern-most port on the Russian island of Sakhalin, from where it's a $140 flight to Vladivostok or about $25 by ship to the mainland.

Warning

This chapter is particularly vulnerable to change – prices for international travel are volatile, routes are introduced and cancelled, schedules change, special deals come and go, and rules and visa requirements are amended. Airlines seem to take a perverse pleasure in making price structures and regulations as complicated as possible; you should check directly with the airline or travel agent to make sure you understand how a fare (and the ticket you may buy) works. In addition, the travel industry is highly competitive and there are many schemes and bonuses. The upshot of this is that you should get opinions, quotes and advice from as many airlines and travel agents as possible before you part with your hard-earned cash. The details given in this chapter should be regarded as pointers and are not a substitute for your own careful, up-to-date research.

Getting Around

This chapter covers transportation options between the various Arctic countries. For information on guided tours, see the Organised Tours & Adventures chapter; information on travelling within individual countries is provided in the introductory Getting Around sections of each country chapter.

ALASKA
To/From Canada

There are five road border crossings between Alaska and Canada: Stewart/Hyder (Glacier Hwy), Skagway/Carcross (Klondike Hwy); Haines/Haines Junction (Haines Cut-Off); Beaver Creek/Northway (Alaska Hwy); and Dawson/Boundary (Top of the World Hwy).

Although the Alaska Marine Hwy ferries follow the Inside Passage from Bellingham, Washington, to Haines and Skagway, Alaska, via Prince Rupert, British Columbia (see the Getting There & Away chapter), they leave you a long way from Arctic Alaska. Check out the Marine Hwy's Web site at www.dot.state.ak.us/amhshome .html.

From Skagway or Haines, Alaskon Express buses run to Whitehorse (daily in summer) or Haines Junction (three times weekly in summer), in the Yukon, where you can take a connecting Alaskon Express bus to Anchorage (US$190) or Fairbanks (US$165). For further information try its Web site at www.yukonweb.com/tourism/westours.

Alaska Direct Busline (USA toll-free ☎ 1-800 770 6652; Canada ☎ 403-668 4833), PO Box 501, Anchorage, AK 99510, USA, has services three times weekly from Whitehorse to Anchorage (US$245) and Fairbanks (US$128).

Greyhound Lines of Canada (☎ 604-662 3222, toll-free ☎ 1-800 661 8747), in Vancouver, heads north several times daily from Vancouver for Prince George and Dawson Creek. There you connect with a three-times weekly bus to Whitehorse (C$292 for the full trip), where you pick up either the Alaskon or Alaska Direct bus into Alaska. If you want further details try its Web site at www.greyhound.ca.

The 30 day Alaskapass bus pass (toll-free ☎ 1-800 248 7598, fax 1-800 488 0303), which includes bus transport from Seattle (or the Marine Hwy from Bellingham, with payment of a US$50 surcharge), via Whitehorse, costs US$899, while a version allowing 12 days of travel in 21 costs US$669 and 21 days in 45 costs US$949. It's good on nine major bus companies statewide and in the Yukon (including a trip to Dawson).

Any of these options will get you within striking distance of Arctic Alaska, but you'll still have to fly from either Anchorage or Fairbanks.

To/From Russia

The only connection between the far north of Alaska and Russia is the flight between Nome and the Chukotka Peninsula town of Providaniya, with Bering Air (☎ 907-443 5620, email info@bcringair.com), PO Box 1650, Nome, AK 99762-1650, USA. The fare is US$250 each way and you're limited to 22.5kg of baggage. From Providaniya, you can organise connecting Aeroflot flights to Anadyr and elsewhere in Russia.

If you're headed for the Kamchatka Peninsula, your only option is Reeve Aleutian Airways' (toll-free ☎ 1-800 544 2248) flight 911, which operates on Wednesday and Saturday between Anchorage, Petropavlovsk Kamchatsky and Yuzhno-Sakhalinsk. Other flights from Anchorage to Russia include Magadan Airlines' (toll-free ☎ 1-800 214 0647) Thursday flight to and from Magadan, Aeroflot's (toll-free ☎ 1-888 340 6400) Monday flight to Vladivostok, and its Wednesday and Friday flights to Khavarovsk and Vladivostok.

Everyone needs a pre-issued Russian visa, available from a Russian consulate.

The nearest are at 2790 Green St, San Francisco, CA 94123, USA (☎ 415-202 9800, fax 929 0306) and 2001 Sixth Ave, Seattle, WA 98121, USA (☎ 206-728 1910, fax 728 1871). Note that Chukotka is 21 hours later than Alaskan time.

CANADA
To/From Alaska
Several bus companies offer transport between Canada and Alaska. For details, see the preceding Alaska section. You can also opt for the Alaska Marine Hwy ferry system (see the Getting There & Away chapter).

To/From Greenland
Between Canada and Greenland, your only direct option is First Air (☎ 613-839 3340, fax 839 5690, email reservat@firstair.ca), 3257 Carp Rd, Carp, ON X0A 1L0, Canada. It flies frequently between Ottawa and Iqaluit, on Baffin Island, and on Monday and Thursday in summer, from there to Kangerlussuaq (approximately C$360 one way between Iqaluit and Nuuk). In winter, there's one flight weekly. Check out the Web site at www.firstair.ca.

GREENLAND
Currently, the only way to Greenland is by air from Iceland, Denmark or Canada; for details see the Canada and Iceland sections.

ICELAND
To/From Greenland
In summer, Greenlandair, in conjunction with Air Iceland (Icelandair's domestic component), flies twice weekly between Keflavík, Iceland, and Narsarsuaq; the cheapest excursion fare is around US$560 return for stays of up to 28 days; for longer stays, the two hour flight costs a rather steep US$960 return. You must purchase tickets at least 30 days in advance. Try www.greenland-guide.dk/gla for further information.

Also in summer, Air Iceland operates day tours from Reykjavík to Kulusuk, in east Greenland, starting at around US$500; these include a Kulusuk tour and the chance to fly on to Tasiilaq (Ammassalik), on

Greenland's east coast. However, Air Iceland isn't permitted to carry transit passengers to Kulusuk, so you can't continue from there to west Greenland or stay more than five days in east Greenland. For that, you'll have to take Greenlandair's weekly excursion flight between Keflavík and Kulusuk, Kangerlussuaq and Nuuk. Greenlandair also has one weekly flight between Keflavík and Nerlerit Inaat.

To/From Norway
The Smyril Line (☎ 55 32 09 70) runs weekly in summer between Bergen and Seyðisfjörður (Iceland), via the Faroe Islands. One-way fares from Bergen begin at Nkr560/780 to Tórshavn in the Faroe Islands and Nkr1190/1710 to Seyðisfjörður, Iceland. These fares are for a couchette, with the lower fares for the first three sailings in June and the last four sailings in August, and the higher fares for midsummer travel. The boat leaves Bergen at 3 pm on Tuesday.

SCANDINAVIA
Air
For those in a hurry, the Nordic Airpass provides an inexpensive air travel option in Finland, Denmark, Norway, Sweden, Estonia, Latvia and Lithuania from 1 May to 30 September. (Local residents may only use it between 15 June and 17 August.) This book of coupons, each good for one flight segment, is available through international travel agents or within Scandinavia. Note that at least one coupon must be used on an international flight and you must purchase between four and 10 coupons; the first four cost US$360, plus US$90 for each additional coupon up to 10 (not including taxes), and unused coupons are refunded. Affiliated airlines are Air Lithuania, Braathens SAFE, Estonian Air, Finnair, Lithuanian Airlines, Maersk Air, Skärgårdsflyg and Transwede.

Land
Numerous buses and trains connect the ample road networks of northern Norway,

Sweden and Finland. There are six crossings from northern Sweden to northern Finland across the rivers Tornionjoki/Torneälv and Muonionjoki. Between Norway and Finland, there are six border crossings along roads plus a few legal crossings along wilderness tracks.

The tour-like Ofotens Bilruter Nordkapp Expressen (☎ 76 92 35 00, fax 76 92 35 30, email ob@ofotens-bilruter.no) does return trips between Narvik and Nordkapp (Nkr1050). It runs via Sweden, Finland and Finnmarksvidda on the northbound route (13½ hours) and via Alta and the E6 on the return (13 hours). If you need further details try the Web site at www.ofotens-bilruter.no (in Norwegian only). Alternatively, you can return on the Hurtigruten coastal steamer from Honningsvåg to Sortland (see Getting Around in the Norway chapter), then travel by bus to Narvik (Nkr1755), or by bus to Moskenes (Lofoten) and ferry to Bodø (Nkr1870).

The excellent value ScanRail Pass for travel within Scandinavia can be purchased in Denmark, Norway, Sweden and Finland. Check out the Web site at www.starnetinc.com/eurorail/scanrail. Children travel at half price, and discounts apply for seniors and travellers aged 12 to 25. The ScanRail Consecutive pass allows 21 days or one month of travel while with the ScanRail Flexipass, you can opt for five days of travel in 15 days or 10 days of travel in one month.

Sweden/Finland Buses from Stockholm follow the Swedish east coast to Haparanda, and farther north along the border to Övertorneå and Karesuando; all three are just a short walk or bus ride from the border with Finland. There's also a daily bus between Abisko and Karesuvanto (the Finnish border town opposite Karesuando), which connects with the Eskelisen Lapin Linjat bus north to Kilpisjärvi and Tromsø and south to Rovaniemi.

Swedish trains travel as far north as Boden; from there you'll have to take the bus (rail passes are valid) to the border town of Haparanda, from where you can easily walk (or take another bus) to Tornio, on the Finnish side. There, you can ride the bus to the railhead at Kemi (buses between Boden and Kemi are covered by rail passes).

Norway/Sweden Nor-Way Bussekspress (☎ 23 00 24 40, fax 23 00 24 49, mobile ☎ 81 54 44 44, email ruteinformasjon@nor-way.no) runs express buses three to four times daily from Oslo to Göteborg (4½ hours, Nkr220) and Malmö (10 hours, Nkr350), with a boat connection to Copenhagen. At 8 am on weekdays, there's a bus from Oslo to Stockholm (nine hours, Nkr320). In the north, however, you are limited to the daily buses between Bodø and Skellefteå (8¾ hours, Nkr320) and along the Blå Vägen, or 'Blue Highway', between Mo i Rana and Umeå (7½ hours, Nkr185). For further information try the Web sites at www.nor-way.no or www.nbe.no.

Daily trains run between Stockholm and Oslo (seven hours, Nkr675), Trondheim (11 hours, Nkr700) and Narvik (22 hours, Nkr1010); the latter is the only rail connection between the Arctic regions of Sweden and Norway.

Norway/Finland The E8 highway runs from Tornio, Finland, to Tromsø and secondary highways connect Finland with the northern Sami towns of Karasjok and Kautokeino. Regular buses serve all three routes. In summer, the daily bus run by the Finnish company Eskelisen Lapin Linjat runs between Rovaniemi and Tromsø (11½ hours, Nkr378), via Karesuvanto and Kilpisjärvi. It leaves at 7.10 am southbound and 11.20 am northbound. Also in summer, the company runs daily buses between Rovaniemi and Tana Bru (9¼ hours, Nkr500), via Inari and Ivalo; and between Rovaniemi, Karasjok (6¾ hours, Nkr267) and Lakselv (7¾ hours, Nkr267), with a connection to Nordkapp (11¾ hours, Nkr464). Four times weekly, buses connect Kautokeino with Enontekiö (2¼ hours, Nkr66), with connections to Rovaniemi.

RUSSIA
To/From Alaska
All connections between Russia and Alaska are by air. See Alaska earlier in this chapter.

To/From Norway
If you're intending to enter Russia independently at Storskog, Russia's only Arctic land border, be sure to have your Russian visa (preferably from your home country) before arriving in the Norwegian border town of Kirkenes. Unless you have an official prearranged invitation, the Russian consulate in town (☎ 78 99 37 37), Arbeidergata 6, does not issue independent tourist visas, and no amount of charm or begging will sway them. Some nationalities may be issued visas at the Russian consulate in Oslo, but USA citizens, in particular, shouldn't count on it. Note that your visa must specify which Russian cities and towns you intend to visit, and without permission to visit Nikel (which is surely the most horrible spot on earth – at least outside major war zones – and deserves a visit for that reason alone), Zapolyarny, Murmansk or another Pechenga or Kola peninsula town, you may not be allowed to cross the border.

For tour participants coming from Norway, visa fees are determined by nationality and also vary according to what sort of urgency is required; all applications require three passport photos and for the best rates, you'll have to wait a minimum of 10 days. Citizens of Canada, the UK, Italy, Japan and India pay just Nkr50 while Norwegians pay Nkr245, other Scandinavians Nkr200, other EU citizens Nkr280 and USA citizens Nkr350. In addition, everyone pays a servicing fee of Nkr50. If you need a visa the next day, you'll pay anywhere from Nkr1000 to Nkr2500. Naturally, this is all subject to change on a whim.

Air The Norwegian airline Widerøe (☎ 67 11 60 00, fax 67 11 61 95, email internetbooking@wideroe.no), based in Lysaker (near Oslo), has services between Kirkenes and Murmansk, Russia, on Monday and Wednesday. Further details can be found on its Web site at www.wideroe.no. Braathens SAFE has twice-weekly flights between Tromsø (☎ 77 66 00 00) and Murmansk (☎ 085-10034).

Bus Those who already have a visa can just hop on the Murmansk Shipping Company's public bus to Murmansk (seven hours, Nkr400), which travels via Nikel and Zapolyarny. It leaves Kirkenes on Wednesday, Friday and Sunday at 3 pm from the Rica Arctic Hotel and from the Hotel Polyarny Zory in Murmansk at 9 am on the same days (thanks to more efficient border crossings, the return trip takes only four hours). Due to military exercises, the route is only open to foreigners (even those in their own vehicles) on Monday, Wednesday, Friday and Sunday, from 7 am to 9 pm Norwegian time (9 am to 11 pm Russian time).

Organised Tours Many visitors who have travelled as far as Kirkenes, Norway, want to visit Russia – or at least sally up to the border – and several local agencies are happy to accommodate them. If you're happy with just a quick hop across the border, you can pop over with a local travel agent, who will organise your visa locally. However, your itinerary will be rather limited and without a great deal of creativity, you probably won't be permitted to continue farther into Russia.

Sovjetrejser (☎ 78 99 19 81, fax 78 99 11 42) organises day trips to the hell-hole Nikel for Nkr480 to Nkr600 per person, including a lunch and guide, and to Zapolyarny for Nkr1100. Day trips to Murmansk run daily except Sunday and Wednesday, from 1 June to 31 August, and cost Nkr1000, while weekends in Murmansk cost Nkr11650 per person plus Nkr400 per night. Straight minibus transfers between Kirkenes and Murmansk are Nkr550.

The other main player offering Russian trips is Pasvikturist (☎ 78 99 50 80, fax 78 99 50 57), which offers adventure tours, including canoeing and camping in the Pechenga wilderness, and longer tours of north-western Russia. An eight day all-inclusive trip visiting Murmansk, the Pomor trading centre of Solovki and Archangelsk costs Nkr5950 per person.

To/From Finland

Air Most international connections to north-western Russia – Murmansk, Petrozavodsk and Arkhangelsk – are through St Petersburg and Moscow. From northern Finland to or from Murmansk, you can fly on Finnair.

Land Along the heavily travelled Helsinki-Vyborg-St Petersburg corridor there are two road crossings between Finland and Russia: Nuijamaa/Brusnichnoe and Vaalimaa/Torfyanovka. Farther north, it may be possible to cross into Russia at the Finnish post of Niirala/Vyartsilya and continue 500km to Petrozavodsk. From Salla, there is a road across the Russian border to Alakurtti, and from Ivalo, a road goes east to Murmansk via the Finnish border post of Raja-Jooseppi.

The Raja-Jooseppi border station, 53km south-east of Ivalo, is a crossing point to Russia for travellers to Murmansk, 250km away. It's also a good starting point for treks into the Saariselkä Wilderness. A post taxi travels between Ivalo and the border station, departing Ivalo early in the afternoon from Monday to Saturday.

Daily express buses run between Helsinki, Turku and other southern Finnish towns and St Petersburg, via Vyborg. Check current timetables and book tickets at the city bus station or a travel agency. From Helsinki to Vyborg, the fare is FMk160, and to St Petersburg, FMk250.

There are also post buses from Joensuu to Sortavala and Petrozavodsk (Finnish: Petroskoi), and from Rovaniemi and Ivalo to Murmansk. To qualify for travel on a post bus, you need a passport and a visa and must pre-pay for your journey at a post office; the receipt is your ticket. Inquire at the local post office about rates and schedules.

Finland uses broad gauge railways simi-lar to those in Russia, and daily trains connect Helsinki with St Petersburg and Moscow. Tickets are sold at the international counter in the Helsinki train station; the route crosses the border at Vainikkala/ Luzhayka. All three trains stop in Lahti and Kouvula in Finland, and Vyborg in Russia. A Russian visa is required.

Organised Tours & Adventures

Thanks to the complications involved in reaching the Arctic and planning the logistics, many people opt for a tour with a tour agency, cruise line, outfitter or guiding company. The following is a selection of companies that specialise in the Arctic regions. Note that inclusion in this list does not constitute a recommendation (unless otherwise stated in the blurb).

ORGANISED TOURS

The following list includes companies that provide sightseeing tours, transport and Arctic cruises for holiday-makers. If you'd prefer more strenuous activity-oriented options, see Adventure Tours later in this chapter.

Australasia

Bentours (☎ 02-9241 1353, fax 02-9251 1574) Level 11, 2 Bridge St, Sydney 2000, NSW. The only Australian agency specialising exclusively in Scandinavia, Iceland and Greenland, including guided excursions, horse riding tours and camping and dogsledding tours.

Gateway Travel (☎ 02-745 3333, fax 02-745 3237, Web site www.russian-gateway.com.au) 48 The Boulevarde, Strathfield 2135, NSW. Russia specialist selling a variety of group and individual tours, including specialist hunting, fishing, mountaineering and ecotourism packages. Also organises Kamchatka and Sakhalin tours.

Saga Holidays Australasia (☎ 02-9957 5660) Level One, 110 Pacific Highway, North Sydney 2060, NSW. Scandinavian holidays for travellers over 50 years of age.

Wiltrans/Maupintour (☎ 02-9255 0899) Level 10, 189 Kent St, Sydney 2000, NSW. Offers a range of pricey luxury tours around Scandinavia.

Canada

Aurora Sport Fishing & Tours (☎ 867-699 3551, fax 867-699 3526) Aurora Marketing, Fort Providence, NWT X0E 0L0. Fishing and leisure cruises along the Mackenzie River.

Great Canadian Ecoventures (☎ 867-920 7110, toll-free ☎ 1-800 667 9453, fax 867-920 7180, email tundra@thelon.com, Web site www.thelon

.com) PO Box 2481, Yellowknife, NWT X1A 2P8. Fly-in Arctic wildlife-viewing tours to observe wolves, muskoxen, snow geese, gyrfalcon and caribou.

Inukshuk Ventures (☎ 867-873 4226, fax 867-669 9665) 49th St, Yellowknife, NWT X1A 3R6. Specialists in easy going adventures in the north – camping, wildlife-viewing and canoeing trips.

Marine Expeditions (toll-free ☎ 1-800 263 9147, fax 416-964 2366, email info@marineex.com, Web site www.marineex.com) 30 Hazelton Ave, Toronto, ONT M5R 2E2. Organises cruises to Arctic Russia, including Wrangel Island, Kamchatka and the Kuril Islands (18 days, US$4795); cruises the Northwest Passage (10 days, US$2095); and runs tours to Baffin Island (US$1945), the Russian Far East and Alaska (13 days, US$3795) and Greenland to Churchill (12 days, US$2195).

Raven Tours (☎ 867-873 4776, fax 867-873 4856, email raventours@yellowknife.com) PO Box 2435, Yellowknife, NWT X1A 2P8. Relatively soft winter dogsledding tours to view the northern lights and watch caribou.

Res Delta Tours (☎ 867-394 3141, fax 867-394 5122) Don Balsillie, Fort Resolution, NWT X0E 0M0. Five to seven-day sightseeing, fishing, and bird-watching cruises through the rich waterfowl nesting grounds of the Slave River delta.

Scanditours (toll-free ☎ 1-800 432 4176 or ☎ 1-800 377 9828, fax 416-482 9447 or 604-736 8311, email toronto@scanditours.com or vancouver@scanditours.com, Web site www.scanditours.com) 308-191 Eglinton Ave E, Toronto, ONT M4P 1K1 or 21-1275 W 6th Ave, Vancouver, BC V6H 1A6. A Canadian company concentrating on northern Scandinavia, as well as historical routes between St Petersburg and Oslo.

Travcoa (☎ 416-927 9610) 112 St Clair Ave W, Suite 400, Toronto, ONT M4V 2Y3. Organises hotel-based tours to Greenland and the Faroe Islands for those after some comfort.

Denmark

Arctic Adventure (☎ 33 25 32 21, fax 33 25 63 08) 30 Reventlowsgade, DK-1651 Copenhagen V. Offers well organised hotel-based tours around Reykjavík, south Greenland and Disko Bay. Also concocts painless winter (April to May)

dogsledding tours in north-west Greenland and Disko Bay.

Germany

Arktis Reisen Schehle (☎ 0831-521 5964, fax 0831-521 5951) Bahnhofstrasse 12-II, D-87435 Kempten. Comprehensive list of tours covering Greenland, Canada, Alaska and Svalbard; all styles of travel, including hiking.

Ísland Reisen (☎ 030-823 1435, fax 030-823 1405) Rheinbabenallee 27, D-14199 Berlin. Specialises in individual itineraries in Iceland and Greenland.

Greenland

Arctic Wonderland Tours (☎ 981293, fax 981393, email arcwon@greennet.gl,) PO Box 117, DK-3913 Tasiilaq. Short hotel-based excursions from Tasiilaq, including cruises, day hikes and dogsled trips.

Greenland Tours Elke Meissner (☎ 944411, fax 944511, email greenland.tours@greennet.gl, Web site iserit.greennet.gl/gtem) PO Box 160, DK-3952 Ilulissat. Disko Bay agency concentrating on shorter trips around Ilulissat, including hiking, dogsledding, cruises and visits to small villages. It's based in the small village of Oqaatsut.

Jacky Simoud (☎ 572571, fax 665001) Qassiarsuk, DK-3921 Narsaq. Mr Simoud organises all sorts of tours, including hiking, kayaking, horse riding, skiing, day cruises and transfers between Narsarsuaq and Qassiarsuk. He also hires out mountain bikes, kayaks and snowmobiles.

Maya Boat Adventures (☎ 946061, fax 946062) Saqqaq DK-3952 Ilulissat. Runs cruises around the Disko Bay area, aimed specifically at the German market. It's based in the tiny village of Saqqaq.

Nielsen Travel (☎ 642913, fax 642987, email ntravel@greennet.gl, Web site www.greenland-guide.dk/south-tourism) PO Box 183, DK-3920 Qaqortoq. Offers a range of tours around Qaqortoq and other areas of south Greenland.

Polar Rejser (☎ 865747, fax 865208) PO Box 329, DK-3911 Sisimiut. Offers hotel-based tours, fishing, hiking, dogsledding and sailing, and also organises mountaineering expeditions.

Iceland

Nonni Travel (☎ 461 1841, fax 461 1843, email nonnitra@est.is) Rådhúsplads, Akureyri. Runs Grímsey tours daily. Flying both ways costs Ikr8125. Monday and Thursday you can take the ferry both ways for Ikr4745. If you opt to fly back it's Ikr7350. Participants get a certificate stating that they've crossed the Arctic Circle. For longer stays, you can leave the tour on the island and return to Akureyri another day.

Norway

Sovjetrejser (☎ 78 99 19 81, fax 78 99 11 42) Kirkenes. Organises Russia day trips to Nikel for Nkr480 to Nkr600 per person, including a lunch and guide, and to Zapolyarny for Nkr1100. Day trips to Murmansk run daily except Sunday and Wednesday, 1 June to 31 August, and cost Nkr1000, while weekends in Murmansk cost Nkr11650 per person plus Nkr400 per night. Straight minibus transfers between Kirkenes and Murmansk are Nkr550.

Russia

Alpha Tours (☎ 41522-50579 or ☎ 41522-55850), international ☎/fax 50901-640081, email tour@alpha.kamchatka.su) 59 Kosmonavtov St, Petropavlovsk-Kamchatskiy 683905. Recommended as a tour company that can cope with independent travellers. It can arrange guides, *vezidkhod* vehicles, fishing, rafting, skiing and helicopter transport around the Kamchatka Peninsula.

Arcsovtour (☎ 3773, fax in Anchorage 907-274 9614) Egvekinot, Chukotka. Organises sightseeing tours around the Chukchi reindeer herding areas of the Chukotka Peninsula.

Kamchatintour (☎ 41522-71034 or ☎ 41522-73776, fax 41522-118007, email intur @svyaz.kamchatka.su) ulitsa Leningradskaya 124b, Petropavlovsk-Kamchatskiy 683003. Handles 300 to 1000 tourists a season, mostly foreigners who come to the peninsula aboard posh cruise ships. Its tours are expensive, and the staff, though friendly and knowledgeable, may be unable to help those who don't give one or two week's advance notice.That said, it may be able to plug last-minute travellers into an existing group or offer something on a smaller scale, like an overnight trip to Esso or Paratunka. Its offices are 150m behind the 16-storey octagonal tower, on the 4th floor.

Snow Leopard (☎ 41500-64254, fax 41500-24364, email service@post.kamchatka.su) 19-29 ulitsa Pogranichnaya, Yelizovo, Kamchatka 684010. Operates organised tours to the volcanoes and geothermal areas of Kamchatka.

Sogjoy (☎ 41500-61493) ulitsa Sopochnaya 13, Yelizovo, Kamchatka 684010. The only company that can organise tours to the Valley of the Geysers.

USA

Alaska Snail Trails (toll-free ☎ 1-800 348 4532, ☎/fax 907-337 7517) PO Box 210894, Anchorage, AK 99521. Offers 10-day Alaska tours for able-bodied and disabled travellers, and others with limited mobility; covers the popular sites, including Denali and Kenai Fjords National Parks.

Backroads (toll-free ☎ 1-800 462 2848 or ☎ 510-527 1555, fax 510-527 1444, Web site www.backroads.com) 801 Cedar St, Berkeley, CA 94710-1800. Offers all-inclusive upmarket six-day cycling holidays around Lofoten and Vesterålen (US$2198), in Arctic Norway.

Bennett Tours (toll-free ☎ 1-800 221 2420, Web site www.bennett-tours.com) Specialises in shorter trips through Scandinavia as well as long-haul trips north to Nordkapp, and Hurtigruten coastal steamer cruises.

Bettles Air Service (toll-free ☎ 1-800 770 5111, summer fax 907-692 5655, winter fax 907-488 7909) PO Box 27, Bettles, AK 99726. Offers fly-in and flightseeing services from Bettles to Gates of the Arctic National Park.

Borton Overseas (toll-free ☎ 1-800 843 0602, ☎ 612-822 4640, fax 612-822 4755, www.borton.com/overseas.html-ssi) 5516 Lyndale Ave S, Minneapolis, MN 55419. Borton's forte is adventure outdoor travel, and offers trips in Scandinavia. It's also the North American agent for DNT, the Norwegian Mountain Touring Club.

Brekke Tours (☎ 701-772 8999 or toll-free ☎ 1-800 437 5502, fax 701-780 9352, email tours@brekketours.com, Web site www .brekketours.com) 802 N 43rd St, Grand Forks, ND 58203. Caters mainly to North Americans of Norwegian, Danish, Finnish, Swedish or Icelandic descent, and cobbles together a host of Scandinavian options – with the two-week US holiday in mind.

Euroseven Tours (toll-free ☎ 1-800 890 3876, ☎ 212-255 8166, fax 212-255 8944, email euro7@concentric.net, Web site www.travelitile.com/get/euro7.html). Runs all-inclusive, hotel-based tours to Scandinavia from the US east coast.

Frontier Flying Service (☎ 907-474 0014, fax 907-474 0774) 3820 University Ave, Fairbanks, AK 99709. In summer, Frontier flies daily to Gates of the Arctic National Park, and also has service to 20 other northern Alaska destinations.

Golden Plover Guiding & Air (☎ 907-659 3991) Colville Village, Pouch 340109, Prudhoe Bay, AK 99734. This company, based at a remote Arctic Lodge, offers boating, sightseeing, and bird-watching tours.

Larry's Flying Service (☎ 907-474 9169, fax 907-474 8815) PO Box 2348, Fairbanks, AK 99707. Larry flies from Fairbanks to Bettles, Fort Yukon, Anaktuvuk Pass and other Arctic Alaska communities.

Mountain Travel Sobek (☎ 510-527 8100, toll-free ☎ 1-800 227 2384, fax 510-525 7710, email info@mtsobek.com, Web site www.mtsobek.com) 6420 Fairmont Ave, El Cerrito, CA 94530. Offers a 15 day cruise that begins in Petropavlovsk-Kamchatskiy and visits Provideniya and Wrangel Island in Arctic Russia. Prices range from $7290 to $9590 excluding air fares.

Russian Nature Travel Company (☎ 603-835 6369, toll-free ☎ 1-800 304 6369, email s.levin2@genie.geis.com) South Acworth, NH. Organises nature tours all over Russia, including the Lapplandsky Zapovednik on the Kola Peninsula and places in the Russian Far East.

Saga International Holidays (☎ 617-262 2262) 222 Berkeley St, Boston, MA 2116. Cobbles together Scandinavia tours aimed at travellers over 50.

Scanam World Tours & Cruises (toll-free ☎ 1-800 545 2204, fax 973-835 3030) 922 Hwy 23, Pompton Plains, NJ 07444. Organises cruises and shorter upmarket tours. Also the North American agent for Fjord Line ferries.

Scantours (☎ 213-451 0911, toll-free ☎ 1-800 223 7226, fax 213-395 2013, email info @scantours.com, Web site www.scantours .com) 1535 Sixth St, Suite 205, Santa Monica, CA 90401. Offers an extensive range of short tours in Scandinavia, including 14 days aboard the Hurtigruten coastal steamer. Also does hotel-based excursions to Iceland and Greenland. As with many operators, the tours aren't too imaginative, but will show you the sights in a measure of comfort. Its Web site includes details and prices for all its offerings.

Society Expeditions (toll-free ☎ 1-800 548 8669, Web site www.societyexpeditions.com) 2001 Western Ave #300, Seattle, WA, 98121. Does upmarket cruises of the northern Pacific rim, including Kamchatka, starting at $5,820 per person.

Trans Arctic Circle Treks (☎ 907-479 5451, fax 907-479 8908, email arctictk@ptialaska.net) 4825 Glasgow Dr, Fairbanks, AK 99709. Cobbles together Alaska itineraries, including several destinations in Arctic Alaska.

Travcoa (☎ 714-476 2800, fax 714-476 2538) S.E. Bristol 2350, Santa Ana Heights, CA 92707. As with its Canadian branch, the American arm of Travcoa provides short hotel-based highlights tours in Greenland.

Zegrahm & Eco Expeditions (toll-free ☎ 1-800 628 8747, email zoe@zeco.com or zdv@deepsea voyages.com, Web site www.deepseavoyages .com or www.zeco.com) 1414 Dexter Ave N #327, Seattle, WA 98109. Offers Kamchatka and other Arctic area cruises. If you are really flush with cash, how about a submarine visit to the Arctic waters near Beechey Island to see the wreck of the HMS *Breadalbane* (this company also visits the undersea volcanoes of the Azores and actually sidles up to the *Titanic*?

UK
Arctic Experience (☎ 01737-218800, fax 01737-362341, email sales@arctic-discover.co.uk, Web site www.arctic-discover.co.uk) 29 Nork Way, Banstead Surrey SM7 1PB. Friendly and popular British tour operator organising trips to Scandinavia, Iceland and Greenland. Offers highlights tours, whale-watching and ice-breaker cruises in Svalbard. It's also started Iceland High Adventures, featuring mountaineering, glacier travel, ice-climbing and other activity-oriented trips.

David Oswin Expeditions (☎ 01228-75518, fax 01228-75427) Millgarth, Kirklinton, Carlisle CA6 6DW, Cumbria. With more than 15 years of experience in Iceland and Greenland, David Oswin is now the foremost UK specialist in North Atlantic photographic tours. Programs include two-week photo tours in Iceland and east Greenland, and winter camping tours in Iceland.

Goodwood Travel (☎ 01227-763336, fax 01227-762417) Flights of Fantasy, Concord House, Stour St, Canterbury, Kent CT1 2NZ. Got a spare £2495? If so, spring for a trip on the Concorde to Greenland (Kangerlussuaq) for three days of icy adventure in Ilulissat.

Flying Ghillies (☎ 01670-789603) PO Box 1, Morpeth, Northumberland NE61 6YX. If you're a fish fan, this is the company to go with. In Norway, its speciality is salmon fishing, combined with other outdoor pursuits.

Russian Nature Tours (☎ 01962-733051, fax 01962-733368) Chautara, Brighton, Alresford, Hampshire SO24 9RB. Focuses on flora and fauna, bird-watching tours around Russia.

Saga Holidays (☎ 0800-300 500) Saga Building, Middelburg Square, Folkestone, Kent CT20 1AZ. Operates tours to Scandinavia, aimed specifically at folks over 50.

Regent Holidays (☎ 01983-864212, fax 01983-864197) Regent House, 31A High Street, Shanklin, Isle of Wight PO37 6JW. Offers comprehensive packages to Iceland, Greenland and all over Russia.

Russia Experience (☎ 020-8566 8846, fax 020-8566 8843, email 100604.764@compuserve .com, Web site www.trans-Siberian.co.uk). These folks have years of experience in Russia, and can help you with putting together an all-inclusive adventure, transport, tours and bookings.

Scantours (☎ 020-7329 2927, email scantour suk@dial.pipex.com, Web site www.scan tours.com). As with the US branch of this company, the Web site includes details and prices for a wide range of options throughout Norway, lasting from four to 14 days.

Taber Holidays (☎ 01274-735611) 126 Sunbridge Rd, Bradford, West Yorks BD1 2SX. Offers a range of highlight-oriented all-inclusive tours around Norway, including cruises, coach tours and self-drive options.

Twickers World (☎ 020-8892 7606, fax 020-8892 8061) 20/22 Church St, Twickenham TW1 3NW. Puts together a range of highlight holidays in Iceland and Greenland.

Wild Oceans (☎ 0117-984 8040, fax 0117-967 4444) Wildwings, International House, Bank Rd, Bristol BS15 2LX. Wild Oceans is a booking agent for Arctic cruises on the *Professor Molchanov*, which does dolphin and whale-watching expeditions worldwide, and frequent runs to Iceland, Greenland, Jan Mayen and Svalbard.

ADVENTURE TOURS
These tours are generally for those with outdoor interests who are prepared to face the elements without any luxuries, and participate in skiing, hiking, camping, canoeing, rafting and dogsledding trips. Note that many of these companies also offer softer options, so it's worth contacting them anyway.

Australasia
Explore Holidays (☎ 02-9872 6722) 1st Floor, Oasis Centre, Carlingford, Sydney 2000, NSW. Runs outdoor and adventure-oriented tours in Scandinavia.

Canada
Adventure Canada (☎ 905-271 4000, toll-free ☎ 1-800 363 7566, fax 905-271 5595, email info@adventurecanada.com, Web site www .adventurecanada.com) 14 Front St South, Mississauga, ONT L5H 2C4. Specialises in rafting on Canadian Arctic rivers. It also guides nine-day hikes to Auyuittuq National Park from Pangnirtung for C$1895.

Alcantara Outfitting (☎/fax 867-872 3701, email alcantara@auroranet.nt.ca) PO Box 909, Fort Smith NWT. Ever want to join a Native trapper on a snowmobile tour to follow his trapline, learn his techniques and gain first-hand experience of Native lifestyles? These trips operate in the Slave River area.

Arctic Chalet Outfitters (☎ 867-777 3535, fax 867-777 4443) 25 Carn St, PO Box 2404, Inuvik NWT X0E 0T0. Hires canoes and kayaks for self-guided adventures, and also does car shuttles and pick-ups.

Arctic Nature Tours (☎ 867-777 3300, fax 867-777 3400, email arcticnt@permafrost.com, Web site www.arcticnaturetours.com) PO Box 1530, Inuvik, NWT X0E 0T0. Does whitewater rafting and wildlife-viewing trips through Ivvavik National Park in the Yukon and along the Horton River in NWT. It also offers lighter trips along the Dempster Hwy, the Richardson Mountains, the Mackenzie Delta and Banks and Herschel Islands, and winter aurora-viewing and dogsledding tours.

Arctic Red River Outfitters (☎/fax 867-633 4934) PO Box 5988, Whitehorse, YT Y1A 5L7. Summer wildlife photo safaris and hiking trips through the McKenzie Mountains.

Arctic Tour Company (☎ 867-977 2230, fax 867-977 2276, email atc@auroranet.nt.ca) PO Box 325, Tuktoyaktuk, NWT X0E 1C0. Camping and whale-watching tours to Herschel Island, Ivvavik National Park and Banks Island, community tours, and camping, hiking and bird-watching along the Dempster Hwy.

Arctic Vision & Go Wild Tours (☎ 867-668 2411, fax 867-668 2642, email arcticv@yknet.yk.ca, Web site www.arcticvision.com) PO Box 31210, Whitehorse, YT Y1A 5P7. Runs seven to 10-day nature tours for bird-watching on Herschel Island, muskox-viewing on Banks Island, rafting in Southeast Alaska, and visits to north-western national parks.

Big John's Tourism Adventures (☎ 867 966 4711) PO Box 96, Fort Providence, NWT X0E 0L0. Snow machining and dogsledding tours in the Mackenzie Sanctuary to photograph migratory birds and other local wildlife.

Black Feather Trailhead (☎ 613-722 8375, toll-free ☎ 1-800 574 8375, fax 613-722 0245, email info@blackfeather.com, Web site www.trailheadcnd.com) 1960 Scott St, Ottawa, ONT K1Z 8L8. Does hiking, canoeing and white-water rafting trips throughout the Northwest Territories, and also does sea kayaking trips in Greenland.

Canada North Outfitting (☎ 613-256 4056, fax 613-256 4512, email larmann@worldnet.att.net)

72 Mill St. Almonte, ONT K0A 1A0. Organises charter fly-in trips and guided hikes through Ellesmere Island National Park.

Canadian Arctic Adventure Tours (☎/fax 867-777 4006, email arnon@internorth.com) PO Box 1701, Inuvik, NWT X0E 0T. If your passion is tearing over the frozen wastes making a lot of noise, here's your chance to take a five day snowmobile tour from Inuvik to Tuktoyaktuk or to Aklavik and the Richardson Mountains. Shorter trips are also available.

Canadian Arctic Holidays (toll-free ☎ 1-877 272 8426, email info@canadianarcticholidays.ca) 151 Basswood, Aylmer, PQ J9H 5E1. This very adventurous outfitter offers ski touring on Axel Heiberg and Ellesmere Islands, hiking, skiing and kayaking around Baffin Island and even a 14 day ski trip to the North Pole!

Cygnus Ecotours (☎/fax 867-873 4782, email cygnus@internorth.com) PO Box 682, Yellowknife, NWT X1A 2N5. Light-hearted and nontechnical natural history field trips revealing the geology, botany and zoology of the Canadian Shield, mostly around Yellowknife.

Ecosummer Yukon Expeditions (☎/fax 867-633 8453, email joycejill@hypertech.yk.ca, Web site www.silasojourns.com) PO Box 5095, Whitehorse, YT Y1A 4Z2. Eight to 12-day backpacking trips in Kluane and Ivvavik National Parks and rafting on the Firth and Tatshenshini Rivers.

Enodah Wilderness Travel (☎ 867-873 4334, fax 867-873 3825, email info@enodah.com, Web site www.enodah.com) PO Box 2382, Yellowknife, NWT X1A 2P8. If you're interested in fishing in the Arctic's largest lake – and have US$1125 for a three day fly-in adventure – this is the way to go. Ice fishing and aurora viewing are available in the winter. Accommodation is in the Trout Rock Wilderness Lodge on Great Slave Lake.

Fresh Tracks Canada (☎ 604-737 8743, toll-free ☎ 1-800 667 4744, fax 604-718 5110, email adventure@freshtracks.com, Web site www .freshtracks.ca) 1823 W 4th Ave, Vancouver, BC V6J 1M4. Fresh Tracks bills itself as the tour company for the un-tourist, and can take you on active outdoor adventures far from the beaten track.

Great Slave Sledging Company (☎ 867-873 6070, fax 867-920 4999) Moraine Point Lodge, PO Box 1978, Yellowknife, NWT X1A 2P5. Winter dogsledding and skiing expeditions from Yellowknife, with camping or lodge accommodation.

Mountain River Outfitters (☎ 867-587 2285) PO Box 449, Normal Wells, NWT X0E 0V0.

Canoe hire for trips on the Natla and Keele Rivers, motorboat transfers to and from put-in points and hikers' transfers to the Canol Trail trailhead.

Nahanni Wilderness Adventures (☎/fax 403-637 3843, toll-free ☎ 1-888 897 5223, email adventures@nahanniwild.com, Web site www.nahanniwild.com) PO Box 4, Site 6, RR1, Didsbury, AB T0M 0W0. Runs thrilling two and three-week white-water rafting and canoeing trips through wild Nahanni National Park, in the Northwest Territories. Trips cost C$2350 to C$3395.

NorthWinds (☎ 867-979 0552, fax 867-979 0573, email plandry@nunanet.com, Web site www.northwinds-arctic.com) PO Box 820, Iqaluit, NT X0A 0H0. A friendly organisation taking groups into Auyuittuq National Park, Ellesmere Island, the Soper River, the North Pole, the Magnetic North Pole and wildflower and cultural tours.

Outdoor Hunting & Safari (☎ 905-727 1956, fax 905-727 1089) 28 Mill St, Aurora, ONT L4G 2R9. Five to 14-day backpacking trips around the Anderson River on Baffin Island.

Qimutsik EcoTours (☎ 514-694 8264, toll-free ☎ 1-888 297 3467, email info@qimutsiktours.com, Web site www.qimutsiktours.com). Inuit-owned company running traditional dogsledding tours at Kuujjuaq, in the Inuit country on Ungava Bay in far northern Quebec.

Raven Eye Outfitters (toll-free ☎ 1-888 463 6736, email raveneyerivers@hotmail.com, Web site www.wilds.mb.ca/raveneye) PO Box 93, Seven Sisters Falls, MT R0E 1Y0. Northern Manitoba company offering guided canoe trips along the Kazan and Thlewiaza Rivers through the barren grounds around Hudson Bay. You'll have a good chance of seeing migrating caribou.

River Trails North (☎ 867-872 2060, email rivertrails@auroranet.nt.ca) PO Box 852, Forth Smith, NWT X0E 0P0. Organises hiking, canoeing and wildlife-viewing on the Little Buffalo River in Wood Buffalo National Park.

Toonoonik Sahoonik Outfitters (☎ 867-899 8366, fax 867-899 8364, Web site www.pondtour.com) Pond Inlet, NT X0A 0S0. Offers ice floe cruises, fishing trips, and wildlife-viewing trips (whale-watching, bird-watching), around the northern end of Baffin Island.

Tununik Travel & Adventure (☎/fax 867-899 8194, email marian@tununiq.com, Web site www.tununiq.com) PO Box 25, Pond Inlet, NT X0A 0S0. Recommended company concentrating on wildlife tours around the northern end of Baffin Island, including the exotic Sirmilik National Park. Options include 10-day

snowmobile sled *(qamutik)* adventures for C$2470; nine-day fishing and narwhal and beluga spotting cruises for C$2340; and nine days of dogsledding for C$2560. All prices are from Pond Inlet.

West to North Tours (☎ 867-587 3043, fax 867-587 2312, email wntours@netcom.ca) PO Box 62, Norman Wells, NWT X0E 0V0. Seven-day guided hiking trips along the Canol Trail and winter snowmobile tours.

Whitney & Smith Legendary Expeditions (☎ 403-678 3052, fax 403-678 5176, email info@legendaryex.com, Web site www.legendaryex.com) PO Box 2097, Banff, AB T0L 0C0. Established company operating guided backpacking, trekking and kayaking trips through the Canadian Arctic, including Banks, Ellesmere and Baffin islands, as well as northwest Greenland. Its fabulous 15 day 'Top-of-the-World Trek' on Ellesmere Island costs US$4000 from Resolute. The emphasis is on Inuit culture and Arctic wildlife: birds and land and marine mammals. An excellent choice.

Denmark

Greenland Travel (Grønlands Rejsebureau) (☎ 33 13 10 11, fax 33 13 85 92) Gammel Mønt 12, PO Box 130, DK-1004, Copenhagen K. Agency affiliated with Greenland Home Rule government and a good source of help for independent travel in Greenland. It arranges hotel-based tours, books ferries and flights, and conducts 'Green Tours': multi-day hiking, dogsledding and mountain-biking tours inherited from the former backpackers' agency, DVL Rejser. The guides, most of whom speak English, German and Danish, are friendly and well-informed volunteers who scout out and organise their own routes and hikes. The result is a slate of refreshingly original options.

France

Grand Nord Grand Large (☎ 01-40 46 05 14, fax 01-43 26 73 20) 15, rue du Cardinal Lemoine, F-75005 Paris. As one of the world's most adventurous agencies, GNGL seeks out the locations and activities that are noticed by only a handful of other companies. GNGL visits all the Arctic countries and are highly recommended, especially for hiking, trekking and sea kayaking tours.

Greenland

Arctic Incoming Vildmarksrejser (☎ 981254, fax 981354, email vildmarksrejser@greennet.gl, PO Box 116, DK-3913 Tasiilaq). Adventure tours in east Greenland, including wilderness hiking and camping, summer or winter trips with local hunters, dogsled trips, boat transfers, and both summer fishing and ice-fishing.

Mt Forel Expedition Support (☎ 981320, fax 981373) PO Box 116, DK-3913 Tasiilaq. Recommended company offering all sorts of expeditions – trekking, sailing, mountaineering, glacier climbing, dogsledding and fishing – either hut-based or camping.

Nonni Travel Greenland (☎/fax 991280, email nonni@greennet.gl, Web site www.est.is/non nitra) PO Box 28, DK-3980 Ittorqqortoormiit. The only local agency that operates organised expeditions into North-East Greenland National Park; choose from dogsledding, kayaking, hiking and Zodiac trips. It also provides support for independent expeditions.

Tuning Incoming Agency (☎/fax 981650) PO Box 81, DK-3913 Tasiilaq. All sorts of tours, mainly in east Greenland: kayaking, hiking, mountaineering, fishing and winter activities.

Netherlands

Travel North (☎ 023-537 7573) Duin-lustparkweg 48 A, NL-2061 LD Bloemendaal. Dutchman Ernest Dixon, a resident of Finland for over 30 years, has guided trekkers on his 'Lap-land Pulka Treks' and 'Lapland Ruska Treks' through the wilds of northern Finland and Russia, and is one of the foremost experts on the region. Ernest takes trekkers to local Sami homes or across the fells in search of reindeer herds, and prepares meals, including freshly-caught local salmon, Sami-style over an open fire. You can either book through Travel North or write well in advance to J Ernest Dixon, SF-99930 Sevettijärvi, Finland.

Norway/Svalbard

Bjørn Klauer (☎/fax 77 18 45 03) Innset, N-0250 Bardu. Winter visitors will have the unique opportunity to join a dogsled trip through Arctic Norway led by resourceful musher, Bjørn Klauer. In addition to tours through nearby Øvre Dividal National Park, he runs expeditions into Finnmark, northern Sweden and Finland, and Svalbard. With two people, seven/10/12 day tours, including meals and hut or tent accommodation, cost Nkr14,500/21,000/25,500 per person.

Engholm's Husky (☎ 78 46 71 66, fax 78 46 71 76, email se.engholm@online.no) Karasjok. Sven Engholm presents Alaskan dogsled demonstrations daily in summer at 10 am and 1 pm (Nkr30). He also offers excellent winter dogsled and cross-country skiing tours, and summer dog-packing tours. Week-long dogsled tours range from Nkr8000 to Nkr12,000. For a

light taste of dog mushing, a short winter spin around the premises costs Nkr150.

Pasvikturist (☎ 78 99 50 80, fax 78 99 50 57) Kirkenes. Offers adventure-oriented tours, including canoeing and camping in Russia's Pechenga wilderness, and longer tours of north-western Russia. An eight day trip visiting Murmansk, the Pomor trading centre of Solovki and Archangelsk costs Nkr5950 per person all-inclusive.

Svalbard Polar Travel (☎ 79 02 34 23, fax 79 02 34 01, email spot@svalbard-polar.no, Web site www.svalbard-polar.com) Næringsbrygget, PO Box 540, N-9171 Longyearbyen. Conducts a range of cruises, including shore excursions and short hikes. The five day Svalbard Adventure Cruise (with three days of actual cruising) departs twice weekly in summer from Longyearbyen and heads northward to 80°N, with two to four landings daily, including Barentsburg, Magdalenefjord, Ny Ålesund and Blomstrandhamna. Single/double cabins cost between Nkr11,050/17,100 and Nkr16,850/26,700. Its wondrous eight day circumnavigation of Spitsbergen also includes a cruise along the western coast of Nordaustlandet and a possible visit to the face of Austfonna glacier. This option greatly increases your chances of spotting polar bears and walrus. The cheapest single/double rates are Nkr28,900/47,180; in a shared triple cabin, you'll pay Nkr20,490. The 13 day 'Trekking at the North Pole Rim' includes either a series of day hikes from the Raudfjord and Blomstrand base camps or a 13 day Nordic ski trek, and costs Nkr18,190/15,190. A 15 day mountaineer expedition to Newtontoppen (1713m) costs Nkr18,050/33,700 for singles/doubles, not including skis or camping gear.

Spitsbergen Tours (☎ 79 02 10 68, fax 79 02 10 67, email info@spitsbergen-tours.com, Web site www.spitsbergen-tours.com) PO Box 6, N-9171 Longyearbyen. Opened in 1987 and the first registered tour operator in Svalbard. Run by Andreas Umbreit, who has written a couple of books on the area, it specialises in small group arrangements (normally fewer than 10 people) and environmentally conscious adventures. An Arctic Week in Longyearbyen, Barentsburg and Pyramiden is offered over New Years (during the polar night), in spring, and during the summer high season for Nkr8100 to Nkr18,000 per person, including dogsledding, snow machining, cruises and treks. For a straight week-long dogsledding tour you'll pay Nkr16,000, while 11-day ski tours are Nkr13,300. Cruises on research vessels start at Nkr21,000 for a one day circumnavigation of Spitsbergen Island, with numerous landings. On a simpler sailing ship, you'll pay just Nkr13,500. In summer, a 15 day hiking and trekking tour around Longyearbyen and Barentsburg costs Nkr13,020, while a more demanding 22 day trek involving an inland crossing with prearranged food caches and two fjord cruises costs Nkr16,500.

Spitsbergen Travel (✆/fax 79 02 24 10, email spitra@mail.link.no) N-9171 Longyearbyen. Offers Hurtigruten cruises between Troms and Longyearbyen. The entire return cruise, including accommodation in a single/double cabin with shared facilities, costs Nkr10,700/15.140. Posher cabins are available for considerably higher rates; the most expensive option is a private single/double suite with a shower and toilet for Nkr19,640/26,180. Alternatively, you can fly between Tromsø and Longyearbyen and only join the Svalbard portion of the cruise for Nkr9485/16,390, in basic single/double cabins. If you join the cruise in Longyearbyen, the minimum cost is Nkr3350/5200 for singles/doubles, including meals and landings.

Svalbard Wildlife Service (✆ 79 02 10 35, fax 79 02 12 01, email wildlife@mail.link.no, Web site www.svalbard.com/wildlife) Longyearbyen. In addition to booking a range of day tours from Longyearbyen, this agency operates a week-long wilderness camp around Isfjorden (Nkr14,875); a week of trekking on Ekmanfjorden (Nkr13,940), and a three day cruise to Ymerbukta (Nkr4400), which includes kayaking and hiking.

Russia
Alpindustriya-Kamchatka (✆ 41522-30246, ✆/fax 41522-72489) Kosmichesky 4-61, Petropavlovsk-Kamchatskiy, 683003. Run by brothers and mountain climbers Vitaly and Sergey Malkov, out of a camping equipment store where you can rent outdoor gear. It's behind Restoran Lonkhey on prospekt 50 let Oktyabrya. For about US$100 for jeep transport, you'll go out to the ski camp in Rodnikovoe, where lodging in wooden huts cost US$10 per night. For about $30, they will drop you off in the evening at the foot of Avachinskaya and Koryakskaya volcanoes and retrieve you the next evening, after your climb. For the same amount, they can arrange for camping on the beach. Three days of rafting on the Bystraya costs US$75 per person, including transportation and food. With advance notice, they can arrange and provide guides for longer expeditions, including ascents of Klyuchevskaya.

Pilgrim Tours (✆ 095 365 45 63 or ✆ 095-207 32 43, fax 095-369 03 89, email pilgrimtours @glas.apc.org), 1-y Kirpichny pereulok 17, Moscow. Locally known as Moskovskoe Turisticheskoe Agentstvo Piligrim, this agency offers excursions, hiking, trekking or mountaineering trips in the Caucasus, Kamchatka and other parts of the ex-USSR, plus kayaking, bicycling, cross-country and downhill skiing, helicopter skiing and what it refers to as a 'leisurely expedition to the North Pole'. Prices are reasonable, and the company comes highly recommended. It's also used by the US travel company, REI Adventures.

Other Moscow firms offering adventure travel include *Travel Russia* (✆ 095-290 34 39 or ✆ 095-290 30 88, fax 095-291 87 83) at korpus 2, Trubnikovsky pereulok 21, Moscow 121069; *CCTE-Intour* (✆ 095-235 44 26, fax 095-230 27 84) Ozerkovskaya naberezhnaya 50, Moscow 113532; and *Sputnik* (✆ 095-939 80 65, fax 095-938 11 92 or 095-956 10 68) Hotel Orlyonok, ulitsa Kosygina 15, Moscow 117946.

USA/Alaska
ABEC's Alaska Adventures (✆ 907-457 8907, fax 907-457 6689) 1550 Alpine Vista Ct, Fairbanks, AK 99712. Good value one-week to three-week backpacking expeditions in Noatak, Gates of the Arctic and the Arctic National Wildlife Refuge (ANWR). A 12 day trip on the remote Hulahula River costs US$2400 and a 10 day backpacking trip through the ANWR to witness the caribou migrations is US$1800.

Alaska-Denali Guiding, Inc (✆ 907-733 2649, fax 907-733 1362, email adg@alaska.net, Web site www.alaska.net/~adg) PO Box 566, Talkeetna, AK 99676. Try these guys for climbing in Alaska; they offer guided expeditions on Mt McKinley and other Alaskan mountains.

Alaska Fish & Trails Unlimited (✆ 907-479 7630) 1177 Shypoke Dr, Fairbanks, AK 99709. Runs guided backpacking, fishing, rafting and skiing expeditions into Gates of the Arctic National Park.

Alaska River Charters (✆ 907-455 6827, fax 907-455 4041) PO Box 81516, Fairbanks, AK 99709. Float trips and motorboat trips on the Yukon and Tanana Rivers and their tributaries, also rafting, backpacking, wildlife-viewing, snow machining and dogsledding throughout Interior Alaska.

Alatna Headwaters/Gates of the Arctic Wilderness Cabins (✆ 907-479 6354) PO Box 80424, Fairbanks, AK 99708. Wildlife buffs will love holing up at these places, about 150km north of the Arctic Circle, to hike, climb and watch wolves, bears and caribou migrations.

Arctic Treks (☎ 907-455 6502) PO Box 73452, Fairbanks, AK 99707. A long-standing company offering very adventurous wilderness trips through Arctic Alaska. A 10 day backpack through Gates of the Arctic costs US$2275 and a 10 day float trip on the North Slope, US$2575.

Brooks Range Wilderness Trips (☎ 907-488 6787) PO Box 80121, Fairbanks, AK. Offers three to 10 day winter dogsledding trips, mushing 35 to 60km in the White Mountains. You'll pay around US$300/400 for one/two people.

Denali Floats (☎ 907-733 2384) PO Box 330, Talkeetna, AK 99676. Guided rafting tours around Alaska and Arctic Russia.

Hugh Glass Backpacking Co Inc (☎ 907-344 1340, fax 907-344 4614) PO Box 11-0796, Anchorage, AK 99511. Guides sea kayaking, rafting, and backpacking trips around Alaska, including the fabulous Arctic National Wildlife Refuge.

Nomad Travel (☎ 907-243 0313, fax 907-243 0333, Web site www.nomad-travel.com) 3200 West 88th Ave, Ste 1 Anchorage, AK 99502. Organises fishing, rafting, sledding and other excursions in the Russian Far East.

REI Adventures (☎ 206-891 2631, toll-free ☎ 1-800 622 2236, fax 206-395 4744, email travel@rei.com/travel) PO Box 1938, Sumner, WA 98930. REI's offerings aren't cheap, but if you want to trek or cycle through Russia, you couldn't do any better than the trips offered by this well-established outdoor recreational equipment cooperative. It's especially recommended for trips to Kamchatka.

Simpson's Alaska Flocations (☎ 402-374 1430, fax 402-374 1430) Rt 1 Box 73, Decatur, NE 68020. Offers sightseeing, fishing, rafting, bird-watching and wildlife-viewing on western Alaska's upper Anvik River.

Sourdough Outfitters (☎/fax 907-692 5252, email sour@niga.sourdough.com) PO Box 90, Bettles, AK 99726. Offers backpacking, trekking, canoeing, rafting, wildlife-viewing, fishing, snow machining and dogsledding trips in and around Gates of the Arctic and Noatak National Parks, and in the Arctic National Wildlife Refuge. Eight days will cost around US$1500 per person. Canoeing on the Noatak will cost from US$1950 for 10 days; five days rafting in the Brooks Range is US$1100 and eight days of backpacking in Gates of the Arctic National Park US$1300.

Wilderness Alaska (☎ 907-345 3567, fax 907-345 3967, email madgill@alaska.net) PO Box 11-3063, Anchorage, AK 99511. Offers several Arctic adventures, including 10-day float trips on the Porcupine River in September (US$2150) and 20-day rafting and backpacking trips in Gates of the Arctic (US$3600).

Wilderness: Alaska/Mexico (☎ 907-479 8203) 1231 Sundance Loop, Fairbanks, AK 99709. Rafting, kayaking and backpacking trips in Noatak, Kobuk Valley and Gates of the Arctic National Parks, as well as the Arctic National Wildlife Refuge.

UK

Arcturus Expeditions (☎/fax 01389-830204), email arcturus@btinternet.com) PO Box 850, Gartocharn, Alexandria, Dumbartonshire G83 8RL. One of Britain's most inventive operators, Arcturus does hiking and trekking tours to far-flung areas of Greenland, including Qaanaaq and the North-East Greenland National Park, as well as trips to Antarctica, Arctic Siberia, north ern Canada, Alaska, Spitsbergen and every other cold and frosty place you could name. This company will take you beyond even the unbeaten track! It's highly recommended.

Mountain & Wildlife Venture (☎ 015394-33285) Compston Rd, Ambleside, Cumbria LA22 9DJ. This is the British agent for DNT, and can organise a good choice of nordic ski tours and alpine adventures. Although its emphasis is on mainland Scandinavia, it also operates adventurous trekking and skiing expeditions in the Cape Farewell region of south Greenland, including trips onto the inland ice.

Paul Walker Tangent Expeditions (☎ 015395 59087, fax 015395-59088, email paul@tan gentexp.demon.co.uk, Web site www.tangent exp.demon.co.uk) 10 Stockdale Farm, Moor Lane, Flookburgh, Cumbria LA11 7LR. Excellent and experienced guide concentrating on the high nunataks of east Greenland, and on unclimbed and unnamed peaks.

Waymark Holidays (☎ 01753-516477) 44 Windsor Rd, Slough SL1 2EJ. Specialists in nordic skiing holidays and other outdoor pursuits.

Way Up North (email wayupnorth@clara.co.uk, Web site www.wayupnorth.clara.co.uk) Quiet Cottage, Hittisleigh Mill, Exeter EX6 6LD. These folks run all sorts of wild adventure tours in Svalbard, Arctic Scandinavia and Greenland, including an inland ice crossing!

ICEBREAKERS – THE NORTH POLE, THE NORTHEAST & NORTHWEST PASSAGES

Icebreakers are vessels specially designed with a reinforced bow and powerful engines that allow them to cut through pack ice.

Their rounded keels allow them to ride up onto the ice, where the weight of the ship then crushes the ice, allowing forward progress. When the ice is particularly thick, or when pressure ridges block the way, the ship's engines cannot make headway, and so the vessel is reversed a short distance to build up momentum and ram into the blockage. On a North Pole voyage in 1998, I/B *Sovetskiy Soyuz* encountered a 12m-high pressure ridge in the pack ice that required 28 attempts before the ship was able to break through. In many icebreakers, powerful compressors shoot streams of air bubbles under the hull, which assists in the break-up of ice and helps ensure that the metal hull does not stick to the ice.

Icebreakers can be powered by diesel or nuclear fuel (there were coal-fuelled icebreakers in the past). Most icebreakers operating today are diesel powered, although these are limited by the amount of fuel they can carry. No such restrictions apply to the nuclear-powered ships, which use roughly 200g of fuel a day when breaking thick ice. This means that the nuclear ships can stay at sea for longer periods – an important consideration for vessels that might spend several months in the Arctic region. Some are able to carry sufficient provisions to operate without resupply for seven months.

Russia is the only country to operate nuclear-powered icebreakers. The largest of these are the Arktika class, which are leased to the Murmansk Shipping Company by the Russian Government. There are five Arktika class icebreakers in operation today – *Arktika* (launched 1975), *Sibir* (1978), *Rossiya* (1985), *Sovetskiy Soyuz* (1990) and *Yamal* (1992). These massive ships are 150m in length, and 55m tall (from the bottom of the keel to the mast head). The engines are 75,000hp (horse-power). The reactors need to be refuelled approximately every four years, an operation usually conducted in Murmansk; refuelling can take several months to perform.

The Russian icebreaker fleet is used mainly for keeping the Northern Sea Route open, a shipping lane that links Russia's northernmost ports. Without the icebreaker fleet, ports like Dikson, Nordvik and Tiksi would be cut off during the winter, since supplies tend to be transported by sea. The Canadian and American icebreaker fleet also maintain shipping lanes through ice-choked waters during winter, particularly in connection with the developing oil and gas industries in the Arctic Ocean. Small icebreakers also work in the great lakes and on northern rivers such as the Hudson.

A number of research ships that operate in the Arctic can also be classed as icebreakers. These include the German *Polarstern*, a state-of-the-art vessel used for oceanographic and meteorological surveys in both polar regions. In recent years, a number of Russian icebreakers have been chartered by western tourist companies to take passengers to the North Pole and the Northeast and Northwest passages. These include diesel-powered vessels like *Kapitan Khlebnikov* and *Kapitan Dranitsyn*.

Travelling North by Ship

A number of voyages on icebreakers and ice-strengthened ships are available to tourists. These range from cruises to Svalbard and Greenland, which may not involve travelling through pack ice, to the grinding two-week voyage to the North Pole on one of the Arktika class icebreakers. There is an increasing demand for adventure travel, and a number of tour companies have responded by offering a variety of High Arctic cruises. It's possible to 'circumnavigate' the Arctic on I/B *Kapitan Khlebnikov*, a Russian-owned Finnish-built ship, launched in 1992. The circumnavigation includes the Northwest and Northeast Passages, and stops in Greenland and Svalbard. The *Kapitan Khlebnikov* measures 121m long, and 48.7m high. Cabins are comfortable, although not all have private facilities.

The only companies to offer trips to the North Pole are Quark Expeditions and TCS Expeditions. Either *Sovetskiy Soyuz* or *Yamal* are chartered from the Murmansk Shipping Company each year. Both are working icebreakers, and the cabins of the senior officers and crew are used to provide accommodation for about 80 passengers. These are comfortable but basic, although this adds to the sense of adventure. Austrian chefs are hired for the season and food is imported from outside Russia. Passengers are welcome on the bridge, and the crew are helpful and friendly, although most do not speak English. Trips start at about $20,000 per person for a shared cabin. Each trip lasts for two weeks, and only the Arktika class icebreakers can reach the Pole in this length of time – although attaining the Pole can never be guaranteed. A heavy ice year might mean that not even 75,000hp engines can cut a path to the top of the world.

It is difficult to plan itineraries in the polar regions, because it's impossible to predict weather or ice conditions. Quark and TCS voyages to the North Pole may also include visits to Franz Josef Land and Novaya Zemlya, as well as helicopter flights and Zodiac cruising. In windy or misty weather, helicopters will not fly, and if there is too much fast ice, Zodiacs cannot be used. Any travellers to the Arctic need to bear in mind that they are at the mercy of the elements, and that their $20,000 does not guarantee a successful arrival at the Pole, nor does it mean that they'll visit every site listed on the itinerary. However, few who invest in a shipboard trip to the Arctic are disappointed. Whether they see deeply crevassed glaciers tumbling into still blue-green fjords, desolate rocky islands swathed in mist and occupied only by birds and seals, become mesmerised by the great white space and its distances, or spend hours watching their ship plough through 1m-thick ice like a knife through butter, they will carry home an unique experience and lifelong memories.

Companies

A number of companies offer ship-based travel to the Arctic. Tours range from short trips to Alaskan glaciers to Norway's Hurtigruten coastal steamers, where passengers can travel from Bergen to Kirkenes or from any of the stops along the way. Short cruises also run to Svalbard, Greenland, and parts of Canada, with longer ones to the High Arctic, such as the Northeast and Northwest Passages. The main companies offering adventure travel to the Arctic are as follows:

Amazing Cruises & Travel (☎ 203-358 9033, fax 203-325 9798, email actusa@aol.com) 980 Post Rd, Darien, CT 06820, USA.

Arcturus Expeditions See UK in the Adventure Tours section, earlier in this chapter.

Explorer Shipping Corporation (☎ 708-954 2944, fax 708-572 1833) 1520 Kensington Road, Oak Brook, IL 60521, USA.

Grand Nord Grand Large See under France in the Adventure Tours section, earlier in this chapter.

Hanseatic Tours GmbH (☎ 49-40 23 91 12 53, fax 49-40 23 21 10) Nagelsweg 55, 20097 Hamburg, Germany.

Marine Expeditions (☎ 416-964 9069, fax 416-964 2366) 13 Hazelton Avenue, Toronto, Ontario M5R 2E1, Canada.

Mountain Travel Sobek (☎ 510-527 8105, email info@MtSobek.com) 6420 Fairmount Ave, El Cerrito, CA 94530, USA.

Quark Expeditions (☎ 203-656 0499, fax 203-655 6623, email 76255.3266@comou serve.com) 980 Post Rd, Darien CT 06820, USA.

Society Expeditions (☎ 206-728 9400, fax 206-728 2301) 2001 Western Ave, Suite 710, Seattle, WA 98121, USA.

TCS Expeditions (☎ 206-727 7300, fax 206-727 7309, email travel@tcs-expeditions.com) 2025 First Ave, Suite 450, Seattle, WA 98121, USA.

Travel Dynamics (☎ 212-517 7555, fax 212-517 0077) 132 East 70th St, New York, NY 10021, USA.

Wildwings (☎ 44 117-984 8040, fax 44 117-967 4444) International House, Bank Rd, Bristol BS15 2LX, UK.

Zegrahm Expeditions (☎ 206-285 4000, fax 206-285 5037, email zegrahm@accessone.com) 1414 Dexter Ave, Suite 327, Seattle, WA 98109, USA.

This list is not complete. A range of companies offer novel and exciting trips that vary each year, depending on projected ice conditions and demand. The best, most up-to-date information is available on the Internet.

Activities

With its vast open spaces and largely un-populated landscapes, the Arctic regions offer a similarly expansive range of outdoor activities, from hiking and trekking through wild mountain and tundra country to moun-taineering on unnamed peaks, dogsledding with local hunters, canoeing wilderness lakes, sea kayaking through isolated fjords and white-water rafting down unbridged rivers. While the costs and logistics of mounting an expedition in the region can seem formidable, many areas of northern Scandinavia and North America are open to more casual travellers, and plenty of tour operators are willing to indulge would-be adventurers with a wide choice of exciting possibilities (you'll find suggestions under Adventure Tours in the Organised Tours & Adventures chapter).

For map information, see Maps under Planning in the Facts for the Visitor chapter. For general guidelines on planning for and coping with wilderness travel, look for the Sierra Club book *Walking Softly in the Wilderness*, by John Hart.

HIKING & TREKKING
Alaska

Alaska is a hiker's paradise, and the south-ern and central areas of the state boast a host of fabulous hiking and trekking routes. For detailed descriptions of these relatively accessible options, see Lonely Planet's *Backpacking in Alaska*, by Jim DuFresne; Falcon's *Hiking Alaska*, by Dean Lit-tlepage; and the Mountaineers' *55 Ways to the Wilderness in South Central Alaska*, by Helen Nienheuser and John Wolfe.

Unfortunately, the Arctic regions of northern Alaska take in much wilder coun-try than the typically tamer south-eastern, South-Central and Interior areas of the state. Although several wilderness routes have been established through Gates of the Arctic and Kobuk Valley National Parks, as well as the Noatak National Preserve and Arctic Na-tional Wildlife Refuge, there are no marked tracks or hikers' facilities anywhere in the region. Therefore, most trips will begin with a bush flight from a road head, such as Fair-banks, or from a bush town or village that's accessible on commercial air routes, such as Nome, Bettles or Kotzebue.

These bush flights, which carry residents and supplies to remote homesteads and fly anglers to uncrowded streams, also drop backpackers off in some of the wildest and most pristine country in North America. Most bush planes are either equipped with floats, for landing or taking off on water; skis, for ice or glaciers; or balloon tyres, for gravelly river bars.

The fares differ according to the type of plane, the number of passengers and the flight time, but you can safely plan on around US$300 per hour of flight time with three passengers and limited gear. If you want to add a kayak, a raft or other serious equipment, the costs will climb into the ozone layer. Bear in mind that you'll have to pay the full flight time both to and from your destination, and the same again for a pick-up at your destination. Make sure you're there at the specified time, or you'll be charged for the flight and perhaps for a search and rescue as well!

Before chartering a bush plane, it's wise to look into all commercial possibilities, in-cluding air-taxis and mail flights, as they're normally considerably cheaper. You'll find a good listing of bush air charter companies in the *Alaska Wilderness Guide* (see Books in the Facts for the Visitor chapter); alter-natively, check out the Web site at www .alaskan.com/outdoors/siteair.htm.

Once you've been dropped off and the bush plane has disappeared from view, it's worth remembering that you're *literally* on your own. On an ideal trip, you won't see an-other person, or even hear the buzz of an-other plane overhead – until yours returns. This situation is of course a vision of nirvana for most wilderness junkies, but it also means that Alaska's back country presents more risks than more accessible venues do.

No amount of wilderness survival or rescue training can replace good, thorough trip preparation. First, you'll need a good solid three or four-season tent, enough food for the intended length of your trip – plus three or four days of extra rations – and a range of clothing to cope with any eventuality. Even then, the unpredictable weather is a major concern when you're a week's trudge from the nearest village or medical help. When you do become socked in (by snow, fog, low cloud, dust, etc), visual navigation with a map becomes impossible. Without a GPS system, you'll simply have to wait until visibility improves. Similarly, if you've booked a pick-up by a bush plane at a specified location, you may have to hole up until the weather clears sufficiently for the pilot to land in the typically marginal terrain.

The best book to use for exploration of protected wilderness areas, including those in the Arctic and other bush regions, is the Mountaineers' *Alaska's Parklands: The Complete Guide*, by Nancy Simmerman. For further information on Alaska's parks, contact the Alaska Public Lands Information Center (☎ 907-271 2737), 605 W 4th Ave, Suite 105, Anchorage, AK 99501-2231 or the US National Park Service (☎ 907-586 7137), 709 W 9th St, Juneau, AK 99801.

Canada

Canada offers a range of walks and hikes, from short to long, gentle to rugged and coastal to mountain. Many of the finest trails traverse provincial, territorial and national parks, as well as conservation areas, wildlife reserves and sanctuaries. As a general rule, the larger the park, the longer the trails and routes, and in the northern part of the country, most hikes will involve multi-day routes. Outside the federal and provincial park systems there are also some extended trails running through a mix of public and private lands.

The information on bush planes included under Alaska in this chapter is also relevant

for most of northern Canada. For lists of charter companies in the Yukon, see the *Canada's Yukon Vacation Guide*, published by Tourism Yukon (☎ 867-667 5340, fax 867-667 3546, email info@touryukon .com); its Web site is at www.touryukon .com. For the Northwest Territories, see the *Explorer's Guide to Canada's Northwest Territories*, published by NWT Arctic Tourism (☎ 867-873 7200, fax 867-873 4069, email nwtat@nwttravel.nt.ca); its Web site is at www.nwttravel.nt.ca. For Nunavut, there's a list of charter companies in the *Nunavut Handbook*, or try the Web site at www.arctic-travel.com.

Work is continuing on the Trans Canada Trail, a 15,000km-long crushed stone path winding from coast to coast with an offshoot from Calgary to Tuktoyaktuk on the Arctic Ocean. It is hoped much of it will be completed by 2000. It will take about 300 days to cycle, 500 days to ride on horseback and 750 days to walk. For the current status and information on completed sections call the trail foundation at toll-free ☎ 1-800 465 3636 or visit www.tctrail.ca on the Web.

Unfortunately, there's a shortage of hiking books dealing with the Arctic regions of Canada (some avid Canadian hiker may want to take the initiative and fill in this market gap!). Most parks sell or distribute booklets describing their own hiking possibilities, but currently, the only widely available publication is the *Kluane National Park Hiking Guide*, by Vivien Lougheed, which details tracks and routes through Kluane National Park in the south-western corner of the Yukon Territory.

Greenland

Trekking in Greenland isn't much like trekking anywhere else. Apart from the odd sheep track in south Greenland, the track to the inland ice at Narsarsuaq, the increasingly popular Kangerlussuaq-Sisimiut route and a growing network of trails around Tasiilaq, Greenland has very few marked walking tracks, and most routes run crosscountry or follow winter dogsled routes. In short, you need to be better prepared for trekking in Greenland than in most other places. You'll need a good GPS system or know how to read a compass and calculate the substantial compass deviations for these latitudes, and also be able to follow a topographic map through some of the most difficult countryside around.

In places, the terrain (even along popular routes) can become suddenly impassable, requiring long detours. Thick low-lying vegetation hides fields of ankle-cracking boulders; mossy bogs and hidden waterholes abound; and walkers must make their way along steep, rocky and slippery mountainsides, climbing and descending often to avoid the rough bits. At times, detours will take them over lofty mountains or up boulder-choked valleys to avoid dangerous stream crossings.

In short, Greenland isn't an ideal country for casual or amateur trekkers but, having said that, it provides some of the world's most magnificent and rewarding walks and also some of its most profound silence. Best of all, it's relatively undiscovered and you're not likely to run into another party, even on the more popular multi-day trips in south Greenland that at the time of writing were attracting 20 to 30 groups per year.

Despite the low numbers, being lost or injured while trekking is a real possibility and the need for caution and precautions can't be overstated. Greenlandic weather can be horrendous, even in summer, with fog and freezing rain that can obscure the terrain for days on end. Under such conditions, even the best map and compass won't help you. In recent years, several trekkers have gone missing in Greenland and have never been found. This shouldn't put you off trekking – there's no better way to appreciate the wilderness – but careful preparation is of utmost importance.

There are plenty of routes throughout Greenland, but don't set off without carefully seeking out local advice. If trekking is your main emphasis, pick up a copy of the Skarv Guide *Trekking in Greenland* (1990) by Torbjørn Ydegaard, which provides details on routes, access and practicalities. It may be ordered directly from Munksgård

International Publishers (☎ 45-33 12 70 30, fax 45-33 12 93 87), Nørre Søgade 35, DK-1370 Copenhagen K, Denmark.

Trekkers, and even day hikers, should tell someone about their plans and estimated time of return (remember to inform them when the trip is complete). Rescue helicopters cost around Dkr40,000 per hour and it is the missing hiker who pays.

More serious adventurers should note that it is illegal to set off on an expedition to the inland ice without first obtaining a permit and purchasing search-and-rescue insurance covering up to Dkr900,000.

Norway

Norway has some of Europe's best hiking, including a 19,000km network of marked trails that range from easy strolls through the green zones around cities to long treks through national parks and wilderness areas. Many of these trails are maintained by Den Norske Turistforening (the Norwegian Mountain Touring Club, or DNT) and are marked either with cairns or red 'T's at 100 or 200m intervals.

The hiking season runs roughly from June to September, with a much shorter season in the higher mountain areas. In the highlands of the Arctic regions, the snow often remains until July and returns in September. Arctic Norway's most popular wilderness hiking areas are the Øvre Dividal, Stabbursdalen, Rago, Reisa, Øvre Pasvik, or any of the vast number of unprotected areas, such as Lofoten. Avid hikers will never run out of options!

Thanks to Norway's 1000-year-old *allemannsretten* ('every man's right') tradition and the *Friluftsleven* (Outdoor Recreation Act), anyone is legally entitled to hike or ski across wilderness areas, including outlying fields and pastures; camp anywhere for up to two days, as long as it's more than 150m from a dwelling; cycle or ride horseback on all paths and roads; and canoe, kayak, row and sail on all rivers and lakes. However, these freedoms come with some responsibilities: not to light fires between 15 April and 15 September; not to litter; to avoid damaging plant or animal life; to leave cultural sites perfectly intact; and to leave the countryside as pristine as it was found.

DNT and its various chapters maintain a network of over 320 mountain huts and lodges throughout the country. For details and prices for the use of these huts, see Accommodation in the Norway chapter. If you're doing lots of hiking, it's certainly worth joining DNT; membership for one calendar year costs Nkr325/160 (Nkr385/220 with catalogues and magazines) for people over/under 26 years of age; members' families pay Nkr125 per person. For further information, contact Den Norske Turistforening (☎ 22 82 28 00, fax 22 82 28 01), Storgata 3, PO Box 7, Sentrum, N-0101 Oslo. DNT also sells hiking maps and topographical sheets. The latter, which are published by Statens Kartverk, cover the entire country at scales of 1:50,000 and 1:100,000; catalogue maps outlining map titles and sheet numbers are available free of charge.

For information about independent exploration in Svalbard, see the boxed text in the Norway chapter.

Sweden

Hiking is popular throughout Sweden and, as in Finland and Norway, anyone may walk, boat, ski or swim anywhere outside the immediate vicinity of a house, garden, fenced area or cultivated land. While you are free to camp anywhere for one night, and to pick and eat berries and mushrooms (only harmless ones, of course), you may not drive a car over open ground or on private roads, leave rubbish or collect living wood, bark, leaves, bushes or nuts. Also, be sure to close all gates and avoid disturbing reindeer or other stock animals. Fires may be set where safe (not on bare rocks and with fallen wood only); when you're finished douse them with water, even if you think they're out.

The best wild camping sites are normally found along unsealed forest tracks, off secondary country roads, but be sure to select a spot that's at least 50m from the track and not visible from any building or sealed road. Dry pine forests are your best bet. It's wise to bring drinking water, although running creek water can normally be used for washing, and even for drinking, if it has been purified.

In northern Sweden, the mountain challenges of the national parks are most compelling. However, these parks are rarely snow-free and the jewel, Sarek, should be considered only by experienced hikers. Having said that, there are also a number of easier walking tracks, such as the long-distance Kungsleden, the Ofoten Navvies' Trail and the several routes in Abisko National Park. In most other regions of northern Sweden, walking routes thread between the finest natural attractions and many *kommuner* (municipalities) maintain their own wilderness tracks. Many of these off-the-beaten-track routes are dotted with huts or rain shelters that may be used free of charge.

For information on organised group walks, contact STF (see Tourist Information in the Facts for the Visitor chapter). The STF mountain huts (about 90 of them are maintained by Naturvårdsverket) are placed at intervals averaging about 20km. You may stay the night (or camp nearby and pay Skr35 to use the facilities) for only slightly more than in the STF hostels. A special card available to those aged under 26 allows hut accommodation for 10 nights (Skr400). You may want to drop by STF or stop at a mountain station and buy a card or up-to-date maps. Accommodation is self-service, and users must provide their own sheets or sleeping bags. The STF hostel guide *Vandrarhem och Fjäll* (Skr98) also includes mountain hut information.

Finland

Trekking, or fell-walking, is one of the most popular summer activities in Finland. National parks offer marked trails, and most wilderness areas are crisscrossed by locally used walking paths. Nights are short or nonexistent in summer, so you can walk for as long as you like (or until your feet blister up). Water is abundant everywhere, and you can camp practically anywhere. In northern

Finland, the trekking season extends from late June to early September, but note that the mosquitoes become a serious bother in July and August (see Dangers & Annoyances in the Facts for the Visitor chapter).

Trekkers are strongly advised not to hike alone; if you insist on going solo, sign a trekking register before you leave, notify someone of your itinerary and when you plan to return, and sign the hikers' register at every hut along the way.

The *jokamiehenoikeus* (or *allemansrätt*) code, literally 'everyman's right', has been in effect in Finland for centuries. As elsewhere in Scandinavia, it guarantees responsible visitors access to all areas of the country, and the right to walk, ski, cycle, or camp anywhere in forests and other wilderness areas – even on private land as long as the owners and their crops and animals aren't disturbed. However, camping is not permitted in town parks or on beaches, and to camp on private property requires the owner's permission.

Under the right of public access, you may not make a campfire on private land unless you have the owner's permission. In national parks, look for designated campfire areas, called *nuotiopaikka* in Finnish, and watch for fire warning signs – the word *metsäpalovaroitus* designates a very high fire risk. When you do light fires, use extreme caution and choose a place near a river or lakefront if possible. Felling trees or cutting brush to make a campfire is forbidden; use downed wood instead. Watch for other regulations regarding access in nature reserves and national parks: in some cases, camping may be forbidden and travel confined to marked paths.

Hikers can pick mushrooms and berries, but not other types of plants. Blueberries ripen in late July; lowbush cranberries are common in late summer; and cloudberries grow in muskeg bogs throughout northern Finland (visitors may not collect them but are permitted to pick and eat them on the spot). Edible mushrooms are numerous in Finnish forests, as are poisonous ones; unless you're a mushroom expert, you'll need a *sieniopas* (mushroom guide). The Finnish words to know are *myrkyllinen* (poisonous), *keitettävä* (has to be boiled first) and *syötävä* (edible).

For further information, your best bet is the Finnish Tourist Board brochure *Hiking in Finland*, which is distributed free through its offices worldwide (see Tourist Information in the Facts for the Visitor chapter).

Russia

Most of Arctic Russia is little more than a wilderness on which humanity has scarcely made a scratch (apart from some world-class environmental contamination – for more information go to www.greenpeace .org). Activities such as hiking, mountaineering, rafting and canoeing have always been popular with Russians and some small towns have well-established outdoor clubs. However, don't expect to be able to just turn up and organise a complicated adventure. Even if you arrive armed with addresses and phone numbers it can take two or three days to make contact with anyone – and then maybe a few more days to communicate exactly what you're on about. Give people as much advance warning as possible and, even if you can't hammer out all the details, try to know the Russian words for the crux of what interests you. Above all, be flexible, be patient, and by all means, don't expect things to go smoothly!

Kamchatka, with its awesome volcanic landscapes, the vast tundra expanses of Chukotka and the wild Khibiny Mountains of the Kola Peninsula are among the best parts of Arctic Russia to explore on foot. Mikhail Skopets (☎ 4132-23 29 90, email ibpn@ibpn.magadan.su) in Magadan is a biologist and avid fisherman whose claim to fame is that he knows the outlying regions of the Magadan district well, including Kolyma and Chukotka. He also speaks English and has worked with many western visitors. Boris Levin of BOL Tours (☎/fax 4132-22 02 96, email bol@online.maga dan.su or bol@asianoffice.com) is reportedly another excellent northern guide. Two brothers and mountain climbers, Vitaly and

Minimum Impact Camping

Wild campers taking advantage of the wonderful Arctic wilderness will help preserve the beauty of the region and foster goodwill by heeding the following guidelines:

• Select a well-drained camp site and, especially if it's raining, use a plastic or other water-proof groundsheet to prevent having to dig trenches.
• Along popular routes, set up camp in sites that have been previously used.
• Ask permission before setting up camp anywhere near a village or within sight of a cabin, lodge or house.
• Carry out all your rubbish, including cigarette butts. Biodegradable items may be buried but anything with food residue should be carried out, lest it attract bears or be dug up and scattered by other animals.
• Use established toilet facilities if they're available. Otherwise, select a site at least 50m from water sources and bury waste at least 20cm below the surface. Carry out, burn or bury used toilet paper.
• Use only biodegradable soap products (they're available at all good camping stores) and use natural temperature water where possible. When washing with hot water, avoid damage to vegetation either by letting the water cool to ambient temperature before pouring it out or by dumping it in a gravelled, nonvegetated place.
• If you're able to build a fire, try to select an established site and keep fires as small as possible. Use only fallen, dead wood and when you're finished, make sure ashes are cool and buried before you leave the site.

Sergey Malkov, can fulfil your every volcanic fantasy, and also run a camping equipment store, Alpindustriya-Kamchatka (☎/fax 4152-27 24 89), Kosmichesky 4-61, Petropavlovsk-Kamchatsky, 683003. Another highly knowledgeable person is Vasily Galichin (☎ 4152-11 25 44).

The best – and only – guidebook for hikers in Russia is the rather phenomenal *Trekking in Russia & Central Asia*, by Frith Maier, which is published by The Mountaineers. It includes good information on Kamchatka and Chukotka, as well as the northern Urals, but for the Khibiny Mountains in the Kola region, you'll need to make your way to either Apatity or Kirovsk and work out your itinerary with local assistance.

CLIMBING & MOUNTAINEERING

While Finland, Sweden and Arctic Russia do offer rock climbs and a few mountain scrambles, none has much in the way of technical mountaineering. Alaska, Canada, Norway and Greenland however, provide some fabulous challenges, including some of the world's most spectacular granite fells (especially in south Greenland and on Baffin Island).

Thanks to its latitude and penchant for inclement weather, climbing and mountaineering in the Arctic regions can be every bit as challenging as climbing in the Andes or Himalaya, and on the higher peaks of the Alaska, Wrangell and St Elias ranges, the altitude must also be considered.

Alaska

For most mountaineers, climbing in Alaska is synonymous with climbing Mt McKinley, the highest peak in North America, which is locally but unofficially called Denali (Athapaskan for 'the great one'), and every year, hundreds of climbers attempt to reach its 6096m summit. However, Alaska is packed with countless more challenging – albeit lower – summits: Bona, Marcus Baker, St Elias, Blackburn, Foraker, the Arrigetch Peaks, and the ultimate, Moose's Tooth. Even a lifetime of climbing could never exhaust all the possibilities.

The main ranges include the ice-capped Coast Range in Southeast Alaska, the vast Wrangell and St Elias ranges, the spectacular Alaska Range (which includes Mt McKinley), and the Chugach, Kenai, Aleutian, Talkeetna and Brooks Ranges. Of these, only the Brooks Range, which averages 2500 to 3000m, lies within the Arctic Circle. However, the harsh climate and lack of vegetation at this latitude have shaped these summits into much more dramatic peaks than their altitudes would suggest.

For further information, you may want to join the Mountaineering Club of Alaska (email mca@alaska.net), PO Box 102037, Anchorage, AK 99510 or check out their Web site at www.alaska.net/~mca.

Anyone hoping to bag McKinley will get the lowdown in the books *Denali Climbing Guide*, by J Secor, and *Denali's West Buttress: A Climber's Guide to Mt McKinley's Classic Route*, by Colby Coombs. Tales from those who've done it are collected in *Alaska Ascents: World-Class Mountaineers Tell Their Stories*, edited by Bill Sherwonit. If you want to join an organised expedition on Mt McKinley or another Alaskan peak, try Alaska-Denali Guiding (☎ 907-733 2649, fax 907-733 1362, email adg@alaska .net), PO Box 566, Talkeetna, AK 99676; Web site is at www.alaska.net/~adg.

Canada

In northern Canada, the finest climbing venues include the Mt Logan area of Yukon's Kluane National Park, the almost-accurately-named Cirque of the Unclimbables in Nahanni National Park, and of course, the fabulous granite fells of Baffin Island's Auyuittuq National Park. Unfortunately, none of these is readily accessible and all will require mounting a major private expedition or organising something through a climbing guide in Whitehorse, Yel-

lowknife or Iqaluit. In the case of Nahanni, access will involve chartering a helicopter from Watson Lake or hiking in from Glacier Lake. For Mt Logan, you'll have to fly in from Haines Junction or Whitehorse.

For some suggestions, see the Organised Tours & Adventures chapter or contact the Canadian Alpine Club (☎ 403-678 3200, fax 403-678 3224) PO Box 8040, Canmore, Alberta. Its Web site is at www.ffa.ucal gary.ca/acc.

Interesting reading for prospective mountaineers in Canada would be *The Canadian Mountaineering Anthology*, by Bruce Fairley and Sid Marty, published by Lone Pine Publishing.

Greenland

For mountaineers who dream of doing a first ascent, Greenland offers plenty of scope, but for serious expeditions outside inhabited areas, the previously mentioned compulsory insurance policy keeps cropping up like a bad dream. Officials just don't like the idea of people risking their lives for the thrill of the experience.

There are four major climbing areas in Greenland: the Stauning Alps in the northeast; around Ammassalik in the east; around Kap Farvel and Nanortalik in the south; and the Kangerlussuatsiaq (Evighedsfjord) in the south-west. Of these, Ammassalik and Nanortalik are the most accessible. Greenland's highest peak, Gunnbjørns Fjeld (3708m), lies between Ammassalik and Ittoqqortoormiit; and Uummannaq, in northwest Greenland, also has an intriguing technical peak.

For rock climbers, Greenland's southern tip offers myriad challenging – and in many cases unclimbed – walls and spires that rival those of Yosemite, Patagonia and the Karakoram. Two of the world's highest and most impressive granite faces, Uiluit Qaaqa (2012m) and Ulamertorssuaq (1830m), rise above Tasermiut Fjord near Nanortalik. Best of all, access is straightforward and no official insurance policy is required.

For specifics on organising a mountaineering expedition in Greenland, contact the Dansk Polarcenter (☎ 45-32 88 01 00, fax 45-32 88 01 01, email dpc@dpc.dk), Strandgade 100H, 1401 Copenhagen K, Denmark. If you prefer a guided expedition, try Paul Walker Tangent Expeditions (see the Organised Tours & Adventures chapter).

Norway

As one would imagine, a country with the astounding vertical topography that Norway enjoys would be a mecca for climbers interested in rock, ice and alpine pursuits. In fact, outside the Alps, Norway is probably Europe's finest climbing venue and it offers a wide range of possibilities. However, due to Norway's climatic and topographic extremes, technical climbers face harsher conditions, shorter seasons and many more concerns and restrictions than hikers and backpackers. The most popular alpine venues include the Lyngen Alps, Jotunheimen, Hurrungane, Lofoten, and just about anywhere in the western fjords.

In addition to the rock climbers' classic *Climbing in the Magic Islands*, by Ed Webster, which describes most of the feasible routes in the Lofoten Islands, prospective climbers may want to look for *Ice Fall in Norway* by Sir Ranulph Feinnes, which describes a 1970 jog around Jostedalsbreen, and the more practical *Scandinavian Mountains*, by Peter Lennon, which introduces the country's finest climbing venues.

Russia

Limited mountaineering is available on the volcanoes of Kamchatka; for contacts, see Hiking & Trekking, earlier in this chapter.

Crossing Streams

Trekkers and mountaineers in the Arctic regions will invariably face unbridged rivers but in most cases they needn't be put off. The sun and heat of the day melt snow and glacial ice and cause water levels to rise, so the best time to cross is early in the morning, and preferably no sooner than 24 hours after a rainstorm.

Remember that constricted rivers passing through narrow passages run deep, so the widest ford is likely to be the shallowest. The swiftest and strongest current is found near the centre of straight stretches and at the outside of bends. Observe the character of the water as it flows and choose a spot with as much slack water as possible.

Never try to cross just above a waterfall and avoid crossing streams in flood – identifiable by dirty, smooth-running water carrying lots of debris and vegetation. A smooth surface suggests that the river is too deep to be crossed on foot. Anything over thigh deep shouldn't be considered crossable without experience and extra equipment.

Before attempting to cross deep or swift-running streams, be sure that you can jettison your pack in midstream if necessary. Put anything that mustn't get wet inside sturdy waterproof bags. Unhitch the waist belt and loosen shoulder straps, remove any bulky clothing that will inhibit swimming, and remove long trousers. Lone hikers should use a hiking staff to probe the river bottom for the best route and to steady themselves in the current.

Never try to cross a stream barefoot. While crossing, face upstream and avoid looking down or you may risk losing your balance. Two hikers can steady each other by resting their arms on each other's shoulders. More than two hikers should cross forming a wedge pointed upstream, with the people behind holding the waist and shoulder of the person at the head of the wedge.

If you do fall while crossing, don't try to stand up. Remove your pack (but don't let go of it), roll over onto your back, and point your feet downstream, then try to work your way to a shallow eddy or to the shore.

SKIING
Alaska

Much of Alaska's cross-country skiing action takes place in urban areas on floodlit tracks, but a few hardier individuals set off on mountaineering skis and tackle long distance winter routes. An exceptional experience is the fly-in ski trip to Ruth Glacier, between soaring granite cliffs on the southern slopes of Mt McKinley, which has been described as a 'frozen Yosemite Valley'. Best of all, it's accessible year-round and Talkeetna has at least five air-taxi companies that can get you there. Similarly, in Kenai Fjords National Park you can climb up the trail that flanks Exit Glacier and leads to the vast, 150km-long Harding Icefield, which offers excellent summer skiing.

Alpine skiing in Alaska is fairly limited. The only real resort is Alyeska, south of Anchorage, but don't expect anything on the order of Telluride or Val d'Isere. There are also a couple of slopes around urban Anchorage (Hilltop and Arctic Valley), one near Juneau (Eaglecrest) and a couple of little hills around Fairbanks.

However, note that none of these options is in Arctic Alaska, where your only hope of finding a good slope will involve a major fly-in expedition. If you're interested, contact one of the adventure outfitters suggested in the Organised Tours & Adventures chapter.

Canada

While Canada in general offers some superb downhill and heli-skiing, most of the skiing areas are concentrated in the south: the Rockies, around Vancouver, and near populated regions of Ontario and Quebec. However, in northern Canada, cross-country skiing isn't a half bad way of getting around most towns in winter, and towns like Whitehorse and Yellowknife even offer floodlit cross-country trails. Otherwise, you'll face wilderness conditions and as with Alaska, cross-country skiing expeditions will involve a fly-in trip and require a great deal of planning and careful preparation.

Greenland

Skiing in Greenland becomes more popular every year. Cross-country skiing is possible nearly anywhere in winter, but there are also several summer ski fields. The most organised are Kangerluarsunnguaq, near Nuuk; Apussuit, near Maniitsoq; and on Disko Island. A gruelling cross-country ski race is held in south-western Greenland along the Kangerlussuaq-Sisimiut route in winter, and the normally 10 to 12-day hike is contracted into a three-day ski.

The largest alpine ski area is Nuuk's Kangerluarsunnguaq summer ski centre, with a 1km run and 300m vertical variation. Apussuit, near Maniitsoq, offers excellent summer skiing and a vast new facility is now being developed on the glacier north of Sisimiut. There are also small winter-only ski lifts at Sisimiut and Tasiilaq (Ammassalik), and two on the slopes of Quassussuaq behind the Nuuk airport.

Norway

'Ski' is a Norwegian word and thanks to aeons-old rock carvings depicting hunters travelling on skis, Norwegians make a credible claim to having invented the sport. Interest hasn't waned over the years and these days, it's no exaggeration to say it's the national pastime. Most of the skiing is of the cross-country (nordic) variety, and Norway has thousands of kilometres of maintained cross-country ski trails. However, visitors should only set off after studying the trails/routes (wilderness trails are identified by colour codes on maps and signposts) and ensuring that they have appropriate clothing, sufficient food and water, and emergency supplies, including matches and a source of warmth, such as a four-season sleeping bag. You can bring your own equipment; rely on friendly locals to loan theirs; or purchase skis, poles and boots on site. You'll probably find the best deals on second-hand gear at weekend flea markets.

Most towns and villages provide some illuminated ski trails, but elsewhere, it's still worth carrying a good light source, as winter days are very short and in the north, there's no daylight at all in December and January. The ski season generally lasts from early December to April. Snow conditions vary greatly from year to year and region to region, but February and March, as well as the Easter holiday period, tend to be the best (and busiest) times. When nature has not provided an ideal skiing surface, many areas use snow cannons to produce more amenable conditions.

There are also scores of resorts with downhill runs, but these are quite expensive due to the costs of ski lifts, accommodation and the *aprés-ski* drinking sessions. Although the most popular ski venues are in southern Norway (Lillehammer for downhill and Jotunheimen and Hardangervidda for cross-country), Arctic Norway also presents some superb cross-country terrain, such as Finnmarksvidda and the wild northern peninsulas. For general information, DNT produces the pamphlet *Welcome to the Norwegian Mountains in Wintertime*.

Sweden

Cross-country (nordic) skiing opportunities vary depending on the snow and temperatures, but the north-west usually has plenty of snow. Practically all town areas (except southern Sweden) offer marked, often illuminated skiing tracks.

Do not leave marked cross-country routes without a good map, local advice and proper equipment including plastic sheet and ropes. Winter wind-chill factors of – 30°C or so aren't uncommon, so check the daily forecasts. Police and tourist offices have information on local warnings. In the mountains there is the risk of avalanche *(lavin)* and susceptible areas are marked by yellow multilingual signs and ominous signs bearing stylised depictions of a buried skier. The national SLAO insurance covers all injuries on marked slopes and lifts run by the national SLAO slalom organisation, and can be purchased for less than Skr100 per season.

Finland

Finland has more than 120 downhill ski resorts – in fact, there are ski lifts in all major

towns with a hill taller than the local apartment buildings. Most Finnish resorts also offer designated runs and halfpipes for snowboarders. The generally low Finnish slopes are excellent for beginners and families. The best resorts are in the far north, where the vertical drop averages 250m over 3km. In Finland, the ski season runs from late November to early May, and slightly longer in Lapland and the North, where it's possible to ski through midsummer. Beware of the busy winter and spring holiday periods – especially around Christmas and Easter – that are too crowded to be appreciated.

You can rent all skiing or snowboarding equipment at major ski resorts for about Fmk80 to Fmk100 per day. A one-day lift pass is typically an additional Fmk100, although it is often possible to pay separately for each ride.

Cross-country skiing is one of the simplest and most pleasant winter activities in Finland, and it's an ideal way to explore the beautiful, silent winter countryside of lakes, fells, fields and forests. Practically every town and village maintains ski tracks around the urban centre, and these are typically in use from the first snowfall in November through early May – although die-hard skiers will grimly continue to ski across bare rock in spring if they feel that the season has been too brief. In many cases, local tracks are illuminated *(valaistu latu)*. Access is always free, and getting lost is impossible on municipal tracks as they are usually loops of only a few kilometres. However, you'll probably have to bring your own equipment.

It's possible to practice cross-country skiing at an organised ski resort, where you'll find longer, well-maintained tracks, instruction and rentals (Fmk80 to Fmk100 per day or Fmk200 to Fmk380 per week). In the far north, where the best skiing lasts from December to April, resorts offer hundreds of kilometres of trails, but only a few are illuminated for night and winter skiing.

Russia

Although the town of Kirovsk on the Kola Peninsula does have a basic downhill resort, most of the skiing done in Arctic Russia is of the cross-country variety. Any local tour agency can help out with finding a pair of skis and point you in the right direction. Alpindustriya-Kamchatka (see Hiking & Trekking in this chapter) can organise skiing and snowboarding on the slopes of the Kamchatka volcanoes as well as at a summer camp in Rodnikovoe.

CANOEING & WHITE-WATER RAFTING

Before any sort of coherent discussion of paddling will be possible, it's essential to define a few terms. For the purposes of this discussion, a kayak is a rigid one-person craft used for running white-water rivers, or a longer rigid or folding one or two person craft with a rudder used for 'bluewater paddling' (that is, in salt water). Either type is steered or propelled using a double-bladed paddle. A canoe, for our purposes, is synonymous with the 'Canadian canoe', which is a long, rudderless open-topped craft holding anywhere from one to four people. Most canoes are propelled or steered using a single flat paddle. A raft is a broad, inflatable rubber boat normally holding between two and 12 passengers; it's steered either with two long oars or an oarsperson seated on a frame in the middle of the boat or by the passengers using long flat paddles.

In the Arctic countries (and much of the rest of the world), white-water rapids are classified on a scale of I to VI, but note that in the High Arctic, one grade is typically added to the white-water class to account for the water temperatures.

By the standard classifications, Class I refers to a simple, lazy rumble in the water; Class II features slightly whiter water and is a bit more exciting, especially if you're in an open canoe; Class III is very challenging for canoes but ideal for rafts; Class IV will give rafters a real thrill and cause kayaks to bob around like corks but is in no way suitable for canoes; and Class V rapids are very dangerous but may be run by experienced paddlers in a sturdy raft or kayak. Although class VI rapids (which are just short of the

barrel-over-Niagara-Falls experience) have been attempted by very experienced kayakers with a death wish, they'd almost certainly be disastrous for anyone else. When the going gets rough, be prepared to portage your canoe, kayak or raft around the unsafe stretches (dangerous rapids, waterfalls, log jams, hydroelectric stations, broken dams and so on).

When you're paddling on white water, a route map and guide with detailed information (including the position of any and all rapids) are absolute essentials for a safe, fun trip. For everything you need to know about white-water rafting, look for the bible on the subject, Jeff Bennett's *The Complete White-water Rafter*, published by McGraw Hill.

Alaska

Alaska is a paradise for canoers, rafters and kayakers. Enthusiasts can choose between anything from lovely tangles of flat-water lakes (such as the Swan Lakes or Nancy Lake systems); nearly stagnant streams (such as Alexander Creek or Birch Creek); and Class I and II afternoon paddles (such as the Eagle River or Kenai River). There are the popular tourist raft trips (such as the Nenana River near Denali National Park); rollicking Class III and IV white-water (such as the Alsek-Tatshenshini or the Gulkana River); and longer expedition-class floats down the wild rivers of Interior and Arctic Alaska (such as the Fortymile, the Yukon, the John and the Noatak).

While the north-flowing rivers of the North Slope may stay iced-up until July, the south-flowing rivers are usually open by June and in Interior and South-Central Alaska, the season lasts roughly from May to September. Note that many rivers, especially those in the Arctic and Interior regions, can be extremely braided, with numerous channels to choose from – and if you choose the wrong one, you may well have to do a bit of pushing, pulling or lining (that is, towing your canoe or raft on a line over gravelly or sandy shallows).

If you're chartering a bush plane into a remote area, remember that all your food, clothing, camping gear and paddling equipment will also have to ride along. Sometimes, lightweight canoes or kayaks can be strapped to the floats on bush planes (if not, you may have to pay for an extra flight), but deflated rafts or collapsible canoes or kayaks generally work much better.

Happily for prospective paddlers in Alaska, there are several excellent books describing the best rivers and routes in great detail. The recommended *Fast & Cold: A Guide to Alaska Whitewater*, by Dr Andrew Embick, directs adrenaline junkies down 79 of the best white-water rafting and kayaking rivers in the state. The tamer *Alaska River Guide*, by Karen Jettmar, includes canoeing streams as well as kayaking and rafting rivers, and even describes the canoe route down Campbell Creek, right through the urban heart of Anchorage. Another popular publication is the *Alaska Paddling Guide*, by Jack Mosby and David Depkus, but the classic reference to use – if you can find a copy – is Sepp Weber's *Wild Rivers of Alaska*, published in 1976. Several of the best lake circuits are described in *55 Ways to the Wilderness in South Central Alaska*, by Helen Nienheuser and John Wolfe.

For further information, you may want to contact Knik Canoers & Kayakers, PO Box 101935, Anchorage, AK 99510. You can also check out the Web site at www.kck.org. A list of outfitters is provided in the Organised Tours & Adventures chapter.

Canada

Canada's canoeing, rafting and kayaking possibilities are almost limitless and range from easy half-day paddles to some highly challenging white waters. In general, the national, provincial and territorial parks are good places to start, and in Whitehorse, Yellowknife and other towns, you'll find outfitters who can organise equipment, transport and other logistics. Tourist offices are also happy to help with information on canoeing areas and outfitters.

When one thinks of white-water in northern Canada, the first word that springs to mind is Nahanni, and this spectacular national park is indeed the favourite rafting venue in the entire region. On the other hand, the more accessible Mackenzie and Yukon Rivers are attracting a growing number of paddlers intent upon a more leisurely, self-organised trip.

Gentle float trips down the Yukon from Whitehorse for a few hours or 16 days, all the way to Dawson, are popular. Many tourists start or end at Carmacks, the half-way point, making an eight-day trip. Boat rental and return charges for such a trip start at around C$200. A good, scenic trip for inexperienced canoeists is the eight days down the Teslin River from Johnson's Crossing to Carmacks. The Nisutlin River offers beginners a good five-day trip along the Canol Road north of Johnson's Crossing to Teslin Village. A three-day excursion on the Takhini River from Kusawa Lake west of Whitehorse offers some white-water and some lake paddling. More challenging is the two-week trip down the renowned Bonnet Plume River in the north-eastern Yukon.

In the Northwest Territories, excellent canoeing is available on the region's typically vast lakes, but the great Mackenzie River also offers fabulous long-distance wilderness options. The logical starting point is Fort Simpson, where you can rent canoes. Some people then spend weeks riding the current all the way to the Arctic Ocean, but it's also possible to put in or take out at Fort Providence. A good source of direction is the guidebook *Canoeing Canada's Northwest Territories: A Paddler's Guide*, by Bruce Cockburn.

In Nunavut, the best white-water streams include the Thelon, the Coppermine, the Sylvia Grinnell (near Iqaluit) and the Soper (near Kimmirut).

Norway

Norway's steep slopes and icy, scenic rivers create an ideal environment for avid rafters, and a number of reputable operators offer trips. These range from short, Class II doddles to Class III and IV adventures and rollicking Class V punishment. While these trips aren't especially cheap, most are guaranteed to provide an adrenaline thrill, and the rates include all the requisite equipment and waterproofing. Among the finest rafting venues are Evje (Setesdalen), Sjoa (Heidalen) and Oppdal (Drivadalen). These rivers are covered by several operators, but are all in southern Norway. In the Arctic regions, you'll find plenty of wild white-water and lots of fine flat-water canoeing on the lakes of Finnmarksvidda. However, that sort of activity hasn't really caught on in northern Norway and there are no rentals available, so you'll probably have to bring your own raft or canoe.

The Norges Padleforbund (☎ 67 15 46 00, fax 67 13 33 35), Hauger Skoleveien 1, N-1351 Rud, can provide a comprehensive list of rafting operators in Norway.

Sweden

Sweden's superb wilderness lakes and white-water rivers are a real paradise for canoeists. The national canoeing body is Svenska Kanotförbundet (☎ 08-605 600, email kanot@rs.se), Storforsplan 44, 12387 Farsta. It also has a Web site at www.svenskidrott.se/kanot. It provides general advice and produces *Kanotvåg*, an annual brochure listing the 78 approved Canoe Centres that hire canoes (Skr500 to Skr950 per week). According to the right of common access, canoeists may paddle or moor virtually anywhere provided they respect the basic privacy of dwellings and avoid sensitive nesting areas within nature reserves. The recommended brochure *Advice for You Who Paddle* is available from Naturvårdsverket (☎ 08-698 10 00, fax 08-698 15 15, email kundtjanst@environ.se), Blekholmsterrassen 36, 10405 Stockholm.

Finland

With its zillions of lakes, Finland offers some of the world's finest and most extensive flat-water canoeing routes. In fact, you're never far from a lake in Finland, and a canoeist could probably traverse a good chunk of the country without having to portage more than a couple of kilometres!

While southern Finland offers lots of popular and established white-water canoe and rafting routes with easy-to-follow route markers and designated camping sites, the northern rivers around Kuusamo and in Lapland, are generally faster-flowing and steeper, with tricky rapids, making them suitable only for experienced white-water enthusiasts.

The best white-water trips in northern Finland include the four Class I to Class II Hossa Trails, which start at Hossa, and range in length from 8½km to 35km; and the 70km route along the Ivalojoki in northeast Lapland, which starts at Kuttura and finishes in Ivalo, passing 30 rapids along the way. If you're uncertain of your paddling skills and just want to experience the thrill and beauty of the mighty northern rivers, contact one of the local tourist offices about joining a white-water rafting expedition with one of the many summer operators that organise tours.

Canoe and kayak rentals are normally available for trips that last several days or weeks. Rentals range in price from Fmk100 to Fmk200 per day and Fmk400 to Fmk900 per week. You'll pay more if you need overland transportation to the start or end point of your trip, if you want to hire a guide or if you need to rent extra gear such as tents and sleeping bags. Try to locate a rental company at both ends of the route, and compare rates (including transport); it's generally more convenient to rent from the end point of your trip so that you will be transported to the starting point first. A couple of good outfitters in northern Finland include Rukapalvelu Oy (☎ 08-860 8600, fax 08-860 8601), 93825 Rukatunturi (near Kuusamo), and Lapin Safarit (☎ 016-331 1200, fax 016-331 1222), Koskikatu 1, 96200 Rovaniemi.

For longer trips you'll need a waterproof plastic barrel or a good set of dry bags to hold your gear, a life jacket and waterproof route maps, which are available from the Karttakeskus mail order service (☎ 0204-45 5911, fax 0204-45 5929, email info @karttakeskus.fi), PO Box 40, FIN-01511, Vantaa, for Fmk25 to Fmk50 (see Maps under Planning in the Facts for the Visitor chapter). Occasionally tourist offices and rental outfits will supply route maps free of charge.

SEA KAYAKING

In all northern areas, the greatest danger is the water temperature, which rarely rises above 2 or 3°C, even in summer (in some areas, the water temperatures are actually below freezing, but the seas remain unfrozen due to the salt content of the water).

Sea ice is one of the greatest dangers. Keep at least 800m away from tidewater glacier faces as they frequently calve whopping big ice cubes and create powerful swells. Also avoid paddling near icebergs, which can roll without warning and knock a boat right out of the water – and bear in mind that nine tenths of the berg lies beneath the surface!

Tides are also a concern; carry a tide table and inquire locally about dangerous rips or currents through narrow passages and try to paddle them during slack tides. Similarly, when the tide is incoming, avoid narrow fjords and inlets containing lots of ice, as the floes and bergs are likely to pack up at the end and will readily crush a kayak. When camping, be sure to secure your boat and gear well above the high tide line for that day.

It goes without saying that you should give wide berth to marine mammals, particularly whales, seals, walruses and *especially* polar bears!

Alaska

Although sea kayaking is certainly possible in northern Alaska, the flat, gravelly Arctic coastline is less than thrilling and the sea kayaking areas for which the state is justifiably famous – Misty Fjords, Glacier Bay, Prince William Sound, Kenai Fjords National Park, etc – all lie in South-Central and Southeast Alaska. Nevertheless, there's no better place to explore the coastal wilderness by kayak, and a kayak trip in these regions will make a great prelude or follow-up to an adventure in the Arctic.

Canada

Some of the finest sea kayaking venues in Canada lie along the Pacific Coast, particularly around British Columbia's Queen Charlotte Islands. Fortunately, however, the great Arctic Archipelago of northern Nunavut also offers fabulous sea kayaking, as the local Inuit, who have historically hunted by kayak, will naturally attest. The best place for embarking on an organised trip is probably Pond Inlet, at the northern end of Baffin Island. Several experienced outfitters are listed in the Organised Tours & Adventures chapter; a recommended operator is Whitney & Smith Legendary Expeditions.

Greenland

Although it was developed in Greenland, the days of the practical hunting qajaq – the sealskin-covered one-person craft that made Greenland famous – are probably numbered, as they've been replaced by the buzzing Mariner-powered speedboats. Thanks to qajaq clubs, however, whose efforts are aimed at a revival of the Greenlandic qajaq for practical, competitive and recreational purposes, it is now making a comeback.

Avid sea kayakers will probably drool as they cruise the Greenlandic coastline. Recreational kayaking (with a 'k', the word refers to the wider canvas or fibreglass varieties) has only recently been introduced, but recreational kayaks and equipment can now be hired in several towns. These are fine for short trips, but for longer expeditions it's best to bring your own equipment. The most convenient are the folding Klepper or Feathercraft models.

Taking into consideration the wind, weather, technical difficulty, exposure, landscapes and accessibility, the most suitable areas for kayaking are Tasermiut Fjord, near Nanortalik; the Narsarsuaq-Narsaq-Qaqortoq region; Kangerlussuaq; Nuup Kangerlua (Godthåbsfjord); and around Uummannaq. The Ilulissat area is also superb, but the icebergs do present dangers, and stories of capsizing and death by rolling icebergs tend to follow kayakers around Greenland.

Qajaq & Umiaq

The *qajaq*, or kayak, the long, narrow boat which is now used recreationally around the world, was originally developed by the Inuit as a hunting boat. It was propelled and steered with a double-bladed paddle and designed without a keel. The traditional Greenlandic qajaq was constructed with a driftwood or whalebone frame, covered with a tightly stretched sealskin and waterproofed with animal fat. It was ideal for hunting walrus, seals, polar bears and whales, as it could be rolled over and then righted by the occupant without taking on water. The original Greenlandic qajaqs were longer and considerably narrower than their modern recreational counterparts. Some measured up to 7m, yet the narrow hull allowed very little space for the occupant's legs.

A similar skin-covered boat, used mainly by women, was called an *umiaq*, or 'women's boat'. It was open and not specifically designed for hunting, although it was sometimes used to take whales. Its purpose was the transport of women, children, older people and cargo.

Although the hunting qajaq is occasionally used around Avanersuaq and on the east coast, skin boats haven't been in common use since the 1950s. However, several towns now have qajaq clubs, which attempt to preserve construction and handling skills and promote qajaq skills among younger people, thereby reviving a bit of Greenland's traditional heritage.

Norway

Norway's hysterically indented coastline is ideal for sea kayaking, but surprisingly, as a sport it hasn't really caught on locally. Currently, most of the takers are foreigners who bring their own equipment and share the seas only with whales and fishing boats. Several companies also organise sea kayaking tours around the spectacular islands of Svalbard.

FISHING
Alaska

Serious anglers in Alaska need to carefully research the areas they plan to fish and make sure they're equipped with the correct gear and tackle. In the streams of Southeast and South-Central Alaska, the most common fish are the cutthroat, Dolly Varden and 'fighting' rainbow trout, while in the Interior and Arctic regions, you can expect to find grayling and Arctic char. Deep sea fishing is also quite popular, and monster halibut are frequently hauled out of Cook Inlet; there are plenty of operators around Homer, Anchor Point and Deep Creek, on the Kenai Peninsula.

Most people, however, come for the five species of salmon – king (chinook), silver (coho), red (sockeye), pink (humpie) and chum (dog) – that are generally plentiful and arrive in Alaskan streams in separate 'runs' between July and September. During summer, salmon runs in some areas, however – particularly on the Kenai Peninsula and in parts of the Susitna Valley – sport fishing would be (and is) better described as 'combat fishing'. Unless you're prepared for tangled lines, riverbanks that look more like trash dumps, fights over parking or fishing spots, and often boozy and aggressive crowds, avoid these areas at all costs and spring for a more solitary fly-in fishing adventure somewhere in south-western, Interior or Arctic Alaska.

A nonresident fishing licence costs US$50 per year (residents pay US$15) or you can purchase a three-day licence for US$15 or a two-week licence for US$30. They're available at bait and sporting gear shops throughout the state. If you're keen on fishing, order a copy of the US$5 *Recreational Fishing Guide*, published by the Department of Fish & Game (☎ 907-465 4112),

PO Box 25526, Juneau, AK 99802-5526. Alternatively, look for the whopping 640-page tome, *Alaska Fishing*, by Gunnar Pedersen and Rene Limeres, or the more down-to-earth *Flyfishing Alaska*, by Anthony Route.

Canada

Freshwater fishing is abundant and a popular activity across Canada and both residents and visitors flock to the lakes and streams to take advantage of the piscine bounty. In winter, people in many northern areas set up 'huts', small wooden fishing shanties, on frozen lakes. Inside there's a bench, sometimes a heater, a hole in the ice and often more than a few discarded beer bottles.

Generally, northern Canadian fish species are the same as those in Alaska, with the exception of salmon, which don't normally spawn in the rivers that empty into the Arctic Ocean (Canadian salmon fishing normally takes place on the Pacific and Atlantic coasts). Anglers must purchase fishing licences that vary in duration and price between the provinces and territories. Any tourist office can help with information and advice on where to buy one, and provide a local guide that includes the various seasons and favoured spots for each local species. Also be sure to check on daily limits and whether there are any bait restrictions; in some areas, minnows or other bait is prohibited.

Greenland

Greenlandic lakes, particularly in the south, are rich in Arctic char; the Kapisillit area near the upper end of Nuup Kangerlua has a salmon run; and many fjords teem with cod that seem to snap at anything, so it makes sense for trekkers to carry a fishing rod and a variety of lures. To fish in lakes and streams, you'll need to buy a nonresident licence from a police station, tourist office or hotel; a one/three-month noncommercial fishing licence costs Dkr200/500. Ask for a list of regulations when purchasing a licence.

Norway

In the 19th century, Norway was a mecca for wealthy anglers, principally European aristocrats. English lords fished the rivers of western Norway, such as the Lågen (Suldal) and the Rauma (Romsdal), but during the 20th century, they were mostly replaced by avid anglers from the USA. Norway's salmon runs are legendary, and in June and July, you can't beat the streams of Finnmark. In addition to salmon, 41 species of fish inhabit the country's 200,000 rivers and lakes.

In the south, you'll normally find the best fishing from June to September, and in the north, in July and August. In Svalbard, the best fishing holes are well kept secrets, but Arctic char inhabit some rivers and lakes. The 175-page book *Angling in Norway*, available from tourist offices for Nkr130, details the best salmon and trout-fishing areas, fees and regulations. In the UK, it's available from MMW Productions Ltd, 26 Woodsford Sq, London, W14 8DP, UK.

Regulations vary between rivers but, generally, from mid-September to November fish under 20cm must be thrown back. At other times between August and May, you can't keep fish less than 30cm in length. For sea or fjord fishing, no licence is required. All river and lake fishing in Norway requires an annual licence (Nkr180 for salmon, trout and char and Nkr90 for other fish), which is sold at post offices. A weekly licence is also available for Nkr45. To fish on private land, you must also purchase a local licence, which is available from sports shops, hotels, camp sites and tourist offices.

Sweden

Sweden has national fishing ordinances, but local restrictions on inland waters may also apply, especially concerning salmon, salmon trout and eel, so check with tourist offices or the county authority before dropping a line. You generally need a permit, but open areas include parts of Vänern, Vättern, Mälaren, Hjälmaren and Storsjön lakes and most of the coastline (except for fishing the

Baltic salmon off Norrland and in some protected areas). Local permits (for inland waters in a specific kommun) are sold at sports or camping shops (or ask at a tourist office) and typically cost Skr50 per day and Skr280 per week.

Three authorities maintaining fishing waters should be noted: Kronopark runs centres of farmed stocks and developed facilities; AssiDomän administers 20% of Sweden, including thousands of lakes and rivers; and Vattenfall, which has salmon farms in south and central Norrland. AssiDomän's annual fishing cards are cheap at Skr200 per family. For brochures call ☎ 021-18 86 70 or write to AssiDomän, 72185 Västerås.

Finland

Finnish waters are teeming with fish – and with at least one million enthusiastic domestic anglers! In general, the northern areas have the finest fishing spots, but most of the best are privately owned. The exceptions are designated as 'Government Fishing Areas', which are stocked by the Forest and Park Service with tonnes of fish each year.

Local tourist offices can direct you to the best fishing holes, and usually publish a regional fishing map. (The Mikkeli tourist office is particularly good.) An annual guide to fishing the entire country is available from the Forest and Park Service at two offices: Tikankontti (☎ 09-270 5221, fax 09-644 421), Eteläesplanadi 20, 00130 Helsinki, and Etiäinen (☎ 016-362 526, fax 016-362 528), 96930 Napapiiri, Rovaniemi.

Foreigners are required to secure several permits before they can fish in Finland, and the regulations are strictly enforced by the 'fishing police'. National fishing licences are sold at post offices and banks; a one-week permit costs Fmk20 while an annual licence is Fmk80. You'll also need a special permit to fish with a rod or lure; they're also sold at banks and post offices and cost Fmk35/150 per week/year. Finally, you'll need a local permit that specifies time and

catch limits (for example, two salmon per day and an unrestricted amount of other species). These cost around Fmk45/130 per day/week and are available at popular fishing spots.

Many camping grounds and tourist offices rent fishing gear in summer. To go ice-fishing in winter, however, you'll either need to buy your own gear or join an organised tour – nobody rents ice-fishing tackle in Finland because every Finn has their own!

Russia

Arctic Siberia, Karelia, the Kola Peninsula and the Russian Far East offer exceptional angling opportunities, and the great northern rivers are swollen with grayling and several salmon species. However, participating in this particular activity (sitting around for hours dangling a line from the end of a pole) can be a bureaucracy-plagued and heart-stoppingly expensive business in Russia. While it is possible to head off alone with rod and tackle, most regions have stringent restrictions on fishing. In fact, US corporations have actually purchased all fishing rights along several Russian Arctic rivers, and access is limited to their paying clients. Rather than facing a white-water torrent of bureaucracy and expense, you may prefer to just read the book *Reeling in Russia*, by Fen Montaigne, who will take you vicariously to Kamchatka, Eastern Siberia and the Russian Far East in pursuit of his greatest passion.

DOGSLEDDING
Alaska

Alaska may be home to the world's best-known dogsled race, the Iditarod, but adventure dogsledding (called mushing in Alaska) has yet to become a major winter tourist activity – perhaps the problem is that Alaska sees so few winter visitors. However, a range of operators from Homer to Bettles offer winter trips, from a two-hour 'taster' to a week-long expedition through the Brooks Range. The best time for mushing in Alaska is normally between late February and early April, when the daylight hours are longer, the snow base is at its best and the temperatures are getting a bit more comfortable.

To take a commercial dogsledding trip, you won't need any sort of experience but you will need good cold-weather clothing and gear, and be prepared to rough it a bit. Accommodation on longer trips is normally in large tents, trappers' cabins or remote lodges and meals are likely to be quite basic.

In Arctic Alaska, recommended operators include Sourdough Outfitters and Brooks Range Wilderness Trips; for contact details, see Adventure Tours in the Organised Tours & Adventures chapter.

Canada

As in Alaska, dogsleds have historically been northern Canada's primary means of winter transport, and the Yukon Quest dogsled race is the second best-known of the unofficial 'triple crown' of mushing (the others are Alaska's Iditarod and Minnesota's Beargrease). As yet, however, winter tourism in the region remains a rather new tourist activity. Several competent outfitters are described in the Organised Tours & Adventures chapter.

Greenland

During the eight or nine months of continuous snow and frozen seas in Arctic and east Greenland, travel by dog sled is the most common method of getting around. For those visitors with money to spend, it's exciting to do a 'winter' tour. Some of the most popular dogsledding venues are Ammassalik, Uummannaq, Ilulissat, Sisimiut, Qasigiannguit and several other smaller places. Most dogsled tours are arranged by the hotels in the respective towns, but individuals may also make arrangements directly with the drivers. The high season runs from March to May when days are longer and temperatures are not so extreme as in mid-winter. However, summer visitors may also sample dogsledding tours on Disko Island.

Greenlandic sled dogs bear little resemblance to the drippy tongued, tail-wagging pooches most visitors probably associate with the breed. Most of these dogs seem to be only a generation or two removed from wolves and their reputation for snarling, howling and a generally ill-tempered demeanour should be taken seriously. To try to pat adult dogs is to court disaster. In many Arctic villages, these dogs spend their days snoozing on the rocks, and they blend in quite well – be especially careful not to trip over one.

Apart from in Ammassalik, Greenlanders may not keep sled dogs in villages south of the Arctic Circle, nor can they keep ordinary domestic dogs north of the Circle. This means you won't go dog sledding in Nuuk, Qaqortoq or elsewhere in southern Greenland. (Nordic skiing is possible anywhere the dog sleds go but, as yet, you'll have to bring your own skis unless you're on an organised tour.)

Tourist dogsled trips range from one-day samplers to two-week expeditions, and some include accommodation in villages or hunting camps along the way. For example, from March to May, a week-long package that includes seven nights in the hotel in Ammassalik, two day-trips by dog sled and an optional overnight village stay and meal, costs around Dkr8000 per person.

Less expensive informal dogsled trips can be arranged spontaneously in such places as Uummannaq, in the north-west, or Qasigiannguit, on Disko Bay. You'll normally pay at least Dkr700 per person per day for a more realistic experience than hotel tours allow. However, many of the coastal ferries don't operate during the dogsledding season from March to May, so at this time of year, you'll be forced to travel about by air.

Norway

Although dogsledding isn't an indigenous Norwegian sport, this Inuit means of transport readily transfers to the Norwegian wilds, and several reputable operators can take you on a range of adventures. While many people are content with just a half-day taster of the sport, keen prospective 'mushers' can jump in on the deep end and opt for a two-week dogsled safari over the Hardangervidda or through Finnmark or Svalbard.

DNT (see Hiking & Trekking earlier in this chapter) organises several trips through southern Norway. In the north, you'll want to contact Bjørn Klauer in Innset or Sven Engholm in Karasjok, and all Svalbard operators can also arrange Svalbard dogsled tours. Arcturus Expeditions in the UK offers extended dogsledding tours in Norway with operator Odd-Knut Thorsen. For contact details, see the Organised Tours & Adventures chapter.

ARCTIC
NATURE
GUIDE

By Dr Graham Bell

INTRODUCTION

Despite its harsh climate, the Arctic is rich in so many forms of wildlife that the following pages can offer only a taste of it in words and pictures. It may seem surprising that such a hostile environment can support so many mammals, birds, plants and even insects, but all natural habitats have their own wildlife communities and the Arctic is no exception. It covers a vast area at the top of the world and is by no means just a bleak desert of bare ground, ice and snow, as many imagine.

The terrain (and therefore the wildlife) is varied, and includes mountain tops and slopes, rocky screes, sheltered valleys, marshes, rivers, lakes, grasslands, heaths, steppes, seashores, snowfields, glaciers and sea ice. All of these habitats support plants and creatures adapted to living there either permanently or seasonally. Winter is a time of dormancy for some forms of wildlife and continued growth and food-searching for others, but it is in the brief Arctic summer – peaking in June and July – that everything surfaces in a burst of exuberant activity and colour.

Millions of migrant birds swarm in from the south to take advantage of the continuous daylight, ample food and wide choice of breeding sites. This is the time when Arctic wildlife comes into its own, where nature rules supreme and humankind easily loses its significance in the vast teeming wilderness of the land of the midnight sun.

It was after the last ice age (which ended some 10,000 years ago) that wildlife succeeded in colonising the Arctic, adapting to its uncompromising conditions. Plants and animals accepted the challenge of the cold, ice, wind, and months of darkness – and won. We humans must ensure that we do not destroy that hard-won success. So far, our impact on the Arctic has been detrimental. However, with current environmental knowledge and awareness, more appreciation, less exploitation, more of the wisdom and feeling of the indigenous peoples and less of the greed and insensitivity of commercial interests, we can and must ensure that this priceless wilderness is preserved intact for future generations of people and wildlife.

SEA MAMMALS

WHALES

Whales are divided into two groups: Mysticeti (baleen) and Odontoceti (toothed). The baleen whales have closely packed rows of comb-like plates – baleen, formerly called whalebone – hanging from the upper jaw, through which they sift out small creatures from mouthfuls of water. The toothed whales – and this includes porpoises and dolphins – have teeth instead of baleen and attack and devour larger prey.

Title Page: Polar bears (photograph by Nicholas Reuss)

Baleen Whales

Humpback Whale Along with the grey whale, the humpback *(Megaptera novaeangliae)* is one of the most commonly encountered whales in the Arctic and one of the easiest to identify. Also like the grey whale, it is often very active at the surface, breaching or lying on its side with jaws open, feeding or sticking one of its long flippers in the air. It is the only whale to have flippers up to 1.8m long, black above and white below: when seen these alone are diagnostic, as are the calluses on its head. When it sounds (dives) you see the very strongly arched back – hence the name 'humpback' – followed by a 'wavy' lower back ridge, and finally the fluke (tail) raised vertically and dramatically as the huge animal goes down. The under side of the fluke is different in each whale, enabling scientists to identify and track individuals.

The humpback is probably most famous for its 'songs' – the most complex and varied vocalisations in the animal kingdom.

Grey Whale Like most whale species, the grey whale *(Eschrichtius robustus)* was hunted nearly to extinction but has managed better than most to recover its numbers. For the last 50 years or so it has been popular with whale-watchers, being regular on its migration from the High Arctic – where it feeds from April to November on both sides of the Bering Strait and in the Chukchi and Beaufort seas – down to its breeding grounds in Mexico and Baja California for the rest of the year. This is the longest migration undertaken by any mammal in the world.

One of the reasons for its popularity is that it provides a great show for whale-watchers: it commonly spyhops (rises vertically to look around) and breaches (leaps right out of the water) or rolls on the surface waving a flipper in the air. Whether this is due to sheer high spirits, or the fact that it is host to more itchy parasites than any other whale species, is anybody's guess! It also loves shallow water, where it vacuums the sea bed for small marine creatures, often sending clouds of mud up to the surface in the process – a feeding technique unique to the species.

Right: Humpback Whale

The grey whale is among the larger whales – up to 13.5m long – and has a narrow head, a low hump (instead of a fin) on its back and a series of low knuckles behind. The mottled grey colour, looking very pale at times, is distinctive, as is the high, sometimes V-shaped, blow. The grey whale is also known as the Californian grey whale.

Fin Whale At 21m or more in length, the fin whale *(Balaenoptera physalus)* is second in size only to the blue whale, and is one of the fastest swimmers (up to 32km/h). With a long, narrow head and sleek body, it is unique in having the lower part of its right lip white in contrast to the uniformly grey left side. When close to the surface this white lip is a diagnostic identification feature. Though not common in Arctic waters, the fin whale takes little notice of boats – its undoing in peak days of whaling – so, with luck, good views are sometimes obtained, though it rarely shows its flukes, even when sounding. The fin whale is sometimes called finback or common rorqual.

Blue Whale Averaging 21-24m in length (up to 33m recorded), and weighing over 150 tons (up to 196 recorded) the blue whale *(Balaenoptera musculus)* has the distinction of probably being the biggest animal ever to have lived on earth. Even the baby is 7m long when born and weighs 2½ tons, drinking over 200L of milk, and putting on 80kg, daily.

This gentle giant – blue-grey in colour above and white or yellowish below – is the ultimate whale to see, though it is much less common than other species previously mentioned. It can be identified by its huge size alone, in particular its enormous broad head (a quarter of its body length), the incongruously tiny fin (30cm high) and the high blow (up to 9m, rising even higher in the wind). Blue whales are most often seen in the gulf of St Lawrence and off Greenland.

Top: Fin Whale

Bottom: Blue Whale

Sei Whale More likely to be encountered in the subarctic than in the high polar seas, the sei *(Balaenoptera borealis)* is not abundant in any particular region. The best place to observe it is probably the Barents Sea, north of Finnmark, Norway. When present, however, its progress in the water can often be followed easily because it stays and swims nearer the surface than most other whales. In appearance it closely resembles the fin whale but does not arch its back when diving and similarly rarely shows its flukes. Its dorsal (back) fin is taller and both sides of its mouth are white. Quite approachable at times, sei whales can swim very fast (up to 50km/h) if alarmed.

Northern Right Whale Called the right whale *(Eubalaena glacialis)* because it was ideally the right whale to hunt – being large, slow-moving and approachable – this species was brought to the brink of extinction in the 19th century by the whaling industry and is now one of the world's rarest whales. However, it can still be encountered in Arctic waters, when it appears as a large (15m-long) whale, black, with no fin at all on the smooth back of its thick-set body. The enormous head supports a highly arched upper jaw and several large crusty lumps or callosities. Its blow is distinctively V-shaped. In many of these features, particularly the lack of dorsal fin, the northern right whale resembles the equally rare bowhead whale, but misidentification is unlikely as their ranges do not normally overlap – both do occur in the sea between Alaska and Kamchatka, but at quite different seasons.

Sperm Whale The easily recognised shape of this whale *(Physeter catodon)*, with its enormous blunt head and tiny lower jaw, is what most people visualise as a typical whale – the original Moby Dick. Though rare through being overhunted, sperm whales range widely, including into Arctic waters. These huge mammals, over 15m long and weighing up to 58 tons, eat up to a ton of squid every day. But their favourite delicacy is the legendary, luminous giant squid, and for this they dive deep – 22km has been proved but it is virtually certain they can go considerably deeper than this. It is almost beyond our understanding that

Right: Sei Whale

they can, and do, lie in wait for an hour at these incredible depths for their prey, in the pitch dark and under tremendous pressure; they suck in huge amounts of water through their enormous nostrils and adjust the density of the spermaceti wax in their skulls, thereby somehow achieving perfect buoyancy.

Minke Whale In comparison with other baleen whales, the minke whale *(Balaenoptera acutorostrata)*, or piked or lesser rorqual, is small – about 9m long. Its size saved it from the whalers' harpoons for many years, but with the dramatic decline in the numbers of larger species, the minke is no longer safe from commercial interests – particularly in the southern hemisphere. Despite this, it is still one of the most encountered whales, occurring over almost all the world's oceans, including the Arctic where they sometimes become trapped in pockets or 'leads' of open water among the ice. The minke whale has a slim body, thin head and diagnostic white bands across its flippers.

Toothed Whales

Narwhal The small narwhal *(Monodon monoceros)* is unique among whales, indeed among all mammals, in having a single (very rarely double) long, spiralling tusk – actually a modified tooth. People used to believe this was the origin of the legendary unicorn, and though nowadays we think more scientifically, we are still not quite sure what the tusk is used for. It could be an indication of strength and dominance (normally only the males have it and they use it in fighting over females): at least a third of the tusks are broken short. The tusk is mainly hollow and spirals anticlockwise.

Characteristic of the High Arctic, narwhals rarely stray south of 70 degrees north. They are common in Davis Strait, and around Baffin Bay and Greenland. Apart from the tusk of the male, when present and visible,

Top: Sperm Whale

Bottom: Minke Whale

narwhals are identified by their bulbous heads (with a very slight 'beak'), rounded bodies, heavily mottled upper parts, short upturned flippers and only a hint of a lump where one would expect the dorsal fin to be.

Long-Finned Pilot Whale Called pilot whales *(Globicephala melaena)* because they travel in large pods with an apparent 'pilot' leading them, these small whales average 5-6m long. They traverse the cool northern waters of the world but without reaching the polar regions. Apart from their gregarious nature, they can be identified by their bulbous forehead overhanging the mouth, long-based and prominent dorsal fin (bluntly rounded, specially in males) and slender, pointed flippers on a mainly black body. They often allow a close approach by boats; look for a long grey streak often present behind each eye and a grey 'saddle' behind the fin.

Orca/Killer Whale It is unfortunate that the orca *(Orcinus orca)* used to be, and often still is, also called the killer whale. Unfortunate, because it has unfairly been regarded as some sort of bloodthirsty monster, endlessly attacking all and sundry. It is, of course, a flesh-eating predator but recent research has shown it also to be an intelligent, sensitive and playful animal with a strong sense of loyalty and concern towards its family unit.

There is no record of it ever attacking humans without provocation, and indeed films like *Free Willy* have shown how friendly orcas can be. Orcas are easily identified by their contrasting black and white pattern – the white oval patch behind the eye being particularly striking. They travel in pods of up to 20 animals, among which the males are conspicuous by their tall (up to 2m), erect dorsal fins, which lack the backward curve of the smaller females. This is one of the most commonly encountered whales in Arctic waters, and an exciting one to watch.

Beluga The beluga *(Delphinapterus leucas)*, or white whale, is virtually impossible to confuse with any other whale because it's the only one that is completely white as an adult. This is a highly sociable species, travelling in pods of females with young, or pods of males, or

Right: Orca/Killer Whale

sometimes combined groups involving hundreds. As they frequently swim slowly just below the surface, they are easy to spot and then the small size, small rounded head on a very flexible neck and lack of dorsal fin, can all be noted. At a distance, however, they can be surprisingly difficult to distinguish from floating bits of ice! They rarely leap out of the water but often spyhop to satisfy their curiosity.

Widely distributed in the Arctic, belugas prefer cold shallow waters and large estuaries and, unlike other whale species, even travel up rivers, often for hundreds of kilometres. They are highly vocal creatures, emitting a variety of clicks, whistles and bell-like notes; hence their nickname, the 'sea canary'.

DOLPHINS & PORPOISES

Porpoises are often confused with dolphins and the two terms used indiscriminately, but in fact they refer to two related but different groups of mammals, even though both are basically very small toothed whales. There are 26 species of dolphin and six of porpoise in the world but only a few of these reach Arctic waters.

As far as the Arctic is concerned, there is only one porpoise – the harbour or common porpoise *(Phocoena phocoena)*. This robust, slow-moving animal is most often observed as it rises to the surface to breathe; there it sluggishly rolls forward, gently arching its dark grey back and showing its low, blunt, triangular dorsal fin. It usually does this several times at intervals of a minute or more before disappearing for long periods.

It sometimes lies on the surface for a while, with only its back and fin visible, but never indulges in displays of acrobatics or follows ships. The head is therefore not easy to observe, but is small, fairly rounded and lacks a prominent beak and forehead. Porpoises are rather solitary animals and it is unusual to see more than two or three together.

In contrast, dolphins are highly sociable animals often travelling in large pods. They move fast, often repeatedly leaping out of the water – confusingly called 'porpoising'! – as they do, for example, on their way to investigate a passing ship and perhaps 'bow ride' there. Characteristically playful and active, they love to swim just in front of a ship's bow, twisting and turning, and periodically swerving off to the side and returning to the point of the bow.

When they 'bow ride', you can obtain excellent views and photographs, while admiring their skill, agility and supreme mastery of the sea. At this close range you will see the angled forehead joining its beak – a quite different outline from the porpoise's head – while its dorsal fin is also distinctly more backward curved than in that species.

There are only three dolphin species that you are at all likely to encounter in Arctic waters and then rarely farther north than 70 degrees. The white-beaked dolphin *(Lagenorhynchus albirostris)* shows not only a white beak but also a white streak the length of its grey body, plus pale patches behind the fin.

The rather similar Atlantic white-sided dolphin *(L. acutus)* has a dark beak and yellowish, instead of greyish, patches behind the fin. The bottlenose dolphin *(Tursiops truncatus)* – the species most often found in sea life tanks and zoos – is a uniform grey over its upper parts, and typically larger than the other two.

PINNIPEDS

As with porpoises and dolphins, the terms 'seal' and 'sea lion' are often confused, especially as both groups of animals are classed as 'pinnipeds' (mammals with flippers or fin-like limbs). However, sea lions *(Otariidae)* have clearly visible external ears.

To swim they use their front flippers to propel themselves forward and their rear ones as a rudder. Out of the water they use both sets of flippers for support – they can rear up on the front ones and swivel the hind ones round; this also enables them to gallop forward with a fast but clumsy lolloping gait.

Seals, on the other hand, though superficially similar, belong to a different family *(Phocidae)*. They have no external ears, and when swimming, propel themselves with alternate swings of their hind flippers combined with undulating movements of the rear end of their bodies; their front flippers are used as rudders only.

Out of the water, seals use neither set of flippers for locomotion, moving forward with slug-like contractions of their bodies. Therefore, they are much slower on land or ice than sea lions.

There are six species of Arctic seal, though only two are present throughout the year. Polar bears and Arctic foxes are adept at locating their lairs, and many pups and adults fall prey to these land predators.

Bearded Seal

The bearded seal *(Erignathus barbatus)*, which lives year-round in the Arctic, is a large, solitary species whose remarkably bushy, walrus-like moustache makes identification easy when it lies on an ice floe, as it often does. It feeds mainly on clams scraped from the sea floor.

Right: Bearded Seal

GRAHAM BELL

Ringed Seal

The ringed seal *(Phoca hispida)*, like the much larger bearded seal, is a permanent resident of the Arctic, and the one most often encountered. It is named after the diagnostic pale, ring-like markings on its grey upper parts. Unique among seals, the pups are born in a lair built by the female deep under the snow, with access through the ice floor to the sea below. They feed on small fish, krill and other small marine creatures.

Harp Seal

The harp seal *(Phoca groenlandica)* is only slightly larger than the ringed seal but easily distinguished by its large, irregular dark patches on a paler background – giving a map-like pattern or, in the imaginative vein of its original name, a harp-like shape. Harp seals are denizens of deep Arctic waters, particular Baffin Bay, but they come inshore farther south in late summer to drop their pups on the ice off Labrador and New-foundland – sites of the traditional but controversial annual cull.

Hooded Seal

The much larger hooded seal *(Cystophora cristata)* has a similar life-pattern to that of the harp seal. Though less often seen by visitors to the Arctic than most other seals, the male hooded is at least easily identified by its remarkable inflatable proboscis that gives a unique outline to its head; moreover, when angry it can extrude a large, red, balloon-like sack from its nasal cavity, offering one of the most extraordinary sights in the animal world – and presumably very off-putting to rival males.

Ribbon Seal

The diminutive ribbon seal *(Phoca fasciata)* is a little-known species apparently resident in Bering Strait. Its coat is chocolate-brown with diagnostic cream-coloured bands round the neck, flippers and pelvis.

Harbour Seal

The only other seal whose distribution extends to Arctic waters is the common or harbour seal *(Phoca vitulina)*. Though more abundant in temperate seas, it is found around the more

GRAHAM BELL

Left: Walrus

southerly rocky and sandy shores of the Arctic region. Common seals have very blunt faces and grey backs heavily marked with innumerable small dark spots.

Steller's Sea Lion

Sea lions are essentially mammals of the southern hemisphere but the Steller's sea lion *(Eumetopias jubata)* does just overlap into the waters of the Bering Sea and off the Alaskan coast farther north. The characteristic sea lion features described earlier readily identify it.

Walrus

The unique and massive walrus *(Odobenus rosmarus)* forms a separate family *(Odobenidae)* from seals or sea lions. As with sea lions, walruses can stand and walk on their front flippers, but like seals, they use their rear flippers for propulsion under water and their front flippers for steering. They live on the Atlantic and Pacific coasts of the High Arctic and along the northern shores of Siberia, but the largest concentrations are in the Bering and Chukchi seas. They prefer shallow water and spend much of their time lounging on land or ice in dense noisy herds. By far the largest and heaviest of the pinnipeds in the Arctic, the walrus measures up to 4m in length and weighs as much as 2200kg.

The walrus is too familiar to require much description but few people realise that both sexes have tusks. As bottom feeders, their favourite meal is clams, and it was once thought that they used their tusks to dislodge or crush these and other bivalve molluscs. We now know that they simply suck out the contents of the shells, presumably using their whiskers to help them locate their food and manoeuvre into position. Walruses use their tusks for fighting, protecting themselves from polar bear attacks and hauling themselves up on to ice floes.

LAND MAMMALS

POLAR BEAR

For most people, the magnificent polar bear *(Ursus maritimus)* typifies the Arctic more than any other form of life. The sight, or even just the thought, of this, the largest living carnivore on earth, wandering over the ice, raising its head to sniff the air for danger or prey, can set the adrenalin flowing and bring a shiver to the spine.

Although generally classified as a land mammal, the polar bear is, as its scientific name implies, just as much at home in the water, being an excellent and tireless swimmer and pursuer of seals. Its huge furry paws are equally adapted as paddles in the sea as snow-shoes on ice and snow.

Exclusively circumpolar in distribution, this magnificent creature cannot be mistaken for any other, as it ambles along the ice or swims

NICHOLAS REUSS

slowly and stealthily from ice floe to ice floe, looking for seals to dislodge and devour – especially ringed seals, their favourite food.

Being so large and imposing, it has no enemies, apart from humans. Low temperatures do not worry it, even in winter, protected as it is by a dense layer of fat and thick white (or creamy-white) hairs. Indeed, the polar bear's problem is not keeping warm in winter but keeping cool in summer – perhaps that is why it moves about slowly and sedately!

The cubs are born in January in a lair under the snow and tended exclusively by the female. Males are solitary for most of the year, and it is usually these lone males that are encountered by human visitors to the Arctic.

GRIZZLY/BROWN BEAR

W LYNCH

The grizzly or brown bear *(Ursus horribilis)* is the world's second largest bear. Though smaller and different in shape and colour from its white cousin, the grizzly or brown bear is closely related, and the two species can interbreed and produce fertile young (as has been proven in captivity). The largest specimens are found on Kodiak Island and the Alaska Peninsula, where they enjoy a diet rich in protein, thanks to spawning salmon, while the bears of interior Canada, Alaska, Siberia and northern Europe are smaller and subsist largely on berries and small mammals. As well as its colour, the grizzly's outline is different from the polar bear's; the head, which is set on a much shorter neck and body, has a broader, flatter profile, and interior grizzlies have a larger dorsal hump than coastal brown bears.

Top: Polar Bear

Bottom: Grizzly/Brown Bear

Grizzly/brown bears are by no means confined to the Arctic, though their range in other areas (central and southern Europe, southern Canada and the contiguous 48 states of the USA) is now much reduced by their conflicts with human civilisation. They certainly stand out conspicuously in their bleak habitat, and identification presents no problem. They are omnivorous, ranging over the tundra looking for berries, small mammals, fish, birds and eggs. Though grizzlies aren't common anywhere, they're often observed in the tundra and taiga regions of Alaska and north-western Canada, and very fortunate observers may also spot them in Arctic Russia, Finland, Sweden or Norway.

CARIBOU

The caribou *(Rangifer tarandus)* is a member of the deer family, and the European version is more often known as reindeer. All male deer have antlers, which are shed and renewed annually, but caribou is the only species where the females also bear antlers.

The human inhabitants of the Arctic, such as the Inuit and the Sami, have long depended on the meat, hides, oil, bones and sinews of these animals for food, clothing, tents, fuel and tools. To do this, they have traditionally hunted and herded caribou and reindeer, and still do so to a great extent.

In the wild these large, graceful herbivores live in herds for much of the year, gathering to migrate south to their wintering grounds in autumn – stopping en route for the rut, when the males fight one another for their harems of females – and then north again in spring to the calving grounds.

In Canada and north-eastern Alaska these migrations can be spectacular, especially when viewed from the air, as the herds move in thousands, or sometimes tens of thousands, over a wide front, using routes that their ancestors also followed since time immemorial. Lone animals and small family groups can also be found in suitable habitats at any time of the year. As well as the European reindeer, there are several other races in Canada, Alaska and Svalbard, some now rare or endangered. All, however, are easily identified, thanks to the traditional Christmas card image we all know.

Right: Caribou

MOOSE

MARK LIGHTBODY

The moose *(Alces alces)*, which is often called 'elk' in Europe, is the other main Arctic deer species. Much larger than the caribou, it has a quite different profile, and males bear distinctively flat, saucer-shaped antlers. The snout is long, heavy and slightly drooping, with a rounded end (not pointed as in other deer). Beneath the chin hangs a distinctive dewlap. This is the world's largest deer – an average human would not even reach its shoulder – and weighs up to 450kg or more. These gentle herbivores live in Arctic forests and wooded valleys, especially in the swampy areas rich in their favourite food, the Arctic willow. They sometimes venture out onto the tundra, particularly in Alaska and Canada, to browse on other vegetation where mosquitoes and other insects are less troublesome.

MUSKOX

Although it's a member of the Bovidae family (as are sheep, goats and cattle), the muskox *(Ovibos moschatus)* bears little resemblance to its nearest relations, or indeed, to any other animal. During the last ice age, it was distributed throughout much of the northern hemisphere's glaciated areas but its current range is much smaller. Nowadays, wild herds are restricted to Kangerlussuaq, Greenland, and North-East Greenland National Park; barren lands in Arctic Canada; Nunivak Island, Alaska; and Dovrefjell and Femundsmarka National Parks, in Norway.

The anatomy of the muskox, which weighs in at between 225 to 445kg, is one of nature's oddities. In front of its incredibly high shoulders, the enormous, low-slung head has two broad, flat horns sweeping across the forehead rather like those of an African Cape buffalo, before curving outwards and downwards, then upwards and forwards. Its incredibly thick and shaggy coat, with a matted fleece of soft hair (commercially known as *qiviut*) underneath, covers the whole body, and hangs down like a skirt to almost reach the ground and swings from side to side when the animal runs. Below this skirt of hair, only the bottom part of the legs protrude, giving the animal a solid, stocky

Left: Moose

appearance reminiscent of a medieval horse dressed for jousting! Indeed, this analogy is especially appropriate because during the rutting season, when the males gather their harems, they repeatedly charge each other, butting their heads together with a crash that's often heard for miles around. This heated battle continues until one animal admits defeat and lumbers off.

Traditionally, wolves have been the muskox's main predator but polar bears have also been known to eat them. Their primary defence is to form a circle with the males on the outside and females and calves inside, trusting in the force of their collective horns to rip open any potential attacker. However, this defence has proven useless against human hunters, especially the Greenlandic Inuit, who love their beef-like meat and prize their warm qiviut hair. As a result, their numbers have been seriously decimated and only with restocking have they been able to thrive in their current range.

Although muskoxen aren't inherently aggressive toward humans, an animal that feels threatened can charge at speeds of up to 60km/h, and woe unto anything that stands in its way. Hikers should stay at least 200m away; if an animal seems agitated or paws at the ground, don't run but back off slowly until it seems relaxed again.

ARCTIC FOX

The Arctic fox *(Alopex lagopus)* is the region's most common and widespread land predator, and also the most frequently observed, particularly as it is bold and inquisitive. At times, it may even approach a human observer. It resembles the more familiar but shy red fox, of more southerly latitudes, but is smaller with shorter tail and legs, and blunter nose and ears. These features are no doubt an adaptation to the cold, since the smaller the surface area of appendages, the less risk there is of heat loss and frostbite. The Arctic fox does not hibernate, thanks to its adaptation to life on the tundra, where it searches for small mammals, birds and their nests, carrion and, in lean times, even insects and berries. It also follows wolves and polar bears to scavenge the remains of their kill.

Right: Arctic Fox

DAVID TIPLING

WOLF

Once you've heard the howl of a wolf *(Canis lupus)* in a bleak Arctic landscape, you'll never forget it, and this haunting sound must strike terror into their prey species. The favourite food of these very strong carnivores is caribou, and the movements of some wolf packs revolve around the seasonal migrations of caribou herds (for example, the Canadian barren ground caribou, or Alaska's Porcupine herd). Wolves hunt in a highly coordinated way, selecting the older, weaker or incapacitated animals, thereby ensuring the health of their prey stock (as is the case generally with all predators).

Although the wolf has historically been hated and persecuted by humans, wolves remain widespread in remoter regions of the Arctic. Although casual visitors are unlikely to see a large pack, odd individuals and family groups can be encountered on the islands and mainland of northern Canada and Alaska. Their appearance – like a huge, mottled grey Alsatian (German shepherd) dog – is familiar to most westerners from childhood stories. A distinctly white subspecies inhabits the remotest regions of Canada's Ellesmere Island National Park.

ARCTIC HARE

The largest of all hare species *(Lepus arcticus)* poses no identification problems as it is the only one resident in the Arctic. It is also fairly easy to observe, owing to its size, colour and behaviour. In the Canadian High Arctic, adult hares are pure white, apart from black tips on the ears. Although they blend into a snowy backdrop, they also inhabit tundra and rocky terrain, where they stand out better, especially when they rear up and hop along on their hind legs. They are not shy, and in the Canadian High Arctic and Greenland they sometimes occur in large groups. Those living on the Canadian mainland are generally more solitary, and turn white only in winter, as does the blue hare of northern Europe. The leaves and buds of the willow are the hare's favourite food.

WOLVERINE

The wolverine *(Gulo gulo)* or 'glutton' is little known and rarely seen, though it ranges widely, if sparsely, over the Arctic taiga and tundra. It looks for all the world like an enormous stoat or weasel – and indeed belongs to that family, Mustelidae. It is basically grey in colour all over, with a light patch on top of the head and crossing the face like a mask, and a yellowish stripe from the shoulders along the side of the body. Though extremely fierce and fearless, like others of its tribe, its weight and stockiness make it considerably less agile. It therefore often depends on ambush to catch its prey – animals up to the size of large herbivores. It is unable to successfully pursue the latter over hard ground or frozen snow, but has a chance on soft snow, where cloven hooves sink in more easily than the wide, furry paws and claws of the wolverine. However, it isn't fussy and can survive on a diet of much smaller animal and vegetable items gleaned from its tundra home.

BEAVER

Beavers *(Castor canadensis)* are not typically Arctic animals, dependent as they are on trees for food and lodging, but their range does extend to the subarctic taiga, where willow swamp prevails. These rodents are not particularly well adapted to very cold conditions, their tails and feet being unprotected by hair. Although they don't hibernate, they are less active in winter than summer. Beavers are best known for their habit of felling trees to construct dams and underwater lodges.

LEMMINGS

There are several species of lemming, but all look similar and have similar lifestyles, living in underground burrows and making tracts through tundra vegetation – a clear sign of their presence. They resemble hamsters or large, dumpy tailless mice. All are basically vegetarian and compulsive eaters. Even people who know nothing else about lemmings have heard about their supposed periodical

mass suicides; a pity, because this is a myth! What actually happens is that populations of these highly active Arctic rodents reach maximum levels every few years as a result of good weather and plenty of food allowing a high survival rate of the young. (Lemmings have long breeding seasons.) When this occurs, food becomes scarce, predators increase and overcrowding induces restlessness and aggression; the animals then 'panic' and set off looking for fresh feeding grounds. If they come to a wide river or lake they will try to cross it and may, unintentionally, drown in the process; they may also be forced over cliff faces, from the sheer press of their numbers.

OTHER SMALL MAMMALS

The Arctic is home to many small animals that are unobtrusive and seldom seen – except perhaps as a flash of brown or white, disappearing under a rock or tussock of tundra grass. They nevertheless form a link in the Arctic ecological chain, as essential meat for larger animals and birds.

Voles are part of this chain. Being small and short-lived (one to three years on average) they succumb to starvation when food is scarce but produce four or five litters when food is abundant. They breed and sleep in underground burrows but have to come above ground to feed on vegetation, furtively, always on the lookout for their many enemies.

Shrews are often confused with voles, but are even smaller and have long, pointed, not rounded, snouts and are largely insectivorous

Right: Lemming

– taxonomists place them in a quite different order (Insectivora) from the rodents (Rodentia).

Voles and shrews do have one thing in common, however, besides their diminutive size: they are both the favourite food of ermines, least weasels and martens – all voracious members of the same carnivorous family (Mustelidae) – as well as being snapped up opportunistically by almost anything else that happens to come across them. No wonder they live their short lives to the full in such a feverish manner!

Ermines and least weasels are usually brown in summer and white in winter. Martens are tree-living carnivores, larger than ermines and weasels, which just reach the Arctic at the edge of the northern forests.

BIRDS
PETRELS
Fulmar

One of the world's most common and widespread sea birds, the fulmar (*Fulmarus glacialis*) resembles a miniature albatross in its effortless gliding flight on stiffly held wings, often accompanying boats for hours on end. In appearance it superficially resembles a gull, but its tubed nostrils show that it is indeed related to the albatross and other members of the petrel group. Its grey tail also distinguishes it from gulls, while in some parts of the Arctic the whole body is grey or brown.

GULLS
Arctic Skua

This fine piratical bird *(Stercorarius parasiticus)* is related to, and rather resembles, a gull, but is bolder, fiercer and more determined in its flight. The central tail feathers project beyond the others, forming a point. It comes in pale and dark forms (called 'morphs') that interbreed randomly. Though Arctic skuas do fish for themselves, they prefer to chase other sea birds, forcing them to drop or disgorge their catch in midair and retrieving it spectacularly before it reaches the water. Look out for skuas wherever other sea birds are fishing.

Two other species of skua may also be encountered, though less commonly: the pomarine *(S. pomarinus)* with wide, twisted tail projection, and the long-tailed *(S. longicaudus)* with very long, flexible projection.

Kittiwake

This small species of gull *(Rissa tridactyla)* has a dark eye giving it a gentle expression and is named after its call 'kitti-i-waake!'. Like most gulls, its body is white and its back and upper wings grey, but the combination of yellow-green beak, black legs and 'dipped-in-ink' black wing-tips (with virtually no white spots) is unique. In its first year it has a beautiful 'W' pattern across the wings.

Unlike most other gulls, which forage inshore or inland, kittiwakes live far out to sea, only coming to land to nest, in the manner of all true sea birds. This is the gull you are most likely to see on Arctic sea cliffs in summer, or from your ship, even though away from land, at any time of year.

Ivory Gull

Of the approximately 50 kinds of gull in the world, the ivory gull *(Pagophila eburnea)* is the only one that is pure white all over as an adult – to camouflage it among the ice and snow where it lives all the year round. It scavenges on the remains of dead birds, mammals and fish; in particular it loves to attend polar bear kills for the bits left over. The young bird's white plumage is scattered with black spots.

The ivory gull is a hardy bird, nesting on remote and inaccessible cliffs and rarely straying south of the Arctic circle even in winter. The edge of the northern pack ice is where you are most likely to see it.

Glaucous Gull

With its white body, grey wings, yellow beak with orange spot and pink legs, the glaucous gull *(Larus hyperboreus)* is like a large edition of its well known counterpart farther south – the herring gull *(L. argentatus)*. However, its white primaries (the main feathers at the end of the wing) easily distinguish the adults from the herring gull and all other gulls of temperate regions. The young bird is a strikingly pale buff-brown all over, with fine barring and vermiculations.

Glaucous gulls can be seen anywhere in the Arctic, particularly around harbours, following ships and scavenging on rubbish tips. In the

GRAHAM BELL

GRAHAM BELL

MIKE WESTON

Top Left: Fulmar

Top Right: Kittiwake

Right: Skua

breeding season they also take many sea birds' eggs and chicks, as well as adult puffins, little auks and anything else similar.

Sabine's Gull

This small, dapper gull *(Larus sabini)* has a dark grey head in summer plumage and a striking unique wing pattern – grey inner wing, black tip (with white spots) and white triangle in between. It is most likely to be seen where there are 'feeding frenzies' involving other sea birds and whales, particularly off the East Greenland, Svalbard and Alaskan coasts. The biggest breeding colonies are on the Alaskan tundra but they can also be seen nesting by the shore on Southampton Island, Canada. In autumn Sabine's gulls migrate south to winter off the coasts of Africa and South America.

This bird is named after Sir Edward Sabine (1788-1883), astronomer to the Arctic expeditions of John Ross and William Parry in 1818 and 1819, and later, with Faraday, scientific adviser to the Admiralty.

Ross's Gull

This little gem of a gull *(Rhodostethia rosea)*, pale pink with a black neck-lace in breeding plumage and a wedge-shaped tail, has long been a bird of mystery. It was named after another redoubtable Arctic and Antarctic explorer, Sir James Clark Ross (nephew of John Ross), who first came across this species on one of Parry's attempts to find the Northwest Passage in the 19th century. It was a long time before any nesting grounds were discovered – early in the 20th century – and to this day only a few are known, mostly in north-east Siberia though scattered and intermittent breeding has been recorded in north-western Greenland and in Canada.

With luck you can come across a Ross's gull anywhere, but thousands regularly pass Point Barrow in Alaska every autumn, peaking in September/October, travelling north to their unknown Arctic wintering areas.

TERNS

Arctic Tern

Renowned as the world's longest-distance traveller, the Arctic tern *(Sterna paradisaea)* nests in the Arctic and winters in the Antarctic – an annual round trip of some 20,000 miles (incredible, particularly

GRAHAM BELL

GRAHAM BELL

Left: Arctic Terns

when one considers that it does not fly in a straight line, but fishes as it goes). Thus it is reputed to see more daylight than any other living organism in the world, swapping the continuous Arctic summer for the equivalent in the Antarctic. Both sexes make this annual pilgrimage but separate for the winter, meeting up again on some sandy or pebbly Arctic beach to lay their two eggs and rear their young. With typical slender tern body and wings, and long forked tail, this species has a red beak and tiny red legs.

AUKS
Brunnich's Guillemot/Thick-Billed Murre

One of the most numerous High Arctic members of this family, this attractive bird *(Uria lomvia)*, in its smart formal dress, black above and white below, and its sharp pointed beak, reminds one of a penguin – though, of course, penguins cannot fly and are confined to the southern hemisphere. Expert swimmers and divers after fish, their low flight and whirring wings indicate effort. They lay their single colourful egg on bare sea cliff ledges.

Two closely related species, the common guillemot/murre *(U. aalge)* and razorbill *(Alca torda)* breed at a slightly lower latitude into the subarctic zone. The former has a narrower, longer beak with no white line down the middle, while the latter has a much wider beak with white lines along the top and around the tip.

DAVID TIPLING

Top: Common Guillemot/Murre

Bottom: Guillemots

GRAHAM BELL

Black Guillemot

Like the other guillemots, the black guillemot *(Cepphus grylle)* is considerably smaller in shape and all black except for large oval white wing patches and red legs. They are more solitary by nature and keep closer inshore, preferring rocky coasts.

Atlantic Puffin

The puffin *(Fratercula arctica)* is everyone's favourite sea bird. With their outsize multicoloured beak, smart black and white plumage, triangular eye ornaments and bright orange legs, puffins look quite comical on land, as they interact with one another in their colonies. Unlike most other auks, they nest in burrows on the grassy sloping part of sea cliffs. Expert fishermen, they can go on catching and holding sprats and sand eels in their beaks to take back to their young without losing the ones they have already caught – the most recorded is 62!

Little Auk/Dovekie

Much smaller than all the other auks described previously, this starling-sized sea bird *(Alle alle)* is similarly black above and white below but with a tiny stubby beak. Nesting in dense colonies among the scree at the base of cliffs their 'elfin laughter' is one of the strangest sounds of the High Arctic summer. They feed on small marine invertebrates.

DIVERS/LOONS

Great Northern Diver/Common Loon

If you've ever sat beside a lake in the northern wilderness, chances are you've heard the wonderfully evocative wail of the diver/loon *(Gavia immer)*, which is known in Inuit languages as *tullik* or *tugdlik*. It inhabits mainly large lakes away from civilisation and calls only during the breeding season. In winter it is pelagic (seagoing), but rarely strays far from inshore waters, estuaries and bays. Perfectly streamlined for diving after

GRAHAM BELL

Left: Atlantic Puffins

fish, it has a long torpedo-shaped body with legs set far back, and a long dagger-shaped bill. A commoner relative, the red-throated diver/loon *(G. stellata)* is distinguished by its smaller size and upturned bill.

SWANS

Whooper Swan

The bugling cry of the whooper swan *(Cygnus cygnus)* rings out over the lakes of the Arctic where it nests in the summer, especially where no trees grow in the southern part of the area.

Lake Myvatn in Iceland is an ideal place to see these beautiful wild swans, either breeding or when gathering in late summer prior to their flight to lower latitudes for winter.

The tundra or Bewick's swan *(C. columbianus)* that nests in the more exposed tundra of the High Arctic is smaller, with less yellow on the otherwise black beak. It too flies to northern Europe for the winter.

GEESE

Snow Goose

Easily identified as the only goose that is all white with black wing-tips, the snow goose *(Anser caerulescens)* breeds on rocky tundra in north-west Greenland, Alaska and Canada, subsequently gathering in large herds to fly south to its wintering grounds off the Atlantic and Gulf coasts of North America. Both parents help rear the family of goslings, which, like their parents, can be either the white phase or the so-called 'blue' phase – in which only the head is white.

The other Arctic-breeding geese you are most likely to come across are the pink-footed goose *(A. brachyrhynchus)*, which is all grey-brown with darker head and neck, and the barnacle goose *(Branta leucopsis)*, with black upper parts, breast and neck, with white face and belly.

DUCKS

Eider

The male of this widespread species *(Somateria mollissima)* is unique among ducks in being white above and black below; the head is tinged

Left: Whooper Swan

Right: Barnacle Geese

GRAHAM BELL

GRAHAM BELL

with green and the breast with salmon-pink. The female is brown but has the same diagnostic wedge-shaped beak – the 'Roman nose' effect. You will see these ducks along most rocky shores throughout the Arctic, where they remain all year. In some places the down from their nests is collected to make the famously valuable eiderdowns – with the finest insulation known.

WADERS

Red-Necked Phalarope

Nothing is more dainty than this tiny wader (*Phalaropus lobatus*) swimming on the sea or some tundra pool, rapidly picking dead mosquitoes off the surface or spinning round and round to stir up invertebrates below. Unlike most shore birds it spends much of its time swimming, and has lobed toes to enable it to do so.

Even more unusual is the sex reversal situation when breeding; the female is the more brightly coloured partner and it is she who initiates the courting and mating, leaving the more sombrely attired male to incubate the four eggs and rear the young.

The less common but closely related grey/red phalarope (*P. fulicarius*) is rusty-red in breeding plumage and has a thicker beak. Both species fly to the southern hemisphere for the winter.

CRANES

Siberian Crane

This imposing bird (*Grus leucogeranus*), with its pure white plumage, black wing-tips and red face, beak and legs, is now an endangered species. Only three isolated breeding populations are known – all in northern Siberia. Its breeding grounds, migration stopover points and wintering grounds – in Iran, India and China – are all under threat from human disturbance. However, great efforts are being made on the Siberian crane's behalf and it has become a symbol of Arctic conservation.

Top Left: Male Eider Duck

Top Right: Female Eider Duck

FALCONS
Peregrine Falcon

The peregrine falcon *(Falco peregrinus)* can appear anywhere, striking terror into almost any other bird as it dashes past. Often the first sign of its presence is when all the birds rise up in the air in alarm; that's the time to look for its rather pigeon-like silhouette but with sharper wings, a black moustache-like stripe and much more powerful flight. The closely related gyrfalcon *(F. rusticolus)* also occurs throughout the Arctic. It is bigger and paler – the Canadian form being almost pure white.

OWLS
Snowy Owl

If you see a large white owl with yellow eyes, it's the snowy owl *(Nyctea scandiaca)* – a daytime Arctic hunter. The female is larger than the male and is peppered with brown spots. Their favourite food is lemmings and in good lemming years the owls take advantage by rearing large broods. Conversely they may not breed at all when lemmings are scarce.

EAGLES
Bald Eagle

DAVID TIPLING

Imperious, impressive, inspiring – no wonder the bald eagle *(Haliaeetus leucocephalus)* was chosen as America's national bird. This status did not, however, prevent it succumbing to pesticide poisons in the 1950s and 60s, absorbed mainly through eating dead fish stranded on riverbanks and beaches. This resulted in infertile or thin-shelled eggs and brought the species close to extinction. Though still officially classed as threatened, these magnificent birds with their 1.8m wingspan are slowly recovering in numbers, particularly in Alaska and Canada.

The bald eagle has yellow eyes, beak and feet. The adult plumage, attained after about five years, is dark brown; the head and tail are contrastingly white, producing an overall piebald effect (the bird is certainly not bald of feathers as its name suggests). Juveniles lack this conspicuous contrast, being dark brown all over, flecked paler.

Living up to 50 years in the wild, they feed on fish, ducks and carrion but are slow and rather lazy hunters, sometimes preferring to rob ospreys of their catch.

The nest is a huge affair atop a cliff or tree and is added to each year if the owners are unmolested. It can eventually weigh a ton or more – what a bird!

Right: Bald Eagle

White-Tailed Eagle

This magnificent eagle *(Haliaeetus albicilla)* – the largest in Europe – adds the final touch of majesty to the rugged coastline and off-shore islands of Scandinavia, Iceland and the west coast of Greenland. Look for it soaring over the fjords or perched on some rock, surveying its domain with huge, cloak-like wings hanging by its sides.

It can be confused only with the golden eagle, but it has a bigger beak and larger and broader wings. Moreover, the adult's head is whitish and protrudes more, while the tail, as well as being pure white, is short and wedge-shaped. It soars high on flat or only very slightly raised wings – a sort of avian flying mattress! Immature white-tails have browner heads and tails, but the latter still show white vanes, conspicuous from below.

Slow (not to say sluggish) hunters, white-tailed eagles (also known as sea eagles) obtain their prey – fish, birds, small mammals – by surprise rather than speed. There is no more dramatic sight than one of these regal raptors silently gliding down to water level, lowering its talons and scooping up an unsuspecting fish swimming near the surface, easily gripping the slippery, struggling creature in one foot, before gradually regaining height and carrying it away to eat on a rocky headland or shore.

CROWS

Raven

The raven *(Corvus corax)*, the largest and most widespread of the crow family, is identified by its huge beak and long wedge-shaped tail. It does not migrate, as, being omnivorous, it can find food equally well near human habitation as in the wilder areas.

GROUSE

Rock Ptarmigan

This is one of the few Arctic birds that stay put all year. When winter comes to the tundra, rock ptarmigan *(Lagopus mutus)* – and the very similar and closely related willow grouse *(L. lagopus)*, or spruce hen – live under the snow, feeding off leaves, berries and young shoots. With their cryptic colouration they are hard to spot when crouching still on the ground, but in flight their white wings make them easy to observe.

Left: White-Tailed Eagle

BUNTINGS
Snow Bunting

Of the few small land birds in the Arctic, the snow bunting *(Plectro-phenax nivalis)* is the one most likely to be encountered, flitting low over the ground, flashing its large white wing patches as it does so and uttering its cheerful, tinkling rattle. There is much white on the body as well, particularly on the male. They prefer treeless landscapes, often near villages.

MARINE LIFE

The Arctic waters are generally rich in sea life, though not uniformly so. In areas of the High Arctic, where the permanent thick ice prevents sun penetration and mixing of the water by wind and currents, the necessary ingredients for life remain on the bottom of the sea or lake. In the Low Arctic, however, where the surface water is ice-free in summer, wind and currents disturb this bottom layer and produce an upwelling of gases, salts, and nutrients, forming a rich mix that enables life to thrive all the way to the surface.

Even in the Low Arctic, water is cold and it may seem strange that this is a suitable habitat for fish but in fact, when well stirred up and mixed like this, it is richer in nutrients than in the tropics. Indeed, some Arctic seas are so full of plankton – vegetable (phytoplankton) and animal (zooplankton) – that they can at times make the water look like pea soup. For example, the Barents Sea has been estimated to produce some 2000-3000 million tonnes of phytoplankton in summer, with perhaps 100 million tonnes of zooplankton feeding on it. This zooplankton is the staple diet of fish.

Fish are not the only cold blooded inhabitants of Arctic waters. The same conditions that enable fish to thrive also enable other sea creatures to do the same – in fact, the fish would not survive without them as a source of food, just as the fish themselves are food for larger creatures. Where sunlight penetrates it provides the power source for photosynthesis by small or microscopic, mostly single-celled, plants (phytoplankton) that absorb minerals, salts, nitrates, phosphates and other nutrients.

The phytoplankton is eaten by small or microscopic animals (zooplankton) which in turn are food for the fish which attract birds and sea mammals to eat both them and the zooplankton. Jellyfish and comb jellies join in the feast too, moving through the water with a rhythmical motion reminiscent of rays. Many of these creatures are brightly coloured but unfortunately they are hard to see when living naturally, and often fade when found dead on the tide line. Most of this activity takes place at or near the sea surface, but it produces a steady 'rain' of debris – dead and damaged animals and plants, skeletons, shells, faeces etc – which sinks to the ocean floor and builds up a layer of nutritious food on which bottom-feeding creatures (collectively called benthos) depend.

Bacteria break down this mass of food debris. Not all is eaten, but even the insoluble and indigestible residue is not wasted – the process of decomposition liberates the nutrient salts and gases essential for plant growth, the wind and currents stir them up and the whole process starts again. The ocean floor, then, is able to be the home of benthic animals, such as mussels, clams and other bivalve molluscs, crabs, sponges, starfish, brittlestars and octopi.

Crabs pick and choose, sponges and molluscs sift out particles in much the same way as, at the other end of the size scale, baleen whales do, while octopi squirm over it all and grab almost anything that moves, themselves falling victim to whales and other large sea mammals.

'Eat and be eaten' is the order of things in the deep dark depths of the Arctic ocean.

FISH

The cold temperatures do not generally worry fish; though some move to less cold areas in winter, most stay. They can produce a sort of antifreeze in their blood that enables them to survive in icy-cold temperatures. Some species go into a state of semi-hibernation or winter dormancy, slowing down their breathing and metabolic rate, and becoming lethargic. Others constantly adjust their metabolic rate in a way that keeps them completely active, whatever the temperature.

Members of the salmon family are the most abundant, well known and sought after fish in the Arctic. Salmon feed exclusively at sea, returning to spawn up the rivers, often travelling many miles to the upper reaches where they lay their eggs in the gravelly bottom. The short-lived Pacific salmon, the pink *(O. gorbuscha)*, and the chum *(Oncorhynchus keta)* – die after spawning once. The Arctic char *(Salvelinus alpinus)* is a member of the same family, many of which have a similar life history, though some, like the Atlantic salmon *(Salmo salar)*, are long-lived and spawn annually. Some char live permanently in freshwater lakes, as do their cousins, Arctic graylings *(Thymallus arcticus)* and also the voracious pike *(Esox lucius)*. There is even a species of shark in the Arctic – the Greenland shark *(Somniosus microcephalus)*.

Even a brief account of Arctic fish must mention capelin *(Mallotus villosus)*. These are small silvery fish that are occasionally found in vast shoals, living in deep water in winter, and swimming to shallower bays and fjords in summer to spawn and where they are caught in large quantities by all kinds of predators, including man. Fish are of commercial value in the Arctic as elsewhere – for example, they account for 95% of all Greenland's exports.

INSECTS

Perhaps surprisingly, insects abound in the Arctic – bumblebees, crane flies, stoneflies, hover flies, blowflies, ichneumon wasps, aphids, midges, mosquitoes, moths and butterflies, to name but a few. They over-winter variously as eggs, larvae or adults, among vegetation, in crevices, under the snow or in the soil. Some remain dormant but some adults emerge from time to time in warm spells. Like plants, and like other cold-blooded creatures, insects can acclimatise to very low temperatures and survive – though ice crystals in the body's cells can be lethal.

Insects share the exuberant activity of all other forms of life in the brief Arctic summer; indeed they are an integral part of it, pollinating flowers and forming a vital link in the food chain. In particular, most nesting land birds and shore birds depend on them to feed themselves and their young at this time. Humans curse the billions of mosquitoes that plague them (and plague animals like the caribou), but the female mosquitoes need the blood to provide protein to lay a large number of eggs. Without mos-quitoes much life in the Arctic would not exist – perhaps some con-solation for those itching bites, which at least do not transmit tropical diseases.

Fortunately, more appealing insects do exist in the Arctic, notably butterflies. It always seems slightly incongruous to see butterflies flit-ting from flower to flower or basking in the sun, against a background of glaciers or pack ice but they too are well adapted to the climate and enjoy their brief lives as imagoes (adult insects) before the winter closes in and they die. Butterfly species to look out for include the clouded yellows or sulphurs *(Colias)* – yellow with black edges – and the fritillaries *(Clossinia)* – an intricate pattern of wavy dark lines and spots on a paler orange-brown background. All Arctic butterflies like to turn their wings towards the sun when settled – either open or closed according to the species.

PLANT LIFE

TUNDRA PLANT COMMUNITIES

The word 'tundra' means 'treeless plain' and is loosely used to describe Arctic terrain above the tree line. Typically it is open, bare ground with a patchy covering of low-growing vegetation – shrubs, grasses, reeds, sedges, flowering plants, lichens, mosses, liverworts and algae. All these plants have a tough time and their hold is precarious to say the least. In winter they are exposed to icy, drying and abrasive winds or are covered in snow, while in the spring thaw the easily eroded thin layer of poor quality soil they grow in becomes waterlogged because of the permafrost below.

To survive in these conditions, plants need to keep low and maintain a good grip with their roots, which can expand only sideways. In the drier and higher parts of the tundra, typical plants include berry-bearing shrubs and a myriad of flowers like purple saxifrage *(Saxifraga oppositifolia)* whose blooms are the first harbingers of spring; moss campion *(Silene acaulis)*, looking like a purple-studded pin cushion; mountain avens *(Dryas octopetala)* with its yellow and white single flowers, and various species of gentian *(Gentiana)*, pushing up their incredibly blue trumpets towards the sky. Dry river beds are the favourite habitat for the broad-leaved willow herb *(Epilobium latifolium)* – sometimes called river beauty or dwarf fireweed – the national flower of Greenland.

Unlike typical sturdy tundra flowers, the Arctic poppy *(Papaver radicatum)* seems to defy the elements with its delicate petals on slender stems – and, perhaps incongruously, is the one Arctic flower that everybody can name.

The damper parts of the tundra are where low-lying land is poorly drained owing to permafrost, where rivers overflow in the spring thaw,

Top Left: Broad-Leaved Willow Herb

Bottom Left: Tundra Landscape

Top Right: Cotton-Grass

Middle Right: Dwarf Birch

Bottom Right: Arctic Willow

or where snow or ice remain well into summer. In such areas the nodding heads of cotton-grasses *(Eriophorum)* abound. Here too you can see the veined white petals of grass of Parnassus *(Parnassia palustris)* – not a grass, but related to the rose family. Also to be found are two remarkable carnivorous plants – round-leaved sundew *(Drosera rotundifolia)* and butterwort *(Pinguicula vulgaris)* – whose sticky leaves produce an enzyme to digest trapped insects. Many other species await the traveller appreciative of botanical beauty.

TAIGA PLANT COMMUNITIES

'Taiga' is the name given to the transitional zone between the boreal forests of the subarctic and the tundra of the High Arctic. It is sharply defined in atlases but rarely so on the ground. It normally extends for many miles with sheltered valleys extending like tongues far into the tundra. Taiga shares characteristics with both forest and tundra; it is the area where trees become more stunted, shrubby and scattered and the surrounding vegetation correspondingly shorter.

Trees can tolerate cold but not the shallow, poor soils, permafrost and very windy conditions of the far north. Trees that do grow in this transitional area suffer from the weight of winter snow on their branches, desiccation from lack of water as well as wind abrasion, and heavy browsing by animals. Nevertheless, some species fare better than others and push as far as they can up to the edge of the tundra zone. Notable among these are the black spruce *(Picea mariana)*, the dwarf birch *(Betula nana)* and – especially in damper parts – various species of willow *(Salix)*.

At the northern edge of the taiga, willow and birch trees become shorter and shorter, finally becoming prostrate along the ground. (It is sometimes said that if you get lost in an Arctic forest, just stand up!) In late summer the leaves of these horizontal 'trees' turn red and gold, just as they do in the tall forests farther south. Among these shrubs and trees a host of other plants grow, many of which are common to both tundra and taiga. The flowering season is short in the Arctic, so if you are there late in the summer a good hint is to search near patches of lingering snow or ice, where the lower temperature will have delayed flowering.

FUNGI, ALGAE AND LICHENS

Fungi are not conspicuous members of the Arctic community; they are hard to identify and are mostly known only by their Latin (scientific) names. Some fungi grow on the stems of Arctic shrubs and are known as bracket fungi.

Lichens are a characteristic feature throughout the Arctic, adding pattern, texture and colour to what otherwise would be just bare ground and rocks. Some are crust-like and very hard, others feathery and soft, some creeping low along the surface, others growing comparatively tall and bushy above it. All lichens are tough, growing in exposed situations where 'normal' plants would die.

They are unique in the plant world in having no roots as such. A lichen is in fact two organisms in one: a symbiotic relationship between an alga above and a fungus below, the fungus providing a spongy base to cling to the rock and store moisture for the alga which, in return, absorbs sunlight, water and nutrients through its leaves and shares these with the fungus. They are incredibly slow-growing – some spreading by only 1mm a year, or not at all in some years if conditions are unfavourable. Some have been estimated to be 4000 years old! However, they have one weakness; they require pure air, succumbing easily to pollution and so are good indicators of air quality.

Lichens are an important part of Arctic ecology: they break up rock surfaces – part of the soil-making process – and provide food and shelter for insects and animals in the harshest parts of this extreme environment.

Algae do not only grow in symbiosis with fungi, of course; they are separate plants in their own right, depending on sunlight and nutrients in order to grow and reproduce. Some live on rocks, usually near water, and others in vast quantities in the sea, where they form part of the plankton mass in the upper layers or cling to the underside of ice.

References

A Naturalist's Guide to the Arctic by E C Pielou
The Whale Watcher's Handbook by Erich Hoyt
Whales, Dolphins and Porpoises by Mark Carwardine
Whales of the World by Lyall Watson
Animals of the Arctic: the Ecology of the Far North by Bernard Stonehouse
North Pole South Pole by Bernard Stonehouse
Kingdom of the Ice Bear by Hugh Miles & Mike Salisbury
Life in the Cold by Peter J Marchand
The Arctic & its Wildlife by Bryan Sage

ARCTIC HISTORY & EXPLORATION

By Robert Headland

The region lying beneath the constellation of the Great Bear (a truly polar one) is much more difficult to define than its antipodes, the Antarctic. Various authors have proposed bounds: the Arctic Circle (66°33'N); the 10°C maximum isotherm; the limits of permafrost, both continuous and discontinuous; the tree line, and several others. These differing limits invariably reflect the nature of the study concerned. From the historical point of view the tree line, although not always clearly defined (tree vs bush), is probably the most efficient and practical one. From the point of view of discovery, the limits of the Arctic have apparently moved north through the ages. In effect, the Arctic boundary has retreated northward with time, as wild and inaccessible territory was explored and settled from the south.

The history of exploration of the Arctic is profoundly affected by its geography, which is essentially that of a frozen ocean (the smallest of all the oceans), the northern extremities of three continents and some diverse archipelagos. The boundaries are not distinct and a subarctic region may be loosely defined.

Of the eight countries which surround the Arctic Ocean, Russia has the longest coast with 164° of longitude facing north. Canada is second with less than half that and the others have much less. Thus, Russia dominates the bulk of the Arctic region, both geographically and historically.

ARCTIC EXPLORATION

Exploration of the Arctic is vastly affected by the extreme and often adverse climatic and topographical conditions. As well as the cold (a minimum of -68°C has been recorded – in contrast, the Antarctic has recorded -89.2°), the extreme difference between summer and winter (where ranges often exceed 50°C) also presents severe problems to exploration and the technical aspects of mapping.

Although the hours of daylight are annually constant throughout the planet, their distribution is increasingly anomalous towards the poles. The time when the sun is below the horizon severely limited any winter survey until many new techniques were invented in the latter part of the 20th century. Conversely, summer navigation and determination of position were difficult when the stars were invisible owing to the unsetting sun. The long day length had the advantage that it made things comparatively less uncomfortable and allowed explorers to work a 24 hour day (sometimes a mixed blessing).

Of course, during winter very long periods of astronomical observations are practical, but this is offset by many other adverse conditions including the frequent impossibility of seeing much else other than one's immediate surroundings.

The low average temperatures, a result of the diminished intensity of solar radiation because of the inclination of the planet's surface from the sun, result in vast ice fields. These reflect what little solar radiation

Title page: Researchers taking a break (photograph by Lawson Brigham)

is received and thus contribute to their own frigidity. One should remember that, in the polar regions, water is far more commonly encountered as a solid rather than as a liquid – about 99% of the ice (thus some 90% of freshwater) of the earth is in the polar regions.

Another effect of this cold is wind; very cold air draining down slopes may develop high velocities, rapidly becoming blizzards during almost any season of the year, especially near the equinoxes. From the point of view of the explorer, navigator or cartographer, the loss of body heat and consequent danger to survival comes more from wind than cold – and the combination may be extreme. As a result, Arctic history has included many accounts of tragedy and many expeditions which never returned.

Geomagnetism is irregular at both polar regions. This makes using a magnetic compass difficult or impossible over large parts of the Arctic and Antarctic. The positions of the magnetic poles are also different from the geographic poles. Because of their importance in navigation, many early explorations set out to chart the positions of the magnetic poles and for a long period this attraction outweighed the importance of reaching the geographic poles.

Another significant factor in Arctic exploration is the Arctic Ocean with its associated seas. Conditions below the surface are usually more comfortable for life than above it. Saltwater freezes at -1.8°C and the sea can never go below this despite very much lower air temperatures. Its surface is insulated by the snow and pack ice of its frozen surface. Although cold, it is highly mineralised (from glacial run-off), well oxygenated (oxygen dissolves far better in cold than in warm water) and has much illumination during summer. These conditions make marine life abundant in the sea compared with the land.

The food chains are short but sustain large mammals of economic importance. Species that have been (and to some extent still are) exploited include: whale for blubber and baleen, seal for fur, narwhal and walrus for ivory and blubber, eider duck for feathers, polar bear and Arctic fox for pelts, and musk ox for *qiviut* wool. All these creatures also provide meat.

Despite these resources, neither polar region has provided explorers much more than basic survival, although their needs have been augmented by local resources. Arctic literature contains many accounts of such survivals – but one is tempted to think there are many more who did not get the opportunity to record their fates.

Exploration of the seas and ocean is severely constrained by the sea ice, both because of the impenetrability of frozen oceans to ships and because of constantly moving ice floes with pressure ridges. From 1958, with the voyage of the *Nautilus*, submarines began to make long voyages beneath the icecap, but it was not until 1977, with the *Arktika*, that the North Pole was reached by a surface vessel. In relatively open conditions a strengthened ship can safely penetrate to many remoter areas. Conversely, with a dense, closed pack ice, it is possible to travel long distances across its surface. The most common circumstance is, however, broken pack ice which is difficult for either method of travel. Many expeditions traversing pack ice have used sleds and kayaks, one being carried on the other as conditions require, but thick brash ice may often stop both.

ARCTIC HISTORY

The Arctic has had an indigenous population for many thousand years. These include: groups of Eskimo (including the Inuit of Canada) which extended from far eastern Siberia across to Greenland; Lapp or Sami who inhabited Arctic Scandinavia and the Kola Peninsula; Samoyeds or Nenets in western Siberia; Yakuts in central Siberia; and Chukchi in eastern Siberia. The divisions between these groups are indistinct and, in modern times, much admixture with many other groups, especially immigrants, has occurred. The most northern indigenes are the Inuit whose settlements have existed beyond 80°N in Greenland.

The contribution to exploration, cartography, or dissemination of knowledge generally, by indigenous populations has been negligible. What they knew, although undoubtedly locally extensive, was not communicated beyond very local circumstances. Interestingly, Inuit peoples in the Canadian archipelagos knew the region sufficiently well to draw maps under the guidance of John Ross in 1831. These included several useful features, but were drawn under quite artificial circumstances.

Several phases in the progressive process of the exploration of the far northern regions have been proposed. These are useful historical divisions, although overlap occurs between some because of geographical differences. The names used to here to distinguish these phases indicate the predominant theme only and are not intended to exclude other activities which occurred during the particular period. The dates are also generalisations – there are no 'watertight compartments' in such a historical continuum.

The Speculative Period (to 1595)

A great variety of conjectural ideas about the northernmost land in the world developed as speculative geographers placed real and hypothetical lands on the globe. The voyage of Pytheas to 'Ultima Thule', as it was known, in about 325 BC was widely commented upon, but how far north he reached remains contentious. The Ancient Greeks were the earliest to record information on this region and bestowed the name 'Arctic' on it.

Reasonably accurate descriptions of Arctic regions and their inhabitants did not emerge until the general form and size of the earth became known. A detailed early account was written in 1555 by Oleaus Magnus, the last Catholic Archbishop of Uppsala in Sweden. This monumental publication, *A Description of the Northern Peoples*, presents an immense store of fact and fantasy, and although it's largely European based, it served as the chief source of knowledge about the North for over two centuries.

The study of geography and exploration of the earth progressed rapidly after the Dark Ages with great voyages to the remotest parts of the planet. During this time, cartographers steadily improved their representations of the continents. The first well known Arctic chart was that in the famous comprehensive atlas compiled by Gerardus Mercator, and published by his son Rumbold in 1595, with many subsequent editions. This chart is based on a complicated mixture of fact and myth. Mercator described the Arctic thus:

> The islands adjacent to the North Pole were formerly called Ciliae and now Septentrionales ... And there are many small rivers ... and they are called the 'indrawing sea' because the current always flows northwards so strongly that no wind can make a ship sail back against it. And there it is all ice from October to March. And in these latitudes the mountains reach up to the clouds and almost all rock is bare of vegetation. And it is almost always misty and dull weather. And it is well known that beyond 70 or 78 degrees of latitude there is no human habitation ... In the midst of the four countries is a whirlpool ... into which empty these four Indrawing Seas which divide the North. And the water rushes around and descends into the Earth just as if one were pouring it through a filter funnel ... Except that right under the pole lies a bare rock in the midst of the sea. Its circumference is almost 33 French miles, and it is all of magnetic stone.

From this well publicised basis, Arctic history became the progressive reduction of the hypothetical landmass around the North Pole and the discovery that the Arctic is largely ocean. It is interesting to note Mercator theorised a magnetic mountain at the North Pole to account for the behaviour of the compass.

Marine Exploitation (1600 to 1860)

One factor in polar exploration which is frequently underestimated is the contribution to exploration made by the sealers, whalers, hunters and trappers who were very active in the Arctic for almost four centuries. The whalers working in Greenland waters knew the seas from Novaya Zemlya to Baffin Island from the 1500s. Some of the earliest voyagers returned with accounts of graves from remote regions proving that others exploiting the resources had preceded them. A good example of this was provided by Willem Barents finding graves with Russian Orthodox crosses over them and wreckage of ships along the north-western coast of Novaya Zemlya in 1596.

Sometimes the advice and charts of whalers and others were used effectively by explorers. William Scoresby provided one of many excellent examples of this. More often this source of information was not appreciated – and several disasters can be regarded as being partly due to lack of such practical information.

Somewhat similar comments may apply to the knowledge held by indigenous inhabitants of the Arctic. Many explorers adapted the best indigenous methods to their techniques, some went almost wholly native, and a few neglected local knowledge and occasionally suffered because of this.

Although not directly concerned with Arctic resources, some of the earliest exploratory interest in the far north was also mercantile, by traders endeavouring to reach the orient by routes other than Cape Horn or the Cape of Good Hope. These voyages were made when both Spain and Portugal endeavoured to exert monopolies over the southern routes, sometimes by force. Dreams of the Northeast Passage, the Northwest Passage, and even a seaway across the pole were numerous.

For both reasons, local exploitation and trade routes, the period marked the beginning of many chartered companies working in the Arctic, some of which still exist. These include Muscovy Company (founded in London in 1555), Vereenigde Oostindische Compagnie (VOC, Netherlands, 1602), Hudson's Bay Company (London, 1670), Compagnie du Nord (Paris, 1684), Den Kongelige Grönlandske Handel (Copenhagen, 1774) and Rossiysko-Amerikanskaya Kompaniya (St Petersburg, 1799). Many of them published charts but a large proportion were kept secret as 'trade, in confidence'.

The Dutch compiled many of the earliest Arctic maps. Much of this cartographic work was associated with the explorations of Jan Rijp and Willem Barents, and several others searching for a route to China. The coast and northern extent of Novaya Zemlya appears with Bjørnøya well defined and Svalbard appears to merge with the east coast of Greenland.

During this phase a dichotomy developed between the Eurasian and the American Arctic with regard to the progress of exploration and cartography. The exploration of these regions took quite different courses resulting in the former becoming reasonably well mapped over a century before the latter. Geography, as well as politics, was a powerful influence on this.

The American Arctic features innumerable islands with small straits between them which retain the winter ice; it is exceptionally difficult for navigation and much of the coast is inaccessible to most vessels. Only one major river, the Mackenzie, enters the Arctic Ocean from America. Only about 60 vessels have ever made a transit of the Northwest Passage.

The Eurasian Arctic coast is considerably more accessible. It has far fewer islands, wide seaways, is often free of pack ice during summer and has many large rivers flowing into it. Currently, almost as many vessels transit the Northeast Passage in a few years than have ever used the Northwest one.

Russian Expansion (1720 to 1830)

The Russian empire had been in a continuing state of expansion from the days of the first campaigns of the Cossack leader Yermak in 1581. This extended the tsar's domain to the Pacific coast of Asia but left the northern regions far less well known. Semyon Dezhnev rounded the extreme eastern cape of Asia, now Cape Dezhnev, in 1648.

Peter the Great, founder of the Russian Navy, was responsible for vast explorations and augmentations of his empire. He set in motion a series of explorations that culminated in the Great Northern Expedition of 1733-43, but died before they came to fruition. The expedition was led by the Dane Vitus Bering. It included 977 men in seven detachments, and its objective was to establish the practicality of the Northeast Passage, exploring western Arctic America, and charting the Bering Strait. The majority of the exploration was by land, in particular by dogsled along frozen rivers and over snow-covered tundra. In 1741 Semyon Chelyuskin reached the most northern point in Asia (later Cape Chelyuskin). These explorations virtually completed the mapping of the Eurasian Arctic coast. Only some of the Eurasian Arctic archipelagos remained to be discovered. The Russian explorations extended beyond the Asian boundaries and reached Alaska – where the tsars ruled until the province was sold to the USA in 1867.

The resulting maps were detailed and informative but proved convincingly that the Northeast Passage was not suitable for navigation at that time. Thus the pressure for finding an efficient route to China from Europe this way collapsed, although some attempts to find one across the Arctic Ocean were made, in a theoretical belief that there might be open water near the pole. It was not until engines were developed that such navigation became commercially practical, over two centuries later.

The Great Northern Expedition produced maps that provided a basis for much local exploration and development of trade routes. It was a hunting expedition, led by Ivan Lyakhov in 1770, which opened up the main group of the New Siberian Islands (Novosibirskye Ostrova) and developed a trade in the fossilised mammoth tusks which abound in the region. During Lyakhov's exploration he found a copper kettle on the western island (named Ostrov Kotelny, 'Kettle Island'), but there was no indication of its origin.

The Northwest Passage (1800 to 1910)

The results of the Great Northern Expedition caused increased interest in the Northwest Passage. At the beginning of the 1800s, in contrast to Eurasia, the large central part of the American Arctic was unknown. Whalers had not penetrated far west from Greenland. They knew that the waters were difficult and dangerous and did not contain profitable quantities of their quarry. The north coast of Alaska was better known – but this barely extended beyond the tsar's domains. The end of the Napoleonic Wars left the Royal Navy with a very large fleet and, to cut a long story short, a question of what to do with it. Exploration had long been undertaken by naval expeditions and discovery of a Northwest Passage was an alluring proposition.

Efforts began early in the 19th century and charting was progressive from both ends. Techniques of polar travel were constantly improved and the navy adopted sledging early. Many of the difficulties were with the weather and ice conditions, as the whalers had experienced; the difference between a good and a severe winter was enormous. More than 30 vessels were forced to endure unexpected winters and some were crushed.

The fate of Sir John Franklin's 1845 expedition still dominates this period of Arctic exploration, but there is the irony that by disappearing he was responsible for a vast improvement of the charts resulting from the activities of several dozen search expeditions. After 15 years of attempts to determine the fate of Franklin's expedition, the majority of the lower American Arctic was mapped, and the Northwest Passage's first transit had been made (Robert McClure aboard the *Investigator*, then sled journeys to the *Polar Star*). It was not until 1903-07 that one ship, *Gjöa*, made the transit. It was commanded by Roald Amundsen whose voyage extended over three winters.

After the Franklin period, the North American Arctic was left comparatively untouched. Sir George Nares' major expedition with HMS *Alert* and HMS *Discovery* along the north-west coast of Greenland achieved another farthest north position. The tragedy of Adolphus Greeley's expedition (1881-84) overshadowed the rest of the International Polar Year expeditions (only seven out of 25 men survived). The last mapping of the extreme north of the Canadian Arctic was done by 1902.

Ocean Exploration & Navigation (1860 to 1930)

By the latter part of the 19th century, only the extreme northern lands, several parts of the high Arctic archipelagos and some isolated islands remained undiscovered. Franz Josef Land was discovered and partly mapped in 1873 after the Austrian ship *Tegetthoff* became beset. Several expeditions then worked there during the last decades of the century.

Of the significant expeditions during this period, one made the first transit of the Northeast Passage between 1878 and 1879. The development which made it possible was the steam engine. A Swedish expedition, led by Adolf Nordenskiöld aboard the *Vega* – equipped with this new invention – left Stockholm, proceeding round Norway and after spending one Arctic winter in far eastern Siberia, returned triumphant around Asia and through the Suez canal. Thus not only was the Northeast Passage transited but Eurasia was circumnavigated. The expedition made detailed surveys of the route and conducted a comprehensive scientific program. One of its most important consequences was to draw attention to the navigation and exploration of the Arctic Ocean.

The next major voyage ended in tragedy but providentially left major clues about the ocean. In 1879 George De Long, of the United States, took the *Jeannette* through the Bering Strait in an attempt to reach the North Pole. The ship became beset in the pack ice and drifted slowly westwards around Wrangel Island and the De-Long Islands (named by subsequent search expeditions), where it was crushed and sank on 2 June 1881. Only 13 of the crew of 33 survived the subsequent arduous journey to the safety of the Siberian coast and settlements (the tsars had begun the convict exile system used to populate these regions).

In 1884, Greenlanders kayaking off southern Greenland found relics of the *Jeannette*. The find generated great interest from the scientific community. It was known that Siberian artefacts occasionally wash up in Greenland but these relics came from a definite location and their speed of transport was known.

This gave Fridtjof Nansen (who was to become one of the greatest Arctic explorers) an idea. The specially designed polar ship *Fram* (Norwegian for 'forward') was built to Nansen's specifications and, in 1893, sailed through the Northeast Passage to a position near the Novosibirskye Ostrova. From here Nansen deliberately sailed north in the *Fram* until she became beset in 25 September 1893 and remained so until 14 August 1896. The drift took her to a farthest north of 85°55.10′N on 15 November 1895. The voyage proved that a suitably built and equipped ship could withstand the ice, and also that the Arctic Ocean was deep, with no findings of land, and depths measured often exceeded 4000 m. Nansen had hoped to reach the North Pole and set off over the ice from the *Fram* with this intention on 14 March 1895. The southern drift of the pack ice was too much for him and his companion Hjalmar Johansen to reach the pole and have sufficient supplies to return. Thus, at a new farthest north position of 86°13.10′N, they were forced to return but, owing to the continued drift, were unable to find the *Fram*. After an exceptionally difficult journey, they wintered in a stone hut they built in a remote part of Franz Josef Land. The next summer they continued south for a most providential rescue at Cape Flora by a British expedition which spent 1000 days exploring the archipelago.

The *Fram* voyage was a major exploratory one which brought back vast amounts of scientific observations. The story of endurance and heroism inspired many of the efforts to attain the North Pole described in the following sections.

Another major exploration was that of the second voyage of the *Fram*, led by Otto Sverdrup. Between 1898 and 1902 he discovered and explored much land in the extreme north of the Canadian Arctic archipelago and claimed it for Norway. At the expedition's conclusion, the North American Arctic had effectively caught up with the Eurasian Arctic as far as mapping was concerned. Mapping was complete to the beginning of the Arctic Ocean. The missing coasts were in the north-east of Greenland and (after misleading maps from Robert Peary had confused and led to the death of the Danish Mylius-Erichsen expedition) these were completed by Johan Koch by 1913.

Right: Fridtjof Nansen

Arctic diplomacy became a significant issue during this period. British and Netherlands whalers abandoned Spitsbergen because of the decline in the whaling trade due to overexploitation. This effectively made Spitsbergen a 'no man's land'. Early in the 20th century, mining interests became stronger and other visitors became more numerous. Even a 'hotel' and hunting expeditions were organised. The 'no government' situation was, in the circumstances, becoming increasingly complicated. Thus, in 1920, an international meeting was convened. After much deliberation the Spitsbergen Treaty was written, giving sovereignty over the archipelago to Norway with the provision that citizens of all contracting parties would have rights equal with Norwegian citizens. There was provision for mining, exploitation of biological resources, and protected areas.

The Spitsbergen Treaty resolved conflicts of sovereignty and was the precursor, to some extent, of the other international polar convention, the Antarctic Treaty. After the treaty came into force, Norway adopted the name Svalbard ('cold rim') for what was generally known as Spitsbergen (the name of the main island). Mining settlements continued at several locations, and some operate today. The largest settlement, Longyearbyen, is now a major Arctic airport.

The North Pole (1895 to 1915)

An unprecedented amount of exploration and adventure was concentrated into the two decades after the voyage of the *Fram*. This affected both the North Pole and South Pole. In both regions there was much exploration of the lands and oceans surrounding both poles. The South Pole was attained twice, but, despite fraudulent claims, the North Pole remained unseen until 1926.

During this brief but intense period, 17 expeditions attempted to reach the North Pole. They came from Italy, Germany, Norway, Russia, Sweden and the United States; sleds, balloons, ships and airships were all tried. All failed. Particularly strong and contentious claims were made by Frederick Cook in 1908 and Robert Peary in 1909; both are now regarded as fraudulent but, incidentally, diverted much attention to the South Pole. (The North Pole was first seen in 1926 but it was 1948 before anyone stood there, 1968 before it was reached by surface, and 1969 before the Arctic Ocean was crossed on the surface.)

Several of the polar attempts ended in tragedy. One of the early ones was so ill-conceived that this was virtually inevitable. Salomon Andree, from Sweden, with two companions, attempted to fly a hydrogen balloon, guided by drag ropes, over the pole in 1897. They crashed and perished on the remote Svalbard island of Kvitøya while trying to sled back. Part of the tragedy was caused by trichinosis from eating inadequately cooked bear meat. It was not until 1930 that their last camp was found, together with notebooks and undeveloped photographic film which revealed their fate.

Other North Pole attempts set out from Svalbard, Franz Josef Land, Greenland, and Ellesmere Island. A Russian attempt, led by Georgiy Sedov, was the last, and it ended fatally for its leader who perished from scurvy on 5 March 1914, before the expedition advanced beyond Rudolf Island in Franz Josef Land. WWI ensured that attempts on the North Pole ceased for over a decade.

The Confrontation Period (1920 to 1991)

The renewal of concentrated Russian attention on the Arctic began after the disastrous defeat of the Imperial fleet by Japan at the Battle of Tsushima in 1907. The problem for Russia had been to reinforce the Vladivostok detachment; support arrived too late by travelling through the Suez Canal. Thus a survey of the possibility of using the Northeast Passage as a strategic waterway was investigated. Two specially built coal-fired icebreakers, the *Taymyr* and the *Vaygach*, surveyed the Bering Strait region for two summers then made the journey to Murmansk between 1914 and 1915.

After the Russian Revolution (beginning in 1917) the Soviet Union consolidated and it was not long before politics in the newly formed state concentrated on the Arctic and increasingly restricted access to it. This period was when the Northeast Passage became commercially navigable and became known as the Northern Sea Route. It was also when politics moved into the 'Cold War' period of confrontation.

Of the many technological improvements in cartography, the one which most profoundly affected the polar regions was undoubtedly the use of powered aircraft. The first Arctic powered flight was part of a series of unsuccessful searches for a lost expedition in 1914. Aircraft use in the Arctic developed rapidly and longer flights allowed local survey of many archipelagos.

The next transit of the Northeast Passage was led by Roald Amundsen aboard the *Maud* from 1918 to 1923. The intention was to repeat the voyage of the *Fram* but to start farther east. Many things went wrong, including serious financial difficulties as the expedition progressed. The transit was completed, the fourth in history, but most other objectives were not realised and the *Maud* was impounded for debt.

Early on, in 1919, an organisation destined to be a major Arctic research establishment was formed – the Commission on the Study of the North, in Leningrad. This became the Northern Scientific-Industrial Expedition in 1920, then the Institute for Study of the North in 1925, and ultimately the Arctic and Antarctic Research Institute. It remains in St Petersburg and is the senior polar organisation in the world.

Roald Amundsen emerged in 1925 as one of the pioneers of Arctic aviation and, cooperating with Lincoln Ellsworth, made an attempt to reach the North Pole from Svalbard using two aeroplanes. This was unsuccessful because of engine troubles, and he had to land on pack ice only 2°10′ from his objective. The expedition, which carried no radios

because of their weight, was regarded as lost. Three weeks later, after much effort and good organisation, the six men managed to return in one aircraft.

This gave Amundsen sufficient reason to abandon attempts in heavier-than-air machines and, instead, he tried a dirigible balloon. On 11 May 1926 he set off from Svalbard aboard the airship *Norge*, reached the North Pole the next day, and continued to Teller, Alaska. The airship caused much consternation to the Eskimo when it reached its destination; they described it as a 'flying whale'. Many difficulties, especially involving ice accumulation and consequent weight gain, beset the flight but were overcome. The worst was the accumulated ice on the propellers becoming detached, flying through the air like scimitars and threatening to puncture the gas bags which kept the airship aloft.

On 9 May 1926 Richard Byrd, from the United States, claimed to have flown an aircraft over the pole, but calculations from available evidence demonstrated it was impossible. This was later confirmed from some of Byrd's notebooks. Amundsen had thus become the leader of the expeditions which first saw both the South Pole and the North Pole, and in both expeditions he had been accompanied by Oscar Wisting.

A comparable airship exploration of the Arctic by General Umberto Nobile of Italy took place in 1928, but it ended in tragedy. Returning from a flight over the North Pole, the airship crashed and broke in two off Svalbard. One part, with some of the crew aboard, was lost, while the other section remained on the ice. Radio apparatus was carried and a major international rescue began. Nobile, with his lap dog, was the first to get out. After several later attempts the Soviet icebreaker *Krassin* effected the major part of the rescue of the survivors. This event demonstrated the power of icebreaking vessels and concentrated the Soviet Union's attention on its northern regions. It also led to the loss of Roald Amundsen with the crew of a rescue aircraft.

Expeditions to establish stations on Wrangel Island, Franz Josef Land, Severnaya Zemlya and several mainland sites took place. The station at Bukta Tikaya on Franz Josef Land was one of the earliest, and in 1931 was visited by the first tourists to the Russian Arctic when the *Malygin* arrived, and the *Graf Zeppelin* 'dropped in' to exchange mail during an exploratory flight. Another such tourist voyage did not occur

Left: Roald Amundsen

until 1990. The east coast of Severnaya Zemlya was discovered in 1913 but its extent was unknown. In 1930 to 1932 a comprehensive land survey was conducted which mapped what was the last major unknown land on earth. In the subsequent years the last of the Russian Arctic islands – the remaining small ones – were discovered.

In 1932, the Soviet icebreaker *Sibiryakov* made the first transit of the Northeast Passage in one summer with no winter stop on the way (the fifth transit in history) but sustained severe damage at its conclusion. This reinforced interest in the seaway. Thus, in 1933, Stalin commissioned a special department, 'Glavsevmorput', to concentrate on opening up the Soviet Arctic. The beginnings of a series of polar stations had been made in 1928, but under Stalin's command the number vastly increased. These stations were initially established as navigation and communication aids and were also for invigilation. Later they were allowed to be used for scientific research. At one time over 100 polar stations operated, the resources of the Arctic coast were investigated and many were exploited. Forced labour was used for much of this work, a system that persisted into the 1960s.

As stations were established, local traffic along the Northern Sea Route increased but through-traffic remained a difficulty. The sinking of the *Chelyuskin* in 1933 and the subsequent amazing rescue of the 'Chelyuskinites' from the ice through aircraft operations was a successful, and very widely publicised, conclusion to a potential tragedy. The next summer *Feodor Litke* made a successful transit with as many as 85 ships operating along different parts of the route. In 1935 four transits were made with local traffic and icebreakers assisting as necessary. Subsequent years showed comparable traffic but severe ice conditions in 1937 resulted in the entrapment of three icebreakers. One, the *Georgiy Sedov*, eventually made a drift comparable to that of the *Fram* and emerged off Svalbard 27 months later.

During this period aviation rapidly increased for exploration and for assisting navigation by spotting ice conditions. Unfortunately, the characteristic Soviet reluctance to let foreigners know what they were doing has resulted in few of these major explorations being known. From the early 1930s surveys and long distance flights rapidly increased as flying expertise improved. Landings were made with increasing frequency on the ice floes which culminated in 1937 in the establishment of the first drift station. This was established by aircraft from Rudolf Island, in the north of Franz Josef Land, as near to the North Pole as conditions permitted (89°26'N on 21 May), and began a drift southwards following the Greenland coast. Four men, commanded by Ivan Papanin, made meteorological, hydrographic and other scientific observations during the drift and were eventually relieved by icebreakers after nine months.

Rudolf Island had become an important centre for air operations. Several Soviet flights fuelled there before penetrating deep into the Arctic. In 1937 two of these, piloted by Mikhail Gromov and Georgiy

Baidukov, started in Moscow and continued over the North Pole to reach the United States three days later. A third trans-Arctic flight was unsuccessful; Sigismund Levenavskiy took off in August 1937 and was never seen again despite searches by many aviators from the North American side. The fate of this flight is another of the unsolved Arctic mysteries.

WWII interrupted nearly all exploratory progress. Just as it began, a German commerce raider, *Komet*, passed through the Northern Sea Route in 1940 to reach the Pacific Ocean. During the rest of the war the route was not used. The polar station on Franz Josef Land was cut off for almost four years but maintained radio contact. At the European side, vast convoys of ships supplied Murmansk – but this is more war history than Arctic history. The German navy needed meteorological forecasting data for many of its operations and covertly established manned and automatic weather stations in several high latitude lands including north Greenland, Nordaustlandet on Svalbard, and Franz Josef Land. These generally lasted only briefly before being detected or were closed for other reasons (one instance was because of an outbreak of trichinosis in Franz Josef Land from eating inadequately cooked bear).

Post-War Developments After the war, the two potential protagonists of any major conflict emerged as the United States and Soviet Union. The shortest routes between them, either absolutely or as measured between major industrial regions, lay across the Arctic. The quantities of long-range weapons, aircraft and missiles available led to the construction, at immense expense, of airfields and chains of radar early warning stations. While the military aspects were dominant, a secondary effect was the opening up of many Arctic regions because of the transport provided. Science, in particular, benefited.

The secrecy and isolation of parts of the Arctic had military significance for another reason: as a test site for nuclear weapons. In 1954 the small civilian population of Novaya Zemlya was removed and a large atomic testing region established there. It was used from 1956 until 1989, during which time 132 bombs were tested. These included submarine, atmospheric and underground explosions. The largest detonation was of a 56 megatonne bomb in the atmosphere, in 1963. This was the most powerful atomic weapon ever tested. The islands and their coasts have also provided disposal sites for radioactive waste.

In 1956 Nikita Khrushchev noted that the Northeast Passage was to become a route for mass transport, and two shipping companies were established to undertake this: in the west the Murmansk Shipping Company and in the east the Far East Shipping Company based in Vladivostok. Improvement in icebreaker technology was essential and nuclear power was the solution to energy requirements. In 1957 the *Lenin* was launched, powered by 32.4MW reactors, and went into service 1959. The experiment was successful and the Soviet

Union developed a major fleet of nuclear icebreakers supplementing a large fleet of diesel powered ones.

The USA specialised in nuclear-powered submarines the first of which, USS *Nautilus*, was launched in 1956. On 3 August 1958 this submarine made a transit of the Arctic from the Bering Sea under the North Pole to the Greenland Sea. On 17 March 1959 the USS *Skate* surfaced at the North Pole, and in 1961 the first Soviet submarine did the same. Covert voyages beneath the pack ice then became regular, with constant improvement of 'cat and mouse' techniques between nuclear submarines of the Soviet, US and British navies.

In the 1950s, defensive and detection stations were established around the entire Arctic by NATO and Warsaw Pact countries. These included large airfields for forward bombing missions, such as on Graham Bell Island in Franz Josef Land and Thule in Greenland. Icebreaker and submarine operations became increasingly common, but all were conducted in great secrecy. The Russian Arctic became virtually closed to foreigners and few Soviet scientists were permitted to visit the stations which became essentially military. One exception was for the experiments of the International Geophysical Year (1957-58) where an unprecedented amount of cooperation in both the Arctic and Antarctic greatly advanced science. In the former it terminated at the conclusion of the programs, but it persists today in the latter, under the Antarctic Treaty system.

North Pole Attained During this period, two notable private expeditions reached the North Pole. In 1968 American Ralph Plaisted, with three companions, used snowmobiles to arrive on 19 April. They abandoned the machines there and flew out. In the next year Wally Herbert, from Britain, led the Trans-Arctic expedition of four men who reached the pole on 6 April by dogsled, while crossing the Arctic Ocean from Alaska to Svalbard. These were the first and second expeditions to have reached that point by surface travel and Herbert's was also the first surface crossing of the ocean. Subsequently several expeditions have crossed the Arctic on the pack ice through the North Pole and many have made one-way surface journeys, leaving by aircraft.

Military aspects dominated the Arctic but the costs of such operations were very severe and became increasingly difficult to sustain. This, and a general change in world affairs, caused the Soviet president, Mikhail Gorbachev, to speak in Murmansk in 1987, promoting international use of the Northern Sea Route and encouraging scientific research in the Arctic. One consequence was the possibility of greater scientific cooperation, which led to the founding of the International Arctic Science Committee (IASC), at Resolute Bay in 1990, by the eight states with territory north of the Arctic Circle. Subsequently another nine states, also involved in Arctic research, have joined.

Many aspects of Arctic research thus became organised in ways not dissimilar to those in the Antarctic where research has been successfully coordinated by the Scientific Committee on Antarctic Research (SCAR) from 1958.

Open Period (1991 to the present)

The enormous and rapid changes in the Soviet Union which began in August 1991, perhaps greater than those which occurred in Russia in 1917, have had profound effects on the Arctic in general and the Russian Arctic in particular. The opening of this previously strongly exclusive region has been a major manifestation of the events. A decade ago the Soviet Arctic was a strictly prohibited region for tourists and other foreigners, and most Russians. Now it is open, although at a price. Passengers, paying in valuta, have been taken to the North Pole on more than 20 voyages, all but one aboard atomic icebreakers, during the decade from 1990, and many groups have visited the magnificent islands and coasts along the Northern Sea Route. Among the many attractions, spectacular geographical features, courageous history, fascinating wildlife and human circumstances are most important.

In the rest of the Arctic, national scientific programs continued, although many suffered from financial shortfalls. On the Russian side, international cooperation and scientific research greatly benefited from the Russian 'openness'. Access for foreigners allowed radio-echo sounding to be conducted through many significant glaciers and similar observations of planetary importance to be made. This aspect of the 'open period' of Arctic history may best be typified by the meeting of three icebreakers at the North Pole on 22 August 1994: *Yamal* from Russia, *Louis S. St-Laurent* from Canada, and *Polar Sea* from the USA.

The current changes also have several adverse ramifications, a large proportion of which affect finance and Russia. All but six of the extensive network of about 100 polar stations, many with excellent long-term meteorological and other data, are now closed (some have been vandalised and become ruined). Many Russian Arctic settlements have recently become wholly or partly abandoned, mainly for economic reasons. In the Arctic in general, the population has declined more than 50% during the 1990s. The reasons elsewhere are: in Canada and Greenland, because of the reduction in military imperatives; in Alaska, because of mineral extraction replacing exploration; and in Svalbard, because of Russian withdrawal from mining. The Arctic population in Scandinavia has, in contrast, remained roughly constant.

INDIGENOUS PEOPLES & CULTURES OF THE ARCTIC

By Dr Mark Nuttall

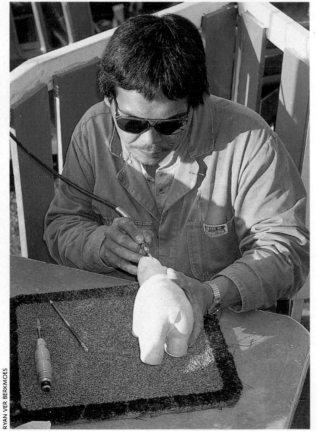

Title Page: photograph by Dr Mark Nuttall

Top: Aleut children in traditional dress, Alaska

Bottom: Inuit craftsman carving local stone, Inuvik, Canada

Often perceived by outsiders as barren, inhospitable and largely un-explored tracts of wilderness, the Arctic regions of Alaska, Canada, Greenland, northern Scandinavia and Siberia are homelands for a diverse number of indigenous peoples who have subsisted for thousands of years on the resources of land and sea, as hunters, fishermen and reindeer herders. In Alaska, these peoples are known as Inupiat and Yup'ik Inuit, Alutiiq (Aleuts) and Athapaskans; in Canada and Greenland they are the Inuit; in Scandinavia the indigenous population is the Sami; while in Siberia indigenous groups include the Chukchi, Even, Evenk, Nenets, Nivkhi, Itelmen and Yukaghir. The Sami also inhabit the Kola Peninsula in north-western Russia, while Yup'ik Inuit also live along the far eastern coasts of Siberia.

The indigenous peoples of the Arctic can all trace similar origins in Central Asia – for example, archaeological research shows that the ancestors of the present-day Greenland Inuit arrived in Alaska from Siberia during the last ice age. These nomadic hunters moved gradually across the vast tundra plains of northern Canada, eventually reaching the mountainous and ice-filled coasts of Greenland some 4500 years ago.

Archaeological and anthropological research also shows that, prior to the arrival of Europeans, Arctic peoples were far from being isolated and many groups came into regular contact with one another, mainly through trade networks. The peoples of north-eastern Siberia and western Alaska, for example, participated in long-distance trade, trade fairs and even warfare. At the same time, they also participated in complex ritual exchanges, festivals and elaborate religious ceremonies. These activities linked them to other ethnic groups in wider-ranging economic, social and ritual and religious networks.

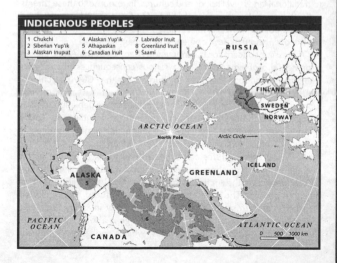

INDIGENOUS PEOPLES

1 Chukchi	4 Alaskan Yup'ik	7 Labrador Inuit
2 Siberian Yup'ik	5 Athapaskan	8 Greenland Inuit
3 Alaskan Inupiat	6 Canadian Inuit	9 Saami

For Alaskan and Siberian peoples, these networks extended across the vast expanses of Siberia, and south to Korea, Japan and China; while Alaskan Inuit and Athapaskans had links with peoples to the east in Canada, and farther south with the numerous Indian groups on the Pacific Northwest coast. Such contacts provided the opportunity for mutual influence in terms of material culture (for example, Chinese pipe styles have been found at prehistoric Alaskan Inuit sites), technology, religious and spiritual beliefs and mythology. The widespread myths about the primeval figure of the Raven, for example, provide strong evidence of contact between the Chukchi and Koryak of Siberia and the peoples of western Alaska.

The indigenous peoples of the Arctic have their own distinctive cultures, economies and forms of social organisation, yet they all share a unique and special relationship to the Arctic environment and to the animals they depend upon which is essential for their economic survival, social identity and spiritual life. This relationship to nature is reflected in a rich mythology and world-view, and in moral and ethical codes that guide people in their relationships to animals and the environment.

Throughout the Arctic, indigenous peoples also share common experiences arising from their encounters with missionaries, traders, whalers, explorers and colonial governments. This is most strikingly evident in the impact of rapid social, cultural and economic change that has swept across the circumpolar north over the last 50 years or so. As they enter the 21st century, the peoples of the Arctic will continue to rely on natural resources for their economic and cultural survival, but they are increasingly tied to the global economy and thus subject to the impact of global processes. Industrial development, oil and gas exploitation, environmental problems, social change, immigration and tourism all pose threats to traditional lands, livelihoods and cultures. In response to these threats, indigenous peoples have fought for, and in some cases have achieved, increased political power and self-determination, as well as a degree of control over resource development and management.

Of pressing concern for the indigenous peoples of the Arctic are environmental problems which have serious consequences not only for traditional livelihoods, but also for human health. PCBs (polychlorinated biphenyls) have already been found in the breast milk of Inuit women and there is concern over the effects of ozone depletion, climate change, transboundary pollution and contaminants in indigenous foods.

Arctic ecosystems are also extremely sensitive to climate change and because of global warming, scientists predict an increase in average Arctic winter temperatures of between three to six times the global average. If these predictions come true, global warming will have a significant impact on the Arctic environment and on the livelihoods of indigenous peoples. The extent of sea ice will be reduced, fish stocks will fluctuate, permafrost will thaw far more quickly in spring, but take longer to refreeze in autumn. Climate change is also likely to disrupt the migration routes of caribou, seals, whales and geese – this will impact upon the hunting, trapping and fishing economies of many small, remote Arctic settlements.

Tourism in the Arctic is also a fast-growing industry, and increasing numbers of tourists regard indigenous cultures as the main attraction in visiting the Arctic, after wildlife and scenery. There is concern, however, over the possible social and environmental impact that may result from tourism development in the Arctic. The first steps have been taken to implement a code of practice for Arctic tourism. For indigenous peoples, tourism in the Arctic offers economic opportunities and there is no doubt that, developed and managed sustainably, it can contribute to small-scale community-based sustainable development.

THE INUIT

The total Inuit population is about 125,000 and occupies a vast geographical area, stretching from east Greenland across the north of Canada to the coasts of Alaska and Chukotka (in the Russian Far East).

For anthropologists, Inuit culture represents one of the most extraordinary environmental adaptations to be found on earth. Traditionally, the Inuit have subsisted on hunting marine and terrestrial mammals and fishing. Today, hunting and fishing remain vital activities for the economies of many communities, but commercial fishing, sheep farming, oil-related business or financial enterprise, among other things, are increasingly important.

The word *Inuit* means 'the people' (singular: *inuk* – 'person') and is applied generally across the Arctic. However, it obscures the diversity of Inuit groups, who are known as Kalaallit and Inughuit in Greenland; Inuit and Inuvialuit in Canada; Inupiat, Yup'ik and Alutiiq in Alaska; and Yup'ik in Siberia. Nevertheless, 'Inuit' as a more general term of reference was adopted by the Inuit Circumpolar Conference (ICC, a nongovernmental organisation (NGO) representing the rights and interests of all Inuit) in 1977 in preference to the term 'Eskimo', which means 'eaters of raw meat' in the Athapaskan language (while 'Eskimo' is seen as a derogatory term in Greenland and Canada, this is not the case in Alaska).

The First Peoples

From the archaeological, linguistic, cultural and physical anthropological evidence, it is the view of most scholars that the Inuit have their origins in Siberia and possibly in Central Asia. Using artefacts found at ancient Siberian sites in the Lake Baikal region, dating back some 12,000 to 25,000 years, archaeologists have constructed a picture of a wide-ranging, seminomadic culture that survived by hunting large animals such as reindeer, woolly rhinoceros, muskox and mammoth. These people lived in semisubterranean houses constructed from sod, stones, reindeer antlers, animal bones and animal skins during winter and in skin tents during summer.

Most likely, some groups moved progressively northward to the coasts of North-East Asia and there is evidence of similar hunting cultures living on the shores of the Bering Sea at least 18,000 years ago. These people, who are now regarded as the Paleo-Inuit ancestors of the present-day Inuit, entered the New World by crossing Beringia, an intercontinental land bridge connecting Siberia to Alaska, although water crossings were also probably made in skin boats similar to the ones still used by Yup'ik Inuit today.

Rather than resulting from a large-scale migration from Asia, the peopling of Arctic North America was a gradual process, beginning with the exploration of new hunting grounds instead of a search for new land to settle. Initially, the Paleo-Arctic hunters probably maintained a home base on the Siberian side of Beringia, with some occasional forays over to the Alaskan side in search of game. As the animals these people depended on for food gradually moved eastward from North-East Asia as a result of major climatic changes during the last ice age and the immediate postglacial period, several waves of Paleo-Arctic peoples did the same and began to range far and wide in search of game in Alaska, eventually moving into Canada and across the tundra and northern shores of the North American Arctic.

The ancestors of present-day Alaska Natives can be traced to two distinct migrations, which occurred between 5000 and 10,000 years ago. The first migration was of inland Na-Dene-speaking groups, which includes the present-day Athapaskans of Alaska, northern Canada, British Columbia and California. The second migration, around 7000 years ago, was of Aleut-Inuit-speaking groups which arrived in North America with a maritime-focused culture and mode of subsistence. Around 4000 years ago, the Aleut and Inuit groups diverged and developed similar, yet distinct, ways of life. This is a crucial date in the chronology of Arctic peoples, because from this time archaeologists and anthropologists have been able to trace, with fair accuracy, the social, economic and technological development of the many Inuit groups of Alaska, Canada and Greenland.

Left: Inuit ice fishing

This development began with the Northern Archaic period, charac-terised by Arctic hunting groups utilising a variety of simple hunting implements made of bone, stone and pebbles. Between 3000 and 2000 BC what is known as the Arctic Small Tool Tradition, a more so-phisticated culture based on the hunting of caribou and other tundra animals (with some limited sea mammal hunting), developed in north-west Alaska. The oldest archaeological sites identified as Inuit in south-west Alaska and the Aleutian Islands date from around 2000 BC, and this period of development is known as the Norton culture. This culture focused almost entirely on sea mammal hunting and spread along the coasts of the Bering and Chukchi seas. A famous example of the Norton culture, although a northern variant and perhaps not typical of the earlier south-western Alaskan sites, is Ipiutak at Point Hope on the North Slope. The Ipiutak site consists of more than 600 houses and is a rich source of information about early north Alaskan life.

Around 1800 BC, at the same time that people were still living at Ipiutak, more socially complex and hierarchical forms of Inuit society, known as the Old Whaling or Bering Sea culture, and other related cul-tures emerged along the coasts of north-eastern Siberia and the Bering Strait region of Alaska. These people hunted sea and land mammals from permanent coastal settlements and their culture and mode of sub-sistence closely resembles that of the Inuit in historical and contact times. They travelled by *qajaq* (kayak) and *umiaq* (skin-covered boats mainly rowed by women) in summer and dogsleds in winter, and were perhaps more dependent on the abundance of walrus populations for their continuous settlement of this area.

Another cultural development was that of the Birnirk people, who coexisted for some time in north-west Alaska with the Ipiutak, but eventually replaced them and became the dominant culture in north-ern Alaska. Their subsistence economy was based on caribou and fish, as well as sea mammals, but declining caribou populations (whether as a result of overhunting or changing ecological conditions) forced the Birnirk people to hone their sea mammal hunting skills and techniques. In particular, captains of whaling boats (as well as their wives) were ac-corded prestige within the society, and were highly respected for their knowledge of whales and for their skill and prowess in hunting. The contemporary Inupiat Inuit culture derives from the Birnirk people, as did the Thule culture which migrated as far as Greenland, and to this day they remain first and foremost highly skilled hunters of the sea.

By the time that the Birnirk people were chasing the mighty bowhead whale off the icy coasts of Alaska, Inuit groups had migrated across the North American Arctic and through central Canada, into Quebec and Labrador, and on to Greenland.

The coastal areas of Greenland have been inhabited by Inuit groups for about 4500 years. The first Paleo-Inuit migrants arrived in the far north of the island between 2500 and 2000 BC. These people were nomads from the Canadian High Arctic who depended mainly on terrestrial mammals such as muskox, and successive waves of migrants exploited both land and sea resources such as caribou, seals, whales and walrus.

What archaeologists call the Dorset culture flourished in eastern Canada and Greenland between 1000 and 1300 AD, but between 1000 and 1200 AD the Thule Inuit had mainly overrun the Dorset in some parts of the High Arctic and had reached northern Greenland. It was in Greenland and Labrador that the first European settlers in North America, the Norse, who had made their way across the North Atlantic in their wooden longboats from Norway to Iceland and beyond, met with the Thule people, whom they called *skrælings*.

Traditional Culture & Subsistence

It is always dangerous to simplify the complex, and in a short chapter it is impossible to discuss all Inuit groups in detail. Inuit cultures, both past and present, are diverse, but there are specific features of Inuit life that can be identified so as to paint a composite picture of the culture of the peoples that Europeans first came into contact with. From the 15th and 16th centuries onward, Europeans came into regular and prolonged contact with Inuit, visiting the Arctic first as whalers and explorers, then as traders, colonisers and administrators. They were able to observe at first hand a superbly adapted culture in what they saw only as a frozen wasteland.

The Inuit depended first and foremost on seals, whales and other sea mammals, caribou and fish. Seals provided the staple food throughout the year, for both humans and dogs, and sealskins were used to make clothing and shelter. Other parts of the seal provided materials for making boats, fishing lines, harpoon lines and, crucially, oil for heating and light.

Social organisation was built around the immediate kin group, and social obligations to help one's kin and to share meat and fish were key cultural principals. Groups were on the whole small in number, based around nuclear families, and largely nomadic. In summer, families travelled over hunting and fishing grounds and lived in skin tents, while in winter families tended to group together and live in semipermanent settlements. Winter houses were semisubterranean and made of stone and sod, with a frame of driftwood, whalebone or caribou antler.

Left: Seals and caribou provided the Inuit with the essentials of survival: food, clothing and shelter.

During long winter journeys, some Canadian Inuit groups built shelters from blocks of snow (the common misconception is that these shelters were called igloos, when in fact *iglu* or *illu* is the Inuit word for 'house'). Summer transportation was by qajaq or umiaq, or by foot across the tundra; while in winter the dogsled was more or less known by all Inuit groups.

Traditional clothing for men and women consisted of watertight boots, trousers and a parka, all made mainly from sealskin or caribou fur.

Traditional Inuit religious beliefs were animistic – they lived in an aware world where everything in the universe had a spirit which could affect the lives and fortunes of humans. Much of daily life was spent not only trying to procure food but ensuring that taboos and rituals were observed so as to avoid harming the spirits of animals. The shaman was a prominent figure in all Inuit communities, someone who had the knowledge and power to influence and control the spirits that were all-pervasive throughout the natural world.

Eskimo or Inuit?

Although they're often referred to as Eskimos by outsiders, most people of that group prefer to be called *Inuit*, which means 'the people'. Alternative words include *Yup'ik* or *Inupiaq*, in reference to groups in Canada and Alaska, or *Kalaallit*, which refers specifically to the Greenlandic people.

The word 'Eskimo' (a disparaging Athapaskan word meaning 'eaters of raw meat') is still considered acceptable in Alaska, where most Inuit people still refer to themselves as Eskimos when they speak English. The Alaskan government and most other Alaskans generally refer to the Yup'ik and Inupiaq peoples as 'Alaska Natives' (with an upper case 'N'), and lump them together with the Athapaskan, Tlingit, Haida, Tsimshian and Aleut peoples as a single indigenous lobbying group. The word 'native' (with a lower case 'n') generally refers to anyone, of any ethnic origin, born in Alaska.

In Canada and Greenland, however, the word 'Eskimo' is normally used exclusively to refer to the early aboriginal Arctic dwellers; for example, any ruins not attributed to Europeans or other Native groups are often locally known as 'Eskimo ruins'. In this book, 'Eskimo' is used only in that context, but in the modern Arctic – among members of those groups – it may also refer disparagingly to individuals who behave crudely or in an uncivilised manner. On occasion, it may also be used in jest, much as an Australian might call their best friend 'ratbag' or 'shit-for-brains'.

To avoid confusion or unintentional offence, visitors would probably do best sticking to simply 'Alaskans', 'Canadians', 'Greenlanders', 'Russians' etc, to refer to Arctic residents of any ethnic origin.

A wealth of Inuit myths have been collected from all over the Arctic by missionaries, travellers and anthropologists, and these deal with the daily concerns of the Inuit – the preparation for a successful hunt, the appeasement of animal spirits, and the intricate relations between humans, animals and the environment. As we shall see later in this chapter, despite the conversion of the Inuit to Christianity, traditional beliefs concerning human-environment and human-animal relations, and about the reincarnation of the human soul, have not entirely disappeared.

The Modern Inuit: Social Change & Self-Determination

Today, there is considerable unity in the diversity of Inuit cultures in that, despite the many regional variations, there are remarkably similar features in all Inuit languages, forms of social organisation and economic activity, and belief systems. The Inuit fall within the following geographical and cultural groupings today: the Greenland Inuit (living on the west, north-west and east coasts of the country); the Canadian Inuit (living in Labrador, Quebec, Nunavut and the Northwest Territories); the Alaskan Inuit, who are divided into Inupiat, Yup'ik and Alutiiq/Sugpiaq peoples (living in the northern, western and southwestern parts of the state); and the Siberian Yup'ik of Chukotka in north-eastern Siberia.

In this section, each of these groups is discussed briefly, with particular focus on recent experiences of rapid social and economic change and movements for self-determination and self-government.

Greenland Inuit In Greenland the Inuit population comprises three distinct cultural and linguistic groups: the majority Kalaallit, who inhabit the west coast from Nanortalik district in the south to Upernavik district in the north; Inughuit (popularly known as the Polar Inuit and famous for being the world's most northerly indigenous inhabitants) in the north around Avanersuaq/Thule; and Iit on the east coast. Since Home Rule was introduced in Greenland in 1979, the country has been known officially as Kalaallit Nunaat (the Greenlanders' Land), although both 'Inuit' and 'Greenlanders' are used as more generic and interchangeable terms to refer to the indigenous population.

European settlement in Greenland can be traced to 985 AD, when the Icelander Erik the Red was banished from his homeland, sailed west to Greenland and established two colonies in the south and southwest. The Norse settlements existed for almost 500 years, longer than the current European settlement of the Americas. They subsisted as farmers, keeping cattle, sheep and goats, and marine mammal hunters.

Contact between Greenland and the rest of the Scandinavian world was severed in the early part of the 15th century, and scholars have put forward several theories in an attempt to discover what happened to the Norse settlements. The Icelandic sagas record that the Norse communities in Greenland knew of, and most likely came into contact with, an indigenous people they called skrælings.

In the 16th and 17th centuries, the Greenland Inuit had experienced contact with European whalers and explorers, and Danish colonisation dates from 1721. For over 200 years the Danes followed an isolationist policy toward Greenland and the indigenous Inuit. The Danes controlled trade and Greenland was effectively a closed country. After WWII, however, Denmark ended its isolationist policy and emphasis was placed on social welfare and on infrastructural change as part of a process of modernisation of both the country and of Inuit society. Commercial fishing was placed at the centre of policies of economic development and people were moved from small hunting settlements and resettled in larger towns on the west coast.

By the late 1960s and early 1970s, Greenlandic Inuit society had been transformed from one based primarily on small-scale subsistence hunting and fishing to a modern, export-oriented economy. The majority of the Inuit population were now living in the fast-growing west coast towns and this demographic transition brought its own problems. Life in the settlements had been characterised by, and organised around, kinship. Movement to the towns led to the disruption of kin-based groups and individuals experienced alienation, social and economic marginality and discrimination, made worse by ethnic tensions and increasing numbers of Danes, who were living in Greenland because of the need for construction workers, teachers, doctors and administrators.

One direct result of these social changes and upheavals was the emergence of Inuit political parties and a heightened sense of Inuit identity. Greenlandic politicians and political activists began to campaign for Home Rule in the early 1970s and by 1979 this had become a reality. Greenlanders thus became the first population of Inuit origin to have achieved a degree of self-government. While Greenland remains a part of the kingdom of Denmark, the Home Rule Authorities have embarked on an ambitious policy of nation building. Fishing for cod and shrimp is vital to the economy of the country as a whole, and many small communities still depend on marine mammal hunting, but in the future Greenland is likely to develop its rich minerals and hydrocarbons.

Canadian Inuit The Canadian Inuit inhabit the entire length of the Canadian north, from the Mackenzie Delta region near the border with Alaska, to Baffin Island and farther south in Quebec and Labrador. The Inuit of the Mackenzie Delta region prefer to call themselves Inuvialuit, while Inuit is used as a term of reference and address elsewhere in the Canadian north. Until the middle of the 20th century many Inuit groups in Canada still retained a seminomadic lifestyle based around the hunting of seals and caribou.

In Canada, the powerful Hudson's Bay Company dominated the country's fur trade from the time it received its charter in 1670 right up to the early 20th century. During this period, the Canadian Inuit became dependent on the Hudson's Bay Company trading posts, cultural values were changed and the spiritual relationship between the Inuit and the animals they hunted was altered.

In the 20th century, the Inuit continued to be dependent upon the fur trade, but their lives were also affected by the expansion of other forms of economic development, such as mining and the exploitation of hydrocarbons. Following WWII, there was an expansion of mining activity and, together with the development of hydroelectric projects, this reinforced a southern Canadian vision of the far north as a vast storehouse of natural resources, the development and exploitation of which was regarded as necessary for the future of the Canadian nation. In recent years, major industrial projects have been opposed by environmentalists and Native peoples, fearful of the social and environmental impacts development may have on the Canadian north.

The effects of economic development on the Canadian Inuit have already been considerable. Government resettlement policies only exacerbated the erosion of the Inuit subsistence hunting culture, and the Inuit have been drawn into a position of greater dependency on Canadian government and institutions. The presence in small Inuit settlements of large numbers of southern Canadians who went north to work as administrators, trade managers, teachers and construction workers caused considerable resentment among Inuit, and ethnic conflict between the two groups was common.

Since the 1950s, the prevailing Canadian government attitude has been one of incorporating the Inuit into the mainstream economic, social and cultural life of Canada. While it is easy to judge this as misguided from today's perspective, it is important to recognise that this was a paternalistic attitude and that successive Canadian governments believed they were doing a good thing for the Inuit. After all, in the popular imagination as well as in official legislation, the Inuit were believed to be living on the edge of starvation in a barren, inhospitable wilderness. Through education and training, the indigenous inhabitants of the Arctic were to become modern Canadians, able to improve their lifestyle options and take their place in the new period of economic development on the Canadian Arctic frontier.

In response to social change and large-scale economic development, the Canadian Inuit have attempted to achieve self-determination in recent decades. Faced with oil and gas development in the Mackenzie Delta, the Inuvialuit formed the Committee of Original People's Entitlement (COPE) in 1969, and in 1971 the Inuit Tapirisat of Canada (ITC) was founded in Ottawa as a voice for Inuit throughout Canada's north. In 1984 the Inuvialuit Final Agreement gave 35,000 sq miles of the Northwest Territories to the Inuvialuit, together with financial compensation and other rights (including gas, petroleum and mineral rights in 5000 sq miles) in return for their surrendering further territorial claims. In 1975 the Inuit of northern Quebec signed a land claims agreement against the backdrop of controversy surrounding hydro-electric development in James Bay.

In 1992 the Tungavik Federation of Nunavut and the government of Canada signed an agreement which addressed Inuit land claims and harvesting rights and committed the federal government to establishing Nunavut (our land) in the Canadian eastern Arctic. Nunavut was inaugurated on 1 April 1999 and comprises some 200 million hectares of northern Canada. The majority population of Nunavut is some 80% Inuit and the government is effectively Inuit-led. However, the settlement did not create a new ethnic Inuit state, but public government within the limits defined by the Canadian constitution. Nonetheless, Nunavut has given the Inuit of the eastern Arctic a greater degree of autonomy and self-government than any other indigenous group in Canada.

Alaskan Inuit The Alaskan Inuit are the most diverse of all the Inuit populations. The Inupiat Inuit (singular: 'Inupiaq') inhabit the Arctic tundra plains of Alaska's North Slope, the boreal forests of the northwest, and the coastal lowlands of the Bering Sea. The other major group, the Yup'ik Inuit, live along the coasts and rivers of south-west Alaska. In the south, around Cook Inlet, the Kenai Peninsula, Kodiak Island and the Alaska Peninsula, live the Alutiiq and Sugpiaq-speaking peoples who have been traditionally referred to in the anthropological literature as Pacific Inuit.

Prior to European contact, the coastal Inupiat Inuit specialised in hunting the bowhead whale, walrus, seal and polar bear, while the social and cultural life of inland groups revolved around caribou hunting. Today, whaling and the hunting of other marine mammals remains a strong part of Inupiat culture and economic life. Whaling has meant that a distinctive and more socially stratified society has emerged on the North Slope. Social status has traditionally been determined by the skill and knowledge of the hunter, and the hunter's ability to catch an abundance of game and thus share out meat throughout the community. The captain of a whaling crew is known as an *umialik* and the umialik and his wife have traditionally held a high social position in Inupiat Inuit society.

In complete contrast to the Inupiat of the North Slope, the Yup'ik peoples of south-west Alaska inhabit a subarctic landscape rich in natural resources. The Yup'ik are seal hunters, although beluga whales and walrus are also harvested, and take advantage of the abundance of different types of fish found at sea and in the many thousands of kilometres of rivers that cut across the Yup'ik homeland. The Yup'ik are renowned for their complex ceremonial traditions. For example, elaborate masks carved from wood, or made from sealskin, and depicting animal spirits and mythical figures, are worn at community feasts and dances to celebrate the memory of the ancestors.

The Pacific Inuit of southern Alaska comprise a number of groups who prefer to see themselves as either Aleut, Koniag, Alutiiq or Sugpiaq-speaking people. They inhabit largely mountainous coastal areas and traditionally combine whaling, sealing and fishing. Traditionally, Pacific Inuit societies had higher population densities and were more hierarchically complex in terms of social organisation.

The European discovery of Alaska is accredited to Vitus Bering, a Danish explorer on a Russian expedition, in 1741. When Bering's expedition returned home with sea otter furs, the subsequent course of Alaska's economic development based on the exploitation of its natural resources was set.

Alaska was prominent in both the Russian and British fur trades and, over a period of 140 years, fur seals, sea otters and some species of fur-bearing land mammal were exploited to near extinction. Beginning in 1847, American whalers from New England hunted the bowhead whale in the waters of Bering Strait, thus seriously affecting the viability of the indigenous Inupiat hunt. From the 1880s, gold mining formed the basis for the expansion of the Alaskan economy and its subsequent settlement by nonindigenous peoples, and the agenda for Alaska's late 20th/early 21st century economic development was fixed with the discovery of vast reserves of oil and gas at Prudhoe Bay on the North Slope in 1968.

The integration of the indigenous Inupiat and Yup'ik Inuit peoples into mainstream American social, cultural and economic life has followed a pattern similar to the experiences of Inuit groups living elsewhere in the Arctic. The encounter with whalers, traders, missionaries and administrators has meant disease, exploitation, rapid social and cultural change, and economic and social dependency. Whalers and traders had already partly disrupted the indigenous Inupiat spiritual belief system by the time the first Presbyterian missionaries arrived on the North Slope at the end of the 19th century. Catholic missionaries, however, who arrived in the Yup'ik area of south-west Alaska at the same time, found that the Native people had been more resistant to the influence of outside religious beliefs and practices, especially those of the Russian Orthodox Church, and traditional spiritual beliefs still provided the foundation of much daily life.

In both the Inupiat and Yup'ik areas, missionaries soon established boarding schools and assumed responsibility for religious and secular education until federal schools were established in the first half of the 20th century. Until the mid-1970s, the education system in rural Alaska's Native communities was assimilationist in aim. Native children were to be educated as citizens of the USA and many had to leave their home villages for a high school education. In 1975 a revision in the administration of education established regional schools districts and village high schools. While this went some way to empowering communities with regard to education, the education curriculum remained the same. Native schoolchildren learned the same subjects as children elsewhere in the USA. Today, while schools in rural Alaska are effectively under local control, they remain institutions that are not really part of the social and cultural fabric of Native communities.

During the 20th century, there were improvements in health care and the Alaskan Inuit population steadily increased, more hunters and trappers moved to larger villages from smaller, remote settlements, customary subsistence activities declined and alternative employment opportunities became available both in the villages and in other parts of Alaska. While hunting and trapping remain an important and integral part of the Inupiat and Yup'ik village economies, many people now find permanent and seasonal employment in commercial fishing, in the oil industry and in urban centres such as Anchorage and Fairbanks.

The discovery of oil at Prudhoe Bay on Alaska's North Slope, together with fears of other large-scale industrial development, resulted in the establishment of the Alaska Federation of Natives (AFN). The AFN lobbied the United States Congress for the appropriate settlement of land claims for Alaska Natives and, in 1971, the US Congress passed the Alaska Native Land Claims Settlement Act (ANCSA). ANCSA did not recognise a Native claim to the whole of the state of Alaska, but it did establish 12 regional Native corporations, giving them effective control over one-ninth of the state. ANCSA extinguished Native claims to the rest of Alaska and US$962.5 million was given in compensation. By doing this, ANCSA made Alaska's Native people shareholders in corporate-owned land.

Siberian Yup'ik The Siberian Yup'ik speak one of four Yup'ik dialects (the others – mainland Yup'ik, Pacific Yup'ik and Nunivak Yup'ik, are spoken in Alaska), but it is a dialect perhaps linguistically more closely related to the language spoken by the Chukchi of Siberia. The Siberian Yup'ik communities are thinly scattered along the isolated coasts of Chukotka in north-western Siberia, and the entire population numbers around 2000 people. The Siberian Yup'ik economy has revolved traditionally around the hunting of bowhead and grey whales, seals, walrus, caribou and polar bears. Like other Inuit groups, their social organisation, culture, spiritual beliefs, religious practices and mythology have been inextricably linked to the animals they depend on for survival.

Contact between Siberian Yup'ik and Europeans first occurred in the 10th century, but it was only in the 18th century that regular and prolonged contact began to take place with Russians. Once this contact was established, a familiar pattern followed, whereby Siberian Yup'ik communities experienced wave after wave of epidemics, including smallpox, mumps, influenza and chickenpox, which seriously affected the demographic composition of north-eastern Siberia.

The Yup'ik also suffered the extreme impact of Soviet economic policies during the 20th century. The Soviets established the Committee of the North in 1928 and Yup'ik economic life was collectivised

through the organisation of boat crews into seasonal hunting coopera-
tives. Following the end of WWII, many Yup'ik villages were closed
down by the Soviet authorities and the inhabitants were resettled in
Chukchi villages. This set in motion a process, which is continuing
today, of social and cultural integration with the Chukchi population.
At this time, Soviet hunting collectives dominated whale and walrus
hunting along the coast of Chukotka, almost decimating stocks, and
this monopolisation of a vital economic activity for the indigenous
population made it extremely difficult for Yup'ik boat crews to land
whales or walrus and thus undermined the subsistence culture.

In the 1950s and 1960s what was left of traditional Yup'ik culture
and livelihoods was marginalised even further, as a process of resettlement reduced the number of Siberian Yup'ik villages from 50 to 12.
Major social, economic and infrastructural changes swept across the
region – roads, pipelines, nuclear power plants and military installations
had a massive impact on the human and physical environment. During
the Cold War, the Soviets were also nervous about the proximity of the
USA to Siberia, and about the Yup'ik population on Big Diomede
Island and the village of Naukan who were related to the Alaskan
Yup'ik on the other side of the Soviet-American border. To prevent
contact (and possible US-inspired espionage) between the Siberian and
Alaskan Yup'ik communities, the Soviets removed the people from Big
Diomede and Naukan.

Through the institutions of Russian society, such as government and
education, attempts were made to bring the Yup'ik into the mainstream of Russian social, cultural and economic life. Yup'ik children, like
children from other indigenous communities, were sent to village
schools or to boarding schools because of a policy of Russification.
They were expected to go through entirely the same education system
as Russian children in urban areas, such as Moscow, Leningrad and
Kiev, and to learn a totally new view of the world which was quite different from the cultural upbringing they had so far experienced as
Yup'ik. Yup'ik children became dependent on the state and, in many
cases, also lost the ability to speak their own language. Yup'ik hunters
and fishers were also deprived of their traditional livelihoods and many
soon had no other choice but to enter the wage economy, mostly by
becoming labourers in menial jobs, either in the villages or in Soviet
construction projects, or by working in collective fox farms.

Despite the tremendous changes that have transformed much of
their traditional life, the Siberian Yup'ik have maintained a distinctive
ethnic identity within Russia. In many ways, this identity has strengthened since the collapse of the Soviet Union in 1991. The Siberian Yup'ik
have formed organisations concerned with cultural survival and self-
determination, which are themselves members of the Russian Association of the Peoples of the North (RAPN). Big Diomede and Naukan were
resettled by Siberian Yup'ik in 1992 and throughout the 1990s economic, cultural and political links have been established with Inuit in

Alaska. Collectivisation is no longer the means by which economic life is organised and the Siberian Yup'ik are free to resume traditional hunting. However, this is also a matter of economic and cultural survival, as the collapse of the Soviet Union and the subsequent economic crisis affecting the Russian Federation has made the links between Siberian Yup'ik villages and the rest of Russia increasingly tenuous. Marine mammal hunting has once again become vital to the Yup'ik coastal communities of the Russian Far East, as it has for the Chukchi (see The Chukchi section later in this chapter). However, because knowledge and skills surrounding whaling had mostly disappeared in the small Siberian Yup'ik communities, in the mid-1990s the Siberians appealed to Alaskan whalers for assistance in obtaining appropriate whaling technology and training in the process of whaling once more. Alaska's North Slope Borough thus set up a project with the American Russian Center of the University of Alaska Anchorage, which aimed to help Siberian Yup'ik document local knowledge about marine mammals and teach local hunters to relearn long-forgotten hunting skills.

Languages & Dialects

The diversity of Inuit culture is reflected in the different languages and dialects spoken across a vast geographical area, extending from the Bering Sea area to the coast of Denmark Strait in east Greenland. Languages and dialects spoken by Inuit represent a sub-branch of the Inuit-Aleut language family.

Linguists have identified a major linguistic division into two languages, Inuit/Inupiaq and Yup'ik. Inuit/Inupiaq is spoken in northern Alaska (where it is called Inupiaq), in Canada (where it is called Inuktitut) and in Greenland (where it is called Kalaallisut). Yup'ik is spoken in south-western Alaska and in the Siberian Yup'ik villages.

However, within these two major languages, there are many variations. In Alaska different dialects are spoken by Inupiat, Yup'ik and Alutiiq peoples; in Canada there are major distinctions between the languages spoken by Inuvialuit in the western Arctic and Inuit in Nunavut Territory; while in Siberia several Yup'ik dialects are spoken. In Greenland, there are major differences in west Greenland, in Avanersuaq (Thule) and Tasiilaq (Ammassalik). In west Greenland alone there are many regional sub-dialects.

Although the various Inuit languages and dialects are all agglutinative and follow similar rules regarding the construction of words from roots and postbases, they differ in vocabulary, pronunciation and variations in the use of the same word. Furthermore, while a Greenlandic speaker from Nuuk may be able to converse with an Inuktitut speaker from Baffin Island, those same speakers may have difficulty conversing in their own languages with a Yup'ik speaker from south-west Alaska.

Inuit languages, like many minority languages, were long perceived as primitive languages, and thus unable to express sophisticated, abstract and intellectual thought. This could not be further from the truth, however, and it is misguided to see Inuit languages as primitive languages. Greenlandic, for example, is able to express complex concepts and has evolved a new vocabulary in response to political, social and economic change. Indeed, Greenland has a long history of publishing works in Greenlandic and a publishing house has been in existence in Greenland since the 1850s. Early on in the 18th century, the missionaries had translated the Bible into Greenlandic. And not only have many classics been translated into Greenlandic, but Greenland also has a rich tradition of novel writing and poetry of its own (see the Arctic Literature chapter).

Rather than using loan words, many imported items have been rendered intelligible in Greenlandic in descriptive terms. For example, when sugar was introduced to the Inuit for the first time, they called it *siorasat* (looks like sand), while coins were called *aningaasat* (looks like the moon). A motorboat is a *pujortuleeraq* (makes a little smoke), while an aeroplane is *timmisartoq* (something that flies).

English remains a direct threat to Inuit dialects in the Canadian north and in Alaska, whereas Greenlandic is a strong language. That it is the everyday language of government, education, commerce, broadcasting and the church has helped in this respect. As Inuit dialects are under threat elsewhere in the Arctic, Greenlandic clearly demonstrates that the language of the Inuit can evolve a more technical, economic and political vocabulary to cope with the challenges and demands of the modern world.

Kinship & the Person

Kinship and family life is the very essence of social organisation in many Inuit communities. Perhaps the most striking aspect of Inuit kinship is that it is not always based on biological or genealogical relationships. Kinship is an inherently flexible way of organising social relationships. In fact, Inuit tend to see social relationships in terms of kinship or non-kinship. In short, if a person considers another person, who is not related by biology or through marriage, a relative, then those people can become relatives if they wish to. All they need to do is consider each other a relative and refer to each other by using an appropriate kin term. This works both ways, of course, and a person can also deny that a kinship relationship exists!

There may be various, and often complex, personal or pragmatic reasons for deciding that someone is a relative or not. Two unrelated persons who have a particularly strong friendship may wish to commemorate it by turning it into a kinship relationship. More practical reasons for choosing one's kin may relate to subsistence activities, where a man may have no brothers but may need to depend on close male kin for participating in hunting and fishing. In this way, friends who help out may be regarded as kin and the relationship established with a kinship term.

The Inuit commonly believe in a multiplicity of human souls as spiritual components of the person. The person consists of three souls: the personal soul, the breath or free soul, and the name soul. Myths and stories surrounding human souls and human reincarnation are universal themes in Inuit culture. In Greenland, for example, Inuit believe that after death the personal soul travels either to the underworld, a place with an abundance of game animals and where the souls of dead kin and friends would be reunited, or to an upper world of starvation and cold. The breath or free soul, however, can leave the body at will, often when a person is sleeping. It may have to be retrieved by a shaman if it strays too far.

Throughout Greenland, Canada, Alaska and Chukotka, Inuit believe that a person's name is also a soul. The name soul is the person's source of life and physical and spiritual strength, important for identity and health. Upon death, the name soul leaves a person's body and is said to remain 'homeless' until it is called back to reside in the body of a newborn child. When a child receives the name of a recently deceased person, the social and spiritual essence of that person is reincarnated in the newborn. Names have immense power and some of the good personal qualities of the deceased are inherited by the receiver of the name. Many myths and stories tell of the name soul's wanderings after death. Through the name soul, the deceased become the guardian spirits of their descendants.

Traditionally, Inuit believed that the body, as the material part of the person, was subject to disease and decay, but that souls were prone to attack by evil spirits. The Netsilik Inuit of the central Canadian Arctic, for example, believed that all physical illness was the result of malevolent spirits inhabiting a person's body and hurting the soul, while Inupiat Inuit believed illness to be the result of the temporary departure of the soul from the body.

If a person's soul happened to stray too far from their body then that person would die unless a shaman could first find and then retrieve the lost soul. After a person's death there were often quite elaborate taboos that had to be observed and rituals that needed to be practised to ensure that the deceased's soul was properly cared for and did not remain cold, lonely and homeless. If taboos and rituals were not correctly observed then malevolent spirits would cause poor health, illness and even famine.

There was a danger that human souls could themselves become malevolent spirits; the shaman, as well as being a benign figure of spiritual strength, also had the power to cause harm and bring illness. The Inupiat of Arctic Alaska, for example, believed illness to be the result of soul loss or the intrusion of a foreign object by a malevolent shaman who used his extensive spirit powers for personal advantage and gain.

In Inuit mythology, when a person dies their souls joins the souls of other deceased persons, which are waiting to be reborn, to form the aurora borealis, the northern lights. A Labrador Inuit myth tells of a great abyss at the end of the world. The souls of the deceased must cross this abyss by a dangerous pathway, which leads to the land of the dead through a hole in the sky. The souls of those who have already crossed over safely light torches, thus forming the aurora borealis, so that the souls of those who have recently died may be guided to the heavens.

In other variants of aurora myths, the souls of those who go to the land of the dead can be seen feasting and playing ball with a walrus skull and this appears as the northern lights. Variants from Greenland and Canada relate how the souls of the dead make a crackling sound as they run over the frost-hardened snow of the heavens. Because the souls of the dead are waiting to be reborn on earth, they do not wish to remain apart from the living for too long and try to communicate with them by whistling. When a living person hears this whistling, they must respond with a soft whistle or whisper, and the northern lights will come closer to earth out of curiosity.

Humans & Animals: The Ideology of Hunting

Hunting animals, particularly marine mammals such as seals and whales, remains the basis for Inuit cultural and economic life across the Arctic. Animals provide meat for food and furs for clothing, and indeed make life in the Arctic possible. But hunting is not just the exploitation of animals for economic reasons. Through hunting, humans interact and engage with the natural world, and Inuit cultural identity is founded upon and derives meaning from this interaction and from the relationships between persons, animals and the environment.

In the Inuit world-view, animals have souls that must be propitiated. Human beings must follow a code of correct ways of acting in relation to animals, and Inuit myths and stories emphasise the spiritual relationship between humans and animals. Animals are conceptualised as nonhuman persons, endowed with consciousness and intelligence and some species of animal are said to live in communities which are similar in social organisation to human communities. For example, the Alaskan and Siberian Yup'ik say that seals live according to the same kinds of rules that humans are subject to. Yup'ik stories describe how young seals learn appropriate rules from their elders, such as knowing the dangers of approaching a hunter who appears to be a careless and disrespectful person.

The dependence on animals for food is reflected in community hunting regulations and in patterns of sharing and gift-giving. In seal hunting households in Greenland and Canada, for example, the meat, fat and skin of the seal is utilised. There is rarely much wasted. Complex and precise local rules exist which determine the sharing and distribution of the catch, and seal meat is commonly shared out to people beyond the household, whether those people are related to the hunter or not.

The cultural expression of respect for animals and animal souls is manifested in first-catch celebrations. At an early age, boys are taken on hunting trips with their fathers, who teach them the skills and impart the knowledge necessary to be a successful hunter. When a boy catches his first seal, he will give gifts of meat to every household in his community and people are invited to his parents' home for coffee or tea and cake. A first-catch celebration is not only a recognition by the community of the boy's development as a hunter, it is a statement of the vitality and cultural importance of the hunting way of life.

Like other Arctic peoples, the Inuit believe that animals and all other aspects of the natural world, such as lakes, rivers, the sun and the moon, have souls, just as humans do. Indeed, this spiritual essence is shared between humans, animals and natural phenomena and reminds human beings that they are not unique, but are part of a transcendent universe in which everything emanates from the same spiritual source.

Among all Inuit groups, the souls of animals are particularly significant, and ritual and ceremonial life is often devoted entirely to ensuring that the souls of whales, polar bears, walrus, seals and caribou receive proper treatment and respect. Because humans, animals and everything in the natural world share the same spiritual essence, the Arctic environment is essentially a dangerous and uncertain one, and not just because of the extreme physical conditions that the Inuit have to endure. Part of this danger is due to the fact that, as all Inuit food consists of souls, offences by an individual against animals and spirits in the natural world can cause pain to the souls of recently killed animals and entice vindictive and malevolent spirits, putting entire human communities at risk. Mistreatment of an animal or the failure to observe a taboo may result in poor hunting, illness, misfortune, famine and bad weather.

Hunters are obliged to see that animals are killed properly and their meat, bones and hide utilised in ways that will not offend the animal's guardian spirit. Traditionally, rites practised both before and after the killing of animals took the form of elaborate ceremonies. The purpose of these ceremonies was for people to honour the animal, for the hunter to ask its forgiveness for killing it, and to return its soul safely to the spirit world.

For the Inuit maintaining balance between the human and natural worlds was often perceived to be a matter of life and death. Disease, illness and misfortune were regarded as resulting from a violation of a taboo, or by offending the souls and spirits of animals. This could happen in a number of ways; for example, by mixing the meat of marine and land creatures, or by failing to propitiate the souls of animals killed by hunters.

For all Inuit groups, the shaman was a central figure in the maintenance of good relations between humans and animals. The shaman acted as intermediary in the transactions between humans, the souls of animals and the guardian of the animals. Inuit myths relate how the shaman would first have to undergo a long, solitary and arduous initiation, in the mountains, on the barren tundra, or in a deep cave, wrestling with spirits and acquiring his or her powers before returning home.

The essence of shamanic practice was the trance and journey to the spirit world. As the shaman went into a trance, their soul would journey to the spirit world and bargain with the guardian of animals for the animals to be sent to the human world to be hunted. The shaman would also go into a trance to search for the souls of human beings that had been captured by malevolent spirits. The shaman also depended on a variety of helping spirits to assist in journeying to the spirit world. Most commonly, the helping spirit was an animal, such as a polar bear, which carried the shaman on its back, flying silently through the air, or swimming effortlessly to the bottom of the sea to take the shaman to visit the Sea Woman (see the following paragraph). It was sometimes the case that a shaman's helping spirit was a human, but whatever form they took they also acted as instructors of magic and spiritual teaching.

A fundamental Inuit belief is that animals have a guardian who releases the animals in their care only if people treat them with courtesy and respect. Because Inuit culture is closely linked to water, the Sea Woman (called Sedna or Nuliayuk) is the guardian of the sea mammals. She embodies their essence and punishes the disrespectful with failure in hunting.

There are several variants of the Sedna myth, but they all share a common motif. The myth relates how Sedna, as a girl, refused to get married and so her father married her to a dog as punishment. The newly married couple then went to live on an island, but Sedna was lonely and longed to return to her family and home community. One day, when her dog-husband was away from home hunting, a tall, good-looking stranger appeared in a boat and called to Sedna to join him. Sedna seized this opportunity to escape from her dog-husband and stepped into the boat. They reached the stranger's village after a long journey, and Sedna soon realised that the stranger was not a man after all, but a petrel who could assume the appearance of a human. Sedna grew afraid and made plans to escape. In the meantime, her father and brothers had been searching for her and, when they eventually found her at the petrel's village, they rescued her when the petrel was away. However, the petrel

Left: Sedna, guardian o
the sea mammals

soon returned, realised what had happened and managed to catch up with their boat. The petrel caused a great storm and, fearful for their own safety, Sedna's father and brothers threw her overboard into the sea. Sedna gripped the side of the boat and, as the storm grew wilder, her father cut off the joints of her fingers. As they hit the water, Sedna's fingers were transformed into seals, whales, walrus and narwhals. Sedna slipped beneath the waves and descended to the lower world at the bottom of the sea, where she became guardian of the sea mammals which had been created from her fingers.

Sedna is usually generous to the Inuit and releases the sea mammals to them so they can be caught for food. Yet there are times when she refuses to let the animals go, especially if hunters have caused pain to an animal's spirit. Sedna's hair can also become dirty if the Inuit violate a taboo and the animals then become entangled. When seals, whales and other sea mammals are scarce a shaman must journey to Sedna's lair and plead with her to release them, or comb her dirty and tangled hair in order to free them.

The Sedna myth reflects a fundamental belief in the unity of all life, both human and animal, but also symbolises the tensions that exist between the human and animal worlds. It also illustrates how, in the distant past, humans and animals were not seen to be as clearly distinguished from each other as they are today. Like the petrel who takes Sedna away from her dog-husband, there are many other characters in Inuit mythology that have a dual existence. Animals can become humans at will, and vice versa. In fact, Inuit myths often relate how all humans have the power and ability to change their form. Similarly, the guardian spirit of an animal not only can assume the shape of the animal it protects, but can take the form of any other animal or person. As the myths and oral histories of the Inuit attest, hunters are faced with a dilemma: when they meet an animal – be it seal, whale, polar bear, caribou or petrel – they can never be entirely sure of its true nature!

Environmental Strategies & Sustainability

Today, like other Arctic peoples, the Inuit face threats to their cultures, livelihoods and homelands from environmental problems, such as transboundary pollution and climate change, large-scale industrial activity, rapid social and cultural change, and other exogenous forces such as the activities of animal-rights groups and environmental movements that are campaigning against traditional Inuit hunting activities, such as sealing and whaling.

Despite the overwhelming social and economic changes that have occurred in the Arctic over the last 50 years or so, many Inuit communities, from east Greenland to the Bering Sea coast of Siberia, continue to rely on the harvesting of terrestrial and marine resources for subsistence purposes. As in the past, the species most commonly harvested are marine mammals such as seals, walrus, narwhals, beluga, fin and minke whales, and land mammals such as caribou and muskox.

The Inuit say that no individual has the right to claim that they own the animals. Access to resources is based on communal rights and hunting is guided by community regulations, which are often unwritten. The sharing of the catch from the hunt remains at the very heart of the hunting culture.

From an Inuit perspective, threats to wildlife and the environment do not come from hunting but from airborne and seaborne pollutants which enter the Arctic from industrial areas far to the south of traditional Inuit homelands. Threats also come from the impact of nonrenewable resource extraction within the Arctic, such as oil and gas development and mining.

In recent years the Inuit have set themselves the challenge to counteract such threats and to devise strategies for environmental protection and sustainable development. The Inuit argue that adequate systems of environmental management and the most appropriate forms of sustainability are only possible if they are based on local knowledge and Inuit cultural values. In this way, the Inuit have claimed the right for international recognition as resource conservationists. The success of this approach has been possible, in part, by the work of the Inuit Circumpolar Conference (ICC).

The ICC is a pan-Arctic indigenous peoples' organisation that represents the rights of the Inuit in Greenland, Canada, Alaska and Siberia. Formed in Alaska in 1977 in response to increased oil and gas exploration and development in the Arctic, the ICC has had NGO status at the United Nations since 1983. The ICC has set about challenging the policies of governments, multinational corporations and environmental movements, and has argued that the protection of the Arctic environment and its resources should recognise indigenous rights and be in accordance with Inuit tradition and cultural values.

Since its formation, the ICC has sought to establish its own Arctic policies, based on indigenous knowledge about the environment, that reflect Inuit concerns about future development, together with ethical and practical guidelines for human activity in the Arctic. The ICC has also played an active role in the Arctic Environmental Protection Strategy, and is a permanent participant at the Arctic Council, which is a high-level forum for discussion and cooperation between the Arctic states on environmental protection and sustainable development.

But the work of the ICC is not just confined to the Arctic. Inuit representatives have been involved in the United Nations working group on indigenous peoples, which was charged with drafting a universal declaration on human rights, and the United Nations Conference on Environment and Development (UNCED) held in Rio de Janeiro in 1992. In this way, through the work of organisations such as the ICC, the Inuit have set themselves at the vanguard of indigenous rights and environmental protection worldwide.

THE SAMI

The Sami are a distinct Finno-Ugrian-speaking ethnic group inhabiting the Arctic regions of Norway, Sweden, Finland and Russia's Kola Peninsula. This vast area of the Nordic and north-west Russian Arctic is usually known as Lapland, and includes the Norwegian counties of Nordland, Troms and Finnmark, the Swedish counties of Vasterbotten and Norrbotten, the county of Lappi in Finland, and parts of the Kola Peninsula. In Sweden, the Sami population extends relatively far south into the county of Jamtland.

Over the centuries, the Sami way of life has been tied to reindeer herding, hunting and fishing and, because the Sami have never been organised at a social and political level into different tribal groupings, Lapland has not been divided into firm Sami territorial boundaries. Nomadic Sami reindeer herders have traditionally ranged far and wide, crossing national borders as they follow their reindeer herds between winter and summer pastures, although political developments have restricted migration routes over the last 100 years or so. However, despite the fact that Sami were not originally reindeer herders and the majority of Sami do not follow reindeer herding as a main source of livelihood today, it is reindeer and reindeer herding that have come to define and symbolise Sami culture.

Lapland covers an area of some 193,000 sq miles and the entire population of Sami is some 61,000, with about 40,000 living in Norway, 15,000 in Sweden, 4000 in Finland and approximately 2000 in Russia. This figure, however, is based on a contested definition of who is ethnically Sami. There has been a long tradition of intermarriage with Norwegians, Swedes and Finns, and some definitions of Sami are also based on language and self-ascription (ie people who consider themselves to be Sami based on particular criteria). The relationship between Sami and other reindeer herding peoples in Siberia has long been an area of contested scholarly debate. However, because the language of the Sami is part of the Finno-Ugrian sub-group of Uralic-Altaic languages, the Sami are related linguistically to Finns, Magyars and Estonians, and not to Siberian peoples.

Economy & Way of Life

Humans were inhabiting the coastal areas of northern Norway some 10,000 years ago, having probably arrived there along the North Atlantic western coast from the south, but also from the east along the shores of the Arctic Ocean. These peoples lived mainly from hunting sea mammals and from fishing, but as the ice sheets receded from the inland areas of northern Fennoscandia, there were further migrations inland and hunting cultures dependent on elk and wild reindeer developed some 9000 years ago. Archaeological evidence suggests that these hunters of Fennoscandia's coastal and inland areas were the direct ancestors of the present-day Sami culture.

Farther to the south in Scandinavia, agricultural societies developed around the same time as the emergence of the early Sami hunting cultures and it is likely that, far from being isolated from one another, these two societies began to trade goods from an early time. The Sami, however, were increasingly marginalised by wealthy Scandinavian farmers during the Viking age (to whom they also began to pay taxes in the form of skins) and were pushed farther and farther to peripheral regions.

Hunting and fishing remained the basis of Sami culture for several hundred years and it was only in the 1600s that reindeer were domesticated and some Sami began to follow the herds on their annual migration routes. However, not all Sami became nomadic reindeer herders, and many fishing communities had developed on lake shores and along the north Norwegian coast.

Yet Sami still faced competition from settlers to Lapland who began to farm land that would otherwise have been used as pasture for the reindeer herds. This was especially the case in Finland, where an official process of internal colonisation and agricultural development took place in the 16th and 17th centuries. In the 17th and 18th centuries some Finnish settlers began to keep domesticated reindeer herds. Industrial development in the 19th and 20th centuries, such as mining, forestry, railways, roads, hydroelectric power and tourism, have all had their impact on traditional Sami livelihoods.

In Sweden and Norway, only Sami are entitled to own reindeer herds and can only do so on land designated officially as reindeer grazing areas. In Finland, however, Finns as well as Sami continue to keep reindeer. Recent transformations in reindeer herding, as well as an increase in the population of some reindeer herds, have increased the risk of overgrazing in northern Fennoscandia. Reindeer herding continues to be central to Sami culture, but it remains possible in some areas of Norway, Sweden and Finland only due to government subsidies, which are mainly intended to maintain traditional Sami livelihoods.

Only a minority of Sami depend on reindeer herding today, but in northern Fennoscandia, the expansion of agriculture and the development of mining, tourism, forestry and hydrocarbon development projects have all encroached upon Sami reindeer herding lands and put further pressure on this way of life.

For the Sami living on the Kola Peninsula, the collapse of the Soviet Union has brought opportunities, but problems and uncertainties as well. Under the Soviets, reindeer herding was collectivised. With the break-up of the Soviet Union and the end of the collective farms, Sami herders now have the right to buy and own reindeer herds privately, although few can afford to do so. Combined with controversies over grazing rights and limited markets for reindeer meat, the reindeer herding economy of the Kola Sami faces a bleak future.

Cosmology & World-View

Contemporary Sami religion is the result of a syncretism between traditional pre-Christian practices and Christian (mainly Lutheran) beliefs. Pre-Christian religion was animistic and similar in many ways to the spiritual beliefs and practices of other circumpolar peoples. Animals, plants, the sun, moon, stars, rivers, lakes, rocks and so on all have consciousness and awareness, and are imbued with a spirit.

For the Sami, many features in the landscape are sacred places, especially along migration routes, where animals reveal themselves to hunters in dreams, or where people encounter animal spirits while travelling. In the past, reindeer antlers would have been placed at sacred sites and adorned with gifts, and sacred stones *(seiteh)* were placed on mountain tops, and near lakes and rivers. Sometimes these stones were sacred in themselves, or incarnated local spirits or deities.

Although Lapland is often called 'Europe's last wilderness', this label ignores the fact that the region is a homeland for the Sami, who have named almost every tree, river, stream, lake, mountain, valley and meadow. Such names are not merely geographically descriptive. Sami place names, like the names the Inuit give to the Arctic landscape in Greenland, northern Canada and Alaska, are multidimensional, in that they contain information about physical features, community history and mythological events.

In traditional Sami belief, everything in the universe has a spiritual essence and, because to some extent human existence was influenced by the forces of nature, great care and attention was made to ensure that spirits were appeased and placated. For example, in Sami tradition hunters who take part in a bear hunt are regarded as unclean and must undergo ritual purification during a period of ritual seclusion.

The central figure in traditional Sami religion was the *noaidi*, or shaman. Chosen by the spirits, novices spent several months in solitude undergoing initiation as shamans. Although the noaidi fulfilled many tasks, their role was mainly as healer, and they also acted as diviners and spiritual facilitators of the hunt, and as sacrificial priests. With the help of guardian spirits, such as fish, birds or reindeer, the spirit of the noaidi would travel to the hidden spirit worlds either to bargain with the spirits and deities with respect to ensuring good weather and good hunting, or to retrieve a soul which may have wandered from a person's sick body.

As the Sami believed that serious diseases had supernatural origins, it was as healer that the noaidi was most often called upon by members of the community. Minor diseases and illnesses could be treated by the patient themselves, their families, or by other traditional medical carers, but only the noaidi had the power and the means to go into a trance and travel to the spirit world, find out the cause of a disease and win back a lost soul. Sometimes, depending on the ailment and the nature of the disease, it was not necessary for the noaidi to travel to the spirit world. The sacrifice of a reindeer, goat or lamb could be offered to the deity or spirit instead – the idea being that one living thing could be exchanged for another – and this was sufficient to aid a sick person's recovery.

Much of what is known about pre-Christian Sami religious beliefs is to be found in the accounts of very early travellers and missionaries in Lapland. The Sami came into contact with Christian missionaries several hundred years before many other Arctic peoples were converted to Christianity. The earliest missionary attempt was in 1050, and by the 14th century Sami were converting to Christian beliefs. During the 1600s a major conversion process took place, during which time many of the old beliefs and practices were abandoned. The Christian missionaries saw the shamans as being in league with the Devil, and attempted to wipe them and their influence out. While many shamans were killed, shamanism survived in some isolated places until the 20th century. In the 1830s, a popular fundamentalist movement known as Laestadianism (after Lars Levi Laestadius) won many converts, and today it is the main faith for many Sami.

Social & Political Change

As the northern lands were settled by Norwegians, Swedes and Finns, the Sami came progressively under the influence of the dominant Scandinavian societies. Sami became involved in trade with southern Scandinavia but were also liable to pay taxes. At the same time as missionary activity became intense in the 16th and 17th centuries, the Sami became subject more and more to administrative influence from the south. The church played a major role in Sami education, and missionary activity became the means by which the Scandinavian monarchies were able to establish and assert political control over Lapland.

In the 20th century, the Sami have been subject to greater legislation which affects grazing rights and the reindeer herding industry. Policies of modernisation have also not left Sami culture unaffected. The nomadic way of life has changed for many reindeer herding families and policies of 'rationalisation' have aimed to raise living standards by settling Sami in permanent communities and bringing them into 'the modern world'. In Norway, for example, a policy of assimilation restricted the use of the Sami language during the first half of the 20th century, and Sami populations elsewhere in Fennoscandia were also subject to processes of cultural and economic integration.

In 1953, Sami from Finland, Sweden and Norway met to discuss issues of common concern to Sami culture and livelihoods, and in 1956 the Nordic Sami Council was established to represent Sami interests. It was not until the 1960s, however, that Sami rights to preserve and develop their own culture were officially recognised. The Nordic Sami Council (now called the Sami Council) joined the World Council of Indigenous Peoples in 1976 and, like the Inuit Circumpolar Conference (see the earlier Inuit section), the Sami Council has NGO status at the

United Nations. Sami have thus been active in the promotion of indigenous rights and are linked to indigenous peoples' networks that work for indigenous causes elsewhere in the Arctic, as well as in other parts of the world.

Conflicts between Sami populations and the dominant Norwegian, Swedish, Finnish and Russian nation-states are not only caused by attempts to integrate the Sami into mainstream society. Conflict and tension also stems from conflicting views on the Nordic Arctic environment. On the one hand, the Sami relate to Lapland as a homeland, an environment with cultural, symbolic and spiritual importance, while national governments view the north lands as economic frontiers, with vast natural resources vital for the development of the nation as a whole.

One example of such conflict has been controversy over hydroelectric projects in northern Norway. In the 1980s, for example, Norwegian government plans to dam the Kautokeino-Alta waterway, which Sami hunters, herders and fishers had depended on for thousands of years, resulted in Sami issues and rights being placed firmly on the Norwegian political agenda. Sami were joined by environmental groups and organised nonviolent protests in Lapland and Oslo.

Although these protests did not stop construction of the dam, a committee to look into Sami rights was appointed. The recommendations of the committee, that the Norwegian government was obliged to protect Sami culture and allow Sami the right to utilise the natural resources of their homeland, resulted in the Norwegian government formulating the Sami Act in 1987. The Act recognised that Sami and Norwegians were two distinct ethnic groups and led to the creation of the Sami parliament in 1989. However, Sami have not been recognised as having the right to self-determination, nor does the Sami parliament in Norway have the right to limit the encroachments on land in northern Norway which threaten Sami land use.

Similar situations are to be found in Finland and Sweden, where committees and acts have also addressed Sami issues. As in Norway, the Swedish and Finnish Sami have their own parliaments, which are, in effect, representative and consultative assemblies. The creation of these assemblies marks a turning point in how Finland, Sweden and Norway view the Sami as an ethnic minority and a separate people within their borders, although they remain citizens of those states. As democratically elected ethnic bodies, the Sami parliaments deal with issues relating to Sami culture and economy. The parliaments have gone some way to ensure cultural survival but are nonetheless limited in their powers, especially in terms of determining land rights and access to resource use.

In Russia, although indigenous minorities of the Russian north were given certain rights and privileges under the Soviets, these rights have not always been recognised. Like other northern minorities, the Sami of the Kola Peninsula are also demanding self-government and regional autonomy. They have formed their own organisation, the Kola

Sami Association, to promote and defend Sami interests and to work for a degree of self-determination. The Kola Sami Association is linked to the Russian Association of the Indigenous Peoples of the North and has recently joined the Sami Council, thereby giving Sami in Russia a greater international voice.

Environmental Change

Environmental problems and resource development place great strain on the Sami. Perhaps one of the best illustrations of the environmental impact of development in the circumpolar north generally is the Kola Peninsula, the most industrially developed part of the Russian Arctic. The total population of the Kola Peninsula is over one million, and the regional capital of Murmansk is the largest city north of the Arctic Circle. The exploitation of natural resources (such as mining for iron ore, nickel and zinc), commercial fishing, timber production and manufacturing form the basis of the Kola economy. The Kola Peninsula has also been of great strategic importance in Soviet and post-Soviet Russia, and still contains nuclear submarine and nuclear bomber bases.

Industrial development on the Kola Peninsula has resulted in a severe ecological crisis unlike any environmental problems facing other Sami populations in Norway, Sweden and Finland. The ecological crisis is especially severe in those areas affected by mining and smelting. But the heavy industrial base of the Kola Peninsula threatens the entire northern part of Fennoscandia and poses great dangers to the economy and health of Sami communities. Nickel smelters, in towns such as Monchegorsk and Zaplolyarny, are possible contributors to Arctic haze and causes of the acid rain which is contributing to the destruction of Russian, Finnish and Norwegian forests. Satellite surveillance, for instance, has revealed that about 100,000 hectares of the Kola Peninsula have almost no living plants as a result of industrial activity, while scientists have observed gradual defoliation of trees, structural changes in lichens and a gradual shift of the boreal forest treeline. Reindeer pasture is under great threat, lakes and rivers are polluted, land is expropriated by oil, gas, mining and timber companies, and local economies are in danger of collapsing.

While land use and land ownership remain crucial issues for Sami in northern Fennoscandia and Russia, and shape indigenous perspectives on self-determination and cultural survival, perhaps the greatest threats now facing the Sami are rapid social, economic and cultural change as the result of major environmental crises.

THE ATHAPASKANS

Northern Athapaskan peoples inhabit a huge expanse of coniferous forest both above and below the Arctic Circle that stretches across Alaska, the Yukon Territory and the Northwest Territories, and down into northern British Columbia, Alberta, Saskatchewan and Manitoba. Athapaskan-speaking peoples also live far to the south of the northern forests, in California and Arizona. In Alaska, the various Athapaskan groups have been known as the Koyukon, Ingalik, Tanacross, Ahtna, Han, Tanana, Denaina, Gwich'in, Holikachuk and upper Kuskokwim; while in Canada they include the Dogrib, Hare, Gwich'in, Dunne-za, Slave, Chipewyan and others. Many northern Athapaskans now call themselves Dene or Dena, which means 'human beings', and speak languages that belong to the Athapaskan branch of the Na-Dene family of languages.

To an outsider, unaccustomed to a life lived on the land, the boreal forest shows few visible signs of long settlement by Athapaskan peoples. Indeed, in their habitation of the land for several thousand years, Athapaskans have exemplified how human beings can live in societies that are in fine balance with the natural world. Traditional Athapaskan subsistence activities centred around the hunting of land mammals, such as moose, caribou and bear, and fishing for salmon, northern pike and other species. Houses, tents, boats and hunting and fishing equipment were made from wood and animal hides, which have, over time, rotted beneath the forest floor, and archaeologists have had to search hard for evidence of ancient Athapaskan settlement. It is easy to see how outsiders can come to the conclusion that the vastness of the northern forest represents an empty wilderness, devoid of any human presence. Yet the northern forest is a homeland for Athapaskan peoples, who have moved around it, inhabited it, named it, and survived from its rich resources, for thousands of years. They have not devastated the natural world but have coexisted with the land and its animals guided by a contract of mutual respect.

Archaeologists say that Athapaskan-speaking peoples probably crossed the Bering Strait from Siberia to Alaska some 10,000 years ago. As these people moved into North America as the great glaciers and ice sheets of the Pleistocene period receded, they encountered a landscape not unlike the one in which they live today. Contemporary Athapaskan culture thus represents an incredible ecological adaptation to an environment that has barely changed over several centuries. The earliest Athapaskan artefacts, however, can be dated to only about 2000 years ago and there are many gaps in the archaeological knowledge of Athapaskan prehistory. Much of what is known about Athapaskan origins comes from both archaeology and linguistic research, which has traced the spread of Athapaskan-speaking peoples eastward across the North American continent.

Economy & Way of Life

The forests and rivers of Alaska and northern Canada have provided Athapaskan peoples with a rich variety of resources which have formed the basis for diverse economies and modes of subsistence.

Traditionally, and in modern times, life in Athapaskan communities has revolved around an annual seasonal round of hunting, gathering and fishing.

Unlike other Arctic hunting peoples, such as Inuit communities which depended almost entirely on seals, Athapaskans exploited a wide ecological niche and hunted, when the need arose, almost every animal in the area. Athapaskan subsistence activities were therefore generalised, rather than highly specialised. Having said that, however, moose and caribou are especially important animals for many communities in providing a source of meat for the entire year. Moose and caribou meat is eaten fresh for a good deal of the year, and is dried for winter consumption. Smaller animals and birds, such as wild geese and ptarmigan, also provide an important part of the Athapaskan diet.

In the Alaskan interior, especially for those villages situated on the banks of the Yukon, Tanana and other rivers, although the hunting of large animals is a vital part of the subsistence economy, it has been fishing which has given particular stability to the Athapaskan way of life all year round. When land animals hibernate or move to winter feeding grounds which are difficult for people to access, fishing remains possible throughout the winter, even when the rivers freeze over. However, fishing has not been of such crucial importance for all Athapaskan groups. For example, the Gwich'in of north-east Alaska and the northern Yukon have depended almost entirely on the porcupine caribou herd.

Traditionally, the Denaina of Cook Inlet and the Kenai Peninsula in southern Alaska (who also hunted moose, caribou and bear, and fished for salmon) depended a great deal on sea mammal hunting and the techniques, technology and boats used for hunting seals, sea otters, sea lions and beluga were not unlike those employed by Pacific Inuit who hunted in a similar south Alaskan environment. Indeed, it is clear that the Denaina were heavily influenced by Pacific Inuit groups.

Traditional social organisation was based around kinship groups and communities consisted of several nuclear families, often connected through various relationships and alliances. Athapaskan society is well known for the potlatch, a ceremony which honours the dead and the connection between the ancestors and the living. The potlatch is also an elaborate form of highly ritualised gift exchange and distribution, of which some extreme examples have been noted among the Indians of the north-west coast of Canada and the USA. The potlatch was often the primary way through which an individual achieved prestige in and beyond their community.

Archaeologists working on Athapaskan sites have found that housing and other structures reflected what was, in traditional times, a highly mobile society. The pattern of settlement corresponds to the annual subsistence cycle and even winter dwellings were either temporary or semipermanent. Today, although Athapaskan hunters and fishers travel great distances in search of game, and often spend the summer in camps, they live in permanent villages and their daily lives are influenced heavily by the institutions of American society.

Cosmology & World-View

Not surprisingly, the archaeological view of Athapaskan origins is at odds with Athapaskan oral history and mythology, which talks of everything in the universe – humans, animals, the forest and so on – as having a common creation, and emerging from the same spot. Like the hazy archaeological knowledge as to the emergence of Athapaskan culture, however, the exact time of this creation is difficult to pinpoint. Athapaskans say that this all happened in the Distant Time. Although the Distant Time is a remote, ancient time, oral history and mythology nonetheless recount the events of the Distant Time in incredible detail. Anyone discovering Athapaskan oral history for the first time will be rewarded with stories that reveal an immensely rich spiritual and cultural heritage.

The stories of the Distant Time represent a culture's view of itself, of its origins and of its place in relation to the natural world. Distant Time stories provide indigenous accounts of the origin of the world, the elements and the animals. These stories also reveal how, like other northern peoples, the Athapaskans live in an aware world, where everything (humans, animals, rivers, trees, thunderstorms etc) has consciousness. Athapaskan oral history describes how features of the landscape, or the elements, such as the moon, sun, wind and stars, were originally human beings, whose spirits are now embodied in aspects of the natural world. Stories about the origin of the elements, the sun, the moon and celestial bodies are often related to myths about the balance between daylight and darkness, time and space, and between the human and natural worlds.

As in many Inuit myths, the Raven (or Raven Man) is a central figure in the Athapaskan accounts of the origins of the world. Before the beginnings of time, in fact even before the beginnings of Distant Time, there existed only darkness until Raven created the world by revealing the daylight. Having revealed the daylight, Raven then created the first people. Several variants of Raven stories tell how Raven either takes a human wife, who bears his children, or how Raven is transformed into a spruce needle and swallowed by a woman who then gave birth to him as a boy. In these myths, Raven's human children become ravens themselves, but retain the power to transform themselves back into human form, just as Raven himself, born as a human, returned to his original form. Raven also appears in variants of stories about a great flood which occurred in the Distant Time, or in stories which account for the origins of the behaviour of animals.

A fundamental theme in the Athapaskan world-view is respect for nature and animals. This is not only found in mythology and stories from the Distant Time, but is reflected in contemporary practice. Animals and humans are similar in many ways, and animals have distinct and unique personalities just as humans do. In the Distant Time, humans and animals were not as clearly distinguished as they are today, however. Stories tell how humans and animals often lived in the same communities, even sharing the same household. As in the Raven myths, humans had the power and ability to transform themselves into animals and vice versa.

From the Distant Time stories, people learn the proper rules and behaviour for interacting with animals and the natural world. Powerful spirits inhabit the natural world, and animal spirits can be particularly dangerous and vindictive if animals are not respected and treated properly. The Athapaskan respect for animals is perhaps most vividly illustrated by the fact that some animals, such as bears and wolverines, are given funeral rituals after being killed. The rituals surrounding the hunt of a bear, for example, symbolise the close yet ambivalent relationship between humans and animals. The bear is human-like, can stand on its hind legs and looks like a human when skinned. The bear is a great hunter and has special power. Although the killing of a bear brings prestige to the hunter, it also brings danger. When a bear has been killed, a feast is held where the dead bear is treated as an honoured guest and asked to give its forgiveness to people for slaying it.

Social Change

Traditional northern Athapaskan culture was initially affected primarily by contact with Russians in Alaska, and with British fur traders in the Canadian north-west in the 18th century. As well as economic, cultural and ideological influences, explorers and traders brought new diseases to which the indigenous peoples had no immunity. The historical record shows that entire communities were wiped out by diseases such as smallpox, influenza, typhoid, tuberculosis and measles. Missionary activity also had a profound impact on the Athapaskan world-view.

Athapaskan life changed as a result of involvement with the fur trade, most noticeably in the way in which trapping fur-bearing animals meant that hunting became more specialised and concentrated on only a few species. However, dramatic changes have swept through Athapaskan villages during the 20th century. Education through formal schooling, together with policies of modernisation and assimilation into mainstream American and Canadian society, have meant that traditional skills and activities have been lost. However, cultural survival has been made possible through land claims in Alaska and Canada and degrees of self-determination.

THE CHUKCHI

The Chukchi live in isolated and remote villages in the north-easternmost part of Siberia – in the Chukchi Autonomous Oblast (an administrative territory within the Russian Federation), although small numbers also

Right: Inuit art

RYAN VER BERKMOES

JOHN BORTHWICK

Top: Archaeologists inspect the reconstructi⬤ of a native house, Nunavut, Canada

Bottom: Sami herder, Finnish Lapland

inhabit the Koryak Autonomous Oblast, and Yakutiia. The Chukchi call themselves the Lyg Oravetlyan, 'the true people', and are closely related ethnically, culturally and linguistically to the Koryak and Itelmen peoples of north-east Siberia.

Excepting the basin of the Anadyr River, most of the oblast is mountainous – it has a severe Arctic climate and only sparse tundra vegetation persists, with some forest in the south (the northernmost vestiges of the taiga). The oblast was formed in 1930 for the Chukchi, although a minority of Evens, Koryaks and Yakuts also live in the territory. However, Russian settlers outnumber these peoples. Russians have developed mining for tin, gold, tungsten and mercury, with some coal near Anadyr, the administrative centre.

Economy & Way of Life

Traditionally, the Chukchi have been divided into two principal economic and cultural subgroups: the nomadic Reindeer Chukchi inhabiting the interior of the region and the Chukchi Peninsula; and the Maritime Chukchi, settled hunters and fishers who live on small peninsulas jutting off the Arctic and Bering Strait coasts.

The economy and mode of production of the Reindeer Chukchi is based on herds of domesticated reindeer, which provide transportation, meat, milk and hides for clothing and shelter. The Maritime Chukchi subsist on the hunting of marine mammals and by fishing. Today they still travel mainly in wooden-framed boats covered with walrus skins.

The reindeer herders of the tundra and the marine mammal hunters of the coast did not live in isolation from one another: the two groups were dependent on each other for trade and mutual exchange (reindeer skins were traded for whale blubber, sealskins and walrus hides), and were linked through marriage and other forms of alliance. The social organisation of the Maritime Chukchi is based on the boat (umiaq) crew and extended kin groups. Hunters from five or six related families normally form a boat crew. The village is the basic territorial unit and comprises kin and unrelated members. The social organisation of the Reindeer Chukchi is centred around the camps of nomadic families who follow their reindeer herds around the landscape.

Cosmology & World-View

Like many other Arctic peoples, the Chukchi believe that the universe is populated with spirits. Everything in the world, be it animate or inanimate, has a life-force and shares the same spiritual nature. In traditional Chukchi religion, shamanism was important for healing and divination, and the shaman made journeys to the spirit world to retrieve the wandering souls of sick people. Under the tsars, attempts were made to convert the Chukchi to Russian Orthodox Christianity, although many of the traditional beliefs and customs persisted alongside Christianity and resulted in a syncretic religious faith.

Traditionally, the Chukchi believed that a great spirit protected the animals they hunted and herded, embodying their essence and supervising their correct ritual treatment after being slaughtered. In Siberian reindeer herding societies, this master or guardian of the animals is protector of the herds and known by the Chukchi as Reindeer Being, while the ritual life of the Maritime Chukchi focuses on the master or mistress of the sea, who is said to rule over sea mammals and punish those who mistreat the souls of seals, walrus and whales with failure in hunting.

The Chukchi also believed in a Supreme Being which they called Creator or Life-Giving Being. But the nature of the Supreme Being is uncertain and difficult to conceptualise and, for the Chukchi, the Supreme Being is indistinguishable from the master of the reindeer herds.

In common with other Siberian reindeer herders such as the Koryak, each Reindeer Chukchi family has a guardian spirit in the form of a sacred wooden fireboard, which is used to light the fire in the hearth of each home. The fireboard represents the deity of the family fire, which protects the family, the home and hearth from malevolent spirits. The sacred fireboard is considered to be an aspect of the master of the herd, and the Chukchi fireboard is carved in the shape of Reindeer Being. The fireboard not only protects the family, but fire ceremonies also play an important part in the welfare and sacrifice of reindeer. In Chukchi myth, reindeer have their origins in fire – the Supreme Being is said to have pulled the first reindeer out of a sacred fire. The return of reindeer from pasture is celebrated in a fire ceremony – a new fire is started with the fireboard and burning sticks are thrown to greet the herd as it approaches the herders' camps. When Chukchi sacrifice a reindeer, its blood is collected in a ladle and fed to the fire.

The bear holds a pre-eminent place in Chukchi mythology, as in that of other Arctic peoples, and in Siberia the bear festival is one of the most elaborate forms of animal ceremonialism anywhere in the Arctic. After a bear has been hunted, a feast is held where the dead bear is treated as an honoured guest and people ask its forgiveness for slaying it. Rituals, myths and stories surrounding the bear and bear hunting clearly express both the desire of the hunter for the bear and the anxiety that surrounds a kill.

Social & Political Change

Although the Soviet Committee of the North had proposed creating reservations for the indigenous peoples of Siberia, where they could continue to pursue their traditional lifestyles, during the 1920s Lenin and other Bolsheviks argued that the indigenous and minority peoples of the Soviet empire should be assimilated into the political, cultural and economic mainstream of the country. Between 1929 and 1932 territorial administrative units known as oblasts, and named after each indigenous group, were formed. The Chukchi did not escape the dramatic upheavals under Stalin – they were settled into permanent coastal villages or collective farms and new economic activities were introduced. The collectivisation of the Chukchi reindeer herding economy, together with the establishment of boarding schools, hospitals and permanent villages, was an attempt to eliminate the traditional nomadic and subsistence activities of the Chukchi. Russian became the language of instruction for all Chukchi schoolchildren and both traditional Chukchi and Russian Orthodox religious ceremonies and festivals were prohibited.

From the 1950s onward, Siberia was central to the economic development of the Soviet Union. Massive industrial projects, mining, and oil and gas exploitation threatened the traditional homeland of the Chukchi, who found themselves struggling to maintain a reindeer herding economy on smaller tracts of available pasture. While some Chukchi still followed the herds, living for a good part of the year in tents, still more moved to the coastal settlements or abandoned reindeer herding and took up jobs in the oil and gas industry, in factories and in construction. The large influx of settlers and migrant labourers from other parts of the Soviet Union also had a considerable social and economic impact on the indigenous populations of north-eastern Siberia.

Although the die was cast and much of the social and economic changes were irreversible, Mikhail Gorbachev's policies of perestroika and glasnost ushered in a new era of political freedom and cultural revival for the Chukchi after 1985. Concerned with the threats posed both to the cultural survival of Siberia's indigenous peoples and to the natural environment, the Chukchi played an active role in the formation of the Association of the Small Peoples of the North (now called the Russian Association of the Indigenous Peoples of the North), an organisation established to represent the rights and interests of Russia's indigenous peoples.

The Chukchi in Post-Soviet Russia

Today, the most complex and unresolved issues relating to the autonomy and self-determination of the Arctic's indigenous peoples are to be found in Russia, and the Chukchi and other indigenous groups are demanding forms of self-government and regional autonomy. Ironically, the collapse of the Soviet Union has left the Chukchi in a vulnerable position and they are faced with as many challenges to cultural and economic survival as during the decades of cultural repression under the Soviets. Environmental problems such as pollution, and large-scale resource development, place great strain on the lands and societies of the Russian Far East. Reindeer pasture is under threat, lakes, rivers and streams are polluted, land is taken over by oil and gas companies, indigenous communities are afflicted by a disturbing range of health problems, and local economies have collapsed.

Cut off from western Russia and essential supply lines, the Chukchi have found themselves having to rely more on traditional subsistence activities. For example, marine mammal hunting has again become vital to Chukchi coastal communities to remedy extreme food shortages and offset the regional economic crisis. Local hunters who have not harvested whales for many years have no choice but to resume whaling, although many have inadequate equipment and have lost the knowledge required for successful and safe hunting.

A recent project initiated by Alaska's North Slope Borough has aimed to assist the indigenous peoples of north-east Siberia in re-learning traditional activities and skills. The future of the Chukchi is dependent on the revitalisation of whaling and reindeer herding, the strengthening of indigenous organisations in north-eastern Siberia, the implementation of local wildlife management strategies, the development of small-scale community-based business initiatives, and the achievement of a degree of self-determination.

References

Polar Peoples: Self-Determination and Development, Minority Rights Group (ed), 1994, Minority Rights Publications, London

Arctic Homeland: Kinship, Community and Development in North-West Greenland, Mark Nuttall, 1992, University of Toronto Press, Toronto

Protecting the Arctic: Indigenous Peoples and Cultural Survival, Mark Nuttall, 1998, Harwood Academic Publishers, Amsterdam

ARCTIC
RESEARCH

By Lawson W Brigham

The Arctic, despite a rich history of exploration and systematic sampling dating back to the International Polar Year of 1882-83, is one of the least studied and understood regions on earth. The extreme climate on land and sea has constrained what and where scientific research could be conducted. The Cold War also limited the exchange of information and co-operation among the circumpolar nations. However, during the decade of the 1990s the Arctic has been transformed from a region of direct confrontation between the superpowers (the USA versus the former USSR) into a region of cooperation among many nations with Arctic territories and interests. There is increasing belief that the Arctic is closely linked to the global climate system, and is a key region for the study of climatic changes. Arctic research not only improves our understanding of physical, chemical, biological, geological and social processes in the far north, but also contributes to knowledge about the earth as a whole.

In 1990 the nongovernmental International Arctic Science Committee, or IASC, was created. As with the Scientific Committee on Antarctic Research (SCAR), the IASC encourages and facilitates cooperation in all aspects of Arctic research. It promotes basic and applied interdisciplinary research in all regions of the Arctic and can also provide scientific advice on Arctic issues. Nations active in IASC have included Canada, China, Denmark (and Greenland), Finland, France, Germany, Iceland, Italy, Japan, Netherlands, Norway, Poland, Russia, Sweden, Switzerland, the UK and the USA.

The Arctic Environmental Protection Strategy (AEPS), initiated in 1989 by Finland and formally launched in 1991 by the circumpolar nations, has provided a renewed impetus for Arctic research. The following working groups have addressed a wide range of environmental issues facing the Arctic: Arctic Monitoring and Assessment Programme; Conservation of Arctic Flora and Fauna; Protection of the Arctic Marine Environment; Emergency Prevention, Preparedness, and Response; Sustainable Development and Utilisation.

The establishment of a governmental Arctic Council in 1996 has led to its assumption of all activities of the AEPS. One priority of the new council will be continuing emphasis on the importance of scientific research in the Arctic.

ARCTIC RESEARCH STATIONS & CENTRES

Canada
Research stations have been located in the Arctic since the last decades of the 19th century. During the 20th century many have been temporary or seasonal stations; some were even located on sea ice as were the USSR's 'drift stations' in the Arctic Ocean from 1937 to 1991. All of the following modern research stations and centres are located near or above the Arctic Circle.

Title Page: Arctic Researchers at work (photograph by Laws(W Brigham)

For the past 40 years the primary organisation supporting Canada's Arctic research has been the Polar Continental Shelf Project (PCSP), a programme of the federal Department of Energy, Mines and Resources. PCSP has coordinated logistics for its two bases at Resolute Bay on the south coast of Cornwallis Island and at Tuktoyaktuk, on the Beaufort Sea in the north-western corner of the Northwest Territories. PCSP charges non-Canadian users for services and shares logistics costs with Canadian research teams. During the 1997 field season (March to September) PCSP supported 1000 scientists who were conducting more than 170 research projects throughout the Canadian Arctic.

Also in the Canadian Arctic, during 1995, the Nunavut Research Institute was established in Iqaluit. The research institute focuses on environmental issues including contaminants and linking Inuit traditional knowledge with western science. The Inuvik Research Center under the Science Institute of the Northwest Territories is an additional support organisation for conducting scientific research. The centre provides technical and logistics support for long-term data collection and focused research projects primarily in Canada's Western Arctic region.

Finland

Finland's major Arctic research institute is the Arctic Centre located on the Arctic Circle in the city of Rovaniemi. Founded in 1988 the centre is a separate institute of the University of Lapland. The centre's central mission is to access, understand and communicate the effects of global changes on Arctic societies and nature. It also services the international scientific community as the site for several secretariats involving global change and social sciences.

Denmark

The Danish Polar Centre (DPC), under the Danish Ministry for Research and Information Technology, supports Danish and international research throughout Greenland. In 1997 the DPC opened the Zackenberg Arctic Field Station on the north-east corner of Greenland (74°2′N, 20°33′W). The station's key research and monitoring programme is named ZERO (Zackenberg Ecological Research Operations). This will be a 50-year monitoring of animals, plants, climate, geology, and permafrost to assess the impacts of global climate change. Research programmes in physical geology, botany, zoology and ecosystems science can be supported. The DPC also supports KISS (Kangerlussuaq International Science Support), a year-round facility just north of the Arctic Circle along Greenland's south-west coast. This site, located near the former Søndre Strømfjord airport, has been a base for glaciological (deep drilling of ice cores) and geological research. Also, the US Thule Air Base (77°28′N, 69°12′W) has support services and capabilities for Arctic logistics for research purposes. In

1994 the Greenland Home Rule Government created the Greenland Institute of Natural Resource with offices in Nuuk. The institute's primary research includes natural resources, environmental protection and biodiversity. Focus is also on selected species valued by Greenland's society; scientific data are gathered for background to decisions regarding sustainable utilisation of Greenland's living resources.

Iceland

Iceland, a relatively small island and circumpolar nation, is uniquely linked to the Arctic environment and surrounding cold seas. The Marine Research Institute in Reykjavik conducts research on northern fisheries and all aspects of the Arctic marine environment. The University of Iceland in Reykjavik, especially it Faculty of Science and Faculty of Social Science, has conducted Arctic research for most of the 20th century. An Arctic Institute has also been established recently in the northern city of Akureyri.

The Stefansson Arctic Institute under the Icelandic Ministry of Environment was established in 1998 in the northern city of Akureyi. The institute's primary tasks will be to coordinate and facilitate Arctic research and northern issues in Iceland.

ARCTIC RESEARCH STATIONS & CENTRES

- ● Major Research Centre
- ○ Field Research Station
- ● Field Support Location

RUSSIA

William Barents
Dikson
Lena-Nordenskiöld
Tiksi
Apatity
Murmansk
FINLAND
Svanhovd Rovaniemi
SWEDEN
Tromsø Kiruna
Abisko
NORWAY
Ostrov Zhukova
Cherskiy

Average summer minimum extent of sea ice

North Pole

ARCTIC OCEAN

Ny Ålesund

Arctic Circle

Zackenberg

ICELAND
Akureyri

Barrow
Toolik
ALASKA
Fairbanks
GREENLAND
Thule
Reykjavik

Inuvik Tuktoyaktuk
Resolute
CANADA
Kangerlussuaq
Nuuk
Iqaluit

0   500   1000 km

Norway

In recent decades Norway has made sizeable investments in Arctic research. Ny Ålesund, Svalbard (78°53′N, 11°56′E) is both a centre for Norwegian Arctic research and an international base for interdisciplinary science. The Norwegian Polar Institute station established there in 1968 conducts year-round research in terrestrial and marine biology, geology, glaciology, meteorology and oceanography.

The universities of Bergen, Oslo and Tromsø also hold science courses at Ny Ålesund. A state-owned corporation (Kings Bay Kull Compani A/S), under the Ministry of Commerce and Energy, owns and operates the Ny Ålesund complex. Additional facilities include a nearby atmospheric research station (Norwegian Institute for Air Research) and a high-precision space geodesy observatory (Geodetic Institute of the Norwegian Mapping Authority). Three international year-round research programmes have been established at Ny Ålesund: Germany's Koldewey Station (Alfred-Wegener-Institute for Polar and Marine Research); Japan's International Arctic Environmental Research Station (National Institute for Polar Research); and the UK's programme sponsored by the UK National Environment Research Council.

In the north-east corner of mainland Norway a government institution, the Svanhovd Environmental Centre, has been established near the Russian border. The objectives of the centre are to gather and distribute information about the Barents Region, to be a research base, and to serve as a conference facility.

Tromsø, on Norway's north-west coast, is also widely recognised as one of the world's leading polar research centres. The federal Norwegian Polar Institute moved its headquarters in 1998 to Tromsø from Oslo. A major satellite receiving station and the University of Tromsø conduct a wide range of polar research programmes. The university has specific Arctic programmes in biology, fisheries, history and anthropology.

Sweden

Sweden maintains the Abisko Scientific Research Station, 200km north of the Arctic Circle on the southern shore of Lake Torneträsk (68°21′N, 18°48′E). The first field station was located in the area in 1903 and since 1935 the station has operated under the Royal Swedish Academy of Sciences. The primary areas of research are plant ecology and meteorology, and the station is open to Swedish and foreign investigators. The meteorological observatory has taken continuous measurements for 80 years.

The city of Kiruna also serves as a major centre of Arctic environmental and space research hosting several key institutions. Included under the Environment and Space Research Institute are four elements: the atmospheric research programme; environmental satellite data centre; climate impacts research centre; and spatial modelling centre on human dimension of environmental change. The Kiruna complex also includes a high-performance computer facility.

Russia

The number and viability of Russia's Arctic research stations and institutions have been changing rapidly since the end of the Soviet Union. For six decades prior to 1991 small research stations and several observatories ringed the Russian maritime Arctic; major observatories were located at Mys Chelyuskin (the northernmost point in mainland Eurasia), Mys Shmidta (in Chukotka on the Chukchi Sea), and in Franz Josef Land (Krenkel Observatory). Many other polar stations, now closed, supported national security, weather observations and shipping along the Northern Sea Route.

Today, two prominent polar research centres operate on the Kola Peninsula under the Russian Academy of Sciences: the Kola Science Centre in Apatity and the Murmansk Marine Biological Institute. Several fisheries research organisations are also located in the Murmansk area. A small research station is located on Ostrov Zochova in the New Siberian Islands, and although Russian funding for Arctic research has greatly reduced from Soviet times, logistic support is available from the Arctic coastal ports of Dikson, Tiksi and Cherskiy (on the Kolyma River and near the East Siberian Sea). Two recently completed research field stations in the Russian Arctic are worthy of note.

The Willem Barents Biological Station was established in 1993 with funding from the Netherlands Ministry of Agriculture, Nature Management and Fisheries to support Russia's Great Arctic Reserve on the Taymyr Peninsula. The main facility is located in a tundra region on Medusa Bay east of the port of Dikson – an ideal location for research on migratory birds. A second site, the Lena-Nordenskiöld Biological Station, located 100km from Tiksi on the Lena River delta, was inaugurated in 1995. The new research station was funded by the Sakha Republic government and the Swedish office of the World Wide Fund for Nature, and will support Arctic ecosystems research, environmental monitoring and management of the Lena Delta Reserve.

USA

The North Slope region of Alaska (a vast marshy tundra with shallow lakes located north of the Brooks Range) provides the United States with a foothold in the Arctic for field research. The Toolik Field Station operated by the Institute of Arctic Biology (University of Alaska Fairbanks) is located in the northern foothills of the Brooks Range on the south-east shore of Toolik Lake (68°38′W, 149°38′W) approximately 275km south of Prudhoe Bay. The station, a US national research facility for the study of terrestrial biology, freshwater biology, geology, hydrology and ecosystems, affords access to the Brooks Range, the Arctic foothills, and the Arctic coastal plain. Toolik Station provides key logistics to academic basic research associated with the Toolik Long-Term Ecological Research project, for more than two decades a multidisciplinary and experimental study of Arctic ecosystems.

Barrow, Alaska (71°17'N, 156°47'W) on the Beaufort Sea is a second site for American Arctic research. The ownership and management of the former (federal) Naval Arctic Research Laboratory has been taken over by the Barrow village corporation (Ukpeaqvik Inupiat Corporation – NARL). Laboratory, residential and telecommunications support are available for scientific research and educational projects. Within the UIC-NARL complex, the North Slope Borough operates a small research station, the Arctic Research Facility, for studies on bowhead whales, fisheries and waterfowl. Since 1973 the federal NOAA (National Oceanic and Atmospheric Administration) has maintained in Barrow the BRW Laboratory as a field site within the national Climate Monitoring and Diagnostics Laboratory. The BRW Laboratory is a key Arctic climate change research facility and provides support to more than 40 US and international projects.

The city of Fairbanks is a major gateway to the Arctic and an important US Arctic research centre. All departments of the University of Alaska Fairbanks conduct Arctic and subarctic studies; the Institutes of Arctic Biology, Marine Science and Northern Engineering are three research units of note. The university's Geophysical Institute is a leading US and international centre; co-located are the Alaska Synthetic Aperture Radar Facility (for receiving high-latitude satellite data) and a new joint US-Japan venture, the International Arctic Research Center. Located nearby is the Poker Flat Research Range that is used for scientific rocket launches for sounding the atmosphere.

ATMOSPHERIC RESEARCH – THE AURORA BOREALIS

The aurora borealis – the magical curtains or ribbons of colour in the northern night sky – is produced by the solar wind. This 'wind' is actually a stream of particles from the sun that collide with oxygen and hydrogen atoms in the upper atmosphere. The collisions produce the distinctive colour of the aurora located 70 to 200km above the earth. The earth's magnetic field, the field lines of which terminate in the Arctic and Antarctic, draws the solar wind particles toward the polar regions. Since the auroras are dependent on the sun, an increase in solar flares usually indicates the intensification of the polar aurora.

Research on the aurora phenomena is focused on predicting such disturbances in space and in the upper polar atmosphere. This is necessary since the auroras can disrupt high-latitude communications, electric power grids (causing blackouts), satellite orbiting and various defence systems.

One US facility for upper-atmosphere and solar-terrestrial research is HAARP (High-frequency Active Auroral Research Program). Built in 1995 near Gakona, Alaska HAARP's objective is to study the properties and behaviour of the ionosphere (see the boxed text 'Do Angels Play This HAARP?' in the Alaska chapter). This work is primarily accomplished using a high power, high frequency radio transmitter which stimulates or excites a small region of the ionosphere. The antenna system is made up of 180 towers in a 33 acre area. A large number of instruments detect the artificial effects produced by the radio transmission.

Near Tromsø, Norway, a five-nation consortium operates the European Incoherent Scatter Radar Site (EISCAT), another ionospheric research facility. Sensitive optical observations of the aurora in daytime are also taken at Ny Ålesund, Svalbard.

Ozone Depletion in the Arctic

The stratospheric ozone layer, located 10 to 50km above the earth, is crucial to the absorption of most ultraviolet (UV) radiation coming from the sun. The layer acts as a shield for the earth's surface from most of the biologically harmful portion of solar radiation. Research in the 1970s suggested that the ozone layer was being damaged by the use of man-made compounds such as chlorofluorocarbons (CFCs) found in air conditioners and refrigerators. Other damaging compounds have since been found. However, the seriousness of this ozone loss was not fully appreciated until the 1980s and the discovery of the well-known 'ozone hole' in the Antarctic.

Ozone depletion has also been observed in the Arctic and research has shown this decrease to have occurred since the late 1970s. During the early 1990s the average yearly ozone values in the Arctic were 10% lower than 20 years earlier. However, different patterns have emerged in the Arctic compared with the distinct Antarctic ozone hole. Arctic atmospheric circulation is less stable and the polar vortex does not normally allow the extremely low temperatures found in the Antarctic atmosphere. Satellite monitoring has shown that in the Arctic smaller 'holes' occur at different times during the late winter and early spring. Decreases of 25% to 40% ozone have been measured in regions over the Arctic Ocean, Greenland, northern Europe and Siberia.

Since the late 1980s UV surface monitoring sites have been established around the Arctic; the site at Point Barrow, Alaska observed that the daily ozone values in March 1997 were 6% below the previous ten year average. Recent satellite instruments have continued to monitor ozone levels in both polar regions. Since ozone depletion has been observed to be most severe in the polar regions, the long-term effects on human beings and Arctic ecosystems are crucial reasons for expanded research.

Arctic Haze

During the 1950s reconnaissance air crews observed an unusual reduction in visibility in the Arctic. Research during the 1970s showed that man-made, mid-latitude emissions were being transported to the Arctic from Europe and Asia. The haze, consisting of sulphate, soot and dust, was found to be seasonal with the highest values measured between December and April. This lower latitude pollution from fossil fuel combustion, smelting and other industrial emissions was being carried to the remotest regions of the Arctic Basin by winter and spring wind patterns.

More than any other observation, the Arctic haze phenomenon led to intensive monitoring and research regarding the pathways by which contaminants can reach the Arctic. Continued research has identified the Arctic environment as a natural sink for certain contaminants. Studies have shown that during winter, atmospheric particles can remain in the air for 20 to 30 days, allowing for long-range transport to the Arctic. Remote sensing research has also shown that Arctic haze is located in the lowest 5km of the atmosphere, with the highest values of contaminants found in the lowest 2km.

SEA ICE, GLACIERS AND PERMAFROST

Sea ice is a dominant feature of the Arctic Ocean and acts as a natural barrier between the atmosphere and the ocean. It undergoes considerable seasonal changes in extent – from a maximum of 16 million sq km in winter (March) to 9 million sq km in September.

Monitoring these seasonal fluctuations and interannual changes has been an important task of satellites during the past two decades. Regional studies using satellite and field data have also become key to understanding which regions are showing lower or shorter ice seasons.

Field measurements, drifting buoy observation (The International Arctic Buoy Programme) and satellite images have been assembled over many years to reveal two major ice circulation systems in the Arctic Ocean – an east to west Transpolar Drift in the Eurasian Arctic (out from the Russian coast) and a clockwise Beaufort Gyre (north of Alaska and Canada). Most ice in the Transpolar Drift eventually exits the Arctic Ocean at Fram Strait located between Greenland and Svalbard.

Recent research has also focused on the transport of sediments and contaminants by drifting Arctic sea ice. The freezing process in shallow Arctic seas results in the incorporation of sediments and other materials into the sea ice. Contaminants such as metals and radionucleides (from nuclear fuel reprocessing) and sediment have been transported hundreds of kilometres from shallow coastal areas to the deep basin of the Arctic Ocean.

In several regions of the Arctic Ocean systematic measurements of sea ice thickness have been taken. Submarines using upward-looking sonars have been used for data on ice thickness and under-ice topography. Upward sonars have also been moored to the sea floor in several projects. A successful experiment using sonars in Fram Strait has provided a valuable record of ice exiting the Arctic Ocean into the Greenland Sea.

The ice masses of the Arctic have attracted significant study and attention because they can be indicators of environmental change – a form of 'early warning' of climatic events. The largest Arctic glacial mass, the Greenland Ice Sheet (representing 10.9% of the world's total glacierized area), is routinely surveyed by aircraft and satellites for evidence of changes in thickness. While many outlet glaciers around Greenland have retreated during the last century, there is much debate about whether the ice sheet has 'lost' or 'gained' mass.

Recent observed temperature increases may result in higher precipitation (snow) on the ice sheet; evidence exists for such increases in snow accumulation from ice cores drilled on the summit. Glaciers in Svalbard, Franz Josef Land and Novaya Zemlya are also being monitored by field measurements and with the use of satellite imagery to determine ice velocities and overall glacial movement.

Permafrost, or perennially frozen ground, can reach 600-1000m depths in the coldest regions of the Arctic. Along the northern coasts of the Arctic Ocean permafrost also reaches out under the seabed of the shallow shelf seas. The study of permafrost has advanced dramatically in recent decades. An example is illustrated by the proceedings of the June 1998 Seventh International Permafrost Conference held in Yellowknife, Canada: included are 188 papers on all aspects of permafrost written by 368 authors from 19 countries! This should not be too surprising since permafrost underlies more than 25% of the earth's land surface.

Significant permafrost research has been conducted in Russia, Canada, Japan and Alaska for several decades. Many studies, some continuing today, are devoted to the practical issues of the construction of roads, buildings and pipelines on permafrost. Climate studies involve boring holes into the permafrost to monitor changes in depth of the frozen layer.

New research using modelling techniques has contributed projections for the reduction of permafrost under global warming. Simulations of various scenarios indicate 12-44% of permafrost may be lost. The active layer thickness (summer upper layer of Arctic soil that thaws) increases by as much as 50% in many Arctic regions. These potential changes in permafrost will have significant implications for local communities and future resource development projects.

Arctic Sea Ice

While high latitude icebergs are composed of ice calved from glaciers and ice sheets, sea ice is in fact frozen sea water. In the Northern Hemisphere sea ice reaches a maximum area during March of 16 million sq km, an area greater than Canada or the United States; in September the area of Arctic sea ice reduces to an average minimum of 9 million sq km.

In winter, sea ice is found as far south as the coast of Labrador, Cook Inlet (Alaska), in the Sea of Okhotsk and in the Baltic Sea. Summer coverage of sea ice is primarily confined to the central Arctic Ocean, the Greenland Sea, and Canada's Arctic Archipelago.

Sea ice is an important cover or 'blanket' over the Arctic Ocean substantially reducing the exchange of heat and mass between the ocean and atmosphere. It also limits the amount of solar radiation reaching the earth by reflecting incoming radiation back into space – while the open sea reflects approximately 10% of incoming solar radiation, snow-covered sea ice can reflect more than 80%.

Sea ice is generally formed in the shallow seas around the Arctic Ocean basin. Two major circulation patterns for Arctic sea ice have been observed: the Transpolar Drift and the Beaufort Gyre.

The Transpolar Drift carries ice westward from the surrounding coastal seas (primarily in the Russian Arctic) across the Arctic Ocean and into Fram Strait between Greenland and Svalbard. It can take one to three years for sea ice formed along the Russian coast to exit the Arctic Ocean into the Greenland Sea.

The Beaufort Gyre, located north of the Alaskan and Canadian coasts, rotates in a clockwise motion, or drift, and carries along ice formed in the Chukchi, Beaufort and East Siberian seas, as well as ice trapped from the Transpolar Drift. Ice caught in the Beaufort Gyre can circulate for more than five years, driven by seasonal winds and surface atmospheric pressures, before being swept into the Transpolar Drift, to eventually exit via Fram Strait.

Due to this constant circulation around the Arctic Ocean, sea ice can transport sediment and contaminants (captured in the freezing process in shallow waters) hundreds of kilometres to the remotest regions of the basin. Evidence of this unusual transport was confirmed during the 1994 US-Canada Arctic Ocean Section Expedition when pockets of 'dirty ice' were sampled along a track from the Chukchi Sea to the North Pole. Other contaminants in the form of atmospheric particles can be deposited on the surface of sea ice and transported across great distances.

Arctic sea ice in confined areas, such as coastal seas, can grow to level thickness of 2m during winter. However, sea ice rarely forms a flat, uniform sheet since the action of winds, waves, currents and
(continued overleaf)

Arctic Sea Ice

tides moves and breaks the ice into floes of various sizes. Because of these forces, ice floe thicknesses can vary between 0.4m and 5m. Old or multiyear ice is found throughout the central Arctic Ocean; it has survived two or more summer melt seasons and is generally more than 3m thick. Winter sea ice north of Greenland and the Canadian Arctic Archipelago can be greater than 6m thick, while winter ice at the North Pole has been found, from submarine sonar data, to be 3 to 4m in thickness. At the end of each winter 2m thick (or less) first-year ice covers most of the shallow, shelf seas around the Arctic Ocean basin.

Considerable research in recent years has revealed the formation process and structure of sea ice to be quite complex. Due to the presence of dissolved salts and other solids in the ocean, the freezing point of sea water is not 0°C, but averages -1.8°C. During sea ice formation, ice crystals develop while salt is rejected and released into the underlying ocean. However, at cooler temperatures some salt is retained in brine pockets within the columnar structure of the sea ice. These pockets migrate down through the sea ice as it ages, and thus the salinity of sea ice decreases through time. Recently formed sea ice can have a salinity of 15 to 20 parts per thousand while old ice can be as low as two parts per thousand. The cold brine or salt that is rejected into the water beneath the sea ice increases the salinity and density of the surrounding surface waters. These denser waters gradually sink and can eventually contribute to the circulation of deeper waters in the Arctic Ocean. This growth process of sea ice in the Arctic and Antarctic is believed to play a significant role in the formation and circulation of bottom water throughout the global oceans.

Satellite remote sensing during the late 20th century has revolutionised the way in which Arctic sea ice can be viewed. Since the early l970s, satellite microwave sensors have provided routine sea ice and polar ocean observations. These sensors have the ability to

SIGNIFICANT ARCTIC RESEARCH PROJECTS OF THE 1990s

This section is a selection of major Arctic research projects, each of which has either taken place or is ongoing at the end of the 20th century. Although most of the projects are interdisciplinary, this is only a sample and not all disciplines are represented. However, those included should provide a glimpse of the variety, complexity and international nature of modern Arctic science and research.

Arctic Sea Ice

monitor the earth's surface day or night and under all weather conditions, including cloud cover (in comparison, satellite visible sensors are greatly limited by clouds and polar darkness). Such large-scale observations of sea ice coverage have become increasingly important to research on global environmental change. A recent study of satellite microwave data reported in *Science* shows that from 1978 to 1996 the extent of Arctic sea ice decreased by 2.9% per decade. Although this is a short record in time, such observations indicating change are invaluable to the continuing research and assessment of the earth's changing climate.

Lawson W Brigham,
Scott Polar Research Institute,
University of Cambridge, UK

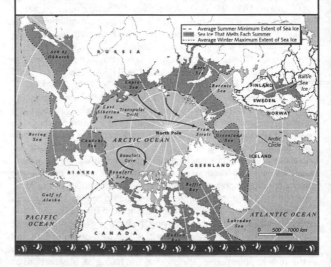

International Tundra Experiment (ITEX)

Since 1990, an international field project under the Man and the Biosphere programme – ITEX – has conducted extensive studies in Arctic ecology. The main objective of ITEX is to assess the potential impact of global warming on Arctic and alpine vegetation. The approach to field research has been two-fold: first, the performance of plant species and communities in undisturbed Arctic habitats is monitored; second, the surface temperature where the plants live is artificially raised 2-3°C. This experiment is an attempt to simulate the climate that may exist in

2050 based on several General Circulation Models. Field monitoring sites ring the Arctic and have also been placed in several alpine areas; sites are located in Canada, Finland, Greenland, Iceland, Japan, Norway, Russia, Sweden, Switzerland and the USA. The ITEX secretariat is located at the Danish Polar Centre in Copenhagen.

Results show that under increased temperatures there is evidence of a disintegration of the plant communities (loss of species and biodiversity) on the tundra. With new plants slow to move into the tundra areas, animal populations using these regions will be at risk. ITEX monitoring and experimental research will continue into the next century and should provide more long-term understanding of the Arctic botanical processes at work under climate change.

Surface Heat Budget of the Arctic Ocean (SHEBA)

In an experiment reminiscent of Fridtjof Nansen's *Fram* drift in the Arctic Ocean (1893-96), the USA established a drifting research station on 2 October 1997 at 75°N, 142°W (300 nautical miles north of Alaska). Project SHEBA's core objective was a coordinated sampling and measurement programme from the drifting ice pack in the central Arctic Ocean. During 13-month drift (aboard the icebound Canadian Coast Guard icebreaker *Des Groseillers*), the SHEBA station meandered 2700 nautical miles along a circuitous route to 80°15′N, 166°1′W.

The primary research, funded by the US National Science Foundation, focused on the interaction among sea ice, atmospheric radiation and clouds. A comprehensive data set was taken from the mixed layer of the ocean (to several hundred metres depth), sea ice, snow cover and into the atmosphere (sampling to a height of several kilometres with balloons and aircraft). The key task was to document the detailed physical processes of this ocean-ice-atmosphere 'column' for a full annual cycle. These observations are important to improving model simulations of the Arctic climate and to the future interpretation of satellite remote sensing data.

Another team of Canadian and American marine biologists and physical oceanographers were studying the biology of the Arctic Ocean (Joint Ocean Ice Study). Measurements were taken of the carbon flux in and out of the ocean, plant productivity, and the entire food chain in this remote polar region. The physical and biological observations of Project SHEBA during an entire year will significantly advance our understanding of the Arctic climate system.

International Northern Sea Route Programme (INSROP)

A landmark interdisciplinary research study – INSROP – was coordinated during 1993-99 by the Fridtjof Nansen Institute in Norway. The work focused on all aspects of the Northern Sea Route (NSR), the Arctic waterways north of Eurasia (and Russia) that allow shipping access to the Russian North and can potentially be an international route between Atlantic and Pacific oceans. The NSR was officially opened to international shipping by the USSR on 1 July 1991.

The programme was led by three main cooperating partners: the Ship and Ocean Foundation of Japan, the Central Marine Research and Design Institute of Russia; and the Fridtjof Nansen Institute of Norway. Sponsors were from these three countries and 468 researchers from 14 nations contributed to the broad research programme. In phase one, INSROP was divided into four sub-programmes: natural conditions and ice navigation; environmental factors; trade and commercial shipping aspects; political, legal and strategic factors.

More than 160 research reports have been published including key topics such as: new icebreaking tanker and cargo ship designs for the NSR; an NSR geographic information system; impact analyses of the NSR on Russian Arctic indigenous peoples; analyses of sea ice variability and distribution in the coastal seas; regional economic studies of trade in the Russian Arctic; analyses of the environmental risks of NSR shipping; and the use of satellite remote sensing of sea ice for NSR navigation.

In phase, two simulations were run of potential cargo flows and NSR seasonal and year-round operations. The information available from INSROP will enable public and private interests to make informed and rational decisions about the use of the NSR for marine commerce.

Mackenzie Basin Impact Study (MBIS)

The Mackenzie Basin region in northern Canada is one of the world's largest high-latitude watersheds (1.8 million sq km). It is subarctic and Arctic, running north from British Columbia and Alberta to the Northwest Territories where the Mackenzie River delta meets the Beaufort Sea.

Federally funded by Environment Canada, the six year (1990-96) MBIS was designed to assess the potential impacts of climate change on this key region of Canada. It was a regional, integrated assessment that included many stakeholders throughout the process – individuals from the federal, provincial and territorial governments, universities, aboriginal organisations and the private sector. Four scenario cases were studied in terms of the impacts to the basin: changing water levels; changing land capabilities; changing fire weather and the effects of renewable resource impacts on nonrenewable resource development.

A vast amount of environmental and socioeconomic data was amassed during the study. The consultation process and participatory approach were challenging when added to the complex, multidisciplinary research necessary to begin understanding the natural processes within the Mackenzie Basin.

Ice Cores of the Greenland Ice Sheet

During the 1990s two long ice cores were drilled and retrieved from the Greenland ice sheet. A European project, GRIP (Greenland Ice Core

Programme), and a US effort, GISP2 (Greenland Ice Sheet Project Two), produced cores that have yielded a unique record of climatic change over the past 110,000 years.

These cores from the summit of the Greenland ice sheet are the oldest environmental records in the northern hemisphere. GISP2 reached the base of the central Greenland Ice Sheet on 1 July 1993 (3053.44m depth) at 72°35′N, 38°29′W.

The ice in the two cores preserves critical information about the chemical composition and physical properties of past atmospheres – a history of volcanic activity, sea ice extent, fires, marine storms and other extreme events. The GISP2 and GRIP cores have been found to be remarkably similar when comparing the two parallel records of such properties as electrical conductivity and oxygen isotopes.

Minor features or events in the records have also been found to match closely. Analyses of both records together have shown that major climatic changes have occurred during the time of human occupation of the Arctic. Measurements of carbon dioxide in the air bubbles of the GISP2 core show abrupt increases in concentration in the early 19th century. These observations correspond well with long-term atmospheric carbon dioxide records in other regions. The GISP2 and GRIP ice cores and others in the Arctic are highly valuable

ARCTIC RESEARCH PROJECTS OF THE 1990s

environmental records since they span several glacial cycles and can be dated precisely.

Nuclear Submarines & Arctic Oceanography

In a sign of extraordinary change in the post-Cold War era, US nuclear submarines have been used during the decade of the 1990s for oceanographic research cruises in the Central Arctic Ocean. Following a trial cruise aboard the USS *Pargo* in 1993, the attack submarine USS *Cavalla* was deployed to the Arctic Ocean for science in April and May 1995. Sailing more than 10,000 nautical miles within the Arctic Ocean, the *Cavalla* collected 4,725 water samples and gathered continuous data on ice draft, bathymetry, gravity, sea water temperature and sea water conductivity.

A significant cross-basin transect from Point Barrow, Alaska to a position north of Franz Josef Land yielded valuable observations on physical oceanographic features, under ice topography and bathymetry. Subsequent cruises of SCIEX – the Submarine Arctic Science Programme – have included geophysical surveys of many of the least explored regions of the Arctic Basin (USS *Pogy* in 1996 and USS *Hawkbill* in 1998). The extraordinary range and mobility of the nuclear submarine, as well as its ability to remain submerged for months, have made it an ideal platform for extensive sampling of the Arctic Ocean.

International Expeditions to the Russian Arctic Coast

Access to the Russian Arctic has been opened to foreign scientists who are collaborating with Russian investigators. During the summer of 1994 a Swedish-Russian Tundra Ecology Expedition sailed across the Russian Arctic aboard the Russian polar research ship *Akademik Fedorov*.

Sixty scientists from seven nations participated in this expedition, the major objective of which was to conduct a detailed survey of the tundra ecosystems of this region. The unusual plan was to sail along a route with the same team of investigators and carry out terrestrial research from the ship. Supported by the Swedish and Russian academies of sciences, the expedition gathered a wealth of ecological information on tundra soils, migratory birds, plant distributions, lemmings and fish populations.

A second major programme involved German and Russian scientific collaboration. During 1992-96 research cruises were conducted in the Laptev Sea by a joint German-Russian team of scientists. The Laptev Sea System Programme was focused on both ocean and terrestrial processes. The Laptev Sea is a major ice-production area for the Arctic Ocean and is also the recipient of large volumes of Lena River water during spring and early summer. Extensive sampling was done for sea ice, sediments, phytoplankton, zooplankton and benthos. Experiments were conducted on the incorporation of sediment into sea ice during the freeze-up process. Studies based on radio carbon dating of bivalve shells in sediment cores provided new information on the recent history of the region.

US/Canada Arctic Ocean Section 1994 Expedition

During July and August 1994 two polar icebreakers, the Canadian Coast Guard's *Louis S. St Laurent* and the US Coast Guard's *Polar Sea*, crossed the Arctic Ocean on an historic scientific voyage. The two ships with an expedition science party of 70 sailed from the ice edge in the Chukchi Sea on 25 July, reached the North Pole on 22 August, and exited the ice edge off Svalbard on 29 August.

The scientific sampling was the first conducted from surface ships along a section into the central Arctic Ocean from Bering Strait to the North Pole. A host of measurements of the atmosphere, sea ice, ocean and seabed were made at each station. Also included were observations of the concentration and distribution of contaminants along the route, a polar bear study, and a ship technology programme focusing on ship performance and ice navigation.

Notable findings included the following: sediment observed along the track on the sea ice from the Chukchi Sea to the North Pole; an Atlantic layer of water in the Arctic Ocean that was found to be 0.5 to 1.0°C warmer than prior to 1993; polar bears and ringed seals observed across the entire Arctic Basin; cloud optical properties linked to marine biogenic sulphur emissions; an active microbial community in the sea indicating bacteria and protists are significant consumers of plant production; meso-zooplankton biomass found to be increasing with latitude (as the ships sailed north); total biological productivity found to be significantly higher than previous estimates in the central Arctic Ocean; and ice thicknesses from 1m in the Chukchi Sea to 2.4m at the North Pole.

Real-time satellite imagery was received aboard the *Polar Sea* and used for ice navigation throughout the voyage. The *Polar Sea* was also linked to a low-orbiting communications satellite (LES), which provided Internet and email connections and allowed the science party to communicate with a host of laboratories.

UNDERSTANDING THE ARCTIC OCEAN

The Arctic Ocean is a 'Mediterranean sea' (a sea surrounded by land) that receives most of its water through Fram Strait, the Barents Sea and Bering Strait. Rivers rimming the basin also contribute 2% of the water inflow. A small amount of water flows out of the straits in the Canadian Archipelago. However, the main outflow is again through Fram Strait via the East Greenland Current. It is this cold current that brings ice and polar water out of the Arctic Ocean into the remaining world ocean. Thus, the Arctic Ocean is strongly linked to the Greenland Sea and by extension, the North Atlantic Ocean. Much research is now focused on understanding better the oceanography of the seas north of Iceland, and on how the Arctic Ocean is linked to the Atlantic (by ice, ocean and atmospheric processes).

During the past 15 years polar icebreakers with oceanographers aboard have probed farther into the Arctic Ocean than ever before. Instruments have been lowered through 4000m to obtain water samples at all depths of the ocean. Advances in chemistry have allowed the detection of very minute concentrations of natural (for example, oxygen and barium) and man-made (radionucleides and chlorofluorocarbons) substances. These water mass 'tracers' have provided new insights into the circulation of the Arctic Ocean by indicating how long it takes to replace or renew water in a particular reservoir or layer. Water has been calculated to reside on the shallow shelves for one to three years while Arctic surface waters may be replaced in ten years. Deeper waters have longer residence times of several decades to a century. Knowledge of these water masses and their residence times are key to determining how sensitive the Arctic Ocean is to environmental change.

As with all natural science today, modelling has become a key research tool for studying the Arctic Ocean. The increase in computer capability has fostered the development of three-dimensional models that connect the ocean and ice environments. Model simulations have recently shown how freshwater from Arctic rivers circulates around the ocean basin. Other modelling efforts have simulated ice extent, motion and growth, and the distribution of many physical, chemical and biological properties of the Arctic Ocean. Future models will be called upon as predictive tools, but the accuracy of their output must be continually compared with long-term field observations of the Arctic marine environment.

ARCTIC CLIMATIC CHANGES

The Arctic in recent decades has been undergoing significant changes. Since 1978, polar-orbiting satellites monitoring Arctic sea ice have observed a 2.9% decrease in ice extent every decade. There have also been notable decreases in ice extent in the Bering and East Siberian seas. Icebreaker expeditions and nuclear submarine cruises have showed that Atlantic water is more widespread and intense in the central Arctic Ocean than previously measured. During the past 30 years Arctic temperatures from meteorological stations (1966-99) have shown regions of significant warming – over northern Canada, Alaska and Eurasia (2°C per decade winter temperature increases in some regions). Annual snowfall has increased by 20% over Canada and 11% over Alaska. And, borehole measurements on permafrost indicate a 2-4°C warming.

Another perspective on Arctic environmental change has involved research on palaeoclimate records, including ice cover from glaciers, tree-ring records, and lake and marine sediments. The analyses, going back 400 years, showed that from 1840 to the mid-20th century, the Arctic warmed to its highest temperatures (over the four century span).

Two major research studies related to the assessment of global change on Arctic regions are ongoing. BASIS – the Barents Sea Impacts Study –

is an integrated assessment of global change impacts on cultural and so-cioeconomic systems (that are dependent on renewable and nonrenew-able resources) in the Barents Sea region. Funded by the European Commission and European Scientific Foundation, BASIS involves 17 in-vestigators from eight nations. BASIS research encompasses ocean climate and fisheries, impacts on major terrestrial natural resources, per-mafrost and hydrology and the integrated effects of global changes on the socioeconomic system and conditions for sustainable development.

BESIS – the Bering Sea Impacts Study – is an interdisciplinary project funded primarily by US federal agencies to: assess the nature and mag-nitude of changes in the western Arctic/Bering Sea; predict the conse-quences of these changes on the region's physical, biological and socioeconomic systems; determine the probable cumulative impacts; and investigate policy options to mitigate the cumulative impacts. The following areas are being studied: fisheries, coastal core, land ecosys-tems, social and cultural conditions, resources and infrastructure. BASIS and BESIS are under the auspices of the International Arctic Science Committee. Both regions are important economically, have local in-digenous populations, and are sensitive to climatic fluctuations.

THE HUMAN DIMENSION

The most striking difference between the two polar regions is that the Arctic has had indigenous human populations for at least 15,000 years. The variety of human cultures and their extraordinary capacity to adapt to the demands of living in the high latitudes are remarkable. As one might surmise, research on the human condition in the Arctic takes in a broad spectrum of disciplines – anthropology, archaeology, eco-nomics, geography, history, linguistics, political science and sociology. However, this research usually cuts across disciplinary boundaries and most programmes have become highly international.

A sampling of general topics for recent research includes: ethnic and regional identities, particularly in the Russian Arctic; development of re-gional Arctic political institutions; the relationships between Arctic cul-tures and the environment; the use of Traditional Ecological Knowledge (TEK) in western science; the changing social conditions of Arctic com-munities; the impacts on Arctic communities of large-scale development in the Arctic; and, key issues related to subsistence hunting.

Selected research projects can provide a cursory perspective on the range of studies undertaken to understand better the linkages between Arctic human populations and their physical/biological environment. In Canada one research study on TEK gathered information from 15 Inuit and 13 Cree communities in the Hudson Bay region. Arctic residents discussed their traditional views and values of the environment and their ecological observations related to the Hudson Bay ecosystem. A database of this information can be helpful during assessments of future development in the region.

Several studies under the International Northern Sea Route Programme were social impact assessments of the Route on indigenous peoples. As an example, along the Yenisey River valley, year-round open sea lanes (maintained by icebreakers) have formed new barriers to the natural caribou migrations; this disruption threatens a key food staple of the local native population. Another study seeks to understand the relationships between sea ice, climate changes and Icelandic fisheries throughout history. The frequent presence of sea ice in past centuries was quite detrimental in that fishing vessels could not put to sea and lower air temperatures were the norm.

Significant research has also been conducted on the collapse of the Norse settlements in Greenland around 1350. Radiocarbon dating and the use of GISP2 ice core climate records indicates that the settlement was abandoned during a series of cold summers and winters during the 14th century. A final example relates to many studies on Beringia – the former land bridge across Bering Strait linking Alaska and Chukotka. Extensive data dating back 16,000 years are used to show vegetation and shoreline changes.

ECOSYSTEMS & BIOLOGICAL RESEARCH

Arctic marine ecosystems research has typically focused in regions where fishing was commercially viable. Decades of studies of the Barents and Bering seas provide a basic understanding of the nutritional levels involved and overall ecosystems dynamics within these regional seas. However, both seas are being impacted by a changing climate and increased fishing, and ongoing research will need to consider such alterations.

Recent studies have highlighted the biological importance of the Arctic Ocean and its surrounding shelves. Ice algae are now believed to be a more significant component of primary production in the central Arctic Ocean. Potential changes in the extent of sea ice will have significant impacts on Arctic marine ecosystems and continued modelling research may be able to predict such climatic impacts. Marine mammal research in all of the circumpolar nations has focused on a range of subjects including: population stability, physiological adaptation, marine mammal interaction with the fisheries, and subsistence hunting.

Much of Arctic terrestrial biology is conducted on the tundra and can involve an important subsistence resource. Arctic terrestrial research has benefited immensely from the use of satellite technology. As an example, caribou migration on the North Slope of Alaska has been studied by tracking satellite-collared animals. Seasonal patterns have been observed with this technique and the research results indicate that climate change may affect caribou movements.

Satellite monitoring has also played a key role in the observation of increased plant growth in the northern high latitudes. Data from meteorological satellites suggest an increase in plant growth associated with a lower growing season (spring warming that causes an early melt of snow). In addition to these regional and global studies, investigators are also looking at tundra plants from a process point of view. The interactions of water, carbon and nutrients are being analysed using ecosystem models.

THE FUTURE OF ARCTIC RESEARCH

The future of Arctic research is promising in view of the expanded international cooperation of the 1990s. Since the end of the Cold War, nearly all of the Arctic has been open for the conduct of science, including the Russian Arctic on occasion for joint foreign-Russian research programmes.

This is in sharp contrast to when these key tundra regions and Arctic coastal seas were tightly controlled under the Soviet Union. There has been a much improved sharing of regional environmental data – the Barents Sea is a good example – and this will be continued into the next millennium. Increased cooperation and a 'pooling' of Arctic logistics capability have also led to successes of complex, multidisciplinary projects taken to the remotest regions of the Arctic Basin. The continued development of the Arctic Council and the International Arctic Science Committee should help to maintain research as a priority within the circumpolar governments, particularly where climate change impacts may be notable.

New and highly capable research tools will become available to Arctic researchers. An entire new generation of remote sensing satellites will be launched. For example, a US satellite named *Icesat* (to be launched in 2001) will be equipped with a sensitive laser altimeter that will precisely measure changes in mass of the Greenland and Antarctic ice sheets. More capable autonomous underwater vehicles (AUVs) can potentially contribute to future Arctic oceanographic operations – sampling deep sea communities, the water column and underwater geologic features. A greater use of improved geographic information systems will assist the merging of an enormous amount of satellite as well as field data taken across the Arctic.

Novel and exciting research programmes are being planned. Marine geologists and geophysicists are preparing for extensive shipboard expeditions into the central Arctic Ocean to unravel the mysteries of Arctic tectonic history. Oceanographers are focusing efforts to understand better the Arctic shelves (30% of the Arctic Ocean's area), especially bio-geochemical cycling, sea ice formation and sediment records. New studies on the health of Arctic marine ecosystems – and the effects of UV radiation and organic contaminant cycling – will be supported. One of the most important activities will be research aimed at providing a better predictive capability to assess future Arctic climate change.

Integral to all change research will be studies related to the impacts of environmental change on the Arctic's human population and how these residents can adapt. There is little doubt continued research will show how even more strongly the Arctic influences the rest of the planet.

ARCTIC LITERATURE

By Norbert Schurer

For a region some consider cold and barren, the Arctic has inspired a surprising amount of literature. As a matter of fact, in proportion to the number of people who have set foot in the area – as indigenes, explorers or visitors – the Arctic has probably produced more literature than any other region on earth.

There are two overarching themes to Arctic literature (meaning works written in, concerned with, set in, or inspired by the Arctic). The first is loneliness: the feeling inspired by the magnitude of Arctic nature and humans' insignificance in it, whether they be indigenous or visitors. The second is mutual understanding. From the earliest times, explorers have attempted to comprehend not only their natural surroundings, but the indigenous people they encountered in the Arctic. In turn, these people have been trying to come to terms with the colonial attacks on their country and culture as well as the more well-intentioned influences of the contemporary world.

Nonfiction

HISTORY & EXPLORATION

Perhaps the best place to start with a survey of Arctic literature is with the history of its discovery by denizens of more southerly regions. Most comprehensively, Richard Vaughan's *The Arctic: A History* (1994) spans the time from 12,000 years ago until the present. Vaughan considers archaeological evidence of early habitation, the history of whaling and the fur trade, exploration and colonisation of all parts of the Arctic – Canadian, Russian and everything in between – and the future survival of the indigenous people of the polar regions in the face of scientific exploitation and environmental destruction.

More narrow in scope, Jeannette Mirsky's classical account of the exploration of the Arctic from ancient Greece to the early 20th century, *To the Arctic* (1934), has recently been reissued in paperback. This volume contains the best published chronology of expeditions – unfortunately not updated since the original edition of 1934. Frank Rasky's *The North Pole or Bust* (1977) is told more like a suspense thriller, sprinkling the stories of Arctic explorers from Sir John Franklin to Vilhjalmur Stefansson with dialogue, mostly from the printed sources, to lighten the reading.

The best history of the race for the North Pole is Pierre Berton's *The Arctic Grail, The Quest for the Northwest Passage and the North Pole, 1818-1909* (1988). In this book, the explorers emerge as heroes in spite of their failings, but the Inuit also receive their due. Berton combines scholarly and more journalistic writing to enthral the common reader without disappointing the specialist.

In *Cook & Peary* (1997), Robert Bryce focuses on the race between Frederick Cook and Robert Peary and comes to the conclusion that neither reached the Pole, knew it and lied about it. The author argues that the quest for the North Pole 'has more rewards than arriving at its destination' and reveals some of the 'inaccessible mysteries that lie within the ultimate enigma of the human heart and mind'.

Another classic is Wally Herbert's *The Noose of Laurels: Robert E. Peary & the Race to the North Pole* (1989), which concentrates on the same subject, emphasising the explorers' need to be not just discoverers, but also heroes. Herbert knows what he is talking about; in 1969, he was the first person to reach the North Pole by dogsled (with the British Transarctic Expedition).

Finally, Mick Conefrey & Tim Jordan's *Icemen* (1998) is the volume accompanying the BBC television series of the same title. Starting with Franklin and the Northwest Passage, the authors follow the various attempts to reach the North Pole and then move on to discuss the contemporary strategic and political importance of the Arctic, and the conflicts between the Inuit and the Canadian government. The book is illustrated with black-and-white stills from early expeditions.

Recently, a number of authors have also tried to raise awareness of neglected aspects of Arctic discovery, or re-evaluate traditional histories. S Allen Counter's *North Pole Legacy: Black, White & Eskimo* (1991) centres on Matthew Henson, Peary's black companion on almost all of his Arctic expeditions. Counter, a descendant of Henson's, not only succeeded in having Henson, who died in poverty, reinterred at Arlington National Cemetery next to Peary, but also organised a reunion of Henson's American and Inuit families.

W Gillies Ross has edited the journal of Margaret Penny as *The Distant & Unsurveyed Country: A Woman's Winter at Baffin Island*. Travelling with her husband, the captain of the whaler *Lady Franklin*, Penny spent the winter of 1857-58 on Baffin Island – the first European woman to spend a winter in the Arctic. Her journals and Ross' annotations provide unique insight into life on a whaling ship and the relationship between the Inuit and Europeans. Not nearly as convincingly, Lisa Bloom's *Gender on Ice* (1990) looks at the typically masculine ideology underpinning the expeditions of Peary and Cook, and examines the role of the National Geographic Society and photography in polar exploration.

Bryan McCannon investigates a frequently neglected topic, the Soviet Union's part in Arctic exploration, in his *Red Arctic* (1994). In clear and well-organised writing, McCannon concentrates on the Stalinist 1930s, when Soviet exploration was at its zenith.

Of course the narratives and journals of many individual explorers (such as Peary, Rasmussen, Nansen, Stefansson and Freuchen) are available as well – on their own, or in excerpts. In 1999, the University of Alaska Fairbanks published a new edition of Knud Rasmussen's beautifully written classic, *Across Arctic America*. The most significant collection of excerpts is the *Top of the World Trilogy*, edited by Farley Mowat. *Ordeal by Ice* (1960) concentrates on the search for the Northwest Passage and takes the reader up to the middle of the 19th century;

The Polar Passion (1967) departs from about that point and traces the pursuit of the North Pole until Cook's 'arrival' there in 1909; *Tundra* (1973) shifts attention to the exploration of the north Canadian Arctic land mass from the end of the 18th to the middle of the 20th century. In *Farthest North: The Quest for the North Pole* (1994), Clive Holland has assembled excerpts from travellers from antiquity to the present.

A classic travel narrative is *Letters from High Latitudes* (1856) by Lord Dufferin, whose full name was Frederick Temple Hamilton-Temple-Blackwood, 1st Marquess of Dufferin and Ava, Earl of Ava, Earl of Dufferin, Viscount Clandeboye, Baron Clandeboye, Baron Dufferin and Clandeboye of Ballyleidy and Killyleagh. Before he became governor general of Canada, British ambassador to Turkey, and viceroy of India later in his life, this scion of an old English family sailed extensively in the North Atlantic at the age of 30. His book, which is still accurate and relevant in large parts, is subtitled *Being Some Account of a Voyage, in 1856, in the Schooner Yacht Foam to Iceland, Jan Mayen, & Spitzbergen.*

Another early travel account is illustrator Rockwell Kent's *N by E* (1930), which recounts Kent's disastrous trip to Greenland via Newfoundland and Labrador in a small schooner. The book stands out for its description of the relationships between the three travellers as well as the Inuit society they encountered, and for Kent's 100 magnificent woodcuts and sketches accompanying the text. Other Greenland-theme works by Kent are *Salamina, Voyaging* and *Rockwell Kent's Greenland Journal.*

The best place to find copies of explorers' books – most of which are out of print – is Colin Bull's Polar Books (☎ 206-842 9660, email gbull@linknet.kitsap.lib.wa.us), PO Box 4675, Rolling Bay, Washington 98061, USA.

Sir John Franklin

Unless one is willing to credit the third, disappeared expedition with the discovery of the Northwest Passage, the three expeditions led by Sir John Franklin between 1819 and 1847 were fairly unimportant with regard to scientific or geographical discoveries. Nevertheless, of all Arctic exploration they seem to have most inspired the imagination of writers in a variety of genres, bridging the categories of fiction and nonfiction.

Franklin's first expedition of 1819-22 to the mouth of the Coppermine River was especially fruitful in this respect. Of the five English participants, four left written (and painted) records of their experiences. The then 33-year-old Franklin wrote the *Narrative of a Journey to the Shores of the Polar Sea*, making use of the notes of his co-explorers as well as his own journals, which have been republished recently.

Over the last decades, scholar C Stuart Houston has edited the journals of the other three Englishmen. The records of Franklin's second-in-command – who went on to become a significant Arctic explorer in his own right – have been made available in *Arctic Ordeal: The Journal of John Richardson, Surgeon-Naturalist with Franklin* (1994). This edition concentrates on Richardson's observations of flora and fauna as well as his geological field work.

The beautiful edition *Arctic Artist: The Journal and Paintings of George Back, Midshipman with Franklin* (1995) is divided into chapters according to steps in the expedition's progress. But the most wonderful parts of the volume are the excellent reproductions of Back's 50-odd paintings and engravings of Stone and Yellowknife Indians, animals, natural scenery and the expedition. Like Richardson, Back stayed in the navy, returned to the Arctic, and died in 1876 as a highly decorated and respected admiral.

To the Arctic by Canoe, 1821: The Journal and Paintings of Robert Hood, Midshipman with Franklin (1974) is a similar edition. Of course, Hood did not make it back to England but died in 1821 under mysterious circumstances. He was probably killed by the Iroquois voyager Michel Terohaute either by accident (this is what Terohaute claimed), or to put him out of his misery (he was dying of starvation), or to eat him (Terohaute almost certainly fed human flesh to Richardson and Hood earlier), or due to competition over a woman. Unfortunately, Houston does not include in his edition Hood's picture of that woman, the Copper Indian Greenstockings, perhaps because only the engraving in Franklin's narrative rather than the original painting has survived.

After the disappearance of the third Franklin expedition after 1845, a continuing stream of expeditions looking for Franklin went to the Arctic for the next 30 years. Many of these expeditions (some of which managed to get lost themselves) left their own records. Most recently, Robert Randolph Carter's *Searching for the Franklin Expedition* (de Haven expedition of 1850-51), Emile Frederic de Bray's *A Frenchman in Search of Franklin* (Belcher expedition of 1852-54) and Francis Leopold McClintock's *The Voyage of the Fox in the Arctic Seas* (1857-59) have become available in contemporary editions.

The events have also been re-examined by David Woodman 'in the light of native traditions and recollections concerning strange white men in the Arctic' in his book *Unravelling the Franklin Mystery* (1991). The same author collected 'some unresolved stories dealing with white men farther east in the Melville Peninsula', probably members of the Franklin expedition trying to make it home, in *Strangers Among Us* (1995). Excerpts from all available records of Franklin's expeditions and the 30 year search have been combined by Paul Nanton into the fascinating account *Arctic Breakthrough* (1970). In *Frozen in Time* (1987), Canadian scientists Owen Beattie and John Geiger describe their exhumation of three graves of members of the Franklin expedition on Beechey Island in the 1980s. These graves of seamen, who died in 1846, had been discovered by the de Haven expedition in 1850. Accompanied by haunting photographs, Beattie and Geiger's research shows that at least one contributing factor to the failure of Franklin's expedition was lead poisoning from newly introduced tin cans (which were sealed with lead).

But next to the literature of exploration and science, the Franklin disaster also inspired imaginative literature almost immediately. As early as 1858, one JA Turner wrote a poem titled 'The Discovery of Sir John Franklin', and one of Algernon Swinburne's first poems was 'The Death of Sir John Franklin' of 1860. Alfred, Lord Tennyson wrote the epitaph for Franklin, and Dickens produced a play about him. In contemporary times, authors such as Gerald St Maur and Gwendolyn MacEwen (the latter including an Inuit perspective) have written more poetry on the same subject.

The Franklin expeditions have also inspired a number of serious novels. German author Sten Nadolny's excellent fictionalised biography titled *The Discovery of Slowness* (1983) concentrates on a particular quality of its protagonist; his slowness, which allowed him to develop extraordinary stamina and made the slow-moving Arctic the perfect place for him. While Franklin's apparent lethargy made him seem out of sync with the European world, it also helped him to recognise structures and patterns in nature and culture that most people in his fast-paced times could not see. Robert Erdric's *The Broken Lands* (1992) tells the story of the third Franklin expedition from the point of view of James Fitzjames and Francis Crozier, the captains of Franklin's two ships *Erebus* and *Terror*. The novel ends with the death of Fitzjames, conjectured to have occurred in May 1848, trapped on his boat by the ice, in the presence of Inuit.

Using the journals of the members of the first Franklin expedition and imagining the experiences of the Yellowknife Indians, Rudy Wiebe has created the stunning *A Discovery of Strangers* (1994). This novel, which won the (Canadian) Governor General's Award, dramatises the relationship between Robert Hood and Greenstockings and imagines their attempts at understanding and communication by alternating passages from a European and an American perspective.

The Rifles (1995) is volume six of a projected seven-volume series of novels by William Vollmann chronicling the encounter of Europeans and Native Americans on the North American continent. In his typical disjointed postmodern collage style, Vollmann constantly switches between the time of Franklin's last expedition and the present. The author of the rather strange *Polar Knight* (1998), BJ Rule, claims to be a descendant of Franklin's. Supposedly, Franklin himself and his wife told their 'real' story to Rule through automatic writing and spirit channelling.

Finally, the Franklin disaster has inspired a number of essays, especially by Canadian authors. Rudy Wiebe's brief but powerful *Playing Dead: A Contemplation Concerning the Arctic* (1989) contains one essay on Franklin, a kind of preparation for *A Discovery of Strangers*. The volume starts with an appropriate disorienting of the reader with a map of the Canadian Arctic from the Inuit perspective (with the north at the bottom) and with the engraving of Robert Hood's *Greenstockings* painting. Wiebe attributes Franklin's failure to his lack of understanding of the Inuit way of comprehending the Arctic in terms of space and movement. The other two essays in this collection deal with the mystery of Albert Johnson, a trapper who was chased and eventually killed by the Royal Canadian Mounted Police, as well as the collision of Europeans and indigenous people in the Arctic. Margaret Atwood's *Strange Things: The Malevolent North in Canadian Literature* (1995) contains four essays covering: 'Franklin and His Gallant Crew'; 'Europeans going native'; the Wendigo, a giant cannibalistic ice-hearted Algonquin Indian monster; and women of the north.

CONTEMPORARY ARCTIC PEOPLE & NATURE

Times have changed since the days of the explorers. In many ways, the Arctic has only recently joined the 20th century, causing its citizens to face a host of new issues and problems. For information on the culture and history of the Inuit, the gorgeous *Inuit: Glimpses of an Arctic Past* (1995), by David Morrison & Georges-Hébert Germain, is indispensable. In eight chapters, the authors alternate the story of a Copper Inuit family's life in 1909-10 with background appropriate to each stage or season – including pages on everything from sex and friendship to building a sled and from hunting a seal to life on the summer tundra. The book is extravagantly illustrated with pictures and drawings that bring the subjects to life; it also contains the best available overview of the various Inuit groups around the Arctic region.

Bryan Alexander's *The Vanishing Arctic* (1996) is the most comprehensive survey of the cultures, landscape and wildlife of the Arctic. Writing from 25 years of experience with the Arctic, Alexander combines his personal and anecdotal text with numerous beautiful photographs. In *Arctic Memories* (1993), Fred Bruemmer follows the decline of traditional Inuit culture by reminiscing with an Inuk friend about a dog team trip they took 30 years previously. He also talks to elders from communities across the Arctic – from Alaska to Greenland – about the disappearance of the 'old ways' and contrasts them with modern Inuit town life. *Contested Arctic* (1997), edited by Eric Alden Smith & Joan McCarter, explores the Inuit reactions to the environmental and industrial developments in their home.

In a category of its own is Barry Lopez's classic *Arctic Dreams* (1986). Part essay, part history, part nature writing, part anthropology, this book is more a celebration than a description of the Arctic. Lopez wants his readers 'to see the subtle graces and mutability of the different landscapes'. In the Arctic, he looks for 'an expression of allegiance with the landscapes' and finds glimpses of a state 'that like light is unbounded, nurturing, suffused with wisdom and creation, a state in which one has absorbed that very darkness which before was the perpetual sign of defeat'.

Jean Malaurie's *The Last Kings of Thule* (1976) is a similarly personal account. Malaurie conveys his surprise and consternation when he returns from a nine month expedition in northern Greenland and

Canada, only to find the US Thule Air Base has appeared without warning, to drastically affect the traditional lifestyles of the local Inuit.

For nature lovers, two books are worth noting, but both are illustrated with drawings rather than photographs. Steven B Young's *To the Arctic: An Introduction to the Far Northern World* (1989) is an elegant volume covering the flora and fauna, the oceans and ice, the geology and environment of the Arctic. Scientific yet readable, Young ends his book with the first conflict between Inuit and Europeans around 1000 AD. EC Pielou does not bother with humans in his *A Naturalist's Guide to the Arctic* (1994), which has chapters on the sky, climate and atmosphere, terrain, seas, plant life, birds, mammals, fish and insects. If this book has a flaw, it is that it's too narrowly focused on the North American Arctic. In the magnificent *Polar Dance: Born of the North Wind* (1997), photographer Thomas Mangelsen has collected over 250 exquisite pictures of polar bears (and a few of other wildlife and scenery) gathered over eight years of travel in the Arctic. The images as well as the accompanying text by Fred Bruemmer describe a year in the life of a polar bear family.

There is also a considerable body of literature dealing with Alaska. The classic of this genre is Hjalmar Rutzebeck's *Alaska Man's Luck* (1920). Told in diary form and mostly autobiographical, it tells the story of the Dane's acclimatisation to Alaska (where he had gone because his lover, Marian, was so enamoured with the place). The same year, Rockwell Kent published *Wilderness*, the journal of his autumn and winter at Resurrection Bay on the Kenai Peninsula with his son, which features Kent's remarkable artwork.

Somewhat more recent is *Two in the Far North* (1962) by Margaret Murie. The author fascinatingly recounts three journeys into the far north with her husband, Olaus (who illustrated the book), in 1924, 1926 and 1956. Perched between an earlier era of dogsled travel with hazards in the wilderness and a contemporary time of modern scientists, Murie has been referred to as the first American conservationist.

Between them, John McPhee in *Coming into the Country* (1977) and Joe McGinniss with *Going to Extremes* (1980) give a fairly complete view of Alaskan life. In a lyrical yet unromantic description of three trips he took — a canoe trip above the Arctic Circle, a helicopter ride with politicians, and a visit to a settlement on the Yukon — McPhee encapsulates his vision of how Alaskans have come to adapt to life in the north. In complementary contrast — and travelling in different areas of the state — McGinniss takes himself back, and hilariously and intimately lets the people of Alaska speak for themselves in a number of vignettes including the tale of a couple of deadheads who took over a Bethel radio station and led locals to believe that Anglo-American music was limited to the wailings of Jerry Garcia and company. It could be said that *Coming into the Country* shows Alaska from above, and *Going to Extremes*, from below. Finally, James Michener offers his usual mix of fact and fiction in the epic *Alaska* (1980), and a similar but even more entertaining angle is taken in *The Great Alone*, by Janet Dailey, which was published almost concurrently.

Contemporary Travelogues

Finally, contemporary travellers are publishing accounts of their trips in a variety of modes (and varying quality) at a rather alarming rate:

By sailboat: *Ice!* by Tristan Jones; *Riddle of the Ice* by Myron Arms
By small boat: *North to the Night* by Alvah Simon
By kayak: *Cold Oceans* by Jon Turk
By umiak: *Arctic Passages* by John Bockstoce
By dogsled: *Running North* by Ann Mariah Cook; *Tracks Across Alaska* by Alastair Scott
By bicycle: *Above the Circle* by Marty Basch
On foot: *Polar Attack* by Richard Weber & Mikhail Malakhov; *Dans les Pas de l'Ours – Une Traversée Solitaire de l'Alaska Sauvage* by Émeric Fisset
Skiing: *Driving to Greenland* by Peter Stark
Mountaineering: *Sea, Ice & Rock* by Sir Robin Knox-Johnson & Chris Bonnington
A variety of means: *Beyond Siberia* by Christina Dodwell

Fiction

SAGAS & MYTHS

The myths and sagas of the northern people form an important part of Arctic literature. In the literature of the Scandinavian people who explored the Arctic around the turn of the millennium, sagas are the most significant literary form. A saga (meaning 'what is said or told') was a narrative in prose imagining the near or distant past as a story, something like a historical novel. In their content, the sagas are characterised by action, tragedy and revenge. Most sagas were probably circulated in oral form for generations before they were written down, frequently by named authors. While the kings' sagas are irrelevant here, the two other saga genres are important.

The two most famous sagas of the Icelanders are *Njáls Saga* and *Egills Saga*. The former depicts life in Iceland at the time of the Althing and is valued for its characterisation of the two heroes, Njál and Gunnar, who are drawn into blood feuds in spite of their peacefulness, good will and honour because of the Icelandic rules of honour and revenge. *Egills Saga*, the story of one of the greatest of Iceland's poets, Egill Skallagrímsson, is attributed to another, his descendant Snorri Sturluson. In contrast to the 13th century Sturluson, who was assassinated on orders of the Norwegian King Haakon IV, 10th century Skallagrímsson lived to a ripe old age. The history of Norse Arctic exploration is preserved in the Vinland sagas, the *Grænlendinga Saga* (Saga of the Greenlanders) and the *Saga of Eiríkur Rauðe* (The Saga of Eric the Red).

The most famous legendary saga is the two part *Edda*. The *Prose* (or Younger) *Edda*, written or collected by Snorri Sturluson around 1225, contains the Norse creation myths, the adventures of the gods, and foretells the end of the world in Ragnarök in a dialogue. The narrative frame for part of the text, which is written in a kind of free metre, is to instruct aspiring poets in Icelandic *skaldic* (court) poetry. In one part, Sturluson lists 102 different metres he knows! The *Poetic* (or Elder) *Edda* dates from the second half of the 13th century, but contains material from the 9th to 12th centuries (hence the alternate name). Again, there are creation myths and poems about the gods – especially Oðinn and Thór. The *Poetic Edda*'s second half gives Germanic tales connected with the hero Sigurd – earlier forms of the stories told in the German epic *Nibelungenlied*.

The *Kalevala*, the Finnish national epos, was compiled in 1835 by Elias Lönnrot from an oral tradition of ballads, songs and incantations. The epos spans the time from the creation of the world to the arrival of Christianity, concentrating on the journeys and adventures of mythical heroes Väinämöinen, Ilmarinen, Lemminkäinen and Louhi. Written in a specific metre known as the Kalevala metre, the epos looks back as much as forward. It fostered a Finnish national spirit and promoted the use of the Finnish language over Swedish.

INDIGENOUS LITERATURE

As a European and American form, written literature is relatively new to Arctic cultures. Nevertheless, two main forms have developed. On the one hand, Europeans as well as the various Arctic people have begun collecting their oral literature, either by simply writing it down, or by transforming it into something closer to European literature in the process. On the other hand, some indigenous people have adopted European forms such as the novel, poetry and drama and made their own unique contributions to these genres.

Inuit Literature

Myths and legends of the indigenous people of the Arctic have been collected and retold many times. The most accessible collection is *Northern Tales: Stories from the Native People of the Arctic and Subarctic Regions* (1998), edited by Howard Norman. In this wonderful volume, Norman brings together over 100 short folk tales and several story cycles from 35 different tribes. The range of Norman's collection is immense, from the Ainu of Hokkaido to the Micmac Indians, from the Chukchi of northern Siberia to the east Greenland Inuit. The book is organised into eight parts, such as 'The Stubbornness of the Bluejays: Stories About Animals' and 'Carried Off by the Moon: Shaman Stories', each with an introduction of its own. The book's only flaw is that the maps don't include Asia, making it difficult to locate some of the tribal homelands.

Another wonderful volume is the gorgeously illustrated *The Epic of Qayaq: The Longest Story Ever Told By My People* (1995) by Inupiaq Lela Kiana Oman. Collected in the 1940s in northern Alaska, these traditional stories follow the wanderings of the hero Qayaq in the north and relate his encounters with other people, animals and nature. The beautiful black-and-white and colour images illustrating the text are reproductions of work by Native artists.

Anthropologist and traveller James Houston (also the author of an autobiography and an Arctic novel) has retold a number of Inuit legends for young adults, including *Tikta'Liktak* (1965), *The White Archer* (1967) and *Akavak* (1968), most of which centre around their heroes' coming of age. In recent years, Velma Wallis has been highly successful with her retelling of Athapaskan legends in *Two Old Women* (1993) and *Bird Girl & the Man Who Followed the Sun* (1996), which are about the life, travails and survival of the Gwich'in people, one of 11 Athapaskan groups.

Except for the Greenlanders, the Inuit do not yet seem to have developed a modern narrative literature in the western sense. Hailed as the first 'Eskimo' novel, Markoosie's *The Harpoon of the Hunter* (1970) is little more than a juvenile adventure story – except for the unexpected ending. The texts collected in *First People, First Voices* (1983) and *Northern Voices: Inuit Writing in English* (1988) by Penny Petrone are more autobiographical and historical than literary. However, there are some excellent Inuit poets in *Poems of the Inuit* (1981), edited by John Robert Colombo. The most distinguished Athapaskan poet (of the Koyukon group) is Mary TallMountain. In her volumes *The Light on the Tent Wall* (1990) and *A Quick Brush of Wings* (1991) she presents poems mostly about nature subjects, introducing characters such as Negoodzegke (the great horned owl) and Gisakk (white people), as well as excerpts from a novel in progress, *Doyon*.

In *Songs Are Thoughts* (1995) folklorist Neil Philip has anthologised 10 children's poems by Inuit writers. These short pieces, intended to be sung, were originally collected by Knud Rasmussen. They are paired with superb and colourful oil paintings by Maryclare Foa.

While there is a surprisingly large amount of Greenlandic literature, only one volume is available in English, the bilingual *From the Writings of the Greenlanders/Kalaallit Atuakkiaanit* (1990), edited by Michael Fortescue. This book presents selections from 11 Greenlandic texts written between 1922 and 1982: three essays, two folk tales and six novels. These excerpts are so intriguing that one can only hope for more soon.

Sami Literature

Like most written literature by indigenous people of the Arctic, poetry, prose and drama by the Sami of northern Scandinavia is a relatively new phenomenon. However, there is some continuity between the oral and written Sami tradition in their unique musical and literary genre, the *yoik*. Historically, the yoik – a kind of aphorism or song – has been a literary expression of the unity of a particular Sami community, sung by the shaman and used to create self-awareness and to pass on rituals as well as practical knowledge. In modern times, the most common form is the personal yoik, which not just describes, but for the Sami actually *is* the person of, or by, whom it is sung. Originally bestowed by shamans, the personal yoik functioned as a kind of confirmation, marking its bearer as a full member of the community. The personal yoik still is an important part of contemporary Sami literature.

Because of the long history of colonisation, Sami literature to this day is not necessarily written in the Sami language. While this is partly due to the effects of the suppression of that language by colonial education, some Sami authors also chose and continue to choose the languages of their colonisers to reach larger audiences. It does not help that among the 50,000 Sami, there are four dialect groups, and not all can understand the other.

Contemporary Sami literature written in the Sami language begins in 1910 with *Turi's Book of Lapland* by reindeer herder Johan Turi. This book, which is something of an autobiography and anthropological account, collects many rituals and legends, such as the one providing the basis for the 1988 Sami film *Pathfinder*. It also supplies the earliest excerpt in the excellent collection *In the Shadow of the Midnight Sun: Contemporary Sami Prose & Poetry* (1998), edited by Harald Gaski, the world's foremost scholar of Sami literature. This volume, the first and only of its kind, gives short samples from the work of more than 20 Sami authors – including all those mentioned here – as well as an extensive and informative introduction on its subject.

Texts by five other Sami authors are available in translation. Ailo Gaup (1944-), winner of the 1986 Nordic Poetry Prize, is the author of the novel *In Search of the Drum* (1988). At the behest of his dreams, the protagonist Jon travels to Sàpmi with his girlfriend Lajla to save a shaman's drum from destruction and regain knowledge of how to use it. On their journey, which is of course also a journey of self-discovery, Jon and Lajla meet a variety of good and bad, real and imaginary characters – and hear a number of yoik songs. Gaup says of his novel, 'For me it is a challenge to integrate dream and reality. One does not know where one ends and the other begins. The storytelling techniques used in myth have helped me do this, involving letting outer world actions be manifestations of inner world experiences'. Unfortunately, the sequel to this work, *Night Between the Days* (1992), has not been translated yet except for an excerpt in Gaski's anthology.

One of the most prolific Sami writers, and the first woman author, is Kirsti Paltto (1947-), who has contributed political tracts, radio dramas, essays and children's stories next to poetry and novels and was the first chairperson of the Sami Writers' Association. Her novels *May Our Reindeer Graze in Peace* (1987) and *Signs of Destruction* (1991, available in German translation), the first two instalments in a trilogy, trace the life of the Finnish Sami Johanas before, during and after

WWII. The novels deal with the Sami's adjustment to modern life and the question of how traditional cultures can survive in modern times, and have been called an epic description of the emergence of a Sami nation, similar to Lönnrot's *Kalevala*.

Two works by poet, musician and artist Nils-Aslak Valkeapää (1943-) are available in English: *Trekways of the Wind* (1985) and *The Sun, My Father* (1988), which won the prestigious Nordic Council's Prize for Literature in 1991. Harald Gaski describes Valkeapää as an artistic polymath who unites words, images, and music in a modern project, aimed at the future and powered by the past'. His published works are based on yoik in that they have text as well as music, but also include Valkeapää's drawings and paintings. Through his work, Valkeapää addresses the formal question of how traditional genres can survive as well as the cultural question of how Sami society must confront modernity.

Finally, the anthology *Aboriginal Voices* (1992) contains the play *Gesat*, by Nils Gaup & Knut Walle, which translates as 'a story about a reindeer calf who grows up among people and becomes domesticated'. This drama, originally written in Norwegian, creates a fictional meeting between two Sami authors, Matti Aikio and John Savio. These two authors have very different attitudes toward cultural assimilation – Aikio supports it, Savio opposes it – and the play uses this confrontation to address, in Walle's words, 'the issues of identity and how one uses oneself as an artist and the whole issue of being of Sami background'.

Yuri Rytkheu

The most significant writer of the Russian Arctic is Yuri Rytkheu (1930-), the first author in his culture of about 14,000, the Chukchi. In his novels, Rytkheu dramatises the Chukchi's confrontation with modernity, either by retelling ancient legends or by fictionalising historical encounters with other cultures. Six of these novels are available in German, and some of Rytkheu's early work was translated into English. In addition, he contributed an article on his people to the February 1983 edition of *National Geographic*, a theme issue on the Arctic.

In his earliest period, Rytkheu wrote in Chukchi and translated his own work into Russian. At this time – the 1950s – he was doing mainly social realist storytelling and propaganda pamphlets. In his next phase, Rytkheu wrote new versions of traditional tales of his people. *When the White Whales Leave* (1975, available in English in the December 1977 issue of the journal, *Soviet Literature*) takes up the myth that the Chukchi are descendants of Nau, a human woman, and Reu, a whale. Nau lives through the ages and has to witness the humans' loss of their connection with the natural world. When this novel was published, Rytkheu commented that it held a 'sometimes startling relevance to our own times'. In *Teryky* (1980), the seal hunter Goigoi lives a myth; he turns into a furry monster called a teryky when he accidentally gets stuck on an ice floe and has to live there for several weeks. After he returns, the prophecy that all teryky must be killed is ultimately fulfilled.

In his more recent oeuvre, Rytkheu addresses the clash of culture through dramatisations of actual events. Most spectacularly, he retells the Semenchukovshchina in *Under the Constellation of Sorrow* (1992) – an episode McCannon relates from a historical perspective in *Red Arctic*. In 1934, the Soviet administration sent a new head to their Wrangel station, one Konstantin Semenchuk. In the following years, Semenchuk turned out to be a tyrant of the worst sort – toward his Russian colleagues as well as toward the Inuit in the area. The station's biologist committed suicide under mysterious circumstances, the doctor was murdered, and Taian, the leader of the Inuit in the area, sent a letter to Moscow complaining about Semenchuk. In 1936, he was recalled, put on trial, sentenced to death, and executed in a kind of dry run for Stalin's show trials.

In Rytkheu's retelling, the main figures are the doctor Vulfson and Atun, the son of Inuit shaman Analko. Vulfson and Atun try to understand each other across linguistic and cultural barriers, but any progress they make is doomed because of the interference of Semenchuk, who is not only unwilling to listen to the Inuit's needs and suggestions, but is too power-hungry to be interested in communication.

Similarly, *The Search for the Ultimate Number* (1986) is based on Amundsen's wintering in the ice north of Russia in 1918. Here, the main Chukchi figure is the shaman Kagot, who was taken on board by Amundsen in order to educate him into being a servant. However, Kagot turns out to be too curious and intelligent to be satisfied with the role Amundsen wants him to play. In *Dream in the Polar Fog* (1968), the Canadian MacLennan is forced to spend a winter with the Chukchi by the forces of nature. In the course of the season, he becomes what the Chukchi consider a 'real human being' and decides to spend the rest of his life with them. Rytkheu's latest novel *Unna* (1992) is something of a departure from his previous writing. This time, the Chukchi protagonist leaves her home country and has to come to terms with living in Russia.

EUROPEAN & NORTH AMERICAN FICTION

In addition to literature by indigenous authors, the Arctic has inspired distinguished authors from other countries. Most prominently, Mary Shelley's *Frankenstein* (1818) is told from the (epistolary) perspective of polar explorer Robert Walton. The final fight between Victor Frankenstein and his monstrous creation takes place in the Arctic, and after he has killed his creator, the monster drifts off on an ice floe.

Only a few years later, Hans Christian Andersen used the Arctic in his fairy tale *The Snow Queen* (1835). Kay, the main protagonist, is transported to the North Pole, where the Snow Queen has her empire. The story constructs a contrast between the abstract rationality of the cold queen and the warm emotionality of God and feeling, which of course wins out in the end.

Wilkie Collins' book *The Frozen Deep* (1857) stands out as a co-production between its main author and Charles Dickens. Dickens – who had written articles on the charge of cannibalism made against the Franklin expedition – conceived the play, Collins wrote it, Dickens revised it, both performed in the first production, and Collins later turned *The Frozen Deep* into a short story. The two protagonists of the story, rivals over a woman's love, accidentally go on the same Arctic expedition in search of the Northwest Passage. They get lost in the ice, but are rescued at the happy ending.

Jules Verne wrote two novels about Arctic exploration: *The English at the North Pole* (1864) and *The Field of Ice* (1866), which were published together as *The Adventures of Captain Hatteras* in 1867. The hero of these novels is a British captain who wants to reach the North Pole before the Americans do and goes mad in the process – a kind of Ahab of the north. Interestingly, Verne mixes fact and fiction in these books, constantly giving precise and correct geographical locations and information on earlier expeditions. The protagonist of Arthur Conan Doyle's short story *The Captain of the 'Pole-star'* (1890) is equally obsessed, but with a woman. He is haunted by the ghost of a woman who is in fact a siren luring him into the ice. In the end, he dies, but over him a woman's figure has formed out of ice and snow.

Northern Writers

The two authors probably most intimately associated with the far north are Jack London and Robert Service. John Griffith London (1876-1916), who was born in California and experienced an impoverished youth (which turned him into a socialist), spent 1897-98 in Alaska as a prospector during the Klondike gold rush in 1897. His experiences in the Yukon provided the material for a number of short stories as well as his most famous novels, *The Call of the Wild* (1903) and *White Fang* (1906) – both of which have dogs as their main characters.

In *The Call of the Wild*, Buck is kidnapped from a California ranch, goes through a series of adventures, serves as a sled dog in a depiction of perfect love and understanding between man and dog, and finally ends up as the leader of a wolf pack. This process of regression from civilisation to brutal, primitive nature is reversed in *White Fang*, where the wolf dog protagonist ends his days domesticated, basking in the California sun. Nevertheless, both books explore similar topics; the influence of the environment over life and character and the ultimate victory of cooperation (socialism) over competition (capitalism).

At the age of 20, Robert Service (1874-1958) migrated to Canada from England, but spent most of his last 40 years in France. He is best known for his poems 'The Shooting of Dan McGrew' and 'The Cremation of Sam McGee' (both 1907). In these poems, consciously anti-intellectual and meant to address the common reader, Service uses flowing cadences and rhymes to re-create the time of the Klondike gold rush in a mythological, heroic form.

Historical Novels

Recently, several books set in the Arctic – mainly historical novels – have received international attention. In 1998, Andrea Barrett, a previous winner of the (American) National Book Award, published *The Voyage of the Narwhal*. The plot, part Arctic exploration and part love story, is based on the journey of the (fictional) ship *Narwhal* in search of Franklin's expedition. While the protagonist Erasmus Darwin Wells is made up, most background characters are real people. In this novel, Barrett uses the Arctic to create a landscape in which individuals can no longer run away from themselves.

Similarly, the two protagonists in James Houston's *The Ice Master* (1997) – a Yankee whaling veteran and a young Newfoundlander – learn as much about themselves as about each other during their year-long stay on Baffin Island in 1875-76. Houston has used his extensive experience of the Arctic to create believable suspense, introduce a variety of characters (from the protagonists to spouses to Inuit), and present information on 19th century whaling.

Two other novels are set at about the same time. In *Journey* (1988), James Michener describes the trek of four English aristocrats and their Irish servant across the Canadian Arctic during the 1897 Klondike gold rush in his typical blend of fact and fiction. Per Olof Sundman's *The Flight of the Eagle* (1967) is a retelling of the disastrous 1897 attempt of Salomon Andrée to reach the North Pole by balloon, told from the perspective of crewman Knut Frankel, who did not leave a diary in real life.

In her novel *Greenlanders* (1988), Jane Smiley provides a fictional treatment of the last decades of Norse presence in Greenland. Using the sparse records of the last years of the Vikings on that island, she constructs a fascinating narrative similar to the Icelandic sagas in style and its concentration on one family. In Smiley's account, the Norse disappear from Greenland because they emigrate to Vinland, join the Inuit, or are wiped out by Bristol pirates. Yves Thériault's *Agaguk: Shadow of the Wolf* (1958, with several spin-off novels) is the story of a young Inuit hunter who leaves his father's tribe to live with his wife and comes into conflict with the white man's law.

The Ice Shirt (1993), the first volume of William Vollmann's previously mentioned series, is a collage of Viking tales and sagas and Inuit traditions describing the travels of the Norse to Iceland, Greenland and Vinland, as well as contemporary observations of Greenlandic and

Canadian life. Christoph Ransmayr's *The Terrors of Ice & Darkness* (1984) is a similar collage, telling three stories: the historical Austro-Hungarian polar expedition of 1872-74, the 1981 disappearance of the traveller Josef Mazzini during his retracing of that expedition's journey, and the contemporary narrator's attempt to find out what happened to Mazzini.

Farley Mowat

The most famous Canadian writer of the north is Farley Mowat (1921-). Mowat has written children's literature, novels, short stories, essays and film scripts on his subject. Best of all, he's known for the book and film *Never Cry Wolf* (1963), describing a summer in the Arctic barrens in which he observed the life of a wolf family and its affects on caribou herds. Combining humour and zoological information, Mowat comes to the conclusion that really, wolves are fairly virtuous creatures, while humans are predators.

In his books on the tribe of inland Inuit called Ihalmiut, *People of the Deer* (1952) and *The Desperate People* (1959), Mowat makes four forces responsible for the problems of the Inuit: the Canadian government, the Protestant and Catholic churches, the Royal Canadian Mounted Police (RCMP), and the Hudson's Bay Company. Predictably, none of these groups were particularly happy about Mowat's books but have at least addressed his accusations to some degree (if only denial).

Mowat has also written many works of fiction. The protagonists of *Lost in the Barrens* (1956, a novel for young adults), a young Canadian and his Cree friend, become separated from their companions and have to fight for survival through an Arctic winter. They learn that it is better to submit to nature than to fight it. The nine short stories and two essays in *The Snow Walker* (1971) similarly deal with the human struggle with the natural environment. Mowat once again displays his admiration for the Inuit, and his disdain for the influences of European culture that have destroyed their way of life.

Contemporary Novels

Of the Arctic novels set completely in modern times, the most recent is Peter Høeg's *Miss Smilla's Feeling for Snow* (1992). It was published in the USA as *Smilla's Sense of Snow*. Under the guise of a murder mystery, Høeg talks about the relationship between Denmark and Greenland, and creates an unforgettable character in the Danish-Greenlandic heroine, Smilla Jespersen.

There are also two novels by Anglo-Canadian writers set in the North American Arctic. The heroine of *The Victory of Geraldine Gull* by Joan Clark (1988) is an Ojibwa woman living in the Cree village of Niska on the shore of the Hudson Bay. She stands as an off-putting example of the problems facing her people: poverty, alcoholism, poor health, prostitution, suicide. The end of the book is anything but upbeat, yet Gull comes across as a strong individual who is at least willing to ask questions and address issues. In Aritha van Herk's *The Tent Peg* (1982), a woman disguises herself as a man to be able to work in a Yukon uranium mining camp. With numerous biblical references and a range of perspectives, van Herk investigates the relationships between men and women.

Finally, there are three mystery series set in the Arctic. The heroes of Sue Henry's *Alex Jensen* series (five novels to date) are the eponymous Alaska State Trooper and his girlfriend, Iditarod musher Jessie Arnold. These novels are set in the Yukon and frequently refer to the Klondike gold rush. The nine novels of the *Kate Shugak* series are centred around a tough Aleut private investigator, and are penned by Dana Stabenow, who in her own words 'was raised on a 75-foot fish tender in the Gulf of Alaska'. In *Blood Will Tell* (1996), Shugak investigates murders on the Aleut Council that are connected with power struggles over land within the tribe, which is led by her grandmother, the matriarch Ekaterina. The protagonist of the two *Matteesie Kitologiak* mysteries, by Scott Young, is an Inuit RCMP inspector who investigates cases in the Canadian Arctic. Young's novels are interesting for their plot as much as for the colourful characters such as the shaman Jonassie Oquatoq, and for their local detail.

FILMS

In addition to written literature, a growing body of films deal with, or are at least set in, the Arctic. Here is a chronological list of some of the most important ones:

Nanook of the North (1922, directed by Robert Flaherty) was the first major anthropological documentary. It follows the Inuit, Nanook and his family through a year in their life, showing a culture almost completely untouched by European civilisation.

The Gold Rush (1925) is Charlie Chaplin's masterpiece on the north. To the background of a slapstick love story, Chaplin shows spectacular and hilarious scenes of the Chilkoot Pass, hunger hallucinations, blizzards, snow-shovelling and a cabin hanging over a precipice.

In their movie versions, Jack London's stories concentrate on humans rather than dogs. *The Call of the Wild* (1935, directed by William Wellman, starring Clark Gable) ends with Buck's and Thornton's friendship, and in *White Fang* (1991, directed by Randal Kleiser, starring Ethan Hawke and Klaus Maria Brandauer), the boy hero Jack decides to stay in Alaska with his trusty canine companion. In *White Fang II* (1994, directed by Ken Olin), which bears no resemblance to Jack London's at all, the dog's new owner (his old one has moved to California without him) meets Haida Indians and saves them from evil miners.

The White Dawn (1974, directed by Philip Kaufman) is based on a novel by James Houston. A group of whalers is stranded in an Inuit community and introduces the European way of life – gambling, alcohol and sex – until tensions mount.

Never Cry Wolf (1983, directed by Carroll Ballard) manages to improve on Farley Mowat's book by adding the visual element of the Arctic's stunning scenery. It was filmed along the border between Alaska and Canada's Yukon Territory.

Pathfinder (1987, directed by Nils Gaup, the author of *Gesat*), originally titled *Ofelas*, was the first major motion picture by and for the Sami. Nominated for the Oscar for best foreign film in 1988, this movie tells the legend of the boy Aigin, whose village is massacred by the invading Tchudes, whom he subsequently has to outsmart. In *Pathfinder*, the Sami are played by Sami (including *Gesat*'s co-author Knut Walle), the Tchudes by Norwegians. The entire film is in Sami with English subtitles.

Salmonberries (1991, directed by Percy Adlon, starring kd lang) is an artsy film by a German director, set in Kotzebue, Alaska. Lang's character, an androgynous pipeline worker, searches for her parents and, along the way, falls in love with the German town librarian. Appreciating this movie certainly requires letting go of American ideas of action cinema and embracing the movie's lesbian themes and lyrical, symbolic vision.

Shadow of the Wolf (1992, directed by Jacques Dorfman, starring Lou Diamond Phillips and Donald Sutherland), the movie version of Thériault's novel, privileges scenery over any serious investigation of the situation of the Inuit.

Arctic Blue (1993, directed by Peter Masterson) stars Rutger Hauer, playing an accused killer who is determined to escape from his environmentalist escort in Northern Alaska.

North Star (1996, starring James Caan and Christopher Lambert) was Nils Gaup's first US release after *Pathfinder*. Set in Alaska in 1899, Gaup's film pits the half-breed Hudson Ipsehawk against a brutally unscrupulous miner who is trying to exploit him and steal his land.

Smilla's Sense of Snow (1997, directed by Bille August, starring Julia Ormond and Gabriel Byrne) loses much of the intricacy of Høeg's plot, but makes up for it with absorbing atmosphere, haunting Greenlandic scenery (the Greenland scenes were filmed near Ilulissat), and Ormond's spectacular performance.

Arctic Alaska

☎ 907

Alaska, the westernmost extent of the Americas, stretches westward from the main body of the continent towards Asia and indeed, it's widely believed that it provided the welcome for the first North Americans. The earliest migrants are thought to have crossed the postulated Bering Land Bridge some 25,000 years ago and eventually spread throughout the Americas. However, the migrations continued by boat even after the sea level rose and closed off the land bridge (for more information, see Inuit History in the Facts about the Arctic chapter).

No other area of the USA possesses the mystical pull that Alaska has. As with all the earth's northern regions, Alaska ignites the imaginations of people in more populated areas who long for space and time to wander through unspoilt country. When its former Russian colonisers began to view their North American foothold as more of a distant liability than an asset, they offered it for sale to the USA for a bargain US$7.2 million – less than 2¢ per acre. In 1867, they signed a treaty with US Secretary of State William H Seward, whose enthusiasm for the purchase met with considerable resistance from the US populace, which derided him for spending good taxpayers' money on a place they disparagingly called Seward's Folly, Seward's Icebox, Walrussia and Uncle Sam's Attic.

However, in the late 19th and early 20th centuries, the promise of adventure and the lure of untold mineral wealth brought the first invasion of miners to the young territory. In the 1970s, just over a decade after Alaska became the 49th state of the USA, it drew even more people with dreams of the absurdly generous wages paid in exchange for facing the gruelling conditions involved in building a pipeline through the wilderness. Now, the equivalent of Seward's modest investment flows through that pipeline every day, and Alaska's value in minerals, fish, timber and tourism potential is scarcely calculable.

Although Alaska's mythical nickname 'The Last Frontier' may seem a bit ludicrous when you're number 2192 in the Friday afternoon motorhome train headed for the recreation lands of the Kenai Peninsula, or sitting in the Anchorage or Fairbanks rush hour traffic, most of the country beyond the highway system – which includes most of Arctic Alaska – remains little altered by modern humanity. In places like Teller and Barrow and Anaktuvuk Pass, it's sometimes hard to remember that you're still in the USA!

In addition to the Arctic regions of Alaska, this chapter covers the gateway cities of Anchorage and Fairbanks and two of the state's most popular and spectacular national parks, Denali and Wrangell-St Elias. The latter is tied with Canada's Kluane National Park to form one of the world's largest and most significant conservation areas.

GETTING AROUND
Air

Over 75% of Alaska is inaccessible by road (including the capital city, Juneau!), which means that many towns and villages rely on air travel for access and supplies. Most of the larger 'bush' towns, including Barrow, Kotzebue, Nome, Bethel and Deadhorse

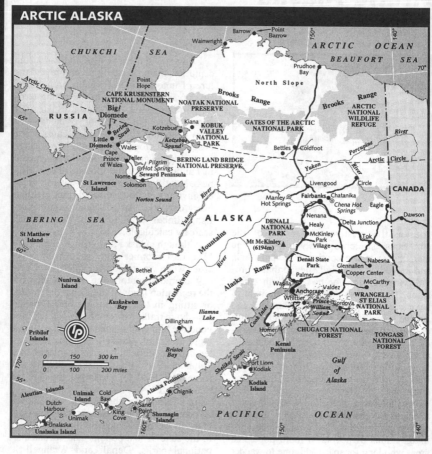

ARCTIC ALASKA

(Prudhoe Bay) are linked to Anchorage and Fairbanks by Alaska Airlines (toll-free ☎ 1-800 252 7522, fax 206-433 3477, email reservations@alaskaair.com, www.alaska air.com), while Era Aviation (☎ 248 4422, toll-free ☎ 1-800 478 1947, fax 266 8350, email airlineinfo@era-aviation.com, www .era-aviation.com), Reeve Aleutian Airways (☎ 243 4700, toll-free ☎ 1-800 544 2248, www.reeveair.com), Penair (☎ 243 2485, fax 243 6848, email info@penair.com, www .penair.com) and Yute Air (☎ 243 1011,

email info@yuteair.com, www.yuteair.com) connect the two main hubs with larger villages throughout Interior, Arctic, western and south-western Alaska. Note that return flights are substantially better value than one way, and that you'll save a bundle with a 14 day advance purchase.

In addition to the scheduled flights, you can choose from a large number of charter operators, which provide 'bush flights' into off-runway locations: river sandbars, wilderness lakes, glaciers and open tundra. Their services are used mainly by folks living in bush cabins, wilderness hunting and fishing lodges, and visitors embarking on wilderness climbing, hiking, rafting and canoeing trips.

You'll find that the man or woman at the controls is normally referred to as a 'bush pilot' and, given the technical nature of the landscape and volatility of the weather conditions, it's worth seeking out a good one. Bush planes include aircraft on floats, which can land on lakes, the sea or larger rivers; those with large balloon tyres, which allow landing on beach sand, tundra or gravel bars; and those equipped with skis, for landing on snow, glaciers and ice caps. Many of these carry special navigational equipment, for coping with stormy or whiteout flying conditions, and outside boat racks, for hauling canoes and kayaks.

The amount you'll pay for a bush flight will be determined by the size of the plane, the number of passengers you have, the distance and time to be flown, and the amount of gear you have. Generally, a Cessna 185, which can carry three passengers and limited gear, will cost around US$250 per hour, while a four passenger Cessna 206 costs around US$300 per hour. A DeHavilland Beaver, which holds five passengers and quite a lot of gear, may cost upwards of US$400 per hour. Bear in mind that you must pay not only for the flight time to your destination, but also for the return flight to the plane's home base. You'll have the same situation with the pick-up run, which must naturally be organised in advance, and if you're not at the designated spot at the designated time, you'll still have to pay for the

The Alaskan Bush Pilot

As you might imagine given its distances and shortage of roads, Alaska has by far the most pilots per capita of any state in the USA, and most likely has the highest density of aviators anywhere in the world. In fact, as early as the beginning of WWII, small airlines in the Alaska territory were hauling 1000 times as much freight per capita as any of the air services in the contiguous 48 states!

If you're heading off to a rural village, taking a wilderness fishing trip or flying in to a remote lodge, chances are you'll come in contact with the breed known as the Alaskan bush pilot. With the designation of Alaska's wilderness as 'the bush', the folks who were able to transport people and cargo to those remote regions naturally enough came to be known as 'bush pilots'. Although Alaskans had dabbled in exhibition aviation as early as 1913, bush aviation didn't really take off until after WWI, when the Curtiss Jenny arrived and pilots began flying between Anchorage and Fairbanks. Among the early pilots, the best-known names include Carl Ben Eielson, Jim Dodson, Noel Wien, Steve Mills, Harold Gillam, Bob Reeve, Archie Ferguson, Jack Jefford, and most recently, Don Sheldon.

These seat-of-the-pants aviators managed to open up the farthest reaches of the state to development, progress and cargo shipments, and the tradition continues to the present day. These days, dozens of small operations haul both passengers and cargo to all parts of Alaska. In winter, they take off and land on skis and in summer, on floats, which allows access to lakes, rivers and bays, or they use large balloon tyres, which allow them to land on open tundra or on river gravel bars.

Even Anchorage International Airport, in Alaska's largest city, is supplemented by the private and commercial seaplane bases at Lake Spenard and Lake Hood. In 1945 the municipal airstrip known as Merrill Field (named for pioneer naval pilot Russell Merrill, who crashed on a cargo run across Cook Inlet in 1929) saw more air traffic than New York's La Guardia airport, and it's still the eighth busiest airport in the USA.

flight (and perhaps a search and rescue operation!). Also, it's worth noting that inclement weather conditions may prevent the pilot from turning up at the arranged time. If that happens, don't panic – they'll be along as soon as it's safe to fly in – but be sure you have sufficient supplies to ride out a bad spell of at least several days.

While it's always wise to book your flights in advance, bush pilots are generally quite flexible and if a plane and pilot are available, you can be winging your way across the wilderness on a half-hour's advance notice. For suggestions, see the Organised Tours & Adventures chapter.

Car & Motorcycle

With your own vehicle, much of Alaska – including the entire south-eastern quarter of the state – will be accessible on your own terms and at your own pace. In addition, you'll be able to head north to the Arctic region on the Dalton Hwy, which connects Fairbanks with Deadhorse and Prudhoe Bay on the Arctic Ocean.

Car rental, however, is rather expensive. Although petrol is very good value – currently US$1.20 (in towns) to US$2 (in remote areas) per US gallon (3.8L) – CDW (insurance) and mileage charges can turn a rental fee of US$50 per day into several times that. If you're going to do a lot of driving, it's worth looking for a deal that includes unlimited mileage. In smaller towns, a good-value rental agency is Affordable New Car Rental, with offices in Anchorage (☎ 243 3370, toll-free ☎ 1-800 248 3765, email ancr@alaska.net) and Fairbanks (☎ 452 7341, toll-free ☎ 1-800 471 3101, email nissan@polarnet.com). Rent-a-Wreck also has offices in Anchorage (☎ 562 5499, fax 562 1156) and Fairbanks (☎ 452 1606).

If you do rent a car, one of the first things you'll discover on the Alaskan highways is that most roads are nothing but an endless stream of lumbering RVs, campers, caravans, trailers and pop-ups. In fact, many people decide they can't beat 'em so they join 'em and rent a self-contained motorhome. A host of companies offer packages. Great Alaskan

Holidays (☎ 248 7777, toll-free ☎ 1-888 225 2752, fax 248 7878) offers packages starting at US$125 per day. Check out the Web site at www.akholidays.com. Other options include Sweet Retreat Motorhome Rentals (☎ 344 9155, toll-free ☎ 1-800 759 4861, fax 344 8279, email sweetretreat @customcpu.com, www.sweetretreat.com), Clippership Motorhome Rentals (toll-free ☎ 1-800 421 3456, fax 562 7053, email clippership@custom cpu.com, www.customcpu.com/commercial /clippership) and ABC Motorhome Rentals (toll-free ☎ 1-800 421 7456, fax 243 6363, email rvalaska@alaska.net, www.alaskan .com/abcmotorhomes).

Note that the Wal-Mart stores in Anchorage, Wasilla, Juneau and Ketchikan offer free overnight parking for motorhomes, as does the Fred Meyer store in Fairbanks.

For road conditions, phone the recorded Department of Transportation message on ☎ 273 6037 in South-Central Alaska and ☎ 456 7623 in Interior Alaska and along the Richardson Hwy, or call up the department's Web site www.dot.state.ak.us.

Bus

Reliable bus services link all the main towns in Alaska – well, at least those that are on the highway system. Every summer, new bus lines pop up, run for a while and then disappear, only to be replaced by a new company. However, on the popular routes, you'll always find something. For example, the Denali National Park Van Service connects the popular park with both Anchorage and Fairbanks. In Anchorage, contact Moon Bay Express (☎ 274 6454), which departs daily from the HI hostel; the Alaska Backpacker Shuttle (☎ 344 8775); or the Parks Highway Express (☎ 479 3065). From Fairbanks, try the Fireweed Express (☎ 452 0521).

From Haines or Skagway, Alaskon Express (☎ 227 5581) has three trips weekly to Anchorage (US$190), which is handy for anyone arriving on the ferry from Seattle. The service runs from mid-May to mid-September and doesn't include accommodation on the overnight stop at Beaver Creek, Yukon. Between Anchorage and

Seward, try the reliable Seward Bus Line (☎ 224 3608).

For more information, see the Getting Around chapter.

Train

The Alaska Railroad (☎ 265 2494, toll-free ☎ 1-800 544 0552) has one main route, between Seward on the Gulf of Alaska and Anchorage (US$40), and north from there to Denali National Park (US$95) and Fairbanks (US$135). During summer, early bookings are essential on this popular route. The narrow-gauge White Pass & Yukon Railway (☎ 983 2217) links Skagway, in Southeast Alaska, with Fraser, British Columbia, where you'll find road connections to Whitehorse.

Boat

The Alaska Marine Highway System is in fact two car ferry systems; one connects Bellingham, Washington, with the towns of Southeast Alaska's Inside Passage, and the other links the coastal towns of Prince William Sound, the Kenai Peninsula, Kodiak Island, the Alaska Peninsula and the eastern Aleutian Islands. Once monthly, the two systems are connected by the MV *Kennicott*, which sails between Juneau, Valdez and Seward. Cabins are available, but many people opt to erect a tent on deck or just throw a sleeping bag down in the heated solarium on the top deck. This is a great way to get around along the Gulf of Alaska coast, but note that advance booking is essential, especially if you're travelling with a vehicle, and that there are no ferry services to the coastal towns of western or Arctic Alaska.

For timetables and booking, contact the Alaska Marine Highway System (toll-free ☎ 1-800 642 0066, fax 277 4829), 1591 Glacier Ave, Juneau, AK 99801-1427. Its Web site address is www.dot.state.ak.us/external/amhs/home.html.

ACCOMMODATION
Camping

If you're on a strict budget in Alaska, don't forget to bring a tent. Although the state lacks cheap B&Bs and has only a few hostels, there are lots of state, federal and private camping grounds where you can pay US$10 to US$15 for a scenic spot to pitch a tent and access to basic facilities. However, on summer weekends, you'll be hard-pressed to find a site in most government camping grounds, so arrive as early as possible.

For Denali National Park (☎ 683 1266), PO Box 9, Denali Park, AK 99755, advance bookings are essential if you have a vehicle or want to stay in one of the camping grounds away from the park entrance. Reservation forms are available on the park Web site www.nps.gov/dena. However, even without reservations, cyclists and campers who arrive on public transport will normally find a tent site at the Morino walk-in camping ground.

Note that access to park camping grounds (except Riley Creek) is available only between around 10 June and 1 September.

Alternatively, you can camp anywhere on public lands (a notable exception is Denali National Park, where you need a backcountry permit) or along hiking routes. In Arctic Alaska, campers will normally have to hike out of town and set up camp along a beach or on the tundra (but beware the mosquito plague!).

Hostels

Hostelling International now operates 11 official hostels around the state, including Anchorage, Juneau, Ketchikan, Sitka, Ninilchik, Palmer and Tok (but none in Arctic Alaska). For information, contact Hostelling International (☎ 276 3635), 700 H St, Anchorage, AK 99501, or check out its Web site www.hiayh.org/ushostel/islreg/ak.htm.

As with many places in the English-speaking world, independent backpackers' hostels are also making their welcome debut in Alaska. You'll find them in Anchorage, Denali Park, Fairbanks, Haines, Homer, Circle Hot Springs and Seward (28km north of town) with more springing up all the time.

B&Bs

In the early 1980s, Alaska had only a handful of B&Bs, but the system now includes a network of hundreds of places in every town and many villages between Ketchikan and Kotzebue (including several hundred in Anchorage alone!). For travellers who'd rather avoid camping, B&Bs can provide a reasonably priced middle ground between hostels and expensive hotels. However, they're not cheap, and in most places, you're still looking at rates of US$55 to US$100 per night for a double. For further information, contact one of the following organisations:

Accommodation in Alaska
   (☎ 345 4279)
   PO Box 11-0624, Anchorage,
   AK 99511-0624
Alaska Bed & Breakfast Association
   (☎ 586 2959)
   369 S Franklin, Suite 200, Juneau,
   AK 99801-1353
Alaska Private Lodging
   (☎ 258 1717)
   PO Box 20-0047, Anchorage,
   AK 99520-0047
Mat-Su B&B Association of Alaska
   (toll-free ☎ 1-800 401 7444)
   PO Box 87-3507, Wasilla, AK 99687
Fairbanks B&B
   (☎ 452 7700)
   PO Box 73334, Fairbanks, AK 99707-3334

USFS Cabins

The Tongass and Chugach National Forests, in Southeast and South-Central Alaska respectively, offer wilderness cabins which may be reached on foot, by boat or by bush flight. Unfortunately, they're quite expensive at US$35 per night and, unlike hikers' huts elsewhere in the world, they may be reserved only by a single party. They tend to fill up quickly, especially at weekends, so be sure to book well in advance. For more information, contact the US Forest Service Information Center (☎ 586 8751), 101 Egan Drive, Juneau, AK 99801 or the Alaska Public Lands Information Center (☎ 271 2737), 605 W 4th Ave, Suite 105, Anchorage, AK 99501-5162.

Lodges & Roadhouses

For a taste of life in rural or wilderness Alaska, you may want to stay at one of the numerous lodges dotted around the state. While some 'roadhouses' lie along the highway system and cater to casual drop-in traffic with basic accommodation, restaurants and bars, the most interesting ones lie deep in the wilderness and offer rustic cabins with saunas and ample opportunities to explore the surrounding areas on foot or by canoe or kayak. Many cater especially to the fishing and hunting crowd. Rates range from US$150 to US$250 per person per day, including all meals. Transfers are normally provided by air at an extra charge.

Hotels & Motels

Although you may find a few bargains, hotels and motels are almost uniformly expensive and in Arctic Alaska, you're looking at rates of well over US$150 per night for a double room. In Anchorage, the nicer places (which are frequented by business travellers) will cost around US$200 per night. Despite the high rates, during summer most places tend to fill up with tour groups and cruise ship passengers so advance booking is advised.

ANCHORAGE

Although it's a long way from the Arctic, Anchorage (population 248,300) serves as a jumping-off point for most visitors to the far north, and Alaska's largest city offers the comforts and problems of a large US city within a 30 minute flight of the Alaskan wilderness.

Founded in 1914 as a work camp for the Alaska Railroad, the city was devastated by the 1964 Good Friday Earthquake. Registering 9.2 on the Richter scale, it was the strongest quake recorded in a populated area. The oil boom made the town an industry headquarters, and oil money has paid for many of the city's modern amenities and assisted its growth. While people in other parts of Alaska love to shop in Anchorage, where prices and taxes are the most reasonable in the state, many still cynically describe this overcrowded urban zone as 'Los Anchorage' or 'a beer can in the woods'. If you're after 'the real Alaska', get out of here as quickly as you can!

Information

The Log Cabin Visitors Center (☎ 274 3531), at the corner of 4th Ave and F St, distributes a guide and walking tour map, as well as a listing of events (☎ 276 3200). Nearby, the Alaska Public Lands Information Center (☎ 271 2737) has park information and excellent displays. If you're looking for outdoor equipment, the widest variety is available from the REI Cooperative (☎ 272 4565) at 1200 W Northern Lights Blvd.

The best bookshops are Borders, on Dimond Blvd (which has an especially good travel section), and Barnes & Noble, on Northern Lights Blvd. The Loussac Library, on 36th Ave, has one of the world's finest collections of Arctic Literature.

For emergency medical care, the two main hospitals are Alaska Regional (☎ 264 1222) and Providence (☎ 562 2211).

Things to See & Do

Most visitors stay in the downtown area, where short walks lead to several sites of interest. On K St is the sculpture known as The Last Blue Whale, and the Captain Cook Monument in nearby Resolution Park marks the 200th anniversary of Cook's visit to Cook Inlet. On M St north of 5th Ave, the wood-frame Oscar Anderson House (☎ 274 2336) is Anchorage's only home museum.

The impressive Anchorage Historical & Fine Arts Museum (☎ 343 4326), at the corner of 7th Ave and A St, features Alaskan history and indigenous culture (admission US$5). The Heritage Library Museum (☎ 265 2834), at the corner of Northern Lights Blvd and C St, displays Native Alaskan costumes, weapons and artwork.

To get in touch with Alaska's aviation history, visit the Alaska Aviation Heritage Museum (☎ 248 5325), south of Lake Hood. A new addition to the Anchorage museum scene is the comprehensive Alaska

Native Heritage Center (☎ 330 8000). Admission is US$19.95 and it's open daily from 9 am to 9 pm.

Bus No 75 will take you to the Elmendorf Air Force Base Wildlife Museum (☎ 552 2282) and the Fort Richardson Fish & Wildlife Center (☎ 384 0431). The nicest city parks include Earthquake Park, Russian Jack Springs (the Municipal Greenhouse) and the 1618 hectare Far North Bicentennial Park, where the Hilltop Ski Area becomes a mountain biker's oasis in summer (bike rentals are available).

Activities include cycling on 200km of paved bike trails; the popular Coastal Trail begins at the west end of 2nd Ave. You can hire bikes at Downtown Bicycle Rental (☎ 279 5293). Alaska's most-climbed peak is Flattop Mountain, a relatively easy two hour hike from the Glen Alps trailhead on Upper Huffman Rd. Maps are available at the Alaska Public Lands Information Center.

Places to Stay

For both tent and RV campers, there is *Centennial Park (☎ 337 9711)*, 7km from the town centre on the Glenn Hwy. It charges US$12 per site, but the 90 sites fill up quickly and advance reservations are essential. You can also opt for the privately run *Anchorage RV Park (☎ 338 7275, toll-free ☎ 1-800 400 7275, 7300 Oilwell Rd)*, north of the Glenn Hwy and west of the Muldoon Rd exit. Its Web site is www.anchrvpark .com. In nearby Eagle River, there's the *Hidden Haven RV Park (☎ 694 7275, 10011 Aleden Lane)*.

The *Anchorage International Hostel (☎ 276 3635, 700 H St)* charges US$15/18 for members/nonmembers. In summer, advance bookings are requisite. The friendly *Spenard Hostel (☎ 248 5036, 2845 W 42nd Place)* charges US$12, while the *International Backpackers Hostel (☎ 274 3870, 3601 Peterkin Ave)* lies 5km east of the town centre and charges US$12. The *Qupqugiaq Inn (☎ 562 5681, 640 W 36th Ave)* offers rooms from US$25.

The large number of B&Bs, which start at around US$75 for a double, can be accessed

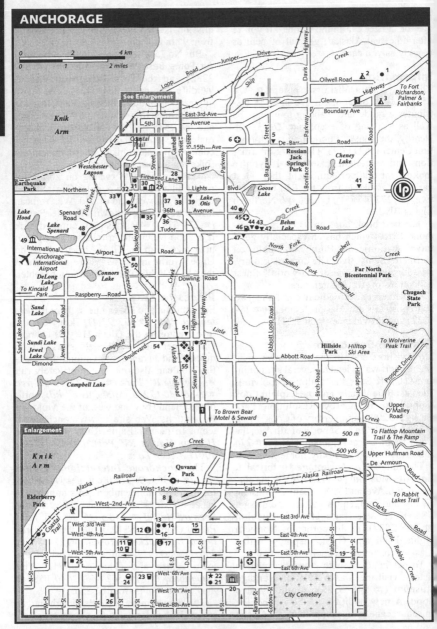

ANCHORAGE

PLACES TO STAY
2 Anchorage RV Park
3 Centennial Park Campground
4 International Backpackers Hostel
19 Econo Lodge
25 Caribou Inn
26 Anchorage International Hostel
30 Midtown Lodge & Cusack's Brewpub
35 Qupqugiaq Inn & Q-Café
48 Spenard Hostel
50 Arctic Inn Motel

PLACES TO EAT
5 Costco
28 Elmer's
33 Carr's
38 Carr's
39 Village Inn
41 Carr's
42 Saigon
44 Thai Kitchen
47 Fu Do

51 Carr's
54 Costco

OTHER
1 Alaska Native Heritage Center
6 Alaska Regional Hospital
7 Alaska Railroad Train Station
8 Alaska Statehood Monument
9 Oscar Anderson House
10 Glacier Brew House
11 Darwin's Theory
12 Old Federal Building, Alaska Public Lands Information Center
13 Alaska Booking & Reservation Center
14 Alaska Airlines
15 Post Office
16 Gray Line, Columbia Glacier Tours
17 Log Cabin Visitors Center
18 Open Door Clinic
20 Anchorage Historical & Fine Arts Museum

21 Fire Station
22 Police Station
23 Humpy's Great Alaskan Alehouse
24 Transit Center
27 Waterfowl Sanctuary
29 Heritage Library Museum
31 Chilkoot Charlie's
32 REI Co-op & Middle Way Café
34 Mr Whitekey's Fly-by-Nite Club
36 Loussac Library
37 Barnes & Noble Bookshop
40 University Of Alaska - Anchorage (UAA)
43 Capri Cinema
45 Providence Hospital
46 Courtney's Petrol Station
49 Alaska Aviation Heritage Museum
52 Borders Bookshop
53 Dimond Center Mall
55 Wal-Mart

through the Log Cabin Visitors Center or via the B&B Hotline (☎ 272 5909).

Many of the town's 50 hotels and motels offer free airport/station pick-up and off-season discounts of 30 to 40%. The *Arctic Inn Motel* (☎ 561 1328), on International Airport Rd, is handy to the airport and charges US$69/79 for singles/doubles. The downtown *Caribou Inn* (☎ 272 0444, 501 L St) has rooms starting at US$69. Amid 5th Ave's cluster of motels is the *Econo Lodge* (☎ 274 1515, 642 E 5th Ave), which charges US$70/80. The *Midtown Lodge* (☎ 258 7778, 604 W 26th Ave) has rooms with shared bath from US$60/70.

Places outside the city are cheaper. The *Brown Bear Motel* (☎ 653 7000), at Indian, 20 minutes south of town on the Seward Hwy, charges just US$38 for a single.

Places to Eat

Anchorage offers a wide range of eateries. Recommended breakfast options include *Elmer's* (☎ 258 2913) and the *Village Inn* (☎ 279 6012). One of the finest informal options for lunch is the *Middle Way Café* (☎ 272 6433), conveniently located beside the REI Cooperative on Northern Lights Blvd, which serves a delicious range of soups, sandwiches and wraps, including many vegetarian options. Also good is the popular *Qupqugiaq Café* (☎ 563 5634, 640 W 36th Ave), more comfortably known as the Q-Cafe, where your sandwiches and home-made sweets may be accompanied by anything from live folk music to lectures on eastern and Native wisdom.

Another fine choice for lunch is any of the *Carr's* supermarket chain, with stores all over town (but unfortunately not downtown). Most Carr's stores have an excellent salad bar, as well as a soup bar, a taco bar, a deli, an oriental takeaway and good-value sushi packages. For the best value on pizza, try one of the two *Costco* stores, where a family-sized combo pizza costs under US$10. If someone asks for a membership card, tell them you just want to buy a pizza – the food court is right at the front of the store.

For something more exotic, you can't beat the *Thai Kitchen* (☎ *561 0082)*, in the back of a convenience shop at the corner of Tudor Road and Dale St; the decor, ambience and authenticity are reminiscent of any 'Mom & Pop' place in central Bangkok. Just across the car park is another superb Asian option, *Saigon* (☎ *563 2515)*, which features genuine Vietnamese cuisine. A friendly Chinese place is the *Fu Do* (☎ *561 6611)*, on Tudor Road just west of Folker St; try the excellent chicken noodle soup.

Entertainment
Check the free weekly *Anchorage Press* (published on Thursday) for entertainment listings. Colourful *Chilkoot Charlie's (2435 Spenard Rd)* features bands and dancing. Nearby, *Mr Whitekey's Fly-by-Nite Club* (☎ *279 7726, 3300 Spenard Rd)* plays jazz, blues and rock but is best known for the annual shows (*Springtime in Spenard, Whale-Fat Follies* etc), which cost from US$12. *Humpy's Great Alaskan Alehouse* (☎ *276 2337)*, on the corner of 6th Ave and F St, is a lively pub with great food. Locals frequent *Darwin's Theory*, on the corner of 4th Ave and G St, while Anchorage's best brew-pubs are *Glacier Brew House (757 W 5th Ave)*, and *Cusack's*, at the Ramada Inn.

If you want to catch a quality film, check out the *Capri Cinema*, in the shopping centre at the corner of Tudor Rd and Dale St, which features art and foreign films.

Getting There & Away
Numerous major US airlines offer reasonably priced services to Anchorage, mainly from Seattle (starting at around US$280 return on Alaska Airlines), but also from Minneapolis (Sun Country Airlines offers a superb US$249 return fare), Portland (starting at around US$300) and San Francisco (from around US$300), among other places.

Alaskon Express (☎ 227 5581) and Alaska Direct (☎ 277 6652) buses head for Beaver Creek, with connections to Whitehorse,

Haines and Skagway. Moon Bay Express (☎ 274 6454) and Alaska Backpacker Shuttle (☎ 344 8775) service Denali National Park (US$35). Parks Highway Express (☎ 479 3065) goes to Fairbanks (US$40) via Denali (US$20) and Nenana (US$40). Seward Bus Line (☎ 224 3608) charges US$35 to Seward, while Alaska Backpacker Shuttle goes to Portage (US$20).

Alaska Railroad (☎ 265 2494) trains go south to Portage (US$25 one way, with connections to the ferry at Whittier) and Seward (US$43), and north to Denali (US$99) and Fairbanks (US$149).

Getting Around
The People Mover (☎ 343 6543) city bus network charges US$1 per ride (US$2.50 all day, and transfers for US$0.10), and also offers 'around Anchorage' options from US$2. The best-value petrol station is Courtney's (the 'Gas you Can't Pass'), on Tudor Rd, which consistently has the lowest prices in town.

AROUND ANCHORAGE
The Seward Hwy runs south of Anchorage, carved into the mountainside beside the water, passing numerous lookouts with scenic views. At Portage, a short railroad runs to Whittier for the ferry to Valdez. South of Portage, the Portage Glacier Access Rd leads 9km to the **Begich-Boggs Visitors Center** (☎ 783 2326), overlooking what's left of the receding **Portage Glacier**; from there, it's an easy 1.5km hike to the more impressive **Byron Glacier**. Gray Line offers hour-long cruises for US$21 and along the road are two Forest Service *camping grounds* which charge US$6 per site.

North of Anchorage, the Glenn Hwy runs 23km north to Eagle River, where the scenic Eagle River Rd leads 20km to the **Eagle River Nature Center** (☎ 694 2108). Here you'll find wildlife displays and access to some wonderful hiking routes, including the 43km Crow Pass Crossing to Girdwood. Near Palmer, 56km north, **Hatcher Pass** is an alpine paradise, with hiking, parasailing, gold-rush artefacts and panoramas of the Talkeetna Mountains. You can stay at the 1930s *Motherlode Lodge* (☎ 746 1464), which charges US$65 for a double, or *Hatcher Pass Lodge* (☎ 745 5897), which costs US$70.

WRANGELL-ST ELIAS NATIONAL PARK

Part of an eight million hectare wilderness area, Wrangell-St Elias National Park sits at the meeting point of the Wrangell, Chugach and St Elias ranges, forming the second-highest mountain massif in North America. Extensive ice fields and 100 major glaciers spill down from the peaks, and harbour diverse wildlife, including moose, bears, wolves and caribou. Along with Canada's Kluane National Park, in the Yukon, and British Columbia's Tatshenshini-Alsek Provincial Park, it's part of one of the world's largest contiguous protected wilderness areas, and has been named a UNESCO World Heritage Site.

From Valdez, the **Richardson Hwy** heads scenically northward to Glennallen, through canyons, over passes and past glaciers. The main headquarters for Wrangell-St Elias National Park (☎ 822 5235) is at Mile 104 on the Richardson Hwy.

Before reaching Copper Center, the Edgerton Hwy heads eastward to the ramshackle village of **Chitina**, where a log-cabin visitors center (☎ 823 2205) dispenses park information in summer; it also has a petrol station and several small shops. For further information, contact the Superintendent, Wrangell-St Elias National Park (☎ 822 5234), PO Box 439, Copper Center, AK 99573.

From Chitina, the Edgerton Hwy becomes a poorly maintained track. After crossing the mighty Chitina River and the once-daunting (but still interesting) Kuskulana Bridge, it winds for 100km through forests and past mountains along the former Kennicott railway route to the rustic village of **McCarthy**. You'll have to leave your vehicle on the western bank of the Kennicott River and cross the footbridge to reach the town. From there, a road continues for 10km to the amazing ruins of the copper-mining ghost town of **Kennicott**, in the national park. From there, excellent hikes will take you along the Kennicott Glacier to Root Glacier or steeply up the mountain to the incredible view from the abandoned Bonanza Mine.

McCarthy

Attractive McCarthy (year-round population 25) just manages to tolerate the growing number of visitors that support it. In 1900 prospectors who'd stayed on after the gold rush discovered the rich Kennicott copper deposit, and a syndicate built 350km of railroad through the wilderness to bring the ore to Cordova. From 1911 to 1938 the company town of Kennicott worked 24 hours a day, but in November 1938, faced with falling copper prices and a possible labour strike, management closed the mine, giving workers two hours to catch the last train out. Despite some pilferage, Kennicott remains a near-perfectly preserved tableau of US mining history.

There's some good **hiking** around the glaciers, peaks and mines, and rafting on the Kennicott River. Chris Richards offers colourful 1½-hour guided walks around the mines for US$12.50. St Elias Alpine Guides (☎ 277 6867 in Anchorage) offers day trips from McCarthy, and the McCarthy Museum has a US$1 walking-tour map. In clear weather, you can take a one hour flight around Mt Blackburn and Mt Wrangell for US$90.

Places to Stay & Eat You can camp along the west side of the river for US$3, but it can get crowded and dusty. Ask at *McCarthy Country Store* for cabins, B&Bs and affordable bunks. *McCarthy Lodge* (☎ 554 4402) offers meals, showers (US$5) and cold beer (US$4). The renovated 1916 *Ma Johnson's Hotel* costs US$95/105 for singles/doubles, without meals. In Kennicott, the *Kennicott Glacier Lodge* (toll-free ☎ 1-800 478 2350) costs US$149/169 and has a good value US$11 breakfast. A *Tailor Made Pizza* costs US$14.

Getting There & Away Backcountry Connections (☎ 822 5292) buses leave

Do Angels Play This HAARP?

What exactly is HAARP, the High-frequency Active Auroral Research Program, you may ask? Well, that's what a lot of people – especially Alaskans – have been asking, and there seem to be several conflicting opinions. On the surface, the HAARP installation, located near Gakona, Alaska, west of the Wrangell-St Elias National Park, consists of miles of ground-based antenna arrays and other impressive bits of equipment, the most prominent of which is the Ionospheric Research Instrument. According to official US government/navy/air force releases, this large high-frequency radio transmitter is capable of concentrating several megawatts of power into an intense ray that heats up and causes vibrations in the electrically charged ionosphere. Focusing this energy onto a specific section of the sky causes the air to heat up dramatically enough to create an 'opaque spot' which can be used to reflect back radar and radio waves, and thereby interfere with radio or other transmissions anywhere in the world.

This technology is based on the work of Serbian researcher and naturalised US citizen Nicola Tesla (1857-1943), who discovered the rotating magnetic field and the terrestrial stationary wave, which demonstrated that the earth could be used as a conductor of electrical vibrations of a specific frequency. (Interestingly, the Belgrade museum dedicated to his work happily escaped destruction in the 1999 NATO attacks on the Yugoslav capital.)

While this project may sound relatively innocuous, Alaskans Dr Nick Begich and Jeane Manning (who co-authored the book *Angels Don't Play This HAARP*) maintain that the project is a 'military Pandora's box', in which the US government is attempting to create the potential for psychological, environmental and geophysical warfare by turning the upper atmosphere into a giant X-ray device that can focus deadly rays on any part of the earth's surface. Is this just an unfounded, paranoid reaction to an innocent research program, or do their fears have some basis in fact? Perhaps it's best to let the records speak for themselves.

The US air force claims that 'the potential applications of artificial electromagnetic fields are wide-ranging and can be used in ... military or quasi-military situations ... including dealing with terrorist groups, crowd control, controlling breaches of security at military installations and antipersonnel techniques in tactical warfare ... In all of these cases, the electromagnetic systems would be used to produce mild to severe physiological disruption or perceptual distortion or disorientation'. The patent for HAARP states the following:

... this invention provides the ability to put unprecedented amounts of power in the earth's atmosphere at strategic locations and to maintain the power injection level ... in a manner far more precise and better controlled than heretofore accomplished by the prior art, particularly by detonation of nuclear devices of various yields at various altitudes ... It is possible not only to interfere with third party communications but to take advantage of ... such beams to carry out a communications network even though the rest of the world's communications are disrupted ...

... large regions of the atmosphere could be lifted to an unexpectedly high altitude so that missiles encounter unexpected and unplanned drag forces with resultant destruction. Weather modification is possible by, for example, altering upper atmosphere wind patterns by constructing one or more plumes of atmospheric particles which will act as a lens or focusing device ...

... molecular modifications of the atmosphere can take place so that positive environmental effects can be achieved. Besides actually changing the molecular composition of an atmospheric region ... for example, ozone, nitrogen, etc concentrations ... could be artificially increased.

Bizarre, eh? For the full official story from the US navy, call up the Web site w3.nrl.navy.mil/haarp .html. For Dr Nick Begich's take on the issue, see www.xyz.net/~nohaarp/pandora.htm.

Glennallen most days for McCarthy via Chitina and cost US$55. There's a five hour stop in McCarthy, enabling you to visit Kennicott; this long day trip costs US$75. Once there, St Elias Alpine Guides rents bikes for US$25 per day.

DENALI NATIONAL PARK

The brilliant but overcrowded Denali National Park, which includes North America's highest mountain, is the Alaska that most tourists come to see. Indeed, the park attracts over a million visitors each summer, and at times it seems they're all milling around the park entrance clamouring for backcountry permits, bus reservations and park access. A single road penetrates about 155km of wilderness through the heart of the park, with camp sites, trailheads, wildlife and stunning panoramas. However, this road can be used only by official shuttle buses, with limited seating. Also severely limited is the number of camp sites inside the park, which means that those who are successful at getting in will enjoy relative solitude.

Most people are interested in wildlife-viewing, and you're likely to see everything from marmots and moose to caribou, Dall sheep, beavers, grizzly bears and possibly even wolves. However, the main attraction is dramatic **Mt McKinley**, a 6096m pyramid of rock, snow and ice rising over 5000m from the 700m-high valley floor (in contrast, even 8700m Mt Everest rises only 3300m from the surrounding plateaux). However, remember that more often than not, the mountain is obscured by fog and cloud, so it's wise to allow time to wait for the big view.

Information

The park entrance is at Mile 237.3 of the George Parks Hwy, lost amid a rapidly growing jumble of tourist facilities, known as McKinley Park Village. The Visitor Access Center (VAC; ☎ 683 2294) is the place to organise your trip into the park, pick up permits and purchase maps. The centre opens at 7 am, but the queues begin to form an hour or two earlier; it stays open until 8 pm. If possible, reserve bus seats and camp sites ahead through the Denali National Park Reservation Service (☎ 272 7275, toll-free ☎ 1-800 622 7275).

For **backcountry camping** inside the park, you must get a free backcountry permit from the VAC one day in advance. The park is divided into 43 zones, each with a regulated number of visitors at any one time. Some are more popular than others. Watch the Backcountry Simulator Program video at the VAC, covering bears, rivers and backcountry safety, and check the quota board for an area you can access. With your permit, you'll get a bear-resistant food container. You then go to the counter to book a camper shuttle bus and buy your maps. Denali is a trailless park, so you must be able to use topographical maps.

Note that you may camp anywhere within your designated wilderness track, but you must be at least a kilometre from the park road and out of sight of any road or building. There are no facilities anywhere in the Denali backcountry.

Activities

For a **day hike**, get off the shuttle bus at any valley, riverbed or ridge that takes your fancy (no permit needed). If you prefer a guided walk, book at the VAC one or two days ahead.

Most cyclists book a camp site at the VAC, then carry their bikes on the campers' shuttle. **Cycling** is permitted only on the roads; you can rent bikes from Denali Mountain Bike Rental (☎ 452 0580), just north of the entrance.

Several **rafting** companies offer daily floats on the Nenana River; Denali Raft Adventures (☎ 683 2234), also near the entrance, has a canyon run through the gorge, and a milder run for US$45.

Places to Stay – Inside the Park

Camp sites inside the park cost US$6 or US$12, plus a reservation fee of US$4. It can be difficult to get a place in the camping ground of your choice, so take anything

Alaska National Interest Lands Conservation Act (ANILCA)

In 1980, when US President Jimmy Carter signed the Alaska National Interest Lands Conservation Act (ANILCA), he designated 42 million hectares (104 million acres) of federal land, or a total of 28% of the state of Alaska, as protected wilderness. The act was controversial in that it highlighted tensions of interest between residents of Alaska and those living elsewhere in the USA. ANILCA added substantial lands – about 22.7 million hectares (56 million acres) – to the US National Wilderness Preservation system, which delighted environmentalists and lovers of wilderness, but dissatisfied many of Alaska's Native peoples, for whom land in Alaska was never viewed as uninhabited wilderness but as a homeland with thousands of years of continued occupancy.

The origins of ANILCA can be traced back to the late 1950s when Alaska became the 49th state of the USA. The Alaska Statehood Act allowed the state of Alaska to select federal lands, but this laid the foundations for lengthy procedures by which lands were selected and redesignated by state and federal institutions and by Native organisations.

It was clear that before the act could be passed, traditional subsistence rights needed to be addressed. When ANILCA was passed in 1980, Title VIII allowed a priority for the subsistence use of fish and wildlife on federal lands (some 60% of total land in Alaska). The state of Alaska was granted authority to manage subsistence hunting and fishing that took place on federal lands, providing that Alaska state laws and US federal laws covering this were consistent. A problem, though, was that ANILCA limited subsistence use to rural residents. Exploiting the fact that there were inconsistencies on this between state and federal law (the subsistence preference being limited to rural residents was not written into state law), legal challenges were mounted. A rural limitation was written into the state law but, following a celebrated case called McDowell vs State, the Alaska Supreme Court found that the exclusion of urban residents from subsistence hunting and fishing was unconstitutional and that, furthermore, many urban residents in Alaska, such as Native people, could claim legitimacy as subsistence hunters and fishers.

Because the federal government has argued that the Alaska Supreme Court ruling conflicted with ANILCA, and that the state of Alaska could therefore not implement a state law that was inconsistent with federal law, the authority to manage subsistence hunting and fishing on federal lands passed back to the federal government. Because the state of Alaska has since ruled that all Alaskans are potentially eligible for subsistence rights on lands covered by ANILCA, the issue of subsistence and the management of hunting and fishing in Alaska remains a contested one.

Dr Mark Nuttall, University of Aberdeen

that's available (in summer you'll be lucky to get anything at all!) and maybe change camping grounds after you arrive.

At the park entrance, *Riley Creek Campground* is open year-round and is overrun by RVs (US$12). Skip the VAC and self-register at *Morino Campground*, a walk-in backpackers' camping ground near the train station (US$6). Other camping grounds are spaced along the park road; the nicest is *Wonder Lake*, with 26 tent sites (US$12) complete with superb views of Mt McKinley.

Denali National Park Hotel (☎ 683-2215), near the entrance, costs $155 a double. Backcountry lodges like *Camp Denali*

(☎ 683 2290) and ***Kantishna Roadhouse
(toll-free ☎ 1-800 942 7420)*** charge over
US$500, including meals.

Places to Stay – Outside the Park

Most places north and south of the park entrance provide courtesy transport to Riley
Creek, at the park entrance. In a pinch, you
can camp on gravel parking bays beside the
highway, but it's definitely discouraged and
you may well have a rude awakening by the
police in the middle of the night. The ***Denali Grizzly Bear Campground (☎ 683
2696)***, 10km south of the entrance, and the
McKinley KOA (☎ 683 2379), 19km north,
near Healy, both charge US$17 for tents or
RVs. South of the entrance, the ***Denali
Cabins (☎ 683 2643)*** cost US$140 and ac-
commodate four. Farther south, ***Carlo Creek
Lodge (☎ 683 2576)*** has creekside cabins
from US$75 and tent sites for US$11. The
Denali Hostel (☎ 683 1295, fax 683 2106),
on Otto Lake Rd north of the park entrance,
has bunks for US$22, including use of the
kitchen, while ***Stampede Hotel (☎ 683
2242)*** charges US$60 for a double.

Places to Eat

There are two restaurants and a bar off the
lobby of the ***Denali National Park Hotel***.
Its ***Whistlestop Snack Shop*** is open early to
late, serving burgers and coffee. Nearby,
McKinley Mercantile sells fresh, dried and
canned food, but it's better to stock up on
supplies in Fairbanks or Anchorage. Outside the park, ***Lynx Creek Pizza*** has excellent offerings – fill yourself up for $12.
Denali Salmon Bake charges $17 for an
Alaskan salmon dinner. South of the entrance, ***The Perch (☎ 685 2823)*** has steak
or seafood dinners from US$16.

Getting There & Away

From the VAC, Alaska Backpacker Shuttle
(☎ 344 8775) makes the run back to Anchorage (US$35), as do several other companies.
Heading north, Fireweed Express (☎ 452
0521) charges US$30 to Fairbanks. The Parks
Highway Express (toll-free ☎ 1-888 600

6001, fax 457 2034, email info@alaskashut
tle.com) runs daily trips between Anchorage
and Fairbanks, via Denali, from 10 May to 25
September. Check out the Web site www
.alaskashuttle.com. Sample fares include Anchorage to Wasilla (US$15), Talkeetna Junc-
tion (US$25), Denali (US$35), Nenana
(US$50) and Fairbanks (US$55). From Fairbanks, you can travel to Nenana (US$15), De-
nali (US$20), Talkeetna Junction (US$35),
Wasilla (US$50) and Anchorage (US$55).

From the train station near Riley Creek
Campground, you can ride the scenic Alaska
Railroad to Fairbanks (US$50) or Anchor-
age (US$95).

Free courtesy buses serve the park entrance area and the nearby highway. Heading north, take the McKinley Chalet bus and
going south, the McKinley Village bus.

Getting Around

Shuttle buses provide access for day hiking
and sightseeing and can be booked up to
five days ahead, but are usually available on
the spot for anyone boarding in the backcountry (note that you'll need a camp site or
backcountry permit for overnight access).
For a day outing on park buses, pack food,
drink and a map. Buses leave the VAC regularly from 6.30 am to 1.30 pm, going to
Eielson Visitor Center (four hours, US$20)
and Wonder Lake (5½ hours, US$26). Spe-
cial campers' shuttle buses, with space for
backpacks and mountain bikes, charge
US$15.50 to any point on the road.

FAIRBANKS

The low-rise and spread-out city of Fairbanks (population 82,500) was founded in
1901, when a trader's riverboat was stalled
by the shallows of the Chena River. A gold
strike 20km north turned the settlement into
a boom town, and by 1908 the population
had grown to 18,000. By 1920 it had
slumped to 1000, but when the Alaska Railroad reached Fairbanks in 1923, major mining companies introduced mechanised
dredges to extract ore from the frozen
ground. Further minor booms were brought
about by WWII, the construction of the

ARCTIC ALASKA

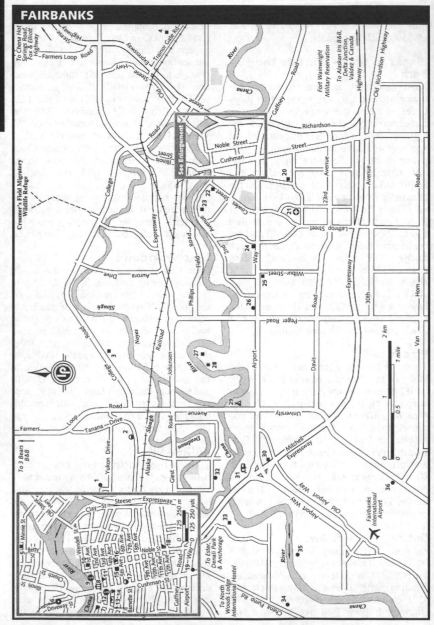

FAIRBANKS

FAIRBANKS

PLACES TO STAY
3 Fairbanks Backpackers'
    Hostel (Billie's Backpackers')
4 Grandma Shirley's Hostel
5 Tamarac Inn
10 Northern Lakes Hotel
15 Alaskan Motor Inn
20 Alaska Heritage Inn
22 Ah, Rose Marie B&B
23 Northern Lights B&B
24 Borealis Inn
25 Super 8 Motel
27 Comfy & Cozy B&B
28 Becky's B&B
29 Chena River State
    Campground

30 Golden North Hotel
31 River's Edge RV Park
33 Arctic Cat B&B

PLACES TO EAT
7 Gambardella's Pasta Bella
11 Soapy Smith's
14 Woolworths
16 Thai House
18 Peking Gardens

OTHER
1 University of Alaska
    Fairbanks
2 Commuter Terminal
6 Train Station

8 Yukon Quest General
    Store & Museum
9 Visitors Bureau
    Log Cabin
12 Alaska Public Lands
    Information Center
13 Post Office
17 Transit Park
19 Gray Line Office
21 Hospital
26 Alaskaland
32 7 Bridges Boats
    and Bikes
34 Chena Pumphouse
35 Riverboat Discovery
36 Frontier Flying Service

Alcan Hwy, and the Eielson and Fort Wainwright military bases, but in the mid-1970s, the town really took off as a construction base for the Trans-Alaska oil pipeline and a gateway to the North Slope. When the pipeline construction was completed, the growth again slumped, and the population has remained fairly stable ever since.

In Fairbanks, the sultry summer days average 25°C and can even reach a stifling 35°C. 'Downtown' is roughly focused on Cushman St and the Golden Heart Park. Most of the downtown restaurants and accommodation options conveniently lie within a 15 minute walk of the train station.

Information

The Visitors Bureau Log Cabin (☎ 456 5774) overlooks the Chena River at the corner of 1st Ave and Cushman St and has courtesy phones to motels and B&Bs. For daily events and attractions, phone the daily recorded update (☎ 456 4636). The Alaska Public Lands Information Center (☎ 456 0527), on Cushman St, sells maps and dispenses information on parks, wildlife refuges and recreation areas.

Things to See & Do

The Golden Heart Park is a pleasant riverside greenbelt. The biggest attraction is Alaskaland (☎ 459 1087), a tourist-oriented

theme park with historical displays, an old stern-wheeler and a railroad car.

At the University of Alaska Fairbanks (UAF), you may want to visit the excellent **University Museum** (☎ 474 7211), which has sections on geology and history, including a 36,000-year-old bison found preserved in permafrost. Admission is US$5.

Canoeing options range from afternoon paddles to overnight trips; ask at 7 Bridges Boats & Bikes (☎ 479 0751), at 4312 Birch Lane near the river. For a guided paddle, call Bull Moose Canoe & Raft (☎ 474 9066) for customised trips from $65 per person.

Travel the Chena River on the historic *Riverboat Discovery* (☎ 479 6673). For organised tours, call Gray Line (☎ 456 7741) or Alaska Sightseeing (☎ 452 8518). Air charter companies fly to the Arctic Circle for around US$200.

Places to Stay

The public *Chena River State Campground*, just north of Airport Way, has sites for US$15, and the *River's Edge RV Park* (☎ 474 0286, 4140 Boat St), near Airport Way and University Ave, charges US$15.50 for tent camping and US$24.95 for RVs.

The best-known hostel is *Fairbanks Backpackers' Hostel* (☎/fax 479 2034, email akbillie@aol.com, 2895 Mack Rd), also called Billie's Backpackers', with

US$18 bunks and US$5 breakfasts. *Alaska Heritage Inn (☎ 451 6587, 1018 22nd Ave)* has rooms from US$40 and some bunks. Alternatively, try *Grandma Shirley's Hostel (☎ 451 9816)*, on Trainor Gate Rd, which charges US$16.25, or the *North Woods Lodge International Hostel (☎ 479 5300, toll-free ☎ 1-800 478 5305, fax 479 6888, Chena Hills Drive)*, where you'll pay from US$15 for a dorm bed, US$12 for camping and US$40/45 for a single/double cabin.

Fairbanks is also replete with B&B accommodation. Most charge from US$55 to US$70 for a double. For a full listing, see the brochure published by the Fairbanks Association of B&Bs, which is available at the airport or the visitors bureau. Among the options are *Comfy & Cozy B&B (☎ 474 0285, email cbean@polarnet.com, 928 Wood Way)*; *Ah, Rose Marie B&B (☎ 456 2040, 302 Cowles St)*; *Northern Lights B&B (☎ 452 2598, fax 452 7247, email nlightsb@eagle.ptialaska.net, 360 State St)*; *Becky's B&B (toll-free ☎ 1-800 474 9569, 1130 Coppet St)*; *Arctic Cat B&B (☎ 455 7625, 4440 Stanford Drive)*; *3 Bears B&B (☎ 457 2449, 1068 Ski Boot Hill Rd)*; and *Alaskan Iris B&B (toll-free ☎ 1-800 474 7262)*, on Porter Ave, North Pole. See the Fairbanks map for locations.

Cheap hotels cluster on Cushman St downtown, but be sure to check the room before signing in. The *Alaskan Motor Inn (☎ 452 4800, 419 4th Ave)* has single rooms starting at US$50; try for the top floor. *Tamarac Inn (☎ 456 6406)*, just north of the river, charges US$74/80 for singles/doubles. *Northern Lakes Hotel (☎ 452 4456, 427 1st Ave)* offers singles starting at US$120. The *Golden North Hotel (☎ 479 6201, 4888 Airport Way)* has small singles from US$69, including transfers from the airport or train station. *Super 8 Motel (☎ 451 8888, 1909 Airport Way)* has big clean double rooms from US$99. In summer, the *Borealis Inn (☎ 456 1100, fax 456 2472, 1500 Airport Way)* charges US$75/95 for singles/doubles; check out the Web site www.alaskaone.com/borealisbb.

Places to Eat

The inexpensive grill at *Woolworths*, on Cushman St, has US$4 breakfasts and cheap, but very standard, dinners. *Soapy Smith's (543 2nd Ave)* offers good burgers, sandwiches and chowder in a saloon atmosphere. Try *Gambardella's Pasta Bella*, on 2nd Ave, for US$12 pizzas in a delightful outdoor setting. Walk south on Cushman St for more restaurants, including *Thai House* on 5th Ave and *Peking Gardens* on 12th Ave.

Fast-food franchises proliferate on Airport Way and in the university area. For meals by the pound, check out the deli at the *Fred Meyer* supermarket on Airport Way.

Entertainment

The *Palace Saloon* at the tourist-oriented Alaskaland has honky-tonk piano and can-can dancers in its Golden Heart Revue. Several saloons offer live music and bar games. If you're approaching along the highway from Anchorage, you might want to stop by for a game of pool at the (self-proclaimed) legendary *Skinny Dick's Halfway Inn*, near Nenana, about 45km south of Fairbanks, which is the spiritual counterpart of Anchorage's renowned Mr Whitekeys Fly-by-Nite Club.

Getting There & Away

Alaska Airlines (☎ 474 0481) has eight daily flights to Anchorage (US$100 to US$150) and two daily flights to Barrow (US$360). For charter travel into Arctic Alaska, try Frontier Flying Service (☎ 474 0014) or Larry's Flying Service (☎ 474 9169), both on University Ave.

From Fairbanks, Alaskon Express (☎ 456 7741) buses stop at Delta Junction (US$40), Tok (US$67) and Beaver Creek (US$80), with connections to Haines (US$180) and Whitehorse (US$120). Alaska Direct Busline (toll-free ☎ 1-800 770 6652) also goes to Whitehorse (US$120). Fireweed Express (☎ 452 0521) and Parks Highway Express (☎ 479 3065 or toll-free ☎ 1-888 600 6001, fax 457 2034, email info@alaska shuttle .com) offer daily connections to Denali

Alaska Native Claims Settlement Act

Demands for land claims from Native peoples arose after the discovery of oil at Prudhoe Bay in the 1960s. In 1971, the US Congress passed the Alaska Native Claims Settlement Act (ANCSA) which established 12 regional and potentially profit-making corporations. ANCSA did not recognise a Native claim to the entire state of Alaska, but the corporations created by the act were effectively given control of one-ninth of Alaska between them. As a land claims agreement, ANCSA extinguished claims to the rest of Alaska and gave Native peoples US$962.5m in compensation. However, ANCSA only gave Alaska's Native peoples ownership rights to land and gave no assurances for the recognition of aboriginal political, cultural and social rights. In addition to the regional corporations, some 200 village corporations were also established.

The US Congress saw the creation of the Native corporations established under ANCSA as a device for the generation of prosperity for Native communities. But ANCSA has its critics, some of whom say that the act amounted to no more than a way of speeding up the assimilation of Native peoples into mainstream American society. Critics say that by making Alaska's Native people shareholders in corporate-owned land, it alienated them from their traditional relationship with the land and shaped their future as one that would be tied increasingly to the global economy. Basically, ANCSA meant that, since Native corporations are legally obliged to make a profit, this is the only way that Native people could benefit from the settlement.

Despite its legal complexities and controversies, ANCSA represented a significant accomplishment at the time that it was passed. While subsistence activities remain important for the economies of remote Alaskan communities, one consequence of ANCSA has been that many of Alaska's Native peoples are increasingly involved in large business ventures. The corporate ownership of land has meant that Native peoples could be involved in the economic development of Alaska on an equal basis with other residents of the state. As a result of some of the economic and business activities in which they are involved, some Native corporations are tied to countries in South-East Asia to where they export natural resources such as timber and salmon. The success of ANCSA is likely to be measured in terms of how far traditional values have been integrated within the framework of corporate management.

Dr Mark Nuttall, University of Aberdeen

National Park at 7 am (three hours, US$20). Parks Highway Express also has daily services to Valdez from 25 May to 5 September. For further information, look up www.alaskashuttle.com on the Web. From Fairbanks, the fares are: Delta Junction (US$20), Paxson (US$35), Glennallen (US$45), Wrangell-St Elias National Park Visitors Center, Copper Center (US$45) and Valdez (US$59).

The Alaska Railroad (☎ 456 4155) services depart at 8.30 am daily for Denali National Park (US$50) and Anchorage (US$135).

Getting Around

Metropolitan Area Commuter Service (☎ 459 1011) provides local bus services on weekdays; day passes cost US$3.

AROUND FAIRBANKS
Chena Hot Springs Road

There's little hiking around Fairbanks, but hikers who head east out to the Chena River State Recreational Area will find pleasant short climbs to Angel Rocks and Granite Tors, or the longer three day circuit past Chena Domes. At the end of the road lies the renowned *Chena Hot Springs Resort*

(☎ 452 7867, toll-free ☎ 1-800 478 4681, fax 456 3122, email chenahs@polarnet.com), where tent or RV camping costs US$15, double rooms are US$105 and basic cabins for two/four people cost US$80/110. All rates include access to the hot springs and hot pools. Day passes to the pools and other facilities cost US$8 per person.

Steese Highway

For a great hiking experience, head northeast on the Steese Hwy to the 45km **Pinnell Mountain Trail**, which begins at Mile 107 (Eagle Summit) and follows an exposed ridge-line back to Mile 84 (12-Mile Summit). It's a superb alpine hike which requires about three days to complete. Along the way, you'll find two basic mountain shelters, but it's still wise to carry a tent and plenty of water, as there's no reliable supply in the summer months.

Along the way, a worthwhile stop is the *Chatanika Lodge* (☎ 389 2164), at Mile 28.6 of the Steese Hwy, where you'll find excellent meals, bizarre decor and a good, short hike to an enormous abandoned gold dredge.

At the village of **Central**, you'll find petrol, a restaurant, a bar, and the *Crabbe Corner Motel* (☎ 520 5599), where single/double accommodation costs US$50/55.

At *Arctic Circle Hot Springs* (☎ 520 5773, fax 520 5116), 12km off the highway, you can enjoy the wonderful atmosphere of this marvellously low-key resort. Here, you can soak up the natural hot water (US$5 per person) and camp for US$5/10 per tent/RV. Hostel accommodation costs US$15 per bed, cabins are US$85/110 without/with running water, and double rooms in the charming Victorian-style hotel start at US$100.

The lazy village of **Circle**, at the end of the road, has little to offer visitors but a basic shop, petrol station and a sweeping view across the Yukon River. Rooms at the *Yukon Riverview Motel* (☎ 773 8439) cost US$60/70. Informal camping is possible at the Birch Creek wayside, about 40km south of town.

The only public transport along the Steese Hwy is the Steese Highway Stage Line (☎ 520 5610, email loki@xyz.net), which runs shuttle buses on Monday, Wednesday and Friday between Fairbanks and Circle (US$80/145 one-way/return), via Chatanika (US$25/45), the Pinnell Mountain trailheads (US$55/75), Birch Creek Access (US$60/80), Central (US$60/100) and Circle Hot Springs (US$60/100). You must reserve seats at least 24 hours in advance.

Elliott Highway

The main reason to drive the Elliott Hwy from Fairbanks is to reach the **Manley Hot Springs**, 245km to the north-west, at the end of the road. The road turns west at the village of Fox, about 15km north of Fairbanks. At Mile 28 (45km), it runs out of tarmac and continues as a basic gravel route for the remaining 200km to Manley. At 118km from Fairbanks, the Dalton Hwy heads north toward Deadhorse and Prudhoe Bay. The village of Manley Hot Springs (population 94) offers basic accommodation at the rustic *Manley Roadhouse* (☎ 672 3161). Access to the concrete baths at the hot springs (☎ 672 3171) costs US$5 per person.

NOME

In 1898 gold was discovered by the 'three lucky Swedes' at Anvil Creek, and the focus of the Klondike Gold Rush shifted westward, turning this remote and lonely coastline into a bustling Wild West boom town of 10,000 people. When gold was discovered in the beach sands in 1899, however, the real stampede was on, and thousands of opportunists poured in on steamships from Seattle and San Francisco. By 1900 Nome's official population had reached 12,500, but a more realistic figure would be around 20,000. As if to confirm the Wild West tradition, even Sheriff Wyatt Earp, who later made his mark in history at Tombstone's OK Corral, lived here from 1899 to 1901, and built the historic Dexter Saloon. The current population is 4000.

In 1925 a diphtheria epidemic in Nome was averted when a dog team, led by the legendary Balto, brought the necessary remedial serum from Fairbanks, 1000km

Denali National Park, Alaska

KRAIG LIEB

The last train to nowhere, Seward Peninsula

DEANNA SWANEY

Abandoned dredge, north of Nome, Alaska

DEANNA SWANEY

Pilgrim Hot Springs, Seward Peninsula, Alaska

DEANNA SWANEY

Aerial view of lakes and shrubland/tundra north of Yellowknife, Canada

Kluane National Park with mountains and glaciers near Haines Junction, Canada

away. This effort provided the inspiration for the annual Iditarod dogsled race, which now runs each February/March for 1680km along the Iditarod Trail between Anchorage and Nome (see the boxed text 'The Last Great Race – The Iditarod').

Information

The very friendly Nome Convention & Visitors Bureau (☎ 443 5535, fax 443 5832, email tourinfo@ci.nome.ak.us) can provide all the help and information you need for a successful visit in the area. On the Net, you'll find Nome information at www.alaska.net /~nome. The Arctic Trading Post has a good selection of books on local topics.

Things to See & Do

The **Carrie McLain Museum**, in the library on Front St, features a range of arte-

facts, photos and remnants from Nome's colourful history. It's open on weekdays from noon to 5 pm. Less than 2km east of town on the Solomon Road, you'll pass the large abandoned **Swanberg gold dredge**, which is only the most accessible of the 40 or so dredges that languish in the vicinity. Once you've learned about the town history, it's worth taking a wander around town to see the many historical buildings which remain from the gold rush days.

A great time to be in Nome – but a hard time to find accommodation – is for the big finish of the **Iditarod dogsled race** in March. The famed 'burled arch', which marked the end of the race, collapsed in 1999, but will be replaced in 2000 by a new arch from the Kenai Peninsula. For information on dates and schedules, contact the

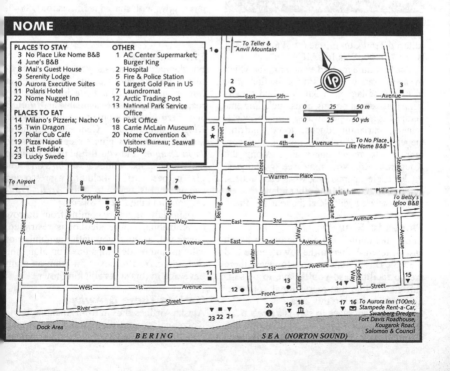

NOME

PLACES TO STAY
3 No Place Like Nome B&B
4 June's B&B
8 Mai's Guest House
9 Serenity Lodge
10 Aurora Executive Suites
11 Polaris Hotel
22 Nome Nugget Inn

PLACES TO EAT
14 Milano's Pizzeria; Nacho's
15 Twin Dragon
17 Polar Cub Café
19 Pizza Napoli
21 Fat Freddie's
23 Lucky Swede

OTHER
1 AC Center Supermarket; Burger King
2 Hospital
5 Fire & Police Station
6 Largest Gold Pan in US
7 Laundromat
12 Arctic Trading Post
13 National Park Service Office
16 Post Office
18 Carrie McLain Museum
20 Nome Convention & Visitors Bureau; Seawall Display

The Naming of Nome

The name of the town dates back to the 1950s, when a British officer scrawled the word 'Name' across an as yet unnamed cape. A future cartographic draughtsman, misreading the word and mistaking the question mark for a 'C', assumed that the officer had knowingly labelled the feature 'Cape Nome'. Some people maintain that the officer had indeed written the word 'Nome', which might have been the transliteration of an Inuit response 'Kin-no-me' (I don't know) to the question 'What is the name of this place?'. Although there was a late 19th century attempt by the mining crowd to rename the place Anvil City, after its first gold strike, the US postal service thought it sounded too much like Anvik, on the lower Yukon, and Nome thereby became the official name of the town.

Iditarod Trail Committee (☎ 376 5155), PO Box 87-0800, Wasilla, AK 99687.

The best time for **bird-watching**, for which the area is renowned, is around the first week in June. The lagoon at Safety Sound attracts large numbers of nesting birds, including emperor geese, whooper swans, Stellar's eiders, scoters, harlequin ducks, loons, puffins, jaegers, crested auklets, murres and cormorants, to name but a few. Along the Kougarok Rd, you may see gyrfalcons, golden eagles, peregrines, wheatears, tattlers, curlews, snowy owls and other inland species. Checklists are available at the tourist office.

Places to Stay

Informal camping is possible on the beach east of town, between the town centre and the Fort Davis Roadhouse. However, there are no facilities, so you'll have to be self-sufficient. Note that recreational gold panning is permitted in this area.

An excellent place to stay is *June's B&B* (☎ 443 5984, toll-free ☎ 1-800 494 6994, email june@gold-digger.com), which is open from 1 May to 1 October and charges US$70/80 for single/double rooms. It's popular so book well in advance. Alternatives include *No Place Like Nome B&B* (☎ 443 2451, 540 Steadman St), which charges US$65/75; *Betty's Igloo B&B* (☎ 443 2419), charging US$55/70; and *Mai's Guest House* (☎ 443 4113), which charges US$55/60. At the rustic and historic *Serenity Lodge* (☎ 443 5972, 222 Seppala Drive) you'll pay US$75/95 for self-contained accommodation.

At the brand new *Aurora Inn* (☎ 443 3838, toll-free ☎ 1-800 354 4606, fax 443 2985) you'll pay US$115/125 in summer for a single without/with a kitchenette; for a double, add US$10. At the affiliated *Aurora Executive Suites*, you'll pay US$99/109 for a single/double studio apartment. The rustic old *Nome Nugget Inn* (☎ 443 2323, fax 443 5966) has rooms right in the centre of town for US$91.50/99.50, and the *Polaris Hotel* (☎ 443 2000, fax 443 2217), has singles with shared facilities for US$40, singles or doubles with facilities for US$80 and self-contained flats for US$90.

Places to Eat

For standard cafe meals, you can choose between *Fat Freddie's* at the Nome Nugget Inn or the *Polar Cub Café* just down the road. Decent pizzas are available at *Milano's* and *Pizza Napoli*. Nome even has a *Burger King* inside the AC Centre supermarket north of town. For Chinese meals, there's the *Twin Dragon*, and you'll find basic Chinese and Mexican specialities at *Nacho's* on Front St. The best coffee, including espresso and cappuccino, is available at the *Arctic Trading Post* and the *Lucky Swede*.

Especially if you're coming from Barrow or Kotzebue, where alcohol is restricted, Nome will astound you with the number of saloons and bottle shops lined up along the main drag. You're never far from an adult beverage in this still rollicking town!

Getting There & Away

Alaska Airlines flies in from Anchorage, via Kotzebue, several times daily, for around US$400 return.

AROUND NOME

It's worth renting a car in Nome in order to drive around the extensive – and detached – highway system of the Seward Peninsula. A good choice is Stampede Rent-a-Car (☎ 443 3838, fax 443 2985), PO Box 633, Nome, AK 99762, based at the Aurora Inn. For a vehicle with unlimited mileage, you'll pay US$75 per day.

Council Road

Skirting the beach east of Nome, the causeway-like Council Rd follows the broad sandbar between Norton Sound and the inland lagoon known as Safety Sound. The latter, a well known bird-watching venue, attracts nesting water birds – and throngs of enthusiastic twitchers – from around the world.

For the first few kilometres out of Nome, you'll pass the informal beach camps of itinerant wildcat dredgers, who still mine the beach sands for alluvial gold. Farther east, you'll pass hundreds of decrepit beachside hunting camps, with spectacular views to the distant ranges of the Seward Peninsula. In May, the seas and sounds remain choked with sea ice, while during the fishing season, you'll see countless wooden racks laden with drying salmon.

At Mile 33, the road crosses a bridge and passes the site affectionately known as **The Last Train to Nowhere**, a string of rusting steam locomotives and rail cars, which are all that's left of the narrow-gauge Council City & Solomon River Railway. **Solomon**, which was originally established as a mining camp in 1900, once boasted a population of 1000, with seven saloons, a post office, a ferry dock and the aforementioned railway that connected it with Council, farther north. The town was destroyed by a storm in 1913 and, although it was relocated to higher ground, it was further decimated by the 1918 Spanish flu epidemic. Today, only four families remain.

The end-of-the-road village of **Council**, with a summer population of about 30, may be visited only when the road is open in the height of summer. To get there, you'll either have to ford the river (seek

local advice regarding the route) or try to catch a ride across in a private boat.

Kougarok/Taylor Road

About 15km north of Nome along the Kougarok Rd, you'll pass the 'suburb' of Dexter, which is little more than a rambling collection of homesteads and artefacts left over from the gold rush days. From here, a winding side road leads to the former White Alice radar installation atop Anvil Mountain and affords a spectacular view across Nome and both Norton and Safety Sounds.

Farther north, the road winds up into the heart of the beautiful **Kigluaik Range**. At Mile 40, you pass the *Salmon Lake Campground*, administered by the Bureau of Land Management (it's normally open from late June to late August). In high summer, you can hike from Salmon Lake through Mosquito Pass, where there's a public cabin at the confluence of Windy Creek and the Sinuk River.

At the 95km (60 mile) point, north of Salmon Lake, you'll pass the turning to **Pilgrim Hot Springs**, which lie 13km off the main road. This interesting oasis of incongruous cottonwood trees in an otherwise treeless landscape contains a lovely hot pool which may be used by visitors whenever the owner is around. However, you may not take vehicles past the entry gate.

Unfortunately, it's not possible to drive all the way to Taylor, as the road is only maintained as far as the Kougarok River Bridge, about 30km past the Pilgrim Hot Springs turn-off.

Teller

Teller is a real end-of-the-road destination and, in fact, lies at the westernmost end of the westernmost road in North America. The town itself, sandwiched between the grey waters of the Bering Sea and a sky that's normally the same colour, stretches along a tapering gravel spit near the head of sheltered Port Clarence. It was here that Roald Amundsen returned to earth after his legendary airship flight over the North Pole on 14 May 1926. More recently, in 1985 it made the headlines when a Teller woman,

The Last Great Race – The Iditarod

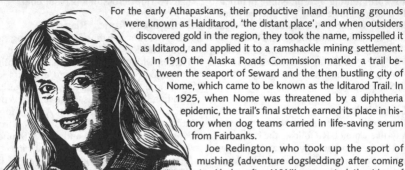

For the early Athapaskans, their productive inland hunting grounds were known as Haiditarod, 'the distant place', and when outsiders discovered gold in the region, they took the name, misspelled it as Iditarod, and applied it to a ramshackle mining settlement. In 1910 the Alaska Roads Commission marked a trail between the seaport of Seward and the then bustling city of Nome, which came to be known as the Iditarod Trail. In 1925, when Nome was threatened by a diphtheria epidemic, the trail's final stretch earned its place in history when dog teams carried in life-saving serum from Fairbanks.

Joe Redington, who took up the sport of mushing (adventure dogsledding) after coming to Alaska after WWII, suggested the idea of starting up a dogsled race between Anchorage and Nome, in honour of both the serum run and the historic trail. By 1973 enough people were attracted to his idea to make it happen.

Libby Riddles

The first race took a leisurely 20 days to complete, but over the next 20 years, tireless dedication to the project by Redington and others turned the annual event into the top mushing event in the world, and by the late 1990s the completion times for the race had been pared down to just over nine days. Joe died in June 1999 at the age of 82.

When Libby Riddles, a 28-year-old woman from Teller, Alaska, became the first woman to win the Iditarod in 1985, the Last Great Race moved from the sports pages of US newspapers to the front pages of papers around the world. Although Joe Redington never came in higher than fifth place, one of his prodigies, Manley musher Susan Butcher, has won the race four times (1986, 1987, 1988 and 1990). This inspired a new (and unofficial) state motto: 'Alaska – where men are men and women win the Iditarod'. Curiously no woman has won the race since but it's expected that Dee Dee Jonrowe from Willow, Alaska, will take the honours in the next few years.

The event's ceremonial start takes place on 4th Ave in Anchorage on the first Saturday in March, and heads up the Glenn Hwy for 20km to the suburb of Eagle River. The following day, the race restarts at Wasilla, following the Iditarod Trail across the wilderness towards the 'burled arch' at the finish line in Nome. Today, there are in fact two Iditarod Trails, and the race path alternates between the northern route through Cripple, Ruby and Galena (in even-numbered years) and the southern route through Iditarod, Shageluk and Anvik (in odd-numbered years). Interestingly, the race isn't officially complete until the last musher passes through the burled arch and gathers up the ceremonial 'red lantern', which signifies a safe end to the year's competition.

The official length of the race is 1678km, or 1049 miles (which adds 49 miles to 1000 in honour of Alaska's status as the 49th state of the USA), but the actual distance travelled is around 1920km (1200 miles). Along the way, mushers must pass through 27 checkpoints, where they can rest and veterinarians can check on the condition of the dogs. Although most contestants are based in Alaska, participants have hailed from all over the USA, as well as Australia, Canada, Switzerland, Norway, Great Britain, New Zealand, Russia, Japan and Italy.

To follow the latest developments – both before and during the race – keep an eye on the Web site www.dogsled.com.

Libby Riddles, became the first woman to win the Iditarod dogsled race across Alaska.

Teller makes an excellent day trip from Nome, about 110km away by gravel road. Along the way, you'll pass all sorts of abandoned gold-mining detritus, and can enjoy the starkly dramatic scenery that's typical of the inland portion of the Seward Peninsula. Overnight accommodation is available at **Blodgett's B&B** (☎ 642 3333, fax 642 3451), which charges US$86.50/120 for singles/doubles. There's also a basic shop and petrol pump.

LITTLE DIOMEDE

The remote island of Little Diomede, just 4km from the Russian island of Big Diomede, is home to 150 Inupiat residents. This remote island is the nearest US landfall to Russia and is accessible only by charter helicopter from Wales, on the western tip of the Seward Peninsula. There are no visitor facilities, but in a pinch, you can stay at the self-contained *flat* provided for visitors by the Inalik Native Corporation (☎ 686 3221).

KOTZEBUE

Kotzebue (population 3200), about 55km north of the Arctic Circle at the northern tip of the Baldwin Peninsula, is most often visited by day tourists who pop in from Anchorage to attend the local cultural program and pick up a certificate verifying that they've crossed the Arctic Circle. However, that distinction belies the scope of possibilities for longer-term visitors, including exploring the remote national parklands that dominate the region and enjoying the warm welcome received by those who want to learn about the local Inupiat culture

The town is named for the Polish explorer Otto von Kotzebue who, in the service of Mother Russia, stumbled upon it in 1816 while searching for the Northwest Passage. The Inupiat name for the town, Kikiktagruk, means simply 'the peninsula'. Recently, the town has received an economic boost from the Red Dog Mine, which

lies 160km north-west of the city and holds some of the richest zinc deposits in North America.

Your best source of tourist information is the Western Arctic National Parklands visitors center (☎ 442 3890, fax 442 8316), near the corner of 2nd Ave and Lake St. It screens video programs on Arctic Alaska and provides some excellent displays on local culture and natural history. It also sells local-interest books and videos.

Things to See & Do

If you don't want to spend any money, the best thing to do is just stroll down Shore Ave and appreciate the historic wooden architecture which survives in these extreme climatic conditions. For a longer hike, stroll across the bridges east of town and along the ridge that dominates the eastern horizon.

At 3.15 pm daily in summer, Tour Arctic (toll-free ☎ 1-800 468 2248 or ☎ 442 3301, www.tour-arctic.com), in conjunction with the Northwest Arctic Native Association (NANA), offers a worthwhile **Inupiat cultural program** at the NANA Museum. The program finishes up with a *nalukataq*, or Inuit blanket toss, which historically allowed people to gain enough elevation to observe vast distances of terrain. The entire program lasts about two hours and is scheduled to accommodate the day tours from Anchorage. The walk-in admission is US$26.50. Tour Arctic also offers a day tour to the Inupiat village of Kiana (US$227, including a bush flight), and a day or evening tour of Kotzebue (US$85).

The **town museum**, Ootukahkuktuvik, or 'the place of old things', lies beneath the Yogi and Boo-Boo sign in the town centre, but it may be visited only by prior arrangement with the town hall.

Wildlife enthusiasts who can manage a short bush flight will probably want to visit the prolific **Selawik National Wildlife Refuge**, to the east of town, which hosts large numbers of nesting migratory birds (including songbirds, raptors, geese, cranes

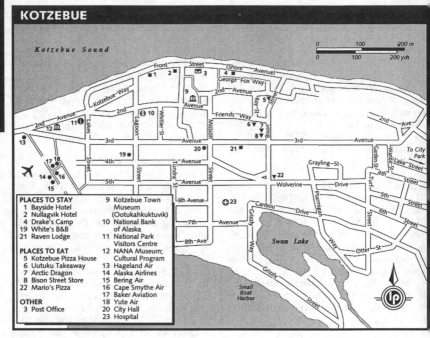

KOTZEBUE

Kotzebue Sound

PLACES TO STAY	9 Kotzebue Town
1 Bayside Hotel	Museum
2 Nullagvik Hotel	(Ootukahkuktuvik)
4 Drake's Camp	10 National Bank
19 White's B&B	of Alaska
21 Raven Lodge	11 National Park
	Visitors Centre
PLACES TO EAT	12 NANA Museum;
5 Kotzebue Pizza House	Cultural Program
6 Uutuku Takeaway	13 Hageland Air
7 Arctic Dragon	14 Alaska Airlines
8 Bison Street Store	15 Bering Air
22 Mario's Pizza	16 Cape Smythe Air
	17 Baker Aviation
OTHER	18 Yute Air
3 Post Office	20 City Hall
	23 Hospital

and ducks), as well as spawning fish, migrating caribou, Arctic foxes, moose, brown bears and large numbers of fur-bearing rodents. For further information, contact the Refuge Manager, Selawik National Wildlife Refuge (☎ 442 3799), PO Box 270, Kotzebue, AK 99752.

Places to Stay & Eat

The reasonably comfortable *Nullagvik* tourist hotel (☎ 442 3331) charges a standard US$141 for singles or doubles, including tax. Nearly as nice is the *Bayside*, which charges only US$85 for singles or doubles. The more basic *Raven's Lodge* (☎ 442 3544, 3rd Ave) charges US$50/65 for single/double rooms with shared bath, as does *White's B&B* (☎ 442 3723). The best alternative to the hotels is the simple but very friendly *Drake's Camp* (☎ 442 2736), which charges US$55/75 for rooms

with shared facilities, including use of the kitchen.

Most eateries in Kotzebue provide free delivery, and indeed, most locals take advantage of their services. The *Uutuku Takeaway* (☎ 442 3337) cooks up and delivers all sorts of Chinese specialities and burgers from US$6 to US$12. Another informal takeaway is the *Bison Street Store*. The *Kotzebue Pizza House* (☎ 442 3432) not only offers pizzas (US$12 to US$20), but also burgers and sandwiches. *Mario's* (☎ 442 2666) also cooks up Chinese dishes (US$8 to US$13) and pizzas (US$10 to US$20).

Getting There & Away

Alaska Airlines has several daily flights to and from Anchorage (US$400 return), as well as all-inclusive day trips which will get you across the Arctic Circle with a minimum of fuss.

NORTHWEST ARCTIC NATIONAL PARKLANDS

The four units of the US National Park Service in north-western Alaska are like no other national parks in the USA – not even those in other parts of Alaska – as they're not accessible by road and as a result, they have very few visitors. However, the difficulty of access means that those who can manage the considerable effort and expense required to visit these areas will enjoy some of the most pristine environments available in North America, and indeed, in all the world. For information on any of these parks, contact the Superintendent, Northwest Alaska Areas, National Park Service (☎ 442 3890 or 442 8300), PO Box 1029, Kotzebue, AK 99752.

Cape Krusenstern National Monument

The broad coastal plain that makes up Cape Krusenstern National Monument consists of alternating beaches, ice-carved lagoons and 114 parallel limestone bluffs and ridges that define the changing shorelines of the Chukchi Sea. In autumn, migrating waterfowl are drawn to Cape Krusenstern by the watery habitats and rich insect life. Most visitors to the park participate in **kayaking trips** along the coast and through the lagoons, or engage in hiking, backpacking and **wildlife viewing** across the wetland landscapes.

Noatak National Preserve

Although stark, the vast open landscapes of the Noatak National Preserve make up what are surely the most beautiful scenes in northern Alaska. This vast, mountain-ringed river basin, bounded by the Baird, DeLong and Brooks ranges, is not only home to the complete gamut of Arctic wildlife, but also straddles the boundary between the taiga and tundra ecosystems. This is truly Big Sky Country, and anyone who wants to experience the best of it can embark on a magical **float trip** by canoe, raft or kayak down the Noatak River, which has been classified as a National Wild and Scenic River.

Kobuk Valley National Park

Between the Baird and Waring mountains, the Kobuk Valley National Park protects the middle reaches of the Kobuk River and the incongruous sand dunes, created by the grinding action of ancient glaciers that flank the Kobuk, Little Kobuk and Hunt rivers.

The placid Kobuk River, which reaches widths of up to 500m, slides along at a negligible gradient of about 6cm per kilometre. An excellent lazy float trip will take you between the villages of Ambler and Kiana. At the **Onion Portage archaeological site** (where there's a seasonal ranger station), you'll find evidence of the Inupiat cultures which have occupied this area for at least 12,000 years. The most dramatic dunes, the **Great Kobuk Sand Dunes**, are accessible on foot along Kavet Creek, about 5km south of the Kobuk River. Caribou migrations pass through between August and October.

Bering Land Bridge National Preserve

The bleak and barren landscapes along the northern shore of the Seward Peninsula reveal evidence of early human migrations between Asia and North America. It's approximately 90km from the easternmost tip of Russia across the Bering Strait to the North American continent, but from 40,000 to 13,000 years ago, so much of the earth's water was locked in ice age icecaps that the sea level was considerably lower than it is today. As a result, the two continents were connected by a 1600km-wide bridge of land that facilitated travel between them. It's theorised that across this bridge passed the Athapaskans and other waves of migrants that would eventually populate much of both American continents.

In the remote 1.1 million hectare Bering Land Bridge National Preserve, visitors can observe more than 170 species of birds which nest in the area, and explore remnants of early Inuit habitation as well as relics from the gold rush at the start of the 20th century. Scattered across the reserve are six shelter cabins, the most popular of which is in a haunting setting at **Serpentine Hot Springs**, which sleeps up to 20 people.

Access is by bush flight from Nome or Kotzebue. Summer use of ATVs (all-terrain vehicles) is prohibited, although snowmobiles may be used during periods of adequate snowfall.

For further information, contact the Superintendent, Bering Land Bridge National Preserve (☎ 443 2522), PO Box 220, Nome, AK 99762.

Getting There & Away

The only access to these parks is by air from Kotzebue or, in the case of the Bering Land Bridge National Preserve, from Nome. From Kotzebue, try Hageland Aviation Services (☎ 442 2936), which charges US$230 per hour between airports and US$250 per hour for off-airport landings. These rates

include a maximum payload of around 310kg. It also offers scheduled flights to Ambler and Kobuk (US$155), Kiana, Deering, Buckland, Kivalina and Selawik (US$90) and Point Hope (US$110), with a luggage allowance of around 20kg, plus US$1.50 for each additional kilogram.

BARROW

The northernmost town in the USA at a latitude of 71°N, Barrow (population 4000) positively brims with pride at its top-of-the-world location and gets a great deal of amusement from the tourists' reactions to the summer midnight sun and the town's rather – shall we say – desultory nature. Yes, junk reigns supreme in this frightfully untidy community, and there's little mystery as to why that's the case. People are happy to pay to ship things in, but once

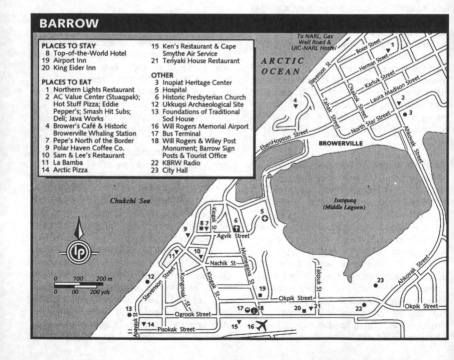

BARROW

PLACES TO STAY
8 Top-of-the-World Hotel
19 Airport Inn
20 King Eider Inn

PLACES TO EAT
1 Northern Lights Restaurant
2 AC Value Center (Stuaqpak); Hot Stuff Pizza; Eddie Pepper's; Smash Hit Subs; Deli; Java Works
4 Brower's Café & Historic Browerville Whaling Station
7 Pepe's North of the Border
9 Polar Haven Coffee Co.
10 Sam & Lee's Restaurant
11 La Bamba
14 Arctic Pizza

15 Ken's Restaurant & Cape Smythe Air Service
21 Teriyaki House Restaurant

OTHER
3 Inupiat Heritage Center
5 Hospital
6 Historic Presbyterian Church
12 Ukkuqsi Archaeological Site
13 Foundations of Traditional Sod House
16 Will Rogers Memorial Airport
17 Bus Terminal
18 Will Rogers & Wiley Post Monument; Barrow Sign Posts & Tourist Office
22 KBRW Radio
23 City Hall

those items have outlived their usefulness, they remain where they fall and simply become just another part of the scenery. The result, once you become accustomed to it, might even be described as interesting – even charming – at least in an odd archaeological or anarchistic sense!

The Inupiat name for Barrow, Utqiagvik, means 'the place to hunt snowy owls'. In summer, the tourist office is open Monday to Friday from 2 to 4 pm.

Things to See & Do

The town's pride and joy is the new **Inupiat Heritage Center**, which contains collections of Inupiat artefacts and traces the history of the local Inuit peoples from the days of subsistence hunting to the emergence of the conveniences of modern life that have been adapted to local needs and the conditions of the harsh landscape. Each afternoon, local people present a cultural program which features traditional singing, dancing and drumming. Near the western end of town, you'll find the less-than-distinct foundations of several early sod houses.

There are several options for hiking. A pleasant one is the 22km trek south of town to the remote spot where Oklahoma Cherokee humorist Will Rogers ('I never met a man I didn't like') and pilot Wiley Post were killed in 1935 when their Lockheed Sirius, crashed into the Walakpa lagoon shortly after take-off. You can see the plane's registration tags at the historic **1889 whaling station** in Browerville (now Brower's Café). There's also a small **Will Rogers and Wiley Post monument** beside the tourist office. Along the route to the crash site, you'll pass the spot known as 'Hollywood', where the Disney studios filmed *The Track of the Giant Snow Bear*. In winter, this trip may be done by snowmobile, and in summer, on foot or by 'four-wheeler' or ATV.

Alternatively, you can slog about the same distance northward along the coast, past the settlement of NARL (Naval Arctic Research Laboratory), now the site of the Ilisagvik College, to **Point Barrow**, the northernmost point in the USA. At the historic hunting camp known as Pigniq, families have hunted polar bears, seals and birds for thousands of years. East of town, along Gas Well Rd, hikers can observe **wildlife** including Arctic foxes, caribou, swans, snowy owls, jaegers, typically testy Arctic terns and numerous other bird species, as well as the untold zillions of mosquitoes that provide nourishment for all the bird life.

If you dare to visit off-season, you can experience the dark days of winter at the **Kivgiq** festival, or 'Messenger Feast', a three day celebration in January or February which takes place every three years and gathers Inuit peoples to Barrow from around northern Alaska and Canada, as well as Russia. In April, when the days are growing longer, you can enjoy the **Piuraagiaqta** spring festival, with parades, foot and snow-machine races, dog mushing and igloo-building contests.

Places to Stay

Most visitors seem to end up at the overpriced *Top-of-the-World Hotel* (☎ 852 3900, toll-free ☎ 1-800 478 8520, email tow@asrc.com), which charges US$179 for a double room with a 'spectacular ocean view' (often frozen solid). Further information is available at its Web site www .alaskaone.com/topworld. The cleaner and more posh *King Eider Inn* (☎ 852 4700, fax 852 2025, email eider@barrow.com), near the airport, has standard non-smoking single/double rooms for US$165/185, and a spacious 'presidential' suite for US$275/ 300, complete with a jacuzzi and stone fireplace.

The pleasant and good value *Airport Inn* (☎ 852 2525, toll-free ☎ 1-800 375 2527) charges US$115/125 for rooms; all have refrigerators and microwaves, and include the use of kitchenettes. The cheapest place to stay is the *UIC-NARL Hostel* (☎ 852 7800) at NARL, where rooms with shared facilities cost US$65 per person.

Places to Eat

Food fans will be pleasantly surprised with the choices that face them in tiny Barrow.

The most renowned restaurant is *Pepe's North of the Border* (☎ 852 8200), run by long-time resident Fran Tate, who is also responsible for the local water haulage services and septic company (the collectible T-shirt reads 'We clean up your act because we've got our shit together'). The Mexican food and breakfasts are great and it's worth stopping by for a chat with Fran, who maintains a museum of artefacts contributed by her many well known friends. If you want to know more, check out the book *Tacos on the Tundra*, which tells the whole story.

If you're after South of the Border Mexican options, you'll want to check out *La Bamba* (☎ 852 6464), which will carry you from the High Arctic straight to the sunny streets of Guadalajara. I'd probably go out on a limb and say that this unassuming place is the best restaurant in the world north of the Arctic Circle and, even better, the prices are very reasonable.

Another great choice is the renowned *Arctic Pizza* (☎ 852 4222). Apart from pizza, it also serves pasta, Mexican-American dishes, burgers and full meat-based dinners. For coffee, your only real choice is *Polar Haven* (☎ 852 2326). *Brower's Café* (☎ 852 3663), at the historic whaling station, has real burgers, sandwiches, pizza, pasta, seafood and beef dishes for US$7 to US$14. On weekends, it serves breakfast from 10 am.

You can also choose between several Oriental eateries: *Sam & Lee's* (☎ 852 5555); the quirky *Ken's* (☎ 852 8888), above the Cape Smythe Air office, which has US$10 lunch specials; *Northern Lights* (☎ 852 3300); and *Teriyaki* (☎ 852 2276), which enjoys an especially pungent setting.

At the AC Value Center supermarket, better known as Stuaqpak or 'big store', you'll find a choice of eateries, including *Hot Stuff Pizza*, *Eddie Pepper's* Mexican takeaway, *Smash Hit Subs*, a *deli* and the *Java Works* coffee shop.

Getting There & Away

Alaska Airlines (☎ 852 8222, toll-free ☎ 1-800 478 0333) has two daily flights between Barrow, Fairbanks and Anchorage.

Getting Around

You can rent four-wheelers (ATVs) from North Slope Auto & Rental (☎ 852 7325) or cars from UIC Auto Rental (☎ 852 2700) and Arctic Airport Truck Rentals (☎ 852 3342). For a taxi, phone Arctic Cab (☎ 852 2227), Quilamik (☎ 852 2020) and City Cab (☎ 852 5050). During the day, city buses (US$1) run every 20 minutes between Barrow, Browerville and NARL.

GATES OF THE ARCTIC NATIONAL PARK

The Brooks Range, which forms the northernmost extent of the Rocky Mountains, makes up the wilderness heart of remote and beautiful 3.4 million hectare Gates of the Arctic National Park. It extends 350km from east to west and lies entirely north of the Arctic Circle. Much of the southern half of the park is vegetated with low shrubbery and thin black-spruce forest, while the northern slope more closely resembles the wild, treeless tundra of Alaska's High Arctic. Wildlife includes wolves, Dall sheep, moose, caribou, wolverines and large numbers of grizzly bears.

For information, contact the Superintendent, Gates of the Arctic National Park (☎ 456 0281), PO Box 74680, 201 1st Ave, Fairbanks, AK 99707, or call up the Web site www.nps.gov/gaar. In Bettles, the address is Bettles Ranger Station (☎ 692 5494), PO Box 26030, Bettles, AK 99726; in Anaktuvuk Pass, it's Anaktuvuk Pass Ranger Station (☎ 661 3520), PO Box 21102, Anaktuvuk Pass, AK 99721.

From late May to early September, the visitors center at Coldfoot (☎ 678 5209), on the Dalton Hwy, provides information and natural history exhibits. Prospective backcountry visitors must participate in a mandatory backcountry orientation program at Bettles, Anaktuvuk Pass or Coldfoot.

Activities

The park lacks trails, organised camping grounds or roads, but visitors who can appreciate the pristine wilderness can trek along the broad, open valleys and raft or canoe down wild, lonely rivers such as the John, Alatna, Tinayguk, Koyukuk or upper Noatak. One of the most popular is the north fork of the Koyukuk, which makes an easy 160km Class I/II paddle, taking you right back to Bettles. Another great float is the five to seven day, 100km trip along the upper Noatak, which begins near Portage Creek and ends at Kacachurak Creek, just outside the park.

One of the most popular hiking trips is the five day hike from Summit to Redstar lakes; less experienced wilderness backpackers often choose to be dropped off and picked up at the same lake (Summit, Redstar, Karupa, Hunt Fork, Chimney etc), spending their time exploring one area well on a series of day hikes.

Getting There & Away

Although drivers on the Dalton Hwy skirt the eastern edge of the park (and can hike in via Nolan/Wiseman), most visitors access it on scheduled or charter flights from Fairbanks to Bettles, south of the park, or the Native village of Anaktuvuk Pass (yes, the name means 'the place of much caribou shit'!). Check out either Frontier Flying Service (☎ 474 0014) or Larry's Flying Service (toll-free ☎ 1-800 478 5169). Plan on spending around US$200 per person for the return flight from Fairbanks to Bettles.

From Bettles/Evansville, air taxi operators, such as Brooks Range Aviation (☎ 692 5444) or Bettles Air Service (☎ 692 5111), can organise landings on remote lakes, rivers or gravel bars and provide access to any of the hiking or float trips. A well known guiding company is Sourdough Outfitters, in Bettles (see the Organised Tours & Adventures chapter). Bettles Lodge (☎ 692 5111) rents canoes and rafts for US$35 and US$45 per day, respectively.

DALTON HIGHWAY

The 670km Dalton Hwy (better known as the Haul Road) connects the Elliott Hwy, near Livengood, with Deadhorse, near the Arctic Ocean coast, via a thin ribbon of gravel. When this truck supply route was

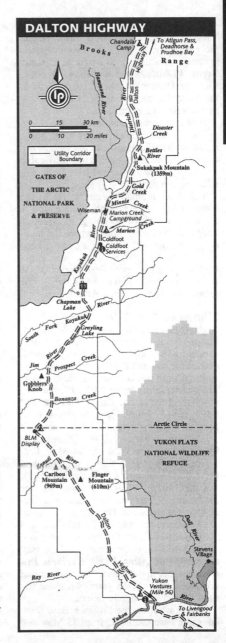

first completed in 1978, all but the first 100km, to the Yukon River, was closed to the public. In 1981, in the face of public pressure, it was opened as far as Disaster Creek, 337km along, but in 1994, the entire route to Deadhorse, about 10km short of the Arctic Ocean, was opened to private vehicles without a permit.

However, prospective drivers should be aware that this gravel road is long, dusty, rutted with potholes and littered with blown tyres from the high-speed truck traffic that constantly places lesser vehicles at the risk of being run down.

The most dramatic scenery lies to the south of Atigun Pass; north of there, you're on the vast, mosquito-plagued, treeless plains of the North Slope, where the landscapes change little. Along the route, keep a lookout for Arctic foxes and other wildlife. You may even find yourself stuck in a caribou traffic jam in the vicinity of the greatest oil field in North America.

Things to See & Do

Highlights along the way include the EL Patton Bridge across the Yukon River, named in 1982 after the death of the president of the Alyeska Pipeline Service Co; the Arctic Circle marker and wayside at Mile 115; and Coldfoot, at Mile 175, where you'll find the *Arctic Circle B&B (☎ 452 0081, fax 479 7306)*. Here, the lowest temperature in North America was recorded (-63°C) on 26 January 1989. Other places worth a look are Wiseman at Mile 178, where there's a gold-mining museum and the *Arctic Getaway B&B (☎/fax 796 9001)*; and the 1463m Atigun Pass, which forms the boundary between the Pacific and Arctic Ocean watersheds. Then there's the town of Deadhorse (population 25 full-time and 2500 part-time), at the end of the road, where you'll find the small Prudhoe Bay General Store, the *Arctic Caribou Inn (☎ 659 2368)* and frustration at the fact that you can't continue on your own along the final 10km to the Arctic Ocean.

If you want to see Prudhoe Bay, four-hour tours are available, from 25 May to 8 September, from the Arctic Caribou Inn/Tour Arctic (☎ 659 2368, fax 659 2289), PO Box 34-0112, Prudhoe Bay, AK 99734. On the tour you'll visit Pump Station 1, the Oilfield Visitors Center and Deadhorse, as well as having a view of the Arctic Ocean.

Getting There & Away

Most people who tackle the Dalton Hwy do so in their own vehicles, but note that petrol is available only in Fairbanks, Fox, Livengood, Mile 56 (just north of the Yukon River Bridge), Mile 175, at Coldfoot, and Mile 414, at Deadhorse. If your vehicle can't handle this long 382km (239 mile) dry stretch, be sure to carry enough jerry cans of fuel to get you through.

For US$169, Arctic Circle Adventures (☎ 474 8600, fax 474 4767, email adventure@alaskasarctic.com) conducts a one day tour from Fairbanks across the Arctic Circle, and for an additional US$20, you can take a short cruise on the Yukon River. For more information, check out the Web site www.alaskasarctic.com. From Fairbanks, the Dalton Highway Express (☎/fax 452 2031) and the Denali Explorer bus (☎ 277 5581, www.inplex.com/gla/gla_nsexplr.htm) head up the Dalton Hwy and cross the Arctic Circle to spend the night at Coldfoot. The next morning, they cross Atigun Pass and continue to Prudhoe Bay, where participants may tour the site before flying back to Fairbanks.

PRUDHOE BAY

In 1968, the Atlantic Richfield (ARCO) Company happily ran across a 10 billion barrel oil reserve on the barren coastal plains at Prudhoe Bay and the next year, the state of Alaska (which had fortuitously selected this land for itself) was auctioning off oil leases to various exploration companies. As fast as you can say 'Get up there and drill', a consortium of the lucky leaseholders were planning a pipeline to carry the crude 1400km from the North Slope southward to tidewater at the ice-free port of Valdez, on Alaska's south coast.

Although the construction was delayed by environmental lawsuits, the disputes were eventually ironed out. The pipeline would be constructed at a level that would not impede caribou migrations, and the ANCSA (Alaska Native Claims Settlement Act) was passed, as was the ANILCA (the Alaska National Interest Lands Conservation Act), which set aside an additional 40 million hectares as National Parks and Monuments. (See the respective boxed texts in this chapter for more information on these acts.) The pipeline construction began in 1971 and was completed, after unimaginable expense (as well as mind-boggling waste, theft and corruption), in 1977.

Profits in the Pipeline

After oil was discovered at Prudhoe Bay in 1968, the 1300km Trans-Alaska pipeline was constructed – at the mind-boggling cost of US$8 billion – to transport the crude to Valdez on Prince William Sound, which is the northernmost ice-free port in the USA. After they've seen Mt McKinley, it's the next sightseeing priority for most Alaska visitors.

The Alyeska Corporation, which constructed the pipeline, is in fact a consortium of British Petroleum (BP), Atlantic Richfield (ARCO), Exxon, Mobil, Amerada Hess, Phillips and Unocal. Alyeska's holdings include not only the line and its pump stations, but also the marine terminal used by tankers hauling crude oil out of the port of Valdez and a fleet of escort and spill response vessels. Thanks to recent mergers and proposed mergers, it's estimated that BP-ARCO will soon hold approximately 72% of the operation, Exxon-Mobil will own 23% and the others will share a mere 5%.

Along its 1300km route, the pipeline crosses more than 800 rivers and streams, including the mighty Tanana and Yukon rivers. For a little less than half its length, the 122cm diameter pipeline is buried in the ground, while the remainder, mostly in areas of permafrost, is well insulated and rests on 78,000 above-ground support posts spaced 30m apart. The design is meant to allow migrating caribou to pass unimpeded. The pipe itself is constructed of coated steel equipped with zinc anodes to prevent corrosion.

It takes just over six days for oil to travel from Prudhoe Bay to Valdez, and at any given time, up to nine million barrels may be flowing through it. At the end of 1998 it was estimated that a total of 12.4 billion barrels had made the trip. In 1988, the throughput peaked at around 2.1 million barrels per day, but currently the figure stands at around 1.2 million barrels per day. Alyeska employs 200 people in Fairbanks, just over 100 in Anchorage and about 500 more scattered between the pump stations and in Valdez. However, many more people are employed by the individual oil companies and their subcontractors.

Without this artery and the money it has generated, modern Alaska would be a very different place. Oil industry workers and supporters maintain that the pipeline, which has carried as much as 25% of the US supply of crude oil and created untold wealth for its shareholders and the Alaskan government, constitutes an essential component of life in modern Alaska and is widely regarded as the best thing that ever happened to the state. For their part, most Alaskans – the majority of whom have been born or migrated to the state since the pipeline was built – have become accustomed to the windfall from the North Slope's black gold.

However, not everyone agrees that it has been a completely positive factor. Many individualists and old-timers feel that the pipeline has produced a bloated state government and attracted crime, corruption and too many people. Environmentalists see the pipeline as a metallic intrusion slicing across an otherwise pristine landscape, and cite the tragic 1989 oil spill in Prince William Sound as an inexcusable – and irreversible – environmental disaster.

Since the oil started flowing, state 'royalties' on the leases have funded Alaska's state government in high style, and financed a number of pork barrel projects (for example, the still unused grain elevators at Valdez). However, a glitch in oil prices in the mid-1980s brought about a devastating economic crash which resulted in a 20% population decline in Anchorage and Fairbanks. Although oil prices bounced back, a similar OPEC-fuelled situation in the late 1990s created a crisis in Juneau, when politicians realised they could no longer fund all their pet government programs with oil money alone.

While Prudhoe Bay oil remains a major factor in the Alaskan economy – and the reserves have defied the original predictions that they'd run out within 20 years – it is no longer its sole driving force. Quite a few workers still enjoy a two-weeks-on/one-week-off work schedule on the bleak North Slope (including generous meal and accommodation programs and airline tickets back to their homes in Anchorage, Texas, Louisiana – or Hawaii – for their off periods), but recent mergers between the big companies have been paring down the workforce and it appears that the 'big bucks' jobs are now a thing of the past.

For information on civilian visits to Prudhoe Bay, see the preceding Dalton Highway section.

Oil Exploration in ANWR

Since oil first began to flow from Prudhoe Bay on Alaska's Arctic North Slope, oil revenues have supplied about 85% of the Alaskan state budget. Now that production from Prudhoe Bay is in decline, the state of Alaska and the various oil companies operating in the north are looking to open up possible new reserves. Situated in north-east Alaska, the coastal plain of the Arctic National Wildlife Refuge (ANWR) is threatened by oil development because it could represent one of the last great oil discoveries in the USA.

Oil development is vehemently opposed by environmentalists, who argue that ANWR also contains some of the last great wilderness areas in North America, which would be seriously disturbed if oil development went ahead. Oil development in ANWR is also opposed by the US federal government, for the time being at least, but supported by the majority of Alaskans. Canada is also against oil development in ANWR's coastal plain, because it would threaten the principal calving grounds of the porcupine caribou herd, a herd which the Gwich'in Indians of north-east Alaska and the Yukon Territory depend on for subsistence. The ANWR issue is complicated by the fact that the Gwich'in stand almost alone as the only Native group not in favour of development. The Inupiat Inuit, who also rely to some extent on the porcupine caribou herd, would stand to benefit financially from leasing lands they hold in ANWR (gained from the Alaska Native Claims Settlement Act of 1971) to oil companies. In 1995, the Alaska Federation of Natives (with the exception of the Gwich'in) signed a declaration in support of opening up ANWR's coastal plain for oil development.

ANWR throws into relief the competing perspectives on the future of environmental protection regarding resource development in Alaska. On the one hand, environmentalists have allied themselves with the Gwich'in to defend ANWR from any oil development and to preserve the area as wilderness, while the majority of Native and non-Native Alaskans look to oil development in ANWR for future economic prosperity.

Dr Mark Nuttall, University of Aberdeen

ARCTIC NATIONAL WILDLIFE REFUGE

On the Arctic Coastal Plain in the north-eastern corner of Alaska lies the three million hectare Arctic National Wildlife Refuge. The main attraction here is the profuse wildlife, and the sheer numbers have been compared to those of the Serengeti Plains in East Africa. The Porcupine River caribou herd, which includes upwards of 100,000 individuals, winters in Interior Alaska, but in spring, migrates northward to give birth on this vast plain in early June. In addition, this is the domain of many other species, including polar bears, moose, wolves, wolverines, red foxes, Arctic foxes and grizzly bears. In some inland areas, it also harbours beavers, coyotes, lynx, Dall sheep, muskoxen and porcupines. It's also home to the world's northernmost population of black bears, which makes it the only place where all three North American bear species are present.

No part of Alaska has experienced greater controversy than this wild country, which is caught in an endless struggle between conservationists, in league with the local Gwich'in people, and the enterprises that would exploit the reserve's supposed oil wealth (see the boxed text 'Oil Exploration in ANWR'). The former faction is concerned that oil exploration and development would disrupt local culture, and affect the caribou migrations and birthing grounds, while the latter sees the area as the economic hope for Alaska in the face of declining oil reserves at nearby Prudhoe Bay. The deadlock between them remains far from resolved, but thus far US federal regulations have prevented any sort of commercial development of the area.

Getting There & Away

Wildlife buffs, birdwatchers, rafters, canoers and backpackers who make the effort necessary to get here will be greatly rewarded. Although private access is impractical, numerous operators offer hiking, rafting and flightseeing tours through the refuge; for suggestions, see the Organised Tours & Adventures chapter.

Arctic Canada

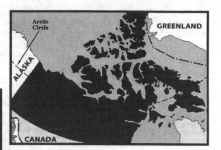

The expansive open spaces of the Canadian Arctic – from the lake-studded Canadian shield of the Northwest Territories to the wild mountains of the Yukon and the nation-sized islands of the vast Arctic archipelago of Nunavut – make up one of the world's greatest wilderness areas. The designation of the Northwest Territories, Nunavut and the Yukon as territories rather than provinces is largely political: it's generally felt that their relatively small populations do not merit equal status in Parliament with the more populous provinces. (And as if to reinforce their northerly locations, their shared area code of 867-spells out T-O-P on the dial.)

Tourism in northern Canada is not especially straightforward and, except for the parts of the Yukon and Northwest Territories that are accessible by private vehicle, travellers need plenty of planning, time and especially money to reach these wild areas.

GETTING AROUND

When you're planning a tour through northern Canada, it's worth remembering that distances are great and the population small. This is naturally part of the region's

The Accidental Tourist

The first Norse seafarer to sight the North American coast was Bjarni Herjólfsson, an Icelander who'd set off to visit family in Greenland in 986 and was blown off course. Instead, he came upon a hilly and wooded land. Disgusted at having missed Greenland, he turned around and left without disembarking. (Had he gone ashore, perhaps a statue of Bjarni Herjólfsson might now grace the lawn of Hallgrímskirkja church in Reykjavík.)

As it happened, Leif Eiríksson, the son of Eiríkur Rauðe, was overcome with curiosity about this new land – and the description 'wooded' sounded particularly alluring in treeless Greenland. He set off on an expedition in abour 1000 and managed to visit places he called Helluland (the land of flat stones, probably Baffin Island), Markland (the land of woods, or Labrador) and Vinland (the land of wine).

The whereabouts of Vinland has never been conclusively determined, but it became the site of the only known Norse colony in North America. This rather half-hearted attempt at colonisation didn't mesh well with the American natives, who were dubbed *skrælings* (those wrinkled by the sun) and the project was abandoned.

According to the solar reckoning described in the sagas, Vinland would have been roughly between the latitudes of Boston and Washington in the present-day USA. However, modern archaeological research has revealed that the Vinland colony was probably further north, at L'Anse aux Meadows (originally L'Anse aux Meduses, meaning jellyfish cove), in Newfoundland, which has now been named a UNESCO World Heritage Site.

appeal, but it also means that transportation is not always frequent, convenient or even available. Hopping on a bus or train on a whim may be possible in much of Europe, but is not realistic here, as the only railway lines are the Yukon & White Pass line from Skagway (Alaska) to Bennett Lake, and the popular line from Winnipeg to Churchill, Manitoba. Buses are also thin on the ground. But as any traveller knows, the greater the hassle and expense to reach a place, the more pristine the experience.

Air

Canada's two major airlines, Air Canada and Canadian Airlines International, both work in conjunction with regional carriers to form widespread domestic networks. Canadian Airlines is also linked with American Airlines, and Air Canada has financial ties and agreements with Continental and United. Other Air Canada partners include Air BC, Air Creebec (northern Ontario and northern Quebec), Air Nova, Air Ontario, Bearskin Airways and First Air. There are also several regional and local airlines which tend to focus on small regions, particularly in the north. The charter airline Canada 3000 consistently offers inviting domestic fares as well as flights to US and Caribbean sun destinations. Inquire about them at travel agencies.

Domestic flights tend to be pricey; your best option is to shop around – directly with the airline or through a travel agent – and be flexible. Waiting a day or two or avoiding a weekend flight could save a lot of cash. Also, bear in mind that Air Canada may be cheap for one flight and Canadian Airlines for another, while First Air is probably the airline that will get you to where you want to go in the Canadian Arctic.

Air fares in Canada are generally quoted as the base fare only and all taxes, including the GST, are an additional cost.

Bus

Buses serve most Canadian highways, and are usually clean, safe and comfortable. The largest carrier is Greyhound, but it concentrates only on routes in the southern part of the country. In the north, services are typically infrequent and normally run only two or three times a week. In more out-of-the-way places there may be no service at all.

A one-way ticket is usually good for 60 days and a return ticket is valid for a year. If you do travel by bus, you may want to pack a supply of snacks, as long-distance halts tend to be at highway stops and lodges where you pay a lot for semi-edible food.

Between Edmonton and Yellowknife, you can travel with Greyhound (toll-free ☎ 1-800 661 8747) and Frontier Coachlines (☎ 867-874 2566) via Enterprise and Hay River. For specific information on buses between British Columbia, the Yukon and Alaska, see the Getting Around chapter.

Car & Motorcycle

If you're headed for the western Arctic – the Yukon and Northwest Territories – driving is surely the best way to get there. You can go where and when you want, use secondary highways and roads and get off the beaten track. It's particularly inviting in summer when you can camp or even sleep in your vehicle.

Canadians drive on the right and use the metric system. The speed limit on highways ranges from 100 to 120km/h and in towns, 50km/h or less. The use of seat belts is compulsory throughout Canada, and motorcyclists must ride with their lights on and wear helmets.

Thanks to peculiar North American sensibilities, the greatest possible motorists' sin – after drunken driving – is passing a school bus with its lights flashing (which indicates that students are getting on or off). Don't do it or you'll be sorry! In cities with pedestrian crossings, cars must stop to allow pedestrians to cross. Providing the way is clear, turning right at red lights (after first coming to a complete stop) is permitted in all provinces and territories except Quebec. Sleeping in your vehicle at roadside parks, picnic spots or other highway parking bays is fine, but you may not erect a tent.

A valid driver's licence from any country is valid for three months in Canada, but an

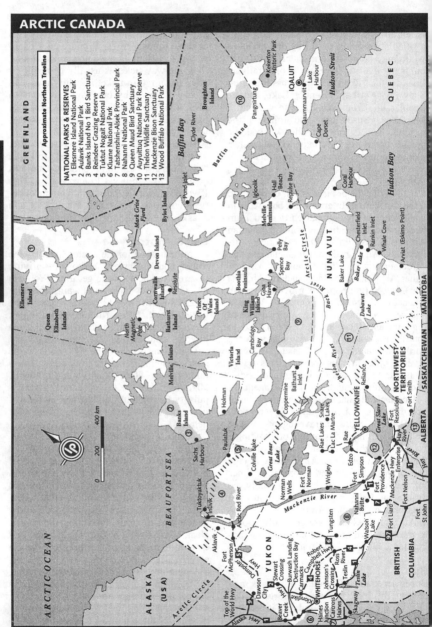

ARCTIC CANADA

NATIONAL PARKS & RESERVES
1 Ellesmere Island National Park
2 Aulavik National Park
3 Banks Island No 1 Bird Sanctuary
4 Reindeer Grazing Reserve
5 Tuktut Nogait National Park
6 Kluane National Park
7 Tatshenshini-Alsek Provincial Park
8 Nahanni National Park
9 Queen Maud Bird Sanctuary
10 Auyuittuq National Park Reserve
11 Thelon Wildlife Sanctuary
12 Mackenzie Bison Sanctuary
13 Wood Buffalo National Park

////// Approximate Northern Treeline

international driving permit from your home-country automobile club allows you to drive for up to a year. Note that foreign-registered vehicles require valid insurance.

Remember that in the north country, distances between petrol stations can be great, so it's wise to carry extra petrol, especially between September and May, when many petrol stations close for the season. Also, ensure that your vehicle is in good condition and carry tools, spare parts, water and food. If you're driving on gravel roads, such as the famed Dempster Hwy, be sure to keep well to the right. You may also want to protect the windscreen and lights with a bug and gravel screen.

In much of the country, wildlife such as deer and moose are a potential road hazard, and most run-ins occur at night when animals are active and visibility is poor. Always scan the verges for animals which may bolt out into the road. At night, vehicle headlights will often mesmerise an animal, leaving it frozen in the middle of the road. Try honking the horn or flashing the lights to encourage it to move away. In winter, watch for caribou, which like to amble down the highways licking off the salt.

Many Europeans who visit Canada head for the Arctic in rented recreational vehicles (RVs). In the west, you'll find the best deals in Calgary, Edmonton and Whitehorse, but they're very popular, so you'll need to book as early as possible. In the high season, a mid to large-size vehicle will cost C$180 to C$220 per day. A company to try is Canadream Campers (toll-free ☎ 1-800 461 7368) with rentals in Toronto, Calgary, Vancouver and Whitehorse. The company also offers one-way rentals. To find out more, try its Web site at www.canadream.com. Another is Go West Campers International (☎ 604-987 5288), 1577 Lloyd St, North Vancouver, BC.

Alternatively, if you're on an extended trip, it may be worth buying a car. Begin searching in the local newspaper or, in larger centres, the weekly *Buy & Sell Bargain Hunter Press, Auto Trader* or an equivalent. Private deals are nearly always the most economical way to buy a car. Used-car businesses must mark up the prices in order to make a profit. Generally, North American cars are lower priced than Japanese and European cars. You may also want to peruse Phil Edmunston's annual *Lemon-Aid*, published by the Canadian Automobile Protection Association. It is available in shops and libraries and details all the used cars on the market, rates them and gives rough price guidelines. Decent older cars should be available for under C$4000. West coast cars last longer because salt isn't necessary on the roads in winter and the cars rust less quickly.

All drivers require Canadian insurance; to organise short-term insurance, phone a Canadian insurance broker, who may be able to help. Bring a letter from your current insurance company indicating your driving record. In addition to making a transaction easier, this might entitle you to some discount as it makes you a more credible risk. You will need an international driver's licence. You may also need to get a local address and a Canadian driving licence.

Bicycle

Those interested in cycling in Canada will want to contact the Canadian Cycling Association (☎ 613-748 5629) 1600 James Naismith Drive, Suite 212A, Gloucester, Ontario, K1B 5N4, or check out the Web site at www.canadian-cycling.com. The Association can supply local contacts, trail information and much more.

Note that buses charge C$10 for the boxed bike and then a weight and mileage fee, which means that to transport a bike on a day-long bus trip would cost around C$70. The major Canadian airlines have a flat fee of C$65 for a one-way flight with just a bag supplied. In all cases some disassembly is required.

Hitching

Hitching in Canada isn't bad, but it's never entirely safe and we don't recommend it. Travellers who decide to hitch should understand that they are taking a small but potentially serious risk. Some travellers still consider thumbing a ride a worthwhile option, and of course they do meet people and see the land at ground level. The ideal hitching situation is two people – ideally a man and a woman. If you're three or more, or a lone woman, forget it.

If you feel you've been waiting a long time for a lift, remember that the ride you eventually get may take you over 1500km. Most people find a cardboard sign indicating their destination helps a lot. However, remember that it's normally illegal to hitch in towns or on limited-access highways.

Boat

If you're headed for Alaska, you may want to use the BC ferries, which connect mainland British Columbia with Vancouver Island, the Gulf Islands and the Queen Charlotte Islands. For schedules and fares, contact BC Ferries (☎ 250-386 3431) 1112 Fort St, Victoria, British Columbia V8V 4V2. Generally, ferry reservations can be made by telephone as little as two days in advance. For further details, check out the Web site www.bcferries.bc.ca.

ACCOMMODATION
Camping

Canada is full of camping grounds – national, provincial and privately owned – but the government sites are nearly always better, cheaper, quieter and more pristine. Not surprisingly, they also fill up first. Most of these sites take advantage of the local landscape, and offer a program of ranger-organised events and talks. Private camping grounds are generally geared to RVs and caravans and often have swimming pools, shops, video arcades and other entertainment facilities.

In national parks, camping fees range from C$10 to C$19 for an unserviced site, and as much as C$23 for sites with power hook-ups. Provincial park camping rates vary from C$10 to C$22, while wilderness camping permits cost around C$5 to C$6. Note that most government sites open in late May and close in early September.

Many people travel around the country camping and never pay a thing. For those with cars or vans, using roadside rest areas

and picnic spots is recommended. You can't set up a tent in these places, but sleeping in your vehicle is just fine.

Hostels

There are some excellent travellers' hostels in Canada, but don't be surprised if locals look askance when you say you're intending to stay at hostels. Few Canadians are aware of the international hostel system, and locally the word is normally associated with shelters for down-and-outs!

Having said that, two hostelling groups operate in Canada. The oldest and best known is Hostelling International (HI) Canada. HI Canada has about 70 hostels with members in all parts of the country. A yearly international membership costs C$27 for an adult. Children under 17 with a parent stay free. Nightly costs range from C$10 to C$23 with most around C$16. At many hostels, nonmembers can stay for an additional C$2 to C$5. A membership can quickly pay for itself and has now been built into the system so that after six nights at nonmember rates, you automatically become eligible for member rates. For more information contact Hostelling International (HI) Canada (☎ 613-237 7884, fax 613-237 7868) National Office, 400-205 Catherine St, Ottawa, Ontario K2P 1C3. Phone (toll-free) ☎ 1-800 663 5777 for the booking network or check out the Web site www.hostellingintl.ca.

The second group is a network of independent hostels collectively known as Backpackers Hostels Canada, which is symbolised by a circled howling wolf with a map of Canada in the background. There are over 100 hostels in the network and membership is not required to use the facilities. The average price is about C$15 for dorms, but doubles or family rooms are often also available. For information, including a list of hostels, contact the Longhouse Village Hostel (☎ 807-983 2042, toll-free ☎ 1-800 705 3666, fax 807-983 2914), RR 13, Thunder Bay, Ontario P7B 5E4. A self-addressed envelope and two international postal-reply coupons should be included with your request for information. You can also take a look at www.backpackers.ca on the Web.

Aside from typical hostels, Backpackers Hostels Canada also has camping grounds, campus and church facilities, organic farms, motels, retreats, and tourist homes which provide budget travellers with inexpensive accommodation.

B&Bs

B&Bs are an established part of the accommodation picture and continue to grow in number. They offer a more personal alternative to the standard traditional motel/hotel and are found throughout the country. Prices of B&Bs vary quite a bit, but average between C$55 and C$75 for two people. The more expensive ones generally provide more impressive furnishings and decor. Many are found in classic heritage houses. Rooms are almost always in the owner's home and are clean and well kept. Note that smoking is almost always prohibited. Breakfast can vary from light or continental to a full breakfast of eggs, bacon, toast and coffee. It's worth inquiring about the breakfast before booking. Several guidebooks dealing exclusively with B&Bs across the country are widely available in Canadian bookstores.

Hotels & Motels

In general, Canada is short on good, inexpensive hotels, and to Canadians, the word 'hotel' generally refers to an expensive place to stay or a cheap place to drink (thanks to Canadian liquor laws, which have historically linked bars with accommodation).

Single rooms normally start at C$25 to C$35, but many rooms are occupied by long-term tenants. Such places may not be suitable for families or females travelling alone. However, there are a few reputable, good-value chains, including Travelodge (toll-free ☎ 1-800 578 7878) and Days Inn (toll-free ☎ 1-800 329 7466).

On the other hand, motels are ubiquitous. They're mostly simple and clean, and are found along most Canadian highways.

Rates range from C$40 to C$75 for singles or doubles. Well known chains include Comfort Inn (toll-free ☎ 1-800 228 5150) and Econo Lodge (toll-free ☎ 1-800 553 2666). Other links in these chains include Quality (toll-free ☎ 1-800 228 5151), the low-cost Rodeway Inn (toll-free ☎ 1-800 228 2000) and the good-value Super 8 (toll-free ☎ 1-800 800 8000).

Lodges & Roadhouses

Along the highways of northern Canada, most petrol stations are linked with simple roadhouse accommodation. These atmospheric places, often constructed of logs, will typically include a greasy-spoon restaurant and bar, as well as basic but comfortable rooms or cabins. They're not as inexpensive as their usual condition would suggest, however, and start at around C$60 for a double.

In roadless areas of the north, you'll also find remote and often rather rugged wilderness lodges, which cater to hunters, anglers and guided hiking, trekking, canoeing and rafting tours. In most cases, guests are flown in on bush flights (at an additional cost), and the substantial prices (usually C$200 to C$300 per person per night) will invariably include a meal plan and often guiding services as well.

Yukon

☎ 867

The Yukon, a 483,500 sq km triangular slice of northern Canada wedged between the Northwest Territories and Alaska, comprises the most mountainous country in northern Canada. It's a scenic wilderness of mountains, forests, lakes and rivers that offer myriad outdoor activities – camping, hiking, climbing, canoeing and fishing. The name of the territory is derived from the word *Yuchoo*, which is not a sneeze, but rather the Athapaskan word for 'great river'. The river in question is the great Yukon itself, which flows for 3700km from the Llewellyn Glacier in north-western British Columbia

Robert Service – the Bard of the Yukon

There are strange things done in the midnight sun
By the men who moil for gold.
The Arctic trails have their secret tales
That would make your blood run cold.
The Northern Lights have seen queer sights
But the queerest they ever did see
Was the night on the marge of Lake Leberge
I cremated Sam McGee.

Robert Service, from *The Cremation of Sam McGee*

On 14 January 1874 Robert W Service was born in Preston, in north-east England. As an adolescent, after spending most of his boyhood in Glasgow, Scotland, he took an apprenticeship as a bank clerk. However, a serious case of wanderlust prompted him, on a whim, to take a passage to Canada and spend the next decade working odd jobs up and down the Pacific Coast of North America.

In 1904 he returned to his former profession and settled down as a bank teller in the wild town of Whitehorse, in Canada's Yukon Territory. Shortly thereafter, however, the bank transferred him to the frontier settlement of Dawson, which was just gaining respectability after the frenetic days of the Klondike Gold Rush.

Inspired by the gold rush tales and myths of hopes, dreams, freedom, riches and wanderlust, in 1907 Service took the lore of the Yukon and spun it into his first collection of verse, entitled *Songs of the Sourdough*, which was published in the USA as *The Spell of the Yukon and Other Verses*. Royalties from this effort allowed him to leave his bank job and concentrate on further poetic expositions of the land he'd grown to love. As a result of his lively and emotional verse, he was awarded the moniker 'Bard of the Yukon', which has stuck to the present day.

Clearly influenced by Coleridge's *Rime of the Ancient Mariner*, his verses, which combined Arctic terminology with Scottish colloquialisms, romanticised the determined, hard-living characters that opened up the wilds of North America's far north. His second book, *Ballads of a Cheechako*, focused on the rollicking camps of scoundrels left over from the gold rush days.

Service's later years, however, carried him away from his beloved Yukon. During WWI, he was dispatched to the Balkans as a correspondent for the *Toronto Globe & Star*, and thence to the South Pacific and France, where he remained until his death in 1958. But if his simplest assessment of the far north accurately reflects his innermost feelings, his heart always remained in the Northland:

Some say God was tired when He made it;
Some say it's a fine land to shun;
Maybe; but there's some as would trade it
For no land on Earth – and I'm one.

Robert Service, from *The Spell of the Yukon*

through Whitehorse to the muskeg (bog) plains of the Yukon-Kuskokwim (commonly called the YK) Delta of south-western Alaska.

From the 1890s until after WWII, the Yukon River was both a vital and dangerous link between Whitehorse and Dawson City. Its turbulent waters are opaque with glacial silt and mud, which hide submerged hazards. Each April or May the break-up of the ice produces earth-moving flows of water which toss about semitrailer-sized chunks of ice like Tonka toys. Dawson City celebrates this impossible-to-schedule event each year and there is a contest to guess when the first cracks will appear. The break-up is not all fun and games, however, and in 1979 an ice jam at Dawson City backed up water and flooded the town.

Yukon's population figure of 30,000 means that every Yukoner enjoys 20 sq km of elbow room, and it's worth noting that 75% of these people huddle in the territorial capital, Whitehorse, leaving the rest of the territory wide open and scarcely populated. Each year, an increasing number of visitors discover the wide open spaces and dramatic beauty of this 'great, big, broad land way up yonder ...' (Robert Service – *The Spell of the Yukon*).

WHITEHORSE

Whitehorse, on the banks of the Yukon River, is by far the largest town in the territory. It sits on the Alaska Hwy and, despite its recent growth, retains somewhat of a frontier feel. The total population amounts to only about 20,000, but people in other parts of the Yukon disparagingly consider Whitehorse residents to be 'soft' urbanites and more like residents of Toronto or Vancouver than 'real' Yukoners.

The Visitor Reception Centre (VRC; ☎ 667 3084) has information on Whitehorse and the Yukon and occupies a new building at the corner of 2nd Ave and Hanson St. It's open from 8 am to 8 pm daily from mid-May to mid-September. Mac's Fireweed Books (☎ 668 6104), 203 Main St, sells a good selection of books on the history,

geography and wildlife of the Yukon plus a section on the Native Indian culture of the region.

Things to See & Do

There's little to see in town, and what there is can be easily covered in a day. For an overview of the city, river and mountains, a steep footpath climbs to a **viewpoint** from the western end of Hanson St.

The **SS** *Klondike* (☎ 667 4511), near the junction of South Access Rd and 2nd Ave, was one of the last and largest stern-wheel riverboats used on the Yukon River. Built in 1937, it made its last run upriver in 1955. Now restored as a museum and National Historic Site, it's open daily from 9 am to 6 pm from mid-May to mid-September.

The **MacBride Museum** (☎ 667 2709), in a log cabin on the corner of 1st Ave and Wood St, holds a collection of materials from the indigenous cultures, the fur trade, the gold rush days and the construction of the Alaska Hwy. It also has displays of Yukon wildlife.

The **Old Log Church** (☎ 668 2555), on the corner of Elliot St and 3rd Ave, was built by the town's first priest in 1900. Reputedly the only wooden cathedral in the world, it is also the oldest building in town. Inside are artefacts from early churches around the territory. Sunday services at 10.30 am are mostly attended by Native Indians and include hymns in the Gwich'in language.

During the last ice age, some 20,000 years ago, a region encompassing the Yukon, Alaska and eastern Siberia was untouched by glaciers. Known as Beringia, the land was home to huge woolly mammoths and many tribes of human hunters. The large **Yukon-Beringia Interpretive Centre** (☎ 667 8855) recreates that time with interactive displays and reconstructions of some of the animals. You'll find it on the Alaska Hwy just south of the airport. From the town centre take the airport bus and then walk south for five minutes.

Nearby, you'll find the **Yukon Transportation Museum** (☎ 668 4792), which

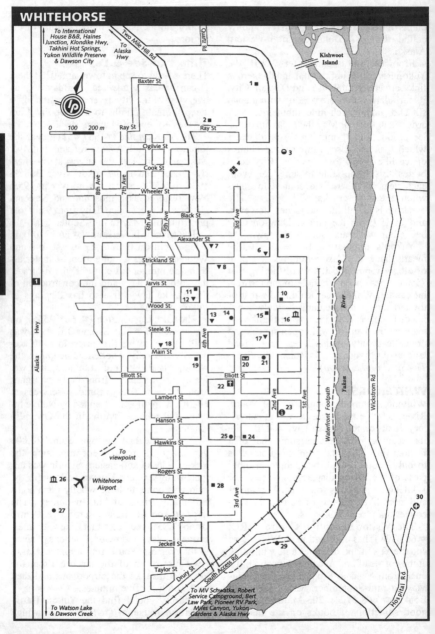

WHITEHORSE

PLACES TO STAY
1 Sourdough City RV Park
2 Stop-In Family Hotel
5 Roadhouse Inn
10 98 Hotel
11 Stratford Motel
15 Westmark Whitehorse Hotel
19 Town & Mountain Hotel
24 Hawkins House B&B
28 High Country Inn

PLACES TO EAT
6 Antonio's Vineyard
7 Alpine Bakery

8 The Chocolate Claim
12 Tung Lock
13 No Pop Sandwich Shop
17 Talisman Café
18 Sam 'n' Andy's

OTHER
3 Greyhound
Bus Depot
4 Qwanlin Mall
9 Kanoe People
14 Yukon Historical &
Museums Association
16 MacBride Museum

20 Main Post Office
21 Mac's Fireweed Books
22 The Old Log Church
23 Visitor Reception
Centre
25 Yukon Conservation
Society
26 Yukon Transportation
Museum
27 Yukon Beringia
Interpretative Centre
29 SS *Klondike*
30 Whitehorse
General Hospital

ARCTIC CANADA

covers the perils and adventures of getting around the Yukon by plane, train, truck and dogsled. Don't miss the photos taken during the construction of the Alaska Hwy or the displays on the Yukon's many historical plane crashes.

The **Yukon Gardens** (☎ 668 7972) are on South Access Rd close to the Alaska Hwy, about 3km south-west of town. The gardens, covering almost 9 hectares, have large displays of wild plants and flowers that can only be found in the north, plus vegetables and fruit trees. At the time of writing, the gardens had been temporarily closed for road construction. Call for new hours and admission details.

The **Yukon Wildlife Preserve** (☎ 633 2922) is about 25km north-west of town, lying off the Klondike Hwy on the Takhini Hot Springs Rd. A fine selection of northern animals such as elk, caribou, Dall sheep, moose, mountain goats, muskoxen and others can be seen on the rolling 280 hectare spread. Call ahead for information on visiting.

About 10km off the Klondike Hwy (Hwy 2) north of town are the **Takhini Hot Springs** (☎ 633 2706). They're open from 8 am to 10 pm daily and cost C$4. There's also a B&B nearby and camping at the site.

For a good walk close to the centre, take the winding footpath through the wooded area of **Bert Law Park**, on a small island connected to the Robert Service Campground by an old military bridge.

Outside Whitehorse, there's plenty of **hiking** and **cycling**, particularly at the Mt McIntyre Recreation Centre, and at Grey Mountain east of town and Miles Canyon south of town. The Ibex River valley is also ideal for cycling. In winter, the hikes become cross-country ski trails.

Whitehorse is also a starting point for the popular **canoe and kayak trips** to Carmacks or Dawson City. It's an average of eight days to the former and 16 days to the latter. Kanoe People (☎ 668 4899), near the corner of 1st Ave and Strickland St, can help arrange your trip. Organised canoe/kayak trips cost C$195/255 to Carmacks, and C$325/450 to Dawson City. Prospect Yukon (☎ 667 4837), 3123A 3rd Ave, and Up North (☎ 667 7905), across the river from the MacBride Museum on Wickstrom Rd, offer similar services. The latter caters to German visitors.

For a lesser adventure, the Rocky Mountain Voyageurs (☎ 633 4836) runs gold-rush-style **raft floats** down the Yukon River daily from May to September. The 2½-hour trips cost C$48. Atsua Ku Riverboat Adventures (☎ 668 6854) is a First Nation (indigenous)-owned company that offers three-hour tours down the Yukon River with nature and history lectures for C$49.

ARCTIC CANADA

Places to Stay

The *Robert Service Campground* (☎ 668 3721), 1km south of town on South Access Rd, is open from late May to early September and has toilets, showers and firepits. Tent sites cost C$9. *Sourdough City RV Park* (☎ 668 7938), at the northern end of 2nd Ave, has a laundry and free showers. It's mainly for RVs but you can pitch a tent on the grassy area behind the office for C$10. *Pioneer RV Park* (☎ 668 5944), 8km south of Whitehorse on the Alaska Hwy, has drinking water, laundry and showers. Tent sites cost C$8.

You can camp for C$8 at *Takhini Hot Springs* (☎ 633 2706), about 30km northwest of town off the Klondike Hwy. South of Whitehorse on the Alaska Hwy there are the *Yukon Government camping grounds* (☎ 667 5648) at Wolf Creek (16km) and Marsh Lake (50km); sites cost C$9.

The *Roadhouse Inn* (☎ 667 2594, 2163 2nd Ave) has hostel rooms with bunks and shared facilities for C$20 per person. Single/double rooms cost C$50/55, but security may not be the best. *International House B&B* (☎ 633 5490, 17 14th Ave), in Porter Creek, north of the town centre, has rooms from C$60/65. Central is the deluxe Victorian-style *Hawkins House* (☎ 668 7638, 303 Hawkins St) which has four distinct rooms with private bath and balcony at C$110 a double.

The *98 Hotel* (☎ 667 2641, 110 Wood St) is basic but central and cheap, with single rooms for C$45, but it's best known for its bar. The well kept *Stop-In Family Hotel* (☎ 668 5558, 314 Ray St) charges C$70/85 for singles/doubles, and has a laundrette and 24 hour restaurant. The good-value *High Country Inn* (☎ 667 4471, 4051 4th Ave) has a range of rooms as well as a restaurant, bar and free airport shuttle. Rooms start at C$100/115. *The Town & Mountain Hotel* (☎ 668 7644, 401 Main St) has single rooms from C$79. The central *Stratford Motel* (☎ 667 4243, 401 Jarvis St) is good, with single rooms from C$69 and some with kitchenettes.

The top hotel is the *Westmark Whitehorse Hotel* (☎ 668 4700, toll-free ☎ 1-800 544 0970), on the corner of 2nd Ave and Wood St, which has 181 rooms at C$135 a single or double, and is home to the Frantic Follies revue.

Places to Eat

The popular *Talisman Café* (☎ 667 2736, 2112 2nd Ave), between Steele and Main Sts, is comfortable and good for any meal. Breakfast costs about C$6, and lunch and dinner fare include Middle Eastern, Mexican and vegetarian dishes, as well as good salads. This is also a fine place for an afternoon cappuccino.

The *No Pop Sandwich Shop* (☎ 668 3227, 312 Steele St) is a long-time favourite with residents. Tasty sandwiches with interesting names like Beltch, Roman or Tel Aviv cost around C$4.50. *The Chocolate Claim* (☎ 667 2202, 305 Strickland St) is known for tasty breakfasts and lunches from C$4. It has its own bakery, makes excellent cappuccino and, as the name implies, produces fine chocolates.

Busy *Sam 'n' Andy's* (☎ 668 6994, 506 Main St) specialises in Mexican food and you can have a beer with your meal in the garden at the front. The nachos are a perennial fave and you can expect to chow down for C$12.

The town's finest dining venue is *Antonio's Vineyard* (☎ 668 6266) which has an excellent Italian-accented dinner menu that averages C$15 for items such as fettuccine alfredo and fresh salmon. The *Alpine Bakery* (☎ 668 6871, 411 Alexander St) has great bread baked from organic ingredients. To stock up for outdoor expeditions, try the *Extra Food Supermarket* (☎ 667 6251) in the Qwanlin Mall at 303 Ogilvie St, which has a huge bulk foods section.

For a taste of what the locals do for entertainment, head for the *Saloon* at the *Roadhouse Inn*, where you'll hear country and western music most nights. Also popular is the pub at the *High Country Inn*, which has good bar food and pints of beer from Whitehorse's own Chilkoot Brewing Co, an excellent microbrewery.

Getting There & Away

In addition to scheduled air services, Whitehorse is the northern 'end of the road' for Greyhound bus services (☎ 667 2223), 2191 2nd Ave, which has services south to Dawson Creek (20 hours, C$165), Prince George (28 hours, C$211), Vancouver (45 hours, C$300) and Edmonton (29 hours, C$230). Norline Coaches (☎ 668 3355) runs three times a week (twice a week in winter) to Dawson City (6½ hours, C$79.50). Gray Line of Alaska (☎ 668 3225, toll-free ☎ 1-800 544 2206) operates Alaskon Express buses to Skagway, Tok, Anchorage, Fairbanks and Haines, all in Alaska, but some journeys involve overnight stops, so you'll have to figure in the cost of accommodation. The two day Anchorage route includes an overnight stop in Beaver Creek and costs US$195.

Alaska Direct Busline (☎ 668 4833, toll-free ☎ 1-800 770 6652), 509 Main St, has buses to Anchorage (17 hours) and Fairbanks (14 hours) and points in-between such as Haines Junction and Beaver Creek, that run at least once a week in summer. The bus to Skagway departs daily (four hours, C$49).

Getting Around

The Whitehorse Transit System (☎ 668 7433) operates buses from Monday to Saturday. There are no buses on Sunday or public holidays. A one-way fare is C$1.25 but a day pass allows unlimited travel for C$3. If you're going to the airport, take the Hillcrest bus from Qwanlin Mall.

Among the local cab companies is Yellow Cab (☎ 668 4811). A trip from the airport into town is about C$10. Kanoe People (☎ 668 4899), at the corner of 1st Ave and Strickland St, rents mountain bikes.

THE ALASKA HIGHWAY

The Alaska Hwy, the main road through the Yukon, extends 2400km between Dawson Creek, British Columbia, and Fairbanks, Alaska. It was originally known as the Alaska-Canada Military Hwy and was built as a joint project between Canada and the USA in 1942, after the Alaskan Islands of Attu and Kiska were occupied by Japanese forces. In summer, it's extremely busy (some would say constipated) with visitors, and although it was recently quite a driving adventure, it's now fully tarred and the only real headaches are construction zones and streams of lethargic RVs. At times, there are 10 of these homes-on-wheels for every car or truck.

Petrol, food and lodging services are found at least every 50km along the route. In summer, hitching is pretty good, but be prepared for the occasional long wait – it's a good idea to carry a tent, food, water and warm clothing.

Watson Lake

Originally named after Frank Watson, a British trapper, and now billed as the 'Gateway to the Yukon', Watson Lake is the first town in the territory north of the British Columbia border. The VRC (☎ 536 7469), at the junction of the Alaska and Robert Campbell highways, has an excellent video show on the history of the territory and the Alaska Hwy.

The town is most famous for its **Signpost Forest** just outside the VRC. The original signpost of 'Danville, Illinois' was put up in 1942 by the homesick Carl Lindlay, a US soldier working on the Alaska Hwy construction. Other people added their own signs and now there are over 22,000 of them, with more being added every day. About 25km west of Watson Lake, the Cassiar Hwy heads south into British Columbia. If you're approaching in the evening, don't miss stopping to camp at the lovely **Boya Lake Provincial Park**, 80km south of the border.

Teslin

Teslin, on the Nisutlin River 280km west of Watson Lake, began as a Tlingit trading post in 1903, but with the Alaska Hwy came both prosperity and outside diseases which decimated the Native population. In the **George Johnston Museum** (☎ 390 2550) you'll see historic Tlingit artefacts and photographs from the gold rush days. There's also canoeing and camping at nearby **Teslin Lake**.

The Alaska Highway

The construction of the Alaska Hwy in 1942 is one of the major engineering feats of the 20th century. Canada and the USA had originally agreed to build an all-weather highway to Fairbanks from the south as early as 1930, but nothing serious was done about it until WWII. Japan's attack on Pearl Harbor, then its bombing of Dutch Harbor in the Aleutians and its occupation of the Aleutian islands of Attu and Kiska increased Alaska's strategic importance. The US army was told to prepare for the highway's construction a month before Canada's prime minister, WL Mackenzie King, signed the agreement granting the USA permission to do so.

The route chosen for the highway followed a series of existing airfields – Fort St John, Fort Nelson, Watson Lake and Whitehorse – known as the Northwest Staging Route.

Thousands of US soldiers and Canadians, including Native Indians, built the 2450km gravel highway between Dawson Creek in British Columbia and Fairbanks in Alaska. They began work on 9 March 1942 and completed it before falling temperatures (in what was to be one of the worst winters in recorded history) could halt the work. Conditions were harsh: sheets of ice rammed the timber pilings; floods during the spring thaw tore down bridges; and bogs swallowed trucks, tractors and other heavy machinery. In the cold months the road crews suffered frostbite while in summer they were preyed on by mosquitoes, blackflies and other biting insects.

In spite of these hardships the single-lane pioneer road was completed at the remarkable average rate of 12km a day. The road crews met a little over eight months after construction began, at Contact Creek close to the British Columbia and Yukon border. The highway cost US$135 million to construct, an incredible sum in those days. It was officially opened on 20 November at Soldiers' Summit (Mile 1061) overlooking Kluane Lake in the south-west corner of the Yukon.

The reason that the original road had so many curves and slopes is that with the bulldozers right behind them, the surveyors didn't have time to determine the best route.

In April 1946 the Canadian portion of the road (1965km) was officially handed over to Canada. In the meantime private contractors kept busy widening, gravelling and straightening the highway; levelling its steep grades; and replacing temporary bridges with permanent steel ones.

The completion of the highway opened the north-west to exploitation of its natural resources, changed settlement patterns and altered the Native Indian way of life forever.

Johnson's Crossing & Canol Road

Just over 50km north of Teslin is Johnson's Crossing, at the junction of the Alaska Hwy and Canol Rd. During WWII the US army built the Canol pipeline at the same time as the Alaska Hwy, to transfer oil from Norman Wells in the Northwest Territories to Whitehorse. The only services on Canol Rd (Hwy 6) are at Ross River, at the intersection with the Robert Campbell Hwy. The road ends near the Northwest Territories' border, and to travel any farther, you'll have to hike the challenging Canol Heritage Trail.

Haines Junction

Haines Junction is close to the Kluane National Park & Reserve. The town may appear large on the map, but on the ground, it's little more than a wide spot on the Alaska Hwy, 158km west of Whitehorse and 256km north of Haines, Alaska via the Haines Cut-Off. The VRC (☎ 634 2345) on Logan St is in the Kluane National Park headquarters building. Haines Junction has two camping grounds and several small hotels and lodges. *The Raven* (☎ 634 2500), on the Alaska Hwy, has comfortable single/double rooms from C$110/125 and the *Vil-*

The Alaska Highway

Thousands died as a result of diseases introduced by soldiers and workers. Others received their first real monetary wages thanks to jobs brought by the road. By 1949 the Alaska Hwy was opened to full-time civilian travel and for the first time, year-round overland travel to Alaska from the south of the continent was possible.

The name of the highway has gone through several incarnations. In its time it has been called the Alaskan International Hwy, the Alaska Military Hwy and the Alcan (short for Alaska-Canadian) Hwy. More irreverently, in the early days it was also known as the Oil Can Hwy and the Road to Tokyo. Officially, it is now called the Alaska Hwy but many people still affectionately refer to it simply as the Alcan.

The Alaska Hwy begins at the 'Mile 0' cairn in Dawson Creek in north-eastern British Columbia and then runs to Fairbanks, Alaska. Actually, the highway officially ends at Delta Junction (Mile 1422) about 155km south-east of Fairbanks (Mile 1523).

Milepost signs were set up in the 1940s to help drivers calculate how far they had travelled along the road. Since then, improvements such as the straightening of the road, mean that its length has been shortened and the mileposts can't be taken literally. On the Canadian side the distance markers are in kilometres. Mileposts are still much in evidence in Alaska, and communities on both sides of the border still use the original mileposts for postal addresses and as reference points.

Until the mid-1970s conditions along the highway were extremely difficult, but the highway is now almost completely surfaced and there are services every 50km or so. Millions of dollars are spent annually maintaining and upgrading the road, especially on maintenance work on potholes and frost heaves (raised sections of pavement caused by water freezing below the road).

Although it's possible to travel the highway throughout the year most visitors do so between May and September when the weather is warmer and road conditions less hazardous. All the attractions, services and accommodation are also open then. During this time the traffic noticeably increases, particularly the number of RVs. In winter the road is left mostly to logging, oil and mining trucks, but if you're well-prepared, it can provide both a spectacular drive and a perspective on the north country as it is most of the year, which few visitors ever experience.

luge Bakery & Deli (☎ 634 2867) offers good meals. Paddlewheel Adventures (☎ 634 2683) arranges tours using canoes, bikes, llamas, horses and more. Kluane Glacier Tours (☎ 634 2916) offers 40-minute C$90 flights over the national park.

Haines Junction is a transfer point for Gray Line Alaskon Express buses (toll-free ☎ 1-800 544 2206) between Whitehorse and Alaska's Haines, Anchorage and Fairbanks.

Kluane National Park & Reserve

The rugged Kluane National Park & Reserve, a UNESCO World Heritage Site,

takes in 22,015 sq km in the extreme south-western corner of the Yukon adjacent to Alaska's Wrangell-St Elias National Park. The name, which means 'many fish', is pronounced 'klu-AH-nee'.

Parks Canada (☎ 634 7201) runs a visitors centre in Haines Junction, with nature displays and an inspiring slide program. There's a second visitors centre at Sheep Mountain, also on the Alaska Hwy.

Kluane's terrain consists primarily of the St Elias Mountains and the world's largest nonpolar ice fields, remnants of the last ice age. Two-thirds of the park is glacier, interspersed with valleys, glacial lakes, alpine forest, meadows and tundra.

From the highway, you'll have a good view of the **Kluane Ranges** (2500m), which shelter vast ice fields, as well as **Mt Logan** (5950m), Canada's highest peak, and **Mt St Elias** (5488m), which straddles the Canada-Alaska border. You'll find the best views of the interior peaks at the km1622 viewpoint between Haines Junction and Whitehorse, and from around the Donjek River bridge.

At the southern end of turquoise-coloured Kluane Lake, the largest lake in the Yukon, a short turn-off to the east of the Alaska Hwy will take you to **Silver City**. In this almost-ghost town, you can poke around the lakeside ruins and see the remains of a trading post and the Northwest Mounted Police barracks.

Most longer-term visitors to Kluane want to head off on a **wilderness hike**, and the park offers both short marked trails and longer unmarked wilderness routes ranging from an hour to 10 days. The official hiking leaflet includes a hiking map and a list of trails, but detailed hiking guides are also sold at the visitors centres. Overnight trekkers must purchase backcountry permits, which cost C$5 per person per night.

At Sheep Mountain, you can embark on the world-class 30km **Slims West Trek** to the **Kaskawulsh Glacier**, which takes three to five days. Hikers on this route need a bear-proof canister from the visitors centre (there are only 50 available, so get there early) and must attend a short orientation talk. Near the Sheep Mountain Visitors Centre, a 500m path leads up to **Soldiers' Summit**, site of the official opening of the Alaska Hwy on 20 November 1942. From here are good views overlooking Kluane Lake.

From Haines Junction, an easy 4.8km loop trail follows the **Dezadeash River**, and the 15km **Auriol Trail**, 7km south of town, makes a great four to six hour hike. Throughout the park, watch for Dall sheep (which abound around Sheep Mountain) as well as moose, brown and grizzly bears, caribou and 150 species of birds, including eagles and the rare peregrine falcon.

Remote Signs of Life

Penetrating the surface of the numerous icecaps of the Arctic regions are rocky peaks known as *nunataks* (an Inuit word for 'land attached') which create isolated islands in the vast seas of ice. From a distance they may appear lifeless, but recent discoveries suggest that many of these outcrops harbour hundreds of plant and animal species, including lichens, mosses and small flowering plants such as forget-me-nots *(myosotis)* which are thought to have blown in from elsewhere. They're also home to castaway colonies of pikas, small rodents that live among the rocks and eke out a spartan existence eating the vegetation and scavenging the bodies of birds which might have landed and lacked the strength to move on.

Surprisingly, in some areas, such as the nunataks of Kluane National Park in the Yukon, archaeologists have discovered evidence of human habitation on these isolated islands, dating back as many as 12,000 years. In fact, it's strongly believed that nunataks have helped to preserve remnants of life that existed prior to the last ice age.

The only *camping ground* technically within the park is at Kathleen Lake, 24km south of Haines Junction off the Haines Hwy. The ground is open from mid-June to mid-September and costs C$10 for a site.

Destruction Bay

Tiny Destruction Bay has a population of about 50 and sits on the shore of Kluane Lake about 108km north of Haines Junction. It began life as a camp and supply depot during the construction of the Alaska Hwy and gained its name after a storm tore through the makeshift camp. The village has a petrol station, motel and camping ground.

Burwash Landing

Just 16km north of Destruction Bay, Burwash Landing is best known for the **Kluane Museum** (☎ 841 5561) with its worthwhile exhibits on local animals, natural history and the Southern Tutchone people (or Dan, as they call themselves – they're in fact a branch of the Dene, or Athapaskan group). The museum is open from mid-May to early September daily from 9 am to 9 pm and admission is C$3. You can visit the church and school of the early mission, and there is also a shop and petrol station.

Beaver Creek

Beaver Creek, Canada's westernmost town, is the last Alaska Hwy town before the US border. The VRC (☎ 862 7321) is open from 8 am to 8 pm daily from mid-May to mid-September, and has information on the Yukon and Alaska. The 24-hour Canadian immigration checkpoint is just north of the town while the US immigration post lies 30km farther west. The *Beaver Creek Hostel & Campground* (☎ 862 7903) has low-cost accommodation from C$10 to C$15 per person.

Tatshenshini-Alsek Wilderness Provincial Park (British Columbia)

Tucked along the southern Yukon border west of Hwy 3, this remote and rugged 958,000 hectare park (☎ 250-847 7320) is also part of the regional UNESCO World Heritage Site designation, together with Kluane and Alaska's Wrangell-St Elias National Park. It's home to thousands of bald eagles, rare 'blue' glacier bears and numerous other species, and attracts about 1200 human visitors a year. It's best accessed along disused roads from the Haines Cut-Off between Haines Junction and Klukwan, Alaska.

However, the park has no facilities of any kind, and most visitors are there on six-day commercial rafting trips from Dalton to face the Class III and IV rapids of the Tatshenshini (to run the river privately, you need to put your name on a waiting list several years long).

ROBERT CAMPBELL HIGHWAY

From Watson Lake, the 588km gravel road known as the Robert Campbell Hwy provides an alternative route north to Dawson City. Named for Robert Campbell, a 19th century explorer and Hudson's Bay Company trader, it's a scenic and little travelled route with few services. The Kasha village of Ross River, 362km from Watson Lake at the junction with the Canol Rd (Hwy 6), serves as a supply centre for the local mines, and has a camping ground and a couple of motels. There's also a small government *camping ground* 13km farther west at Lapie Canyon. From Ross River, the lonely Canol Rd heads north-east to the Northwest Territories border and the beginning of the Canol Heritage Hiking Trail.

Faro, 10km off the Robert Campbell Hwy on the Pelly River, was created in 1968 to support the huge copper, lead and zinc mine in the Anvil Mountains, which has closed and re-opened several times due to the fluctuating world markets. It has a camping ground, a couple of motels, the worthwhile 8km Sheep Trail walking track and other short hiking routes.

KLONDIKE HIGHWAY

The 716km Klondike Hwy links Skagway, Alaska with Whitehorse and Dawson City via the north-western corner of British Columbia, roughly following the route of the 40,000 Klondike prospectors in 1898. The stretch between Skagway and Carcross is a scenic marvel of lakes and mountains in myriad greens and blues.

Part of the 180km Klondike Hwy route from Skagway to Whitehorse runs parallel to the White Pass & Yukon Rail Line (☎ 907-983 2217, toll-free ☎ 1-800 343 7373), a tourist train which may also be used by hikers on the world-famous Chilkoot Trail. From Lake Bennett, they can either take the train back to Skagway or catch a bus to Whitehorse or Skagway. Chilkoot Water Charters (☎ 821 3209) has a water shuttle (C$50) on the lake to Carcross where visitors can also connect with buses. There are also plans to extend some rail services over the scenic but currently unused stretch to Carcross.

Several bus companies offer services between Skagway and Whitehorse. Alaska Direct (☎ 668 4833, toll-free ☎ 1-800 770 6652) charges C$49 or US$35; Alaska Overland (☎ 667 7896) charges C$40 or US$30; and Gray Line's Alaskon Express (☎ 907-983 2241, toll-free ☎ 1-800 544 2206) charges US$56.

Carcross

Carcross, 74km south-east of Whitehorse, was once a Tagish seasonal hunting camp. The name is an abbreviated version of Caribou Crossing – so called because caribou herds once crossed the narrow isthmus between Bennett and Lares lakes – but the name remains applicable because plenty of cars now cross through every summer. The VRC (☎ 821 4431) is in the old train station. You may want to stop 2km north of town for a look at the **Carcross Desert**, the sandy bed of a glacial lake which disappeared after the last ice age.

Whitehorse to Carmacks

North of Whitehorse, between Carmacks and the Takhini Hot Springs Rd, the highway passes through dry, scrubby land with several cattle and horse ranches, and skirts several lakes which are suitable for swimming, boating and fishing in summer. The largest is Lake Laberge, 40km north of Whitehorse, where the narrator in the Robert Service poem 'cremated Sam McGee'. Near Carmacks the mountains grow lower and more rounded and forested, and along the way to Dawson City, petrol stations have taken to selling mutant cinnamon buns the size of bear cubs.

Carmacks

Sitting on the banks of the Yukon River, Carmacks was once a fuelling station for riverboats and a stopover on the overland trail between Whitehorse and Dawson City. It's now a small community of around 400 people with a service station, camping ground, hotel, motel and other services.

Originally known as Tantalus, the name was changed to Carmacks to honour George Washington Carmack who, along with two Natives, Skookum Jim and Tagish Charley, discovered gold at Bonanza Creek near Dawson City in 1896 and sparked off the Klondike gold rush.

About 25km north of town, at the Five Finger Recreation Site, a set of stairs (a hell of a lot of stairs) leads to a view of the rocky Yukon River outcrops which once caused no end of strife for riverboats.

Stewart Crossing & the Silver Trail

Stewart Crossing, once a supply centre between Dawson City and Whitehorse, sits at the junction of the Klondike Hwy (Hwy 2) and the silver prospectors' route known as the Silver Trail (Hwy 11). This is the main put-in point for the excellent five day **canoe trip** down the Stewart River to the Yukon River and on to Dawson. Although this is a wilderness trip, it's still reasonably accessible to inexperienced canoeists; you can make arrangements in either Whitehorse or Dawson City.

The Silver Trail heads north-eastward to the three old mining and fur-trading towns of Mayo, Elsa and Keno City. The region offers some good, accessible outdoor possibilities, such as the 6km trail to the summit of **Mt Haldane** (26km beyond Mayo) as well as several camping grounds and lodges. However, there are no services in Elsa.

Keno Hill in Keno City (population 50) has a signpost measuring distances to cities all over the world. It also offers good views of the mountains and valleys, while several local hiking and driving routes provide access to alpine meadows and old mining areas. **Tintina Trench**, a distinctive geological feature which reveals evidence of plate tectonics, is visible from an overlook about 60km south of Dawson City.

DAWSON CITY

Little Dawson City, with just 2000 people, occupies the confluence of the Yukon and Klondike rivers, 240km south of the Arctic

kon Territory, Canada

pitan Khlebnikov from a helicopter, Baffin Bay, Canada

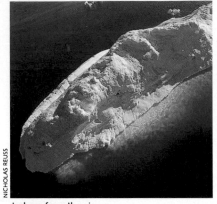

NICHOLAS REUSS

Iceberg from the air

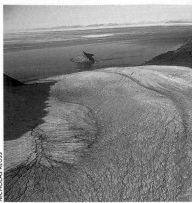

NICHOLAS REUSS

Dodge Glacier, Greenland

DEANNA SWANEY

The icy coast of East Greenland, near Ammassalik (Tasiilaq)

DEANNA SWANEY

The mouth of Ilulissat Kangerlua, Disko Bay, Greenland

Circle. Once (rather preposterously) nicknamed the 'Paris of the North', it boasted deluxe hotels and restaurants, plush river steamers and shops stocking luxury imports from around the world.

Today, Dawson is probably the highlight of any visit to the Yukon. Here, numerous historical remnants bring back visions of the town's fleeting but frenetic fling with world fame and infamy, and many of the original buildings still stand. Built upon the permafrost which begins just a few centimetres below the surface, their plank foundations rest on gravel and many show evidence of the seasonal heaving and thawing. Parks Canada is currently restoring or preserving those which are considered historically significant.

Outside the town, early gold dredging is evident from the eerie mounds of tailings which look like the work of mammoth gophers. The old dredges sucked up the swampy earth at one end and left it behind sans gold as they made their circuitous paths across the land. A century after the original gold rush, as many as 100 small, often family-owned, enterprises still mine for gold in the surrounding region.

On the corner of Front and King Sts is the good VRC (☎ 993 5566). It's open from 8 am to 8 pm daily from mid-May to mid-September. There's also a Parks Canada counter which sells passes to the National Historic Sites (C$15) and a Northwest Territories Visitors Centre (☎ 993 6167) opposite the VRC which has maps and information on the territories and the Dempster Hwy.

Things to See & Do

Diamond Tooth Gertie's Gambling Hall is a re-creation of an 1898 saloon, complete with small-time gambling, honky-tonk piano and dancing girls. It's open daily from 7 pm to 2 am and admission is C$5. Note that the casino's winnings go towards town restoration, so go ahead - lose a bundle.

The large and flamboyant **Grand Palace Theatre**, which served as an opera house and dance hall, was built in 1899 by 'Arizona Charlie' Meadows. At night the

Gaslight Follies (☎ 993 6217) presents remarkably corny stage shows vaguely (very vaguely) based on the gold rush era.

The **Dawson City Museum** (☎ 993 5291) on 5th Ave, houses a collection of 25,000 gold rush artefacts and displays on the district's people which capture the feel of a bygone era. The **SS Keno**, one of the last Yukon riverboats, is on display as a National Historic Site off Front Sts in the Yukon River.

In a typical gold rush cabin on 8th Ave, Robert W Service, the 'Bard of the Yukon', lived from 1909 to 1912. Don't miss the captivating recitals (C$6) of Service's poems by Tom Byrne at 10 am and 3 pm. The Yukon's other most famous resident, Jack London, lived in Dawson in 1898 and wrote many of his popular animal stories, including *Call of the Wild* and *White Fang*. At the cabin and interpretative centre on 8th Ave, you can hear recitals and talks about his works at noon and 2.15 pm daily.

To the north the quarried face of **Midnight Dome** (880m) overlooks the town. Its name is derived from the fact that on 21 June the midnight sun barely sinks below the Ogilvie Mountains to the north before rising again. To reach it, travel 1km south of town to the Crocus Bluffs, turn left off the Klondike Hwy onto New Dome Rd and continue for 7km. The Dome offers good views of the Ogilvie Mountains, Klondike Valley, the Yukon River and Dawson City.

Outside the town, two National Historic Sites reveal aspects of the Klondike mining days. **Dredge #4**, 12km south of the Klondike Hwy on Bonanza Creek Rd, is a massive dredging machine which tore up the Klondike Valley and left piles of tailings which remain as a landscape blight. The **Bear Creek Mining Camp**, 13km south of town, is the site of the large community and shop complex which sprang up around the Klondike gold dredges in 1905 and lasted for 60 years. Admission is covered by the Parks Pass.

When the Klondike Hwy was completed, the **paddlewheel ferries** were sent

Tipped Scales & Greased Palms

Pity the poor gold miner during the Klondike gold rush; having survived the odds to stake a claim and beaten the odds to actually find some gold, the miner would head to Dawson City where the deck was stacked heavily against him.

One of the major scams was practised by the gold buyers who would 'tip the scales' in their favour when it came time to weigh the hapless miner's gold. In the scores of dubious saloons, bartenders would encourage payment in gold. These characters would invariably have heavily greased hair. Before inspecting a miner's nuggets or gold dust, they would wipe their hands in their hair, knowing that a little gold would stick to the grease on their palms. The bartenders would then wipe their hands in their pockets and by the end of the night have a sizeable haul. From this came the phrase 'grease my palms'.

With whatever they had left, miners often went to one of the gambling joints where stacked decks were just one of the many scams aimed at tapping into their hard-earned booty. In the town's back alleys, hundreds of prostitutes had their own schemes to separate a miner from his assets. Given all this, it's no surprise that few miners left the Yukon any better off than when they'd arrived.

downstream and abandoned to rot on the bank. Now overgrown, they make a fascinating destination for a short hike. Take the George Black Ferry across the river, walk north though the camping ground for 10 minutes and then a further 10 minutes north along the beach.

Dawson Trading Post (☎ 993 5316) rents canoes and offers wilderness camping trips. One of the main do-it-yourself **canoe float trips**, suitable for inexperienced canoeists, heads downstream from Dawson for three days to Eagle, Alaska.

Special Events

Beginning in 1996, the Yukon launched an annual series of gold rush centennial celebrations with a different theme each year. Based on the success of these festivities, Yukon Tourism seems likely to continue the series until at least 2096 when the theme may well be 'Milking the Tourist' in honour of 100 years of centennials.

The premier annual event in Dawson City is the Discovery Days Festival, which is held in mid-August in honour of you-know-what that happened in 1896. Over several days there are parades, picnics, a really neat demonstration of gold smelting and a bang-up demolition derby. Don't miss the pancake breakfasts sponsored by the curling club.

Places to Stay

Accommodation fills up quickly in July and August so book early. The tourist office can help you find a place to stay, especially on busy weekends. The *Yukon River Campground*, on the west bank, is 250m up the road to the right from the ferry landing, and has shady sites for C$8. You can also pitch a tent at Dieter Reinmuth's *Dawson City River Hostel* (☎ 993 6823) which lies across the river from town and five minutes up the hill from the ferry landing. This rustic and funky place has a communal bath house, tent sites, dormitories, a cooking area, canoes and bicycles for hire. It also has great views, but no electricity. Camping costs C$9 per site for one person plus C$6.50 for each additional camper, and dormitory beds are C$13/16 for HI members/nonmembers. A free shuttle meets the Norline bus from Whitehorse.

At the corner of 5th Ave and York St, the *Gold Rush Campground RV Park* (☎ 993 5247) is really an RV car park with spots from C$15. *The Dawson City RV Park* (☎ 993 5142) 1km south of town, charges the same. The VRC can book B&Bs around town, which average C$69/79 for singles/doubles. The *White Ram Manor B&B* (☎ 993 5772, cnr Harper St & 7th Ave) is a friendly, easy-going place with a laundry, kitchen and hot tub. Staff will pick you up from the airport. *Dawson City B&B (☎ 993 5649, 451 Craig St)* also offers lunch, dinner and airport transport. Another fine spot is the *5th Ave B&B (☎ 993 5941, 702 5th Ave)* which offers cooking facilities.

The basic *Gold Nugget Motel (☎ 993 5445, cnr Dugas St & 5th Ave)* has single/double rooms from C$46/50, and the frontier-style *Dawson City Bunkhouse (☎ 993 6164, fax 993 6051)* on Princess St, charges C$45/50 for singles/doubles with shared bath and C$75/80 with a private bath. Note that it can get noisy when 'likkered up' guests arrive back after a night of Klondike carousing.

The upmarket *Midnight Sun Hotel (☎ 993 5495, fax 993 6425, cnr Queen St & 3rd Ave)* has a licensed restaurant, a bar and singles/doubles for C$108/118. The *Triple J Hotel (☎ 993 5323, fax 993 5030, cnr Queen St & 5th Ave)* has motel rooms and self-catering cabins from C$107/117. The year-round *Eldorado Hotel (☎ 993 5451, toll-free ☎ 1-800 661 0518, fax 993 5256)* dresses its staff in silly period costumes and charges C$112/122 in summer.

Places to Eat
Klondike Kate's (☎ 993 6527, cnr King St & 3rd Ave) offers great breakfast specials for C$5 with unlimited coffee. Sandwiches go for C$8 and pasta platters average C$12. The best of several places along Front St, *River West (☎ 993 6339)* has excellent coffee, bagels, health foods and sandwiches (C$4.50). *Bonanza Meat Co (☎ 993 6567)* on 2nd Ave near Princess St, sells deli items and has recommended sandwiches from C$4 on fresh baked bread. *Dawson City General Store (☎ 993 5475, cnr Queen & Front Sts)* is the largest supermarket north of Whitehorse.

Getting There & Away
The airport is 19km east of town off the Klondike Hwy. Air North (☎ 993 5110, toll-free ☎ 1-800 661 0407) flies to Whitehorse, Fairbanks, Old Crow and Inuvik. Note that fares and timetables vary by season.

Norline Coaches (☎ 993 6010, Whitehorse ☎ 668 3355) runs buses to and from Whitehorse (6½ hours, C$79.50) three times a week from June to August and twice a week at other times. Buses stop at the Shell station at the corner of 5th Ave and Princess St. The VRC can advise you on an on-again-off-again bus service to Inuvik, along the Dempster Hwy.

The free George Black Ferry (☎ 993 5441) connects Dawson with the Top of the World Hwy and runs 24 hours a day when the Yukon River is not frozen.

DEMPSTER HIGHWAY
The Dempster Hwy begins 40km south-east of Dawson City off the Klondike Hwy and heads northward across the Ogilvie and Richardson mountains, beyond the Arctic Circle, and on to Inuvik, in the Northwest Territories near the shores of the Beaufort Sea.

The Dempster Hwy opened in 1979 and makes it possible to travel the full length of North America by road (as does Alaska's Dalton Hwy). From Dawson City, it's a long 741km of gravel road to Inuvik, but the landscapes brim with mountains, valleys, rivers and vast open tundra. Although it's open most of the year, the best time to travel is between June and September, when the ferries operate over the Peel and Mackenzie rivers. Once the rivers freeze over, vehicles simply drive across on the ice, but the road is closed during the spring thaw and the winter freeze-up, which may occur anywhere from mid-April to June and mid-October to December, respectively.

Accommodation and other services are few. At the southern end, there's a petrol station at the *Klondike River Lodge (☎ 993 6892)* where you can rent jerry cans of petrol to haul north and return on your way back. It's then 370km to the next services at Eagle Plains, where there's the year-round *Eagle Plains Hotel (☎ 993 2453)*. After 180km, you reach Fort McPherson (home of Fort McPherson Tent & Canvas, which makes popular travel bags) in the Northwest Territories, and 216km later, you'll rumble into Inuvik.

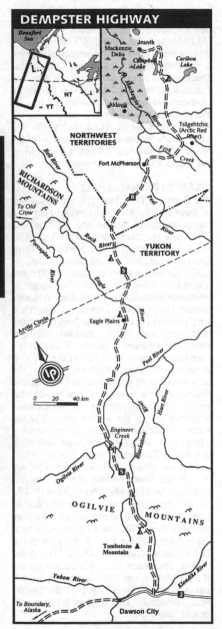

The Yukon government maintains three basic *camping grounds*: Tombstone Mountain (km73), Engineer Creek (km194) and Rock River (km447). There's also a Northwest Territories' camping ground at Nitainlaii Territorial Park 9km south of Fort McPherson. For road and ferry reports, call ☎ 979 2678 or toll-free ☎ 1-800 661 0752.

For information on Inuvik, see the Northwest Territories section later in this chapter.

TOP OF THE WORLD HIGHWAY
At the northern end of Front St in Dawson City, the free ferry crosses the Yukon River to the start of the scenic Top of the World Hwy (Hwy 9). Open only in summer, this gravel road extends 108km to the Alaska border. The small customs and immigration checkpoint is open daily from June to mid-September from 9 am to 9 pm. Once in Alaska, the Taylor Hwy (Hwy 5) continues south for 108km to meet the Alaska Hwy at Tetlin Junction.

VUNTUT NATIONAL PARK
Vuntut (a Gwich'in word meaning among the lakes) is north of the Yukon's most northerly settlement, Old Crow, and was declared a national park in 1993. Each spring, the 160,000-strong porcupine caribou herd follows its migration route north across the plain to the calving grounds near the Beaufort Sea. In Canada these calving grounds are protected within Ivvavik National Park and extend into Alaska where they are part of the Arctic Wildlife National Refuge.

With its countless kettle lakes and ponds, Vuntut National Park is also visited by half a million waterbirds each autumn. Archaeological sites contain fossils of ancient animals such as the mammoth, as well as evidence of early human occupation.

The only access to the 4345 sq km park is by chartered plane from Old Crow, which can only be reached by air. The park has no services or facilities of any kind. For more information, contact the Canadian Heritage Yukon District (☎ 667 3910) No 205-300 Main St, Whitehorse Y1A 2B5.

IVVAVIK NATIONAL PARK

With a name meaning 'a place for bearing and raising the young', Ivvavik, situated along the Beaufort Sea and adjoining Alaska, covers 10,170 sq km. The park is dominated by the British Mountains and its vegetation is mainly tundra. It's on the migration route of the porcupine caribou (see the previous section) and is also a major waterfowl habitat. Access is by charter plane from either Old Crow or Inuvik. For information, contact Parks Canada (☎ 979 3248) Box 1840, Inuvik, NT, X0E 0T0.

Off the coast lies **Herschel Island**, the Yukon's first territorial park, which is a former whaling station and rich in bird and other wildlife. This desolate and foggy place was once an Inuit settlement, which literally died out after westerners brought foreign diseases. At Pauline Cove's protected harbour, camping is available during the short summer season. Amenities include fire rings, wind shelters, outhouses and a limited water supply. Access is by chartered plane, usually from Inuvik, 250km to the south-east. For further information, contact the Yukon Department of Renewable Resources (☎ 667 5648) Box 2703, Whitehorse Y1A 2C6.

Northwest Territories

☎ 867

Canada's northern territories make up a vast tract of land stretching from the northern boundaries of the provinces to within 800km of the North Pole and from the Atlantic Ocean to within a few kilometres of the Pacific Ocean. A third ocean, the Arctic, links Alaska and Greenland across the many islands of the Arctic Archipelago.

In 1999 this vast region underwent a major political change with the hiving off of the 2.2 million sq km territory of Nunavut, leaving the Northwest Territories (NWT) with 1.17 million sq km. Although by reputation the region is a barren, treeless, perpetually frozen expanse of tundra, that's most emphatically not the case, and much of the territory lies south of the tree line. Although we're not talking big timber here, the landscape is dominated by boreal taiga forests and thousands of lakes.

Around the Mackenzie River and Great Slave Lake, most indigenous people refer to themselves as the Dene, or Athapaskans. While the Canadian Inuit live mainly in Nunavut, a few also inhabit the Arctic Ocean coast of the Northwest Territories.

The rolling hills left by retreating glaciers are rich in oil, gas, diamonds and gold, but increasing accessibility, together with the lure of pristine wilderness, means that tourism represents an increasing proportion of the local economy. Other economic pursuits include fishing, trapping and local art.

Slicing across the territory is the mighty Mackenzie River (Deh Cho or 'big river' in the Dene language) which flows 1800km from Great Slave Lake in the south-east to the Beaufort Sea and Arctic Ocean in the north-west. Near its end it fans out into one of the world's largest deltas, encompassing over 16,000 sq km of channels and islands.

YELLOWKNIFE

Rising out of the wilderness, the city of Yellowknife takes its name from the copper-bladed knives used by the Slavey Athapaskans. Although gold was first found here in 1898 by Klondike-bound prospectors, it wasn't until the discovery of richer veins in 1934 and 1945 that European outsiders were attracted to the area in large numbers.

With a population of 17,000, Yellowknife is by far the largest town in the Northwest Territories. This modern, fast-growing settlement on the northern shores of Great Slave Lake (just 1508km from Edmonton by road!) is not only the NWT capital, but also serves as the commercial and service hub for the entire region. For visitors, it's an ideal base to use for hiking, camping, canoeing and fishing trips into the wilderness hinterlands.

ARCTIC CANADA

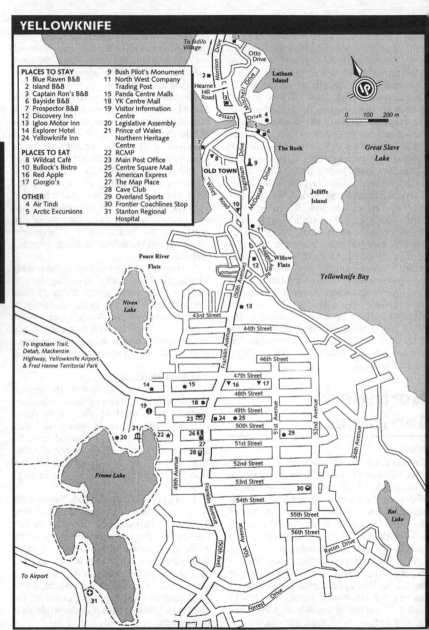

YELLOWKNIFE

PLACES TO STAY
1 Blue Raven B&B
2 Island B&B
3 Captain Ron's B&B
6 Bayside B&B
7 Prospector B&B
12 Discovery Inn
13 Igloo Motor Inn
14 Explorer Hotel
24 Yellowknife Inn

PLACES TO EAT
8 Wildcat Café
10 Bullock's Bistro
16 Red Apple
17 Giorgio's

OTHER
4 Air Tindi
5 Arctic Excursions

9 Bush Pilot's Monument
11 North West Company
  Trading Post
15 Panda Centre Malls
18 YK Centre Mall
19 Visitor Information
  Centre
20 Legislative Assembly
21 Prince of Wales
  Northern Heritage
  Centre
22 RCMP
23 Main Post Office
25 Centre Square Mall
26 American Express
27 The Map Place
28 Cave Club
29 Overland Sports
30 Frontier Coachlines Stop
31 Stanton Regional
  Hospital

The Visitor Information Centre (☎ 873 4262, fax 873 3654) is at 4807 49th St near 49th Ave (confusing, eh?). It distributes maps, canoe routes and a guide to settlements across the territory, as well as fishing, canoeing and motoring guides. Be sure to ask for the free metered-parking pass issued to tourists. At night, you may want to avoid 50th St between 50th and 52nd Aves, where the effects of alcohol abuse are often laid bare.

Things to See & Do

Arm yourself with a copy of *Four Historical Walking Tours of Yellowknife*, which masterfully guides you through the town's many historic structures. The heart of the historic action is **Old Town**, down Franklin Ave, and the wooden houses along Ragged Ass Rd – remnants of the 1934 gold rush – actually live up to the appeal of the street name.

The Rock, a nub of land near the tiny bridge to Latham Island, affords good views of the town from the Bush Pilot's Monument, where you can watch the buzzing float planes and the polychrome house boats on the lake. At the northern end of the island, you can check out **Ndilo** (end of the road), which is Yellowknife's Dogrib Dene aboriginal community. You're welcome to stroll around and often the older men like to chat and can tell you about the old days and ways. One of the best places to choose from a range of local crafts is the **North West Company Trading Post** (☎ 873 8064) near Old Town at 5005 Bryson Drive.

Frame Lake, at the western edge of town, is circled by a 5.6km track which is popular with hikers and joggers. The **Prince of Wales Northern Heritage Centre** (☎ 873 7551) beside Frame Lake off 49th St, is a fine introduction to the Northwest Territories with diorama displays on the lifestyles of the Dene and Inuit, and European development. It also has galleries on the natural sciences and the history of aviation in the Northwest Territories. Admission is free.

In 1993, the NWT government built the striking, domed **Legislative Assembly** (☎ 669 2200) which contains an impressive collection of Native art. Free summer tours are conducted at 10.30 am, 1.30 and 3.30 pm weekdays and 1.30 pm on Sundays.

In **Fred Henne Territorial Park** (☎ 920 2472) off the Mackenzie Hwy, opposite the airport, you'll find the sandy **Long Lake Beach** and the 4km **Prospector's Trail**. The latter leads over rocky outcrops and past a microcosm of northern Canadian topography, including lakes, bush and muskeg.

Overland Sports (☎ 873 2474) 5103 51st Ave, rents canoes, kayaks and winter sports gear. A basic canoe costs C$30/150 per day/week. Narwhal Ltd (☎ 873 6443) charges the same rates, and will also help organise your trip and provide basic lessons. Sail North (☎ 873 8019) charters sailboats on Great Slave Lake and can provide crews, provisions and other services.

There's no shortage of fishing guides. One of the better-known companies is Bluefish Services (☎ 873 4818) which charges C$65 for four hours of battling northern pike on Great Slave Lake. It also offers bird-watching tours.

Special Events

In March, the **Caribou Carnival** provides three festive days in which locals shake off winter with fireworks, games and contests. A highlight is the 240km dogsled race on Great Slave Lake. In July, the seven day **Festival of the Midnight Sun** celebrates local art and culture, and is followed by the **Folk on the Rocks** festival, which draws folk musicians and entertainers from all over North America as well as Inuit and Dene musicians and dancers.

Places to Stay

The camping ground nearest town is at the *Fred Henne Territorial Park*, which has full facilities and costs C$12 per site. From here, the centre of town can be reached in 40 minutes by using the track around Jackfish and Frame Lakes. If you have transport, you can also camp at *Prelude Lake Territorial Park* or *Reid Lake Territorial Park*, respectively 31km and 61km from town along the Ingraham Trail. Sites at either cost

C$12. You can check on availability at all three places on ☎ 920 2472.

The tourist office will book B&Bs. *Island B&B (☎ 873 4786, 34 Morrison Drive, Old Town)* has a comfortable living room with a view of Back Bay and charges C$60/80 for single/double rooms. Nearby, *Captain Ron's B&B (☎ 873 3746, 8 Lessard Drive)* has smoke-free rooms from C$72/88. Also on Latham Island, *Blue Raven B&B (☎ 873 6328, fax 920 4013, 37-B Otto Drive)* has nice rooms from C$60/75. On The Rock by the float-plane terminal, *The Bayside B&B (☎ 920 4686, fax 920 7931, 3505 McDonald Drive)* has great views of Yellowknife Bay and rooms from C$60/70. Just around the corner, *The Prospector B&B (☎ 920 7620, fax 669 7581, 3506 Wiley Rd)* is almost a hotel with well-equipped rooms from C$75/90 and a noted restaurant for fresh-fish dinners.

The friendly *Igloo Motor Inn (☎ 873 8511, fax 873 5547, 4115 Franklin Ave)* between the town centre and Old Town, charges C$95/104. At the *Discovery Inn (☎ 873 4151, fax 920 7948, 4701 Franklin Ave)* rooms cost C$98/113. *Yellowknife Inn (☎ 873 2601, toll-free ☎ 1-800 661 0580, fax 873 2602)* on Franklin Ave between 49th and 50th Sts, is the largest hotel in town. Rooms with all the amenities cost C$130 for a single or double. Looming over everything is the high-rise *Explorer Hotel (☎ 873 3531, toll-free ☎ 1-800 661 0892, fax 873 2789, 4823 48th St)* with standard modern rooms from C$157/172 (this is where the Queen stays in Yellowknife!).

Places to Eat

Upstairs in the Panda II Mall, *The Picnic Nook (☎ 873 6292)* is a lunchtime favourite with locals who wolf down the C$4 sandwiches. Just downstairs, *Ryan's Family Restaurant (☎ 873 2363)* has lunches for about C$7 and a popular Oriental buffet. *The Red Apple (☎ 873 2324, cnr Franklin Ave & 47th St)* has a broad diner-style menu but is acclaimed for its rib-sticking breakfasts.

The best local Italian cooking is at *Giorgio's (☎ 669 2023, 5022 47th St)* where the owner's mother, Cosimina Meraglia, runs the kitchen. Meals cost around C$20 per person. At the famous *Wildcat Café (☎ 873 8850)* in a 1937 log cabin in Old Town, the changing menu focuses on such local specialities as caribou, fish and Arctic berries. Prices range from C$7 to C$20.

For a meal that may inspire a second visit to Yellowknife, head for *Bullock's Bistro (☎ 873 3474, 4 Lessard Drive, Old Town)*. Here only the freshest fish make the daily menu and everything, right down to the incredible garlic-ginger salad dressing, is just plain fabulous. Book at one of the tables or nab a stool at the counter where you can engage in cheery banter with the staff and watch the cook work her magic. Expect to pay about C$15 per person.

Self-caterers can try *Extra Foods* in the YK Centre Mall on 48th St near Franklin Ave.

Getting There & Away

Yellowknife is the hub of air service for much of the NWT and western Nunavut, but fares aren't subsidised for visitors and can seem staggeringly high. Since it purchased NWT Air, First Air (☎ 873 6884, toll-free ☎ 1-800 267 1247) monopolises the transport scene, providing links to/from Edmonton, Fort Resolution, Hay River, Fort Simpson, Whitehorse, Inuvik, Cambridge Bay, Resolute, Rankin Inlet and Iqaluit. Canadian North (☎ 873 4484, toll-free ☎ 1-800 661 1505) is a division of Canadian Airlines and has services to/from Edmonton, Norman Wells, Inuvik and various Nunavut destinations such as Cambridge Bay, Resolute, Rankin Inlet and Iqaluit. Smaller airlines serve towns in the NWT and sometimes offer good special fares. Northwestern Air (☎ 873 8739) serves Fort Smith, Buffalo Air (☎ 873 6112) flies to Hay River with DC-3s, and Air Tindi (☎ 669 8260) serves Fort Simpson.

Frontier Coachlines (☎ 874 2566) has bus services to/from Enterprise and Hay River (eight hours), where it connects with Greyhound (toll-free ☎ 1-800 661 8747) services to/from Edmonton. The bus stop is at the corner of 53rd St and 52nd Ave.

Getting Around

The City of Yellowknife Public Transit System is operated by Arctic Frontier Carriers (☎ 873 4437). Fares are C$2. Route No 1 serves the airport, Old Airport Rd, the town centre on Franklin Ave and Old Town. This bus runs hourly from roughly 7 am to 7 pm on weekdays and for just a few hours on Saturday.

Bikes can be rented from the tourist office for C$20 per day.

AROUND YELLOWKNIFE

The small Dogrib Dene village of Detah is 25km by road south-east of town across Yellowknife Bay. Here you can have a look at traditional life and meet local people and purchase their handicrafts. However, there are no formal tourist facilities.

The 71km **Ingraham Trail** (Hwy 4) extends east of Yellowknife to Tibbitt Lake, where fittingly, a stop sign marks the end of the road and the **Pensive Lake canoe route** begins. The road passes through superb, hilly, rocky Canadian Shield topography dotted with lakes. There are great views and good fishing, hiking, canoeing, camping and picnicking. Cycling is also possible. **Prelude Lake**, 30km east of Yellowknife, has camping, a beach and a short nature trail. A popular hike leads to **Cameron Falls**. At **Reid Lake**, 59km from Yellowknife, you can camp, swim or canoe, but the *camping ground* gets busy on summer weekends.

Surrounded by classic northern Canadian lakes, *Blachford Lake Lodge (☎ 873 3303, fax 920 4013)* offers a variety of fishing and nature tours and accommodation ranging from small rustic cabins to a rather plush lodge. A five day summer package costs C$875/1150 without/with meals, including a bush flight from Yellowknife.

MACKENZIE HIGHWAY

The southernmost stretch of the Mackenzie Hwy follows the Hay River, which flows north into Great Slave Lake. The North of 60 Information Centre (☎ 920 1021) near the Alberta border, dispenses highway information and has an exhibit of northern arts and crafts. Nearby is a *camping ground* with a kitchen shelter and water.

About 75km north of the border is **Twin Falls Gorge Territorial Park** (toll-free ☎ 1-800 661 0788) where 33m Alexandra Falls (named for Britain's Princess Alexandra) is accessed on a short trail. A farther 2km north is the car park for Louise Falls (15m) where you'll find camping for C$10. A 45 minute walking trail along the Hay River gorge links the two falls. Just a few kilometres farther north is Escarpment Creek, a good picnic place with views of the gorge.

Enterprise (population 60) has an Esso petrol station with a shop and motel. North of there, the Mackenzie Hwy is paved most of the way to the Hwy 3 junction, which leads to Fort Providence. At **McNallie Creek Falls**, north of Enterprise, a picnic site enjoys views of a waterfall tumbling into a water-worn bowl of rock. About 9km north, the **Hart Lake Fire Tower** has views as far as Great Slave Lake.

Before the village of Kakisa, 9km off the highway, *Lady Evelyn Falls camping ground* makes a nice stop with good fishing. Sites cost C$12, but it's often full at weekends. Some 105km beyond Enterprise, Hwy 3 branches north for 31km to the free ferry (toll-free ☎ 1-800 661 0751) over the Mackenzie River, which operates from about mid-May to mid-December. In winter, vehicles cross on the ice, but there's no crossing at all for the several weeks during the winter freeze-up and spring thaw.

The Slavey community of 700 people at Fort Providence huddles on the banks of the Mackenzie River, 6km from the ferry and 312km south of Yellowknife. The site was settled in 1861 when a Roman Catholic mission was established, followed soon after by a Hudson's Bay Company trading post. There's a *camping ground* on the banks 2km off Hwy 3, on the access road into town. Also on the fringe of town is the charmless *Big River Motel (☎ 699 4301)* with a petrol station and cafe. Rooms are priced from C$60. The larger *Snowshoe Inn (☎ 699 3511)* charges C$90/110 for singles/doubles, and also serves as the bus terminal.

For nearly 100km north of Fort Providence, Hwy 3 follows the western boundary of the **Mackenzie Bison Sanctuary**, which is home to the world's largest herd of free-ranging wood bison. Hiking isn't recommended as there are no trails and the bison tend to get irritable in summer, thanks to the menacing swarms of bugs.

Continuing on, the road passes through scraggly forests and hilly terrain into the twin **Dogrib communities** of Edzo (214km from Fort Providence) and Rae. Apart from its *camping ground* south of town, there's little call to stop at Edzo, but Rae has a petrol station and a basic shop. Between here and Yellowknife (98km) you'll clearly see the distinctively rounded, copper-coloured rock outcrops that characterise the Canadian Shield.

HAY RIVER

Hay River, with 3200 people, sits on the southern shore of Great Slave Lake, 38km north of Enterprise on Hwy 2. This is the heart of Big River Country which surrounds the Mackenzie, Hay and Slave rivers and Great Slave Lake. In this relatively important distribution centre, barges load up for trips to settlements along the Mackenzie River and up to the Arctic coast. There's also a significant commercial fishery here, including packing and shipping, primarily of whitefish and lake trout.

The town itself is divided into two distinctive parts: the old town, at the northern end of Vale Island; and the newer section, where Hwy 2 is ushered into town. The Visitor Information Centre (☎ 874 3180) is on the corner of Mackenzie Hwy and McBryan Drive.

Across the Hay River, the Dene Reserve operates the **Dene Cultural Institute** (☎ 874 8480). This excellent centre offers tours of the Dene village and has good displays on their culture. It is open from 9 am to 5 pm on weekdays and 1 to 5 pm on Saturdays from June to mid-September.

Places to Stay & Eat

The *Hay River Campground* (☎ 874 3772) on Vale Island has sites for C$12, and staff will always find an empty spot for another tent. Nearby, the *Harbour House B&B* (☎ 874 2233) has great views at the end of the beach road and charges C$45/65 for singles/doubles, with use of the kitchen. The *Cedar Rest Motel* (☎ 874 3732) near the bus stop, has rooms from C$55/62.

Some 24km south of Hay River just off Hwy 2, *Paradise Garden Campground* (☎ 874 6414, fax 874 4422) is a delightful place on a sweeping bend of the Hay River. In summer, staff sell beautiful organic produce and provide a lovely camping ground (C$12 per site) with a good kitchen (for preparing the veggies?).

For meals, there's a surprising number of choices in the commercial centre. The local favourite is the *Boardroom Restaurant* (☎ 874 2111) where the extensive menu spoils guests with Mexican, Chinese, Italian and northern specialities.

Getting There & Away

Buffalo Airways (☎ 874 3333) and First Air (☎ 874 2847, toll-free ☎ 1-800 267 1247) connect Hay River's Vale Island airport with Yellowknife. Canadian North (☎ 874 2434, toll-free ☎ 1-800 661 1505) flies to Edmonton. Greyhound (☎ 874 6966, toll-free ☎ 1-800 661 8747) has daily services to Edmonton (16 hours, C$130). Frontier Coachlines (☎ 874 2566) serves Yellowknife, Fort Smith, Hay River, Fort Providence and Fort Simpson. The bus station is at 39-141 Mackenzie Hwy.

FORT SMITH

This town of 2400 sits astride the Alberta border on Hwy 5, 333km east of Hay River. There is a visitor information centre (☎ 872 2515) at 56 Portage Ave. Among the attractions are the **Northern Life Museum**, with exhibits on local history and a trail to the evocatively named Rapids of the Drowned. **Fort Smith Mission Historic Park** is the site of the 1912 Catholic mission, and you can also visit a **pelican nesting site** south of town.

On the Slave River, west of town, lies the Queen Elizabeth Territorial Park, which has a *camping ground*. At Liz's Corner Store is the *Fort Smith International Hostel (☎ 872 3097, 376 Cedar Ave)* where you can sleep for C$15 or hire a canoe. The *Pinecrest Hotel (☎ 872 2320)* has comfortable rooms for C$75/85, as well as a bar and restaurant. If you're headed for Wood Buffalo National Park, be sure to pick up your food in town.

WOOD BUFFALO NATIONAL PARK

The 45,000 sq km Wood Buffalo National Park, one of the world's largest parks, was established in 1922 to protect its few hundred surviving wood bison. It's now a UNESCO World Heritage Site and much of its seemingly endless boreal forests, bogs and river channels are inaccessible. Camping is available at **Pine Lake**, 60km south of Fort Smith, and in winter, an ice road connects the park with Fort MacKay, Alberta. The park visitors centre (☎ 872 2349) at the corner of McDougal Rd and Portage Ave in Fort Smith, can help you make sense of this fascinating and confounding park.

WEST OF GREAT SLAVE LAKE

From its junction with Hwy 3, the Mackenzie Hwy (Hwy 1) continues 300km west to Fort Simpson and beyond. At about two-thirds of the way to Fort Simpson, it's worth breaking your trip at the **Sambeh Deh Falls** and gorge, which has a *camping ground*. South of Fort Simpson, a free ferry (toll-free ☎ 1-800 661 0752) crosses the Liard River.

Fort Simpson

Established in 1804 as a fur-trading post, Fort Simpson once served as the district headquarters for the Hudson's Bay Company. Today, most of its 1200 residents are Dene, while the rest are Métis and European Canadians. Not only is it the main town of the Deh Cho region, but it's also a main staging point for visits to **Nahanni National Park**, 145km to the west.

The visitors centre (☎ 695 3182) at the entrance to town greets travellers approaching

from the south. Camping is available at the *Fort Simpson Territorial Park* for C$10. Among the handful of small lodgings, *Nahanni Inn (☎ 695 2201, fax 695 3000)* is probably the best, with a restaurant and rooms from C$100.

First Air (☎ 695 2020, toll-free ☎ 1-800 267 1247) stops in Fort Simpson en route between Whitehorse and Yellowknife, and Air Tindi (☎ 669 8260) flies to and from Yellowknife. Frontier Coachlines (☎ 874 2566) has bus services to Hay River.

If your budget won't stretch to a fly-in trip to Nahanni, you may want to consider the *North Nahanni Naturalist Lodge (☎ 695 2116, fax 695 2118)* which is run by a Dene family and offers day trips along the Mackenzie to the North Nahanni River. The five-hour option takes you through lovely scenery along the North Nahanni and Tetcela Rivers, and is priced from C$150. There are also boat trips to Dene outposts, stopping at homes, old cabins and traditional hunting camps. The trips start at the Ndulee Ferry Crossing on the Mackenzie Hwy, 78km north of Fort Simpson.

Liard Highway & Fort Liard

The Liard Hwy branches off the Mackenzie Hwy 65km south of Fort Simpson and follows the Liard River valley to **Nahanni Butte**. It then crosses into British Columbia and joins the Alaska Hwy at Fort Nelson, 487km from Fort Simpson. At km110, near Nahanni Butte, lies the **Blackstone Territorial Park**, where you'll find information, camping, hiking trails and fine views of the Liard River. This is a popular take-out point for river trips through Nahanni.

At the traditional town of Fort Liard (population 500), have a look at the two storey log building erected by Roman Catholic missionaries in 1921. Watch for the characteristic birch bark baskets, woven and adorned with porcupine quills by local Dene women. The town also serves as a minor gateway to Nahanni National Park, and there's a small *camping ground*. The *General Store & Motel (☎ 770 4441)* is just that, and there's also a petrol station.

NAHANNI NATIONAL PARK

Lovely Nahanni National Park, a UNESCO World Heritage Site and one of the Northwest Territories' greatest attractions, protects a superb portion of the Mackenzie Mountains and the spectacular canyons of the turbulent South Nahanni River. It's best known to canoeists, kayakers and rafters who come to challenge some of the finest whitewater on the continent. Other highlights include the waterfalls, particularly 96m **Virginia Falls** (twice the height of Niagara!) and the hot sulphur springs at Rabbitkettle and Wildmint. The vast **Ram Plateau**, immediately to the north, has been slated as a possible territorial park.

Much has been written about the park since the early 1900s when the discovery of the decapitated corpses of two prospector brothers conjured up tales of enormous mountain men, wild native tribes, white Amazon women and other fanciful horrors.

Subsequent casualties and disappearances, mostly among miners, only enhance Nahanni's reputation, which is reflected in colourful names like the Headless Range, Broken Skull River and Deadmen Valley. Even if you don't encounter Amazons, any lust for wildlife will be satisfied by the Park's substantial population of bears, mountain goats, moose, wolves and more.

Thanks to a lack of roads, access is not cheap, and the only way in is by air, usually with a tour group or on an individually arranged charter flight. Nahanni visits come in two main varieties. The water-bound version will normally include a six day to three week canoe or raft trip. The 'classic' trip takes 14 days, allowing for nine days of paddling and five for hiking and delays. All canoeists and rafters wind up at Blackstone Territorial Park on the Liard River. The second type of visit ranges from a simple 30 minute flight over the park to a landing from which you can embark on a hike. The basic option is a one day stroll around Virginia Falls and camping at one of the seven primitive sites.

All independent visitors must register with the park office (☎ 695 3151, ☎ 695 2310),

Superintendent, Nahanni National Park, Box 348, Fort Simpson, NWT X0E 0N0. The entrance fee for the park is C$10 for a day, with higher rates for overnight stays.

Organised Tours

Most organised trips depart from Fort Simpson. While the guided canoe and raft trips offer fantastic experiences, they're not cheap, averaging from C$2200 to C$3600 and beyond. Because park access is limited, you really need to pre-book, preferably months in advance. The canoe trips are best for people with some basic experience while the raft trips are more relaxing and open to anyone. The lines are blurred between the various Nahanni tour operators, outfitters, guides and charter aircraft services; you'll find some suggestions in the Organised Tours & Adventures chapter.

THE MACKENZIE RIVER

Across the broad landscapes of the northwestern Northwest Territories flows the Mackenzie River, swollen by waters which drain from one-fifth of Canada. In places, it meanders along at a width of up to 3km, making it popular with canoeists and kayakers, and an increasing number of hardy souls take advantage of the long summer days to paddle the entire 1800km from Fort Providence to Tuktoyaktuk on the Arctic Ocean.

Norman Wells

Norman Wells, on the northern shore of the Mackenzie River, lies mid-way between Fort Simpson and Inuvik, and its 800 people are largely involved in the oil industry. It has a convenient *camping ground* as well as several hotels, including the *Yamouri* (☎ 587 2744, fax 587 2262) where you'll pay C$100 for a simple room.

Canadian North Airlines (☎ 587 2361, toll-free ☎ 1-800 661 1505) calls in here en route between Yellowknife and Inuvik, while North-Wright Airways (☎ 587 2333) serves the even more isolated communities along the river. The only road access to Norman Wells is by ice road in winter.

The main attraction is the **Canol Heritage Trail**, a hiking trail which leads 372km south-west to the Yukon border and has been designated a National Historic Site. It was built at enormous monetary and human cost during WWII to supply oil to White-horse but in 1947, after the war ended and cheaper ways were found to get oil to Whitehorse, the project was abandoned. Today, it's lined with derelict army camps and equipment and should really be desig-nated as a monument to North American tax-payers, who forked out C$300 million (in 1945) for its construction.

The route traverses peaks, canyons and barrens, and hikers normally see a lot of wildlife. However, there are numerous deep river crossings and although you can sleep in abandoned huts along the way, there are no facilities. The Canol Rd (Hwy 6) from Ross River meets the trail on the Yukon bor-der. Hiking the whole length takes about four weeks and requires food drops along the way. For more information, see the Nor-man Wells Historical Centre (☎ 587 2415).

Inuvik

Although it wasn't founded until 1955, Inuvik is the Northwest Territories' second largest town, with 3000 people. It lies on the East Channel of the Mackenzie River, about 90km south of the Arctic coast and has the shoddy appearance shared by most northern towns.

For nearly two months each year, the mid-night sun shines over Inuvik, but the first snows may fall as early as late August. The population is roughly divided between Inuit, Dene and non-Native people. The Western Arctic Visitors Centre (☎ 777 4727, in win-ter ☎ 777 7327) is on Mackenzie Rd at the eastern end of town. For a selection of north-ern-theme books and maps, stop by Bob Rowe's Boreal Bookstore (☎ 777 3748).

The unusual **Our Lady of Victory Church**, with a lovely interior designed by local artists, is known as the 'Igloo Church' for reasons which will become obvious to vis-itors. At the nearby **Carving Corner**, local artists create works from ivory and stone. At **Chuk Park**, 6km south of town, a lookout

tower affords wide-ranging views of the Arctic terrain.

Having said that, the main reason to visit Inuvik is to get out of town as quickly as possible on an **Arctic Tour**. Most of these in-volve flights over the convoluted Mackenzie Delta. Prices start at around C$150 for three hours. Arctic Nature Tours (☎ 777 3300) be-side the church, also offers trips to Herschel and Banks islands, but the most popular is an excursion to the village of Tuktoyaktuk. Beaufort Delta Tours (☎ 777 4881) 163 Mackenzie Rd, offers C$20 van tours of In-uvik, as well as longer river trips and other regional tours. Canadian Arctic Adventure Tours (☎ 777 4006) specialises in winter snow mobile expeditions and Western Arc-tic Adventures (☎ 777 2594) rents canoes and kayaks from C$200 per week.

The **Great Northern Arts Festival** (☎ 777 3536) is a major show of Native art held annually during the third week of July. Many of the artists travel from tiny remote villages to display and sell their works.

Places to Stay & Eat *Chuk Park Camp-ground* (☎ 777 3613) about 6km down the Dempster Hwy, provides hot showers and firewood and charges C$12/15 without/with electricity. The camping ground has a good view of the delta and the breeze keeps the mosquitoes at bay.

In town, *Robertson's B&B* (☎ 777 3111, 41 Mackenzie Rd) has laundry and kitchen facilities and rents out bikes and canoes. *Polar B&B* (☎ 777 2554, fax 777 3668, 75 Mackenzie Rd) has similar facilities and rents canoes and kayaks. Both charge C$75/85 for singles/doubles.

All three hotels – the recommended *Mackenzie Hotel* (☎ 777 2861, fax 777 3317), the *Eskimo Inn* (☎ 777 2801, toll-free ☎ 1-800 661 0725, fax 777 3234) and the *Finto Motel Inn* (☎ 777 2647, toll-free ☎ 1-800 661 0843, fax 777 3442) – charge about C$120 for a single or double room.

Muskox and caribou burgers are on just about every menu in town. For less carniv-orous fare, *Café Gallery* (☎ 777 2888, 28 Mackenzie Rd) has a bakery with muffins featuring local blueberries. It also has local artwork on display. Next door, *Tamarack Health Foods* (☎ *777 2730*) serves organic and other foods. The *Green Briar Restaurant* in the Mackenzie Hotel offers local specialities and on some nights a popular prime rib special for C$10. It also has a popular pub and *The Zoo* dance club.

On Thursdays, the striking *Ingamo Hall* (☎ *777 2166, 20 Mackenzie Rd*) serves lunches to village elders and visitors are welcome to join them and listen to the story-telling. For a wild time, *The Mad Trapper* (☎ *777 3825, 124 Mackenzie Rd*) traps locals and visitors alike in an often raucous pub setting.

Getting There & Away The Mike Zubko Airport is 12km south of town. Canadian North (☎ 661 2951, toll-free ☎ 1-800 661 1505) flies to Norman Wells and Yellowknife; First Air (☎ 777 2341, toll-free ☎ 1-800 661 0789) flies to Yellowknife; Air North (☎ 668 2228, toll-free ☎ 1-800 661 0407) flies to Dawson City and Whitehorse; and Aklak Air (☎ 777 3777) has scheduled and charter service to the small Arctic communities. A cab for one to/from the airport costs C$25; try United Taxi (☎ 777 5050). For information on the Dempster Hwy, see the Yukon section earlier in this chapter.

THE ARCTIC COAST
Aklavik
Aklavik, 113km north of the Arctic Circle and about 50km west of Inuvik, is home to 700 Inavaluit and the Gwich'in people who, over the centuries, have traded, competed and battled. For a time, Aklavik was the administrative centre for the area, but serious flooding and erosion in the Mackenzie Delta prompted the national government shift to Inuvik in the mid-1950s.

The **Mad Trapper Jamboree**, held at Easter, keeps alive the memory of Albert Johnson, the Mad Trapper of Rat River, who murdered other trappers for their gold fillings. He was finally gunned down in 1932, in a shootout with the Mounties at Eagle River after he'd killed one of their of-

ficers. For local information, call the hamlet office (☎ 978 2351). Most visitors arrive on tours from Inuvik, but it's also accessible by ice road in winter.

Tuktoyaktuk
About 137km north-east of Inuvik in Kugmallit Bay on the Arctic coast is the village of Tuktoyaktuk, better known to tongue-tied outsiders as just Tuk. The surrounding landscape is dotted with *pingos* – huge mounds of earth and ice caused by frost heaves. Originally the home of the whale-hunting Karngmalit or Mackenzie Inuit, it's now a major land base for Beaufort Sea oil and gas explorations. Pods of **beluga whales** migrate past in July and August, and there's an old military base that dates from the Cold War. You can also visit several **old whalers' buildings** and two charming churches dating from an early rivalry between Catholic and Anglican missionaries.

Land access is limited to winter ice roads and most tourists arrive in summer on half-day tours from Inuvik, which invariably feature the chance to plunge your feet into the Arctic Ocean. The hamlet office (☎ 977 2286) can provide more information on the area and services.

Paulatuk
The small Karngmalit community of Paulatuk (population 110) lies at the southern end of Darnley Bay near the mouth of the Hornaday River, about 400km east of Inuvik. Its name, which means 'soot of coal' is derived from the nearby **Smoking Hills**, which contain smouldering sulphide-rich slate and coal seams. For more information, contact the hamlet office (☎ 580 3531).

Paulatuk lies just 60km west of the wild and untouched **Tuktut Nogait National Park Reserve**, which is a major staging ground for caribou migration. For information, contact Parks Canada (☎ 777 3248, fax 777 4491) Box 1840, Inuvik, X0E 0T0.

Banks Island
Banks Island, one of the few Northwest Territories' islands in the Arctic Archipelago,

has probably been inhabited for at least 3500 years. Today, Arctic wildlife is abundant and it's certainly one of the best places in northern Canada to see muskoxen, snow geese and sea birds. The only settlement is Sachs Harbour (Ikaahuk), an Inavaluit community of 140 people.

Aulavik National Park, at the northern end of the island, takes in 12,300 sq km and features the world's greatest concentration of muskoxen, as well as some lovely badlands, tundra and archaeological sites. Arctic Nature Tours (☎ 777 3300) in Inuvik operates guided tours. Locally, accommodation is available at *Kuptana's Guest House* (☎ 690 4151) which organises nature tours and charges C$175 per person with meals. For more information, contact the Sachs Harbour hamlet office (☎ 690 4351) or Parks Canada (☎ 777 3248, fax 777 4491), Box 1840, Inuvik, X0E 0T0.

Nunavut

☎ 867

Until the end of WWII, the Canadian far north was seen as a barren and desolate place, inhabited by primitive peoples and containing vast mineral resources that were there only to be exploited. After 1945, however, these far-flung fringes of the former Northwest Territories (NWT) became strategic. Weather stations were established and war-related accelerations in air travel, radar and turbine technology brought outside contact to previously remote communities.

However, to the politicians in southern Canada, the vast north remained an untapped mineral resource. Prior to 1967, the NWT was governed by a non-resident Commissioner and a council based in Ottawa, but in that year, a planeload of administrators arrived in Yellowknife to establish a new capital. For the first time, local residents had a say in the future of their territory.

In 1982, after much debate and argument, it was decided to divide the NWT into two sections: the eastern part would be known as Nunavut – which means simply 'our

land' – while the western section would remain the Northwest Territories. On 1 April 1999, Nunavut came into existence, with a population that was roughly 80% indigenous (in the new NWT it's only 52%).

For most outsiders, the size of Nunavut is mind-boggling. It comprises a total of about 2.2 million sq km and stretches from Ellesmere Island in the north and Baffin Island in the east to Victoria Island in the west. In the south, it dips down into Hudson and James Bays to Belcher, Akimiski and Charlton islands, just off the Ontario coast.

Nearly every known mineral is found in the region and mining is likely to play a major part in its development. Because indigenous peoples have negotiated royalties on profits derived from natural resource extraction (oil, natural gas and mining) as well as cash compensation for the use of their land, the people are looking at a great deal of potential wealth.

In addition to hydrocarbons and other mineral resources, Nunavut also intends to develop its renewable resources. Fur trading is perhaps the region's oldest 'industry' and was once commercially significant for the local people. Caribou, moose, muskoxen and game birds all provide food, while their antlers and horns are used for carving and, in the case of the muskoxen, their wool *(qiviut)* is used for clothing. Marine mammals are also exploited, but public opinion in many places opposes the seal harvest. Fishing and forestry are also developing, although agriculture generally adds little to the northern economy – mainly due to permafrost and the Arctic climate.

Tourism in the north is also growing economically important. Not only does it provide employment for the local people in the service industries, but it also improves sales of local crafts, such as soapstone carving and leather working, which have long proven to be popular with visitors. Hunting is also being exploited to bring in funds. Each Inuit village is permitted to kill a specified number of polar bears, and these hunting rights may be sold to non-residents. Given that polar bear hunting is legal nowhere else in the world, this has the potential to become a very lucrative business.

When Nunavut was established, most of its indigenous people harboured hopes that it would become a rising force in Canadian politics. Far from being a lone voice from above the tree line, it will have considerable control over its lucrative mineral resources. The indigenous peoples of Canada will at last be heard.

BAFFIN REGION

Politically, Nunavut revolves around the Baffin Region, which is home to the capital, Iqaluit. Not a single tree grows in this lonely country, but numerous flowers bloom during the short summer, and in the autumn, the tundra bursts into vibrant colours.

Iqaluit

In 1984, the town that was formerly known as Frobisher Bay changed its name back to Iqaluit (pronounced ee-KAL-oo-it), its original Inuit name meaning 'salmon trout'. (Make an effort to avoid the English-language habit of inserting a 'u' after the 'q', as it means something quite rude.) With a population of 4000, it's the new capital of Nunavut and although there's little to do in the town itself, there are a number of worthwhile day trips and several excellent hiking trails. These are marked by *inukshuks* (meaning 'human-like' but actually referring to cairns) and lead past archaeological sites and out onto the tundra.

The Unikkaarvik or Baffin Regional Visitors Centre (☎ 979 4636, fax 979 1261) has information on the entire territory, as well as displays on local wildlife and culture in the adjoining museum.

Things to See & Do The **Qaummaarviit Historic Park**, 12km by boat or dogsled from Iqaluit, preserves an historic settlement, complete with reconstructed sod houses and artefacts, which lasted for 750 years. The visitors centre can organise transport and tours from town.

The reputable Eetuk Outfitting & Equipment Rental (☎ 979 1984, fax 979 1994)

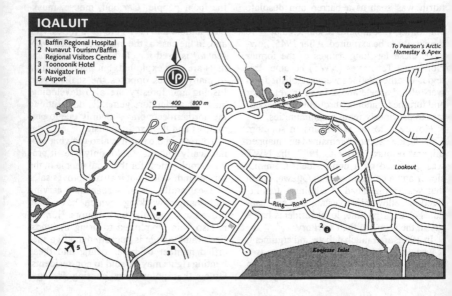

IQALUIT

1 Baffin Regional Hospital
2 Nunavut Tourism/Baffin Regional Visitors Centre
3 Toonoonik Hotel
4 Navigator Inn
5 Airport

0   400   800 m

To Pearson's Arctic Homestay & Apex

Ring Road

Lookout

Ring Road

Koojesse Inlet

can custom design any kind of Arctic journey. Inuit Sea Kayaking (☎ 979 2055, toll-free ☎ 1-888 850 0059, fax 979 2414) arranges trips around South Baffin Island.

In April, the week-long **Toonik Tyme festival** (☎ 979 5617) celebrates Inuit culture with games and contests (including igloo-building!).

Places to Stay & Eat *Pearson's Arctic Homestay (☎ 979 6408)* run by a colourful former mayor, offers B&B for C$100 per person. The *Toonoonik Hotel (☎ 979 6733, fax 979 4210)* has a dining room and charges C$100/125 for singles/doubles. The recommended *Navigator Inn (☎ 979 6201, fax 979 0427)* has rooms from C$139/154, and its restaurant stages a popular Saturday night all-you-can-eat pizza feast.

Pangnirtung

Pangnirtung (commonly called Pang) has about 1100 residents and lies alongside a lovely, mountain-flanked fjord at the entrance to Auyuittuq National Park. Located at the southern end of Pangnirtung Pass, 40km south of the Arctic Circle, it serves as a launch point for park visitors. The Angmarlik Visitors Centre (☎ 473 8737, fax 473 8685) provides the chance to meet the locals and examine displays of Inuit life. It also dispenses information on local guides and outfitters.

The **Uqqurmiut Centre for Arts & Crafts** is an excellent place to look for woven tapestries. There are also a couple of worthwhile hiking trails. One three-hour option follows the Duval River, while the track along the Ikuvik River takes about six hours and provides fine views of the fjord. About 50km south of town, an old whaling station is preserved in the **Kekerten National Historic Park**, where trails lead past the remains of 19th century houses, tools and graves. An interpretative centre provides background information. From Pangnirtung, the return trip by boat takes about 12 hours, including a tour.

Accommodation options include the *Pisuktinu-Tungavik Campground* and the *Auyuittuq Lodge (☎ 473 8955, ☎ 473 8611)*

which charges C$120 per person. Both First Air (☎ 473 8960, toll-free ☎ 1-800 267 1247) and Air Nunavut (☎ 979 4018) connect Pangnirtung with Iqaluit.

Auyuittuq National Park

Auyuittuq National Park, with an area of 21,500 sq km, encompasses a pristine wilderness of mountains, valleys, fjords and meadows. Pronounced 'ah-you-EE-tuk', the name means 'the land that never melts'. The most popular activity in the area is the 97km **Akshayuk Pass hiking route**, which is open between late June and early September, while intrepid climbers head for Mt Thor, with its incredible 1500m granite cliff face.

For information, contact Parks Canada (☎ 473 8828, fax 473 8612, nunavut_info @pch.gc.ca) which has an office in Pangnirtung. Park entry costs C$15 per day. Hikers

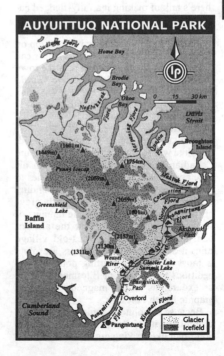

AUYUITTUQ NATIONAL PARK

and climbers who get into trouble are responsible for rescue expenses, so make sure you have insurance.

The park has primitive *camping grounds* at Overlord and Summit Lake, both on the Akshayuk Pass route, and there are also seven emergency shelters along the way. The southern end of the park is best reached from Pangnirtung, 25km away. For much of the year, this entails a C$75 snow mobile trip, but in July and August, you can hike it in two days.

Pond Inlet

Amid peaks, glaciers and icebergs, this town of 1200 at the northern tip of Baffin Island is also the access point for the renowned bird sanctuary on **Bylot Island**. Each summer, this offshore nesting ground attracts snow geese and numerous sea birds such as murres and kittiwakes. The surrounding waters are rich in marine life and there's talk of making it a fully-fledged national park.

The Nattinnak Centre (☎ 899 8226, fax 899 8246) in Pond Inlet has information on the area and on local outfitters. Visitors can camp at the *camping ground* near the town or stay at the shockingly expensive *Sauniq Hotel (☎ 899 8928, fax 899 8364)* which charges C$230 per person, with meals.

Resolute

On the southern tip of Cornwallis Island, Resolute was founded after WWII when the Canadian government established an air base and moved in several Inuit families to protect territorial claims. The surrounding land resembles a moonscape with grey-brown rocks, interrupted by the remains of several crashed planes (near the airport, oddly enough) and centuries-old village ruins near the beach. For visitors, Resolute is most useful as a starting point for expeditions to Bathurst or Ellesmere islands, or excursions to the magnetic and geographic North Poles.

Because Resolute (population 200) isn't brimming with visitor activities, those who don't feel like striking out across the tundra on day hikes may want to pay a visit to **Beechey Island**, south-west of town. In this desolate site, the ill-fated Franklin expedition wintered in 1845-46 before vanishing forever. Many traces of these men and their unsuccessful rescuers remain.

Jessco Logistics (☎ 403-282 2268, fax 403-282 2195) handles expedition support and also runs tours through its Arctic Watch subsidiary. Terry Jesudason organises all forms of travel from Resolute and manages *Tudjaat Inns North (☎ 252 3900, fax 252 3766)* a delightful family-style lodge which charges C$185 per person including home-cooked meals; don't miss the pecan pie.

Thanks to its 'hub' status, Resolute is well-served by air. Canadian North (☎ 252 3880, toll-free ☎ 1-800 665 1177) flies jets to Cambridge Bay and Yellowknife. First Air (☎ 252 3981, toll-free ☎ 1-800 267 1247) flies to these towns plus Iqaluit, and also offers charters. Kenn Borek Air (☎ 252 3845) serves Pond Inlet and offers charters.

Haughton Crater

About 160km east of Resolute on Devon Island is a desolate place called Haughton Crater that was formed 23 million years ago when a meteorite hit the earth here with the force of a 1000-megaton nuclear bomb. Despite the bland featureless terrain, increasing numbers of scientists visit the area, excited to find a place that is probably the closest replica of Mars on earth.

The otherwise arid landscape bears some of the same patterns of seasonal water flow that can be found on the Martian surface, which, like Haughton Crater is largely formed of material from meteor impacts. Teams from NASA and other scientific agencies are finding that the 24km-wide crater is an ideal place to test equipment that will be used on future probes to the red planet.

Grise Fjord

Grise Fjord (population 148) at the southern tip of Ellesmere Island, is the northernmost civilian community in Canada and rivals Pangnirtung as the most beautifully located

From Cornwallis to Lewinsky

Who would have guessed that the sex scandal involving US President Bill Clinton and Monica Lewinsky would have an Arctic angle? But it does and the story begins in 1845 with the loss of the Franklin expedition.

The failure of Sir John Franklin and his 129 officers and seamen to return to England from their search for the Northwest Passage caused several rescue parties to be dispatched over the next few years. None was successful in finding traces of what has become one of the great Arctic mysteries and many were lucky not to suffer the same fate as Franklin and his men. One ill-fated mission consisted of four British ships that were frozen solid in ice off Cornwallis Island during the winter of 1854. That summer the crews were themselves rescued; one later described the island as 'one of the most dreary and desolate spots that can well be conceived'. The ships were left in the ice, where it was assumed they would eventually be crushed and sink.

However, one – the HMS *Resolute* – proved aptly named because the following year it was found floating over 1900km east by American whalers. The small sailing ship was in excellent condition given the rigours of its recent past. The whalers sailed the boat to Connecticut where it was purchased by the American government. To show that there were no hard feelings over 30 years after the British Army had torched the then-new White House during the War of 1812, the US government spent $40,000 restoring the *Resolute*. In 1856, the US returned the ship to Queen Victoria as a gift. This gesture was warmly received and long remembered by the monarch. In 1880 a huge box arrived at the White House (long since rebuilt) containing a massive oak desk built from the timbers of the *Resolute* when it was finally scrapped.

Tipping the scales at almost 600kg, the Resolute desk (as it was named) proved more than able to hold the weighty affairs of state and was used as a personal desk by every president until John F Kennedy was assassinated in 1963. Lyndon Johnson, however, tried to put his mark on the White House by banishing anything Kennedy had used and the desk was exiled to the Smithsonian Institution which placed it on display.

In 1977 the newly elected Jimmy Carter had the desk returned to the Oval Office where it has since been used by Presidents Ronald Reagan, George Bush and Bill Clinton. It's while in service with the latter that one of the most colourful moments of its career occurred. On the evening of 15 November 1995, the president made several calls to members of Congress. It was later revealed during the Senate impeachment hearings in 1998 that while Clinton had been chatting, Monica Lewinsky had been conducting her own business with the head of state. The Resolute desk had no problem supporting this affair, either.

---

village in Nunavut. Oddly enough, its Inuit name is Aujuittuq, which (as with the national park) means 'the land that never melts'.

Local boat owners can arrange tours to the spot where the sea ice meets the open water, about 50km east of the village. Here, you'll have a good chance of seeing walrus, belugas, seals, polar bears and a variety of sea birds. Along **South Cape Fjord**, 40km west of town, the seas are often choked with

icebergs, ensuring interesting photography. The area is also dotted with **archaeological sites,** including an ancient polar bear trap, abandoned Inuit camps and the cross erected to a sailor who died on the Otto Sverdrup expedition.

The *Grise Fjord Lodge (☎ 980 9913, fax 980 9954)* charges C$195 per person, including meals. Alternatively, you can camp free of charge at several inviting streamside sites outside the village. Access is with Kenn Borek Air (☎ 252 3845, fax 252 3777) from Resolute.

Ellesmere Island National Park

Right up at the top of the world is Ellesmere Island National Park, which surely represents one of the world's most pristine wilderness areas and is for wealthy wilderness seekers only.

The park became known to the world when *National Geographic* published a haunting story and photos of its packs of pale-coloured Arctic wolves. Because so few folk can afford to get there, there's no need to be concerned with crowds. While most areas of the park are worthwhile, some highlights include **Cape Columbia**, the northernmost point of North America; **Mt Barbeau**, one of the highest peaks on the eastern side of the continent; several irregular geothermal oases; lovely **Lake Hazen**; and numerous High Arctic icecaps and glaciers.

Several adventure tour companies stage park trips from Resolute, but note that a 10-seater chartered plane starts at around C$18,000, and that's just for transport. For information, contact Parks Canada (☎ 473 8828, ☎ 473 8612) in Pangnirtung.

KITIKMEOT REGION

This seemingly limitless area of tundra encompasses the Arctic coast of the mainland as well as nearby islands. Cambridge Bay (population 1400) in the south-east of Victoria Island, is the administrative centre for the Kitikmeot region and home to a large military early-warning radar station. In the early days, it was frequented by explorers in search of the Northwest Passage and the remains of Roald Amundsen's schooner *Maud* still languishes in the harbour. On a short hike from town, you can climb **Mt Pelly** (220m) and perhaps observe muskoxen. The **Queen Maud Bird Sanctuary**, south across Queen Maud Gulf, is the world's largest migratory bird sanctuary.

The Arctic Coast Visitors Centre (☎ 983 2224, fax 983 2302) has displays on the exploration of the Northwest Passage and

organises tours. The *Arctic Islands Lodge (☎ 983 2345, fax 983 2480)* is relatively swank by Nunavut standards and charges C$205 per person, with meals.

KIVALLIQ REGION

In the south, the Kivalliq Region sprawls across the broad, rocky tundra plateaux and countless lakes of the Canadian Shield. Although its boundaries take in much of the former District of Keewatin, along the shores of Hudson Bay, it's home to only 4800 people. Most of the predominantly Inuit population lives in settlements along the western shores of Hudson Bay.

Rankin Inlet

Founded in 1955 as a mining centre, Rankin Inlet, with 2000 people, is Kivalliq's largest community and also its government and transport centre. Rankin Inlet's few visitors are mainly intent on fishing – either in Hudson Bay or in the myriad rivers and lakes. **Meliadine Park**, 5km from town, is popular for hiking and berry-picking. You can also hike to the **Ijiraliq Archaeological Site**, at the mouth of the Meliadine River, to see some ruined 15th century underground houses.

Out in Hudson Bay, about 50km from Rankin Inlet, lies **Marble Island**, where Northwest Passage aspirant James Knight and his crew met their demise in the 18th century. It's also the site of several ruined 19th century whaling ships. The Kivalliq Regional Visitors Centre (☎ 645 5091, fax 645 5067) has area information and historical displays. The *Nanuq Inn (☎ 645 2513, fax 645 2393)* offers basic single/double rooms for C$99/152, without meals.

First Air (☎ 645 2961, toll-free ☎ 1-800 267 1247) and Canadian North (☎ 645 2746, toll-free ☎ 1-800 665 1177) fly between Rankin Inlet and Yellowknife, Winnipeg and Iqaluit. The commuter affiliate Calm Air connects it to Arviat, Baker Lake and Repulse Bay.

Arviat

The town of Arviat, formerly Eskimo Point, is Nunavut's most southerly settle-

The Canadian Shield

The Canadian Shield, one of Canada's most prominent physical features, surrounds Hudson Bay on the east, south and west in a vast U-shaped chunk of real estate which more or less resembles a shield. In the north, it stretches 3000km north-westward from the Atlantic Ocean on the coast of Labrador, past Lake Winnipeg, to Lake Athabasca, Great Slave Lake, Great Bear Lake and on to the Arctic Ocean. From the Hudson Bay area, it stretches southward all the way to Lake Superior, on the US-Canada border, and south-east to the St Lawrence River around Kingston, Ontario.

And just what is it? Well, it's best described as a mass of ancient, stable rock, the first region of the continent raised permanently above the sea. The predominantly igneous, fossil-free, stratified rock from the archaeozoic period is among the world's oldest. The entire region was scraped and gouged by glaciers, resulting in an almost uniformly flat to undulating rocky surface very sparsely and intermittently covered with soil. Rarely across its expanse does it rise more than 500m above sea level. Many of the dips, dents, cracks and pits in the surface are filled with water – lakes, rivers and ponds of every shape and size. In several sections, as much as 40% of the surface is fresh water.

The southern sections tend to be forested, and in Manitoba, these boreal woodlands extend as far north as Churchill. Further north the trees diminish, and eventually disappear altogether, leaving lichen and mosses as the principal vegetation.

The southern areas, bordering as they do much of the heavily populated regions of the country, have become part of the Canadian mental landscape. Synonymous with outdoor living, camping, cottages, hiking, fishing and wildlife, this generally inhospitable but wildly beautiful land is part of the quintessential Canada.

ARCTIC CANADA

ment. Originally, it served as a summer camp site for Inuit groups living along the western shore of Hudson Bay. Today, its 1100 people rely on fishing, hunting and trapping. The Margaret Aniksak Visitors Centre (☎ 857 2698) provides information and displays on vibrant local artwork.

From Arviat you can arrange a trip south to **McConnell River Bird Sanctuary**. From June onwards, it serves as a nesting site for 400,000 snow geese, as well as snowy owls, Arctic terns, falcons and other birds.

Baker Lake

Geographically, Baker Lake is just about in the heart of Canada. It's best known for its fishing opportunities and also serves as a departure point for canoe or raft trips on the Kazan and Thelon Rivers. A worthwhile excursion will take you to the **Thelon Game Sanctuary** west of town, which was founded

in 1927 by the federal government to save the then-endangered muskox.

The Akumalik Visitors Centre (☎ 793 2456) is open in summer only and has area information.

Repulse Bay

Straddling the Arctic Circle at the southern end of the Melville Peninsula, Repulse Bay's natural harbour has long been a launching point for whaling expeditions. Today, it's known as a whale-watching venue, and the Arviq Hunters and Trappers Association (☎ 462 4334, fax 462 4335) can organise cruises to see belugas and narwhals (August is the best time). Fishing trips are also on offer.

Gjoa Haven

Dubbed 'the finest harbour in the world' by Roald Amundsen, Gjoa Haven, on King

William Island, was named for the ship that carried the intrepid explorer through the Northwest Passage. The original Norwegian pronunciation (GYEW-ah HAH-ven) has been replaced by 'Joe Haven', but it's better known by locals as Uqsuqtuuq, the 'place of much fat'.

An interesting short excursion is to the **Northwest Passage Territorial Historic Park,** just over 3km from the village. Here you can see the 'magnet', a shelter constructed from packing crates and filled with sand, where Amundsen and his men could make magnetic observations, and the 'observatory', where he stored his scientific instruments. Nearby, Amundsen erected a cairn in honour of his mentor, George von Neumayer, as well as a marble slab which he used to support his delicate instruments. The site also contains the grave of William Harold, a Hudson's Bay Company employee who froze to death here in 1905. There are also several other graves, some of which are thought to contain members of the crew from the Franklin expedition. The old wooden ship on the shore is the *Qingalik,* which was hauled in by barge in 1993.

A good *camp site* is Swan Lake, about 2km north of the village. The *Amundsen Hotel (☎ 360 6176, fax 360 6283),* charges C$210 per person, including meals.

Northern Manitoba

☎ 204
CHURCHILL
After Winnipeg, Churchill is Manitoba's greatest tourist draw, and nearly every photo you've ever seen of polar bears was taken in this ursine paradise. The best news is that this is one of northern Canada's few outposts which are readily accessible: you can get there on the rail line that heads north from the Manitoba capital, Winnipeg.

Despite its remote location and climatic extremes – July and August are the only months without snow – the Churchill area is one of the oldest European settlements in Canada. The first Hudson's Bay Company

(HBC) outpost was set up here in 1717 and named for Lord Churchill, Governor of the HBC and later the first Duke of Marlborough.

Much of the exploration and settlement of the Canadian west began here, and at one time, it also served as one of the largest grain-handling ports in the world. The railway was completed in 1929, providing the prairie regions with easy access to an ocean port that's nearer to Europe than Montreal is. After some years of decline, grain is again flowing through, thanks to new management. About 20km east of town, on the site of the former Churchill Research Range, the government recently constructed a C$250 million communications satellite launching and monitoring station, but unfortunately, the project was declared a bust after just one launch.

Nowadays, Churchill's 1000 people are relying more on tourism and rightfully bills itself the Polar Bear Capital of the World. Indeed, it lies right on a major polar bear migration route, which means the great white bears often wander into the township. During September and October, visitors ride out onto the tundra in large motorised buggies to see them doing their polar bear thing.

The tourist information office is on Kelsey Rd, opposite the train station. Towards the town centre, in the Royal Bank building, Parks Canada (☎ 675 8863) operates a visitors centre and a small museum showing polar bear films and displaying articles relating to the history of the Hudson's Bay Company. So ubiquitous was this enterprise that it's been said that HBC actually stands for 'Here Before Christ'. The knowledgeable park staff answer questions and sometimes perform live shows (appalling but humorous) about the history of the region.

Wildlife
The area around Churchill is wild and starkly beautiful. The coastline is heaped with huge quartzite boulders worn smooth by the retreating glaciers, and in summer the tundra is covered in red, orange and violet wildflowers. There is an incredible variety of wildlife to see, from polar bears to beluga whales,

and during winter it's one of the best places in the world for watching the aurora borealis (northern lights). Other wildlife in the Churchill area includes seals, beaver, caribou, grey wolves, lemmings and Arctic foxes.

In late September and into October, as many as 150 **polar bears** begin making their way from their inland summer retreats to the coastal areas, where the ice is beginning to form on the sea. After a summer diet of berries and grasses, they're keen to start hunting seals again. Around this time, local authorities maintain a 24-hour vigil to protect humans and would-be urban bears from each other. Bears that do lumber into town are trapped and carted off to the out-of-town polar bear 'jail' before being released onto the ice. If you see a bear in town, phone their hotline (☎ BEAR or 2327).

The safest way to see polar bears at close range is on a tour. Tundra Buggy Tours (☎ 675 2121, toll-free ☎ 1-800 544 5049) and Great White Bear Tours (☎ 675 2781, toll-free ☎ 1-800 765 8344) charge C$165 with lunch. Some trips include an overnight stay in a Tundra Buggy Lodge. In summer, prices drop to C$75 for a four-hour excursion to watch caribou, birds and foxes.

During summer, from around mid-June until the end of August, up to 3000 **beluga whales** move into the Churchill River, drawn by warmer water and large schools of capelin. Belugas were heavily hunted right up until 1968, but hunting is now limited to the Inuit, who are permitted to take a small number. The whales are readily spotted from the shore, but you'll have an even better view from a boat tour. Normally, the whales swim right up to the boat and a special underwater microphone allows passengers to hear the extraordinary song which inspired early whalers to call them 'sea canaries'.

From late May, it's possible to see up to 200 species of birds around Churchill, including the rare Ross's gull. More common visitors include Pacific and red-throated loons, Smiths' longspurs, Arctic terns, yellow warblers and snow geese. From late June to mid-August it's also possible to see up to 40 species of rare tundra butterflies. Cape Merry,

the Granary Ponds by the port, Bird Cove and Akudlik Marsh, 4km south of Churchill, are all excellent **bird-watching** spots.

Sea North Tours (☎ 675 2195) is run by Mike and Doreen Macri and specialises in boat and sea-life tours. A 2½ hour boat tour, which includes Fort Prince of Wales and most likely dozens of whales at close range (no guarantee) costs around C$50. Scuba diving tours with the whales can also be arranged. Another recommendation is Churchill Wilderness Encounter (☎ 675 2248) run by Bonnie Chartier who uses her extensive knowledge of local flora, birdlife and history on mini-bus tours which vary with the season and the clients' interests. Trips average around C$35.

Things to See & Do

The **Inuit Museum**, on La Verendrye Ave, has an excellent collection of Inuit artefacts and carvings, including kayaks from as early as 1700 BC. There are also northern fauna displays and various articles and books for sale. With the establishment of the Hudson's Bay Company outpost, Lord Churchill became the Duke of Marlborough. **Thanadelthur's Cairn** honours the Chipewyan woman who made the outpost possible by arranging a peace treaty between local warring tribes. The small cairn is located behind the Anglican church.

Four **National Historic Sites** around Churchill are administered by Parks Canada. The partially restored **Fort Prince of Wales**, built on the peninsula head opposite Cape Merry, was intended to protect the HBC's fur trade from potential interlopers. It took 40 years to build but was never seriously active, and was surrendered to the French without a shot fired.

Sloop's Cove, 4km upriver from the fort, was used by European whaling and trading boats. Names of some of the early Hudson's Bay Company people, including that of 18th century governor Samuel Hearn, are carved into the rocks there.

The third site, **Cape Merry**, a 2km walk west of town, bears the remains of a stone battery built in 1746. In summer it's a good spot for whale watching and along the way you'll see lots of birds, but check first on the bear situation and don't forget your bug repellent.

Bird Cove, 15km east of town, offers superb bird-watching, and along the way, you can see the wreck of the *Ithaca*, a freighter which went down in a 1961 storm. The decks of the freighter are rusted through and unsafe to explore.

The **Boreal Gardens** are about 1.5km east of town on Shore Rd. These local gardens and greenhouses produce vegetables for local consumption. In July and August, free tours are offered on Sunday afternoons from 2 to 4 pm. Housed on the site of the old rocket range 25km east of town, the **Northern Studies Centre** (☎ 675 2307) houses researchers from around the world and offers a variety of Arctic studies courses.

In 1996, 11,000 sq km **Wapuska National Park** was created 45km south-east of town along the shores of Hudson Bay. This massive wetland area protects polar bear breeding dens and habitat for hundreds of thousands of birds. Public access and the level of tourism to be permitted was still being determined at the time of writing. For details, visit the Churchill Parks Canada office (☎ 675 8863).

Farther afield, 250km south-east of Churchill, lies **York Factory**, which operated as a fur trading post for 250 years and in the 18th and 19th centuries, served as a major focus of HBC activities. The remaining wooden building, built around 1832, has no foundations so it can 'ride' the permafrost. There are also other ruins, a cemetery and quite a few artefacts. It's accessible only by air or canoe.

Places to Stay

The best value option is *Vera Gould's B&B* (☎ 675 2544, 87 Hearne St) where a modern bungalow costs C$30 per person (C$40 in bear season), including a superb Canadian-style breakfast. Comfortable *La Peruse* (☎ 675 2254, 100 Button St) run by the same family, charges C$36/50 for singles/doubles

from June to September and C$45/70 during bear season. Both of these places rent old bicycles.

The *Bear Country Inn* (☎ 675 8299, 126 Kelsey Blvd) is recommended for its friendly, casual atmosphere and charges C$68/78 (C$10 more at bear time). More expensive is the *Polar Inn* (☎ 675 8878, 15 Franklin St) where rooms cost C$77/84 and mountain bikes can be rented for C$22 per day. It also operates a big-bucks lodge across the Churchill River, where you can watch the bears right outside this heavily-screened former brothel. On the corner of Kelsey Blvd and Franklin St is the straightforward *Churchill Motel* (☎ 675 8853) with rooms at C$75/85 all year.

Places to Eat

Gypsy's Bakery, east along Kelsey Blvd, serves good soups, sandwiches and pastries. It's open daily until 8 pm. The attractive, log *Lazy Bear Café*, on Kelsey Blvd at Button St, serves chilli in a bowl of bread for C$6 and often sizzles up wild meat, including caribou and muskox. The *Traders' Table*, at the other end of Kelsey Blvd, is the most pleasant restaurant for dinner. On the menu, you'll find steak, Arctic char (the local fish) and desserts featuring locally grown berries. An evening meal costs around C$24.

Getting There & Away

Access to Churchill is by air or rail. For the former, book with Canadian Airlines (☎ 632 1250) or Calm Air (toll-free ☎ 1-800 839 2256) at least two weeks in advance or you'll pay a bundle.

Between Winnipeg and Churchill, northbound trains run at 10 pm on Sunday, Tuesday and Thursday, arriving at 8.30 am two days later, while southbound services depart at 10 pm on Saturday, Tuesday and Thursday, also arriving at 8.30 am two days later. You can choose between seats, berths and small rooms. If you book a week in advance, the fare is C$250. With less advance notice, it climbs to C$410. Normally, it's only full in midsummer and during bear season.

Greenland

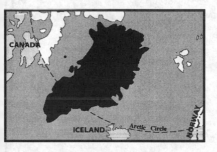

It's said that once a traveller has seen the world, there's always Greenland. Even today, as international travel grows more commonplace, the world's largest island continues to loom distant and mysterious on the travel horizon. Anyone who has ever flown between Europe and North America has probably heard the pilot announce that Greenland lies 35,000 feet below, and then looked out the window to see either a rugged coast, studded with icebergs, or a vast sheet of seemingly dimensionless ice. Understandably, many folk would question why anyone would want to visit such a place on purpose!

The dramatic landscape seems forbidding at times and expresses itself in variations on Arctic conditions: rocky snow-topped peaks; thousands of lakes; fields of both dry and boggy tundra; long, sinuous fjords; and expansive sheets and tortured rivers of ice. Because the Greenlandic interior lies locked beneath the original deep freeze, a 3000m-thick blanket of ice, the population is concentrated near the coasts, where the seas are just a degree or so above freezing and are infested with icebergs and floes. The effect is awe-inspiring. As one Greenlandic poet put it, 'I get dizzy of all this beauty and shiver with happiness'.

What you don't see from the air are the dozens of tiny, far-flung towns and villages, none of which are connected by roads. Here

live Greenland's 55,000 residents, who ironically call their scarcely populated country Kalaallit Nunaat (KHLAKH-let NOO-naht), the 'land of the people'. Not surprisingly, Greenland remains one of the emptiest countries on earth, with about 40 sq km of elbow room for every person. These friendly folk, 80% of whom claim Inuit heritage, take great pride in their country, and visitors from more crowded and less scenic countries may even detect a touch of sympathy from the locals.

Greenland is in a state of transition. As part of the Kingdom of Denmark, it struggles to reconcile its resourceful and independent past with a modern European present. Locals may drive dogsleds and snowmobiles in winter, but in summer they hop into Saabs and Toyotas and buzz down to the supermarket, where they can buy frozen seal steaks from the nearest fjord, mangoes from Mexico and packaged junk food from the USA. They may live in brightly painted Scandinavian-style bungalows or crowd into 100-unit apartment blocks (one such block in Nuuk houses 1% of the national population!) For work, they may spend their days on a fishing boat, working at a computer, or hunting seals amid the icebergs.

GETTING AROUND

Getting around in Greenland will probably be your biggest expense and your greatest source of uncertainty. The key to coping is to remember the word *immaqa* (maybe), which seems to have been invented specifically for the Greenlandic transport system. In fact, Greenlanders will tell you the name of their national airline is actually 'Immaqa Air'!

Air

Given the climate, Greenland is well served by its national airline, Grønlandsfly (Greenlandair; ☎ 328888, fax 327288, email

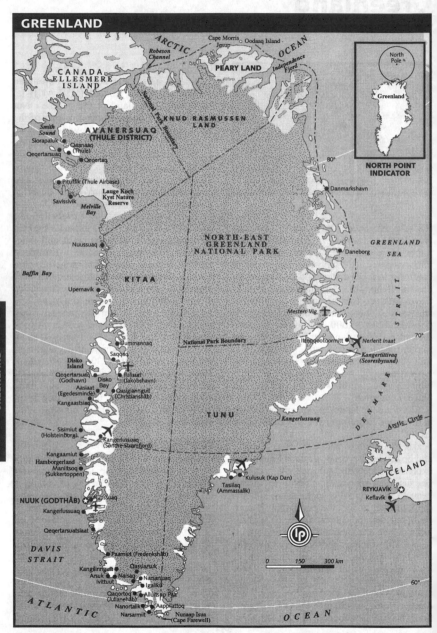

GREENLAND

GREENLAND

NORTH POINT INDICATOR

glsales@greenlandair.gl), with its fleet of Sikorsky S-61N and Bell helicopters, as well as De Havilland Twin Otters and Dash-7 fixed-wing aircraft. However, the inordinately high cost of flying means that budget-conscious travellers will want to do as little of it as possible. Grønlandsfly links the towns of Kangerlussuaq, Nuuk, Ilulissat, Narsarsuaq, Pituffik (Thule airbase), Nerlerit Inaat and Kulusuk using fixed-wing aircraft. As yet, other major towns have only helicopter service, but at the time of writing new airports were under construction at Aasiaat, Maniitsoq and Sisimiut, and were planned for Uummannaq, Upernavik and Paamiut. The possibility of an airport at Qaanaaq (Thule) was also being discussed.

The fickle Greenlandic weather prevents a rigid interpretation of flight schedules. Timetables exist mainly for convenience, but to rely on them may well amount to inconvenience. Allow plenty of leeway when booking connecting flights and remember that the weather has the final word. In winter, flights are less frequent and immaqa really comes into its own.

Around Disko Bay and south Greenland, several seats on each flight are reserved as 'Green Seats' and are discounted by about 30%. Naturally, they are snapped up quickly, so book early. Also ask about 'harpoon' or tuukkaq fares, which must be purchased 14 days in advance and offer good value, subject to certain restrictions. Grønlandsfly also has a special Max-2940 fare, which allows travel between any two Greenlandic towns, regardless of the distance or number of connections, for a maximum of Dkr2940 one way. If that seems too good to be true (as it would if you're looking at a trip from, say, Nanortalik to Qaanaaq), it may well be. To qualify, you must have confirmed advance bookings for each leg of the flight, which is almost impossible with Grønlandsfly, even at the best of times.

Grønlandsfly also operates a charter service, GLACE (☎ 328888, fax 320898, email glcharter@greennet.gl) which charters five-passenger fixed-wing aircraft to all towns with airports. For further information on Grønlandsfly, see the Web site www.greenland-guide.dk/gla.

Boat

Most independent travellers who can't afford plane and helicopter fares will probably use the west coast ferries. There's no better way to go, as they allow you to meet local people and cruise past some of the world's most breathtaking scenery. The KNI trading cooperative operates the Arctic Umiaq Line (☎ 325211, fax 323211, email aulpas@greennet.gl or kniship@greennet.gl), PO Box 608, DK-3900 Nuuk, Greenland. Its fleet of coastal ferries transports passengers up and down the west coast between Aappilattoq (near Nunaap Isua, or Cape Farewell) in the south and Upernavik in the north. They're not cruise ships by any stretch, but the three largest ferries, which handle long-distance runs, have couchettes, cabins (more like dormitories with space for four people and no locks on the doors), cafeterias and showers. The smaller ones do shorter runs and have seating room only.

For the latest schedules, bookings or updates on new vessels and routes, contact the Arctic Umiaq Line directly (the Web site at www.greenland-guide.dk/kni-ship is your best bet!) or try the Grønlands Rejsebureau (☎ 45-33 13 10 14, fax 45-33 13 85 92), Gammel Mønt 12, PO Box 130, DK-1004 Copenhagen, Denmark. You can also check out the Web site www.greenland-guide.dk/greenlandtravel.

KNI also operates a fleet of cargo boats based in district towns, which service local villages once or twice weekly. They carry up to 12 paying passengers, but limited capacity means that passengers must book well in advance.

The Norwegian company OVDS and Greenland Tourism operate tourist cruises up the west coast between Kangerlussuaq and Uummannaq (and, occasionally, all the way to Qaanaaq). Contact Greenland Cruise/OVDS Markedsafdelingen (☎ 47-76 96 76 96, fax 47-76 96 76 11, email booking@ovds.no), Havnagata 2, PO Box 43,

N-8501 Narvik, Norway, or check out the Web site at www.greenland-guide.dk/cruise.

To reach villages and points of interest not accessible by ferry or KNI cargo boat, you'll probably have to charter a boat. Most Greenlandic families own powerboats, and organising private charter to remote places shouldn't be too difficult. However, it will be expensive, as the Greenland Home Rule government has devised a complex fee schedule. Alternatively, you can find someone who's going anyway and wants to make a little extra money. For very short hauls, where the minimum official charges would be unrealistic (such as between Narsarsuaq and Qassiarsuk in south Greenland) you'll pay only several hundred kroner per person.

Car

Thanks to valley glaciers and rugged terrain, only two Greenlandic settlements – Ivittuut and Kangilinnguit – are connected by road. The longest drives in Greenland include the 70km of roads around Kangerlussuaq, the 5km between the Narsarsuaq harbour and Hospital Valley, the 8km route from Qassiarsuk to Tasiusaq, the 7km road from Nuuk to its airport, and the short routes around Arsuk and Kangilinnguit.

Even so, Greenlanders do a fair amount of driving, and even in smaller towns that can be crossed on foot in five minutes people take the car whenever they set foot out the door. Car hire is available in Nuuk and Kangerlussuaq, but otherwise, local drivers have the streets to themselves. In most towns, visitors rely on taxis, buses or their own two feet.

Dogsled

In Arctic Greenland and on the east coast, winter travel by dogsled is a common mode of transport. Individuals may privately arrange trips with local drivers, but most tourist dogsled trips are arranged by hotels and tourist offices in the respective towns. The most popular venues are Tasiilaq (Ammassalik), Uummannaq, Ilulissat, Sisimiut, Qasigiannguit and several smaller places. The high season is from March to May, when days are longer and temperatures not

as extreme as in midwinter. However, summer visitors may also sample dogsledding on Disko Island.

ACCOMMODATION
Camping

Narsarsuaq, Ilulissat and Kangerlussuaq have organised camping grounds, while most other towns have designated camping areas without facilities or charges. There are no restrictions on wilderness camping, so you can simply strike out into the bush and camp wherever you like. However, in the interests of the fragile Arctic ecosystems, you should practise minimal impact camping. If you're using a mountain stove, the local name for Coleman fuel (white gas, Shellite) is *rense bensin* or *lampeolie*. It's available from many youth hostels, tourist offices, shops and even petrol stations.

Greenland on a Shoestring

It is possible to see Greenland on a limited budget, minimising transport and accommodation costs and limiting food expenses by self-catering using food purchased from the harbour markets and supermarkets or from the bush or the sea.

The best way to keep accommodation costs down is to bring a tent. You can camp anywhere in Greenland outside villages and, although there are no facilities available, water is normally plentiful and camp sites are free (the only exceptions are at Ilulissat, Narsarsuaq and Kangerlussuaq, which have organised camping grounds). Those who prefer solid shelter can resort to youth hostels, STI hostels and sheep farmers' huts. For more information, refer to the Accommodation section within this chapter.

The only way to avoid transport costs is to walk, bring your own sea kayak or fly into a particular region and fully explore it. However, the Thule area and any of east Greenland apart from Ammassalik will be off limits to budget travellers.

Hostels

Most budget travellers wind up staying in the pleasant youth hostels, or *vandrehjemmene*. They're maintained independently by villages, tourist offices, travel agencies or private individuals, and nearly every city and town has one. Most have kitchens and hot showers, some offer laundry facilities, and they aren't overly concerned with rules, regulations and curfews. You'll normally need your own sleeping bag, although some places provide bedding for an additional Dkr50 per night. The least expensive hostels charge around Dkr120 per night, but the average cost is Dkr150. The hostels in Narsarsuaq, Narsaq and Ilulissat are loosely affiliated with the Danish Youth Hostel Association, but there's no discount for association members.

The hostels formerly owned by Nuna-Tek, the Greenland Home Rule government institution responsible for public works, have been transferred to another Home Rule entity, *Sanaartortitsiviit* (STI for short) or 'building services'. They now provide housing for STI students, but during the summer holidays (from late June to mid-August), some of these hostels are open to travellers. Some STI hostels serve officially as summer youth hostels, while in others accommodation may only be arranged through local tourism authorities. Their prices are roughly the same as youth hostels and some offer meals and laundry services.

Seamen's Homes

A mid-range option is the Greenland seamen's missions or seamen's homes *(sømandshjemmene* in Danish or *umiartortuq angerlarsimaffii* in Greenlandic). As missions of the Danish Lutheran church, their original purpose was to provide clean, safe lodging for sailors and fishermen while they were in port. The Christian staff begin the day with formal prayers and hymn-singing. If you can accept this – and the regulations against alcohol and carousing – they're a viable alternative to hotels.

All seamen's homes have a cafeteria which serves snacks and *smørrebrød* (open-face sandwiches) all day, and set menus at meal times. Some rooms have private baths and hot showers; there's also a common TV room open to guests. Double rooms without/with bath cost around Dkr475/600.

Mountain Huts

In south Greenland, sheep stations in the Narsaq, Qaqortoq and Nanortalik districts make hostel-like huts available to hikers. In fact, they're locally known as 'youth hostels'. Basic dormitory-style accommodation costs an average of Dkr125 per person.

These relatively opulent huts offer comfortable accommodation, including cooking facilities (some even have video players!) and should not be confused with the more spartan shepherds' huts, which are basic little shelters where herders sleep during roundup and patrol. These are found scattered around sheep-grazing areas of south Greenland and can be used by walkers as emergency shelters. Nevertheless, remember that Greenlandic weather can be vile and never set off hiking without a tent.

The Ammassalik and Sisimiut districts have also established several mountain huts and base camps for hikers, and other areas may follow suit. Hut accommodation is also available in several abandoned villages, which are used as summer camps for hunters or schoolchildren.

Hotels

Most Greenlandic towns have at least one upmarket hotel. Though typically rather drab, they are comfortable and their restaurants and pubs may even serve as town social centres. The cheapest double rooms start at around Dkr600, while tourist-class hotels may charge over Dkr1000. Normally, rates include a continental breakfast.

South Greenland

In Greenlandic, south Greenland is sometimes known affectionately as 'Sineriak Banaaneqarfik' (banana coast), but don't be fooled – it was also the source of the island's verdant-sounding name. Many visitors to

Greenland get their first taste of the country here in the south and it's an overwhelming introduction. Nestled amid the spectacular scenery are hundreds of Norse and Eskimo ruins, colourful towns, tiny villages, sheep farms and even a hot spring in which you can bathe while watching icebergs drift past in the fjord.

NARSARSUAQ

The name of this settlement of 180 people means 'the big plain'. In fact, it's a small flat area – just big enough for the international airport – combined with a braided river delta. In April 1941, after the Nazis invaded Denmark, the USA and Denmark signed a treaty calling for temporary US supply bases in Greenland. The one at Narsarsuaq, known as 'Bluie West One', was constructed practically overnight in July 1941, five months before the USA officially entered WWII. From 1943 to 1944, a hospital was constructed on the site, which subsequently became the focus of much controversy and rumour (see the boxed text 'The Mystery of Bluie West One').

On 11 November 1958, the USA closed the Narsarsuaq hospital, and Denmark established a civilian airfield on the site the following year. On 1 January 1987, the airfield came under the jurisdiction of the Greenland Home Rule Administration. Today, all activity in Narsarsuaq revolves around the international airport, and only people who are employed in the town may live there.

For tourist information, contact the office near the museum (☎ 572493). Your best option for exchanging cash or travellers cheques is the Hotel Narsarsuaq. Foreign currency exchange is also available at the KNI Administration, which acts as the bank.

Things to See & Do

The worthwhile **Narsarsuaq Museum** includes a variety of historical exhibits on the Norse, sheep farming and the US presence in south Greenland.

There are also several great hikes, including **Signalhøjen** and **Hospital Valley**. The wonderful trek through **Flower Valley**

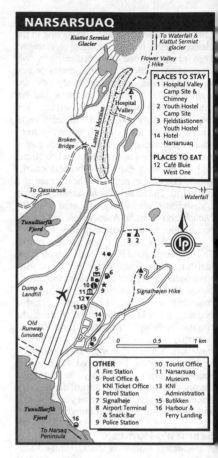

NARSARSUAQ

Kiattut Sermiat Glacier

To Waterfall & Kiattut Sermiat glacier

Flower Valley Hike

PLACES TO STAY
1 Hospital Valley Camp Site & Chimney
2 Youth Hostel Camp Site
3 Fjeldstastionen Youth Hostel
14 Hotel Narsarsuaq

PLACES TO EAT
12 Café Bluie West One

Hospital Valley

Lateral Moraine

Broken Bridge

To Qassiarsuk

Tunulliarfik Fjord

Waterfall

Dump & Landfill

Signalhøjen Hike

Old Runway (unused)

0   0.5   1 km

OTHER
4 Fire Station
5 Post Office & KNI Ticket Office
6 Petrol Station
7 Signalhøje
8 Airport Terminal & Snack Bar
9 Police Station
10 Tourist Office
11 Narsarsuaq Museum
13 KNI Administration
15 Butikken
16 Harbour & Ferry Landing

Tunulliarfik Fjord

To Narsaq Peninsula

goes up a 300m waterfall and past a prehistoric-looking lake to the snout of the **Kiattut Sermiat** glacier. From Qassiarsuk, across the fjord, you can also set out on a number of excellent hiking routes on the **Narsaq Peninsula**, including one which will take you all the way to Narsaq. Hikers should pick up the *Hikers' Guide – South Greenland*, which includes three detailed hiking maps and a descriptive booklet. It's sold at the Fjeldstastionen Youth Hostel for Dkr200.

The Mystery of Bluie West One

During WWII, an immense 250-bed hospital was constructed in Hospital Valley, north of Narsarsuaq, and the purposes of this installation remain a matter of hot contention. Rumour has it that during the Korean War, the Narsarsuaq hospital received the US military's hopeless casualties – those so badly injured they would have dampened public war enthusiasm had they gone home. Families received bottles of ashes and were told their soldiers had been killed in action.

Recent Danish research has determined that this is all rumour, and maintains that the hospital was used only for US personnel and as a way-station for Greenlandic tuberculosis patients. To support these findings, the museum in Narsarsuaq displays photos of the hospital in action and contains letters from personnel who vouch that there was no activity there during the Korean War.

However, the hospital remained well-guarded and off limits to civilians during this time, and although US Defense Department documents about the base have now been declassified, anything relating to the hospital remains classified. The official US line is that the facility was intended for rehabilitation purposes and as a medical unit for base personnel, and that it was completed but never opened.

A recommended tour operator is Jackie Simoud (☎ 572571, fax 665001, VHF radio 10, 'Puttut'), who is based across the fjord in Qassiarsuk. He runs transfers and tours of the **Norse ruins** at Qassiarsuk (formerly Brattahlid), which was founded by Eiríkur Rauðe (Eric the Red). Prices are Dkr100/200 one-way/return aboard the old wooden boat, M/B *Puttut*. Numerous other trips in the area are also on offer.

Places to Stay & Eat

The most pleasant accommodation is the sparkling *Fjeldstastionen Youth Hostel* (☎ 665221) which costs Dkr180 for beds and Dkr90 per person for camping. Unfortunately, it closes around 31 August and doesn't reopen until mid-June. Qassiarsuk, across the fjord, also has a *youth hostel* (☎ 572555) where you'll find a bed for Dkr125.

Other inexpensive hikers' huts and hostels are found along the Narsaq Peninsula like at *Tasiusaq* (☎ 572475), *Nunataaq* (☎ 572539), *Sillisit* (VHF radio 0084, Sillisit 29) and *Ipiutaq* (VHF radio 0084, Ipiutaq 19). All of these charge Dkr125.

Hotel Narsarsuaq (☎ 665253, fax 665370, email narsarsuaq@glv.gl) is often packed with tour groups and charges Dkr850/1050 for singles/doubles with breakfast. The cafeteria has a limited menu, but the dining room serves up à la carte meals for Dkr175 to Dkr200.

Café Bluie West One, beside the museum, serves up coffee, sandwiches, cakes and alcoholic drinks, and the supermarket, marked *Butikken*, sells everything from groceries to socks and rifle ammunition.

NARSAQ

Narsaq (the plain) sprawls across level land at the end of the Narsaq Peninsula. This invitingly flat space couldn't have been ignored by the 10th century Norse colonists and, indeed, it's dotted with their ruins. The present town was founded in 1830 and, thanks to its deep-water harbour, it became a Royal Greenland Trade Department (KGH) station in 1833, gaining town status in 1959.

The friendly Narsaq tourist office (☎ 661325, fax 661394, email narsaq .tourist .office@greennet.gl) is helpful with brochures and information.

GREENLAND

Things to See & Do

The **Narsaq Harbour Museum** (☎ 661666) takes in the old 1883 Nordprøven trading station buildings beside the picturesque old harbour: a cooperage and blubber storage house, stable, chapel, shop, Frederik Høegh's printworks, several stone houses and a recent replica of a traditional sod hut. The **Henrik Lund Museum** (☎ 31616) was the home of Greenlandic priest, poet and painter Henrik Lund and his wife, Malene.

There are also several **Norse ruins** scattered around the town, but the most interesting site is **Dyrnæs**, about an hour on foot north of town. The prominent 685m summit of **Qaaqarsuaq** (big mountain) behind the town makes a popular day hike, or you can just climb up to the 400m-high saddle for great views. For a longer hike, tackle the peak of **Kvanefjeld** (879m) 8km from Narsaq, which is the site of uranium deposits too remote for commercial exploitation. The neighbouring peak, **Illimmaasaq** (1390m) is known for its deposits of *tuttupit*, a rare pink gemstone found only here and in Arctic Russia.

Places to Stay & Eat

Independent travellers love the cosy old *youth hostel* (☎ 661665) which sits on a ridge with a great view of the town. The Dkr135 charge gives you rooms with only one set of bunk beds and access to the hot showers and cooking facilities. Camping outside is Dkr65. Alternatively, you can stay at the 20 bed *Narsaq Farm House* (☎ 661049, fax 661064) north of town towards the Narsaq valley. Beds cost Dkr140.

The *Hotel Perlen* (☎ 31675), run by Arctic Adventure, has single/double rooms for Dkr650/900 with breakfast. For snacks, try the fast food at *Lene's Grill-baren* near the *qajaq* (kayak) harbour. The *Hotel Narsaq* restaurant is pretty good, but meals must be booked in advance.

QAQORTOQ (JULIANEHÅB)

With a population of 3500, the town of Qaqortoq (which means 'the white place' and is pronounced like a very throaty KRA-kror-tok) is the big city and hub of

---

Precious Stones

In 1957, the beautiful soft mineral *tuttupit* was discovered by the West almost simultaneously in two sites: the Ilimmaasaq intrusion, a uranium-bearing geological formation near Narsaq, and on the Kola Peninsula in Arctic Russia. It's found nowhere else.

Most stones from the Narsaq deposit, which is the larger of the two, have a deep red colour, but may also appear in pink, blue or white forms. They're often infused with dark green ægirne, white albite and analcime, and yellow pyrochlore and zincblende.

Due to microscopic impurities within the crystal structure, tuttupit may become faded when stored in the dark, but when exposed to sunlight, the colour is revived. If the stone is boiled, however, the colour may be lost forever. The Russian variety, which is often violet, may be brightened by exposure to x-rays.

The Inuit name, which means 'reindeer blood', is derived from a legend of a girl called Tuttu, or 'reindeer', who fled to the mountains to give birth to her child in solitude. When the blood and placenta fell upon the ground, it seeped into the earth and turned to tuttupit stone. Oddly, a similar legend appears among the Sami of the Kola Peninsula. Among New Age cultures in the USA and Europe, the tuttupit crystal is thought to hold spiritual powers and is highly sought after.

It's technically illegal to remove tuttupit from Greenland, but locals have noted the tourist market for this beautiful stone and either sell it outright or produce unique tuttupit jewellery. So far, the government hasn't attempted to control the trade.

south Greenland. Many visitors find it the cleanest and tidiest of all Greenlandic towns, and in midsummer it explodes with wildflowers.

The original Qaqortoq was founded by Norwegian trader Anders Olsen in 1775 and named Julianehåb after Queen Juliane Marie of Denmark. Over the following decades, Qaqortoq developed into a trading station between the Danes and increasing numbers of Greenlanders. Modern Qaqortoq is an active port town and trade remains its mainstay. It's also home to Greenland's only tannery.

The tourist office (☎ 642913, fax 642987, email ntravel@greennet.gl) is worth visiting to book the youth hostel, pick up brochures or cruise through the well-stocked souvenir shop which sells T-shirts, carvings, maps and books. Staff also organise excursions.

Things to See & Do

No discussion of Qaqortoq would be complete without mentioning the **Torvet fountain** which dates from 1928 and is the only one in Greenland. Thanks to the efforts of archaeologist and former curator Joel Berglund, the **Qaqortoq Museum** is one of Greenland's finest. Exhibits include drawings and photos of early Qaqortoq, indigenous sealskin qajaqs and other hunting and fishing implements, as well as artefacts from the Dorset, Thule, Norse and Greenlandic cultures. You can also visit the beautiful **Frelserens Kirke** (Saviour's Church) if you pick up a key at the tourist office.

Perhaps the most interesting feature of Qaqortoq is the brilliant **Stone & Man project**, the brainchild of Greenlandic artist Aka Høegh, which attempts to turn amphitheatre-shaped Qaqortoq into a sculpture gallery that will constantly evolve.

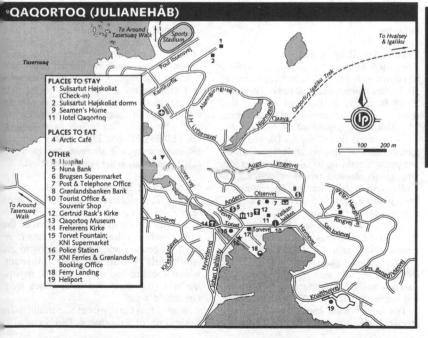

QAQORTOQ (JULIANEHÅB)

PLACES TO STAY
1 Sulisartut Højskoliat (Check-in)
2 Sulisartut Højskoliat dorms
9 Seamen's Home
11 Hotel Qaqortoq

PLACES TO EAT
4 Arctic Café

OTHER
3 Hospital
5 Nuna Bank
6 Brugsen Supermarket
7 Post & Telephone Office
8 Grønlandsbanken Bank
10 Tourist Office & Souvenir Shop
12 Gertrud Rask's Kirke
13 Qaqortoq Museum
14 Frelserens Kirke
15 Torvet Fountain; KNI Supermarket
16 Police Station
17 KNI Ferries & Grønlandsfly Booking Office
18 Ferry Landing
19 Heliport

GREENLAND

Høegh has commissioned artists from around Scandinavia and beyond, who have created shapes and reliefs from natural stone formations all over town. A map and directory to the sculptures is sold at the tourist office shop for Dkr10.

There are plenty of short hikes around town, but the finest is probably the challenging four to five day **Qaqortoq to Igaliku Trek**, which offers a combination of Norse history and wonderful scenery. The route begins at the end of Qaava street in Qaqortoq. On the second day, you'll pass the ruins of **Hvalsey**, or Qaqortukulooq, which was first inhabited in the late 10th century. Its church was one of the last built during the Norse era. For the full story, see *Hvalsø – the Church and the Magnate's Farm* by Joel Berglund, which is available from the souvenir shop for Dkr58. At the end of the hike you'll reach Igaliku, where you'll see the ruins of Garðar, which was the episcopal seat of Norse Greenland. Alternatively, you can choose from numerous possible hiking routes on the Vatnahverfi Peninsula.

Places to Stay & Eat

The *youth hostel* (☎ 642913, fax 642987) has dorm beds for Dkr175 in a collection of six houses scattered around town. These are likely to change at any time, and for this reason, beds must be booked in advance. The *Sulisartut Højskoliat* (☎ 642466, fax 642973) offers dorm beds for Dkr165. Singles/doubles are also available from Dkr165 per person, right up to Dkr875 per person, with meals. Amenities include cooking facilities and a video lounge. There's also a cosy *youth hostel* (☎ 642510, fax 665151) at the village of Igaliku.

The friendly *Seamen's Home* (☎ 642-239, fax 642678) has small single/double rooms with bath for Dkr595/795. The sparkling *Hotel Qaqortoq* (☎ 642282, fax 641234, email hotelsyd@greennet.gl), perched on the hill overlooking the harbour, has rooms for Dkr845/1075 with breakfast.

The best budget eatery is the friendly *Arctic Café*. There's also the *Seamen's*

Home cafeteria, but for a splurge and a great view, try the Thai restaurant at the *Hotel Qaqortoq*.

ALLUITSUP PAA (SYDPRØVEN)

Imaginatively named Alluitsup Paa (outside Alluitsoq) is Greenland's largest village, with 800 people. It was founded as a Royal Greenland Trade Department trading station in 1830 but is now sustained by fishing activities. It's known for its aloof manner, but is worth visiting if you want to reach the **40°C hot springs** on Uunartoq Island. When there's sufficient interest, the Qaqortoq tourist office organises day tours (Dkr800) to Uunartoq Island. Tours from Nanortalik cost Dkr500.

NANORTALIK

Although it's Greenland's southernmost community, the hunting and fishing town of Nanortalik has more in common with the traditional hunting districts of the far north than it does with other towns in south or south-west Greenland. It lacks a tourist-class hotel, but has gained a reputation as a mecca for hikers, trekkers, kayakers, rock climbers and mountaineers. The main draws are the imposing granite peaks and spires of the Nunaap Isua (Cape Farewell) and the Tasermiut Fjord and Lindenow's Fjord regions, where the scenery is comparable to that of Patagonia or Yosemite.

The Nanortalik Tourist Service (☎ 613633, fax 613425), PO Box 43, DK-3922 Nanortalik, can assist you in arranging transport and accommodation in the outlying districts.

Nanortalik Island

Nanortalik's picturesque old harbour area resembles a reconstructed film set, complete with a painted backdrop. Most of the stone and heavy timber buildings date from the 19th century and several belong to the worthwhile **Nanortalik Town Museum**, which contains lots of old photos, qajaqs, *tupilaks* (carvings) and other relics from Greenland's past.

West across the bay from Nanortalik is the Eskimo site of **Sissaritoq**, or Old Nanortalik which once had a shop, manager's residence and blubber storage facilities as well as lots of old stone and peat dwellings. It's recognisable by the large white cross crowning a knoll. While hiking there, watch for an odd upright basalt pillar from one of the ruins known as the **Bear Stone**, which was once used by a spoilt Inuit boy to tie up his pet polar bear cub.

A good, clear trail will take you to the summit of intriguing **Quassuk** (308m) or Ravnefjeldet (ravens mountain) immediately north-west of town. The lovely 559m **Qaqaarssuasik** (Storefjeldet, or big mountain) is the island's highest peak, and its summit presents quite a surprise. After you've slogged up the rockfields, you're met by several cairns and a breathtaking drop-off into the sea. About 175m below the summit is a crater-like formation which contains a mysterious Greenland-shaped lake.

Places to Stay & Eat

Nanortalik's best accommodation is the cosy little *youth hostel (☎ 613441, fax 613442)* between the old harbour and the sea. Dormitory beds cost Dkr120 and camping is Dkr50, with use of cooking facilities. There's also a *hostel annexe*, where you'll pay Dkr175. Camping outside costs Dkr35 per person, including the use of hostel facilities.

Eating at the *Hotel Kap Farvel* bar-cum-dining room is always an unconventional experience, and often involves chasing up the chef (who incidentally does an excellent job). The more dependable *Hotel Tupiluk (☎ 613294, fax 613131)* also serves meals, but it's still wise to book in advance.

TASERMIUT FJORD, NUNAAP ISUA (CAPE FAREWELL) & LINDENOW'S FJORD

One of south Greenland's most spectacular wonders is the 75km Tasermuit Fjord, which winds its way north-east from Nanortalik and ends at the face of the tidewater **Tasermiut glacier**. You can reach it by charter boat from Nanortalik and along the way you'll be treated to some of the world's most dramatic

granite fells, especially the hulking mass of **Ulamertorsuaq** (1830m). Hikers will find interest around the base, but for world-class rock climbers its sheer 1000m walls and the bizarre columnar turret appended to its western face represent a sort of Nirvana. Not surprisingly, it's the most popular climbing destination in south Greenland. Behind it rise the sheer faces of **Nalumaasortoq** (2045m) and other spectacular granite peaks, offering further challenges.

The valley Uiluit Kuua (Klosterdalen), 14km south of the Tasermiut glacier face, holds the ruins of a **14th century Augustinian monastery**, and above the landing site rises the **Uiluit Qaaqa** (2012m), or 'Ketil' as the Norse knew it. Its sheer 1400m wall is one of the world's highest cliff faces, and is considered one of the ultimate climbing thrills.

Tasermiut Fjord also offers loads of hiking possibilities, but its greatest curse, which cannot be taken lightly, is the profusion of bushes and shrubs which proliferate up to 150m elevation. At low tide you can follow the beach, but otherwise, you'll need sterling patience, a will to succeed, and perhaps even a machete. In places, you won't manage more than 1km per hour. Basic accommodation is available around Tasiusaq, and may be arranged through the Nanortalik tourist office.

Nunaap Isua, the 'Cape Horn' of Greenland's 'Patagonia', may be difficult to reach, but the wonderful nearby villages of **Aappilattoq**, with its stunning backdrop on Torsukaataaq Fjord, and **Narsarmiit**, with several Norse ruins, are reached by ferry from Nanortalik. Basic accommodation is available at the *Service House* in Aappilattoq for Dkr125 and can be booked through the Nanortalik tourist office, which can also arrange hostel-style accommodation at Narsarmiit.

Lindenow's Fjord, which is technically on the east coast, has attracted polar bear hunters and mineral investigations, but as yet, the area remains uninhabited. This 65km ice-choked fjord is typical of the rugged local landscape and is worth the effort and expense of getting there. Near its head rises the spectacular granite face of **Apostelens Tommelfinger** (2300m), which means `the apostle's thumb'.

South-West Greenland

The south-western coast of Greenland stretches from Ivittuut in the south to beyond the Arctic Circle, which crosses between Maniitsoq and Sisimiut. The latter is the southernmost town to permit sled dogs and to experience the true midnight sun in late June. Many people catch their first glimpse of Greenland at the international airport at Kangerlussuaq, which has direct connections with Denmark.

PAAMIUT (FREDERIKSHÅB)

Paamiut, or 'those at the mouth', which refers to its position at the mouth of Kuannersooq (Kvanefjord), has a population of around 2800. It's informally known as Greenland's 'artists' colony' for its quality tupilak and other carvings, and is also the site of a maritime training school. The efficient Paamiut tourist office (☎ 681277, fax 681448, email paaehv@greennet.gl) distributes maps and town plans, sells books and souvenirs and arranges tours.

The **Paamiut Museum**, housed in the old trading company buildings, displays Eskimo and Inuit artefacts, qajaqs and historical photos, and has a historical exhibit, a 'whaling in Paamiut' room and a geology section with one of the best stone collections in Greenland. The colourful **town church** is flanked by a churchyard decorated with plastic blooms. The tourist office can arrange boat tours along the picturesque **Kuannersooq** or charter boats to visit the 20km-wide face of the **Frederikshåbs Isblink glacier**.

For accommodation, you can choose between the *Hotel Paamiut* (☎/fax 681798), Dkr495/645 for singles/doubles, or the seedier *Petersens Hotel* (☎ 681299) where you'll pay Dkr475/800.

NUUK (GODTHÅB)

Nuuk, with around 14,000 people, proudly claims to be the world's smallest capital city. Its name means 'the promontory' and is pronounced 'nuke' (thereby inviting some ribbing from English speakers).

Nuuk's founder, Hans Egede, originally named the town Godthåb (good hope) but sadly his optimistic vision has been dashed by sometimes overwhelming social problems. Modern Nuuk houses 15% of Greenland's population in monumental housing projects and the current sprawl spawned by urban drift has lent it a non-Greenlandic air

The Nuuk Tikilluarit tourist office (☎ 322700, fax 322710, email nuuktou @greennet.gl) in the Santa Claus house at Hans Egedesvej 29, Kolonihavnen, distributes maps and brochures and runs city tou programs.

Things to See & Do

The huge triangular cultural centre, **Kulturip Illorsua Katuaq** (Katuaq Cultural Centre dominates central Nuuk and encompasses over 4000 sq metres of airy open space fo art exhibitions, conferences, concerts and other cultural performances.

Quiet and picturesque **Kolonihavne** (colony harbour) is juxtaposed against the apartment blocks looming on the hill. Mos of the buildings date from the 18th and 19th centuries and form the heart of old Nuuk You can still imagine it as the heart of the set tlement before the new industrial harbou was constructed. It was here that the hunter set out in their qajaqs and the whaler brought their victims for flensing. Koloni havnen was also once the central busines district.

The lovely **Frelserens Kirke** (Church o Our Saviour) was consecrated on 6 Apri 1849, and is worth a quick visit en route to the **National Museum**, which depicts 450 years of Greenlandic culture. One hall i filled with historical dogsleds, qajaqs and *umiaqs* (boats), and other exhibits includ artefacts from the earliest Greenlandic cul tures: traditional hunting methods and tools historical and modern Greenlandic dress

NUUK (GODTHÅB)

PLACES TO STAY
2 Godhåbshallen Youth Hostel
15 Hotel Hans Egede
26 Seamen's Home
27 Kujalliit Youth Hostel

PLACES TO EAT
4 Brædtet Market
16 Tulles Rock Café
17 Kristinemut
19 Café Crazy Daisy

OTHER
1 Grønlandsbanken Bank
3 Frelserens Kirke &
   Jonathon Petersen Memorial
5 Greenland Home Rule
   Administration
   (Capitol Building)
6 National Museum
7 Tourist Office
8 Police Station
9 Katuaq Cultural Centre
10 Nuna Bank

11 Grønlandsbanken Bank
12 Post Office
13 Brugsen Supermarket
14 KNI Supermarket
18 Hans Egede's Kirke
20 Old Cemetery
21 Spar Supermarket
22 Ilisimatusarfik/Greenland
    University (New
    Herrnhut Mission)
23 Hospital
24 Charter Boat Dock
25 Ferry Landing

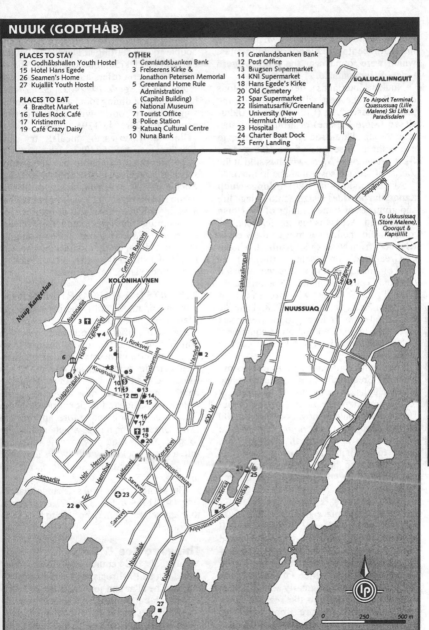

GREENLAND

geology, Eskimo and Inuit art, and Norse history. However, the best known pieces are the 15th century **Qilaqitsoq mummies**, which were found near the north-western town of Uummannaq.

Nuuk's hinterlands offer some fabulous day hikes. The best will take you up the peaks **Quassussuaq** (Lille Malene), **Ukkusissaq** (Store Malene) or around Quassussuaq through **Paradisdalen**. The best map to use is the reverse side of the *Hiking Map West Greenland – Nuuk*, which is sold at the tourist office and several shops in town.

An excursion up 120km-long **Nuup Kangerlua** provides insights into village life and glimpses of some remains of the **Norse Vesterbygd**. Access is via charter boat, the tourist office helicopter tour or the weekly KNI boat from Nuuk to Kapisillit (the home of Greenland's only salmon run). At the head of Ameralla Fjord is **Austmannadalen** (east man valley), named by Norwegian explorer Fridtjof Nansen, who crossed Greenland from east to west in 1888. Here he descended from the icecap to the west coast and broke up his sled and other equipment to build a rowing boat to take him back to Nuuk.

The **hiking route** from Nuuk to Qoorqut is one of Greenland's most challenging and popular treks. It passes through extremely remote and rugged country. All but about 10km of this route is shown on the 1:75,000 *Hiking Map West Greenland – Nuuk*. To tackle the 14 day route all the way from Nuuk to Kapisillit and Austmannadalen, you'll also need the DVL-Rejser 1:100,000 *Nuuk-Godthåbsfjorden* walking map.

Places to Stay & Eat

The most basic place to stay is the *Godhåbshallen Youth Hostel*, in the sports hall at Vandsøvej 2, which is very simple and charges Dkr95. A better choice is the *Kujalliit Youth Hostel*, which must be booked through the tourist office (☎ 322700, fax 322710). It sits magically on a quiet promontory jutting into the sea and is an easy walk from the centre. Rooms with access to cooking facilities cost Dkr200.

The mid-range choice is the *Seamen's Home* (☎ 21029, fax 22104) with single/double rooms starting at Dkr395/620 without bath and Dkr595/860 with bath. The attached cafeteria offers solid set meals. The *Hotel Hans Egede* (☎ 24222, fax 24487) has an elegant dining room and comfortable single/double rooms with all the conveniences for Dkr1045/1295.

For down-to-earth meals, try the *Kristinemut* (☎ 325040) which serves up large portions and simple but good-value specials. Attached is the pub-style *Tulles Rock Café* (☎ 321240) where you'll find bacon and egg breakfasts (Dkr25) as well as a wide range of meals and snacks. The unassuming family-oriented *Café Crazy Daisy* (☎ 323636) offers a menu ranging from hot dogs, burgers and chips to full meals of fish, steak, pasta, pizza, chicken, and Chinese and Thai cuisine.

MANIITSOQ (SUKKERTOPPEN)

Sukkertoppen, the old Danish name for Maniitsoq (population 4100), means 'sugar loaf', after a prominent mountain which dominated the town's former location. Sukkertoppen was founded by Norwegian trader Anders Olsen in 1755. It was relocated in 1781, and with it went the name. The mountain now towers over the village of Kangaamiut, 65km north of the present-day Maniitsoq. More appropriate is the Greenlandic name, which means 'the rough place', as the new town is squeezed into a basin backed by cliff walls and split by gash-like canyons and low, rugged hills.

The Maniitsoq Turismeselskap tourist office (☎ 813899, fax 813877, email mantour@greennet.gl) may be able to help with queries.

Things to See & Do

Maniitsoq's **1864 church** is of historical interest, but its 1981 replacement is also worth a look. The altar and font are made of beautiful rough-cut stone, the altarpiece is a driftwood cross created by Greenlandic artist Aka Høegh, and the altar itself is carpeted

The Petrified Warriors of Ikka

Ikka Fjord, across the peninsula from Kangilinnguit in south-west Greenland, is known in Inuit legend as the place where invading warriors – presumably Norse – crashed through the thin ice to their deaths in the frigid sea water. It's said they descended to the sea floor and were petrified into stalagmite-like stone pillars.

In 1963, Danish geologist Hans Pauly and Danish Navy divers recovered one of these 'invaders' from the sea bed. They dubbed it *ikaite* and left it lying on their boat deck, but when they returned after a lunch break, the pillar had disintegrated into a puddle of water and loose white sand. Information on the phenomenon was published in Danish, but didn't receive outside attention until 1995, when the Imperial College, London, along with the University and Museum of Copenhagen, attempted to map the ikaite formations using sonar, GPS and diving apparatus.

Ikaite, it turns out, is a form of calcium carbonate that is stable only under extremely high pressure – such as at the multiple atmospheres of pressure found beneath the sea. Its occurrence in Ikka Fjord is due to the presence of calcium springs, which issue from the seabed, combined with the 2°C temperature and pressure of the fjord water. In places, the formations measure from 2 to 20m in height. Due to the temperature imperative, researchers are fairly certain they developed since the end of the last ice age, 10,000 years ago. Currently, there are moves to preserve Ikka Fjord as a national marine park and nature reserve.

Although ikaite pillars haven't been found anywhere else in the world, minerals with the same chemical composition exist in Japan, Alaska and Antarctica.

with sealskin. If it isn't open, phone ☎ 813-284 to see if you can arrange something.

The Maniitsoq Museum (☎ 813277) lies in a valley 1km north-east of the centre and is comprised of a number of buildings from the 1870s, including a work shed, bakery and blacksmith's shop. Displays include artefacts dating from Saqqaq times right up to the early 20th century. Another section is devoted to local art and features the work of Kangaamiut artist, Jens Kreutzmann.

Hikers will be impressed with Maniitsoq Island's **labyrinth of narrow gorges**. Most of the valley floors are soggy, claustrophobic and plagued by mosquitoes, but the stunning landscape of crisscrossing gorges makes the trek worthwhile. For winter skiing, Maniitsoq Island also has 100km of cross-country ski track and 500 sq km of cross-country terrain. You'll probably want to pick up the *Hiking Map West Greenland – Maniitsoq* to explore this area properly.

The island of **Hamborgerland**, or Sermersuut, has nothing to do with fast food. It's simply one of the most incredible sights on the west coast of Greenland: an island of sheer and jagged granite spires, tangled glaciers and forbidding terrain. It's best viewed on the coastal ferries between Maniitsoq and Sisimiut.

Places to Stay & Eat

The best place to camp is about 3km from town, just beyond Kig pass, which connects Blomsterdalen and Langedalen. The unofficial summer *youth hostel* is at the only six storey building in town, the Aalisakkanik Tunusassiornermik Ilinniarfik school on Pavia Petersen-ip Aqqutaa. Single rooms with shared facilities cost Dkr210 and can be booked through the tourist office. The *Hotel Maniitsoq* (☎ 813035, fax 813377) which overlooks the harbour has single/double rooms with private baths, telephones and TVs. Prices start from Dkr750/1100, and its dining room is the best restaurant in town. *Guesthouse Kangaamiut (☎ 819422, fax 819482)* near the water charges Dkr425/600, and the friendly *Seamen's Home (☎ 813535, fax 813553)* has a cafeteria, single rooms with shared facilities for Dkr395, and singles/doubles with bath for Dkr595/860.

SISIMIUT (HOLSTEINSBORG)

With 4400 residents, Sisimiut (the fox hole burrowers) lies 75km north of the Arctic Circle and is Greenland's northernmost ice-free port. The harbour is bright and colourful and the weather is better than most other parts of the west coast. The friendly Sisimiut Tourism (☎ 864848, fax 865622), PO Box 65, Jukkorsuup 6, DK-3911 Sisimiut, actively tries to develop the area's adventure tourism potential, and does a fine job. A large number of organised tours are available, including boat tours, hiking, skiing and dogsledding.

Things to See & Do

Sisimiut's **old town** dates from the mid-18th to mid-19th centuries, and you enter it beneath a whale-jawbone arch. The **Gammelhuset** (old house) which contains most of the **Sisimiut Museum**, was originally prefabricated in Norway and erected at Isortoq in around 1756. Other exhibits are housed in the **Gamla Materialhandel** (old general shop) which was built in 1846.

The **kindergarten building** beside it was built at Assimmiut in 1759 and moved to Sisimiut eight years later, where it served as the vicarage. Behind it are two stone buildings; one was a blacksmith and the other a laundry, post office and jail.

The blue **Bethel Church**, Greenland's oldest, was consecrated in 1775. The red church farther up the hill, which looks slightly oriental with its upturned eaves, was designed and built by Bojsen-Møller in 1926 and extended to its present size in 1984.

There are a number of possible walks from Sisimiut. The 775m peak **Nasaassaq** (Kællingehætten, meaning the witch's cowl) dominates the view inland from Sisimiut.

The climb to the top is quite steep and will take an entire day. The best map to use is the westernmost sheet of the *Hiking Map West Greenland – Kangerlussuaq-Sisimiut.*

Places to Stay & Eat

South of the centre is the comfortable *youth hostel (☎ 864848, fax 865622)* which operates from 14 June to 15 August. Beds cost Dkr190, including the use of cooking facilities. The *Hotel Sisimiut (☎ 864840, fax 865615)*, an adequate mid-range hotel, charges Dkr805/1120 for single/double rooms with bath and Dkr285 for a dormitory bed.

Another option is the *Seamen's Home (☎ 864150, fax 865791)* which charges Dkr415/615 for singles/doubles without bath and Dkr595/795 with private facilities. The attached cafeteria serves up good set meals.

The recommended *camp site* is at the lake Nalunguarfik (Spejdersøen) 1km east of town. There are also several *mountain huts* on Kangerluarsuk Ungalleq and along the Kangerlussuaq to Sisimiut trek, as well as a *youth hostel* in Sarfannguaq village, which charges Dkr150 for beds.

Near the old town is the basic *Restaurant Tugto*, which serves full, good-value meals. The dining room in the *Restaurant Kællingehætten* is the best place to eat in town. For inexpensive snacks, try the *Grill & Burgerbaren* on the main road. Daily from noon to 1.30 pm, the *Community Centre* serves up real Greenlandic fare for down-to-earth prices. Dishes include whale, seal, muskox, caribou and fish. If you're tired of the touristy Greenland buffets, this is a super choice.

KANGERLUSSUAQ TO SISIMIUT TREK

The 150km trek or ski between Kangerlussuaq and Sisimiut is an increasingly popular route and it seems destined to become one of the great walks of the world. This is due mainly to its relative accessibility; the route begins at Greenland's largest international airport and ends at a lovely town which is well served by coastal ferries.

The trek takes from 10 to 14 days and requires careful planning, but anyone with some stamina who can carry 20kg on their back and is reasonably good at route finding can probably handle it. The trip normally begins in Kangerlussuaq. All hikers need the essential three part 1:100,000 *Hiking Map West Greenland – Kangerlussuaq to Sisimiut*, which shows the route in detail. Note that the compass deviation in this area is approximately 41.8°W.

Essentially, there are two routes – a High Route and a Low Route. The former is more challenging and its use is discouraged by hunters, who fear that hikers may spook the caribou that provide their bread and butter. Therefore, Greenland Tourism promotes the increasingly popular Low Route. On the third or fourth day hikers reach the western end of the vast lake Amitsorsuaq where there's a canoe centre, a big 14 person hut where beds cost Dkr100, and a small shop where you can stock up on supplies. Canoes can be hired (Dkr200 per day) for paddling around the lake.

KANGERLUSSUAQ (SØNDRE STRØMFJORD)

Kangerlussuaq (the big fjord) lies just north of the Arctic Circle in Greenland's widest ice-free zone (200km) at the head of its third longest fjord. Thanks to its inland position, the continental effect provides a stable climate and some of the island's most extreme temperatures, which range from -50°C in winter to 28°C in the 24 hour summer daylight. It's also the best place in Greenland to observe caribou and muskoxen.

On 9 April 1941, after the German occupation of Denmark, a defence treaty between the USA, the Greenland governor Eske Brun and the Danish ambassador Henrik Kaufmann handed the security of Greenland over to the US military. On 7 October 1941, they set up Bluie West Eight, better known as the Sondrestrom airbase. During the war, it became the main way-station for bombers and cargo carriers flying between North America and Europe.

In 1950, the defence treaty expired and the base was handed back to Denmark, but due to the Cold War threat, it was returned to the US military on 17 April 1951. Three years later, Scandinavian Air Systems (SAS) was granted permission to use Sondrestrom as a stopover on its transatlantic flights between Copenhagen and Los Angeles.

From 1958, the USA set it up as a supply base for its four DEW-line (Distant Early Warning) radar bases in Greenland, but these became redundant after the collapse of the USSR, and on 30 September 1992 the base was closed and handed over to the Greenland Home Rule government.

The Greenland Tourism Information Office (☎ 841098, fax 841498, email kangtour@greennet.gl) in the airport terminal is one of Greenland's most efficient. It not only provides tourist information and organises a wide range of tours, but also hires out vehicles and camping gear.

Things to See & Do

At the community centre, the municipal council holds **local arts and crafts exhibitions**. In the former base commander's office on the old Sondrestrom US airbase is a **museum** dedicated to the history of the base.

Kangerlussuaq is the Arctic equivalent of a Club Med, thanks to the US military, which left behind a host of **recreational facilities**, including a gymnasium, a bowling alley, an indoor swimming pool and an 18 hole golf course! There are also several local clubs, including the Sondrestrom Rowing Club on Tasersuatsiaq (Lake Ferguson); the Rifle Club, which stages shooting competitions on weekends; the Diving Club, which has a wealth of information on Arctic diving; and the Sondie Aero Club, which owns a plane and organises expeditions in the air.

The best tours are the **Musk Ox Photo Safari** (Dkr150) which takes you into the hinterlands on a quest for photogenic muskoxen and caribou; and the **Sandflugtdalen jeep**

KANGERLUSSUAQ (SØNDRE STRØMFJORD)

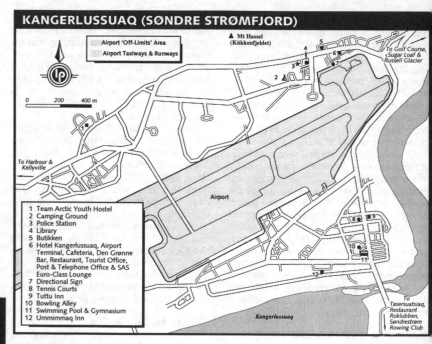

Airport 'Off-Limits' Area

Airport Taxiways & Runways

▲ Mt Hassel
(Kükkenfjeldet)

To Golf Course,
Sugar Loaf &
Russell Glacier

0   200   400 m

To Harbour &
Kellyville

Airport

Kangerlussuaq

To
Tasersuatsiaq,
Restaurant
Roklubben,
Søndrestrøm
Rowing Club

1 Team Arctic Youth Hostel
2 Camping Ground
3 Police Station
4 Library
5 Butikken
6 Hotel Kangerlussuaq, Airport
   Terminal, Cafeteria, Den Grønne
   Bar, Restaurant, Tourist Office,
   Post & Telephone Office & SAS
   Euro-Class Lounge
7 Directional Sign
8 Tennis Courts
9 Tuttu Inn
10 Bowling Alley
11 Swimming Pool & Gymnasium
12 Ummimmaq Inn

tour (Dkr550) which features a barbecue at Russell Glacier.

Although the Kangerlussuaq to Sisimiut trek is the star hiking venue (see earlier in this chapter) numerous other hikes are on offer and you could easily spend an entire holiday exploring this area. The best hikes include the easy 20km return route to **Sugar Loaf** and the straightforward three or four day return trip to **Russell Glacier**.

Places to Stay & Eat

At the organised *camping ground*, west of the airport terminal, camping costs are Dkr40 per person. The *Team Arctic Youth Hostel* (☎ 841433, fax 841417, email team.arctic@greennet.gl) at Old Camp, 2km west of the airport terminal, offers beds with the use of communal facilities for Dkr200.

Down the main road from the airport terminal, but in the same building, is *Hotel Kangerlussuaq* (☎ 841180, fax 841284). With three buildings – Hotel Kangerlussuaq, Ummimmaq and Tuttu – it accommodates up to 400 guests in varying degrees of comfort. Single/double rooms without bath cost Dkr520/580, including breakfast. With private facilities, they're Dkr850/1050. Dormitory accommodation costs Dkr235. You'll find the reception desk at the airport terminal.

For meals, your main choices are the *Hotel Kangerlussuaq restaurant* and *cafeteria*. Alternatively, you can check out the new *Restaurant Roklubben* at the Sondrestrom Rowing Club on the shore of Tasersuatsiaq. Groceries are available at the *Butikken* opposite the airport terminal.

(continued on page 342)

GREENLAND

Greenland Norse Colonies

Between the 8th and the 14th century the Scandinavian Norsemen, popularly known as Vikings, explored and settled land throughout the North Atlantic: the Faroe Islands, Iceland, Greenland and parts of North America. Even today, the reasons for this large-scale expansion are not quite clear. One thing is certain, curiosity was a factor. Irish monks had probably visited some of the North Atlantic islands as early as 700, and it was only a matter of time before the Vikings heard about it and followed them. Another reason was probably a shortage of land in Scandinavia. This shortage could be alleviated by emigration to the north because the common form of agriculture was not crops, but animal husbandry, which was still possible in the harsher climate of the north. In addition, the younger sons of the gentry were able to pursue their desire for wealth, status and adventure there, which they could not do in Norway.

Another reason for emigration to the North Atlantic could have been the changing political structure in Scandinavia. In Norway, Harald Hårfagre (880-930) was the first king to establish a central authority, from which aristocrats of the middle ranks might well have fled. Finally, chance was a significant factor in the expansion of the Vikings into the North Atlantic – according to the sagas, Iceland, Greenland and North America were all originally discovered by sailors who had been driven off course by winds.

Stepping Stones Of the North Atlantic islands, only Greenland had an indigenous population, and because the Norse settlers kept no records of their exploits until several generations later, it is difficult to reconstruct the history of this emigration and colonisation. What we know must be pieced together from the sagas, which – while certainly based on fact – are far from reliable; from scattered church records, which are difficult to understand without a context; and from archaeological evidence, which is almost always open to a variety of interpretations. From the 825 *Liber de mensura orbis terræ* (Book of the Measurement of the Earth) by the Irish monk Dicuil and the *Færeyinga Saga* (Saga of the Faroe Islanders) we know that the Vikings followed Dicuil's fellow monks to the Faroe Islands, where they established sheep and cattle farms in the most hospitable parts.

The next stepping stone to Greenland was Iceland, where Irish monks had established residence, too. The *Íslendigabók* (Book of the Icelanders), written by Icelandic historian Ari Þorgilsson in about 1125, and the *Landnámabók* (Book of the Settlements), probably compiled around the same time, give competing versions of the island's history, especially concerning the very first settlers. While the *Íslendigabók* is more of a narrative following the establishing of civilisation on Iceland, the *Landnámabók* is a list of the 400-odd people who supposedly were the first settlers, complete with details of marriages, slaves and personal anecdotes. In any case, some 20-30,000 emigres came to Iceland from Norway between 870 and 930 and laid the foundations for a flourishing society – one that was extraordinary for its quasi-democratic system of government, and for its quality of poetry and literature.

Greenland Unlike Iceland, southern Greenland lacked previous inhabitants – no monks had established residence, and the Inuit had not yet migrated that far south. According to the *Grænlendinga Saga* (Saga of the Greenlanders), the first Viking to sight Greenland was Gunnbjörn Ulf-Krakuson, who was blown off course to its east coast while trying to travel from Norway to Iceland in around 900. His discovery is not really surprising, considering the distance from Iceland to the closest point in Greenland is only 306km. Next, the *Landnámabók* mentions Snæbjörn Galti, who supposedly established a colony in the area of Ammassalik on the west coast some 80 years later, in 978. However, the members of this settlement feuded until they either died or returned to Iceland.

Greenland Norse Colonies

The *Eiríkurs Saga Rauðe* (Saga of Erik the Red) tells us that Greenland was permanently settled (at least until the end of the Norse colony) several years later by a fugitive from Norway and Iceland. Eiríkur had already fled from Norway in around 970 and had come to Iceland. But by this time – 40 years after the end of the major colonisation period – land was scarce, and Eiríkur soon got involved in a blood feud with his neighbours, which led to his being banned for three years. In about 983-986, Eiríkur followed his predecessors' route, moved to Greenland, and founded a farmstead, probably in the location known today as Qassiarsuk.

At the end of his banishment, Eiríkur returned to Iceland briefly to recruit settlers for the new colony. The *Eiríkur's Saga Rauðe* claims that he chose the name 'Greenland' because 'men would be all the more drawn to go there if the land had an attractive name'. But the name was more than a sales pitch! At the time, the North Atlantic was experiencing a spell of fairly mild weather, which made Greenland greener than today, and it's certainly green compared to Iceland.

Whatever Eiríkur's motivation for the name, he succeeded in his goal. In 986, he set sail for Greenland with 25 boats, and although only 14 of those arrived (according to the *Grænlendinga Saga*) it was still a significant beginning for a population. In the following years, two areas developed in which farms were concentrated – the east and west settlement, both of which were on the east coast. The former (which was more southerly) was in the region of today's Qaqortoq, the latter (more northerly) near Greenland's present-day capital, Nuuk. In addition, the Vikings travelled north along the coast on hunting expeditions. They definitely reached the hunting grounds around Disko Island – where they first would have encountered the Inuit, who were moving south about the same time. They might even have travelled as far as the Arctic Circle.

While no significant legal structure developed in Greenland, the church seems to have become increasingly important (although this is disputed among historians). Supposedly, Eiríkur's wife Þóðhildur was the first in the country to convert to Christianity – the remains of 'her' church can be seen in Brattahlid. When Eiríkur did not follow suit, she refused to have sex with him until he did. A bishop was installed at Garðar in 1124. At the height of the Viking presence in Greenland, there were around 450 farms with 4000-5000 Norse in the eastern settlement and 150 farms with 1000-1500 in the western. These were served by at least 12 and four churches, respectively. The largest remaining Viking structures in Greenland are the churches in Garðar and Hvalsey, and much of the information we have on Greenland in the post-saga age comes from church communication.

Vinland The westward exploration of the Vikings was not finished with Greenland, however. According to the *Grænlendinga Saga*, Bjarni Herjólfsson was blown off course when he followed his parents to Greenland from Iceland in 986. He sighted a wooded coast which he named Markland, but instead of landing made his way first northward, where he came upon a barren place he called Helluland, and then eastward back to Greenland.

Several years later, around 1000, Eiríkur's son Leifur the Lucky decided to trace Bjarni's route in reverse. However, after reaching Markland, Leifur kept on going for several more days until he discovered a land promontory he named Vinland, probably because of wild berries or grapes he found there. Before returning to Greenland, he spent the winter in Vinland. This lore is gathered in the *Grænlendinga Saga* and in *Eiríkur's Saga Rauðe*, which together are known as the Vinland Sagas.

In the following years, a number of Viking expeditions visited the land he had discovered. Leifur's brother Thorwald tried to establish a settlement, but was killed in a fight with Native

Greenland Norse Colonies

Americans. This was the first spot in the colonisation of the North Atlantic where the Vikings actually encountered and had to deal with an indigenous population. The *Grænlendinga Saga* further relates that Þorfinn Karlsefni established a colony with around 100 settlers.

Unfortunately, it has proven difficult to correlate the Norse sites with their contemporary names. It is fairly certain that Helluland is Baffin Island, since that is the first place the Vikings would have seen sailing westward from their traditional hunting grounds around Disko Island. Markland might very well have been Labrador, but it is unclear whether enough trees grew there at the time to warrant the name 'Land of Woods'. Finally, Vinland could have been Newfoundland – although the identity of the berries remains unclear – or it could have been somewhere around Nova Scotia, Prince Edward Island or Northern New England.

For a long time, the archaeological evidence in this matter was inconclusive. In the 1960s, however, archaeologist Helge Ingstad followed a trail of local traditions to find the ruins of a settlement on the northern tip of Newfoundland. The architectural ruins and artefacts at this site, L'Anse-aux-Meadows, prove beyond doubt that the Vikings did spend significant amounts of time on the North American continent-even if they still cannot tell us where Vinland was.

The Decline In spite of their early fierce independence, the islands of the North Atlantic came under Norwegian influence again in the 13th century. Greenland was annexed in 1261, although it is difficult to establish to what extent Norway was able to exert any kind of control. If the relationship was anything like that with Iceland, Norway probably imposed a trade monopoly that limited the number of ships which were allowed to bring supplies from Scandinavia.

At the same time, the Greenlanders became less and less self-sufficient because they were running out of wood with which to build boats and maintain their own independent connections to Europe. Although the distances between the individual islands of the North Atlantic are not very large, most traffic was not between them, but back and forth from Norway, which made good ships all the more necessary. Furthermore, the 'little ice age' set in the North Atlantic, reducing the areas available for agriculture.

The first colony to be abandoned was probably Vinland. It is unknown when the last trips there were made, but in a roundabout way the lure of the American continent may have even contributed to the decline of the Norse colonies in Greenland. It is quite conceivable that when conditions worsened, settlers moved west (where wood was available), as they had done so many times before. In Greenland itself, the western settlement was abandoned around the middle of the 14th century – according to the priest Ívar Bárdarsson's 1360 *Description of Groenland* – due to increasing conflicts with the Inuit and worsening climate. Like the first, the last contact with Greenland happened by chance. A group of Icelanders was blown off course to Greenland in 1406 and spent several years there.

The ultimate reasons for the end of the Greenland colony remained undocumented, and are a mystery to this day. Probably, the Vikings were unable to survive because of a combination of factors. Their numbers were insufficient to sustain a population; they never adapted their habits to the climate of the 'little ice age'; they suffered from the economic consequences of losing contact with Europe; they came into conflict with the Inuit, who were pushing south to avoid the climate changes; and they became victims of sailors from Bristol, who were pirates as well as whalers. Whatever the reason, no Vikings were there when the next European expeditions visited Greenland in the 17th and 18th centuries.

Norbert Schurer

GREENLAND

(continued from page 338)

Disko Bay

The largest and newest island off the Greenland coast shelters Disko Bay (Qeqertarsuup Tunua in Greenlandic), an iceberg-studded expanse 300km north of the Arctic Circle. The five main towns of Disko Bay – Kangaatsiaq, Ilulissat, Qeqertarsuaq, Qasigiannguit and Aasiaat – have a combined population of about 12,000. Visitors heading north up the coast normally feel they're getting their first real taste of the High Arctic here. During winter, Disko Bay normally marks the southern extreme of the pack ice. In summer, the northern hemisphere's most prolific tidewater glacier advances up to 30m a day and calves formidable bergs – some weighing up to seven million tonnes – filling the Ilulissat Kangerlua (Jakobshavn Icefjord) and spilling them into Disko Bay to wander for centuries around the Arctic.

AASIAAT (EGEDESMINDE)

Aasiaat, Greenland's fifth largest community and one of its friendliest settlements, sits amid low, stark and rocky islets near the southern entrance to Disko Bay. The area is short on rugged peaks, but its relative flatness makes a pleasant change. The name Aasiaat means 'the spiders', but was probably originally intended to be 'Aasiat' or 'the gathering place'. Although its coat of arms depicts a spider web, Aasiaat spiders don't spin webs, instead contending with the climate by burrowing underground.

The friendly tourist information service (☎ 892540, fax 892545, email aasiaat .tourist@greennet.gl), PO Box 241, DK-3950 Aasiaat, in this little visited town remains quite informal.

In 1982, the town established the **Aasiaat Systue leather-craft shop** which emphasises traditional tanning, drying, sewing and embroidery skills. Occupying the residence of the poet, merchant and parliamentarian Frederik Lynge is the **Aasiaat Museum**, which is small but well-presented.

Frozen Assets

Most visitors to Disko Bay come to see its world-famous icebergs, but did you know that 'bergy bits' of Disko Bay ice – that is, semi-trailer-sized chunks – are towed into harbours, chipped into cubes and exported to Japan and Europe to chill drinks? That scotch you order in a Tokyo pub may contain 25,000-year-old cubes from the frozen heart of Greenland's icecap, and the air that fizzes out as they melt was trapped long before anyone ever heard of smog alerts.

Though Aasiaat lacks a hotel, there's a comfortable **Seamen's Home** (☎ 892711, fax 892910) near the harbour tanks. Single/double rooms start at Dkr410/620. The only other formal accommodation is the **Aasiaat Hotellejligheder** (☎ 871035, fax 892987, email vinther@greennet.gl), PO Box 66, DK-3950 Aasiaat, which charges Dkr575/995 for single/double apartments. It also offers **youth hostel** dormitory accommodation for Dkr275.

QASIGIANNGUIT (CHRISTIANSHÅB)

Qasigiannguit (small spotted seals) sits at the foot of a long escarpment which rises almost vertically above its well-sheltered small-boat harbour. There's evidence that the area has been inhabited for over 4000 years, and remnants of the Saqqaq, Thule and Dorset cultures have been found here. The small tourist office (☎ 911081, fax 911524, email qts.tourist.service@green net.gl) is at the Hotel Igdlo, PO Box 140, DK-3951 Qasigiannguit.

Things to See & Do

The **Qasigiannguit Museum** has an excellent collection of relics from the Saqqaq through to the Inuit culture. Hikers may want to make the steep two hour climb up the mountain ridge south of town, via a walking track from the southern end of

Flyversøen. It affords a broad view over Disko Bay.

Other worthwhile day hikes will take you north to **Eqaluit** or south to **Illukut** (Bryggerhusbugten), the site where Old Qasigiannguit was founded in 1734. There, the colonial governor's house and several other log buildings and foundations are still visible. About 20 minutes walk to the south, over a low pass, is the cave **Bings Hule**, which was the site where ancient shamans were initiated. The more adventurous walk from Qasigiannguit to Ilimanaq takes about four days.

In 1989, near the head of the bay Orpissooq, the remains of an ancient **Saqqaq autumn camp site** were excavated by the Qasigiannguit Museum. Orpissooq is accessible by charter boat from Qasigiannguit. At the western end of the lake Ilulialik, up the valley from the head of Orpissooq, is the **Qasigiannguit Canoe Centre** (☎ 911-539), Kirkevej 19, Dk-3951 Qasigiannguit, where you can hire canoes to explore the lake and get good close-up views of the glacier flowing into its eastern end. For Dkr2950, you get a package which includes boat transfers from Qasigiannguit, three days of canoe hire, a guide, a hiking map, camping and cooking gear, and half-board.

Places to Stay & Eat

The *DiskoBay Hotel* (☎ 911081, fax 911524, email diskobay@greennet.gl) near the ferry landing, has single/double rooms with bath for Dkr740/940. The best free *camp sites* are around the former reservoir lakes east of Qaerssorassat, which are surrounded by vegetation and low hills. The DiskoBay Hotel has *camp sites* for Dkr50 per person, or you can camp at Flyversøen, a tidal lake north of the inlet. The *Youth Hostel Akulliit* has dorm beds for Dkr200, which you can book through the hotel.

The DiskoBay Hotel has both a cafeteria and an upmarket restaurant. The only alternatives for meals are the grill bar *Mikisoq* in the centre and the *Royal Greenland Cantine*, near the museum. The *KNI supermarket* sells groceries and has an excellent *bakery*.

ILULISSAT (JAKOBSHAVN)

However scruffy and unkempt, Ilulissat (the icebergs) is the Arctic you came to see – cold, mirror-like seas crowded with icebergs and floes, an often unrelenting grey sky and a disorderly spirit noticeably missing from the tidier towns farther south. Not surprisingly, it's now Greenland's most popular tourist destination, not only attracting summer visitors on the ferries and flights, but also a swelling number of cruise ships and spring dogsled tourists. The official Ilulissat Tourist Service (☎ 944322, fax 943933, email ilulissat.tourist@greennet.gl), Kussangajannguaq B447, PO Box 272, DK-3952 Ilulissat, organises a plethora of tours, and sells souvenirs and foreign-language books on Greenland.

Things to See & Do

The lovely red house that once served as the town vicarage was also the home of Greenland's favourite son, Arctic explorer, anthropologist and author Knud Rasmussen (Kununnguaq or little Knud), who was born there on 7 July 1879. It now houses the **town museum**, which is dedicated to his Arctic explorations. Most of the works in the **Emanuel A Petersen Art Museum** are by its Danish artist namesake, who was born on 18 February 1894 in Frederiksberg, Denmark. A great body of his work features Greenlandic themes.

Ilulissat's main tourist attraction is the **Ilulissat Kangerlua** (Ilulissat Icefjord). The glacier face of the Sermeq Kujalleq (Jakobshavns Isbræ), the world's most prolific tidewater glacier outside Antarctica, measures 5km wide and 1100m thick. At the glacier face, the sea is about 1500m deep, but the ice rises only 80m above the surface. It flows an average of 25m daily and is the source of 10% of the icebergs floating in Greenlandic waters, amounting to 20 cubic km annually or about 20 million tonnes per day – enough to supply New York with water for a year.

The largest bergs actually rest on the bottom, with 90% of their mass typically floating beneath the surface. Many settle on the

260m-deep underwater moraine across the mouth of the fjord, until they break up or enough pressure builds up behind them to shove them out to sea. The icefjord is most easily reached from the old heliport, 1.5km from Ilulissat, where a 15 minute track leads to the shore, via the ruins of the Eskimo village of **Sermermiut**.

Local hiking clubs have now marked a series of **walking routes** with blazed cairns. There's a surprisingly adequate tourist office sketch map (Dkr5) but your best source of information is the 1:75,000 *Hiking Map West Greenland – Ilulissat*, which covers numerous routes through Ilulissat's typically haunting surroundings. A challenging loop hike will take you to the mysterious-looking **Akinnaq region** east of the airport.

Places to Stay & Eat

Ilulissat is packed with tourists from mid-July to mid-August, and last-minute accommodation may be hard to find. Campers can go to the organised *camp site* at the old

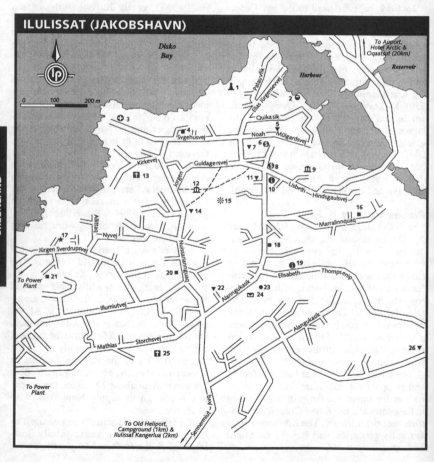

heliport, where they'll pay Dkr35 per night. Pick up keys at the Ilulissat Tourist Service (and don't leave valuables in your tent). Note that camping is prohibited in the Sermermiut Valley.

The friendly *Ilulissat Youth Hostel* (☎ 943377, fax 944577) offers dorm beds for Dkr195/250 in summer/winter. *Disko Bay House* (☎ 944411, fax 944511, email greenland.tours@greennet.gl) has single/double rooms for Dkr395/495, and also offers accommodation in Oqaatsut (Rodebay), a village north of Ilulissat, for Dkr250 per person. The tourist office can also arrange B&B accommodation in private homes in town or in outlying villages for Dkr200.

ILULISSAT (JAKOBSHAVN)

PLACES TO STAY
- 4 Hotel Hvide Falk
- 16 Ilulissat Youth Hostel
- 18 Hotel Naaleraq,
     Cafeteria & Restaurant
- 20 Skolehjemmet
- 21 Disko Bay House

PLACES TO EAT
- 5 KNI Shop & Bakery
- 7 Grill-baren Centrum
- 11 Brædtet Market
- 14 Ristorante Pizzeria Panorama
- 22 Sporthallen & Cafeteria
- 26 KNI Kiosk

OTHER
- 1 Knud Rasmussen Memorial
- 2 Ferry Landing
- 3 Hospital
- 6 Nuna Bank
- 8 Grønlandsbanken Bank &
     Airport Bus Stop
- 9 Emanuel A Petersen
     Art Museum
- 10 Ilulissat Tourist Service
- 12 Knud Rasmussen Museum
- 13 Zion's Church
- 15 Viewpoint
- 17 Police Station
- 19 Greenland Travel
- 23 KNI Supermarket
- 24 Post Office
- 25 Naalakkatta Illua

The tourist-class *Hotel Arctic* (☎ 944153, fax 943924, email hotel-arctic@greennet.gl) occupies an isolated promontory with a view over the bay and charges Dkr925/1245 for singles/doubles. More central is the less pretentious *Hotel Hvide Falk* (☎ 943343, fax 943508) with rooms for Dkr890/1190. The *Hotel Naaleraq* (☎ 944040, fax 944360) is a small and cosy place with character and has single/double rooms starting from Dkr450/ 550.

For hot dogs, snacks or coffee, try the *Grill-baren Centrum* or the more down-to-earth *Cafeteria Sporthallen*. Fine dining is found at the *Arctic* and *Hvide Falk* hotels. Both offer fine views, and the latter has an especially ice-choked vista. For good cafeteria meals and reasonably priced restaurant fare, nothing beats the homy cafeteria and restaurant at the Hotel Naaleraq. A great new place is the *Ristorante Pizzeria Panorama*, which offers pizzas, pasta and salads.

DISKO ISLAND
Geologically, Disko Island (along with the adjacent Nuussuaq Peninsula) is the newest land in Greenland – only 50 million years old – and is comprised of the same igneous basalt formations typical of the Faroe Islands and Iceland's Westfjords. The island's main attraction is hiking through its high, striated, mesa-like mountains.

The flora is also of interest, especially around several 'warm' springs (3°C to 10°C) which contain high concentrations of radioactive fluoride. Around Englishmen's Harbour spring grow three species of orchid as well as the carnivorous plant, penlngula.

Qeqertarsuaq (Godhavn)
The Greenlandic name of both Disko Island and its main town means 'big island', while the Danish name simply means 'good harbour'. The town itself is of limited interest, but it's a good staging point for hikes around Disko Island. The Qeqertarsuaq Tourist Service (☎ 921196, fax 921198, email qtser @greennet.gl) is found at the town museum.

Qeqertarsuaq's odd-looking **church** dates from 1915. Locals like to call it 'God's

GREENLAND

Knud Rasmussen

If Greenland has a favourite son, it's Arctic explorer Knud Rasmussen, who was born in Ilulissat on 7 June 1879. The son of local pastor Christian Rasmussen and his wife Sophie, his ancestry was Danish, Norwegian and Greenlandic, and the people of Ilulissat came to know him as Kununnguaq, 'little Knud'.

Rasmussen hadn't made any career plans early on and after completing school in Copenhagen, he began looking around for something that suited him. Among his pursuits were opera singing and medicine, both of which were quickly abandoned. His talent as a writer was discovered in accounts of his journeys to Lapland and Iceland. In 1902, he joined the Danish Literary Expedition to north-west Greenland, led by Ludvig Mylius-Erichsen. This resulted in his first book, *The New People*, about the traditional polar Eskimos of the Melville Bay area.

From 1906 to 1908, Rasmussen was invited to join the Ethnographical Expedition to north-west Greenland, which attempted to find the route travelled by early migrants to Greenland from Canada's Ellesmere Island.

By 1910, Rasmussen had clearly found his calling in life and, together with fellow Arctic enthusiast Peter Freuchen (who later wrote the book *Arctic Adventure*, which details many of their exploits together) he established a trading company in Qaanaaq (Thule), with the objective of funding subsequent expeditions. Freuchen wrote: 'Rasmussen was something of a dandy and always carried a pair of scissors for cutting his hair and beard. Even in the most biting cold, he washed his face every day with walrus blubber, and his footwear was the most beautiful in the Arctic.'

Their joint business was successful, and between 1912 and 1919 Rasmussen conducted four more expeditions to Greenland. The objectives of these trips were, among other things, to ascertain the existence of the Peary Channel, search for missing explorers, chart the northern coastline of Greenland and perform an ethnographical study in east Greenland.

It was the experience gained from these trips that led to what he hoped would be the fulfillment of his dreams – to trace the migration of the Inuit peoples from Siberia all the way to Greenland. The 5th Thule Expedition set out in 1921 to gather ethnographical, archaeological, geographical and natural history data from Greenland right across the North American Arctic. He visited all the Inuit communities in Arctic Canada and Alaska, collecting myths, legends and linguistic studies, and would have continued across to Arctic Russia, but was denied permission by the Soviet authorities.

The result of this expedition was *The 5th Thule Expedition – The Danish Ethnographical Expedition to Arctic America*, which detailed linguistic and cultural differences between the Inuit groups across the region. It was also the basis for Rasmussen's best-known book, *Across Arctic America*, which has recently been reissued by the University of Alaska-Fairbanks. These projects earned him an honorary doctorate from Copenhagen University.

Two subsequent expeditions, the 6th and 7th Thule Expeditions, involved surveying, aerial photography and geological, zoological, ethnographic, botanical and glaciological studies on the east coast of Greenland. Rasmussen also tried his hand at film direction with the making of *Palos Brudefærd* (Palo's Wedding) in the summer of 1933 in Ammassalik. Sadly, during the filming he contracted food poisoning from pickled auks and died shortly afterwards, on 21 December 1933.

inkhouse', and the bell tower resembles a storybook wishing well. The **Arctic Research Station** was founded by Morten Porsild of the University of Copenhagen in 1906 for scientific investigation of Arctic ecosystems.

A 30 minute walk south of town lies **Qaqqaliaq** or Udkiggen (the lookout) where you'll find a tower which was used by early whalers as a lookout. Whenever a whale was spotted, a cannon was fired to alert the fleet and set the hunt into action.

Disko Island is a vast and uncompromising wilderness, measuring 120km from north to south and the same from east to west. Trekking is limited to the most accessible areas on the southern peninsula near Qeqertarsuaq: west towards Itilleq (Laksebugt) and north towards Diskofjord. The most worthwhile tours – which would be difficult to organise on your own – are the two to seven-day trips to Disko Island's 1500 sq km icecap, **Sermersuaq**. One/two-day tours start at Dkr1350/1895, while a week on the ice plus a village visit in **Kangerluk** is Dkr5590. Rates include transport, meals, mountain huts, skis, snowmobiles and dogsled travel.

Places to Stay & Eat

The *Siorarsuit, Napasunnguit* and *Naja* hostels offer comfortable dormitory accommodation, showers and cooking facilities for Dkr195. Free camping is available at any of the hostels, but campers pay Dkr30 to use the hostel showers. The *Hotel Disko* (☎ 47310, fax 47313) looks more like a grill bar (which it also is) than a hotel and single/double rooms with shared bath cost a rather extortionate Dkr800/1100.

Meals are available at the *Hotel Disko* and the *Godhavn Grill-baren*. Trekkers may want to bring supplies from the mainland.

North-West Greenland

North-west Greenland is finding its way into more and more tourist itineraries. Uummannaq is now a standard cruise and tour group destination; lots of independent travellers ride the boat to Upernavik, Greenland's northernmost ferry terminal; and the increasing access to the Avanersuaq (Thule) district is helping to satisfy long-standing outside interest in the region.

However, it's worth noting that the traditional Arctic cultures described by Knud Rasmussen and other polar explorers and researchers are changing fast. Only 40 years ago, this society still lived and hunted as it had for thousands of years, but in the intervening period, the Danes introduced formal education, western health care, the Danish language, new social values and economic dissatisfaction. The US base at Pituffik introduced an entirely different dimension. Although the traditional hunting culture hangs on, particularly in the Avanersuaq and Upernavik districts, it has now been affected by outside influences like junk food, alcohol, videos, snowmobiles, cellular phones, speedboats and prefab housing.

UUMMANNAQ

Uummannaq (population 1300), meaning 'heart-shaped' (more like a seal heart than a Valentine greeting), sits at 70° north latitude, the same as North Cape, Norway, and Prudhoe Bay, Alaska. Even so, nearly half of Greenland is still north of it. Wonderful Uummannaq Mountain (1175m), which is one of the most unusual and colourful sights in the Arctic, provides both a backdrop for the town and constant entertainment as it changes colours from dull cloud-wrapped grey to pastel rose to carrot orange, back to sepia, pale violet and grey. The mountain and the entire island is composed of a geological formation known as basement gneiss, granite which has been metamorphosed by intense pressure and heat into wild black, white and rose swirls, whorls and stripes.

The Uummannaq Tourist Service (☎ 951-705, fax 951475, email uummannaq @uumkom.ki.gl), PO Box 202, DK-3961, at the Hotel Uummannaq, provides tourist information and monopolises the local tourism scene.

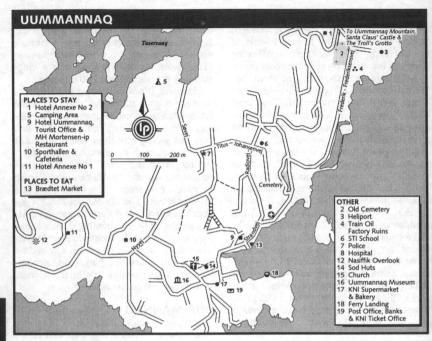

UUMMANNAQ

Tasersuaq

To Uummannaq Mountain,
Santa Claus' Castle &
The Troll's Grotto

PLACES TO STAY
1 Hotel Annexe No 2
5 Camping Area
9 Hotel Uummannaq,
   Tourist Office &
   MH Mortensen-ip
   Restaurant
10 Sporthallen &
   Cafeteria
11 Hotel Annexe No 1

PLACES TO EAT
13 Brædtet Market

0   100   200 m

Savej

Titus- Johansensvej

Radloevej

Cemetery

Frederik · Frederiksensvej

OTHER
2 Old Cemetery
3 Heliport
4 Train Oil
   Factory Ruins
6 STI School
7 Police
8 Hospital
12 Nasiffik Overlook
14 Sod Huts
15 Church
16 Uummannaq Museum
17 KNI Supermarket
   & Bakery
18 Ferry Landing
19 Post Office, Banks
   & KNI Ticket Office

Nyvej

Stradvej

GREENLAND

Things to See & Do

The unique **Uummannaq church**, consecrated in 1935, was constructed of granite
boulders chipped from the nearby hillside.
The three **traditional sod huts** on the
church lawn date from 1925 to 1949 and
one was inhabited as recently as 1982.
Near the heliport are the ruins of the **old
train oil factory**, where whale blubber was
boiled down into lamp oil. Because of the
smell, it was located well away from the
centre.

The main building of the **Uummannaq
Museum** (☎ 48104) was constructed in
1880 as a home for the Royal Greenland
Trade Department clerk. You'll find interesting background information on the
Maarmorilik mine, Greenlandic archaeology and history, the Qilaqitsoq mummies,
the whaling era, the history of the museum
and a library of Arctic-interest books.

Hikers can ramble up into the hills above
the reservoir and up to the shoulder of **Uummannaq Mountain**. With extreme caution,
some people make it as far as the uppermost
black stripe, but it's wise to aim for a lesser
goal. On the lower shoulder of the mountain
are several small but deep mountain lakes
which vary in colour from emerald to azure.

An easier destination is **Santa Claus'
Castle**, a traditional sod hut which was
built near the shore at Spraglebugten for a
Danish children's TV program. From town,
it's a leisurely two hour return walk. Less
than an hour's walk farther along the coast
is a cave known locally as **the troll's grotto**.

Popular tours, run by the Uummannaq
Tourist Service, include nine-hour boat trips
to the prolific **Store Qarajaq glacier**, which
advances 7.5km per year; excursions to the
Eskimo ruins and **mummy cave at Qilaqitsoq**; and **whale-watching** by boat around

The Mummies of Qilaqitsoq

Qilaqitsoq ('where the sky is low') was catapulted to international fame in 1977 when the National Museum in Nuuk – and through it, the archaeological world – learned of the discovery of eight mummies in a cave there. *National Geographic* did a cover story on the find and suddenly, people everywhere were captivated by the haunting face of the six-month-old boy who had lived and died in 15th century Greenland.

The mummies were originally discovered in 1972 by ptarmigan hunters Hans and Jokum Grønvold from Uummannaq, who photographed the site and reported their find to government authorities. However, nothing more was said about the discovery until 1977, when Claus Andreasen took over the director's post at the National Museum.

In addition to the famous six-month-old baby, there was a four-year-old boy, apparently with Down's Syndrome, and one of the six adults (all women) suffered from a debilitating disease. According to Greenlandic custom, the bodies were dressed in heavy clothing suitable for the long, cold journey to the land of the dead. There was no evidence of violence, famine, accident or epidemic which may have caused their deaths. Food poisoning has been suggested, as has drowning and hypothermia. It is most probable, however, that they were considered burdens on the society of the day and were sent off to die of exposure.

Several of the mummies are displayed in the National Museum in Nuuk, and you can read more about the discovery and subsequent research in the February 1985 issue of *National Geographic*. The museum in Nuuk also sells the booklet *Qilakitsoq – the Mummy Cave*, available in English, Danish or Greenlandic for Dkr10.

Qaarsut, where you can also find handmade clothing and Inuit art.

Places to Stay & Eat

At the *Sporthallen Youth Hostel*, dorm beds with the use of cooking facilities cost Dkr200, and can be booked through the Hotel Uummannaq. The *Hotel Uummannaq* (☎ 951518, *fax 951262*) has a superb view over the harbour and charges Dkr825/1050 for single/ double rooms in the main building or Dkr575/ 725 in either of the two annexes north-west and north-east of the town centre. Bed & breakfast accommodation in town (Dkr225 to Dkr275) and beds in outlying villages (Dkr100) can be arranged through the tourist office.

For a great meal and an iceberg-studded view, go to the *MH Mortensen-ip Restaurant* at the Hotel Uummannaq, which frequently puts on Greenland buffets. Otherwise, try the *grill-baren* at the harbour or the *Sporthallen cafeteria*.

UPERNAVIK

Upernavik (meaning the spring place) is the most northerly ferry terminal in Greenland, and many travellers sail up just for curiosity value. A 13th century rune stone found on the island, which bears record of a visit by three Norse, provides evidence that Norse hunters ventured at least this far north. Here, you're nearly 800km north of the Arctic Circle at a latitude of 72° 50' north, and the average summer temperature is 5°C.

With a population of 1100, or 2600 in the district, the economy is based on fishing (several Upernavik district settlements have fish-processing plants) but many of the locals still rely on sealing and polar bear hunting.

The Upernavik Tourist Service (☎ 961-700, fax 961112, email turist@green net.gl) at the museum is headed by the friendly tourist officer and museum curator, Ms Pauline Knudsen.

Things to See & Do

Upernavik's **Old Town Museum** is Green-land's oldest, and the new visitors' book, which was started in 1980, was still only half-full at the time of writing. The previous one, which remains on display, lasted over 60 years and contains inscriptions from numerous Arctic explorers and scientists. Most interesting is the original qajaq ensemble complete with harpoon, throwing stick, bird skewer, knife, seal-stomach float (to prevent seals diving after being hit or sinking after being killed) and line made of leather thong. Other historical paraphernalia includes a collection of Greenlandic money which was in use until Danish notes became the standard currency in the 1950s. Some examples date back to 1911.

At Amerivik, the **skin house**, you can watch local women making skin clothing and purchase handmade pillows, skin bags and boots. Also have a look at the cemetery, where the raised graves are covered with rock and concrete and decorated with plastic flowers, providing a rare splash of colour in this rather drab, untidy town. Downhill from the main cemetery is the **grave of Navarana Freuchen**, the wife of Peter Freuchen. She died on the fifth Thule expedition with Rasmussen.

It's also worth exploring Upernavik island, but its small size means that the new airport will dramatically alter its ancient landscapes. The three hour return walk to the northern tip, **Naajarsuit**, takes you through a gash-like valley, which slices across the island and contains the **Qataarmiut Eskimo ruins** and a couple of nice lakes. Thanks to the acoustics in this valley, you can hear a whisper from several hundred metres away.

Places to Stay & Eat

All accommodation in Upernavik must be booked through the tourist office. From 1 to 31 July, you can stay at the **Kolligiet**, opposite the KNI shop. The clean and spacious rooms cost Dkr150 per person, but there are no cooking facilities. Rooms at the **STI School** (☎ 51099, fax 51478) are available in summer for Dkr350 per person, including the use of kitchens and TVs.

If you book in advance, the tourist office can arrange accommodation in **private homes** for around Dkr200 per person. The hills and valleys north of town offer scenic **camp sites**, but many level areas can be soggy.

The only meal choices are the basic **Pølsebaren**, which does the usual hot dogs, and the **B-747 Cantine**, which serves set lunches and dinners comprised of a greasy meat dish, boiled potatoes and once-frozen vegetables for Dkr40.

AVANERSUAQ (THULE DISTRICT)

Named after the 4th century geographer Pytheas' land of Ultima Thule (the farthest north), the Avanersuaq (the great north) or Thule district is an enigma. It was the first part of Greenland to be colonised by Eskimo people from the west, and modern

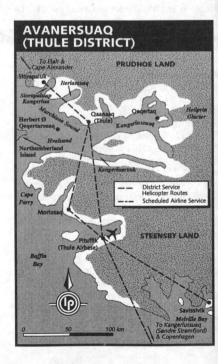

Thule Airbase Permits

Visitors to the US base in Thule (that's Pituffik, not Qaanaaq) are required to obtain a permit to enter the base area. Danish citizens must apply to the Ministry for Foreign Affairs, Asiatisk Plads 2, DK-1402, Copenhagen K. Others should contact the US Air Attaché, 24 Dag Hammarskjölds Alle, DK-2100, Copenhagen Ø, Denmark. A permit is not required by transit passengers through the airport at Pituffik.

Thule Inuit refer to themselves as Inukuit, the 'great people'. Avanersuaq is among the northernmost inhabited places on earth, encompassing 297,000 sq km. It has a population of just 850 and is also the last bastion of the US military in Greenland. Artistic talent runs high and it's an excellent place to look for traditional Inuit art.

Note that foreigners may not enter the Avanersuaq district between 15 September and 15 April. However, as dogsledding and hunting tourism increase in popularity, this may change.

Pituffik (Thule Airbase)

The US military airport at Pituffik serves as a transportation link to the communities of the Avanersuaq district, but you'd be hard-pressed to find a less inspiring place. All visitors and transit passengers visiting Thule airbase require a visitors' permit issued by the US Air Attaché, the Danish Ministry of Foreign Affairs or a Danish embassy. For details, see the boxed text 'Thule Airbase Permits'. Accommodation is available only to holders of visitors' permits. Tourists are confined to the *Transit Guesthouse*, while business visitors and others are housed at the *Base Hotel/Hostel* and allowed more freedom of movement.

Qaanaaq (Thule)

Qaanaaq, the world's most northerly palindrome, was moved 200km north to its present location in 1953 after being displaced by the US airbase at Pituffik. Its population stands at around 400. Tourist information is available from the Avanersuup Kommunia (☎ 971077, fax 971073), PO Box 95, DK-3971 Qaanaaq.

The **town museum** is dedicated to Knud Rasmussen, who spent much of his career researching and exploring in the district. Displays include items relating to his work and archaeological finds from around the area. The attached **Ultima Thule handicraft centre** sells local artwork typical of the Avanersuaq district.

Spring dogsled trips with local hunters may be arranged through the tourist office (or Greenland Travel in Copenhagen). An eight day trip between Qaanaaq and Siorapaluk costs Dkr9500 and includes meals, seal and walrus hunting, and accommodation

Plutonium Peril in Pituffik

The Thule Airbase is a bone of contention in international relations between Greenland, Denmark and the USA. The greatest controversy involves the US B-52 bomber that crashed near Pituffik (Thule Airbase) in 1968 which was later revealed to have been carrying four hydrogen bombs with nuclear detonation devices.

Of the 1000 individuals who worked on the two-month clean-up operation, 118 have since died, half of them from cancer. In 1988, health problems prompted 166 workers to file a joint complaint, but only in 1995, with the declassification of related US documents, was it confirmed that the plane did indeed carry 6kg of plutonium. Upon this revelation, the Danish government paid US$9000 tax-free compensation to each of the 1500 Danish and Greenlandic workers and residents of the base area.

In 1996, the US Air Force awarded a US$268 million contract to Greenland Contractors of Denmark to maintain the Thule Airbase for the next five years.

in cabins and igloos, while an incredible (and challenging) 15 day hunting trip over the sea ice to several Avanersuaq district villages costs Dkr18,950. For warmth on these trips, the Kommunia office hires out traditional fur-lined anoraks, polar bear-skin trousers, and sealskin boots for Dkr150 per day.

Hotel Qaanaaq (☎ *971234, fax 971264*) charges Dkr450 per person and full board in the hotel dining room is Dkr200 per day. Alternatively, basic, inexpensive accommodation at the *Telegraph Station* (☎ *971055*) or *Ionosphere Research Station* (☎ *971027*) can be booked through the Kommunia office. The *Polar Grill* serves snacks and fast food and the *KNI supermarket* is stocked whenever the flight comes in. Note that visitors may not bring alcohol into the Avanersuaq district.

Siorapaluk

Siorapaluk, the third most northerly civilian settlement in the world, after Longyearbyen and Ny Ålesund in Svalbard, has neither electricity nor running water. In winter, temperatures reach -50°C and lower, and water is obtained by melting ice. People survive by hunting seals, narwhals, walrus, birds and polar bears, and fishing for halibut. The area is also known for its agate deposits.

East Greenland

Culturally and linguistically, the isolated eastern coast of Greenland, known to Greenlanders as Tunu or Tunua (the back side), differs greatly from west Greenland. Noticeably more laid-back than the more populous west coast, it remains dependent on subsistence hunting and fishing, and families may spend over half the year at remote hunting camps. Although tourism is big business around Tasiilaq (Ammassalik) the people seem well equipped to handle it, and it will be a while before radical changes come to this beautiful area.

KULUSUK (KAP DAN)

For many years, tourism in Greenland was well contained, and over 30% of the coun-try's annual tourist count visited only the small island village of Kulusuk. Although it's now being overshadowed by Ilulissat as the main tourist draw, it remains a popular destination, mainly due to the international airport, which was built in 1958 to service the US DEW-line radar station. The ease of access is increased by the fact that Kulusuk is just a 1½ hour flight from Reykjavík and several Icelandic airlines offer day tours.

Don't miss the beautiful, haunting **cemetery**, which is festooned with plastic flowers and set against a stark and icy Arctic backdrop. For day tours, Icelandair organises an informal qajaq demonstration and drum dance performance. Worthwhile **hikes** include the 40 minute stroll between the airport and Kulusuk village, and the gravel track to the site of the old DEW-line radar station which lay across the low pass from the airport. Another great walk will take you straight up the hill, south of the airport, to an eerie mountain lake.

The 35 room *Hotel Kulusuk* (☎ *986-993, fax 986983, email kushot@greennet. gl*) charges Dkr795/985 for single/double rooms with breakfast. The tourist office in Tasiilaq can sometimes arrange hostel-style accommodation at the *Kulusuk Youth Club* for around Dkr200 per person.

TASIILAQ (AMMASSALIK)

Tasiilaq, on Ammassalik Island, is the largest community on Greenland's east coast and the administrative centre for the Ammassalik district (population 3000) Like Kulusuk, it enjoys stunning surroundings, and most of its 1600 people still practise subsistence hunting and fishing.

For tourist information, speak with Gerda Vilholm at the bookshop Neriusaq (☎ 981-018) from 2 to 6 pm daily. The Tasiilaq tourist office (☎ 981311, fax 981711, email tasiilaq.museum@greennet.gl) at the museum can arrange hire of two/four-person tents, sleeping bags, backpacks and stoves/cooking pots. Methylated spirits and Coleman fuel for mountain stoves are sold at the bookshop for Dkr25 per litre.

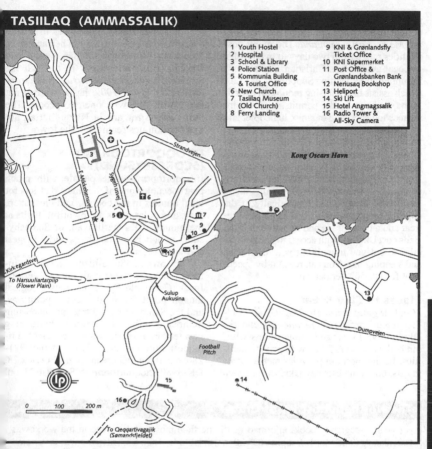

TASIILAQ (AMMASSALIK)

1 Youth Hostel
2 Hospital
3 School & Library
4 Police Station
5 Kommunia Building
  & Tourist Office
6 New Church
7 Tasiilaq Museum
  (Old Church)
8 Ferry Landing
9 KNI & Grønlandsfly
  Ticket Office
10 KNI Supermarket
11 Post Office &
   Grønlandsbanken Bank
12 Neriusaq Bookshop
13 Heliport
14 Ski Lift
15 Hotel Angmagssalik
16 Radio Tower &
   All-Sky Camera

Kong Oscars Havn

Strandvejen

E Mikkelsenivej

Kirkegardsvej

To Narsuuliartarpiip
(Flower Plain)

Sulup
Aukusina

Football
Pitch

Dumpvejen

0   100   200 m

15

16

14

To Qeqqartivagajik
(Sømanckfjeldet)

GREENLAND

Things to See & Do

The **Tasiilaq Museum** is housed in the old church, which was constructed between 1903 and 1908 and expanded in the 1950s. It now contains a wealth of information on the history and culture of east Greenland, including an early hunting tent, several qaaqs and lots of old photographs.

Upstream along the river, beyond the cemetery, is **Narsuuliartarpiip** (the flower plain) which refers to its variety of Arctic flora. On this easy walk, there are some

wonderful lakes and waterfalls, and you'll be inspired to keep exploring. From the radio tower near the hotel, it's a stiff but straightforward climb up 679m **Qeqqartivagajik** (Sømandsfjeldet). Fit hikers can do the return trip in three hours and on clear days the summit view encompasses Tasiilaq, Kong Oscars Havn, the inland ice and the wild iceberg and floe-studded coastline.

The Tasiilaq tourist office, which promotes the area's substantial **hiking** potential with some zeal, has constructed several mountain huts and produced an incredible double map and booklet, the 1:100,000 *Hiking Map – East Greenland*. The many possibilities range from two days to two weeks.

Local guide Hans Christian Florian runs Mount Forel Expedition Support (☎ 981320) which assists in organising **mountain expeditions**, and can handle permits, fuel and insurance logistics, and organise helicopter and dogsled transport. Florian specialises in the Stauning Alps, Mt Forel (3360m), the inland ice crossing between Isortoq and Kangerlussuaq, day climbs of Polham's Fjeld (across Kong Oscars Havn from Tasiilaq) and unnamed first ascents. His mountain hut at Tasiilap Kuua, perched dramatically at the edge of a glacier tongue, makes an ideal retreat and a base for ice and mountain hiking. Beds cost Dkr100, with access to cooking facilities, but you must bring your own food and sleeping bag. You can reach it by speedboat for Dkr500 per person.

Places to Stay & Eat

Hotel Angmagssalik (☎ 981293, fax 981-393, email arcwon@greennet.gl) charges Dkr495/695 for single/double rooms without bath and Dkr795/985 with private facilities. Its dining room provides meals for its guests, but nonguests pay Dkr115 for lunch or dinner. The *youth hostel* at the secondary school is open from the last week in June to the first week in August. For a bed and basic facilities, including a kitchen, you'll pay Dkr150. Book and check in through the tourist office. The *Neriusaq Bookstore (☎ 981018, fax 981009)* has a two bed flat for Dkr100/500 with one/two people. The best *camp sites* are in Narsuuliartarpiip, 1km to 2km upstream from the town.

ITTOQQORTOORMIIT (SCORESBYSUND)

Ittoqqortoormiit (the people with much peat) occupies one of the finest districts for local hunters in the country and muskoxen, seals and polar bears are plentiful. It sits at the mouth of Kangertittivaq, or Scoresbysund, which is by far the world's longest and widest fjord.

This town of 480 residents holds little interest, but the nearby airport at Nerlerit Inaat (Constable Pynt) provides a logical launch point for wilderness expeditions, and the Stauning Alps attract an increasing number of climbers seeking challenging new terrain. For information, contact the Ittoqqortoormiit Tourist Office (☎/fax 991-280, email nonni@greennet.gl), PO Box 28, DK-3980 Ittoqqortoormiit. See also Nonni

---

The Northernmost Bit of Gravel

For years, geography books informed us the northernmost point of land in the world was Greenland's Cape Morris Jesup, at 83° 20' north latitude. Then a small island was discovered off the north coast – a speck of land way up north of Peary Land called Kaffeklubben Ø, 'coffee club island'. It was named by Danish geologist Dr Lauge Koch after the afternoon coffee club at the Geological Museum in Copenhagen, where Dr Koch enjoyed the company and professional discussions of his colleagues.

Kaffeklubben Ø's day in the sun was not to last, however. Further north, amid the ice floes, a scrap of gravel less than 100m across was discovered peeping out of the sea. It was named Oodaap Qeqertaa or Oodaaq Island, and at 83° 40' north, it usurped the title of the world's northernmost land.

The island is now protected within the North-East Greenland National Park. The very wealthy may be able to reach it by charter helicopter, but Oodaaq is scarcely large enough for a heliport, and is unlikely to ever become a tourist destination.

Travel's Web site at www.est.is/nonnitra. It can arrange trekking, sailing, kayaking, skiing and dogsledding tours in the North-East Greenland National Park.

There are no hotels but you may find accommodation at *Leo's Guesthouse* (☎ 991-018, fax 991118), formerly Simonsen & Holtz, which costs Dkr350/500 for single/double rooms, including self-catering facilities. It lies on the hill near the school, a 10 minute walk from the post office. At *Nukissiofiit* (☎ 991066, fax 991121), near the harbour, you'll pay Dkr450 per person. At the airport in Nerlerit Inaat, accommodation is available for Dkr260 per person, with breakfast. Lunch and dinner cost Dkr110 and Dkr160, respectively.

Note that all flights to Nerlerit Inaat are with Flugfélag Íslands (Icelandair) via Reykjavík, Iceland. Helicopter transfers between Nerlerit Inaat and Ittoqqortoormiit cost Dkr395 one way.

NORTH-EAST GREENLAND NATIONAL PARK

The world's largest national park, established in 1974 and expanded in 1988 to encompass a total of 972,000 sq km, takes in the entire north-eastern quarter of Greenland and extends 1400km from south-east to north-west.

UNESCO has recently named it a Man and the Biosphere Reserve. Described as an 'Arctic Riviera' or 'Arctic Shangri-La', its tundra expanses are home to muskoxen, polar bears, caribou, Arctic wolves, foxes, hares and a variety of delicate plant life, while the fjords shelter seals, walruses and whales. Most of the park, however, lies on the icecap.

There are no facilities and the difficulty of access means that most park visitors are professional botanists, biologists, geologists and other Arctic researchers. In the far north-east, at Danmarkshavn and Daneborg respectively, are a weather station and a Danish military installation where the Sir-

The Sirius Sledge Patrol

During WWII, it became apparent that the long and uninhabited coastline of northeast Greenland required military protection. From a military sledge patrol that had operated during the war evolved the Sirius Sledge Patrol, which was officially established at Daneborg in 1950.

Its task is to patrol 160,000 sq km along the entire north-east Greenland coastline – in summer by boat and plane, and in winter by dogsled. After the creation of the North-East Greenland National Park on 22 May 1974, the patrol members inherited the job of park rangers.

Patrol members are selected from the officers' corps of the Danish army and do two-year stints on the patrol. They work in pairs, often moving through some of the planet's most remote wilderness for several months at a time. Their only company is a team of sled dogs and the only contact with the outside world is by radio. It may sound romantic, but combine tent camping and draughty abandoned hunting camps with temperatures of -50°C and you begin to wonder what motivates some people!

ius Sledge Patrol rescue rangers are stationed. The best source of information is the book *Frozen Horizons – The World's Largest National Park*, by Ivar Silis. Traditional hunters and government officials have unlimited park access, but other visitors require permits issued by the Dansk Polarcenter (☎ 45-32 88 01 00, fax 45-32 88 01 01, email dpc@dpc.dk), Strandgade 100H, DK-1401 Copenhagen K.

Applications must be made by December of the year prior to the intended visit, in plenty of time for the Polarcenter's annual meeting which determines who gets the year's permits.

GREENLAND

Arctic Iceland

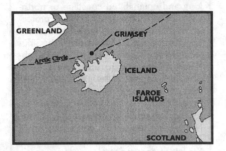

Although Iceland is generally considered a northern country, only two tiny scraps of it – half the island of Grímsey and the rock known as Kolbeinsey – actually extend north of the Arctic Circle.

GRÍMSEY

The northern tip of the 5.3 sq km island of Grímsey, 41km north of the mainland, constitutes Iceland's only real bit of Arctic territory. Yes, Grímsey is dissected by the Arctic Circle, and only here will you see the real midnight sun in Iceland. Although the attention span of most tourists falters there, the island's 100m cliffs harbour extensive bird colonies, accommodating at least 60 different species. Of these, 36 nest on the island – kittiwakes, puffins, razorbills, fulmars, guillemots, Arctic terns etc. Historically, Grímsey provided an abundant supply of birds and fresh eggs, and its waters were some of Iceland's richest in fish.

Sandvík (population 120) is the island's only settlement. Services are limited to a church, swimming pool, guesthouse and community centre.

Nonni Travel (☎ 461 1841, fax 461 1843, email nonnitra@est.is), on Ráðhúsplads in Akureyri (on the mainland), runs Grímsey tours daily. Flying both ways costs Ikr8125. On Monday and Thursday, you can take the ferry both ways for Ikr4745. If you opt to fly back, it's Ikr7350. Participants get a certificate stating that they've crossed the Arctic Circle. For longer stays, you can leave the tour on the island and return to Akureyri another day.

Places to Stay & Eat

You can camp nearly anywhere away from the village; the best sites are at the southern end of the island but the only fresh water is in small ponds and must be boiled. Sleeping bag accommodation costs Ikr750 in the *Múli* community centre (☎ 467 3138). Beside the airfield is the *Gistiheimilið Básar* (☎ 467 3103), which has single/double rooms for Ikr2700/4000 and sleeping bag accommodation for Ikr1500. Meals are also available but they're not cheap. At *Ragnhildur's Appartment* (☎ 467 3148) you'll get a three-bed apartment for Ikr2000; sleeping bag accommodation can be arranged in winter.

GRÍMSEY

1 Gistiheimilið Básar
2 Airport
3 Post Office
4 Swimming Pool
5 Múli Community Centre
6 Miðgarðakirkja Church

Grímsey's Checkmate

Grímsey is known as the home of Iceland's most avid chess players and, historically, many a poor performance at this sacred pastime resulted in messy dives from the sea cliffs; on Grímsey, failure at chess was equated with failure in life. Enthusiasm for the game might have dampened in the past two generations, but everyone on the island knows the story of its rather unconventional American benefactor, Daniel Willard Fiske.

During the late 1870s, Fiske, a millionaire journalist and chess champion, set himself up as the island's protector after hearing about its passion for the game. He sent badly needed firewood (as well as chess supplies!), financed the island's tiny library and bequeathed part of his estate to the community, without ever making a visit.

In the library at the community centre, you can see a portrait of Fiske and some of his donations. Grímsey celebrates his birthday on 11 November. For more on the amusing Fiske story, read Lawrence Millman's account of a visit to the island in his book *Last Places – A Journey in the North*.

There's also a well stocked food shop just uphill from the harbour.

Getting There & Away

Roughly between 9 June and 17 August, Flugfélag Íslands (☎ 460 7000) flies between Akureyri and Grímsey at least once every evening (except Saturday). The trip costs Ikr8000 return; this includes taxes, a short guided hike to the bird cliffs and an Arctic Circle certificate.

The ferry *Sæfari* sails to Grímsey from Akureyri on Monday and Thursday at 9 am, with stops at Hrísey and Dalvík, and returns from Grímsey at 7 pm. The trip takes five hours each way and costs Ikr4160 return, and yes, you can get an Arctic Circle certificate (Ikr300).

KOLBEINSEY

The islet of Kolbeinsey, 100km from the mainland, is Iceland's most northerly scrap of land. Early records describe it as 200m long, but rough sea conditions and ice floes have eroded it down to a mere speck in the Arctic Ocean, and it currently measures just 42 x 38m.

Because Kolbeinsey's existence adds 9400 sq km to Iceland's territorial fishing grounds, the cause of saving it sits high on the parliamentary agenda. A concrete, steel-reinforced wall has been proposed to shelter the vulnerable shoreline, but Kolbeinsey's status is already in dispute, and if it were to be officially classed as just an offshore rock, the cause of saving it would become academic.

ARCTIC ICELAND

Arctic Norway

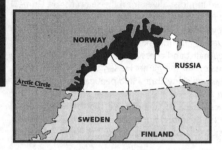

Northbound drivers on the Arctic Hwy enter northern Norway beneath the Nord Norge arch, which represents the aurora borealis, and as one moves northward, the fields give way to lakes and forests, vistas open up, the peaks sharpen and the tree line descends ever lower on the mountainsides. In summer, northbound travellers get their first taste of the midnight sun and won't fail to be impressed by the razor peaks, Caribbean-coloured seas of Lofoten, the broad fjords of the Arctic Ocean coast and the wild forests of Finnmarksvidda. While the mainland is impressive, the Arctic archipelago of Svalbard is an assault on the senses. This wondrous land is not only the world's most accessible bit of the polar north, but also one of the most spectacular places imaginable.

GETTING AROUND

Norway's domestic public transport systems include trains, buses and ferries that run efficiently and are often timed to link with each other. The *NSB Togruter*, available free at train stations, details rail timetables and includes information on connecting buses. For a list of ferry, bus, train and air schedules, fares and reservation phone numbers, get hold of the Nkr210 *Rutebok for Norge*, which is sold in bookshops and some Narvesen kiosks, or order it from Norsk Reiseinformasjon (☎ 22 33

01 92, fax 22 41 60 04), Tollbugt 32, N-0157 Oslo. Boat and bus departures vary with the season and the day, so pick up the latest timetables *(ruteplan)* from tourist offices.

Air

In northern Norway, even budget travellers may want to save travel time and do some segments by air. With the main airlines, SAS and Braathens SAFE, typical one-way fares from Oslo are Nkr1215 to Trondheim and Nkr2305 to Tromsø, but there are several discount programs that make air travel more feasible. You can find further information at www.sas.no and www.braa thens.no. With Widerøe (☎ 67 11 60 00, fax 67 11 61 95, email internetbooking @wider oe.no), which flies small planes, the flights are more like flightseeing trips than mere transport from A to B and even standard fares are considerably lower than on the big airlines. Check out the Web site at www .wideroe.no.

All three airlines offer good value air passes. To all domestic fares, add a commuter tax of Nkr71 to fly between any two cities also served by rail (except Bodø).

Bus

Buses on Norway's extensive long-distance bus network are quite comfortable. Tickets are sold on the buses and fares are based on the distance travelled, averaging Nkr112 per 100km. Many bus companies offer student, child, senior and family discounts of 25 to 50%, so it pays to ask. In northern Norway, holders of InterRail and ScanRail passes are often also eligible for discounts.

Nor-Way Bussekspress (☎ 23 00 24 40, mobile ☎ 81 54 44 44, fax 23 00 24 49, email ruteinformasjon@nor-way.no) operates the largest network of express buses in Norway, with routes connecting every main city and extending north all the way to Nordkapp and Kirkenes. If you want further nformation try its Web site at www.nor way.no.

There are also a number of independent ong distance companies that provide similar prices and levels of service. In addition, NSB (Norwegian State Railways) runs several Togbuss ('train-bus') routes. In Nordland, they run between Fauske and Bodø, Narvik, Tromsø, Svolvær, and Å. Holders of Eurail, Interrail and ScanRail passes pay half-price.

Train

Only three main towns in Arctic Norway are served by rail: Fauske and Bodø (on the line that heads north from Trondheim), and Narvik (on the iron ore line from the mines in Kiruna, Sweden). For timetable information and bookings phone NSB (☎ 81 50 08 88).

Reservations (which are required on some routes) cost an additional Nkr20, and are mandatory on many long-distance routes. Three-berth 2nd class sleepers cost Nkr100 and two-berth cabins are Nkr200/250 in old/new carriages. Students get a 50% discount on departures denoted by green dots in the NSB timetable and 40% on other departures.

The good value Norway Rail Pass allows unlimited 2nd class travel within the country and the ScanRail pass, which is valid on most railways in Norway, Denmark, Sweden and Finland, plus many bus and ferry discounts, are inexpensive ways to cover lots of ground.

Car & Motorcycle

Main highways, such as the E6 from Oslo to Kirkenes, are open year-round. The road network is constantly improving, and more bridges and tunnels are constructed every year. In longer tunnels, motorcyclists must be wary of fumes and may want to avoid them.

If you're expecting snowy or icy conditions, it's wise to use studded tyres or carry tyre chains. The Statens Vegvesen Vegmeldingssentralen, or Road User Information Centre (☎ 22 65 40 40 or ☎ 175), provides 24-hour advice on road closures and conditions. In several places in Arctic Norway, the road network includes vehicle ferry links.

Traffic keeps to the right. The use of dipped headlights and seat belts is obligatory at all times and children under the age of four must have their own seat or safety restraint. Note that the very low speed limits are zealously enforced, and even 5km/h over the limit will elicit a punitive on-the-spot fine of at least Nkr700. Similarly, watch for signs designating *Automatisk Trafikkontrol*, which means there's a speed camera ahead. Drunken driving laws are also strict in Norway; the maximum permissible blood alcohol content is 0.05% and violators are subject to severe fines (a blood alcohol level of 0.08% or greater warrants a fine of Nkr10,000 and a 21 day prison sentence). Third party insurance is also required.

Note that car hire is very expensive; walk-in rates for a compact car with unlimited kilometres start at Nkr800 per day (including VAT and insurance), although some companies advertise a friendlier 'hotel' rate of Nkr600. It may well be cheaper to book through an overseas company before you leave home.

Bicycle

Given its great distances, hilly terrain and narrow roads, Norway is not ideally suited for extensive cycle touring. The biggest headache (sometimes literally) for the long-distance cyclist will be tunnels, and many are closed to nonmotorised traffic due to the danger from hydrocarbon emissions and carbon monoxide fumes. Statens Vegvesen distributes the comprehensive booklet, *Tunnelguide for Syklister*, which lists all the tunnels in Norway, their lengths, whether they have lights and/or fans and whether they're open to cyclists.

Hitching

Norwegian motorists may well look askance at anyone who can't afford a vehicle, and hitching isn't popular. Norwegians are friendly, however, so with luck and patience, most hitchers do find lifts.

ARCTIC NORWAY

Boat

Due to Norway's rugged geography, ferry links are crucial, and an extensive network of car ferries and express boats links the country's offshore islands, coastal towns and fjord districts. Most ferries on the highway system accommodate vehicles, but express coastal services normally take only foot passengers and cyclists.

Hurtigruten Coastal Steamer

For over a century Norway's legendary Hurtigruten coastal steamer route has served as a lifeline linking coastal towns and villages. One ship heads north from Bergen every night of the year, pulling into 33 ports on its six-day journey to Kirkenes, where it then turns around and heads back south. The return journey takes 11 days and covers a distance of 2500 nautical miles. In agreeable weather, the fjord and mountain scenery along the way is nothing short of spectacular.

Sample deck-class fares from Bergen are Nkr1159 to Trondheim, Nkr1973 to Stamsund, Nkr2374 to Tromsø, Nkr2992 to Honningsvåg and Nkr3685 to Kirkenes. One en route stopover is allowed on these fares. Accompanying spouses, as well as children and seniors over the age of 67 receive a 50% discount. For a cabin, you'll pay an additional Nkr250 to Nkr1100 per night in summer and Nkr105 to Nkr525 in the off season.

There's a toll-free number (☎ 81 03 00 00) for information and bookings; otherwise, contact Troms Fylkes Dampskibsselskap (☎ 77 64 81 00, fax 77 64 81 80, email booking @tfds.no or gruppebooking@tfds.no), PO Box 548, N-9001 Tromsø; or the Ofotens og Vesterålens Dampskibsselskab (☎ 76 96 76 00, fax 76 11 82 01, email booking @ovds .no), PO Box 43, N-8501 Narvik. In North

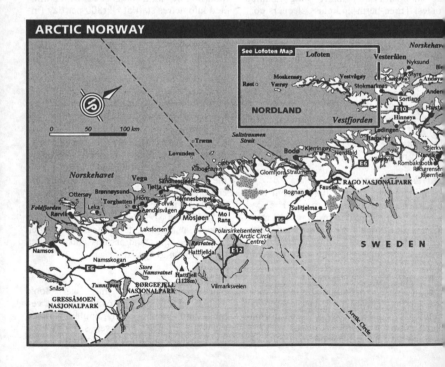

America, book through the Bergen Line (☎ 212-319 1300); in the UK, Norwegian Coastal Voyages (☎ 020-7371 4011); and in Australia, Bentours (☎ 02-9241 1353).

Organised Tours

In every tourist office, you'll find an exhaustive collection of leaflets, folders and brochures outlining organised tours in the immediate area. Typical offerings include bird or whale-watching cruises, lighthouse cruises, mine tours, glacier-walking tours, city and town tours, mountaineering tours, dogsledding trips, white-water rafting trips and excursions to sites of interest. Most tourist offices will book tours for a fee of Nkr20.

ACCOMMODATION
Camping

As with other Scandinavian countries, Norway has an *allemannsretten* (everyman's right) law, which allows you to pitch a tent anywhere for two nights, as long as you camp at least 150m from the nearest house or cottage and leave no trace of your stay. From 15 April to 15 September, lighting fires is prohibited. Most towns have private camping grounds, where tent space costs from Nkr50 to Nkr150 and simple cabins start at around Nkr250 for a very basic two or four-bed bunkhouse. Bring a sleeping bag. More deluxe cabins range from Nkr400 to Nkr800.

Summer Homes & Cabins

Most tourist offices in popular holiday areas keep lists of private huts, summer homes and cabins that are rented out to holiday-makers when the owners aren't using them. Prices for a week's rental start from around Nkr1300 for a simple place in the off season and go up to about

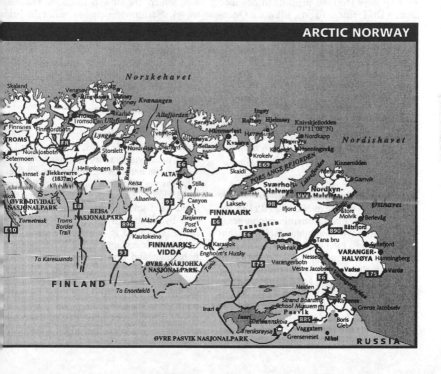

ARCTIC NORWAY

Nkr5500 for something more elaborate in midsummer.

DNT & Other Mountain Huts

Den Norske Turistforening (Norwegian Mountain Touring Association), or DNT, maintains a network of mountain huts of varying standards, but in northern Norway nearly all are small, unstaffed huts. Cooking facilities are usually available but in most places you must have your own sleeping bag or a hostel-style sheet sleeping bag. There are also numerous private hikers huts and lodges peppered around most mountain areas.

At staffed huts, nightly fees for DNT members/nonmembers in a room with one to three beds is Nkr150/220; rooms with four to six beds, Nkr105/175; dormitories, Nkr75/145 and overflow on the floor, Nkr50/120. For unstaffed huts, you must pick up keys (Nkr100 deposit) in advance from a DNT office. To pay, fill out a Once-Only Authorisation slip and leave either cash or a valid credit card number in the box provided. Self-service chalets are stocked with blankets and pillows, and have wood stoves, firewood, gas cookers and a wide range of food supplies for sale (on the honour system). In these, DNT members/non-members pay Nkr105/175 for a bed and Nkr50/120 for overflow space on the floor. At other unstaffed huts, users must carry in their own food. Most DNT huts are closed between 15 October and 15 February.

Hostels

'Youth' hostels, or *vandrerhjem*, offer good value, starting at Nkr100/Nkr125 for hostelling association members/nonmembers. Most have communal facilities that often include a kitchen where you can prepare meals. Normally, guests must bring their own sleeping sheet and pillowcase or linen. The Norwegian Hostelling Association, Norske Vandrerhjem (☎ 22 42 14 10, fax 22 42 44 76, email hostels@sn.no), at Dronningensgata 26, N-0154 Oslo, also publishes a free 156-page directory, *Vandrerhjem i Norge*. You can check out its Web site at www.vandrerhjem.no. Some are open year-round, while others occupy school dorms and are open in summer only.

Private B&Bs/Pensions

Next to camping and hostels, the cheapest places to sleep are in private rooms booked through tourist offices, which average Nkr150/250 for singles/doubles. Most towns also have pensions and guesthouses in the Nkr250 to Nkr400 range, but linens are included only at higher-priced places. Along the highways, you'll also find lots of *Rom* signs, indicating a basic place to crash for Nkr75 to Nkr200.

Hotels

Although normal hotel prices are high, some hotels offer reasonably discounted rates on weekends and in the summer season, which are slow periods for business travel. Nationwide chains maintain high standards of quality. One consideration in this land of daunting food prices is that hotel rates normally include a substantial all-you-can-eat breakfast buffet. If you're travelling with children, ask about family rooms, which accommodate two adults and up to two children for little more than a regular double.

Rorbuer & Sjøhus

Around northern Norway, especially in Lofoten, many visitors stay in either *rorbuer* or *sjøhus*. The name of the former means literally 'rowers' dwelling', and originally they were small red-painted fishing huts that lined the fishing harbours and were occupied by visiting fishermen. Nowadays, the name is applied to a range of structures, from historic cottages formerly occupied by fishermen and dire little prefab camping cabins to simple holiday homes and fully-equipped modern self-catering units. Sjøhus, on the other hand, are normally bunkhouse-style buildings on the docks where fishery workers processed the catch, and for convenience, they also ate and slept there.

Nordland

For general Nordland travel info, contact Nordland Reiseliv (☎ 75 54 52 00, fax 75 52 83 28, email ntravel@online.no) or try its Web site at www.nordlandreiseliv.no.

ARCTIC CIRCLE (POLARSIRKELEN)

Along the Arctic Hwy between Mo i Rana and Fauske, a big deal is made of the Arctic Circle for tourists with exhibits on Arctic phenomena, and the bleak moors adjoining Saltfjellet National Park provide the appropriate polar illusion. But the effect is more a factor of the 600m altitude than the latitude, and northbound travellers quickly descend into the relatively lush, well-vegetated environment that's more typical of northern mainland Norway. At the Polarsirkelsentert, visitors can pay Nkr45 to learn what the Arctic Circle is, peruse a collection of stuffed wildlife specimens and watch an audiovisual presentation on the Arctic regions. Perhaps the most worthwhile feature is the memorial to the forced labourers who, during WWII, constructed the Arctic Hwy for the occupying German forces.

BODØ

Bodø, at a latitude of 67° 17', is not only Nordland's largest town with a population of 40,000, but also serves as the northern terminus for the Nordlandsbanen railway. Because it was levelled on 27 May 1940 and rebuilt in the 1950s, Bodø looks shabby, but its open backdrop of distant rugged peaks and vast skies provide one of Norway's nicest locations. Destinasjon Bodø (☎ 75 52 60 00, fax 75 52 21 77, email destinasjon.bodo@nl.telia.no), at Sjøgata 21, is just five minutes on foot from the railway station and bus terminal.

When you're there, the **Norwegian Aviation Museum** (☎ 75 50 85 50) shouldn't be missed, and if you have even a passing interest in flight and aviation history, allow at least half a day to see it all. Note that the structure is built in the shape of an aeroplane propeller. It's open from 10 am to 8 pm weekdays and Sunday and from 10 am to 5 pm on Saturday from June to August, with shorter hours the rest of the year. Admission costs Nkr65.

The lovely 19th century trading station **Kjerringøy**, 40km north of Bodø, lies on a sleepy peninsula beside luminescent turquoise seas with a backdrop of soaring granite peaks. Most of the timber-built historic district has been preserved as an open-air museum. Buses from Bodø (1½ hours, Nkr65) leave on summer weekdays; fares include Festvåg-Misten ferry.

The **Saltstraumen Strait** connects Saltenfjord and Skjerstadfjord, where the tides cause one fjord to drain into the other and create a swirling, churning, 20-knot watery chaos that shifts 400 million cubic metres of water every six hours. The maelstrom can be viewed from the Saltstraumbrua bridge. From Bodø, bus No 19 frequently does the 33km from Bodø to Saltstraumen (50 minutes, Nkr39). The Bodø tourist office keeps tide tables and can tell you when to expect the best shows.

NARVIK

Narvik was established in the late 1890s as an ice-free port for the rich Kiruna iron mines in Swedish Norrland, and the current city is bisected by a monstrous transshipment facility where the ore is off-loaded from rail cars onto ships bound for industry around the world. However, Narvik was decimated between 28 May and 8 June 1940 and the Germans were in control until 8 May 1945. Although the town was rebuilt, modern Narvik's main draws are several in-town museums, the cable car up Fagernesfjellet, the exciting Ofotbanen railway to Sweden (and the adjacent Navvy's Trail hiking route) and the surrounding fjord, forest and mountain country.

The helpful Narvik og Ofoten Reiseliv tourist office (☎ 76 94 33 09 or ☎ 90 12 55 46, fax 76 94 74 05), Kongens gate 44, can answer all your questions.

Nordland Boats

No visitor to northern Norway will fail to notice the uniquely shaped Nordland boat, which takes its inspiration from the early seafaring Viking ships and has served the local fishing community from the earliest days of settlement in this region. In fact, these boats have now come to symbolise the earthy and self-sufficient lifestyles followed by the hardy coastal folk of the northern regions. Today, they remain in use from Namsos, in Nord Trøndalag, right up to the Kola Peninsula in Arctic Russia, but the greatest concentrations are found in the tiny villages of Lofoten.

The smallest versions are known as *færing*, which measure up to 5m, while the larger ones are called *hundromsfæring* (6m), *seksring* (7m), *halvfjerderomning* (7.5m), *firroing* (8m), *halvfemterømming* (9m), *åttring* (10m to 11m) and *femboring* (11m to 13m).

Traditionally, the larger the boat, the greater the status of its captain, or *høvedmann*. However, all boats of this construction are renowned for being excellent for both rowing and sailing, even in rough northern seas, and the fishing community historically took great pride in joining sailing competitions against their neighbours. A good place to see museum-quality examples is in the harbour at Å in Lofoten.

LOFOTEN

The unearthly glacier-carved peaks of the Lofoten islands, separated from the mainland by tapering Vestfjorden, rise straight out of the sea and from a distance, this so-called Lofoten Wall appears as an unbroken mass. This is Norway's prime winter fishing ground, thanks mainly to the Gulf Stream, which draws spawning Arctic cod from the Barents Sea southward each winter. Although cod stocks have dwindled dramatically in recent years, fishing remains Lofoten's largest industry, as evidenced by the innumerable wooden drying racks that lattice every village.

The islands are dotted with numerous rorbuer and sjøhus, which have been converted into summer tourist lodges and apartments. Tent and caravan camping are available at Unstad, Kabelvåg, Kleppstad, Laukvik, Ramberg, Strandslett (Stamsund) and Svolvær.

Austvågøy

Many visitors make their acquaintance with Lofoten on Austvågøy, the northernmost island in the group and the one with the most people and visitor facilities.

Svolvær

By Lofoten standards, the modern and busy port town of Svolvær is as exciting as it gets. Daredevils like to scale **Svolværgeita** (The Goat), a distinctive two-pronged peak visible from the harbour, and then jump from one horn to the other. If you're keen, see the Nord Norsk Kaltreskole in Henningsvær, who can set you up with a guide and equipment.

The narrow **Raftsund channel**, which separates Austvågøy and the Vesterålen island of Hinnøya, emerges as a highlight for through passengers on the Hurtigruten coastal steamer route, and the most memorable section of the trip is the short jaunt into constricted 2km-long **Trollfjorden**.

Kabelvåg

Kabelvåg presents a more intimate face than its larger neighbour, Svolvær. A few old timber buildings remain, and the small town square wraps around the harbour and features an informal outdoor market. At Storvågan, the **Lofoten Museum** (☎ 76 07 82 23) contrasts the lifestyles of the commoners and that of the Lofoten squires; the seafront **Lofoten Aquarium** (☎ 76 07 86 65), beside the Lofoten Museum, brings to the surface some of the fishy faces that made Lofoten great, and **Gallery Espolin** (☎ 76 07 84 05) features the works of artist Kaare Espolin-Johnson, which reveal the lives and hardships of the Lofoten fishermen; you won't soon forget the haunting quality of his monochrome themes.

Henningsvær

Few people would disagree that bohemian Henningsvær is the lightest, brightest and trendiest place in Lofoten. The **Nord Norske Klatreskole**, or North Norwegian Climbing School (☎ 76 07 49 11, fax 76 07 46 46), N-8330 Henningsvær, offers a wide range of technical climbing, kayaking and skiing courses all around Arctic Norway. If you want to tackle Svolværgeita or any other Lofoten peak, climbing with an experienced guide, including equipment, costs Nkr900/1000 per day for one/two people; you must book one day in advance. For ideas, check out the school's own publication, the 320-page *Climbing in the Magic Islands*, by Ed Webster. It also rents kayaks and runs the local hostel.

Vestvågøy

Vestvågøy may be known as the 'flattest' of the Lofoten islands, but it's far from level, and holds several interesting surprises, especially around the edges. It's also the site of the main airport, at Leknes, and at nearby

Borg, you can visit the worthwhile **Lofotr Viking Museum** (☎ 76 08 49 00, email lofotr@lofotposten.no), which offers a glimpse of life in Viking times, complete with a full-scale reconstruction of the building, costumed interpreters and a Viking ship reconstruction.

The traditional fishing village of **Stamsund** makes a fine destination largely because of the *Justad Vandrerhjem/Rorbuer* (☎ 76 08 93 34), which is a magnet for independent travellers; some have loved it so much that they've lingered for weeks on end. Scenic little **Mortsund** rates a mention mainly because it's home to the friendly *Statle's Rorbusenter* (☎ 76 08 75 55, fax 76 08 71 11), where the 40 cabins and 28 rooms sprawl across a rocky promontory.

Flakstadøy

Tourist information for Flakstadøy is available from Flakstad Brunestrand (☎ 76 09 34 50), in Ramberg. If you're tempted to skip Ramberg, you may want to think again. Imagine a vast arch of white sand along a

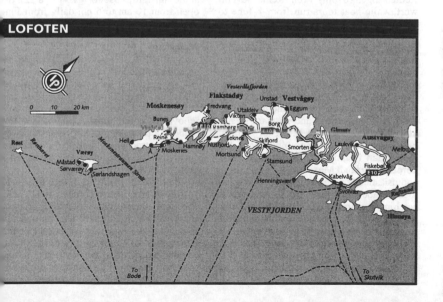

sparkling blue-green bay (that should, by all rights, be about 50° of latitude farther south) against an irreconcilable backdrop of snow-capped Arctic peaks. At the recommended **Ramberg Camping & Gjestgård** (☎ 76 09 35 00, fax 76 09 31 40), right on the beach, you can stay in a cabin or camp within spitting distance of the sand.

Moskenesøy

The 34km long glaciated island of Moskenesøy is unique – a series of pinnacled igneous ridges rising directly from the sea, separated by deep lakes and fjords, and indeed, it would make an ideal location for the film version of a Tolkien fantasy. You'll find tourist information at the Fiskeværsferie Lofoten Turistkontoret (☎ 76 09 15 99, fax 76 09 24 25, email touroff@lofoten-info.no), at the harbour at Moskenes.

Delightful **Reine**, which sits beside a calm turquoise lagoon backed by pinnacled peaks, has recently been voted the most scenic place in Norway. The best way to get its measure is to climb the precipitous track from the village to the summit of Reinebringen (670m). From Reine, several worthwhile boat tours run from 1 June to 31 August; book through the tourist office in Moskenes. **Hamnøy**, which shares a similar backdrop, also boasts a colourful fishing harbour and traditional timber buildings.

The fair village of **Å**, at the end of the road, is truly a living museum – a preserved fishing village with a shoreline of red rorbuer, cod drying racks and postcard scenes at every turn. Most of Å's 19th century buildings have been combined into the **Norwegian Fishing Village Museum**. The **Lofoten Stockfish Museum** (☎ 76 09 12 11) enthusiastically reveals all you ever wanted to know about Lofoten's mainstay, which is catching and drying cod for southern European markets. Beyond the camping ground, south of the village, you'll have excellent views of the **Moskenesstraumen strait**, which is fraught by mighty maelstroms that have inspired tales of maritime peril by Jules Verne and Edgar Allen Poe.

Southern Islands

Lofoten's southern islands of Værøy and Røst offer some of the finest bird-watching opportunities in Norway. Most people come for the clumsy little puffins but as a result of dwindling herring stocks, their numbers have dropped by more than 50% in the past decade. Although Værøy is mainly high and rugged and Røst is flat as a pancake, both islands offer good hiking and you'll also find a rare measure of solitude here, in well-touristed Lofoten.

VESTERÅLEN

The islands of Vesterålen, which are the northern continuation of the archipelago that includes Lofoten, are divided between the counties of Nordland and Troms. A good information source is the book *An Encounter with Vesterålen – Culture, Nature & History*, which outlines Vesterålen's history sites and walking routes. It's sold at tourist offices for Nkr117.

Stokmarknes

You can learn all about Hurtigruten history at the **Hurtigrutmuseet** (☎ 76 15 28 22). It's open from 10 am to 6 pm daily from June to September, admission costs Nkr35.

Nyksund

No one will regret a visit to Nyksund, an abandoned fishing village which is re-emerging as an artists' colony and whale watching centre. From the crumbling and collapsing old structures to the faithfully renovated commercial buildings, every scene is a photo opportunity and the lively youthful atmosphere belies the fact that only recently, Nyksund was considered a ghost village.

Whale Tours (☎ 76 13 11 66, fax 76 13 14 08) is the most recommended whale watching operator in Vesterålen, and the charm of Nyksund itself adds another dimension to the experience. Over the squid-rich banks off Andenes, you're almost certain to see sperm whales lounging and sounding, but you may also spot minke and pilot whales. The all-day cruises, which begin with a quick tour of Nyksund and include a light lunch on board, cost Nkr550. On the way back, you chug past a small island that is abuzz with squawking sea birds and lounging seals. If you don't see whales, which is rare, you can choose between another trip free of charge or a 50% refund.

Andenes

Andøya may not be as high or rugged as the rest of Vesterålen, but this long, narrow island has it own charm. The dark, cold 1000m deep waters off its north-western shore attract abundant stocks of squid – including some very large specimens – which in turn attract squid-loving sperm whales. The result is a reliable summer whale-watching venue. Andenes, especially its jumble of wooden harbourfront boat sheds and nautical detritus, also exudes an appealing nostalgic atmosphere.

Whale Safaris' (☎ 76 11 56 00, fax 76 11 56 10) popular **whale-watching cruises** operate from Andenes between 25 May and 15 September and guarantee sightings of sperm whales. Trips depart at 10.30 am and cost Nkr595.

Troms

ØVRE DIVIDAL NATIONAL PARK

A wild, roadless and lake-studded 750 sq km chunk of Norway between Setermoen and the Swedish and Finnish borders comprises Øvre Dividal National Park. While it lacks the spectacular steep-walled scenery of coastal Norway, this remote semi-forested upland wilderness still enjoys lots of alpine peaks and views. The most popular hike is the eight day Troms Border Trail, which laces seven unstaffed DNT huts. The map to use on the Troms Border Trail and the Abisko Link is Statens Kartverk's *Turkart Indre Troms*, at a scale of 1:100,000. In summer, hikers cannot underestimate the mosquito nuisance in this area; use a head net and carry plenty of repellent!

Access to Innset from Setermoen is by private vehicle, taxi (Nkr150 each way) or summer shopping bus that runs on Thursday (one hour, Nkr47), leaving Innset at 9 am and Setermoen at 1 pm.

TROMSØ

Tromsø (population 58,000), easily the largest town in northern Norway, claims lots of northernmost titles – the world's northernmost 18-hole golf course, botanical garden, university, Protestant cathedral, brewery (they ignore the one in Murmansk) and even the most boreal Burger King, among other

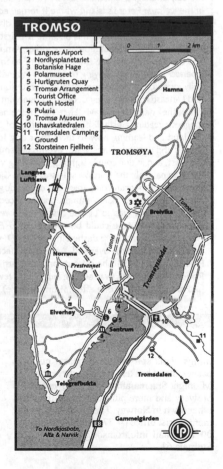

TROMSØ

1 Langnes Airport
2 Nordlysplanetariet
3 Botaniske Hage
4 Polarmuseet
5 Hurtigruten Quay
6 Tromsø Arrangement Tourist Office
7 Youth Hostel
8 Polaria
9 Tromsø Museum
10 Ishavskatedralen
11 Tromsdalen Camping Ground
12 Storsteinen Fjellheis

Roald Amundsen

If Nansen had the biggest heart of any polar explorer, fellow Norwegian Roald Amundsen had the most determination and grit. Born in 1872 at Borge, near Sarpsborg, he dreamed from an early age of becoming a polar explorer, and spent his early days getting his body into shape and devouring every bit of literature he could find on the subject of polar exploration. He was especially enthralled by the journals from the ill-fated 1845 expedition of Sir John Franklin, who had sought the Northwest Passage. In deference to his mother's wishes, he dutifully studied medicine, but when she died in 1893, he returned to his dream and never looked back.

Applying the same methodical approach he'd taken all his life, Amundsen decided that most failed polar expeditions stemmed from captains' errors, and decided to study for his master's licence. In 1894, he went to sea and three years later, sailed to the Antarctic as first mate on the Belgian *Belgica* expedition led by Adrien Gerlache de Gomery. However, the ship froze fast in the ice near Peter I's Island where it remained for 13 months. When the captain fell ill with scurvy, Amundsen took over command and displayed his ability to handle a crisis. Although there wasn't much choice, this became the first expedition to overwinter in the Antarctic.

Having gained a reputation as a captain, Amundsen set his sights on the Northwest Passage, and decided to justify the expedition with scientific studies of the Magnetic North Pole. After a period in Hamburg studying the earth's magnetic field, he selected a 47 tonne sloop, the *Gjöa*. Fully loaded, the expedition set out from Oslo in June 1903, passing Greenland, Baffin Island and Lancaster Sound. They decided to overwinter in a natural harbour on King William Island, which they named Gjöahavn. Here they remained for two years, building observatories, taking magnetic readings, establishing the position of the Magnetic North Pole, studying the lives of the Inuit and learning how to drive their dog teams. By August 1905 they'd completed their studies and continued westward, eventually emerging into waters that had been charted from the west, and in due course sighting a whaling vessel from San Francisco. Having been the first vessel to navigate the Northwest Passage, the Gjöa froze fast in the ice, and in October Amundsen and an American companion set off by dogsled to the telegraph station at Eagle, Alaska, over 900km away. There Amundsen announced the news of his success.

His next goal was to be the first man to reach the North Pole, and he asked his friend Fridtjof Nansen if he could borrow the ship *Fram* for the expedition. Nansen agreed, but Amundsen's hopes were dashed in April 1909, when American Robert Peary announced that he'd reached the pole overland. Amundsen decided to change directions and make the South Pole his goal. In 1910 he set out, only to learn that the British *Terra Nova* expedition, under Robert Falcon Scott, was setting out from New Zealand with the same idea in mind (Scott had already failed at one attempt on the pole).

things. This spirited town boasts cultural bashes, street buskers, a lively street scene, a Midnight Sun marathon, the hallowed Mack brewery and more pubs per capita than any other town in Norway. The Tromsø Arrangement tourist office (☎ 77 61 00 00, fax 77 61 00 10, email info.tromsoe@tosarr.no) is at Storgata 61.

Things to See

Tromsø's most striking church is the **Ishavskatedralen** (Arctic Ocean Cathedral) on the mainland, which is designed to reflect the ice and the aurora borealis of the Arctic regions. The harbourside **Polar Museum** (☎ 77 68 43 73), housed in a restored customs house on Søndre Tollbugata, con-

Roald Amundsen

In January 1911 the *Fram* dropped anchor at Roosevelt Island, which was 60km closer to the South Pole than Scott's Ross Island base. With four companions – Olav Bjåland, Helmer Hanssen, Sverre Hassel and Oscar Wisling – and four light sleds pulled by 13 dogs each, Amundsen set out overland on 19 October. Although they met with some difficulty passing the crevasses of the vast Axel Heiberg glacier, the expedition reached the South Pole on 14 December 1911. Famously, Robert Scott arrived on 17 January 1912, only to discover the Norwegian flag already there. Many historians feel that the hardy Amundsen had made the trip look too easy, especially because Scott's expedition met its end when five members – Edgar 'Teddy' Evans, Lawrence Oates, Henry Bowers, Edward Wilson and Scott himself – died of cold and starvation on the Ross Ice Shelf, while en route back to civilisation.

After two abortive attempts to make further oceanographic, meteorological and geophysical studies in the Arctic aboard the ship *Maud*, which involved three winters frozen into fast ice, Amundsen decided to mount an attempt to be the first person to successfully fly over the North Pole. On a lecture tour in North America, he met the American Lincoln Ellsworth, who was interested in purchasing two flying boats and sponsoring the expedition, in exchange for taking part in the expedition. On 21 May 1925, the two planes took off from Svalbard bound for Alaska, but thanks to a leaking fuel tank on one and engine trouble on the other, they were forced to land on sea ice about 150km from the pole. After using hand tools to hew out a runway, the pilot Hjalmar Riiser-Larsen managed to take off with all six crew members and return one plane to Nordaustlandet, in Svalbard, where they ditched in the sea and had to be rescued.

Having decided that fixed wing aircraft were unsuitable for polar exploration, the following year Amundsen tried again, this time aboard the airship *Norge* with Lincoln Ellsworth, the Italian Umberto Nobile and pilot/navigator Hjalmar Riiser-Larsen. They left northern Spitsbergen on 11 May 1926 and 16 hours later dropped the Norwegian, American and Italian flags on the North Pole. On 14 May, they landed triumphantly at Teller, Alaska, having flown 5456km in 72 hours and completed the first flight between Europe and North America. They also determined that the Arctic Ocean area was all water, with no landmasses embedded in it. (Note: Robert Peary's claim to have been the first at the North Pole, and subsequent claims by Dr Frederick Cook and Robert Byrd, have since been disputed, and it hasn't yet been determined who was the first; in fact, the Amundsen expedition was the first one with indisputable evidence of its success.)

In May 1928, Nobile attempted another expedition in the airship *Italia*, but it crashed in the Arctic. Amundsen volunteered to join the rescue expedition and took off from Tromsø. Although Nobile and his crew were rescued on 22 June, Amundsen's last signals were received three hours after takeoff, and he was never seen again.

centrates on polar research and exploration – particularly Roald Amundsen. Most summer visitors love to complement the 24 hour daylight with a glimpse of the winter-only aurora borealis at the **Northern Lights Planetarium** (☎ 77 67 60 00).

Those toppled dominoes marching up from the harbour are the architecturally daring **Polaria** museum (☎ 77 60 69 00), dedicated to Arctic phenomena, human habitation, marine environment and wildlife; the highlight is Ivo Caprino's audiovisual program on Svalbard. For information on the annual **Midnight Sun Marathon**, in July, contact Midnight Sun Marathon (☎ 77 68 40 54, fax 77 65 56 35, email post@msm.no).

Finnmark

Norway's northernmost mainland county, Finnmark, has been inhabited for 10,000 to 12,000 years, first by the Komsa hunters of the coastal region and later by the Sami fishing cultures and reindeer pastoralists, who settled on the coast and in the vast interior, respectively. Virtually every Finnmark town was decimated at the end of WWII by retreating Nazis, whose scorched-earth policy intended to delay advancing Soviet troops. Towns were soon rebuilt in an unfortunate boxy architectural style, leaving most of them less than memorable. For tourist information, see the Finnmark Travel Association (☎ 78 43 54 44), Postboks 1223, 9501 Alta.

ALTA

The beautifully sheltered fishing and slate quarrying town of Alta (population 17,000) has two main centres, Sentrum and Bossekop, 2km apart, but the town's various other shopping centres, business districts and residential developments actually stretch for at least 15km along the E6. The Destination Alta tourist office (☎ 78 43 77 70, fax 78 43 51 84) is in the shopping centre near the Bossekop bus stop.

Alta's main attraction is **Hjemmeluft**, a concentration of prehistoric rock art at the western end of town, which in December 1985 was named a UNESCO World Heritage Site. The estimated 2500 to 3000 individual Stone Age and Iron Age carvings are thought to date from between 6200 and 2500 years ago. The Nkr40 admission includes the adjacent **Alta Museum** (☎ 78 45 63 30). It's open daily from 8 am to 11 pm from 15 June to 15 August, with shorter hours the rest of the year.

The **Altaelva hydroelectric project**, on a dramatic stretch of the Altaelva, which slides through 400m deep **Sautso-Alta canyon**, northern Europe's grandest canyon. The easiest way to see it is on a four hour Destination Alta tour (Nkr295). There's also a challenging hiking route.

HAMMERFEST

Hammerfest, with a population of 10,000 people, is another predominantly fishing and fish processing community – with a bit of oil drilling for good measure. It was founded in 1789 and for over two centuries, proudly claimed to be the northernmost town in the world. Its lasting legacy is Europe's first electrical street lighting, which dates from 1890 and has proven a blessing in the long winter nights. As an assessment of its character, Bill Bryson noted of Hammerfest in *Neither Here nor There*, on a trip north to see the aurora borealis: 'I began to feel as if a doctor had told me to go away for a complete rest ... Never had I slept so long and so well.' Hammerfest Turist (☎ 78 41 21 85, fax 78 41 19 00), on Com Moesgata, provides tourist information and books local activities.

The Hammerfest town hall houses the renowned **Royal & Ancient Polar Bear Society**, which features exhibits on Arctic hunting. Membership in the club – and a smart certificate, sticker and pin to prove it – costs Nkr150. Hammerfest's **Reconstruction Museum** (☎ 78 42 26 30) celebrates the period following the German bombings of 1944, and discusses the 'Norwegianisation' of the Sami.

NORDKAPP

Nordkapp (North Cape), a high rugged coastal plateau at 71°10'21", is the main destination for most travellers in far northern Norway, but it would be more appropriately regarded as a nice view at the end of a long and scenic tour. But don't let anyone tell you it's the northernmost point in Europe. Those honours go to the promontory Knivskjellodden, a few kilometres to the north-west (see later in this chapter).

Nowadays there's a tourist complex, **Nordkapphallen** (☎ 78 47 68 60, fax 78 47 68 61), with polar exhibits, the posh Compasset restaurant and Grotten bar, a Thai museum (of all things), the St Johannes chapel, a post office (tourists love the Nordkapp postmark) and various souvenir shops. Don't miss taking a walk along the cliffs,

AROUND NORDKAPP

promoters, the signpost there doesn't identify it as such, but at 71°11' 08" N latitude, Knivskjellodden is the real northernmost point in Europe. It's not a difficult walk but does require a few ups and downs and takes about five hours return.

KIRKENES

During WWII, the industrial and iron ore mining port of Kirkenes (population 4500) probably suffered the worst bombings of any town in Norway. In spite of its remote northerly location, its rock and forest studded surroundings are surprisingly lush and not at all bleak. It also serves as a staging point for trips into Arctic Russia, just over the border (but if you're approaching the Russian border, don't even think about popping across for a photo; fines start at Nkr5000!) The helpful Grenseland Tourist Office (☎ 78 99 25 01, fax 78 99 25 25, email grenseland@online.no) is at Storgata 10, in the centre.

Things to See

Kirkenes' attractions include the **Hagenes Monument**, dedicated to the Soviet Red Army troops who liberated the town in 1944 and an underground cave, the **Andersgrotta** bunker, which was used as an air-raid shelter during the war. The well-done **Sør-Varanger Grenseland Museum** (☎ 78 99 48 80), 1km from the centre, deals with the geography, culture, religion and WWII history of the Norwegian, Finnish and Russian border regions. The worthwhile **Savio Museum** (☎ 78 99 25 01), at Kongensgate 10B, is dedicated to the Sami inspired work of artist John A Savio. If you can't wait for a Russian visa (see the Getting Around chapter), Barents Safari (☎ 90 19 05 94, fax 78 99 80 69) offers a **boat trip** up the Bøkfjorden to the Russian border at Boris Gleb (Borisoglebsk in Russian).

where you can gaze at the wild surf 307m below, watch the mist roll in and perhaps even dream of Svalbard, far to the north. Unfortunately, the complex imposes an unpopular admission fee of Nkr175 per person, and the only way to avoid it is to walk to Nordkapp (access to the nature reserve is free) and forego visiting the tourist complex (alas, no embossed Nordkapp certificate). The nearest car park lies 2km back along the road and bus passengers are discouraged from disembarking there, so you'll need your own vehicle and enough energy for a short slog.

KNIVSKJELLODDEN

From an unassuming car park about 9km south of Nordkapp, you can hike the marked 9km track to the lovely Knivskjellodden promontory. Thanks to an apparently unspoken agreement with Nordkapp

ØVRE PASVIK NATIONAL PARK

Even when the diabolical mosquito swarms make life hell for warm blooded creatures, the lakes, tundra bogs and Norway's largest stand of virgin taiga forest lend a strange appeal to odd little Øvre Pasvik National Park. This is the last corner of Norway where wolves, wolverines, lynx and brown bears still roam freely, and it seems more like Finland or Siberia than anywhere else in Norway. The park is also home to moose and a host of birds that are rare elsewhere in Norway. And then there are mosquitoes ...

Hikers can douse themselves in repellent and follow the poor road that turns southwest 1.5km south of Vaggatem, where there's a coffee shop and camping ground, and ends 9km later at the car park near the north-eastern end of the lake Sortbrysttjørna. There, a marked track leads southwestward for 5km, passing scenic lakes, marshes and bogs to end at the Ellenvannskoia hikers' hut, beside the large lake, Ellenvatn. The topographical sheet to use is Statens Kartverk's *Krokfjellet 2333-I*, which conveniently covers the entire park.

KAUTOKEINO

Desultory Kautokeino (Guovdageainnu in Sami), with its decidedly non-European ambience, is the heart of the 'big sky country' of northern Scandinavia and the cultural heart of Norway's portion of the semi-political entity known as Sápmi, the 'land of the Sami'. While tidier Karasjok has made concessions to both prevailing cultures – Sami and Scandinavian – Kautokeino remains emphatically Sami, and resembles no other town in Norway. The Kautokeino tourist office (☎ 78 48 65 00) offers town information.

The fascinating **Kautokeino Outdoor Museum** (☎ 78 48 60 43) presents a traditional Sami settlement, complete with a variety of buildings. Also check out the sculpture *Flyvesjamanens Fugl*, the 'flying shaman's bird', at the entrance to the secondary school. The world's only **professional Sami theatre**, *Beaivváš* operates through the Kautokeino Sami Cultural Centre, which also houses the Nordic Sami Institute. The highly acclaimed **Juhls' Solvsmie** (☎ 76 48 61 89) creates traditional and modern silver and gold jewellery and Sami handicrafts.

KARASJOK

Although Kautokeino is the most Sami settlement in Norway, Karasjok (Kárášvjohka in Sami) is the indisputable capital of Sami Norway and home of the recently established Sametinget, the Sami Parliament. The Karasjok Opplevelser tourist office (☎ 78 46 73 60, fax 78 46 69 00), has a desk in the Samelandsenteret, at the junction of E6 and the Rv92.

The worthwhile **Sami Museum** provides an easily digestible rundown of Sami history and culture from ancient times to the present day. At Engholm's Husky (☎ 78 46 71 66, fax 78 46 71 76, email se.engholm@online.no), 6km from town on the Kautokeino road, Sven Engholm (☎ 78 46 71 66) presents Alaskan dogsled demonstrations daily in summer at 10 am and 1 pm (Nkr30). He also offers excellent winter **dogsled and cross-country skiing tours**, as well as summer dog-packing tours. Pick up from town is free.

Svalbard

The Svalbard archipelago, which is about the size of Ireland, consists mainly of glaciated and eroded sedimentary layers that were laid down beneath the sea up to 1.2 billion years ago (although remnants of material up to three billion years old have been found in the rock). Between 300 million and 60 million years ago, Svalbard lay in the lush warm tropics, where rich layers of organic matter built up on the surface and eventually metamorphosed under great heat and pressure into the coal seams that now drive the islands' economy. Thanks to continental drift, however, Svalbard has migrated northward to its current polar location, and most of its present-day landforms were created during the ice ages of the past two million years. Although the west coast remains ice free for most of summer, pack ice hovers just north of the main island year round and vast sheets and rivers of ice cover approximately 60% of the land area.

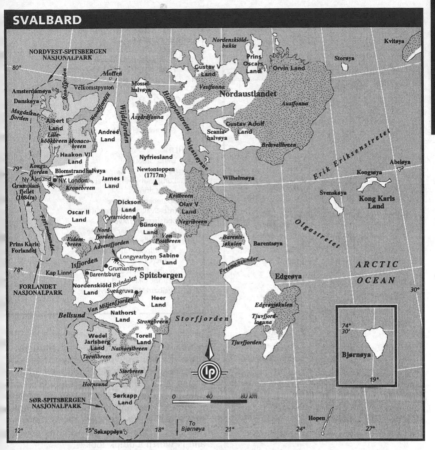

SVALBARD

LONGYEARBYEN

With a population of 1200, Longyearbyen is the capital and 'metropolis' of Svalbard. This practical-looking community on Adventfjorden (a branch of Isfjorden) had its beginnings as the main export site for the rich coal seams that characterise the island. The modern town, which is strewn with all sorts of abandoned coal mining detritus from mines No 1a, 1b, 2a, 2b and 4, also enjoys a superb backdrop that includes two tongues of the Longyearbreen glacier.

Information

The friendly and helpful Info-Svalbard tourist office (☎ 79 02 23 03, fax 79 02 10 20) is on 'the pedestrian street' (Gågata). Note that local decorum dictates that people remove their shoes upon entering homes, offices and hotels (but not shops or eateries).

For hiking and other independent expeditions in Svalbard, the law requires that you carry a firearm to protect yourself from polar bears. You'd naturally be more comfortable and familiar with your own firearm,

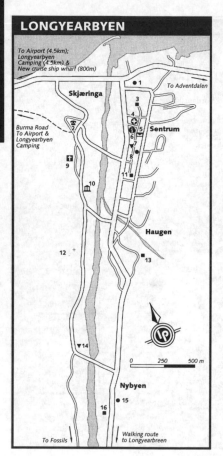

LONGYEARBYEN

PLACES TO STAY
3   Svalbard Polar Hotel
11 Svalbard Kro og Motell
13 Funken Hotel
16 Nybyen Gjestehus

PLACES TO EAT
7   Café Busen
14 Huset Restaurant; Nightclub
    & Convenience Shop; Cinema

OTHER
1   UNIS University
2   Telephone Office
4   Longyearbyen Hospital
5   Post Office &
    Sparebanken Norge
6   Info-Svalbard Tourist Office,
    Spitsbergen Travel,
    Norwegian Polar Institute
8   Svalbardbutikken Supermarket
    & Nordpolet Off-licence
9   Church
10 Svalbard Museum
12 Historic Graveyard
15 Svalbard Wildlife Service

which is one of the oldest buildings in town. Exhibits cover not only the history, climate, geology, wildlife and exploration of the archipelago, but also include some detail on the mining activities that form Svalbard's economic base. The haunting **graveyard** on the hillside above the town dates from the early part of this century and is worth a quick look.

Places to Stay & Eat

Your cheapest option is *Longyearbyen Camping* (☎ 79 02 14 44), near the airport, where a nice marshy bit of turf for your tent and use of the service building, washing rooms and heated toilets costs Nkr70. In town, the budget choice is the *Nybyen Gjestehus* (☎ 79 02 24 50, fax 79 02 10 05), in the suburb of Nybyen. Single/double rooms cost from Nkr350/490 to Nkr495/795, but cheaper rooms are sometimes available at late notice, so it may be worth checking. The *Funken Hotel* (☎ 79 02 24 50, fax

but as few visitors own such weapons and transporting one across international borders would be complicated, it is possible to hire one at either Svalbard Safari (☎ 79 02 13 22) or Svalbard Wildlife Service (☎ 79 02 10 35). Insist that they provide enough ammunition to allow you to practise and get a feel for the gun before heading off.

Things to See

Longyearbyen's **museum** (☎ 79 02 13 84), at Skjæringa, occupies a former pig sty,

79 02 10 05), between the centre and Ny-byen, has comfortable rooms for Nkr1045/1345, plus Nkr175 for extra beds. The poshest digs are in the well-appointed new *Svalbard Polar Hotel (☎ 79 02 35 00, fax 79 02 35 01)*, near the centre. Rooms cost Nkr1060/1320, plus Nkr50 for a room with a view. All the hotel rates include breakfast.

Although it's away from the centre, a good choice for meals and night-time entertainment is *Huset (☎ 79 02 25 00)*, which also houses a popular pub, bar and convenience shop. For lunch, the main local meeting place is the *Café Busen (☎ 79 02 17 07)*, in the Lompen Senteret, which has daily specials as well as typical cafeteria fare. It's open from 10 am to 6 pm Monday to Saturday and from 1 to 6 pm on Sunday.

Although alcohol is duty-free in Svalbard, it's rationed for locals, and visitors must present a valid airline ticket off the archipelago in order to buy it. The Nordpolet beer, wine and spirits outlet is at the back of the Svalbardbutikken.

Getting There & Away

Air In clear weather, the flight between Tromsø and Longyearbyen provides otherworldly views of Svalbard. SAS (☎ 79 02 16 50) flies this route on Monday and Friday and Braathens SAFE (☎ 79 02 19 22) flies daily. The full price return fare is Nkr3930, but you can also get special mid-price and mini-price deals for Nkr2955 and Nkr2360, respectively. Discounts are also available in Braathens SAFE's no-frills Braathens Back class, which eliminates meal and drinks services. The wealthy can charter a helicopter from Airlift (☎ 79 02 10 00, fax 79 02 14 30), but visitors may land only in official settlements.

Boat Troms Fylkes Dampskibsselskap, in conjunction with Spitsbergen Travel (☎ 78 02 24 10, fax 79 02 10 10), runs the M/S *Nordstjernen* ferry between Tromsø and Svalbard on Sunday from 22 June to 28 August. The boat arrives in Longyearbyen on Tuesday around noon and returns from its cruise around northern Spitsbergen at

10 pm on Thursday. It then sails back to Tromsø, via Nordkapp, to arrive on Friday night. The return cruise, including a single/double cabin with shared facilities, costs Nkr10,700/15,140 (these rates include the entire Spitsbergen cruise). Posher cabins are available for considerably higher rates; the most expensive option is a private single/double suite with a shower and toilet for Nkr19,640/26,180.

Getting Around

For a taxi between the town and the airport, the Longyearbyen Buss & Taxi (☎ 79 02 13 75 or ☎ 79 02 13 05) charges Nkr75. The airport bus (Nkr35) runs between the airport and the Nybyen Gjestehus, via the Svalbard Polar Hotel, the Svalbard Kro og Motell and the Funken Hotel, to connect with arriving and departing flights.

AROUND LONGYEARBYEN

The vast upland region overlooking Long-yearbyen to the west is known as **Platåberget** ('The Plateau'), and it makes a popular day hike. You can either ascend from near the Sysselmann's office in town, which is a steep and scree-covered route, or sneak up Blomsterdalen. You can also get onto Platåberget via Bjørndalen, south of the airport. Once on Platåberget, you can continue to the summit of **Nordenskiöldsfjellet** (1050m), where a Swedish observatory operated from 1931 to 1932. Note that bears occasionally wander onto the plateau area (there was a well-publicised death in 1996), and hikers need to carry a firearm.

The glacier tongues that lick at the upper outskirts of Longyearbyen have gouged through layers of sedimentary material, including fossil layers created when Svalbard had a more tropical climate. As a result, the terminal moraine is littered with **plant fossils** – leaves and twigs that left their impressions between 60 and 40 million years ago. There aren't yet any restrictions on collecting them but in the interest of conservation and future visitors, it's best to just have a look and leave them where they lie. The 5km return hike from Huset takes about 1½ hours.

The **Burma Road**, which is now just a walking track, follows the old coal mining **Taubanen cableway** to the processing plant and Mine No 3, near the airport. It makes an easy and casual half-day hike and doesn't require a firearm.

The stark and open landscapes of Adventdalen beckon visitors from town, and indeed, these wild landscapes are the Arctic you came to see. Most people want a photo of the **polar bear crossing sign** at the town end of the valley and hiking is pleasant, but more than a kilometre from town, a firearm is recommended. After leaving town, you'll pass the pungent husky kennels; the freshwater lake, Isdammen, which provides drinking water for Longyearbyen, and a northern lights station that is linked to similar facilities in Alaska and Tromsø.

BARENTSBURG

Against all odds, anachronistic and fascinating Barentsburg, Svalbard's only remaining Russian settlement, continues to mine and export coal. Although economic problems in Russia have translated into neglect and conditions are worsening, for most people, they're preferable to those at home in Russia (or the Ukraine, where many Barentsburg people come from) and most people do what they can to remain beyond their standard initial two-year contracts. On the world's northernmost farm, they grow greenhouse tomatoes, onions, potatoes, cabbage and other Russian staples, and raise chickens, pigs and cattle for meat and milk.

The simple **Pomor Museum** outlines (in Russian) the Pomor trade and Russian coal mining in Svalbard, and also has historical, geological and natural history exhibits. Admission costs Nkr20 and the ticket heartily thanks you for your visit.

At the charming ***Barentsburg Hotel*** (☎ 79 02 10 80 or ☎ 79 02 18 14), you'll pay Nkr440 for a double room. Traditional breakfasts (Nkr60), lunches (Nkr80) and dinners (Nkr90) are also served and in the bar, you can also enjoy a deliciously affordable shot of Stolichnaya vodka for a bargain Nkr10.

Barentsburg is most readily accessed on a tourist cruise, but in summer, hardy travellers can hike from Longyearbyen. Use the Norsk Polarinstitutt map *Nordenskiöld Land*, at a scale of 1:200,000, but seek local advice before you set out. A firearm is required for this trip.

PYRAMIDEN

Pyramiden, Russia's other Svalbard settlement, was named from the impressive Pyramiden mountain, which rises nearby. Around 1915, coal was discovered here and operations continued until the late 1990s, when it became apparent that the complex geology wasn't yielding enough coal to make the operation profitable. Operations ceased on 31 March 1998 and the settlement was abandoned in October of the same year. Until 2001, however, Trust Arktikugol funding during the summer months will maintain a basic infrastructure for workers cleaning up the site and the mining detritus.

The area offers superb hiking opportunities, and Trust Arktikugol, in conjunction with Spitsbergen Tours, is considering a joint management scheme that will involve ecotourism and the establishment of a small international community. The intent is to cooperate with the WWF to resurrect abandoned buildings and pipeline routes as tourist accommodation and walking tracks. One can only wish them well.

In addition to the day tours offered by various Longyearbyen agencies, Spitsbergen Tours runs longer hiking tours based at the Pyramiden Hotel and in remote cabins.

NY ÅLESUND

At 79°N, the scientific post of Ny Ålesund, founded in 1916 by the Kings Bay Kull Compani, isn't the most hospitable spot, but you'd be hard pressed to find a more awesome backdrop anywhere on earth. Ny Ålesund likes to claim that it's the world's northernmost permanently inhabited civilian community and it may be if you can ignore the fact that it lacks children and pensioners. It's now a prominent scientific post with a year-round population of about

Independent Expeditions in Svalbard

The easiest way to visit Svalbard and enjoy its wilderness is with an organised tour, which will handle the logistics and provide access to the islands' finest sites. Virtually everything in Svalbard is controlled by the office of the governor, the Sysselmann (☎ /9 02 31 00), and independent travellers are not only discouraged, but they face a host of regulations aimed at protecting this fragile environment from the ravages of mass tourism (tourism operators are subject to the same regulations). As a result, only a relatively small portion of the archipelago (mainly Nordenskiöld Land, Bünsow Land and Dickson Land) is open to independent travellers without expedition credentials, comprehensive rescue insurance and specific government approval.

Even in these open areas, logistics are complicated. Hikers and boaters must carry firearms to protect themselves from polar bears, and permission and insurance may be required for mountain climbing or sea kayaking trips. Transport can also be a problem, as tourist-chartered helicopters may not land outside of settlements and public transport is limited to boats between Isfjord settlements and flights between Longyearbyen and Ny Ålesund. Tour operators are reluctant to sell partial passages (except at the last minute), as it means losing a full fare, and similarly, they prefer not to commit to pick up groups at remote places which may be inaccessible due to drift ice, weather or other factors. If you're headed for a remote area, therefore, you'll probably have to get there on foot or skis, or use private charter boats or sea kayaks.

If you're set on a remote trekking or boat trip, or wish to independently visit a national park or reserve in Svalbard, contact the Sysselmann's office well in advance (about six months) and post or fax a detailed description of your plans, itinerary, equipment and experience of the participants and apply for permission. In most cases, the Sysselmann will then fix a maximal coverage sum required for search and rescue insurance (this may require coverage of up to Nkr300,000) or a bank guarantee, which must also amount to the recommended total to cover possible rescue costs.

Once the Sysselmann's office has received proof of this insurance or bank guarantee, the issuer may be required to sign a no-fault agreement guaranteeing payment in any case required by the Norwegian regulations for Svalbard. Norwegian insurance companies selling special comprehensive insurance for Svalbard are Europeiske Reiseforsikring (Uni Storebrand) and Gjensidige Forsikring, both in Oslo. You may also need proof that you have the required equipment and firearms, including a rifle with a minimum calibre of 7.62mm. You can import your own weapon with a special licence or hire one in Longyearbyen. Although it's possible to organise all this on site (that is, at the Sysselmann's office in Skjæringa, Longyearbyen), insurance companies may equate such lack of preparation with expedition incompetence and respond accordingly.

Note also that all cultural remains dating from prior to 1945 (including rubbish tips) are protected by law, and other relics, such as the Taubane cableway in Longyearbyen and various animal traps and hunting sites, are protected regardless of their age. Modern visitors on the other hand may not leave any evidence of their own visit, nor can they pick flowers, trample vegetation, or feed, chase or otherwise disturb wildlife. You may only shoot a bear as a last resort, when there is a clear attack and the animal cannot be frightened away by other means – screaming, flares, sound grenades and a number of warning shots. A bear standing nearby or destroying nonvital equipment is no excuse for shooting it and if you do, the fines will be severe.

As an aside, it's worth noting that government, economic and scientific interests enjoy a lot more latitude than tourists and tour operators. In the interest of the environment, visitors should not only follow the rules closely, but they should also make note of any violations by other parties and report them to the Sysselmann in Longyearbyen. For further direction, look for the pamphlets *Responsibilities & Resources*, *Regulations Relating to Tourism and other Travel in Svalbard* and *Take the Polar Bear Danger Seriously!* available at the airport, tourist office and Sysselmann's office, all in Longyearbyen.

25 and in summer, as many as 100 researchers from Norway and other countries descend to work on specific projects.

There's no tourist office and unfortunately, visitors may receive a less than warm reception from the local scientific community and the Arctic terns that nest in town. For the latter, it's wise to pick up a tern stick (available free at the dock) to hold over your head and prevent a vicious pecking by a paranoid mother.

Things to See

In the early 20th century, several polar explorers set off from Ny Ålesund, including the likes of Roald Amundsen, Lincoln Ellsworth, Admiral Byrd and Umberto Nobile, and you can see the **anchor pylon** used by Nobile and Amundsen to launch the airship *Norge* on their successful flight over the pole to Alaska in 1926. There are also several **memorials** commemorating Arctic exploration. Perhaps the most unusual sight is the oft-photographed **stranded locomotive** near the dock, which is the world's northernmost railway relic. In 1917, a 90cm-gauge railway was constructed to connect the coalfields with the harbour and remained in use until 1958. Ny Ålesund also supports the very nice little **Gruvemuseum** (mining museum), in the old Tiedemann's Tabak (tobacco) shop, which concentrates on coal mine history. Admission costs about Nkr7.

The only place to stay is the *camping ground* (the world's northernmost, of course), near Nobile's airship pylon, which has only a long-drop toilet and a trash can. Near the locomotive is the *Bar & Café Mellageret*, but watch for terns, who nest here. Basic snacks are sold at the *Kongsfjord Butikken*, but there's no supermarket, so bring your groceries from elsewhere.

Getting There & Away

Most visitors arrive on tourist cruises and only linger for an hour or two. Alternatively, in July and August, Lufttransport (☎ 79 02 16 60, fax 79 02 17 28) has a 25 minute scheduled daily air service between Longyearbyen and Ny Ålesund. From 1 May to 30 June and 1 to 30 September, it operates on Monday, Wednesday and Thursday. The return fare is Nkr2500 and the 20kg baggage allowance is strictly enforced. You can either book through Lufttransport or the King's Bay Kull Compani (☎ 79 02 71 11, fax 79 02 71 13), N-9173 Ny Ålesund.

AROUND NY ÅLESUND

Ny Ålesund's spectacular backdrop, Kongsfjorden (the namesake for the Kings Bay Kull Compani), contrasts bleak grey-brown shores with the expansive white Kongsbreen, Kronebreen and Kongsvegen ice fields. The distinctive Tre Kroner peaks, Dana (1175m), Svea (1226m) and Nora (1226m), named in honour of Denmark, Sweden and Norway, respectively, which rise from the ice, are among the most recognised landmarks in all of Svalbard.

Gravelly Blomstrandhalvøya was once a peninsula, hence its name, but in the early 1990s, it was released from the icy grip on its northern end and it's now an island. In summer, the name Blomstrand, 'flower beach', would be appropriate, but it was in fact named for a Norwegian geologist. At Ny London, at the southern end of the island, Ernest Mansfield of the Northern Exploration Company unsuccessfully attempted to quarry marble in 1911. Only too late did he discover that the stone had been rendered worthless by aeons of freezing and thawing. Only a couple of buildings and some decrepit machinery remain.

AROUND SPITSBERGEN
Kap Linné

Kap Linné, at the entrance to Isfjorden, consists of little more then the Isfjord Radio installation, but the enterprising facility also offers remote tourist accommodation (☎ 79 02 27 90, fax 79 02 17 82). Here you'll pay Nkr890/1380 for a single/double room, including full board. Transport is by boat, snowmobile or helicopter from Longyearbyen or Barentsburg, and both independent hiking and guided day tours are available in the area. All bookings for accommodation, transport and tours can be made through Isfjord Radio. Note, however, that much of the area lies within a bird reserve and is off limits in summer. With at least four people, helicopter transfers between Longyearbyen and Kap Linné cost Nkr1500 per person return.

Sveagruva

Coal was first discovered at Sveagruva, at the north-eastern end of Van Miljenfjorden, in the early 1910s. The operations were levelled by a submarine attack in 1944, but activity snapped back after the war and by the late 1970s, Sveagruva had grown into a well-appointed settlement of 300 workers and enjoyed nearly as many amenities as Longyearbyen. Over the following years, however, increased production around Longyearbyen resulted in declines at Sveagruva and by the mid-1990s, it had dwindled to just a handful of miners and administrators. Currently, with only one working mine around Longyearbyen, Sveagruva is the last gasp for coal mining in this area, and new buildings have been constructed to handle its anticipated resurrection. From March to May, hikers, snowmobilers and skiiers have access to the *Polartun Gjestehus* (☎/fax 79 02 5112), which has single/double rooms for Nkr525/700.

Prins Karls Forlandet

As you're cruising north along the west coast of Spitsbergen, it's worth noting the oddly-shaped 86km long island of Prins Karls Forlandet, which is a national park set aside to protect breeding pinnipeds. The alpine northern reaches, which rise to Grampianfjellet (1084m), are connected to Salfjellet (430m), at the southern end, by a long flat plain called Forlandsletta.

Krossfjorden

Thanks to its grand tidewater glacier, Lillehöökbreen, and several cultural relics, Krossfjorden also attracts quite a few cruise ships. At Ebeltoftbukta, near the mouth of the fjord, you can see several

whalers' graves as well as a heap of leftover junk from a 1912 German telegraph office that was shifted wholesale to Ny Ålesund in 1914 and kicked off that town's reputation as a scientific post. On the opposite side of the entrance rise some crowded bird cliffs, which overlook one of the most verdant spots in all of Svalbard. Here grow a variety of flowers, mosses and even grasses.

Magdalenefjord

The lovely blue-green bay Magdalenefjord, flanked by towering alpine peaks and intimidating tidewater glaciers, is the most popular anchorage along the western coast of Spitsbergen and for most visitors, it's also the most inspiring. In the 17th century, this area saw heavy Dutch whaling activities and at Graveneset, near the mouth of the fjord, you can still see the remains of two stoves used to boil down the blubber. Between the early 17th and mid-18th centuries, numerous whalers were buried at this site, which is now protected as a cultural monument and marked with a 1930 memorial honouring these early adventurers.

For better or worse, this site is extremely popular and if you're there with (or at the same time as) a large cruise ship, your enjoyment of the place may be affected. Be warned that ships' crew members frequently enhance their beach barbecues by dressing up as polar bears or penguins (clearly lost ones) and dancing on a convenient ice floe.

Danskøya

One of the most intriguing sites in northwestern Spitsbergen is Virgohamna, on the bleak and gravelly island of Danskøya. This was the site of several historical enterprises, and ample remains of several broken dreams now lie scattered across the lonely beach.

The ruins include the ruins of **three blubber stoves** from the old 17th century whaling station; remains of a **cottage** built by English adventurer Arnold Pike; and detritus from the ill-fated 1897 balloon

Fridtjof Nansen

Anyone looking for a modern hero need not look further than the Norwegian explorer, Fridtjof Nansen (1861-1930), who not only exceeded many of the frontiers of human endurance, but also of human compassion. Nansen grew up in the rural area of Store Frøen, at the edge of the Nordmarka woods outside Oslo, in a relatively wealthy family. Perhaps his interest in exploration was derived from this setting, as well as the influence of his father, Hans Nansen, who had once served as the mayor of Copenhagen and explored the shores of Russia's White Sea.

As a young man, he won the national Nordic skiing championships 12 times and broke the world record for the one mile skating course. When he entered the University of Christiania, his interests were in physics and mathematics, but he elected instead to study zoology, as he thought it would allow him to spend more time outdoors.

At the suggestion of a tutor, in 1882 he took passage aboard the sealing ship *Viking*, to sail to the Arctic Ocean and study ocean currents, ice movements and wildlife. During this voyage, he had tantalising glimpses of the eastern coast of Greenland, and he was seized with the desire to undertake a journey across the unexplored central icecap of that island continent. After six more years of study in Bergen, these dreams came to fruition when he led a six man expedition from the east to the west coasts of Greenland, between 18 June and 19 September 1888. He chose this direction, from the wild, uninhabited east coast to the more populated west coast, because there could be no retreat, and although he was only 27 years old, the expedition was completed without mishap. As there was no ship to take them back to Norway that year, Nansen remained in Greenland through the winter observing the Inuit peoples and gathering material for his 1891 book *Eskimo Life*.

In order to mount his next expedition, which aimed to use the Arctic Ocean currents and the westward flow of ice to reach the North Pole, Nansen commissioned shipbuilder Colin Archer to design a ship which would survive being frozen fast in pack ice. The result was the 400 tonne vessel *Fram* (Norwegian for 'forward'), which had a three layered oak hull reinforced with steel. He selected Otto Sverdrup, who had accompanied him to Greenland, to captain the ship and in June 1893 the expedition left Christiania with provisions for six years and fuel for eight. Nansen also left his wife Eva and six-month-old daughter Liv, with no idea when he would return.

After realising that the ship wouldn't come as close to the North Pole as hoped, Nansen decided to make a bid on foot for the pole, and on 14 March 1895 he and Hjalmar Johansen left the *Fram* and its mission in the hands of Otto Sverdrup. After a five month, 550km journey over the ice, they were turned back by ice conditions and low supplies, at the northernmost point ever reached at the time. The two men retreated south to one of the islands in Franz Josef Land, where they holed up for nine winter months in a tiny stone hut they'd built. The following May they continued southward, and in June ran into British explorer Frederick Jackson (for whom

expedition of Swede Salomon August Andrée and the 1906 expedition of US journalist Walter Wellman, who attempted and failed to reach the North Pole in a zeppelin. Most of the junk that now litters the beach are the remains of these attempts on the North Pole, and it's all protected as a historical monument (including dozens of rusted 44-gallon fuel drums).

Amsterdamøya, Fairhaven & Moffen

The offshore island of Amsterdamøya was the site of the large Smeerenburg whaling

Fridtjof Nansen

Nansen later named the island where they'd spent the winter). Nansen and Johansen headed south with Jackson, and arrived back in Vardø, just a week before the *Fram* arrived in Skjervøy.

By 1905 Sweden and Norway faced a political crisis that stemmed from Norway's bid for independence from the union with Sweden, and Nansen, who was by then a national hero, was dispatched to Copenhagen and Britain to represent the Norwegian cause. When Norway achieved its independence, Nansen was asked to act as the prime minister of the new country (there are rumours that he'd turned down the position of king or president) but declined, wishing only to continue as a scientist and explorer, and eventually mount an expedition to the South Pole. However, he did accept the offer from King Håkon to serve as the Norwegian ambassador to Britain. In 1907, Nansen's wife died suddenly, and he permitted fellow Norwegian explorer Roald Amundsen to use the *Fram* on an expedition north of Siberia, which meant that he had to abandon any hopes of reaching the South Pole.

After WWI, Nansen worked tirelessly for the newly organised League of Nations, and took up the cause of half a million German soldiers who'd been imprisoned in the Soviet Union and no longer had a homeland. Although the USSR would not recognise the League of Nations, Nansen set off in April 1920 to plead the case of these dispossessed soldiers. By September 1922, he'd successfully repatriated over 400,000 men or found countries willing to accept them.

Even before this project was finished, a failed grain crop in Russia threatened 20 million people with both famine and pestilence and the International Red Cross asked Nansen to lead an aid project. He soon discovered, however, that the League of Nations was unwilling to help a communist country, and resorted to private fundraising missions to help as many Russians as possible. At the same time, he identified that two million Russians who had fled the 1917 Bolshevik revolution remained stateless; the result was the 'Nansen Passport', which enabled thousands of stateless Russians and Ukrainians to travel and settle in other countries.

Nansen's greatest diplomatic achievement, however, was probably the resettlement in their home countries of several hundred thousand Greeks and Turks who had been displaced after the defeat of the Greek army by the Turks in 1922. As a result, in 1922 he was awarded the Nobel Peace Prize, and donated his prize money to international relief efforts. After 1925 his efforts were concentrated on international disarmament and lobbying the League of Nations to provide a non-Soviet homeland for Armenian refugees in Turkey, Syria and other countries. Although this latter project failed, his name is still revered by Armenians around the world.

On 13 May 1930 Fridtjof Nansen died quietly at his home in Polhøgda, near Oslo. If you wish to learn more about the life of this extraordinary man, look for the biography *Nansen* by Roland Huntford, published in the UK in 1997, or the earlier book of the same title by EE Reynolds, first published in 1932.

station, which was co-founded in 1617 by Dutch and Danish concerns, but all that remains are seven ovens and some graves. All around the nearby sound, Fairhaven, which lies between the mainland and the four small offshore islands, are scattered numerous whalers' graves. Known for its walrus population, most tourist cruises attempt to approach flat and gravelly Moffen Island, but the majority are turned back by pack or drift ice. In any case, between 15 May and 15 September, boats can't approach within 300m of the island, lest they disturb the walruses' breeding activities.

OUTER ISLANDS

Bjørnøya

Svalbard's southernmost island, 178 sq km Bjørnøya, is home to a tiny museum, the Norwegian Bjørnøya Radio meteorological station and a couple of historic buildings. The most interesting is a former pig sty known as **Hammerfesthuset**, which was constructed in 1823 and is the oldest surviving building in Svalbard. The island's name is derived from an errant bear who inhabited the island when Willem Barents first landed there.

Hopen

In 1942, the narrow and lonely island of Hopen saw the wreck of the Soviet freighter *Dekabrist*, only three of the 80 passengers and crew members survived the near-impossible winter conditions. The fol- lowing year, the island was occupied by a German meteorological station, which was later rebuilt by the Norwegians to monitor climatic conditions and later, to study ice movements and the aurora borealis. It's now home to a handful of scientific personnel.

Nordaustlandet

Vast Nordaustlandet, Svalbard's second largest island, takes in over 14,700 sq km, about 75% of which is covered with ice. The lonely eastern coast is dominated by the vast Austfonna ice sheet, which forms the longest tidewater glacial face in the Arctic region.

Although the island is currently uninhabited, it's littered with the ruins of past activities, including the former German weather station at Rijpfjorden and the once unsightly Kinnvika weather station on Murchisonfjorden. Fortunately, the Sysselmann cleaned up the mess left at this installation and now maintains a helicopter fuel depot there.

Kvitøya

The 700 sq km island of Kvitøya, or 'white island', is aptly named, as only three tiny headlands are free of ice and it's almost perpetually surrounded by either pack ice or drift ice. Not surprisingly, it's uninhabited, but there is an unstaffed radio transmitter and the odd icebreaker does call in from time to time. Its 15 minutes of fame, however, came when the Swedish balloon expedition of Andrée, Frænkel and Strindberg crashed here after their failed attempt on the North Pole in 1897. All three died, probably of food poisoning from eating infected bear meat.

Jan Mayen

Norway's 'other' Arctic territory, the island of Jan Mayen, lies in the Norwegian Sea 600km north of Iceland, 500km east of Greenland and 1000km west of the Norwegian mainland. It sits squarely on the northern end of the mid-Atlantic ridge and at its northern end, known as Nord-Jan rises Norway's only active volcano, Beerenberg (2277m).

The island measures 54km long by up to 16km wide, and covers 380 sq km, including a 3.5 sq km slice called Nylandet, which was added by an eruption of Beerenberg in September 1970. During WWII, it served as a headquarters for Norwegian forces in exile, but nowadays, it has only a small Norwegian meteorological post.

Although Arctic cruise ships call in occasionally and a couple of specialist tourism operators offer fleeting visits to the island, independent travel is all but nonexistent. Prospective visitors must obtain permission from the Ministry of Defence in Oslo. If you're intent on visiting Jan Mayen, check with Spitsbergen Tours in Longyearbyen, who may be able to arrange something.

Arctic Sweden

It would be difficult to imagine more starkly beautiful landscapes than those of northern Sweden, one of the last remaining wilderness areas in Europe, with its Sami culture, reindeer, and midnight sun. It is no coincidence that Sweden led Europe in setting up national parks, and that the country's largest and grandest are in Norrland. Sweden has around 20 national parks in all kinds of landscapes, but the best places to admire the mountains are the giant Sarek and the tiny Abisko in the far north. The Sami minority includes around 15,000 individuals living in the far north of the country.

Perhaps no other nation has been so international for such a long time. Today Swedes are everywhere: doing aid work in Africa, selling mobile telephones in Shanghai, backpacking in Borneo, modelling in California and drinking in Torremolinos. Swedes tend to think of themselves as observers rather than the ones to be observed; they visit other countries, they've accepted a larger percentage of immigrants than most European countries, and with their multicultural society, they enjoy ethnic cuisines as well as the best French wines. Ecological consciousness is high and reflected in concern for native animals, clean water and renewable resources.

While Sweden boasts a rather socialist system and the general quality of the available goods is high, when you pay, you pay dearly. No, it's not as expensive as Norway, but if you're coming from central or western Europe, it will take some mental adjustment to get used to the prices.

GETTING AROUND

Public transport in Sweden is well organised and heavily subsidised. The regional air, rail and bus networks, which are tied together with the *länstrafik* system, offer some of the best bargains, as well discount schemes. On the Tågplus, one ticket is valid on trains and on any länstrafik service, but it's not valid with other discount schemes.

Air

SAS has daily flights between all major centres, from Malmö in the south to Kiruna in the north, and the domestic airline Skyways runs an even larger network. Flying is expensive, but substantial discounts are available, such as return tickets booked at least seven days in advance or low-price tickets for accompanying family members and seniors. Those under 25 years of age should go to the airport just in case; one-way stand-by tickets with SAS between Stockholm and Kiruna cost just Skr200.

Bus

You can travel by bus either on national long-distance routes, or using any of the 24 regional länstrafik networks. In Sweden, each bus line has a route number. Länstrafik is usually complemented by regional trains, and one ticket is valid on any bus, local or regional. Rules vary but transfers are usually free within one to four hours. Most counties are divided into zones. Travel within one zone costs from Skr12 to Skr17, with a maximum applicable fare for each network.

Each county has its own timetable, which is normally free of charge and details not only bus timetables, but also the various applicable discount schemes. There are usually daily, weekly or monthly

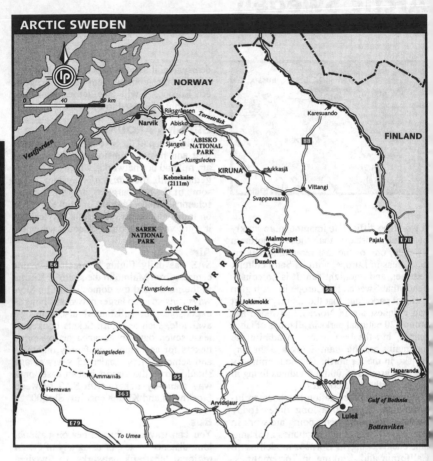

ARCTIC SWEDEN

passes, which are always good value. Value cards are also good; you pay, say, Skr200 for over Skr250 worth of travel. Be sure to ask how the regional discount pass works and how it's validated.

Long-distance buses are either extended regional services (prices vary) or truly national networks. The largest are Swebus, Svenska Buss (reservations required ☎ 020-67 67 67), Linjebuss (from Sundsvall) and the Postens Diligenstrafik postbuses that operate around Norrland. Passengers under 21 or over 60 years of age receive a 30% discount, but student concessions require a Swedish student card.

Train

Sweden has an extensive railway network, and trains are certainly the fastest way to explore. Surprisingly, there are several dozen train operators in Sweden, although the national network of Sveriges Järnväg (☎ 020-75 75 75) covers all the main lines. Further information can be obtained from the Web site www.sj.se. Several of the counties also run regional train networks.

In summer, most visitors want to take the renowned Inlandsbanan to the north country. This 1000km route from Mora to Gällivare costs Skr481, but a special card allows two weeks' unlimited travel on the route for Skr700. It's a bit slow, however – five hours from Mora to Östersund and 14 hours from Östersund to Gällivare. Inter-Rail is the only rail pass that's valid on the Inlandsbanan.

Individual 2nd class tickets are expensive, but discounts are available and all tickets include a seat reservation (night trains include a sleeper or a seat). Discount rail tickets have so many strings attached that most travellers find them inconvenient. The Reslust Card allows discounts of up to 50%, while the Reslust Max 25 Card for young travellers gives a discount of up to 65%; both cards cost Skr150 and are valid for one year. You must book and pay at least seven days in advance. Cheapest are the limited issue Röd (Red) Reslust tickets, but the more expensive Rosa (Pink) Reslust tickets still offer good value. The annual Affärståget card costs Skr1500 and gives a 25% discount on all länstrafiken and SJ (but not Reslust) tickets, without having to book and pay in advance. If you're over 26 and don't have a rail pass, it's a pretty good bet. Students and people under 26 years of age always get a 30% discount on the adult fare.

Inter-Rail, Eurail and ScanRail passes, and Rail Europ S cards are accepted on SJ services and nearly all regional trains. The X2000 trains require a supplement of Skr125 (Skr30 for Eurail Pass holders if they reserve a seat). On most InterCity and InterRegio trains you pay a Skr30 supplement for seat reservations, but there are no supplements on regional trains. Rail passes are also accepted on SJ-run buses, and on buses between Boden/Luleå and Haparanda.

Car & Motorcycle

Sweden has an excellent national highway system and you need only a recognised driving licence (however, an international driving licence from your local automobile club is required by car hire agencies).

The national motoring association is Motormännens Riksförbund (☎ 08-690 38 00, email melem@motormannan.se), Box 23142, S-10435 Stockholm. If your vehicle breaks down, telephone the local number of the Larmtjänst 24-hour towing service. Insurance Green Cards are not required but can be reassuring.

Road rules conform to EU standards, using international road signs. Swedes drive on and give way to the right. Headlights should be dipped but must be on at all times when travelling on the roads. Seat belts must be worn in all seats, and children under seven should be in appropriate harnesses or child seats.

The blood-alcohol limit is a trifling 0.02%, which most people will reach with a single beer or glass of wine. The maximum speed on the motorway is 110km/h. Speeds on other roads are 50km/h in built-up areas and 90km/h on highways. The speed limit for cars towing caravans is 80km/h.

On many highways broken lines define wide-paved edges, and the vehicle being overtaken is expected to ease into this area to allow faster traffic to pass comfortably. In the far north, reindeer and moose present road hazards, and all incidents involving large animals must be reported to the police. Sandbags and sandboxes provided on many roads may be a help in mud or snow.

Automatic ticket street parking is common and small signs point to the nearest *parkeringsautomat* (ticket machine). This generally costs around Skr10 per hour on weekdays and may be free in the evening and on weekends. Parking garages in larger towns charge around Skr15 per hour.

Car hire is quite expensive, starting at around Skr450 per day for a compact car with unlimited kilometres and third-party insurance. Railway and fly-drive packages can bring some savings, and weekend or summer packages are also offered at discount rates (although these are not always available at airport branches).

To rent a car you normally have to be at least 21 (sometimes 25) years of age and show an international driving licence; you may also have to make a deposit by credit card. An inexpensive agency is Happy Rental (☎ 020-99 55 99), which charges as little as Skr200 per day and Skr2 per kilometre. Other small operators offer similar rates. Mabi (☎ 08-612 60 90) at Roslagsgatan 38 in Stockholm rents 650cc motorcycles for Skr595/day, plus 50 öre per kilometre.

Bicycle

The cycling season in northern Sweden runs roughly from July to August. There are over 20 off-road and signposted national routes. If you want an epic challenge, follow the green signs along Sverigeleden, the national circuit linking up over 6000km of tracks. For detailed maps and free route suggestions, write to Svenska Cykelsällskapet (☎ 08 751 62 04), Box 6006, S-16406 Kefta. In towns, follow the marked bicycle paths, or signs for long-distance bicycle routes to leave the urban area. You must turn on lamps after dusk.

Bicycle hire costs anything from Skr70 to Skr150 per day, or Skr250 to Skr600 per week. Taking a bicycle on public transport is easy on länstrafik routes, including some trains and most regional buses. The fee ranges from free up to Skr40 per trip. SJ trains are more difficult, as you must book in advance and pay Skr150. Dismantled bicycles, however, can be taken as luggage. Ferries carry bicycles for a fee, but long-distance buses may not.

Hitching

Hitching is not popular in Sweden, and you'll probably have less luck here than in other European countries. The good news is that Norrland is probably the best region for hitching and you may get short-distance lifts off the main highways.

Boat

The national road authority, Vägvärket, operates about 90 highway ferries that are part of the road network and are usually free.

Local Transport

Local transport is always linked with the regional länstrafik – rules and prices for city buses may differ from long-distance transport, but a regional pass is valid on both city and rural routes.

ACCOMMODATION
Camping

Sweden has some 700 camping grounds and a free guide with maps is available. Some camping grounds are open in winter, but the best time for camping is from May to August. Prices vary with facilities; from Skr80 to Skr150 for a basic site with electricity. Most camping grounds have kitchens and laundry facilities. For camp cooking, look for Primus or Sievert gas products, which are available at service stations.

To stay at Swedish camping grounds, you need the free Svensk Campingkort. Apply at least one month before your journey at Sveriges Campingvärdars Riksförbund (fax 0522 64 24 30, email ck@camping.se), Box 255, 45117 Uddevalla. If this is not possible, you will be given a temporary card on arrival. You can also check out the Web site at www.camping.se. The annual stamp on your card costs Skr49 and is obtainable at the first camping ground you visit.

Thanks to the *allemannsretten* (everyman's right), everyone may walk, boat, ski, swim or camp anywhere in Sweden, except in the immediate vicinity of a house, garden, fenced area or cultivated land. You are allowed to camp for more than one night in the same place, and may pick berries and mushrooms.

You'll normally find good informal camp sites around unsealed forest tracks from secondary country roads. Make sure your spot is at least 50m from the track and not visible from any house or building or a sealed road. You may not leave any rubbish nor take living wood, bark, leaves, bushes or nuts. Fires may be set where safe (not on bare rocks) with fallen wood, but be sure to douse your fires with water.

Hostels

Sweden has well over 400 hostels. Of these, some 305 are 'official' hostels affiliated with Svenska Turistföreningen (STF, part of Hostelling International), which produces a detailed guide for Skr98. Holders of HI cards get a Skr40 discount each night and can stay for the budget rates of Skr75 to Skr150. Nonmembers can join up at hostels.

More than 100 private hostels belong to the 'rival' Sveriges Vandrarhem i Förening (SVIF). No membership is required and rates range from Skr90 to Skr160. Pick up the free guide at tourist offices or SVIF hostels. Also look out for other hostels not affiliated with either STF or SVIF.

Note that reception hours are short and the rest of the time, you'll normally find the hostels locked up tight (especially in winter). The secret is to phone and make a reservation during the reception hours, which vary, but are generally from 5 to 7 pm. Write down the four-digit entrance door code and ask where the room key will be. Theoretically, you could stay overnight without seeing another person until you pay in the morning. Written reservations are recommended but they carry the threat of a Skr50 cancellation penalty! Breakfast is often available for Skr35 to Skr45, but normally has to be arranged the night before. Always carry sheets to save money. Many hostels have kitchens, but you sometimes need your own utensils.

In December, check that hostels you intend to visit are indeed open, especially around Christmas and New Year. In June, July and August you can expect longer reception hours but a reservation is recommended because many hostels are full. The principle is that you should clean up after yourself, but some hostels push optional 'cleaning fees' of up to Skr200! Mountain huts and stations affiliated with STF also charge overnight fees.

Cabins

Daily rates for cabins at camping grounds offer good value for small groups and families. Regional tourist offices and some national agencies rent cabins and cottages by the week – there are detailed listings.

Hotels

There are few cheap hotels in Sweden. Budget travellers may find weekend and summer (June to mid-August) rates reasonable, often below Skr600 for a double. Some packages are good value if you plan ahead. Stockholm, Göteborg and Malmö offer cut-price 'packages' that include a hotel room, free entry to the main city attractions and free local transport – plus an optional discounted return train ticket. Tourist offices and travel agents can usually give details.

Sometimes prices are expressed as 'per person in a two-bed room', so be careful. Some of the discount vouchers available are Scandinavia-wide and run by the big chains. Others, such as the Pro Skandinavia or Biltur Logi packages, are available through travel agents.

ARVIDSJAUR
☎ 0960

Welcome to Lappland. Although it's still south of the Arctic Circle, the small settlement of Arvidsjaur on Inlandsbanan was an early Sami market and today, the **Lappstaden museum village** and **Sita Sameland**, which combine almost 100 buildings as well as forestry and reindeer-breeding concerns, are run by the Sami community. The Skr25 tours run in summer at noon and 3 pm. From early July to early August the old **Ångloket steam train** makes return evening trips to Slagnäs on Friday and Moskosel on Saturday (both Skr120). The tourist office (☎ 175 00, email info@arvidsjaurturism.se) at Garvaregatan 4 books accommodation. The Inlandsbanan take you north to via Jokkmokk to Gällivare (Skr136). Useful Web sites for further information include www.lappland.se and www.arvidsjaurturism.se.

JOKKMOKK
☎ 0971

The village of Jokkmokk, reached by Inlandsbanan, lies just north of the Arctic Circle and started as a Sami market and mission.

ARCTIC SWEDEN

The tourist office (☎ 121 40, email jokk mokk.turistbyra@jokkmokk.se) at Stortorget 4 is open daily from 9 to 7 pm (to 4 pm in winter) and the Old Pharmacy cybercafe nearby offers affordable Internet access.

The **Ájtte museum** at Kyrkogatan 3 (Skr40), open daily in summer, provides a thorough introduction to Sami culture and offers exhaustive information on Lappland's mountain areas. It's a great spot to research wilderness trips and sample local fish or a reindeer sandwich.

Naturfoto, at the main Klockartorget, exhibits and sells work by local wilderness photographer Edvin 'Sarek' Nilsson. The beautiful **wooden church** on nearby Storgatan should be seen; the **'old' church** on Hantverkargatan has been rebuilt, as the original was burned in the 18th century. The Fjällbotanisk trädgård by the lake introduces mountain trees and other local flora. The four day **Sami winter fair** takes place from the first Thursday in February, and offers serious handicraft *(sámi duodji)* shopping.

GÄLLIVARE
☎ 0970

The town of Gällivare (official spelling Gellivare) and its northern twin Malmberget are surrounded by Norrland wilderness and dwarfed by the bald Dundret hill. It isn't the world's most exciting spot, but it has some of the best budget accommodation in Sweden – just bring your own sheets.

The helpful tourist office (☎ 166 60, email touristinfo@gellivare.se) also hires bicycles and can organise wilderness excursions. Check out its Web site at www.gellivare.se. The tourist office also houses the free **Hembygdsmuseum**, which displays local artefacts, and the **Sportfiskemuseum**, a private collection of fishing equipment, admission is Skr20. The **hembygdsområde**, near the camping ground, collects pioneer and Sami huts in a small open-air museum (open mid-June to mid-August).

The summit of Dundret hill is a **nature reserve** and the view reputedly encompasses one twelfth of Sweden. It also contains four nordic ski courses and 10

downhill runs of varying difficulty. Day lift tickets cost Skr180 and ski hire starts at Skr100/150 per day for full nordic/downhill gear. Halfway up, **Vägvisaren** exhibits Sami traditions, and has reindeer (open daily from late June to late August).

In Malmberget, 5km north of Gällivare on bus No1 (Skr13), the free **Kåkstan** museum is a renovated 'shanty town' dating from the 1888 iron-ore rush. Also of interest is **Gruvmuseum**, which covers 250 years of mining.

KIRUNA
☎ 0980

Kiruna, the northernmost town and largest *kommun* (municipality) in Sweden (19,446 sq km), takes in the country's highest peak, Kebnekaise (2111m), and several fine national parks and trekking routes, making this architecturally interesting town an excellent base for wilderness tours. The tourist information centre (☎ 188 80, email lapp land@kiruna.se) is at Lars Janssonsgatan 17 and you'll find Internet access at the library behind the bus terminal.

A highlight of any visit would be a plunge into the bowels of the **LKAB iron ore mine**, 350m underground. The 2½ hour tours, which cost Skr100, depart from the tourist office daily in summer at 9.30 am, 12.15 and 3 pm. The **Kiruna church** has an intriguing history and is one of the most interesting buildings in all of Scandinavia.

Every winter at Jukkasjärvi, 20km east of Kiruna on bus No 501, the amazing **Ishotellet** is reconstructed from hundreds of tonnes of ice. This 'igloo' has a chapel, bar and exhibits sculptures by international ice-artists. Admission costs Skr60. Some 20km farther out is the aurora borealis *(norrsken)* research station **Esrange**, where you can watch a slide show on the phenomenon. The Skr20 tours run daily at 1 pm.

A superb place to stay is the *Yellow House (☎ 137 50, email yellowhouse @mbox301.swipnet.se)* at Hantverkaregatan 25, with dorm beds for Skr100 and singles/doubles for Skr200/300. Advance booking is recommended. There's also a

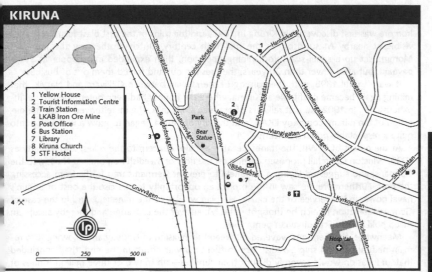

KIRUNA

1 Yellow House
2 Tourist Information Centre
3 Train Station
4 LKAB Iron Ore Mine
5 Post Office
6 Bus Station
7 Library
8 Kiruna Church
9 STF Hostel

Park

Bear Statue

0   250   500 m

hostel in the centre of town, which lies within easy walking distance of transport terminals.

ABISKO & THE KUNGSLEDEN
☎ 0980

The 77-sq-km Abisko National Park occupies the southern shore of the scenic Lake Torneträsk and is well served by buses, trains (the tourist-oriented Abisko Turiststation and the more practical Abisko Östra) and a mountain highway between Kiruna and Nurvik.

Abisko has a tourist office (☎ 402 00), and the **Naturum**, beside the provisions shop (both open daily), provides natural history information and film shows. *Camp Abisko* ☎ *401 48)* near Abisko Östra train station has beds from Skr125. *Abisko Fjällstation* ☎ *402 00, email info@abisko.stfturist.se)*, open from mid-February to mid-September, offers beds from Skr220 (Skr150 for HI members) and singles/doubles for Skr365/ 20. You can hire trekking gear here and lunch/dinner costs Skr65/175. The **Linbana chair lift** (Skr60/75 one-way/return) climbs

1169m **Njulla fell**, where there's a cafe open from 9.30 am to 3 pm.

Hiking
Less rugged and more accessible than other parks in Arctic Sweden, Abisko is full of excellent day hikes. Popular routes lead up the Abiskojåkka valley, to the rock outcrop Paddis, which is sacred to the Sami, and to the distinctive mountain notch known as Lapporten.

The 500km Kungsleden trekking route leads south from Abisko and offers diversions to the summit of Kebnekaise and the magical **Sarek National Park** (no huts and few bridges). Waterproof boots are essential at any time of year, especially during the thaw between May and June. July to September are recommended for hiking, but beware that the boggy ground nurses zillions of mosquitoes. Huts along Kungsleden are spread at 10 to 20km intervals between Abisko and Kvikkjokk. You need a sleeping bag only as there are blankets and gas inside. HI members/nonmembers can stay for Skr130/180 in the southern sections, but

Kiruna – The Ore that Fuelled a War

Iron ore was first discovered in Kiruna in 1647, and the ruins of the first blast furnace are still visible at nearby Masugnsby. In the mid-17th century, Dutch brothers by the name of Momma set up a small-scale iron mining operation, then expanded into copper at Svappavaara, but after fewer than 20 years, the ores ran out and forced them out of business.

It wasn't until 1898, with the coming of the railway between Gällivare and Narvik, that mining again became profitable at Kiruna, where the bounty had been determined to be 'inexhaustible'. In 1902 the first rail cars of ore reached Narvik, the mine thrived under the direction of the mining company LKAB, and the city of Kiruna began to grow and develop into quite a respectable population centre.

At the outset of WWII, the mines became a major concern to the Allies, and as early as 1939, Winston Churchill proposed cutting off the flow of Swedish iron ore, via Narvik, to the Germans, and suggested laying a minefield to prevent German cargo traffic from accessing the port. Furthermore, he saw in the project an opportunity to exercise the best of Britain's naval power in the service of the cause. His plan was to lay the minefield, and in the case of German retaliation (which he thought unlikely), answer the challenge and thereby secure an Allied hold on the Scandinavian peninsula.

Meanwhile, the Germans wavered between the invasion of Norway and allowing it to remain neutral and still ship Swedish ore to fuel their war effort. In the end, they concluded that an invasion would severely disrupt their supplies – up to two or three million tonnes of ore per year – but that the threat of a full British blockade of Norway was considerably more serious and decided to invade. On 9 April 1940 they moved into Oslo and within two months Narvik was decimated. However bravely the Allies attempted to defend the port, on 8 June they accepted orders to surrender Narvik to the occupying forces. The Nazis remained in control of Narvik – and the supply of iron ore – until they were defeated on 8 May 1945.

Over the following years, Kiruna continued to produce but in the 1970s, the steel markets declined and half of LKAB's workers in Kiruna found themselves unemployed. In a rather visionary program, the company set up Future City, which brought aerospace and computer operations into Kiruna to make up for the shortfall. Fortunately, the industry and markets have slowly bounced back and by LKAB's 100th year of operations in 1990, the company had taken 800 million tonnes of ore from the ground. The good news is that it's estimated that two billion tonnes of ore remain and the company is currently investing Skr4 billion on new mills and procedures to open up a 300m deep seam which is projected to hold 400 million tonnes.

around Kebnekaise and Abisko, fees increase to Skr190/245.

A good alternative to the Kungsleden is a trek to **Sjangeli**, south-west from Abisko. It was an unsuccessful mine in the 17th century but is now a Sami-run wilderness centre. A 70km loop route connects Sjangeli with both Abisko and Riksgränsen.

For any of these hikes or treks, fill out the sheets and books *(färdmeddelande)* pro-

vided at mountain huts with your details as you go. The 1:100,000 *Fjällkartor* maps usually cost Skr98. Most huts are equipped with phones. The 100km trek from Abisko to Nikkaluokta runs via the mountain hostel *Kebnekaise Fjällstation (☎ 550 00 email info @kebnekaise.stfturist.se)* with beds from Skr250. It's 130km from Abisko to the Vakkotavare wilderness hut, or a little over 200km to *Kvikkjokks Fjällstation*

(☎ 0971 210 22, email info@kvikkjokk.stf turist.se), which has beds from Skr150 in summer.

RIKSGRÄNSEN
☎ 0980

Riksgränsen is the last station in Sweden before the train rushes through tunnels and mountain scenery back to sea level at Narvik in Norway.

The historic 'Navvy Trail' hiking route roughly parallels the railway line and will take you either to Narvik or Abisko. The best midnight (or daytime) skiing in June in Scandinavia awaits you at this rugged frontier area, the name of which means simply 'national border'. Daily rental of downhill gear costs around Skr200, and a day lift pass, Skr190. In summer visit Sven Hörnell's free **wilderness photography exhibit** or watch the Skr45 audiovisual program. The well-run **Katterjokk** (☎ 431 08) hostel, 2km south of Riksgränsen, has beds for Skr130.

Arctic Finland

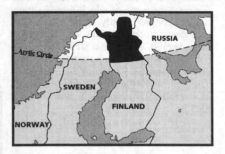

Covering nearly half of Finland, the sparsely populated province of Lapland, with just 200,000 people and a population density of 2.1 per sq km, offers some of the best preserved wilderness in Europe.

Whether you just pass through or set off on an extensive trek, allow enough time to get out into this wide open wilderness country. The information in this book covers only those regions of Lapland that lie north of the Arctic Circle.

GETTING AROUND

For accurate details of every train, bus, flight and ferry route in Finland, you should outlay Fmk110 for the *Suomen Kulkuneuvot*, which is published four times a year. The summer edition, *Kesäturisti*, includes a summary in English. It's sold in bookshops and transport terminals around the country.

Air

Finnair is the principal domestic carrier, with services between southern Finland and Lapland. Although air travel within Finland generally isn't economical, a number of discount schemes offer reasonable fares.

One of the best deals is the discounted return between Helsinki and Ivalo, which compares with rail or bus fares. Stand-by fares also offer substantial savings. For information, phone the Finnair general booking office toll-free (☎ 9800-3466).

One of the best deals is the stand-by youth fare, available for travellers aged 17 to 24, which offers fares of just Fmk249 on any domestic flight. Tickets must be purchased at an airport ticket office within one day of departure. On regular return or one-way fares, travellers aged 17 to 24 receive 50% discount; for seniors and children aged two to 16, the discount is 70%.

Advance-purchase return tickets give up to 50% discount, although restrictions apply. A number of special discounts are offered on selected routes in summer, and 'Snow Fares' offer discounts of 50 to 70% on selected flights between Helsinki and Lapland during non-holiday periods from January to May. The VAT (sales tax) and Fmk56 domestic departure taxes are included in the listed fare.

Bus

Finland's comfortable bus services run efficiently and on schedule, and connect all major centres and most smaller towns and villages. There are two kinds of intercity service: regular buses that plod along, stopping at every post, and express buses that travel swiftly between cities. The latter is handled by Oy Matkahuolto Ab (☎ 09-682 701, timetable information ☎ 0200-4000) Lauttasaarentie 8, 00200 Helsinki, while private companies handle regular bus services. For further information try www.matkahuolto.fi or www.expressbus.com.

Each town and municipal centre has a *linja-autoasema* (bus terminal), where you can verify bus schedules. Most buses run from Monday to Friday with limited services on Saturday and only a few on Sunday. Note that bus stations close at 6 pm Monday to Saturday and at 4 pm on Sunday.

A Coach Holiday Ticket, valid for two weeks and up to 1000km, costs Fmk350 Used wisely it's much cheaper than purchasing individual bus tickets. It's valid for two weeks from the date of the first trip or

The tiny village of Qaarsut huddles beneath the peaks of the Nuussuaq Peninsula, Greenland

DEANNA SWANEY

DEANNA SWANEY

Ųamertorsuaq, Tasermiut Fjord, Greenland

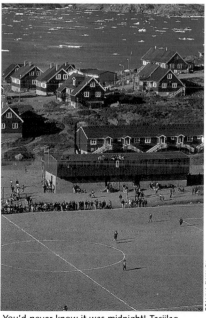

DEANNA SWANEY

You'd never know it was midnight! Tasiilaq

NED FRIARY

Reine, Lofoten Islands, Norway

all buses in Lapland (and throughout most of Finland) and may be purchased at most Finnish bus terminals and travel agents.

Bus reservations are advised for travel on weekends and holidays; you can book at any bus station ticket counter or travel agency. Tickets are valid for one month from date of purchase. A reserved seat is optional and carries a Fmk12 surcharge. One-way bus tickets may be purchased on board the bus at departure if seats are available.

Ticket prices depend on the number of kilometres travelled and return tickets are usually about 10% cheaper than two one-way fares (the fare from Helsinki to Rovaniemi, for example, costs Fmk442/796 one way/return). There is no difference in price for express and regular buses, but discounts are normally available for students, seniors and children. On some routes, buses may offer discounts to holders of rail passes, so it doesn't hurt to ask. Bicycles are transported on buses for Fmk10 to Fmk20, space

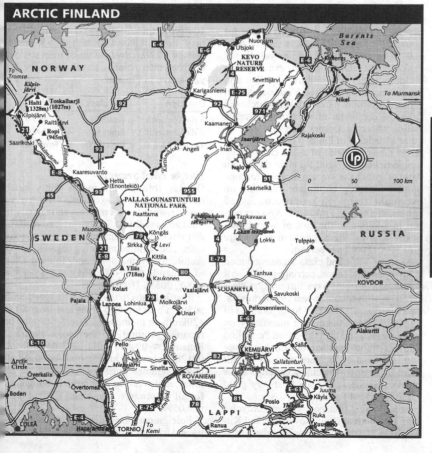

ARCTIC FINLAND

permitting; surcharges are usually at the discretion of the driver.

Train

Trains of the State Railways of Finland, or Valtion Rautatiet (VR), are clean and efficient. The main rail route into Lapland is the Pohjanmaa line, which connects Helsinki with Oulu and continues to Kemijärvi, via Rovaniemi. The rail timetable, *Taskuaikataulu*, is available in English at major stations, where you'll also find VR (☎ 09-707 3519) travel bureaux, which can advise on all schedules and tickets. Check out the VR Web site also at www.vr.fi.

A one-way ticket for a 100km train journey costs Fmk50/75 in 2nd/1st class; for 500km, it's Fmk224/336 (between Helsinki and Rovaniemi, for example, you'll pay Fmk320/608). Discounts are available for children under 17, seniors, families and Finnish students, and there are occasional summer discount fares. Tickets purchased from the conductor after boarding from a station where the ticket office was open require a 'penalty' of Fmk5. The 1st class fare is 1½ times the price of a 2nd class ticket. Single tickets are valid for eight days from date of purchase, return tickets for one month. Sleeping berths are available on overnight trains in one/two/three-bed cabins, at a cost of Fmk250/120/60 per person in addition to the cost of an ordinary ticket. During the ski season prices are Fmk350/ 180/90 per person.

Most of VR's 2nd class accommodation is in open 2nd class carriages with soft chairs. Many trains have just one 1st class carriage, with small six-seat compartments. Seat reservations (Fmk25/30 for journeys of less/more than 200km) are mandatory on Intercity (IC) and the high-speed Pendolino Express trains (neither of which operate within Lapland), but are advised for all trains in summer. The dining carriages serve snacks and meals that are relatively good value at around Fmk35.

Some trains transport cars/motorcycles from the south to Oulu, Rovaniemi and Kittilä; from Helsinki to Rovaniemi the cost is Fmk650/325; with a passenger, it's Fmk800/ 400, and with a sleeping berth, Fmk1160/ 580. Prices increase on weekends in winter and spring and on holidays. On regular trains, you can transport a bicycle/canoe for Fmk50/100.

Valid international rail passes include the Eurailpass, Eurail Flexipass, InterRail Pass and ScanRail Pass (see the Getting Around chapter).

The Lomapassi rail pass is valid for seven days anywhere within Finland from 1 June to 31 August. The cost for an adult is Fmk690, and for students, seniors and children aged 6 to 16, it's Fmk345. The national Finnrail Pass, valid for three, five, or 10 days of travel within a one month period, may be purchased from the VR travel agency *Matkapalvelu* at major train stations or from international travel agents before you arrive in Finland:

Duration	1st class	2nd class
3 days/month	Fmk860	Fmk570
5 days/month	Fmk1140	Fmk770
10 days/month	Fmk1570	Fmk1040

Car & Motorcycle

Driving through Finland is pretty much hassle-free and an excellent, well-marked road network connects most centres; only in rural areas will you find unsurfaced roads or dirt tracks. What's more, there are no road tolls. The national motoring organisation is Autoliitto (Automobile and Touring Club of Finland, ☎ 09-774 761) at Hämeentie 105A, 00550 Helsinki.

Traffic keeps to the right. The speed limit is 50km/h in built-up areas and from 80 to 120km/h on motorways. Accidents must be reported promptly to the Motor Insurers' Bureau (☎ 09-680 401) at Bulevardi 28, 00120 Helsinki. Outside built-up areas all motor vehicles must use headlights at all times, and wearing seat belts is obligatory for all passengers. The blood alcohol limit is 0.05%.

Foreign cars must display their nationality and foreign visitors must be fully insured

– bring a Green Card if you have one. Foreign drivers should keep in mind that in Finland, cars entering an intersection from the right always have right of way, even when that car is entering the highway from a minor road.

In rural areas beware of moose and reindeer (caribou), which may stroll onto the road at any time. Police must be notified about accidents involving moose and reindeer; to take meat is illegal.

Snow and ice can make driving hazardous from September until as late as June, and it's wise to have at least radial snow tyres, and preferably, 'studded' tyres (tyre chains are illegal), which are allowed from 1 November to the first Sunday after Easter and at other times when justified by road conditions.

Petrol is expensive, even by European standards, but if you're coming from Norway, it will seem a real bargain. There are petrol stations throughout the country, although in Lapland it's wise to fill up the tank whenever you can (especially in winter).

On Sunday and at night you can use the *Automaatti* or *Seteli/kortti* automatic petrol pumps. Bank notes and major credit cards (especially Visa) are always accepted. Some stations have instructions in English; essentially, all you have to do is insert bank notes, press *setelikuittaus* after the last note, choose the right pump, choose the right petrol type, and fill the tank.

Car rental in Finland is much more expensive than just about anywhere outside Scandinavia, and a stripped-down compact car costs from Fmk170 per day and Fmk2 per kilometre. Weekly rentals with unlimited mileage start at around Fmk2300. Parking isn't a problem in the north, but metered spaces normally cost a few Fmk per hour. Currently, cars with foreign number plates aren't ticketed for parking violations, but this generous situation probably won't last.

Bicycle

Finland is bicycle friendly, with miles of designated bike roads. Daily hire costs about Fmk50 and is available at tourist offices,

train stations, hostels and camping grounds, and there are bargain weekly rates. Additionally, the Finnish hostelling organisation (SRM) offers a cycling and hostel package that takes in the flat south and lake regions. New bicycles range from Fmk1000, but good second-hand models may cost less than Fmk500.

Hitching

The first rule for hitchers in Finland is to look clean. While few Finns pick up hitchhikers, those that do will do so with enthusiasm and Lapland is probably the best part of the country to stick out your thumb. Drivers may ask *Minne matka*? (Where are you going?); it isn't normally necessary to carry a sign bearing your destination, especially if your route is obvious. Any secondary road, or a crossing at a mid-sized village, will be easy for hitchhiking. The best time to hitchhike is Monday to Friday, when traffic is heaviest.

Local Transport

Most Arctic cities and towns have public bus routes, with services every half-hour or so and fares normally less than Fmk10 per ride. As a rule, train and bus stations are located reasonably close together, and always within walking distance.

Hail taxis at bus and train stations or by telephoning; they're listed in the Yellow Pages under *Taksi*. Typically the flagfall fare is Fmk19, plus a per kilometre charge and a surcharge of Fmk10 at night and on weekends. Shared taxis are available only from airports in larger cities and for local services in remote areas of Lapland. However, if you have a group of four people and want to cover a lengthy distance, most taxi drivers are willing to negotiate a decent price.

Organised Tours

Many Finnish towns offer a great variety of tours, but in the north, your best bet is Rovaniemi. In addition to regular sightseeing tours, local tour operators take groups into the Finnish wilderness for trekking,

ARCTIC FINLAND

white-water rafting, fly-fishing, dogsledding and a range of other activities. Normally, tours will run with a minimum of two participants, but may require as many as four, so be sure to phone ahead to confirm your reservations, or the tour may be cancelled. For details on specific offerings, contact the local tourist offices.

ACCOMMODATION

Accommodation in Finland doesn't necessarily have to be expensive. In fact, most of the wilderness huts along trekking routes are absolutely free. Hostels are probably a bit cheaper than in the USA or western Europe on average, and several people can share cottages at camping grounds. Hotels are more expensive but there are discounts in summer. The Finnish Tourist Board publishes an annual budget accommodation guide, available at local tourist offices.

Camping

There are more than 200 official camping grounds in Finland. They tend to cater for caravans rather than those carrying their own tents, but are still fine if you're looking for somewhere to sleep on the cheap. Note that the majority are open only in summer, eg late May to mid or late August at the latest, and some only open during June and July. Tent sites cost from Fmk35 to Fmk80, with discounts given for camping cards which are sold at most Finnish camping grounds for Fmk20. Typical camping ground facilities include a kitchen area, laundry, sauna, children's play area, boat and bicycle rentals, and café or *grilli*. The majority lie near rivers, lakes or the sea.

What makes camping grounds in Finland so recommendable is the availability of pleasant cabins and bungalows. If you have a group of two to six, prices are comparable to hostels, typically starting at Fmk100 for two-bed cottages and Fmk150 for four-bed cottages. Amenities vary, but a kitchen, toilet and shower are not uncommon. Some even have microwave ovens and televisions.

The Right of Public Access *(jokamie-henoikeus)* grants you legal permission to temporarily pitch your tent in a wide range of places and has been in effect in Finland for centuries. Basically, it gives travellers the right to go anywhere in Finland by land or water – as long as they agree to behave responsibly. You may walk, ski or cycle anywhere in forests and other wilderness areas, and even cross private land as long as you don't disturb the owners or damage crops.

Canoeing, rowing, and kayaking on lakes and rivers is also unrestricted; travel by motorboat and jet ski, on the other hand, is severely limited. Likewise, restrictions apply to snowmobiles, which are allowed on established routes only.

You can rest, swim, and pitch a tent for one night almost anywhere, but camping on private property requires the owner's permission. Camping is not permitted in town parks or on beaches. Fishing is not restricted if you are only using a hook and line, but you will need a permit if you plan to use a reel (see the Fishing section in the Activities chapter). Hunting is only permitted with a licence. Watch out for stricter regulations regarding access in nature reserves and national parks, where camping may be forbidden and travel confined to marked paths.

Hostels

Hostels in Finland offer the best value for money, in most cases. There are close to 150 hostels in Finland, and about half are open all year. No two are similar and you'll find them at university dorm buildings, in manors or schoolhouses, in the heart of big cities and way, way out in the boonies.

The majority of Finnish hostels are run by the Finnish Youth Hostel Association (SRM) and are affiliated with Hostelling International (HI). The average cost is less than Fmk100 per person per night. Most hostels offer private single and double rooms as well, at higher rates (but still much cheaper than hotels), and there are often 'family' rooms and special discounts for families.

If you have an HI card you'll receive a Fmk15 discount on the normal rates. O course, you may stay at a hostel even without an HI card, and there are no age restrictions, despite the term 'youth' hostel.

You should also bring your own sheets (or sleeping sheet) and pillowcase, as linen rentals cost Fmk15 to Fmk30 extra. Sleeping bags are not considered acceptable substitutes. Breakfast is generally not included in the price, but is available for Fmk25.

Often you may use the kitchen, although youth hostels in farmhouses or rural locations may not have a kitchen. In ordinary town hostels (normally student dormitories), the kitchen may not have any utensils. Saunas are common at hostels – although there may be a small surcharge to use them. Laundry facilities can also be used for a small additional fee.

The free publication *Hostellit* gives a full listing of all HI-affiliated Finnish hostels.

Guesthouses

Guesthouses in Finland, called *matkakoti* or *matkustajakoti*, are usually slightly run-down establishments meant for travelling salespeople and other more dubious types. They're usually in town centres near the train station.

However, there are a few guesthouses out there – usually in smaller villages – that just don't fit the category. These places are exceptionally clean and offer pleasant, homey accommodation in old wooden houses. Ask to see a room before paying, so you'll know what you're getting.

Hotels

Most hotels in Finland cater to upmarket businesspeople. They are quite luxurious, service tends to be good and the restaurants and nightclubs may be some of the most popular in town. Prices start from around Fmk450 for a single.

However, hotels offer the best rates on weekends, usually Friday to Sunday, and after midsummer, rates drop drastically and remain that way through to the end of summer. At that time, you can get a Fmk600 room for as little as Fmk350. A bargain in practically all Finnish hotels is the buffet breakfast. Hotel guests will need no lunch!

The Finncheque plan, available between mid-May and late September in most chain hotels, allows accommodation in 140 designated luxury hotels at the discounted price of Fmk200 per person in a double room. Each Finncheque is a 'coupon' good for one night's stay at a participating hotel (you purchase as many as you need), and any supplements are paid directly to the hotel. They may be purchased at a participating hotel or through a travel agency in your home country. If you're travelling during July and August, however, when hotels offer discounted summer prices, you may find Finncheques unnecessary.

Wilderness Huts

The Forest and Park Service maintains most of the country's wilderness huts. Many of these are free – Finland may be the only country in the world to provide such an extensive network of free, well-maintained wilderness huts – and others require advance booking and payment of Fmk50 per person per night.

Huts typically have basic bunks, cooking facilities, a pile of dry firewood and even a wilderness telephone. You are required to leave the hut as it was – ie, replenish the firewood and carry away your rubbish. The 'wilderness rule' states that the last one to arrive is given the best place to sleep.

The largest network of wilderness huts is in Lapland. Outside Lapland, trekking routes generally have no free cabins, but you may find a simple log shelter, called *laavu* in Finnish. You can pitch your tent inside the laavu or just roll out your sleeping bag.

A 1:50,000 trekking map is recommended for finding wilderness huts.

Holiday Cabins & Cottages

There are thousands of cabins and cottages for rent around Finland. They can be booked through regional tourist offices, generally for Fmk1200 a week or more for four people. Rarely are these available on a nightly basis, although weekend rentals are possible. Holiday cabins and cottages are terrific if you'd like to settle down to enjoy a particular corner of the Finnish country-side. They are usually fully equipped with cooking utensils, sauna and rowing boat, although the cheapest, most 'rustic' ones may lack electricity and require that you fetch your own water at a well. However, this is considered a true vacation, Finnish-style.

Prices are highest during midsummer and the skiing holidays, when you'll need to book well in advance. Tax is not necessarily included in quoted prices.

Farmstays

Many farmhouses around Finland offer bed and breakfast accommodation, a unique opportunity to meet local people and experience their way of life. They offer plenty of activities, too, from horse riding to helping with a harvest. Some farmstays are independent, family-run affairs, while others are loosely gathered under an umbrella organisation. In general, prices are good – from around Fmk150 per night, country breakfast included. The drawback is that farms are – by their very nature – off major roadways and bus routes, so you'll need your own transport (or enough money for the taxi fare) to reach them. However, a night at a Finnish farm is certainly a worthy addition to any trip and can be arranged through local tourist offices or by contacting one of the organisations listed.

Lomarengas
(☎ 09-3516 1321, fax 09-3516 1370),
Malminkaari 23C, 00700 Helsinki
Suomen 4H-Liitto
(☎ 09-645 133, fax 09-604 612),
Bulevardi 28, 00120 Helsinki

Rental Accommodation

Rental apartments start at something like Fmk2000 per month, including utilities. Student apartments rent for as low as Fmk500 per month, including utilities, for a *solu* room with a shared kitchen and bathroom. You must be enrolled at a Finnish university or some other educational institution to qualify for student housing.

ROVANIEMI
☎ 016

After its complete destruction by Germans in 1944, the Lapland capital, Rovaniemi, was built from a plan by Alvar Aalto, with the main streets radiating out from Hallituskatu in the shape of reindeer antlers. Until that time, Rovaniemi had been classified as a *kauppala*, or a trade centre. Hidden landmines remained for years following WWII.

Rovaniemi's proximity to Napapiiri (the Arctic Circle) means that tour buses thunder through year-round. Rovaniemi is also a good base for activities such as dog or reindeer sledding, white-water rafting, skiing and touring by snowmobile. It's also a friendly place for the budget traveller.

The tourist office (☎ 346 270) at Koskikatu 1 is an excellent source of information for all of Lapland. Etiäinen (☎ 362 526) at Napapiiri is the information centre for the national parks and trekking regions, with information on hiking and fishing in Lapland.

Things to See & Do

The glass-roofed **Arktikum** at Pohjoisranta 4 (☎ 317 840) is one of the best museums in Finland. Exhibits and interactive displays focus on Arctic flora and fauna as well as the Sami and other people of Arctic Europe, Asia and North America. It's open from 10 am to 8 pm daily in July and August, and to 6 pm daily in May and June. At other times it's open from 10 am to 6 pm Tuesday to Sunday. Admission is Fmk50. The **Rovaniemi Art Museum** at Lapinkävijäntie 4 has temporary exhibitions of contemporary art. It is open from 10 am to 5 pm Tuesday to Sunday. Admission is Fmk20.

Rovaniemi is as busy in winter as in summer – and perhaps even busier. With the Arctic Circle – and Santa Claus – close by there are plenty of festive activities in December celebrating Christmas. The Arctic Circle (Napapiiri) crosses the main Rovaniemi-Sodankylä road about 8km north of town (take bus No 8 or 10), and

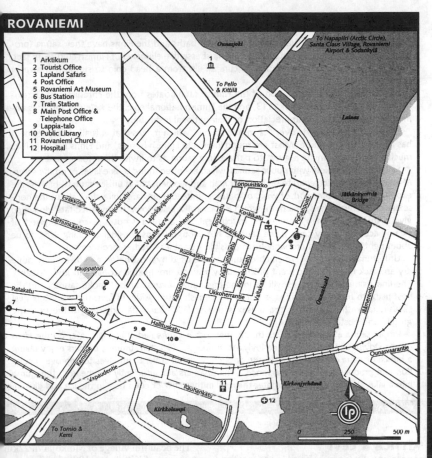

ROVANIEMI

1 Arktikum
2 Tourist Office
3 Lapland Safaris
4 Post Office
5 Rovaniemi Art Museum
6 Bus Station
7 Train Station
8 Main Post Office &
   Telephone Office
9 Lappia-talo
10 Public Library
11 Rovaniemi Church
12 Hospital

features an official **Arctic Circle marker** and the 'official' **Santa Claus Village** and gift shops. The **Northern Lights Festival** in February offers a variety of sports and arts events. In March Rovaniemi hosts the **Ounasvaara Winter Games**, with skiing and ski jumping competitions. **Jutajaiset**, a festival in June, showcases folk music, dance and other Sami traditions.

Lapland Safaris (☎ 331 1200, fax 331 1222), beside the tourist office, is the largest and best established of Rovaniemi's tour operators. It has a weekly tour program for winter and summer. There are many other tour operators near the main hotels, offering river cruises, white-water rafting, fishing, visits to reindeer farms and so on. To tour a **reindeer farm**, book with any of the tour offices near the main hotels. Snowmobile, husky and reindeer **safaris** are popular in winter. Summer tours include river cruises, **white-water rafting** and **fishing**. Tours range from Fmk200 to Fmk700 per person.

Hot & Steamy Times in Finland

The ancient Romans had their steam and hot-air baths and the Finns have their sauna (pronounced SOW-oo-nah), and it's one of the most essential elements of Finnish culture. In fact, Finns will prescribe a sauna session to cure all ills, from a head cold to sunburn (however painful the experience may be!).

The earliest written description of the Finnish sauna dates from the chronicles of Ukrainian historian Nestor, written in 1113, and the Finnish national epic, the *Kalevala*, includes numerous references to the appreciation of their national institution.

Today, Finland supports over 1.2 million saunas, which means that virtually every resident has access to one or more. Most are found in private Finnish homes, and Finns consider it as much a courtesy to invite a guest to partake in a sauna as to invite them for a meal.

Finland is also replete with public saunas, which are often found beside lakes or on the shore. Most are divided into separate sections for men and women, but in unisex saunas, bathers are expected to wear some sort of wrap or clothing. Indeed, Finns are quite strict about the non-sexual character of the sauna bath, which is above all a place to bathe and meditate (and even give birth). Despite many foreigners' misconceptions, a sauna is not a place for any sort of steamy activity. In any case, if the sauna is hot enough (Finns consider a stifling 90°C to be about right!), sex would probably be impossible – or at least rather inconvenient.

Unfortunately, the modern electric sauna stoves used by most hotels and hostels are quite dry and lack the authentic scent produced by a wood fire, heated stones and *löyly* (steam). The finest sauna experiences will be in the traditional *savusauna*, or 'smoke sauna', and the best place to find the real thing is out in the Finnish countryside. In fact, the world's largest savusauna, with 60 seats, is the unisex sauna at Jätkänkämpälä, adjacent to the camping ground and hostel at Kuopio.

Proper sauna etiquette dictates that bathers use a *kauha* (ladle) to cast water on the *kiuas* (sauna stove), which produces the löyly, At this point, at least in summer, bathers enjoy taking a bunch of *vihta* or *vasta* (leafy *koivu*, or birch twigs) to strike themselves to improve circulation and produce a pleasant fragrance. When bathers are sufficiently overheated, they jump into a lake, river or the sea; in winter they roll in the snow or cut a hole in the ice and dive in.

KITTILÄ & LEVI

According to legend, Kittilä was named after Kitti, a daughter of the mighty witch Päiviö, who appears in local fairy tales.

The old wooden **church** was designed by CL Engel and completed in 1831. The **Taidemuseo Einari Junttila** commemorates a local artist, who once lived in that place (closed Sunday). The **Kittilä open-air museum**, 3km south of the village, features a collection of traditional buildings. It's open from Tuesday to Sunday in summer. In early July, Kittilä hosts a traditional **market** that attracts folks from all over Lapland.

The beautiful village of Molkojärvi, 22km south-east of Kittilä, has 100 inhabitants, an old village shop and the excellent **Kittilän Eräkeskus** (π/fax 655 323) with clean B&B accommodation for Fmk105/140. The estate has two small museums and a cafe. Activities include fishing, hunting, berry picking, skiing and snowmobile safaris.

Levi, east of Sirkka (a typical Sami village), is a major skiing centre that lies about 20km north of Kittilä. Skiing is the main activity in the winter months, and the ski season usually runs from November to May. In summer and autumn, trekking and mountain biking are the main outdoor activities.

The long Ounasjoki, one of the best canoeing rivers in Lapland, runs from Hetta in the north to Rovaniemi in the south, and passes Raattama, Sirkka, Kittilä and Kaukonen. Canoes and equipment can be rented at Pole Star Safaris (☎ 641 688 or ☎ 049-391 090, fax 641 687) at the Levin Portti tourist centre, in Levi. Companies in Kittilä also offer equipment rentals.

MUONIO

Although Muonio is nothing special, it's a major centre in north-eastern Lapland. The wooden **church** dates from 1817 and it was somehow spared when the village was burned during WWII. The Muonio tourist office (☎ 534 305 or ☎ 534 213) is in the village centre at Puthaanrannantie 15. South of the centre on road No 21, the **Harriniva Holiday Centre** (☎ 532 491, fax 532 750) rents out canoes and kayaks for exploring the Muonionjoki, as well as fishing equipment for those who'd like to catch salmon or grayling. It also rents mountain bikes, and runs guided mountain bike and hiking tours. Guided tours of Harriniva's husky farm cost Fmk35, and in winter, it runs dogsled safaris.

HETTA (ENONTEKIÖ)

Hetta, previously known as Enontekiö, is the centre of Enontekiö municipality, and is a good base for treks into the surrounding area. Hetta is not a big place, with just a few dozen houses on either side of the road, but it does offer relatively good travel services. There's a municipal tourist office (☎ 556 211) at the crossroads of the Hetta main road and the route toward Karasjok, in Norway.

The nearby **Pallas-Ounastunturi National Park**, established in 1938, protects the area surrounding **Pallastunturi Fell**. The main summer attraction is the excellent 50km trekking route from Hetta to Hotel Pallastunturi inside the park, but the area also offers excellent winter skiing.

The **Pallastunturi Visitor Centre** (☎ 532 451) at Pallastunturi Fell sells trekking maps, makes reservations for locked huts (Fmk50 per night) and provides facts about

the region, and its flora and fauna. The 60km **trek** from Hetta village to Hotel Pallastunturi is one of the easiest in the country and takes three to four days to complete. The route is well marked, with poles every 50m or so, and several wilderness huts along the way. To get started, take the Fmk40 boat-taxi across the lake to the national park entrance.

KILPISJÄRVI

Right at the end of the 'thumb' in Finland's north-western 'arm', tiny Kilpisjärvi lies tucked between the lake of the same name and the highest fells in the country. In fact, Kilpisjärvi consists of two 'villages' several kilometres apart – one has a pair of hotels and a supermarket, and the other has the Kilpisjärvi Trekking Centre (Kilpisjärven Retkeilykeskus) and a petrol station.

The area offers fantastic trekking. The village lies within spitting distance of both Norway and Sweden, and a popular trek leads 11km from the village to the **Treriksröysa**, the three-way border monument, which rises from a dark lake. Other routes range from easy day hikes to demanding two-week mountain treks. A marked loop route to Saana Fell starts at Kilpisjärven Retkeilykeskus. This route takes the better part of a day. Another popular day route is the 15km route through **Malla Nature Park** to the Treriksröysa, where you'll find a free wilderness hut. From the village of **Saarikoski**, 35km south of Kilpisjärvi, is a 45km walking route to the traditional Sami village of **Raittijärvi**.

In midsummer every year, the folk of Kilpisjärvi put on a ski race at Saana Fell, where the snow may not melt until mid-July.

Kilpisjärven Retkeilykeskus is a central meeting place for trekkers, and is also the best place to find advice on routes and to buy maps and supplies. All trekking routes and wilderness huts around the Kilpisjärvi area are clearly displayed on the 1:100,000 *Käsivarsi* map (Fmk50). The 1:50,000 Kilpisjärvi topographical sheet (Fmk25) covers a small area. You can also pick up fishing permits and book wilderness huts (Fmk35 per person).

KEMIJÄRVI

With the northernmost railway station in Finland, Kemijärvi sees a steady flow of travellers. Unfortunately, it's a bit of a disappointment for anyone hoping to catch an instant glimpse of traditional Sami life. The tourist office (π 813 777), in the Torikeskus building at Kuumaniemenkatu 2A, is open from 8 am to 6 pm Monday to Friday, and from 9.30 am to 3 pm Saturday from June to mid-August. At other times, it's open from 8 am to 4 pm Monday to Friday.

The local museum, **Kotiseutumuseo**, features a collection of artefacts and old houses – including a *kota* (Sami hut). It's open from 10 am to 4.30 pm Monday to Friday and from 10 am to 6 pm weekends, from June to late August. Entry is Fmk10. The **Kemijärvi church**, built in 1951, has a wooden bell tower dating from 1774. The church is open daily in summer.

The **Kemijärvi Sculptural Week**, a festival of woodcarving, is held during July. It draws artists from many European countries and is an interesting event as all the woodcarvers work outside, in view of the public. In mid-September, Kemijärvi hosts **Ruksa Swing**, a festival of swing dancing and swing music. Participants come from around the world, and there is a special 'Swing Train' from Helsinki.

SALLA

Salla was entirely rebuilt after WWII, when it was destroyed, and its 1951 **church** is an attractive example of post-war architecture. **Sallatunturi**, 10km from the village, is a small downhill skiing area which also offers activities such as reindeer sleigh rides. The tourist office (π 832 141), called Yrityspalvelukeskus, is on the road to Sallatunturi. At the ski resort, *Sallatunturin Tuvat* *(π 831 931, fax 837 765)* has a restaurant-cafe and two-person cottages priced from Fmk330 in the ski season, and from Fmk245 at other times. The better cottages include a sauna.

SODANKYLÄ

The village of Sodankylä is a busy commercial centre for the surrounding area, which has a population density of just 0.9 people per sq km! The tourist office (π 618 168) at Jäämerentie 9 is open weekdays. Also in the tourist office building, the **Andreas Alariesto Art Gallery** displays paintings by the famous Sami painter who favoured a primitive style to depict images of traditional Sami life.

The **old wooden church** near the Kitinen riverside, built in 1689, is the oldest in Lapland and is one of the few buildings in the province to survive the massive destruction of WWII. It's open daily in summer. Several kilometres south of the village, the **local museum** exhibits typical Sami arts and tools in weathered old buildings. Hours are noon to 5 pm daily from early June to late August and entry is Fmk10.

PYHÄ-LUOSTO REGION

The area between the fells of Luosto (514m) and Pyhä (540m) forms a popular winter sports centre midway between Kemijärvi and Sodankylä. The high season extends from February to May, but in summer, it's also excellent for trekking, particularly in the 43 sq km **Pyhätunturi National Park** that surrounds **Pyhä Fell**. The most notable sight is the steep **Pyhäkuru Gorge** between the Kultakero and Ukonhattu peaks. According to local legend, **Lake Pyhänkasteenlampi** (Lake of Holy Baptism), in the gorge, was where EM Fellman, the 'Apostle of Lapland', forcibly baptised the Sompio Samis in the 17th century to convert them to Christianity. For hiking, look for the 1:40,000 Luosto-Pyhätunturi map, which is sold at the Nature Centre and in local hotels and resorts.

Pyhä and Luosto each have resort 'villages' with full services. In Luosto, the travel agency Pyhä-Luosto Matkailu (π 020-838 4248, fax 624 261) at Pyhä-Luostontie 2 has accommodation and tourist information for the region, and books cottages. In Pyhä, the Pyhähippu Reservation Centre (π 882 820, fax 882 853) also offers tourist information and books accommodation.

For information on Pyhätunturi National Park, as well as summer activities, drop by the park's Pyhätunturi Nature Centre (☎ 882 773, fax 882 824), adjacent to the Pyhä downhill ski centre; follow signs from the main Kemijarvi-Sodankylä road (road No 5).

SAARISELKÄ WILDERNESS (URHO KEKKONEN NATIONAL PARK)

The Saariselkä Wilderness – which includes Urho Kekkonen National Park, the Sompio Strict Nature Reserve, Nuortti Recreational Fishing Area and also large tracts of protected forestry lands – extends all the way to the Russian border and is by far the most popular trekking area in Finland. The large network of excellent wilderness huts is one reason for the area's popularity; another is the beauty of the low tunturi hills.

Villages

Saariselkä village is a winter sports centre and also a base for trekkers heading into the Saariselkä Wilderness area, but be warned that this is one of the busiest yuppie resorts in Lapland. For tourist and accommodation information, contact Pohjois-Lapin Matkailu Oy (☎ 668 400, fax 668 405) at Honkapolku 3.

The Forest Research Institute operates the Saariselkä Information Cabin (☎ 668 122), with plenty of free information for trekkers. Tankavaara, 30km south of Saariselkä, is locally famous as the 'Gold Village'. It also has an Urho Kekkonen National Park Visitor Centre (☎ 626 251) with information about wilderness activities. The Gold Museum (Kultamuseo), open daily, displays tools and other paraphernalia from Lapland's crazy gold-fever years. Admission is Fmk35 and gold-panning costs Fmk20.

The village of Savukoski serves as a base for visits to the isolated south-eastern part of the Saariselkä Wilderness. The National Park Visitor Centre (☎ 841 401) at Samperntie 32 is open daily and has a superb

wilderness exhibition and slide show. It offers park information, and sells maps and permits.

Tulppio, south of the Urho Kekkonen National Park boundary, is a stepping stone to one of the finest fishing rivers in Finland, the Nuorttijoki. In the early 20th century, the old steam locomotive now on display in the centre was transported from the USA in pieces, first by ship to Hanko, then by rail to Rovaniemi, and finally from Rovaniemi to Tulppio by horse sleds over frozen bogs and forests, at temperatures as low as -30°C. It was used by loggers for many decades.

Note that hitching is easiest on weekend afternoons, when people drive to Tulppio for the Tisko, a sort of lumberjacks' disco.

Hiking

The park is divided into four zones, each with different rules; you'll get details from the national park visitor centres in Saariselkä, Tankavaara and Savukoski. Hikers need to carry all their food, as wilderness huts in the park are not stocked with supplies. Note that hiking in Saariselkä can be challenging, as many marked trails are either faint or almost nonexistent. A map and compass are essential for much of the park. The three maps to have include: the 1:50,000 *Sompio-Kiilopää* map, that will do for short hikes from Saariselkä; the 1:50,000 *Sokosti-Suomujoki* map, that takes in lake Luirojärvi; and the 1:100,000 *Koilliskaira* map, that shows the entire park.

There are lots of possible walking routes around Saariselkä, using wilderness huts as bases. The main attractions are the Rumakuru Gorge, Lake Luirojärvi (a hike to the latter normally includes a climb up nearby Sokosti (718m), Paratiisikuru (Paradise Gorge), and Lumikuru (the Snow Gorge). There are also two historical Scolt fields, with restored old houses, 2km south of Raja-Jooseppi, and 2km west of Snelmanninmaja hut, respectively.

The four to six day loop from the main road to lake Luirojärvi is the most popular route, and can be extended beyond the lake. To reach more remote areas, you can take

ARCTIC FINLAND

the week-long trek from Kiilopää to Kemi-
haara, but the least crowded option follows
old roads and walking routes all the way
from Raja-Jooseppi in the north to Kemi-
haara or Tulppio in the south-east.

Within the park are 200 designated free
camp sites and 30 free wilderness huts, while
a handful of huts carry a Fmk50 nightly
charge and must be booked in advance
through any of the park visitor centres.

IVALO

Ivalo (Sami: Avvil) is the undisputed administrative and commercial centre of the
surrounding region. Its airport makes Ivalo
the major transport hub for East Lapland as
well as a hub for many of the prospectors
who spend their time panning the Ivalojoki
for alluvial gold.

Hotel Kultahippu is one place where any
gold found is traded for booze and where
incredible tales are told before panners return to their solitary, secretive hunt for the
mother lode.

The tourist office, open daily in summer,
is at Neste petrol station on the main street.
The public library in the town centre has
some English-language magazines.

A good way to see the Finnish wilderness
in winter is on a husky safari. In Ivalo,
Kamisak (☎ 667 736, fax 667 836), 99800
Ivalo, run by Eija and Reijo Järvinen, offers
just such a tour. Safaris range in length from
five hours to six days and cost from
Fmk690 to Fmk5900 per person. The price
includes transportation, equipment, insurance and meals, plus accommodation in
wilderness cabins on overnight tours.

Participants are taught how to drive their
own husky team of five to 12 dogs. The
Järvinens take solo travellers as well as
groups.

INARI

The small village of Inari (Sami: Anár) is
the main Sami community in the region and
you can easily spend a day sight-seeing –
take a morning trek to the **Pielpajärvi
Wilderness Church** (7km each way), which
was built in 1646; an afternoon cruise to

Ukko (Äjjih) island on lake Inarinjärvi; and
then visit the superb **Saamelaismuseo** in the
evening.

The tourist office, Inari Info (☎ 661 666,
fax 661 777, northern-lapland.tourism@co
.inet.fi) is open from 9 am to 8 pm daily
from mid-June to mid-September. At other
times it's open from 9 am to 5.30 pm Monday to Friday. The museum is open from 9
am to 9 pm daily from June to August. At
other times it's open from 10 am to 5 pm
Tuesday to Sunday. Admission is Fmk20.

LEMMENJOKI NATIONAL PARK

At 2855 sq km, Lemmenjoki (Sami:
Leammi) is the largest national park in Finland. Saariselkä is probably more popular
with hikers, but the Lemmenjoki experience
is more diverse: slush through desolate
wilderness rivers, explore the rough Arctic
landscape and bump into isolated gold panners in the middle of nowhere. In the main
gold-panning area of Morgamjoki, prospectors still occupy several old huts in summer.

An information hut (☎ 673 411) at the
village of Njurgulahti, 50km south-west of
Inari, sells maps and fishing permits, and is
open from June to late September. All services are available in Njurgulahti village.

The Sallivaara Reindeer Roundup site,
70km south of Inari, was used by Sami reindeer herders twice yearly until 1964.
Roundups were an important social event
for the people of northern Lapland, usually
lasting several weeks and involving hundreds of people and animals. The Sallivaara reindeer corrals and cabins were
reconstructed in 1997, and there are plans to
once more stage roundups here in autumn
and spring. Park at Repojoki then follow the
marked trail, 6km one way.

Hiking

Almost all trails start from Njurgulahti, including a 4km marked nature trail suitable
for families with children. The majority of
the trekking routes lie within the relatively
small area between the Lemmenjoki and the
Vaskojoki rivers. A 18km loop between
Kultala and Ravadasjärvi huts takes you to

some of the most interesting gold panning areas. As you can do this in two days, many trekkers head over Ladnjoaivi Fell to Vaskojoki hut and back, which extends the trek to four to five days. For any serious trekking, you will need the 1:100,000 *Lemmenjoki* map, available at the Njurgulahti information hut.

In summer, a local boat service cruises the Lemmenjoki valley, from Njurgulahti village to the Kultahamina wilderness hut at Gold Harbour. A 20km marked trail also follows the course of the river – so you can take the boat one way, then hike back. You can also get on or off the boat at other jetties along the route. There are daily departures from mid-June to mid-September and fares are Fmk60 each way.

ANGELI

This remote village of 70 inhabitants, 70km west of Inari, makes a base for exploring the northern section of Lemmenjoki National Park. The village's greatest claim to fame is as home to the musical duo, Angelin Tytöt. They have been responsible for getting the loud yoik singing – the traditional Sami music style – listed in the 'world music' chart, by combining it with the driving energy of Finnish hard rock.

An Alaskan couple, Todd and Gerry Nolen, runs *Hello Holidays* (π/fax 672 434, *gerry.nolen@pp.inet.fi*), a superb, isolated farmhouse that offers homely accommodation, good food and lots of sheep for Fmk250 per person; airport pick-ups are available.

KEVO NATURE RESERVE

Kevo Nature Reserve was established in 1956 and is 712 sq km in size. Within its boundaries you'll find some of the most breathtaking scenery in Finland along the splendid gorge of the Kevo River (Sami: Geävu), which features some spectacular waterfalls.

Rules for visiting the Kevo reserve are stricter than those concerning national parks: hikers cannot hunt, fish or collect plants and berries, and *must* stay on marked trails. The gorge area is off-limits from April to mid-June.

The main trail runs through the canyon from the Utsjoki-Kaamanen road to the Karigasniemi-Kaamanen road and is 63km long. The trek is rough and takes about four days one way. Use the 1:100,000 *Kevo* topographical sheet, which costs about Fmk50. Camping is permitted within the reserve only at designated camp sites, and there are many. You'll also find three free wilderness huts along a north-western path that does not descend into the gorge.

KARIGASNIEMI

The small village of Karigasniemi (Sami: Gáregasnjárga) is a crossing point from Finland to Norway along the popular Nordkapp route. It has services such as a bank and a post office. Fell Sami, the language of the local people of Karigasniemi, is also the main dialect spoken across the border in Norway.

UTSJOKI

It would be misleading to call the village of Utsjoki (Sami: Ohcejohka) an attractive place, but it has a certain interest as a border town and as the home to a relatively large Sami population. The tourist office, Utsjoki Info (π 686 234 or π 686 111) is jointly run by the municipality and Metsähallitus (the Forest and Park Service).

NUORGAM

Nuorgam (Sami: Njuorggan) is the northernmost village of Finland, and the fact that it's the country's John o'Groats or Point Barrow may be its only true appeal. However, the majority of the 200 residents are Sami, the fishing is good and the village lies at the northern end of the Sevettijärvi trekking route.

SEVETTIJÄRVI

A good road heads from Kaamanen eastwards along the shore of Inarinjärvi to the village of Sevettijärvi (Scolt Sami: Ce'vetjäu'rr), in the far north-east of Finland. The inhabitants are a distinctive Sami group called the Scolt *(kolttalappalaiset)*, who speak Scoltish, Finnish and Russian. **Perinnetalo** is a small museum devoted to Scolt traditions.

The Orthodox **tsasouna** (church), built in 1951, is dedicated to Father Trifon from Petsamo (now in Russia). The altar has beautiful icons, some of which were brought from the Soviet-occupied monastery of Valamo. The oldest graves in the church cemetery are marked by wooden *grobu* (markers) with wooden birds attached. The church is open on weekdays; knock first at the warden's door.

The Dutch resident, Ernest Dixon, has guided 'Lapland Pulka Treks' and 'Lapland Ruska Treks' for over 30 years, and has the best local knowledge in the region. Treks include visits to Sami homes and across the fells in search of reindeer; meals include fresh salmon purchased from local people; and the food is prepared over an open fire. If you're interested, book well in advance: J Ernest Dixon, SF-99930 Sevettijärvi, Finland, or contact Travel North (☎ 31-023 537 7573), Duin-lustparkweg 48 A, 2061 LD Bloemendaal, Holland.

Hiking

The Sevettijärvi region has more lakes per square kilometre than any other region in Finland. Few trekkers see this remote wilderness, yet it's well worth the effort it takes to reach it. The track from Sevettijärvi to Nuorgam is covered on the 1:50,000 *Karttakeskus* topographical sheets. The best place to begin is at Saunaranta, north of Sevettijärvi (look for the sign reading 'Ahvenjärvi 5', and a trekking sign – 12km to Opukasjärvi, 69km to lake Pulmankijärvi). There are six mountain huts along the route.

Another worthwhile trek leads from Sevettijärvi to Kirakkajärvi, across the rocky region across the lake from Sevettijärvi. It takes at least two days and is covered on a 1:20,000 trekking map.

The exciting hiking route from Näätämö to Sevettijärvi begins at the former and leads through a very remote area via Jankkila, Routasenkuru, Vätsäri, Tuulijärvi and Sollomisjärvi to Sevettijärvi, taking you to an region where very few people go. There are a few huts along the way and the gorge Routasenkuru extends north-south for over 5km.

Arctic Russia

Arctic Russia – from the Norwegian and Finnish borders eastward across northern Siberia to the Chukotka and Kamchatka peninsulas – is a fabric of pine and birch forests, marshes, bogs, tens of thousands of lakes and, in the far north, tundra and taiga forests. Kamchatka adds an intense volcanic element.

Here the nearly useless rivers run north to the Arctic Ocean, producing icy blockages in the spring and exceptional bird-watching combined with inhospitable mosquito bogs through the brief summer season. The region not only holds vast untapped petroleum reserves, but is also a potential – if challenging – paradise for hikers, boaters, campers, skiers and other outdoors enthusiasts.

GETTING AROUND

Although Siberia is often considered a polar destination, only a small portion of it lies north of the Arctic Circle, so we don't include information on the Trans-Siberian Railway. If you're approaching on that route, see the *Trans-Siberian Rail Guide* by Robert Strauss, *The Trans-Siberian Handbook* by Bryn Thomas, and/or Lonely Planet's *Russia, Ukraine & Belarus*, which includes a full chapter on the railway.

Air

Because of the vast distances involved in travelling in the Russian Arctic and the Far East, and the limited extent of the road and rail network, flying is sometimes the only practical way of getting around. In many places aircraft take on the role of buses, especially on short-haul flights. Passengers frequently have to carry their own baggage aboard and dump it at the rear before scrumming for seats, and those who lose out end up standing for the duration of the flight.

Almost every small town has its airport (although 'airport', which tends to connote a great, high-tech temple to air transport, is perhaps a misleading term, as most of these places have fewer facilities than the average bus shelter). If nothing else, it will at least have frequent flights to the nearest big town or city, and from there you'll be able to make nationwide connections.

The former Soviet state airline, Aeroflot (Air Fleet) has been decentralised into hundreds of smaller airlines (baby-flots) at such an alarming rate that not even the Russian Department of Air Transport (RDAT) can say how many exist (the estimated number is 300). These came about when Aeroflot left aircraft parked at airfields around the country – in many cases, employees or managers of an airfield with a couple of Aeroflot planes on its tarmac simply commandeered them and started an airline. The upshot of all this is virtually unregulated skies and the world's worst regional air safety record. Cheap flights are available, but given the safety issue, we recommend that you fly only when necessary, and then choose internationally certified carriers (a list of such Russian-owned carriers is available from US Embassy Consular Information in Moscow).

Timetables are often fantasy-based and many flights are delayed, often for hours, without explanation. Rerouting of aircraft *in mid-flight* is not uncommon, as many airports are now demanding hard-currency payment for landing fees (which is illegal but still practised). On timetables, all the airlines are listed together (if you look very closely you'll see that each has a different flight code). You may never actually know which airline you're flying on because they generally share the same ticket outlets and check-in facilities – and many of them still haven't got round to writing their own names on their planes in place of 'Aeroflot'. Some routes are served by two or even three different airlines, others by just one. Aeroflot no longer flies any internal Russian routes, though it flies a few routes between Russia and other ex-Soviet republics.

Some airports have special check-in and waiting-room facilities for foreigners, which make procedures easier. To minimise the danger of loss or theft, try not to check in any baggage: many planes have special stowage areas for large carry-on pieces. Flights are generally one class only and seating is usually a free-for-all. Unless you can manage to fly Transaero, you'll get only a cup of mineral water, and even on the 11-hour flight between Moscow and Petropavlovsk-Kamchatsky, you won't get more than a chicken leg or a hard-boiled egg, so be sure to pack a lunch!

Air tickets for virtually all domestic Russian airlines, and airlines of former Soviet republics, can be purchased from Aeroflot offices in cities all over Russia and through travel agents in Russia or abroad. Generally speaking, you'll do better booking internal flights once you arrive in Russia, where more flights and flight information are available, and where prices may be lower.

Whenever you book airline tickets in Russia you'll need your passport and visa. Most Aeroflot offices in the country have a special window for foreigners and international flights, so you won't have to wait in huge queues, but you'll also have to pay foreigners' rates, which is up to three times the rate for Russians. Flight tickets can also be purchased at the airport right up to the departure time and sometimes even if the city/town centre office says that the plane is full.

Bus

Except in the Kola Region, the distances are too great and the roads too bad for buses to be viable as intercity transport in Arctic Russia. The good news is that foreigners may now use all Russian buses, which are a great way to travel between smaller towns, and in Karelia and the Kola Peninsula, they're probably your best option. There are no foreigners' prices on buses – you pay the same as Russians, but note that the bus stations are scoundrel magnets, and are rarely places you'd want to hang around.

Most cities have a main intercity bus station *(avtovokzal, 'af-toh-vahk-ZAHL')*, usually called the *tsentralnyy avtovokzal* (central bus station) even if it's on the edge of town. From these, several daily services connect to main regional destinations. Tickets are sold at the station, where smouldering queues wait quasi-patiently for the window to open and begin selling seats. This usually happens an hour or two before a bus is scheduled to depart.

Ticket prices are usually listed on the timetable and posted on a wall. As often as not you'll get a ticket with a seat assignment. If tickets seem to be sold out, you can, of course, negotiate with the driver. There will be competition for the remaining floor space, and you'll need to act sharp and stay alert. Find out what platform your bus is leaving from and get there NOW. Proffer the correct ticket price – many drivers will let you buy the ticket without a mark-up if you keep your mouth shut and act as though you do this every day. If that's refused, work your way upwards. Note that it's illegal for buses to carry more passengers than they have seats; drivers may ask those standing to duck when the bus passes road checkpoints.

Train

The only railways in Arctic Russia are the ones connecting Nikel with Murmansk and Murmansk with St Petersburg. They aren't uncomfortable but they are excruciatingly slow. If you like trains, and if you or your travelling partner speaks good Russian, they're an excellent way to get around, see the countryside and meet locals. A good 1st or 2nd class berth on a Russian sleeper train could prove more civilised than one in Western Europe as they're often larger and more comfortable. Note that the whole Russian rail network runs on Moscow time (which seems ludicrous, especially when you're travelling around Vladivostok!), as evidenced in timetables and station clocks.

Outside of St Petersburg and Moscow, getting tickets for the Russian price is generally no big deal, though getting tickets for Russian trains is an art in itself. Most train station ticket windows are maddeningly inefficient, and long waits are the rule. But as far as paying the Russian price, it's quite a simple matter as long as you're willing to do what Russians do to get *their* tickets. You'll need to have your destination, the train number, the date and time of departure, the type of accommodation and the number of tickets – preferably written down in Cyrillic. Use ordinary (Arabic) numerals for the day of the month and Roman numerals for the month. If you get a reservation, your ticket will normally give the numbers of your 1st, 2nd or 3rd class carriage *(vagon)* and seat *(mesto)*.

Take as much food and drink with you as you think you'll need for the whole trip. The food in restaurant cars, if there is any, is repugnant, and you're unlikely to find much that's edible at halts along the way. On long trips Russian travellers bring great bundles of food which they spread out and – as dictated by railway etiquette – offer to each other; you should do the same. Good rail foods include sausage, Marmite, Vegemite and peanut butter, ham, pot noodles, bread, cheese and chocolate: basically, any filling food that doesn't require refrigeration. Always remember to bring along bottled water for the trip as there'll be none available on the train.

Almost every train in Russia has a samovar at the end of the carriage filled with boiling water. The *provodnik* or *provodnitsa* (male or female train attendant) may not smile too often, but they are generally among the best hearted service workers in the country, providing cups of tea from their samovars (though you shouldn't rely on these for all your liquid intake) and often a wake-up call (or bellow) on arrival. On long trips it's well worth your while to foster a good relationship with this attendant.

Car & Motorcycle

Driving in Russia isn't everybody's cup of tea but if you've got a sense of humour and don't mind some fairly rugged road conditions, a few hassles finding petrol, and getting lost now and then, it's a great way to see the country.

Russians drive on the right. Traffic lights that flicker green are about to change to yellow, then red; flickering yellow traffic lights mean that the junction isn't regulated by the lights. As will be painfully (hopefully not too painfully) obvious, vehicles have right of way over pedestrians.

Don't expect to find many places for a decent meal between towns. Petrol *(benzin)* supplies are erratic, and are marked by long queues at petrol stations. Petrol comes in four main grades – 76, 93, 95 and 98 octane. Unleaded is virtually nonexistent. Most western engines prefer 95, but 93, or even only 76, is often all that's available. Petrol stations aren't usually more than 100km apart, but don't rely on it. Oil is *maslo (MAHS-lah)*; the Russian version of Multigrade is called M10GI. Transmission oil is TAD-171 and antifreeze is TOSOL A-40. Air is *vozdukh (VOZ-dukh)* and water is *voda*.

Radar detectors are legal in Russia, and may be a handy piece of equipment to have. Speed limits are generally 60km/h in towns and 110km/h on the open highway, though sometimes signs indicate other limits. There may be a 90km/h zone, enforced by speed traps, as you leave a city. Technically the maximum legal blood-alcohol content is 0.04%, but in practice it is illegal to drive after consuming *any* alcohol at all, and it's strictly enforced.

The normal method of establishing alcohol in the blood is by a blood test (so carry your own syringes to prevent potential exposure to health hazards). However, apparently drivers can be deemed under its influence even without any test.

The State Automobile Inspectorate, GAI (*gah-yee*, short for Gosudarstvennaya Avtomobilnaya Inspektsia) skulks about on the roadsides, waiting for speeding, headlightless or other miscreant vehicles. Officers of the GAI are authorised to stop you (they do this by pointing their striped, sometimes lighted, stick at you and waving you toward the side), issue on-the-spot fines (in roubles only, so get a receipt) and, worst of all, shoot at your car if you refuse to pull over. While shooting is not common, neither is it uncommon. One trouble-making expatriate US resident had 18 bullet holes in his car after he refused to stop! The GAI also hosts the occasional speed trap.

There are permanent GAI checkpoints at the boundary of every Russian city and many Russian towns. For serious infractions, the GAI can confiscate your licence and you'll have to retrieve it from the main station. They've also been known to shake down foreigners – never hand over any hard currency and get a receipt for any legitimate fine you pay. If you've been ripped off, get the shield number of the officer (if they don't have one, they're an imposter), then complain at the nearest GAI office. If you're very sure you've been pulled over by a fake, make sure – *very* sure – that the fake is not armed, then pull away as soon as you can and head for the nearest town border, where you'll find a real GAI station at which to report the incident. They actually do care.

Hitching

Hitching in Russia is a very common method of getting around, and in remote areas, it's a major mode of transport. Rides are hailed by standing at the side of the road and flagging passing vehicles with a low, up-and-down wave (not an extended thumb). You're expected to pitch in for petrol by paying roughly the equivalent of a bus fare for the ride. However, hitching is never entirely safe, and we don't recommend it; travellers

who decide to hitch should understand that they are taking a small but potentially serious risk. People who do choose to hitch will be safer if they travel in pairs and let someone know where they are planning to go. Use common sense and avoid hitching at night. Women should exercise extreme caution and everyone should avoid hitching alone.

Boat

Considering that most of the Russian wilderness was first opened up by boat, the great rivers of the Arctic region are very much under-used. The main reason, of course, is that for six to eight months of the year they're all solid.

During summer, though, the Ob/Irtysh, Yenisey and Lena rivers are put to use as liquid highways, and from June to September, regular services run up the Irtysh from Omsk via Tobolsk and farther north along the Ob to Salekhard. On the Yenisey, regular passenger services run between Krasnoyarsk and various points north as far as Dudinka, and upstream from Kyzyl in Tuva. The Lena provides the main supply route for Yakutsk, a city isolated in the taiga 1000km north of any railway line. Boats moving along the Irtysh and Ob rivers from Omsk via Tobolsk to Salekhard could also provide an interesting trip.

For the truly adventurous – with a month or so to spare – it is possible to hitch a lift on one of the supply ships that sail out of Nakhodka and Vladivostok up to the Chukotka Peninsula towns of Anadyr and Providenia.

ACCOMMODATION

Gone are the days when tourists were restricted to specified hotels and a few grotty camp sites, all of which had to be booked before you could even get a visa. That's the good news. For the rest of the story, read on …

Camping

Camping in the wild is legal in many places, and if you're off the beaten track it is usually fine to put up a tent and hit the hay. Check with locals if you're in doubt.

Organised camp sites *(kempingi)* are increasingly rare (some now house troops returned from abroad) and are usually open only from some time in June to some time in September. They're not quite like western camping grounds: much of the space is occupied by small wooden cabins, with little room for tents. Some lie just outside cities, but others occupy attractive woodland settings. Facilities in these places are few and often filthy.

Hostels & Guesthouses

While larger Russian cities now have youth hostels and backpackers' accommodation, there's no such thing in Arctic Russia. For more information, contact the Russian Youth Hostel Association (RYHA; in Russia ☎ 812-329 80 18, in the USA ☎ 310-618 2014, fax 310-618 1140, email ryh@ryh .spb.su), which acts as a coordinating body for reservations, advance payments and information on its member hostels, and can arrange visa invitations and paperwork for travellers intending to stay in them.

Private Homes

Because of the dire economic condition of most Russian families, in many places, they will be happy to rent out rooms in their private flats. The best thing about this type of informal accommodation – often referred to as 'bed & breakfast' (B&B) or 'homestay' – is that it lets visitors glimpse the way Russians really live. Again, however, this program is restricted to larger cities or popular tourist areas, and the chances of readily finding anything in Arctic Russia aren't very good. If you'd like to try, you can contact one of the following agencies:

Australia
Gateway Travel
   (☎ 02-9745 3333, fax 02-9745 3237, email agent@russian-gateway.com.au, Web site www .russian-gateway.com.au), 48 The Boulevarde, Strathfield, NSW 2135

USA
American-International Homestays
   (toll-free ☎ 1-800 876 2048), PO Box 7178, Boulder, CO 80306-7178

Helen Kates
   (☎/fax 603-585 6534), PO Box 221, Fitzwilliam, NH 03447
Home & Host International
   (☎ 612-871 0596, fax 612-871 8853) 2445 Park Avenue, Minneapolis, Minnesota 55404
International Bed & Breakfast
   (toll-free ☎ 1-800 422 5283, fax 215-663 8580), PO Box 823, Huntingdon Valley, PA 19006

Hotels

Russian hotels run the gamut from flyblown roach motels where for a few dollars you can share a room (and a single unflushable toilet down the corridor) with a gang of male market traders from the 'southern republics', to international five-star palaces full of western business people whose sweet slumbers cost their expense accounts US$400 a night. Most hotels have one price for Russians and another – about 400% higher – for foreigners. The only exceptions are a few hotels, mostly in out-of-the-way places, that get very few foreigners and haven't heard about the gouge-the-foreigner rates. (Don't tell them!)

In most places, you can just walk in and get a room on the spot. If you can't, it will probably be for one of four reasons:

* they're genuinely full (extremely rare)
* the receptionist/administrator thinks that because you haven't got their town named on your visa you can't stay there (almost as rare) – they're wrong, but there isn't much you can do about it
* they say they don't take foreigners – either because they think it's so dire you couldn't possibly want to stay there (they may be persuaded otherwise, but once you've seen the place, you may agree with them); or because they didn't take foreigners in Soviet times and they haven't noticed any changes (this does happen in some remote places)
* the hotel belongs to some institute or organisation and only takes people booked in through special channels

At check-in, you'll have to show passport and visa, and they may keep it until the following day to register your presence with the local OVIR (Otdel Viz I Registratsii or Department of Visas and Registration). You may get a slip of paper with your room number and the hotel's details on it. Carry this with you, as you may be asked to show it to get back into the hotel after you've been out.

In nicer hotels, rooms may have their own toilet, washbasin or shower, or you may have to use facilities shared by the whole corridor. In Arctic Russia you'll be lucky – even in the more expensive places – to have a room with hot water, a toilet that flushes or a TV that receives any stations (well, a few upmarket places do get CNN ...)

Turbazas

A *turbaza* (tour-base) is a holiday camp for Russians, usually owned by a factory or large company for the use of its employees. They range from absolutely spartan to somewhat luxurious, and many are now open to foreign tourists. Lodging usually consists of a large common room with six or more beds, smaller doubles and private cottages. All are cheap – usually US$10/15 or less – but there are reasons. Many have no indoor plumbing, and usually the only place to eat is a *stolovaya* (canteen). But, if you bring a good supply of food and a sense of adventure, these are a great way to get a feel for the average Russian's holiday. Here you can often arrange outdoor sport tours, such as boating, skiing, hiking or mountaineering, and set out on group treks for periods of five to 30 days. Equipment rental is usually available, and trained guides lead the groups.

Kola Peninsula

The White Sea, which cuts deeply inland from the Barents Sea, defines the geography of north-western Russia. The Kola Peninsula (Kolsky Poluostrov), dominated by the port of Murmansk (the largest town north of the Arctic Circle), is a 100,000 sq km knob of tundra, forest and low mountains between the White Sea and the Barents Sea.

Originally populated only by Sami reindeer-herders and a few Russian trappers and fishermen, the discovery of a northern sea route in the 16th century turned the tiny settlement of Kola into an Arctic trading post. In 1916, under pressure from the British to establish a supply port, Murmansk was founded (the first buildings being British-built wooden houses).

The Kola Inlet from the Barents Sea (which is ice-free year-round thanks to an eddy from the Gulf Stream) was the ideal site for the port of Murmansk, and now, at nearby Severomorsk, for the Russian Northern Fleet's home base. Thanks to the latter, the Kola Peninsula now has the somewhat dubious distinction of being home to the world's greatest concentration of military and naval forces. The discovery of ore and mineral deposits sped up growth and generated an environmental mess in many areas, and thousands of square kilometres of forests are dying of sulphur poisoning from nickel smelters in the towns of Nikel and Monchegorsk.

In addition to its geological interest, the area also offers outdoor activities. The Khibiny mountains have some fine hiking and mountaineering opportunities (new granite up to 700m high), cross-country skiing is possible anywhere, and budget skiers will love the downhill runs at Kirovsk. North and west of the ecologically devastated city of Monchegorsk lies the relatively pristine Laplandsky Zapovednik, a 3000 sq km natural wonderland.

MURMANSK
☎ 8152

The most novel thing about Murmansk is its location – halfway between Moscow and the North Pole. It's also the largest city north of the Arctic Circle, with 380,000 to 400,000 people (no one knows for sure) Temperatures range from -8°C to -13°C in January and 8° C to 14°C in July. The nearby port of Severomorsk is home to the Northern Fleet and Murmansk is the home port of Russia's nuclear icebreakers. Perhaps they're hoping the glow will light up the long polar night!

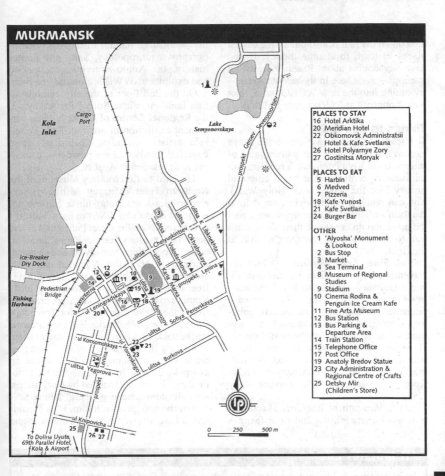

MURMANSK

PLACES TO STAY
16 Hotel Arktika
20 Meridian Hotel
22 Obkomovsk Administratsii Hotel & Kafe Svetlana
26 Hotel Polyarnye Zory
27 Gostinitsa Moryak

PLACES TO EAT
5 Harbin
6 Medved
7 Pizzeria
18 Kafe Yunost
21 Kafe Svetlana
24 Burger Bar

OTHER
1 'Alyosha' Monument & Lookout
2 Bus Stop
3 Market
4 Sea Terminal
8 Museum of Regional Studies
9 Stadium
10 Cinema Rodina & Penguin Ice Cream Kafe
11 Fine Arts Museum
12 Bus Station
13 Bus Parking & Departure Area
14 Train Station
15 Telephone Office
17 Post Office
19 Anatoly Bredov Statue
23 City Administration & Regional Centre of Crafts
25 Detsky Mir (Children's Store)

Most of Murmansk's permanent residents are Russians; many more temporary residents are lured by high pay and other perks to work in fish processing or ship repair. The local Sami people are rarely seen except during the Festival of the North, when they come to compete in traditional games.

The city occupies three levels: the port, the centre and the surrounding heights, crowned with dozens of bland housing blocks. Dominating the centre is the ploshchad Sovietskoy Konstitutsii, also known as Five-Corners

(Pyat-Ugla). To the north of the centre lies Lake Semyonovskaya and an immense concrete soldier named 'Alyosha', that could only have been constructed in Russia. A taxi from the airport to the centre costs around US$16. Bus Nos 106 and 106 (express) run between the airport and the train station every 20 to 30 minutes for less than R1; the express takes half an hour.

Limited tourist information is available at Intourist (☎ 454385), in the Hotel Polyarnye Zory, but for the best results, you'll need to speak Russian. The exchange window down the hall is also one of the easiest places in town to change money. If you have any doubts about Russia's westward leanings – even here in the remote Arctic – try tuning into the new WOKO radio, 'Hot New Country', at 98.9 on your FM dial.

Things to See & Do

St Nicholas Church (Svyatoy-Nikolskaya tserkov), named after the patron saint of sailors, is the Kola Peninsula's religious administrative centre, and it has a colourful history (see the boxed text 'Holy War'). You can reach it on trolleybus No 4 from the train station; after four stops, walk past the pond and up the stairs, then along a dirt trail to the main road, and the church is to the right.

The **Fine Arts Museum** (Khudozhestvenny muzey), ulitsa Kominterna 13, was established in Murmansk's oldest stone building in 1989, and in 1994 received a permanent collection of graphic arts, paintings, decorative applied arts and bone carvings, all on an 'image-of-the-north' theme. However, some of the works seem more than a little tragic (see boxed text 'Art Imitates Life'). It's open Wednesday to Sunday from 11 am to 6 pm and foreigners pay US$2.

In the **Museum of Regional Studies**, at prospekt Lenina 90, the 2nd floor features geology (minerals are a major resource on the peninsula), natural history and oceanography. Anthropology, Sami and Pomor history, the Anglo-American occupation and exhibits of WWII are on the 3rd floor.

On the 2nd floor of the city administration building, ulitsa Sofiya Perovskaya 3, the **Regional Centre of Crafts** holds a permanent exhibition of art from Kola Peninsula artists, including 'paintings' from coloured crushed stone powder – a technique developed in Apatity.

The hard-to-find **Military Museum of the Northern Fleet** (Muzyey Militarny Severnogo Morskogo Flota), ulitsa Tortseva 15, is a must if you're a WWII or naval buff. It's got six rooms on the Great Patriotic War and one on the modern fleet, including torpedos, mines, model ships, and diving and chemical warfare paraphernalia. A guided tour costs around US$2.50, but otherwise admission is free. Take trolleybus No 4, from along ulista Kominterna, north to the last stop, cross the street, then take bus No 10 for four stops (look for the smokestack). Walk towards the smokestack, and turn left at the *tovari* shop.

Anatoly Bredov, a hero of the Great Patriotic War, is honoured with a statue on prospekt Lenina in front of the stadium. Finding himself surrounded by Nazi troops, Anatoly detonated a grenade, taking several of the bad guys with him. He's considered a hero all over the Kola Peninsula and

---

Art Imitates Life

For an emotionally-charged exposé of the modern sentiments of northern Russia, visit Murmansk's Fine Arts Museum, where much of the work brings home the sometimes tragically fatalistic perspective of most people in this neglected region.

Look for the paintings by V. Kumashov, such as *V Sverye* (*In the North*), which depicts a typical Soviet-era statue of a family rising over a huddle of forgotten pensioners on a bench, beside a sleeping stray dog. *Idut v Kino* (*Going to the Cinema*) shows people strolling past broken benches and mounds of trash, concealing bottles of vodka in brown paper bags, carrying Marlboro Man shopping bags, and queuing up to catch the latest pornographic flick. Another, *Return to the Past*, depicts a historic village overlooked by banks of kiosks, while *Old Music* reveals a scene of town square musicians entertaining people queuing up to buy their daily anaesthetic dose of alcohol.

thanks to this character, Murmansk is nick-named the Gorod Gyeroy, the 'hero city'.

In summer, you may see one of the four atomic-powered icebreakers of the Murmansk Shipping Company (Murmanskoye Morskoye Parokhodstvo) at the dock. Photography, except in the port itself, is now permitted. The lake Semyonovskaya is named after the unfortunate would-be hermit Semyon Korzhnev, an old tsarist soldier who retired, at the end of the 19th century, to a cabin on the shore, and was the only resident for miles around. Imagine his disappointment when Murmansk appeared on his utopian horizon! The lake and the monumentally ludicrous statue of 'Alyosha' occupy the plateau above town. To get there, take trolleybus No 3 up prospekt Lenina.

Festival of the North

The annual Festival of the North, held since 1934, takes place the last week in March (although it often goes on longer), with each area town hosting its own events. Murmansk has reindeer and deer-plus-ski races (in which a reindeer pulls a contestant on skis), an international ski marathon and biathlon, ice hockey, 'polar-bear' swimming and a general carnival atmosphere. Hotels get booked up well in advance. Most events in Murmansk are held at the south end of town in Dolina Uyuta (Cosy Valley), a 25 minute ride from the train station on bus No 12. There's through-the-ice swimming at Lake Semyonovskaya, and snow-mobile rides can be arranged through Intourist Murmansk.

Places to Stay

The *Hotel Polyarnye Zory* (☎ 289505, *ulitsa Knipovicha 17, fax – on the Norwegian exchange – 47-78 91 01 91, email po larzor@murmansk.rosmail.com*), near the Detsky Mir bus stop on prospekt Lenina, has large, clean single/double rooms for US$45/56, with cable TV. This is considered *the* westerners' hangout in town, and it has a lively bar and buffet restaurant.

At the nearby *Gostinitsa Moryak* (☎ 455527), you'll find simple but ade-

Holy War

The site of the present cathedral in Murmansk was first occupied by a wooden church, built in 1946.

In 1984, the rather low-profile congregation decided they needed a new church, but thanks to the Soviet government, which allowed no other gods above itself, the work had to progress clandestinely. Not surprisingly, however, it was difficult to hide a cathedral, and when the government learned of the effort in 1985, they sent in miners with orders to dynamite the structure. This raised a holy ruckus, and demonstrators descended upon the site, blocking the miners, while simultaneous protests were held outside the Moscow city executive committee. The government eventually capitulated to some extent, allowing what remained of the building to stand, but forbidding any further work on it.

However, in 1987, after perestroika allowed the exiled Christian God back into the Soviet Union, construction resumed and over the next five summers, the project was completed.

quate rooms for US$26/30. Another option in the city centre is the *Meridian Hotel* (☎ 288694, *ulitsa Vorovskovo 5/23*), opposite the hulking Hotel Arktika. Run-down but clean and comfortable, singles/doubles are US$53/59. It has very friendly service, and the buffet on the 4th floor serves up a great ham and egg breakfast.

Somewhat out of the centre is the *69th Parallel Hotel (Gostinitsa Shestdesyat-Devyataya Parallel, ☎ 565643, Lyzhny proezd 14, postal index 183042)* in Dolina Uyuta (Cosy Valley). Take trolleybus No 1 or 6 from the centre for about 10 minutes. Rooms cost US$23/32 with phones and TVs (some even have balconies and fridges). There's also a cafe in the lobby.

An excellent but pricier option is the *Obkomovsk Administratsii Hotel* (☎ 459278, *ulitsa Sofiya Perovskaya 3)*. Decent rooms cost US$64/68.

At the overpriced **Hotel Arktika** *(☎ 57988, prospekt Lenina 82, postal index 183038)* on Five-Corners, dingy and drafty rooms with bath cost US$95/100. The exception is the 4th floor, which has been renovated and furnished by a Swedish firm to western business standards, but these rooms cost US$110/120 with satellite TV and a satellite phone and fax near the dezhurnaya's desk. All major credit cards are accepted.

If you are determined to spend that much money, do what Mr and Mrs Ted Turner did and stay at the sinfully luxurious (but inconvenient) **Ogni Murmanskaya** *(☎ 553-862, Finnish fax 358-9 4929 2459, ulitsa Furmanova 11)*, with good city views. Single/double rooms cost US$100/110 including breakfast, and all are western-standard luxury – even the bathroom floors are heated. Nicer suites cost US$120/130. The security is relatively good and the restaurant is thankfully short on thugs.

Places to Eat

A seasonal item is reindeer meat, and of course there are lots of fish, especially cod. Try the *severyanka*, which is the local chowder. For self-caterers there's a small market at the bottom of ulitsa Volodarskovo.

For an upmarket feast in the company of movers and shakers in Murmansk, go to the relatively posh **Medved**, at the upper end of prospekt Lenina. For Chinese specialities, try the **Harbin**, around the corner on ulitsa Papanina.

Burger Bar *(prospekt Lenina 72)* has good hamburgers at an expensive US$7. The cafe in front is non smoking, and the bar and restaurant are to the rear. If your idea of pizza is sausage and eggs on a greasy cracker, then try the **Pizzeria**, on prospekt Lenina north-east of ulitsa Voiodarskogo, while the **Kafe Yunost**, behind the Arktika, is OKAY for ice cream and coffee.

Kafe Svetlana, at the Administratsii Hotel, Sofiya Perovskaya 3, is very clean and good, with stingy portions of fresh fish with vegetables for US$0.50, and *plov* (pilaf) for about US$1 – it's non smoking and entry is at the side of the building. There's a surprisingly clean and cheerful **buffet** at the Passenger Ferry Terminal, with sandwiches, hard-boiled eggs and so forth, while the **Pingvin** ice cream cafe at the Rodina cinema is popular and crowded.

Getting There & Away

From the train station, snail-pace trains can get you to Nikel (eight to 12 hours), Apatity (four hours), St Petersburg (eight to 27 hours, US$94on the express train), Moscow (12 to 34 hours, US$134 on the express train) and beyond. Ostensibly, tickets are sold from 8 am to 11 pm. Services to other Kola Peninsula towns leave from the bus station next door.

KOLA

In the Murmansk suburb of Kola, which is pretty much a city in its own right, little of the past remains but the homely **Annunciation Cathedral** (Blagoveshchensky sobor) which dates from 1809. Inside, there's a museum on Pomor life. It's open from 10 am to 5.30 pm (4 pm on weekends), and is closed on Monday. (You can see a more comprehensive display on this subject at the Murmansk Museum of Regional Studies.)

From Murmansk, take bus No 106 (not No 106-Э) from the train station for 15km to the Kola stop, then walk for 10 minutes to the west from the Lotta turn-off.

SEVEROMORSK

The headquarters of the Russian Northern Fleet is mostly closed to foreigners, but with lots of time and some stressful effort, it's possible to visit. What you need is a good reason, and there seem to be three of them. The WWII-era submarine K-21 saw quite a bit of action and is now a museum. The Military Aircraft Museum in Safonovo, near Severomorsk, is said to house a spectacular exhibition of military aviation. Intourist Murmansk can arrange tours of either place with 'lots of notice' and heavy bureaucratic intervention. The Apatity City Administration can arrange a look at the atomic cruiser *Admiral Khimov* when it's in port at Severomorsk, but at least one month's notice is required. For any of these trips, no one will mention prices or guarantee anything until each case is reviewed.

NIKEL

There's nothing to prepare a visitor for Nikel. Even the slums of the teeming Indian cities emit some sense of hope, while this particular suburb of hell seems to be past despising its own condition. And for that – as well as for the emotional wrench you're sure to experience – Nikel is most emphatically worth visiting. The scope of its environmental and architectural disaster – and the depths of its despair – must be experienced to be believed. If Greenpeace needs a poster child or some Hollywood director wants to film a vision of post-nuclear apocalypse, Nikel is all prepped and ready for the cameras to roll.

Nikel was founded in the 1930s when Finns discovered rich deposits of nickel, but in 1939, the original plant was destroyed. However, it was quickly rebuilt, as nickel became essential to the Nazi war effort. In September 1944, Finland capitulated and handed the entire Pechenga region over to the Soviet Union. The following month, however, the plant was destroyed by the German forces and wasn't rebuilt until 1951 when it was taken over by Pechemnikel. Over the years, strip mining operations ripped up the landscape; enormous amounts of sulphur dioxide spilled into the environment, destroying the vegetation for 50km in all directions; and the Soviet regime prevented any sort of artificial enhancements – such as pleasing architecture – that might have awakened some sense of hope.

The small **local museum** features a collection of minerals from the Kola Peninsula, as well as the historical links between Norway, Finland and north-western Russia. If for some reason you want to stay the night, pre-booked rooms with shared facilities at the very simple *Nikel Hotel* cost US$39 per person. If you just turn up, however, you're sure

to pay considerably less. The town also has a small and very, very simple Russian eatery.

ZAPOLYARNYE

The nickel-mining town of Zapolyarnye, which is only marginally more tolerable than Nikel, is the proud home of the world's deepest hole, which extends 12km beneath the surface. While there's little else to see, the town does have a decent hotel, the *Hotel Pechenga* (☎ 81554-36500), and would be a happier place than Nikel to spend the night. Single/double rooms cost US$70/110. The high prices are due mainly to the fact that most of the takers are short-term Norwegian visitors (for whom these rates seem a bargain!), and individual travellers are likely to get a much better deal. In addition to the hotel dining room, there's also a basic Russian restaurant.

BORISOGLEBSK

Borisoglebsk, on the Pasvik River at the Norwegian border, was named after the 1565 church which inspired its inclusion in Russia when the boundary was drawn in 1826. The original church, named in honour of the saints Boris and Gleb, fell into disrepair in the mid-19th century and was replaced in 1872. While the original church burned down in 1944, its replacement was restored by Norwegian donors and is now a pleasant and distinctive attraction. From 1958 to 1963, a Norwegian-Soviet joint project also created the power station and workers' housing projects at Skoltefossen, on the Pasvik River. Special permission is required to visit Borisoglebsk, which is best done with one of the tour agencies in Kirkenes, Norway.

MONCHEGORSK
☎ 81536

If you've ever had a notion to visit Hell, Monchegorsk is pretty close (but not as close as nearby Nikel), and the ground here is literally black. Ironically, the Sami name of the town means 'beautiful tundra'!

The culprit was the glorious Soviet regime, which aimed to dominate nature with its high-blown delusions. Unfortunately, nature refused to submit without dire consequences. In the case of Monchegorsk, its brainchild was the Severonikel Kombinat plant. Between 1980 and 1993, this plant and its sister, Pechemnikel, in Nikel (which makes Monchegorsk look like the Garden of Eden – see earlier in this chapter), processed copper and nickel, and spewed 600,000 tonnes of sulfur dioxide into the atmosphere, along with 10,000 tonnes of nickel powder and other heavy metals. In 1994 and 1995 emissions were cut roughly in half, due mainly to lower production, but given the current state of these places, it was clearly too late to make much of a difference.

The irony is, since the fall of the Soviet Union and the related decline in military orders, the plant's main clients are now subcontractors for US and Japanese auto manufacturers, who use its products to manufacture catalytic converters that reduce emissions on western cars. If there's any good news, it's that reduced demand by the military has led to a 30% reduction in pollution. However, over 1000 sq km of forests have been destroyed and it's unlikely that the damage can ever be reversed. Ironically, the vicinity's only visitor attraction – unless you're curious about the outer limits of possible ecological devastation – is the nearby Laplandsky Zapovednik, which is Arctic Russia's most accessible nature reserve.

Places to Stay & Eat
The town's two hotels are the *Lapplandia* (☎ 24526, prospekt Metallurgov 32), which has singles/doubles from US$14.25/20, and the somewhat nicer *Sever* (☎ 22091, prospekt Metallurgov 45A). The latter is cheaper, for singles/doubles you'll pay US$5.75/7.75. The restaurant at the Lapplandia is open from noon to 11 pm, and the Sever has a buffet on the 1st floor.

Getting There & Away
Buses leave to/from Murmansk's bus station several times a day (three hours, US$4.50).

LAPLANDSKY ZAPOVEDNIK (LAPLAND BIOSPHERE RESERVE)
☎ 81536
South of Monchegorsk, and spanning north and west towards Norway and Finland, the UNESCO-protected Lapland Biosphere Reserve (☎ 50080, fax 57199, email Gilyasovaev@monch.mels.ru) consists of 2784 sq km of almost pristine wilderness. About half of it is virgin tundra, and the rest consists of alpine grasslands, marshes, rivers, lakes and five small mountain ranges (the highest peak being 1114m). The reserve was founded in 1930 to protect the area's reindeer herds; over 1000 reindeer live on the biosphere's territory today, making it among the largest concentrations in Europe. Along with 33 species of mammals (including brown bears, elks, and wolves), 201 bird species and 15 species of fish, there are more than 900 species of higher plants, mosses and lichens.

The threat to the ecological balance of the park's flora and fauna is multi-faceted. On one hand, while the Khibiny mountain range manages to stave off most of the damage that Monchegorsk's nickel plant threatens to inflict, the easternmost section of the park has been decimated. Inside the park itself, poachers and careless trespassers inflict damage too (each year, forest fires from illegal campfires destroy hectares of forest). These miscreants, along with the usual culprits – local and regional government corruption, lack of funding – make keeping the park alive more difficult. While the Russian government provides minimal funding, and the US-based Global Ecological Fund has provided support for an ecological education program, the reserve must mainly rely on itself for maintenance.

Inside, visitors can trek through the wilderness – the best times to visit are March-April, June, and August-September – or traverse it on skis, snowshoes or snowmobiles. The possibilities for adventure tourism are endless, ranging from hiking (the views of seemingly endless stretches of mountains are breathtaking), camping and relaxing nature walks, to winter igloo-building expeditions. There are several waterfalls on the territory, and even a German war plane resting where it fell from the skies during WWII.

Individuals or groups of less than 10 people can visit the reserve any time of the year with advance notice. There are comfortable guest cottages at the reserve's main base on the quiet banks of Chuna Lake, but visitors should expect to 'rough it' in tents on longer expeditions. You can rest those weary bones in the base's heavenly banya on Fridays along with the friendly forest rangers who live and work there. Costs vary depending on the kind of experience you're looking for, but expect to pay US$20 to US$40 per day.

What to Bring

It's important to have warm clothes, in layers – and the outer layer should be waterproof. You'll also need good, comfortable trekking boots, as much of this landscape is wet, soggy muskeg and even in summer, it can get mighty wet. Visitors are also responsible for their own food and equipment – trail mix and high-protein snacks work best. Don't expect anything to be available at the reserve (one trekking group ran out of Snickers bars after two days and had to rely on the rangers' and guides' own meagre rations). Locals maintain that most of the surface water here is clean and drinkable – which is hard to believe when you consider the nuclear presence and utter devastation so near at hand – so if it may be an idea to carry a means of purification. It's also wise to bring navigational equipment, although the guides are quite well-equipped.

Getting There & Away

The easiest access is through Monchegorsk. Arrangements to visit the reserve must be made in advance, either directly (the most effective route), or through Eco-Nord (in Apatity ☎ 81555-79762, Norwegian ☎ 47-78 91 41 18).

APATITY
☎ 81555

Apatity, founded in 1966, is the world's greatest source of apatite ore and the Kola Peninsula's second-largest city. While the city itself isn't that attractive to nonscientific types, Apatity makes an excellent jump-off point for hiking, climbing and skiing expeditions in the nearby Khibiny mountains. You may even spot the Yeti, the Big Foot-like forest loiterer (42cm-long footprints have been found) who is said to put in an occasional appearance and leave his mark. The town is also emerging as a cultural arts and crafts centre.

Apatity has two main sections, the Akademgorodok (Academic Town) and the city proper. The main shopping streets are ulitsa Fersmana and ulitsa Lenina. The train station lies south-west of the centre, while the bus station is north of the centre, east of the Akademgorodok.

Econord, formerly the Scandinavian Study Centre (☎/fax 78586, fax – in Norway – 47 78 91 41 18, email econord@inep .ksc.ru), PO Box 176, Apatity 184200, is a good source of information, and is in the Akademgorodok, in the same building as the Museum of the History of the Research & Exploration of the North. Khibiny TS tour service (☎ 30116, fax 34750, email hts @khibiny.murmansk.ru), at ulitsa Lenina 9-a, 184200 Apatity, which operates tours around the Kola Region, can also offer limited tourist information.

You can change money at one of the two banks on ploshchad Geologicheskaya: Sberbank, open Monday to Friday from 8 am to 8 pm, Saturday 11 am to 5 pm; and Apititkom Bank, open Monday to Friday from 9.30 am to 12.30 pm. Maps of the region (1:1,000,000) are available from Khibiny TS.

Things to See & Do

The best museum in town is the **Museum of the History of the Research & Exploration of the North** (☎ 79255), which was founded in the 1970s and features exhibits on Russian Arctic expeditions, both scientific and

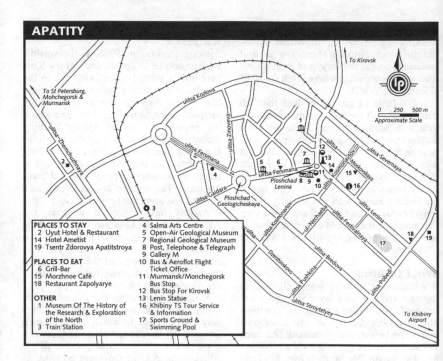

APATITY

To Kirovsk

To St Petersburg,
Mohcheqorsk &
Murmansk

To Khibiny
Airport

0 250 500 m
Approximate Scale

PLACES TO STAY
2 Uyut Hotel & Restaurant
14 Hotel Ametist
19 Tsentr Zdorovya Apatitstroya

PLACES TO EAT
6 Grill-Bar
15 Morzhnoe Café
18 Restaurant Zapolyarye

OTHER
1 Museum Of The History of
 the Research & Exploration
 of the North
3 Train Station

4 Salma Arts Centre
5 Open-Air Geological Museum
7 Regional Geological Museum
8 Post, Telephone & Telegraph
9 Gallery M
10 Bus & Aeroflot Flight
 Ticket Office
11 Murmansk/Monchegorsk
 Bus Stop
12 Bus Stop For Kirovsk
13 Lenin Statue
16 Khibiny TS Tour Service
 & Information
17 Sports Ground &
 Swimming Pool

exploratory, as well as the Solovetsky Monastery, unique drawings of Novaya Zemlya and 5000-year-old Sami rock carvings, tools and other instruments. It's open weekdays from 2 to 5 pm, but will open any time for interested visitors.

Rock fans may enjoy the user-friendly **Regional Geological Museum** at ulitsa Fersmana 16, which has fine exhibitions of local rocks and minerals, as well as some local crafts. It's open Monday to Friday from 9 am to 6 pm. You may also want to stroll through the **Open-Air Geological Museum**, farther west on ulitsa Fersmana, which features a few paths lined with local rock samples.

The **swimming pool** is open daily from 8 am to 10 pm except Monday; a 45-minute session costs US$0.50. Staff may ask for a Health Certificate (which all Russians carry), but if you're clean and look healthy,

you probably won't have any problems. Another building worth noting is the **library** which – yes – resembles the pages of an open book.

Apatity is an artistic centre, and a locally invented method of 'painting', using coloured dust from crushed local minerals, is now catching on all over the Russian north. The **Salma Art Centre**, at ulitsa Dzerzhinskovo 1, is a private cooperative outlet for over 200 Kola Peninsula artists. Prices are low, and the management can arrange the paperwork to expedite customs procedures. The exhibition hall to the front holds new art exhibitions and the sales outlet is at the back. The Salon holds occasional church choir presentations and piano recitals. During the third week in January, the city hosts the Stone Flower Exhibition, in which local minerals are turned into flowery works of art. **Gallery M**, on the 2nd floor of the Polyarny building on ploshchad Lenina, features a changing exhibit of artworks by local artists; it's open Monday to Saturday from 2 to 6 pm.

Places to Stay & Eat

The *Hotel Ametist (☎ 33201, ulitsa Lenina 3)* has clean singles/doubles for US$26/32. Okay, there's no toilet paper or hot water and they scrub the hallways with petrol daily, but you may get lucky and have a room with a mountain view. There's a smoky buffet/bar on the 2nd floor, open until midnight, and a passable dining room on the main floor that's big, loud and very red.

The Apatitstroy Health Centre, or *Tsentr Zdorovya Apatitstroya (☎ 31181)*, at the eastern edge of town, is sometimes known as *Isobela* or the *Dom Otdikha* (rest home). It formerly served as the rest and health clinic of the Apititsroy construction company, but has now been opened to the public. This spotless resort features a nice pool and sauna/banya, winter garden and two restaurants. Here you'll pay US$38/66 for single/double accommodation, with meals and access to the pool and sauna. To get there, take bus No 8 from the train station or ploshchad Lenina. The adjacent *Dacha*, a four-room hotel with queen-sized beds, a lounge, winter garden, sauna and cold-pool, is fine for groups and costs just US$50 per person. A servant is provided to clean the room and cook up meals using any raw materials you can provide.

If you don't mind a worthwhile walk from the centre, try the *Zapolyarye*; whenever it's open, it serves up fairly decent fare. At the *Gril-Bar (ulitsa Lenina 20)* US$1 will buy half a hot dog without a bun and for US$1.50, you'll get microwaved Cup-o-Soup served in its original packaging (they even let you stir it up yourself). 'Coffee' is a spoonful of powder, a spoonful of sugar and a cup of hot water; from there, you're on your own.

If you can live by bread alone (a real plus in these parts), look for the locally made, round-loaf bread, Pomorsky Khleb or the ubiquitous Rom Baba (which is notably de-

void of rum and normally makes its public debut when it's several days old).

Getting There & Away

There are no flights from Murmansk, but Apatity's new Khibiny Airport is served from Moscow (US$124) daily except weekends, and from St Petersburg (US$106) on Monday, Tuesday, Friday and Sunday. From Murmansk, buses leave at least twice daily (four hours, US$9). Most trains between Moscow, St Petersburg and Murmansk stop at Apatity; take any train headed south from Murmansk (five to eight hours). From the St Petersburg-Murmansk Hwy, Apatity lies 30km down a well-signposted eastward spur road, 35km south of Monchegorsk.

Bus Nos 5 and 13 (not 13K) run between the train station and the centre. There's an hourly bus to Khibiny Airport. Bus Nos 101, 102 and 105 travel between Apatity and Kirovsk.

KIROVSK
☎ 815231

Although it's rapidly fading, the main attraction at Kirovsk is its ski hill, which offers the finest skiing in north-western Russia. In winter, the city hosts the annual All-Europe Downhill Freestyle Competition, and the city's five ski schools hold lessons in ballet skiing, ski-jumping and mogul skiing as well as annual giant slalom and speed ski competitions. If you break your leg while you're at it, the city's newest church boasts a 'healing' icon that will ostensibly have you fixed up in a jiffy!

The Kirovsk 'microregion', nestled in the Khibiny mountains, is known not by its Russian name, Kukisvumchorr, but simply as 'Kirovsk-25'. This is in reference to its distance in kilometres from Apatity, a convention adopted by geological crews who identified dig sites by the nearest milepost. Maps are available at the city administration building, and the best bookshop (which isn't saying much) is at ulitsa Lenina 22. You can change money next door at the Sberbank.

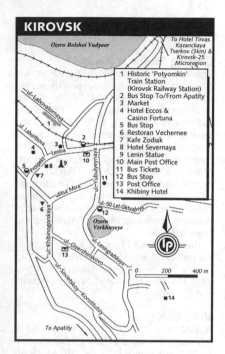

KIROVSK

Ozero Bolshoi Vudyaer

To Hotel Tirvas
Kazanckaya
Tserkov (3km) &
Kirovsk-25
Microregion

1 Historic 'Potyomkin'
   Train Station
   (Kirovsk Railway Station)
2 Bus Stop To/From Apatity
3 Market
4 Hotel Eccos &
   Casino Fortuna
5 Bus Stop
6 Restoran Vechernee
7 Kafe Zodiak
8 Hotel Severnaya
9 Lenin Statue
10 Main Post Office
11 Bus Tickets
12 Bus Stop
13 Post Office
14 Khibiny Hotel

Ozero
Verkhnyeye

0   200   400 m

To Apatity

Things to See & Do

The new orthodox **Kazanskaya Church**
(Kazanskaya tserkov), en route to Kirovsk-
25, is built on the site of another church that
had been moved from Kirovsk, and is un-
orthodox in that it was converted from a typical north Russian wooden house. The inside
is lovely, however, with an impressive
iconostasis and the allegedly miraculous
Icon of St Nicholas. On the night of 21 May
1994, the icon incredibly restored itself, and
now works its miracles Monday to Friday
from 9 am to 6 pm with a break between 2
and 3 pm. Take bus No 1, 12 or 105 from
Kirovsk centre towards Kirovsk-25, and ask
for the church. From the bus stop, walk west
(back towards Kirovsk), turn south (left),
then turn east (left again) and the church is
200m on the right-hand side of the road.

The most impressive building in town is
the white elephant **Kirovsk Railway Station**,
which, like many of the 'Potyomkin villages' that would pop up around Russia
(constructed only to impress visiting officials), is an unused and ludicrous monument
to Soviet anti-logic. Locals joke that its first
and last passenger was Joseph Stalin.

The **Kirovsk-25** 'microregion' has a **Regional Museum** that seems to be perpetually closed, but it's still worth a slog out
there to see the surrounding mountains – or
rather, the awesome gap where they used to
be. A veteran geophysicist for a major western minerals concern said that he knew of
no way to accomplish such a neat removal
of literally half a mountain (they look like
those models you used to see in school of a
cutaway section of a volcano), other than a
nuclear detonation, but local scientists insist
the feat was accomplished with earth
movers and heavy equipment – right. Take
bus Nos 1, 12 or 105 from Kirovsk to the
northern end of Kirovsk-25.

The 17 tow ropes up the city's ski slopes
cost around US$0.50 to US$1 per ride, or
US$4.50 to US$10 for a day pass. Although
limited rentals are available, it's best to
bring your own equipment. Ski packages
can be arranged through the tour agency
Khibiny TS in Apatity.

The region also offers the best hiking in
all of north-western Russia. The most popular destination is the **Khibiny Mountains**,
where the highest point, Judychvumchorr,
rises 1200m above sea level, and the adjacent Lovozero massif, just to the east.

Places to Stay & Eat

The Hungarian-built *Hotel Severnaya*
(☎ 20442, prospekt Lenina 11) is more or
less a western-standard hotel (except for the
tiny Russian hotel beds) right in the town
centre. Single or double rooms cost US$30
per person, but if you're alone, you may be
asked to share the room with a stranger.
There's also a lobby bar and a restaurant
with okay food and loud music.

The new *Hotel Eccos & Casino Fortuna*
(☎ 20234), in a castle-like building in the
centre, has new single/double rooms for
US$13/19 and luxury rooms for US$55. For

breakfast and dinner, you'll pay an additional US$18/24 for one/two people. Construction is still ongoing and it's wise to assume that when it's complete, prices will increase.

The institutional-looking **Khibiny Hotel** (☎ 21256) is a large turbaza on the slope about 1km from the centre. Very basic single/double rooms cost US$11/17.

At the **market** on ploshchad Lenina opposite the Lenin statue you'll find imported food and drinks; it's open from 11 am to 7 pm.

Kafe Zodiak (ulitsa Lenina 13, the sign says Morozhenoe Kafe), is somewhat pricey and doesn't offer much. *Restoran Vechernee (ulitsa Khibinogorskaya 29)* is the best place in town with a café upstairs; it's open daily from noon to 8 pm except Monday.

Getting There & Away

Bus Nos 101, 102 and 105 (US$0.80) and minibuses marked Kirovsk-Apatity (US$1) travel between Apatity and Kirovsk. Bus Nos 1, 12 and 105 run between Kirovsk and Kirovsk-25.

POLYARNYE ZORY
☎ 815233

This 'energy city' is right chuffed to be home to the Kola Nuclear Power Plant, a VVER-440-213 and VVER-440-230-type plant. Throughout the town, cheerful references to the wonders of Mr Atom abound, with slogans like 'An Atom Should be a Worker, not a Soldier' decorating local apartment blocks. Polyarnye Zory lies between Apatity and Kandalaksha, and can be reached by both train and bus, several times a day.

Things to See & Do

Beside the train station is an exhibit optimistically labelled the **Museum of the Polar Partisan**, open daily from 10 am to 7 pm except Wednesday and Thursday.

For something a bit different, the public relations director (☎ 68140 or ☎ 63910) at the **Kola Nuclear Power Plant** may be able to arrange a tour with five days' notice. That way, you can marvel at the fish (trout, salmon and others) that swim in the tank

filled with the plant's output coolant water (purportedly demonstrating the plant's safety standards).

Places to Stay & Eat

The town's hotel, the **Nevsky Berega** (☎ 64151, ulitsa Lomonosova 1) is spotlessly clean, with comfortable doubles for US$25. Most rooms have terraces overlooking the forest and there's a fair restaurant. The **Pivnoy Bar** next to the market isn't bad for a snack.

KANDALAKSHA
☎ 815233

The Kola Peninsula's most important port after Murmansk, Kandalaksha is now a rather grim industrial city, and home to one of the military's most important aluminium plants. The Pomor fishing village, around which the town was founded and which dates from the 17th century, is still inhabited. Kandalaksha is served by several daily buses from Apatity, and at least one daily bus from Murmansk. In addition, any Murmansk train will stop here. Local buses run between the train and bus stations, northeast of town, and the centre, which lies to the south-west, over the railway line.

Things to See & Do

The large **nature reserve & sea-bird sanctuary** (Kandalakshisky Gosudarstvenny Zapovednik), on the White Sea islands southwest of the town, is home to more than 250 species of sea birds. Most prominent are the eider ducks, gulls, murres, kittiwakes, razorbills and black guillemots, which nest in the rookeries of the Kuvshin and Kharlov islands. Summer visits can be arranged through the city administration (☎ 4957), the city excursions bureau (☎ 50396) or the reserve administration centre, at the southern end of town.

To reach the reserve, take bus No 1 from the train station to the last stop and walk toward the port; the administration centre will be on the left-hand side, across the river from the Pomor village. For more information, you can contact the American Association for the Support of Ecological Initiatives (☎ 203-347 2967, fax 8459, email wwasch @eagle.wesleyan.edu), 150 Coleman Rd, Middletown CT 06457, USA.

Places to Stay & Eat

The *Belomore Hotel (☎ 23100 or ☎ 22013, ulitsa 50-letia Oktyabrya dom 1)*, opposite the tank, has surly staff and grotty singles/doubles for US$26/35, with a restaurant that opens 'in the evening' (better opt for the *Gril-Bar*, next door). Much better – but quite dumpy – *Hotel Spolokhi (☎ 55768, ulitsa Naberezhnaya 130)*, east of the centre, towards the riverbank, has rooms for US$25/36 as well as a restaurant that's open on weekends and a buffet that operates on weekdays until 4pm. (The desk clerk thought the author was using a compass to measure background radiation and she did not seem surprised in the least that someone would measure radiation in the hotel lobby.

THE SOLOVETSKY ISLANDS

The isolated Solovetsky Islands, a tiny 300 sq km archipelago in the White Sea between Karelia and Arkhangelsk, are home to the monastery in which Stalin's government housed one of the Soviet Union's most infamous Gulag camps until the late 1930s. Many Russians refer to the islands by their diminutive nickname, Solevki (see the boxed text 'Solovetsky Monastery – From Paradise to Purgatory').

The Solovetsky Monastery – From Paradise to Purgatory

The Solovetsky Islands were settled in the 1420s and 1430s by two monks from the Kirill-Belozersk Monastery, Zosima and Savvaty, who found the lack of hideous monsters there reassuring enough to build a monastery. Over the next hundred years, the monks' dedication and ingenuity resulted in the construction of a huge stone kremlin, factories and smelters; the island's fortress proved good fortification against attacks from Livonians and Swedes (in 1571, 1582 and 1611).

By the 1660s, the monastery owned over 50 saltworks, and by the mid-17th century the island's industry employed 600 workers, and it was home to over 300 monks. The monks had also, inadvertently, become prosperous enough to ensure that they would be the subject of attacks from tsars and Soviet forces for years to come.

In 1668, the monks took advantage of the ousting of Patriarch Nikon to announce their independence from the central church control. Over the next eight years, the monks and their allies (mainly disgruntled workers and Old Believers, with a few fugitive Cossacks thrown in for good measure) held out against constant attacks by the tsar's armies.

They probably could have held out for a good deal longer if it weren't for the turncoat monk, Feoktist, who led tsarist troops to an undefended section of the monastery's White Tower, from where they launched a decisive offensive. The monks were defeated in January 1676; tsarist forces killed almost every participant.

On 6-7 July 1854, at the outset of the Crimean War, the English ships *Eurydice*, *Brisk* and *Miranda* were sent to the White Sea area to look for an auxiliary port for the English navy. When they got to Solevki they engaged in a battle in which both the Russians and the English claimed decisive victory – the Russians said that a hail of cannon fire from the monastery sank one ship, while the English aver that they lost interest after firing red-hot shots at the monastery, landing forces, blowing up buildings and sailing away, fleet intact.

Under the Soviet regime, the seemingly made-to-order prison (what better use for a good, strong stone fortress in Soviet Russia?) was converted into a gulag (forced labour camp), and became one of the most feared and infamous. The gulag closed in 1939.

eitvågen, north of Bodø, Norway

aditional Nordland fishing boats in the harbour at Å in Lofoten, Norway

Lake amidst Finland's highest mountains

Cabin at the edge of a forest, Finland

Boggy lands in Arctic Finland

Typical forest road, Finnish Lapland

Things to See & Do

The **Solovetsky monastery grounds**, on the largest of the islands, are surrounded by formidable stone walls ranging from 8 to 11m high and 4 to 6m thick, with seven gates and eight towers. In 1974, the island was designated an architectural, historical and nature reserve. Inside the 16th century **kremlin**, you can tour the buildings and churches, including the **St Nicholas Church** (Glavny Nikolsky tserkov) which was built between 1831 and 1833; the **refectory** (a massive single-pillared chamber) which connects to the **Assumption Cathedral** (Uspensky sobor), built between 1552 and 1557; and the **Transfiguration Cathedral** (Preobrazhensky sobor), built between 1556 and 1564.

Day tours run to the island, and also visit Sekirnaya Hill and the Khutor Gorka botanical gardens.

Places to Stay

The best option in Solovki village is the *Hotel Priyout* (☎ 297), where clean rooms for one to four people cost US$15, or US$35 with meals. The hotel has lovely and helpful staff.

Getting There & Away

From Kem, you can either book a tour with Turbaz Kem (☎ 81458-20385). Or take bus No 1 for 35 minutes to Rabotcheostrovsk, where boats leave for the islands on Wednesday and Sunday at 4 pm. They take three hours and cost US$11. From Arkhangelsk, you can fly three times weekly for US$18 each way.

Taymyr Peninsula

The Taymyr Peninsula, the world's most northerly continental land, stretches 1200km north of the Arctic Circle to its northernmost point at Cape Chelyuskin. It is washed by two Polar seas, the Kara and the Laptev and is bounded on the west by the Yenisey River and on the east by the Khatanga.

The habitat ranges from polar desert to forest tundra, and about 60% of the land is covered by vast areas of swampy tundra dotted with glistening lakes and sliced by meandering rivers. This is the breeding ground for numerous waders, geese and other birds and in the short summer is covered with wild flowers. Herds of wild reindeer migrate north across the tundra every spring to escape the flies and mosquitoes. The Byrranga mountains have northern slopes which reach the Arctic ocean and it is on these that the muskoxen, which were reintroduced to Russia in the 1970s, roam. Lake Taymyr, Lake Logata and the surrounding rivers are the breeding grounds of the rare red-breasted goose. At Ary Mas on the Novaya River, the edge of the most northerly taiga forest in the world can be found. Farther south-west the Putorana plateau lies 75km east of Norilsk and extends easterly for 350km. It rises to about 1700m and is characterised by flat windswept summits, steep 200-300m scarps, magnificent waterfalls and canyons.

The Kotuy and Kureyka rivers which dissect it have exciting white water rafting possibilities and there is excellent fishing. There are brown bears and snow sheep and the area may be reached by small boat along the rivers and lakes from Norilsk or by helicopter. The Great Arctic Nature Reserve includes large areas of Taymyr which have been set aside to protect the wildlife and the way of life of the indigenous peoples.

The administrative centre of the territory is Dudinka, a port on river Yenesey. It is linked by road and rail to Norilsk which was built in the 1920s by the inmates of one of the largest of Stalin's Gulags to exploit the enormous deposits of copper, nickel, cobalt and coal in the area. It is one of the most polluted cities in the world and its inhabitants live under a cloud of acrid sulphuric smog. For kilometres around, the trees are dead. Its a museum is devoted mainly to the native peoples, the geology and the Gulag.

Norilsk airport lies between Norilsk and Dudinka and a railway connects them. There are fairly regular scheduled flights from

Moscow. Dickson, on the coast farther north, was the first port to be constructed on the Siberian coast. It was a centre for the servicing of a series of polar weather stations but is now a town in decline with streets full of rubbish, although from the coast nearby, it is sometimes possible to watch belugas swimming through the ice floes.

Out of a total population of approximately 300,000 people in the region there are 8000 indigenous people – Dolgans, Nenets, Evenks, Nganasans and Ents. Some of them still engage in reindeer breeding, hunting and fishing. Access to the region is extremely difficult due to the current economic situation. It is possible to reach Norilsk from Moscow by scheduled flights (although the tickets can only be purchased in Russia) but the services to Dickson and Khatanga have been greatly reduced and are extremely unreliable.

Travel outside of the towns is difficult due to the lack of roads. Helicopters are still the most common form of transport but they are expensive and can be unreliable due to poor weather conditions. In summer it may be possible to hire small boats locally for travel on the rivers and lakes. Hotel accommodation, if any, is variable. Communication with the region is extremely unreliable and difficult. Special permits from various agencies for travel within the region are usually required. These have to be obtained locally and may be refused on an apparent whim. For the determined, an organisation such as the Ecological Travels Centre in Moscow (π/fax 095-939 4238, email etc @rc.msu.ru) can help with obtaining permits for nature reserves, travel to the region and local contacts.

Russian Arctic Islands

Off the Russian coast, in the Arctic Ocean, lie five ice-bound archipelagos – Franz Josef Land, Novaya Zemlya, Severnaya Zemlya, the New Siberian Islands (Novosibirskye Ostrova) and Wrangel Island (Vrangelya Ostrov) – which present some of the wildest, most inhospitable and least accessible landfalls on the planet. Any wealthy traveller in search of solitude won't find better venues.

Lying in a sea of ice, Franz Josef Land was not even discovered until at least the 1860s. Like the other Russian Arctic islands, it then became a target for hunters, sealers and whalers but none of these islands were considered of much commercial or economic use until the 1940s. Weather stations along the northern coast of Siberia allowed the development of a Northern Sea Route, at which point these various island groups became strategically important.

FRANZ JOSEF LAND
Farther north than any of the other Russian Arctic islands, Franz Josef Land comprises 191 islands that stretch 375km from west to east and 234km from north to south. The largest is George Land (2741 sq km), followed by Wilczek Land (2054 sq km), Graham Bell Island (1708 sq km) and Alexandra Island (1051 sq km).

About 85% of the land is covered by glaciers, and the area that is ice-free tends to be barren and without soil. Despite this, the vegetation in the archipelago is varied and each island is different. There are no trees, and the most common forms of vegetation are lichens and mosses, which turn the land green, orange and yellow in the summer months. Cape Flora, on Northbrook Island, was named after the richness of its plant life.

No serious studies of the birds on Franz Josef Land occurred until the 1920s, mainly because of the area's harsh and unpredictable climate. Some 41 bird species have been observed, although only 14 species breed here. This is mainly because of the climate, along with the fact that the scanty vegetation and limited snow-free land do not provide an attractive venue for geese, waders and passerines (perching birds). Hungry polar bears and foxes also make ground nesting hazardous. There are, however, large colonies of sea birds that make

THE RUSSIAN ARCTIC ISLANDS

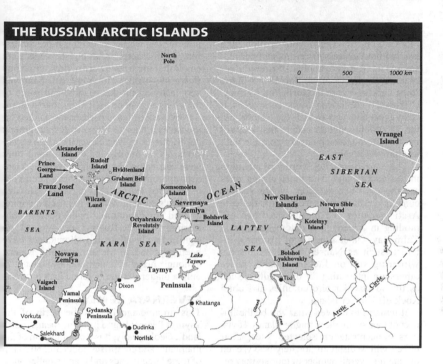

use of the rocky cliffs, especially kitti-wakes, auks and guillemots.

Seals and walruses are numerous all around the islands, particularly since hunting has been banned. Whales can also be seen, including the two most Arctic of cetaceans – the beluga and the narwhal. Meanwhile, polar bears are common – not for nothing is Franz Josef Land often referred to as the 'polar bear capital of the world' – and it is an unlucky visitor who leaves without seeing any. Bears were never seriously hunted in Franz Josef Land, and since the international ban on hunting in 1973, the population has thrived.

Ever since its discovery, possibly by sealers in 1865, Franz Josef Land has remained a land of mystery. Its location far to the north of the mainland, and its inhospitable nature, have meant that little research has been conducted, and the 19th century exped-itions, such as the Austro-Hungarian Exploring Expedition in the ship *Tegetthoff* from 1872 to 1874, chanced upon the archipelago, rather than made it an objective in its own right. After visits by Benjamin Leigh Smith, Frederick Jackson, and Fridtjof Nansen, Franz Josef Land became a popular starting point for attempts on the North Pole, such as the Wellman expedition of 1898-99, and the American Baldwin-Ziegler expedition of 1901-02. In 1926, Russia laid claim to the islands bit by bit (following the example set by Canada with its own Arctic archipelago), and by 1930 the archipelago was closed to outside visitors.

By 1990, the Soviet grip on its Arctic islands began to loosen, and several joint expeditions were permitted, most of them exploring the history of the area. In the following years, a number of ship-bound tours have taken non-Russian visitors to the area.

Fragile and vulnerable places like Cape Flora are protected and no one is allowed to land without express governmental permission. The Russian nuclear-powered icebreaker *Sovietsky Soyuz* travels to Franz Josef Land as part of its North Pole journey, chartered by American tourist companies. It is an expensive way to visit the islands, but the 750,000hp engines ensure that ice will not thwart you, which is very possible with less-powerful ships.

There are many sites worthy of attention in the archipelago. The most visited ones are those with vegetation, where visitors can see verdant moss beds with delicate Arctic poppies and purple saxifrage exploding in a blanket of colour, such as at Calm Bay. Other sites are of historical interest, such as Nansen's and Johansen's wintering site on Jackson Island, while others are interesting for the wildlife, such as the spectacular bird colonies at Rubini Rock off Hooker Island.

It remains to be seen what will be the impact of tourism on these fragile islands. If visitors concentrate on selected sites, their effects will be disproportionately heavy, even though the overall number of tourists may remain low. The future really lies in the ability and willingness of the Russian authorities to regulate and monitor tourist activities, and impose environmental restrictions on the ships and crew that carry them there. In 1994, Franz Josef Land was part of a new 42,000 sq km nature reserve that was given special protection by the government, thus leading the way in nature conservation in the Eurasian Arctic. If the recommended guidelines are followed, Franz Josef Land's continued survival as an area of natural beauty and scientific interest should be assured.

NOVAYA ZEMLYA

Novaya Zemlya comprises two islands separated by a narrow fjord-like strait called Matochkin Shar. Both islands are mountainous, the highest peak reaching 1109m. The northern island is 55,038 sq km, slightly larger than the southern one, which covers about 40,975 sq km. The north is

barren and littered with glaciers that tumble into the sea, while the south is more tundra-like in character, and boasts vegetation cover that includes dwarf willow, birch and flowering plants. There are still Samoyed people living on the islands, and some of the villages may be visited by tourist ships.

Novaya Zemlya is perhaps most noted for its use as a nuclear weapons testing ground during the Cold War. Several surface explosions and a number of underground ones were carried out. Meanwhile, western scientists and environmentalists have been concerned to learn that parts of Novaya Zemlya's coast have been used as a dumping ground for decommissioned nuclear submarines from the Russian navy. As yet, no significant elevations in radionuclides have been detected in the surrounding waters, although many scientists believe that it is only a matter of time before a leak occurs.

SEVERNAYA ZEMLYA

This archipelago lies to the north of the Taymyr Peninsula and its name means 'north land'. Geologically, it is a continuation of the mainland, and comprises about 36,260 sq km of three large islands and many smaller ones. They are subject to severe weather, including blizzards and high winds, and can be hazardous to the shipping along the Northern Sea Route. They are mountainous and severely glaciated, and are home to only 40 or so species of vascular plants. Despite this, huge colonies of birds flock to them for the breeding season, so that, in summer, they ring with the honks and cries of a wide variety of sea birds and geese.

NOVOSIBIRSKYE OSTROVA

The scattering of islands that lie directly north of the Lena and Yana deltas comprise three large islands called Kotelnyy, Faddeevski and Novaya Sibir, with a group of islets to the north-east called the De-Long Archipelago, and another to the south called the Liakhovs. Like Severnaya Zemlya, Novosibirskye Ostrova forms a continuation of the mainland. They are desolate scraps of rock in hostile waters, and it is easy to imagine how their discoverer, George W De Long, died of starvation and exposure in this area.

Although this island group is not on the itinerary of most tourist ships, they became known for the remarkable discoveries of fossils, including mammoths, in their ice. The ice, particularly in the southern islands, is thought to date from the last ice age.

WRANGEL ISLAND

Wrangel Island and its neighbour Herald Island lie in the East Siberian Sea, and are appearing increasingly on the itineraries of cruise ships that explore the Bering Strait and Chukchi Peninsula area. Wrangel takes in about 5180 sq km and enjoys a dry and relatively mild climate for its latitude. It has a varied landscape, with regions of lowland and mountain ranges that reach heights of about 1100m.

Named after Ferdinand von Wrangel, the Arctic explorer, Wrangel Island boasts a great variety of wildlife. There is a large polar bear denning site, and, in the 1970s, muskox were introduced and seem to be thriving. There are

also large colonies of birds, ranging from breeding populations of lesser snow geese sand grey phalarope to sea birds.

Chukotka Peninsula

On the rugged Chukotka Peninsula, in the north-easternmost corner of Russia, the tangle of mountain ranges that extends northward from central Siberia becomes the 2000m-high Anadyrskiy ranges. In the seas, whales, seals and walrus abound; the cliffs are alive with nesting sea birds; and inland, the Chukchi people's extensive reindeer herds graze in the tundra valleys.

At Cape Dezhnev, the Russian mainland faces Alaska's Seward Peninsula, only 89km away across the Bering Strait. Although explorer Vitus Bering got the credit, in the mid-17th century the Cossack Semyon Dezhnev (for whom the cape was named) sailed through this gap and demonstrated that the Eurasian landmass ended there.

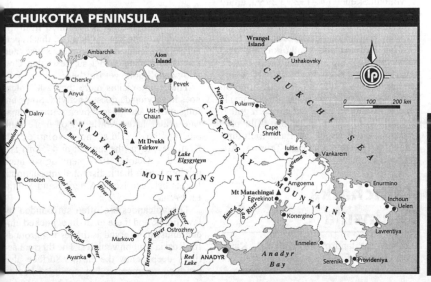

CHUKOTKA PENINSULA

During the Soviet era, this far-flung outpost became a nuclear test site, and the modern populace has been subjected to as much radiation as those who lived in Chernobyl in 1986. In recent years, there has also been a high incidence of tuberculosis and a child mortality rate of 10%.

The US airline Bering Air (☎ 907-443 5620, email info@beringair.com), in Nome, Alaska, flies between Nome and Chukotka's main town, Providenia. It can also help out with visas and invitations through its Russian agent. Note that Chukotka lies across the International Date Line from the USA; when it's noon on Tuesday in Chukotka, it's 3 pm on Monday in Nome (that is, a 21 hour difference in 89km!)

If you're interested in some wild exploration, the book *Trekking in Russia & Central Asia* includes descriptions of a seven day hike around Cape Dezhnev and a rafting trip from the lake Elgygytgyn to the Anadyr River. However, visitors to Chukotka should either be self-sufficient in food and other supplies for the duration of their stay (be sure to bring a tent!) or organise their visit through a reputable agency.

Mikhail Skopets (☎ 4132-23 29 90, email ibpn@ibpn.magadan.su) is a biologist and avid angler who's quite familiar with the outlying regions of the Magadan oblast, including Kolyma and Chukotka. He also speaks English and has worked with quite a few foreigners. Boris Levin of BOL Tours (☎/fax 4132-22 02 96, email bol@online.magadan.su or bol@asianoffice.com) is reportedly another excellent northern guide. Several US tour companies also offer programs in the Russian Far East, including Chukotka (see the Organised Tours & Adventures chapter).

Kamchatka Peninsula

Dubbed 'the land of fire and ice', Kamchatka is one of Russia's least explored but most scenically spectacular regions. A

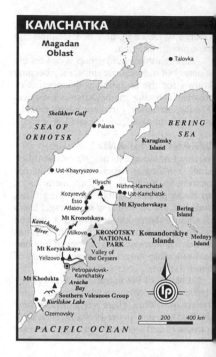

KAMCHATKA

1000km-long peninsula separated from the mainland by the Sea of Okhotsk, this hyperactively volcanic land bubbles, spurts and spews in a manner that suggests that Creation hasn't quite yet finished.

The region claims more than 200 volcanoes in varying degrees of activity. Some are long extinct and grassed over, with aquamarine crater lakes, while 20 or more rank among the world's most volatile. Mt Klyuchevskaya (the highest at 4750m) last erupted in October 1994, sending so much ash into the air that it disrupted international flights between North America and South-East Asia.

The volcanoes are often surrounded by lava fields, and these lunar-like, pocked cinder landscapes served as the testing grounds for Russia's moon vehicles. The thermal activity deep below the earth's surface also produces numerous hot springs, heated ivers and geysers. The most spectacular examples are to be found in the Valley of the Geysers (Dolina Geyzerov) in the Kronotsky National Park, where around 200 funaroles sporadically blast steam, mud and water from the canyon floor.

Away from the volcanoes, Kamchatka is covered by large areas of mixed forests and plains of giant grasses, home to a vast array of wildlife including between 10,000 and 20,000 brown bears and the sable, the animal that provided much of the impetus for early Russian explorations of the peninsula.The man credited with the discovery of Kamchatka, in 1697, was the Cossack Vladimir Atlasov who, like most explorers of his time, was motivated by visions of new lands to plunder. He established two forts on the Kamchatka River which became bases for the Russian traders who followed, looking to exact tribute from the locals in the form of furs.

The native Koryaki, Chukchi and Itelmeni warred with their new self-appointed overlords, however, they fared badly and their numbers were greatly diminished. Today, the remnants of the Chukchi nation inhabit the isolated north-east of Kamchatka, while the Koryaki live on the west coast of the peninsula and have their territorial capital at Palana. These peoples still maintain traditional reindeer herding and sea hunting lifestyles, and use the animals as a source of food and clothing. While much of their culture and language has been

Independent Travel in Kamchatka

Officially, visitors need an invitation specifically for Kamchatka, but Aeroflot rarely asks for any documentation before selling domestic tickets to Petropavlovsk-Kamchatsky and the local OVIR has been known to register foreigners even when the city isn't listed on their visa. To avoid problems, however, it's wise to include Petropavlovsk-Kamchatsky as one of your proposed destinations when applying for your Russian visa and hope it appears on your document.

Once you've arrived at Petropavlovsk, the major problem is getting around. With only one major road on the peninsula and no railways, the most common means of reaching A from B is flying. Lumbering Mi-8 helicopters operate like minibuses, ferrying scientists, volcanologists and hunters between remote settlements and isolated cabins. For an hour's ride in a helicopter you're looking at a minimum of $1200 split between a maximum of 20 people. Even areas that don't require helicopter transfers can only be accessed in a *vezdekhod* (tracked all-terrain vehicle).

In the past, scheduled, short-hop flights around Kamchatka were available for a pittance, but now cost as much as a flight to Moscow and are used mainly by locals who've struck it rich ferrying Korean popsicles from Petropavlovsk to isolated villages. For example, a flight from Petropavlovsk to the west-coast Koryaki settlements of Palana and Ust-Khayryuzovo will cost US$260. Flights are slightly cheaper to Ust-Kamchatsk, a small fishing town at the mouth of the Kamchatka River; Kozyrevsk, a village 40km from the Klyuchevskaya volcano; and Ozernovsky, toward the southern tip of the peninsula and just 15km from Lake Kurilskoe.

A regular bus runs from Petropavlovsk to Klyuchi, via Esso. Depending on the road conditions, the journey takes anywhere from 12 to 15 hours, and a one-way ticket costs US$33. However, none of these places is set up to receive tourists and it's recommended that you make local enquiries before descending on any of these places.

Above all, bear in mind that it's a tough world out there and lots of locals have met their demise attempting to explore Kamchatka overcome by sulphurous fumes on the volcanoes, crashing through thin crusts into boiling pits below, caught by winter avalanches, or mauled by one of the region's many bears.

lost, their storytelling traditions, which include mime, dance and song, have survived.

Kamchatka was long regarded as the least hospitable place in the Russian Empire – a primeval wilderness inhabited by a few primitives, half a year's journey distant and with nothing to offer but a dwindling supply of furs. When Alaska was sold off in 1867, Kamchatka might also have been up for grabs if the Americans had shown any interest. Some 53 years later there was a taker, when an American named Washington Baker Vanderlip wanted to buy the province. He was offered a 60-year concession by Lenin but they could never agree on the terms and the deal fizzled.

After WWII, Kamchatka took on new strategic importance and became a base for military airfields and early warning radar systems, while the coastline sheltered parts of the Soviet Pacific Fleet. Isolated regions served as target areas for missile testings. No foreigners, not even non-resident Russians, were allowed near the peninsula. That all changed in 1990. These days the only hint of past paranoia is that visitors must have 'permission' to visit Kamchatka, which means having it listed on your visa.

There seems to be no attempt to hide the silver snouts of fighter aircraft that protrude from the large grassy hummocks along the runway at the airport in Petropavlovsk-Kamchatsky, but the main volcanoes, geysers, lakes and all the region's most breathtaking scenery lurk well away from the regional capital. Without advance planning, you're unlikely to even get out of Petropavlovsk, and to reach the areas of greatest interest, you'll have to charter a helicopter or engage in some serious hiking and many nights of wilderness camping.

Petropavlovsk-Kamchatsky is reasonably well served by air from other parts of Russia. For details on reaching Kamchatka from Alaska, see the Getting Around chapter.

PETROPAVLOVSK-KAMCHATSKY
☎ 4152

Petropavlovsk-Kamchatsky is the administrative centre of the Kamchatka oblast and the peninsula's only settlement of any size. The huddles of low-rise concrete blocks that make up the town contrast sharply with the brooding active volcanoes, Avachinskaya and Koryakskaya, which make up the backdrop. Both of these irritable peaks have erupted since 1990, but Petropavlovsk residents seem to fear earthquakes more than the wrath of their belching mountains.

Petropavlovsk was founded in 1741 by Vitus Bering, the Danish-born Russian captain who discovered the straits that bear his name. The town was named after Bering's two ships, the *Svyatoy Pyotr* (St Peter) and *Svyatoy Pavel* (St Paul) – the suffix Kamchatsky was added to distinguish it from Russia's various other Petropavlovsks. The settlement eventually became the tsars' major Pacific seaport and was used as the base for the explorations which extended the Empire right along the Aleutian chain to mainland Alaska. By 1866, it remained little more than a cluster of log cabins and a small, green-onion domed church.

There were unlikely visitors in 1779 when a Captain Clerke sailing under the British flag entered Petropavlovsk harbour in command of the *Discovery* and the *Resolution* (formerly commanded by the late Captain James Cook). Clerke had inherited Cook's intention to explore the Arctic, but shortly after setting out from Petropavlovsk he was stricken with consumption and returned there to die that same year. During the Crimean War, the British sailed into Avacha Bay, this time accompanied by the French and intent on a less benign mission. However, this attempt to open up a Pacific theatre of operations was unexpectedly repulsed by the small Petropavlovsk garrison.

During the Soviet era the town retained its military role and became a sizeable Pacific Fleet submarine base, but its present prosperity is owed completely to the fishing industry. Rust-bucket trawlers currently haul in a million tonnes of fish annually, and nearly half of it is sold to Japan for good, hard currency.

Modern Petropavlovsk is strung along one main axis; the road that runs in from the

Volcano Glossary

As you're travelling around Kamchatka, you may encounter some of the following volcanic and geothermal phenomena:

aa – sharp, rough and chunky lava from gaseous and explosive magma. An alternative is the Icelandic *apalhraun*.

basalt – a rock material that flows smoothly in lava form. Some of the most interesting rock formations are columns of basalt cooled into rosette patterns and polygonal shapes

bombs – chunks of volcanic ejecta that cool and solidify in mid-air

caldera – the often immense depression formed by the collapse of a volcanic cone. into its magma chamber.

dyke – a vertical intrusion of igneous material up through cracks in horizontal rock layers.

ejecta – material ejected during a volcanic eruption, especially an explosive eruption.

fissure – a break or fracture in the earth's crust where vulcanism may occur.

fumarole – gas vent in a geothermal field.

geyser – spouting hot spring; pressure from boiling water deep in the ground builds until the force is sufficient to displace cooler surface water, resulting in a sudden explosion. The name is derived from the now dormant example at Geysir, in Iceland.

graben – a valley formed by spreading and subsidence of surface material.

hornitos – small vertical tubes produced in lava by a strong ejection of gases from beneath the surface.

laccolith – a mushroom-shaped dome of igneous material that has flowed upward through rock layers and then spread out horizontally, often causing hills to appear on the surface.

lava cave or *lava tube* – a tunnel or cavern caused by a lava stream flowing beneath an already solidified surface.

maar – a lake in a volcanic explosion crater.

magma – molten rock before it reaches the surface and becomes lava.

mudpots – deposits of boiling mud in a geothermally active area.

obsidian – naturally formed volcanic glass.

pahoehoe – ropy, smooth-flowing lava derived from non-gaseous magma. The Icelandic name is *helluhraun*.

pillow lava – lava formed in underwater or subglacial eruptions. It is squeezed out like toothpaste in pillow-like bulbs and solidifies immediately.

plug – material that has solidified in volcanic vents revealed by erosion.

pseudocraters – small craters formed by steam explosions when molten material flows into a body of water.

pumice – solidified lava froth. Pumice is so light and porous it will float on water.

rhyolite – light-coloured acid lava solidified into beautifully variegated rock

scoria – porous and glassy black or red volcanic gravel formed in fountain-like eruptions.

shield volcano – flattish cones of oozing pahoehoe lava. The name was derived from the classic example, Skjaldbreiður (meaning 'white shield'), near Tingvellir in Iceland.

sill – a finger or vein of molten material that squeezes between existing rock layers and solidifies.

solfatara – a volcanic vent emitting only gases, primarily such acidic gases as sulphur dioxide and hydrochloric acid. Solfataras are often characterised by sulphur-encrusted earth and boiling mud.

table mountain – the result of an eruption inside a glacier which subsequently retreats or melts. Material flows upward and solidifies as in a mould, giving many table mountains their characteristic 'birthday cake' shapes.

tephra – a collective term for all types of materials ejected from a volcano and transported through the air.

PETROPAVLOVSK-KAMCHATSKY

PLACES TO STAY & EAT
2 Hotel Edelveis
4 Hotel Petropavlovsk
6 Restoran Lonkhey
8 Hotel Avacha
10 Hotel Oktyabrskaya

OTHER
1 10 km Bus Station
3 Museum of Volcanology
5 Farmers' Market
7 Telephone &
  Telegraph Office
9 Traders' Market
11 Holkam Supermarket
12 Main Post Office
13 The Regional Museum

airport 30km east, enters the city limits as prospekt Pobedy and changes its name no less than 11 times (prospekt Pobedy, ulitsa Tushkanova, prospekt 50 let Oktyabrya, ulitsa Vladivostokskaya, ulitsa Leningradskaya, ulitsa Ozernovskaya, ulitsa Leninskaya, ulitsa Krasnaya Sopka, ulitsa Sapun Gora, ulitsa Okeanskaya, Petropavlovskoe shosse, ulitsa Industrialnaya) before winding up at the small fishing harbour, Rakovaya (Seashell) Bay, on the southern edge of the town. Town maps are sold at the Re-

gional Museum and the newspaper kiosk in the Oblast administration building on Teatralnaya ploshchad.

Things to See & Do

While Petropavlovsk is primarily a gateway to the surrounding volcanic region, there are a few things to do in town. The **Regional Museum** (Kraevedchesky muzey), housed in an attractive half-timbered building overlooking the bay at Leninskaya 20, provides a beautifully presented history of the region focusing mainly on prehistory and geology, indigenous peoples and early settlers. There's an extremely interesting section on early Russian settlers in America with reconstructions of the first settlements.

There's also a **Museum of Volcanology** at bulvar Piypa 9 and a **Museum of Geology** at ulitsa Beringa 117.

In front of the classically styled regional administration building at Leninskaya 14 is the **monument to Captain Clerke**, a small obelisk erected by a delegation from the British Admiralty in 1913. On Nikolskaya Hill there sits a small chapel and monuments to those who fell in the failed Crimean War invasion of 1854.

Places to Stay & Eat

Accommodation choices are scant, but so is the number of visitors, so you shouldn't have any trouble finding a room, especially since no one lingers very long anyway. The recently renovated *Hotel Avacha (☎ 227-331, ulitsa Leninskaya 61)* has single/ double rooms for US$50/65. It's opposite the T-34 tank monument. The *Hotel Oktyabrskaya (☎ 112684, ulitsa Sovietskaya 51)* is recommended for its location, close to Teatralnaya ploshchad in the prettiest part of town. The hotel has been recently upgraded. Rooms with separate bath are US$76/80. You can also try *Edelveis (☎ 253324, prospect Pobedy 27)*, but it's definitely past its prime; rooms cost US$22/32.

The hotel favoured by tour companies is the *Hotel Petropavlovsk (☎ 250374, prospekt Karla Marxa 31)*. It's a squat concrete block facing the volcanoes, with its back to the main road, about 100m back from ulitsa Tushkanova just north of the major road junction marked by a large obelisk. Singles/doubles cost US$42/55.

The best place for meals, atmosphere and cocktails (with names like *zhurnalistochka*!) is the *Press Klub*, on ulitsa Lukashevskogo in the *Argumenty i Fakty* newspaper building. It's open from 10 am to 4 pm and 4.30 pm to midnight. Despite its rather gloomy atmosphere, the restaurant in the *Hotel Petropavlovsk* basement

serves well-presented fish dishes at reasonable prices. Upstairs, on the ground floor, there's a cheerful cafe-bar with an English-language menu which does decent meals. The respectable-looking *Restoran Lonkhey, (prospekt 50 let Oktyabrya 24)* is open from noon to 5 pm and 7 to 11.30 pm.

A snack bar on the 1st floor of the *Holkam supermarket (ulitsa Leninskaya 62)* serves sandwiches, pastries, cakes and coffee until 7 pm. The supermarket, a sparkling Dutch-Swiss-Russian venture, is also a good place to shop for food supplies. There's also a row of 24-hour shops near the Hotel Petropavlovsk, the best of which is the *Slavyansky*. Other places include the *traders' market* just south of ploshchad Komsomolskaya and the *farmers' market* on ulitsa Voitsesheka.

Getting Around

Buses run to most areas of Petropavlovsk, from the 10-km station (avtostantsiya desyaty kilometr), on prospekt Pobedy at the north end of town, to the Regional Museum. Other transportation is provided by mikriki (minivans), which charge from US$0.50 to US$1. The 45-minute, US$0.50 ride to the airport is served by buses and mikriki from the 10-km stop; take anything marked 'Aeroport' or Yelizovo. Arriving passengers can reach the town on any bus from the bus stop across the car park from the airport entrance, though it may be necessary to change at 10-km. Airport taxis cost around US$10.

AROUND THE PENINSULA

Several excursions can be made from Petropavlovsk without inordinate effort or expense. The hot springs at **Paratunka**, 25km south of the airport town of Yelizovo, is accessible by mikriki (US$2 one way), from the Yelizovo bus station and will stop at request at the three no-frills resorts along the way. Although they're heavily frequented by locals, the Paratunka springs aren't particularly attractive, but there is a lovely set of natural springs some 15km farther south on the slopes of Goryachaya, opposite the volcanology centre.

A 30 minute drive from Petropavlovsk-Kamchatsky lies an interesting black-sand beach where sea lions gallivant in the 6°C Pacific Ocean waters, and the twisted birch groves behind the beach dunes are a favourite camping spot for the locals.

It's also possible to hike up the slopes of **Mt Avachinskaya** and **Mt Koryakskaya**, the two volcanoes that loom over Petropavlovsk. The base for the 2km ascent lies about 30km from the town, but there's no public transportation, so you'll probably have to get there through a local agency. An ascent of Avachinskaya should take about four to six hours, and hikers should be aware of fissures in the glaciers, high winds and the thick fog which often covers the steep upper slopes of the mountain in the late afternoon. Koryakskaya is more difficult and should not be attempted by inexperienced climbers.

Another place worth visiting is the **Valley of the Geysers**, which lies 150km north of Petropavlovsk. This is an expensive excursion as the only access is by helicopter, special permission is required, and the valley is closed for 40 days between May and June due to nesting birds. Currently, Sogjoy is the only agency permitted to issue access permits, but other companies can arrange visits through them. If you go, the best place to touch down is the otherworldly **Uzon Caldera**, which is the remnant of an ancient volcano. This 10km crater now features steaming lakes, enormous mushrooms and prolific berry bushes which are well-attended by local bears. This is not a place to go traipsing around without a guide as the ground is delicate in places, and lies over a particularly uninviting inferno.

Another spectacular region is the cluster of southern volcanoes, including **Mt Mutnovskaya**, which erupted in 1994, and the intermontane valley filled with thermal rivers and boiling lakes. There's skiing and snowboarding from June to August in **Rodnikovoe**, in the Vilyucha valley about 15km north of Mutnovskaya on the north side of Mt Vilyuchinskaya. It's a three hour drive to Rodnikovoe which also has hot springs on a dirt road.

Lake Kurilskoe, near the southern tip of Kamchatka in the Yuzhno-Kamchatsky reserve, serves as a spawning ground for over one million salmon annually, which attract the stellar sea eagle, a bird with a wingspan of around 2.5m. For rafting, the **Bystraya river** is the easiest to reach; the best-known section is the 120km south-west-flowing stretch between the village of Malki, 80km west of Yelizovo, and the Ust-Bolsheretsk bridge just before the Bystraya empties into the Sea of Okhotsk. The name means fast but there are only a few rapids, making for a leisurely two day journey.

North from Petropavlovsk, the towns of Kozyrevsk and Klyuchi are convenient bases to explore the **Klyuchi volcanoes**, a wild, active grouping containing the region's giant Klyuchevskaya (4750m) and its near twin Mt Kamen (just a little lower at 4617m). Along the way, drop in on the village of Esso, best known for its Alpine setting and thermally-heated greenhouses which provide Petropavlovsk with tomatoes year-round. Esso also has a museum and nearby Anavgay is an interesting Eveny village.

LONELY PLANET

Phrasebooks

Lonely Planet phrasebooks are packed with essential words and phrases to help travellers communicate with the locals. With colour tabs for quick reference, an extensive vocabulary and use of script, these handy pocket-sized language guides cover day-to-day travel situations.

- handy pocket-sized books
- easy to understand Pronunciation chapter
- clear & comprehensive Grammar chapter
- romanisation alongside script to allow ease of pronunciation
- script throughout so users can point to phrases for every situation
- full of cultural information and tips for the traveller

'...vital for a real DIY spirit and attitude in language learning'
— *Backpacker*

'the phrasebooks have good cultural backgrounders and offer solid advice for challenging situations in remote locations'
— *San Francisco Examiner*

Arabic (Egyptian) • Arabic (Moroccan) • Australian *(Australian English, Aboriginal and Torres Strait languages)* • Baltic States *(Estonian, Latvian, Lithuanian)* • Bengali • Brazilian • British • Burmese • Cantonese • Central Asia • Central Europe *(Czech, French, German, Hungarian, Italian, Slovak)* • Eastern Europe *(Bulgarian, Czech, Hungarian, Polish, Romanian, Slovak)* • Ethiopian (Amharic) • Fijian • French • German • Greek • Hebrew phrasebook • Hill Tribes • Hindi/Urdu • Indonesian • Italian • Japanese • Korean • Lao • Latin American Spanish • Malay • Mandarin • Mediterranean Europe *(Albanian, Croatian, Greek, Italian, Macedonian, Maltese, Serbian, Slovene)* • Mongolian • Nepali • Papua New Guinea • Pilipino (Tagalog) • Quechua • Russian • Scandinavian Europe *(Danish, Finnish, Icelandic, Norwegian, Swedish)* • South-East Asia *(Burmese, Indonesian, Khmer, Lao, Malay, Tagalog Pilipino, Thai, Vietnamese)* • South Pacific Languages • Spanish (Castilian) *(also includes Catalan, Galician and Basque)* • Sri Lanka • Swahili • Thai • Tibetan • Turkish • Ukrainian • USA *(US English, Vernacular, Native American languages, Hawaiian)* • Vietnamese • Western Europe *(Basque, Catalan, Dutch, French, German, Greek, Irish)*

LONELY PLANET

Lonely Planet Travel Atlases

Lonely Planet has long been famous for the number and quality of its guidebook maps. Now we've gone one step further and produced a handy companion series: Lonely Planet travel atlases – maps of a country produced in book form.

Unlike other maps, which look good but lead travellers astray, our travel atlases have been researched on the road by Lonely Planet's experienced team of writers. All details are carefully checked to ensure the atlas corresponds with the equivalent Lonely Planet guidebook.

- full-colour throughout
- maps researched and checked by Lonely Planet authors
- place names correspond with Lonely Planet guidebooks
- no confusing spelling differences
- legend and travelling information in English, French, German, Japanese and Spanish
- size: 230 x 160 mm

Available now: Chile & Easter Island • Egypt • India & Bangladesh • Israel & the Palestinian Territories • Jordan, Syria & Lebanon • Kenya • Laos • Portugal • South Africa, Lesotho & Swaziland • Thailand • Turkey • Vietnam • Zimbabwe, Botswana & Namibia

---

Lonely Planet TV Series & Videos

Lonely Planet travel guides have been brought to life on television screens around the world. Like our guides, the programs are based on the joy of independent travel, and look honestly at some of the most exciting, picturesque and frustrating places in the world. Each show is presented by one of three travellers from Australia, England or the USA and combines an innovative mixture of video, Super-8 film, atmospheric soundscapes and original music.

Videos of each episode – containing additional footage not shown on television – are available from good book and video shops, but the availability of individual videos varies with regional screening schedules.

Video destinations include: Alaska • American Rockies • Australia – The South-East • Baja California & the Copper Canyon • Brazil • Central Asia • Chile & Easter Island • Corsica, Sicily & Sardinia – The Mediterranean Islands • East Africa (Tanzania & Zanzibar) • Ecuador & the Galapagos Islands • Greenland & Iceland • Indonesia • Israel & the Sinai Desert • Jamaica • Japan • La Ruta Maya • Morocco • New York • North India • Pacific Islands (Fiji, Solomon Islands & Vanuatu) • South India • South West China • Turkey • Vietnam • West Africa • Zimbabwe, Botswana & Namibia

The Lonely Planet TV series is produced by: Pilot Productions
The Old Studio
18 Middle Row
London W10 5AT, UK

Lonely Planet On-line

Whether you've just begun planning your next trip, or you're chasing down specific info on currency regulations or visa requirements, check out Lonely Planet On-line for up-to-the minute travel information.

As well as mini guides to more than 250 destinations, you'll find maps, photos, travel news, health and visa updates, travel advisories, and discussion of the ecological and political issues you need to be aware of as you travel. You'll also find timely upgrades to popular guidebooks which you can print out and stick in the back of your book.

There's also an on-line travellers' forum where you can share your experience of life on the road, meet travel companions and ask other travellers for their recommendations and advice.

And of course we have a complete and up-to-date list of all Lonely Planet travel products including travel guides, diving and snorkeling guides, phrasebooks, atlases, travel literature and videos, and a simple on-line ordering facility if you can't find the book you want elsewhere.

Lonely Planet Diving & Snorkeling Guides

Beautifully illustrated with full-colour photos throughout, Lonely Planet's Pisces Books explore the world's best diving and snorkeling areas and prepare divers for what to expect when they get there, both topside and underwater.

Dive sites are described in detail with specifics on depths, visibility, level of difficulty, special conditions, underwater photography tips and common and unusual marine life present. You'll also find practical logistical information and coverage on topside activities and attractions, sections on diving health and safety, plus listings for diving services, live-aboards, dive resorts and tourist offices.

LONELY PLANET

Guides by Region

Lonely Planet is known worldwide for publishing practical, reliable and no-nonsense travel information in our guides and on our Web site. The Lonely Planet list covers just about every accessible part of the world. Currently there are nine series: travel guides, shoestring guides, walking guides, city guides, phrasebooks, audio packs, travel atlases, diving and snorkeling guides and travel literature.

AFRICA Africa – the South • Africa on a shoestring • Arabic (Egyptian) phrasebook • Arabic (Moroccan) phrasebook • Cairo • Cape Town • Central Africa • East Africa • Egypt • Egypt travel atlas • Ethiopian (Amharic) phrasebook • The Gambia & Senegal • Healthy Travel Africa • Kenya • Kenya travel atlas • Malawi, Mozambique & Zambia • Morocco • North Africa • South Africa, Lesotho & Swaziland • South Africa, Lesotho & Swaziland travel atlas • Swahili phrasebook • Tanzania, Zanzibar & Pemba • Trekking in East Africa • Tunisia • West Africa • Zimbabwe, Botswana & Namibia • Zimbabwe, Botswana & Namibia travel atlas
Travel Literature: The Rainbird: A Central African Journey • Songs to an African Sunset: A Zimbabwean Story • Mali Blues: Traveling to an African Beat

AUSTRALIA & THE PACIFIC Australia • Australian phrasebook • Bushwalking in Australia • Bushwalking in Papua New Guinea • Fiji • Fijian phrasebook • Islands of Australia's Great Barrier Reef • Melbourne • Micronesia • New Caledonia • New South Wales & the ACT • New Zealand • Northern Territory • Outback Australia • Papua New Guinea • Papua New Guinea (Pidgin) phrasebook • Queensland • Rarotonga & the Cook Islands • Samoa • Solomon Islands • South Australia • South Pacific Languages phrasebook • Sydney • Tahiti & French Polynesia • Tasmania • Tonga • Tramping in New Zealand • Vanuatu • Victoria • Western Australia
Travel Literature: Islands in the Clouds • Kiwi Tracks • Sean & David's Long Drive

CENTRAL AMERICA & THE CARIBBEAN Bahamas and Turks & Caicos • Barcelona • Bermuda • Central America on a shoestring • Costa Rica • Cuba • Dominican Republic & Haiti • Eastern Caribbean • Guatemala, Belize & Yucatán: La Ruta Maya • Jamaica • Mexico • Mexico City • Panama
Travel Literature: Green Dreams: Travels in Central America

EUROPE Amsterdam • Andalucía • Austria • Baltic States phrasebook • Barcelona • Berlin • Britain • British phrasebook • Brussels, Bruges & Antwerp • Canary Islands • Central Europe • Central Europe phrasebook • Corsica • Croatia • Czech & Slovak Republics • Denmark • Dublin • Eastern Europe • Eastern Europe phrasebook • Edinburgh • Estonia, Latvia & Lithuania • Europe • Finland • France • French phrasebook • Germany • German phrasebook • Greece • Greek phrasebook • Hungary • Iceland, Greenland & the Faroe Islands • Ireland • Italian phrasebook • Italy • Lisbon • London • Mediterranean Europe • Mediterranean Europe phrasebook • Norway • Paris • Poland • Portugal • Portugal travel atlas • Prague • Provence & the Côte d'Azur • Romania & Moldova • Rome • Russia, Ukraine & Belarus • Russian phrasebook • Scandinavian & Baltic Europe • Scandinavian Europe phrasebook • Scotland • Slovenia • Spain • Spanish phrasebook • St Petersburg • Switzerland • Trekking in Spain • Ukrainian phrasebook • Vienna • Walking in Britain • Walking in Italy • Walking in Ireland • Walking in Switzerland • Western Europe • Western Europe phrasebook
Travel Literature: The Olive Grove: Travels in Greece

INDIAN SUBCONTINENT Bangladesh • Bengali phrasebook • Bhutan • Delhi • Goa • Hindi/Urdu phrasebook • India • India & Bangladesh travel atlas • Indian Himalaya • Karakoram Highway • Mumbai • Nepal • Nepali phrasebook • Pakistan • Rajasthan • South India • Sri Lanka • Sri Lanka phrasebook • Trekking in the Indian Himalaya • Trekking in the Karakoram & Hindukush • Trekking in the Nepal Himalaya
Travel Literature: In Rajasthan • Shopping for Buddhas

LONELY PLANET

Mail Order

Lonely Planet products are distributed worldwide. They are also available by mail order from Lonely Planet, so if you have difficulty finding a title please write to us. North and South American residents should write to 150 Linden St, Oakland, CA 94607, USA; European and African residents should write to 10a Spring Place, London NW5 3BH, UK; and residents of other countries to PO Box 617, Hawthorn, Victoria 3122, Australia.

ISLANDS OF THE INDIAN OCEAN Madagascar & Comoros • Maldives • Mauritius, Réunion & Seychelles

MIDDLE EAST & CENTRAL ASIA Arab Gulf States • Central Asia • Central Asia phrasebook • Hebrew phrasebook • Iran • Israel & the Palestinian Territories • Israel & the Palestinian Territories travel atlas • Istanbul • Jerusalem • Jordan & Syria • Jordan, Syria & Lebanon travel atlas • Lebanon • Middle East on a shoestring • Syria • Turkey • Turkish phrasebook • Turkey travel atlas • Yemen
Travel Literature: The Gates of Damascus • Kingdom of the Film Stars: Journey into Jordan

NORTH AMERICA Alaska • Backpacking in Alaska • Baja California • California & Nevada • Canada • Chicago • Florida • Hawaii • Honolulu • Los Angeles • Louisiana • Miami • New England USA • New Orleans • New York City • New York, New Jersey & Pennsylvania • Pacific Northwest USA • Puerto Rico • Rocky Mountain States • San Francisco • Seattle • Southwest USA • Texas • USA • USA phrasebook • Vancouver • Washington, DC & the Capital Region
Travel Literature: Drive Thru America

NORTH-EAST ASIA Beijing • Cantonese phrasebook • China • Hong Kong • Hong Kong, Macau & Guangzhou • Japan • Japanese phrasebook • Japanese audio pack • Korea • Korean phrasebook • Kyoto • Mandarin phrasebook • Mongolia • Mongolian phrasebook • North-East Asia on a shoestring • Seoul • South-West China • Taiwan • Tibet • Tibetan phrasebook • Tokyo
Travel Literature: Lost Japan

SOUTH AMERICA Argentina, Uruguay & Paraguay • Bolivia • Brazil • Brazilian phrasebook • Buenos Aires • Chile & Easter Island • Chile & Easter Island travel atlas • Colombia • Ecuador & the Galapagos Islands • Latin American Spanish phrasebook • Peru • Quechua phrasebook • Rio de Janeiro • South America on a shoestring • Trekking in the Patagonian Andes • Venezuela
Travel Literature: Full Circle: A South American Journey

SOUTH-EAST ASIA Bali & Lombok • Bangkok • Burmese phrasebook • Cambodia • Hanoi • Healthy Travel Asia & India • Hill Tribes phrasebook • Ho Chi Minh City • Indonesia • Indonesia's Eastern Islands • Indonesian phrasebook • Indonesian audio pack • Jakarta • Java • Laos • Lao phrasebook • Laos travel atlas • Malay phrasebook • Malaysia, Singapore & Brunei • Myanmar (Burma) • Philippines • Pilipino (Tagalog) phrasebook • Singapore • South-East Asia on a shoestring • South-East Asia phrasebook • Thailand • Thailand's Islands & Beaches • Thailand travel atlas • Thai phrasebook • Thai audio pack • Vietnam • Vietnamese phrasebook • Vietnam travel atlas

ALSO AVAILABLE: Antarctica • Brief Encounters: Stories of Love, Sex & Travel • Chasing Rickshaws • Lonely Planet Unpacked • Not the Only Planet: Travel Stories from Science Fiction • Sacred India • Travel with Children • Traveller's Tales

FREE Lonely Planet Newsletters

We love hearing from you and think you'd like to hear from us.

Planet Talk

Our FREE quarterly printed newsletter is full of tips from travellers and anecdotes from Lonely Planet guidebook authors. Every issue is packed with up-to-date travel news and advice, and includes:

- a postcard from Lonely Planet co-founder Tony Wheeler
- a swag of mail from travellers
- a look at life on the road through the eyes of a Lonely Planet author
- topical health advice
- prizes for the best travel yarn
- news about forthcoming Lonely Planet events
- a complete list of Lonely Planet books and other titles

To join our mailing list, residents of the UK, Europe and Africa can email us at go@lonelyplanet.co.uk; residents of North and South America can email us at info@lonelyplanet.com; the rest of the world can email us at talk2us@lonelyplanet.com.au, or contact any Lonely Planet office.

Comet

Our FREE monthly email newsletter brings you all the latest travel news, features, interviews, competitions, destination ideas, travellers' tips & tales, Q&As, raging debates and related links. Find out what's new on the Lonely Planet Web site and which books are about to hit the shelves.

Subscribe from your desktop: www.lonelyplanet.com/comet

Index

Text

Boxed Text

MAP LEGEND

BOUNDARIES

▬·▬··▬·	International
▬··▬··▬·	State
▬ ▬ ▬ ▬	Disputed

HYDROGRAPHY

	Coastline
	River, Creek
	Lake
	Intermittent Lake
	Salt Lake
	Canal
◎ ⟶≫	Spring, Rapids
⥊	Waterfalls

ROUTES & TRANSPORT

	Freeway
	Highway
	Major Road
	Minor Road
======	Unsealed Road
	City Highway
	City Road
	City Street, Lane

	Pedestrian Mall
⟹ = = =	Tunnel
⊢⊢⊢⊢─●─⊢	Train Route & Station
─ ─ ─ Ⓜ ─	Metro & Station
	Tramway
╫─╫─╫─╫─╫	Cable Car or Chairlift
─ ─ ─ ─ ─ ─	Walking Track
─ ─ ─ ─ ─	Ferry Route

AREA FEATURES

	Building
✿	Park, Gardens
+ + + + + +	Cemetery

	Glacier
	Pedestrian Mall
	Urban Area

MAP SYMBOLS

✪ CAPITAL	National Capital	✈	Airport	▲	Mountain or Hill
◉ CAPITAL	State Capital		Ancient or City Wall	🏛	Museum
● CITY	City	∴	Archaeological Site	)(	Pass
● Town	Town	⊖	Bank	★	Police Station
● Village	Village	⅄	Beach	✉	Post Office
○	Point of Interest	↘	Bird Sanctuary	⌂	Shelter
		⁘	Border Crossing	❖	Shopping Centre
■	Place to Stay	ᾱ	Castle or Fort	⚜	Ski field
▲	Camping Ground	⌒	Cave	🏛	Stately Home
ⵁ	Caravan Park	⊞ 🕆	Church	▭	Swimming Pool
⌂	Hut or Chalet	⌒⌒⌒	Cliff or Escarpment	✡	Synagogue
		◑	Embassy	☎	Telephone
▼	Place to Eat	⊕	Hospital	ⓘ	Tourist Information
▮	Pub or Bar	※	Lookout	●	Transport
		⚊	Monument	🐘	Zoo

Note: not all symbols displayed above appear in this book

LONELY PLANET OFFICES

Australia
PO Box 617, Hawthorn, Victoria 3122
☎ 03 9819 1877 fax 03 9819 6459
email: talk2us@lonelyplanet.com.au

UK
10a Spring Place, London NW5 3BH
☎ 020 7428 4800 fax 020 7428 4828
email: go@lonelyplanet.co.uk

USA
150 Linden St, Oakland, CA 94607
☎ 510 893 8555 TOLL FREE: 800 275 8555
fax 510 893 8572
email: info@lonelyplanet.com

France
1 rue du Dahomey, 75011 Paris
☎ 01 55 25 33 00 fax 01 55 25 33 01
email: bip@lonelyplanet.fr
minitel: 3615 lonelyplanet *(1,29 F TTC/min)*

World Wide Web: www.lonelyplanet.com *or* **AOL keyword: lp**
Lonely Planet Images: lpi@lonelyplanet.com.au